JOHN PAUL JONES

FIGHTER FOR FREEDOM AND GLORY

PLASTER BUST OF JOHN PAUL JONES BY JEAN ANTOINE HOUDON IN
CRYPT OF NAVAL ACADEMY CHAPEL
Presented by "The Friends of the United States Navy"

John Paul Jones

FIGHTER FOR FREEDOM AND GLORY

By

LINCOLN LORENZ

Author of

THE LIFE OF SIDNEY LANIER

UNITED STATES NAVAL INSTITUTE

Annapolis, Maryland

1943

KRAUS REPRINT CO.
New York
1969

920
J77L0

TO
JOHN L. SENIOR

FOR HIS DEVOTION TO THE MEMORY OF
JOHN PAUL JONES
AND
FOR HIS GOOD WILL TOWARDS
THE AUTHOR

Preface

THE CAREER of John Paul Jones is one of the most distinguished as well as eventful in American history. Nevertheless, during not only his life but also a century and a half after his death, truth in the portrayal of him often has been more honored in the breach than the observance. The misunderstanding and, in some cases, the deliberate falsification, which began early in his varied fortunes and persist even today, apply in some measure to his historical background and deeds and in far greater degree to his personality.

The life of this ardent citizen of the United States lent itself to startling misconception not alone because of hostility by the British, his countrymen against whom he fought, and rivalry and sensationalism by fellow Americans, but likewise because of treachery by Russians and Russo-Germans. The misrepresentation found an initial pretext when as a young master of a merchant vessel he moderately punished an intractable sailor with the cat-o'-nine-tails and suffered the charge of having occasioned his death. It grew when in self-defense he accidentally killed with his sword a mutineer who had tried to kill him. It developed afresh when he made his astounding raids early in the Revolution on the coasts of Britain to burn the shipping and to seize a hostage for the exchange of prisoners. It spread wider and wider, in step with his fame, when he gained his memorable victories first with the *Ranger* and later with the *Bonhomme Richard*. It reached a definite climax when he prepared to escape from the Texel in command of the *Alliance* with the American flag still flying. It acquired new roots in America, apart from Europe, from the calumnies of jealous officers like Simpson and Landais and from the manœuvres of hostile politicians, aiming at Franklin as well as Jones, like Arthur Lee, Richard Henry Lee, and Samuel Adams. And it discovered in Russia, dominated by the German born and bred usurper,

Catherine the Great, so-called, the most fertile ground of all for
what Jones himself described as "the dark intrigues and mean
subterfuges of Asiatic jealousy and malice."

The record of personal and historical falsification, even in instances favorable as well as adverse to Jones, does not imply, of
course, that books of authority concerning him have failed to
appear. The accompanying bibliography and other references are
sufficient to attest to the contrary. For longer than a century, in
fact, the gradual clarification more than offset the persistence of
false traditions. At the same time such misrepresentation is token
of the measure of error, conscious and unconscious, which besets
the biographer of Jones and which he may too readily pass on to
his readers.

The publication in 1900 and the republication in 1905 of
Augustus C. Buell's *Paul Jones, Founder of the American Navy:
A History* probably turned back the clock of authenticity regarding Jones even farther than it had previously advanced. This purported "history" or biography is such a tapestry of fiction and fact
as to be the more deceiving in its dishonest intention. It is not
unworthy of comparison, as my bibliography, appendix, and biography proper contribute further to explain, with literary forgeries
like those of Chatterton and Macpherson. Even the historical novel
should observe greater fidelity to fact.

During more recent years the influence of Buell has become evident in both direct and indirect form. In 1927 Phillips Russell
stated in his *John Paul Jones, Man of Action* that Buell "has been
assailed by Mrs. De Koven [the author of *The Life and Letters of
John Paul Jones*] for alleged inventions," and he refrained from
taking a stand himself. Russell depended at the same time upon
Buell for some of the incidents in his volume.

The still later biographies by Valentine Thomson, it should be
said, appear to revert, knowingly or unknowingly, both to some
of the episodes traceable primarily to Buell and to other unreliable material. Miss Thomson's two separate biographies of Jones,
the first *Le Corsaire chez l'impératrice* published in Paris and the
second *Knight of the Seas* published in New York, are in some
respects even irreconcilable with each other as well as inconsistent with known, reliable sources. In the former volume, to

cite a conspicuous instance, she characterizes Jones as "corsair," while in the latter she describes him as "knight." Again in the one she fully certifies to the truth of an elaborately told romance between Jones and the Russian princess Anna Kourakina, while in the other she retracts her previous assurances of the veracity of the narrative and sets it apart in an appendix as a plausible but unauthenticated legend. And in comments upon her sources, she alludes, for example, several times to "Professor Samuel Eliott [sic] Morison's bibliography of Paul Jones," which along with another reference book, according to her words, "enabled me to determine precisely not only Jones's maritime career, but also his life as a rover." This volume, however, does not exist, if the reply I received upon an inquiry to Professor Samuel Eliot Morison of the History Department in Harvard University, apart from my own investigation, is evidence enough: "Not guilty of a J. P. Jones bibliography." More definite particulars occur in these pages, as occasion warrants, concerning her representation of Jones.

Apart from these books just specified, no considerable biography of Jones, with the exception of Mrs. Reginald De Koven's in 1913, has appeared during the past forty years. And in fact, with only a second additional exception, a volume published as long ago as 1830, there has been no full-length history of the naval officer, undertaking to present a complete and authentic portrait of all the varied aspects of his life, during the one hundred and fifty years that have elapsed since his death.

It may be desirable to indicate the extended and new material concerning Jones in the present biography. Appendix IV describes its scope in relation to past volumes. The bibliography, with added comments, indicates the extent of the first hand and other trustworthy sources. The reference notes, with detailed identification, supplement the bibliography. As changes in subject matter naturally promote changes in emphasis and interpretation, the augmented material may be found to pervade almost every facet of Jones' life.

For most of the information, especially the first hand in general and the new in particular, I heartily express my obligation to the following libraries, to which my indebtedness appears in detail in the bibliography: The Library of Congress and the Office of

Naval Records and Library of the Navy Department in Washington; the Harvard College Library in Cambridge; the American Philosophical Society, the University of Pennsylvania, and the Historical Society of Pennsylvania libraries in Philadelphia; the Massachusetts Masonic Grand Lodge, the Massachusetts Historical Society, and the Boston Public libraries in Boston; the Naval Academy Museum Library in Annapolis; and the Pierpont Morgan, the New York Historical Society, the New York Society, and the New York Public libraries in New York. For extensive use of general facilities under circumstances of importance to me, I note separately my gratitude to the Columbia University Library.

I desire to record the debt which a biographer of Jones must owe, aside from that to the autobiographical *Mémoires de Paul Jones* edited by André, to the three early volumes based on family records: John Henry Sherburne's published in 1825 and 1851, Robert C. Sands' in 1830, and the anonymous author's at Edinburgh also in 1830. Mrs. De Koven's biography deserves to be named with them in respect to the letters which she first published. I have, however, consulted the letters and other documents in these volumes at their sources in almost every instance in the case of Mrs. De Koven's book and generally in such instances as they were available in the case of the others.

I greatly appreciate the helpfulness in various form and degree of the following persons, some of whom are associated with the libraries just mentioned: Captain D. J. Munro, R.N. (Ret.) of Clearwell, New Galloway, Scotland; Sir C. D. Hope-Dunbar (Bart.) of St. Mary's Isle, Kirkcudbright, Scotland; Messrs. Charles W. Mixer and Louis H. Bolander, Librarian and Assistant Librarian of the United States Naval Academy Library; Drs. St. George L. Sioussat and Thomas P. Martin, the Chief and the Assistant Chief of the Manuscript Division, and Mr. John T. Dorosh of the Slavic Division, of the Library of Congress; Dr. C. O. Paullin, naval historian, of Washington; Dr. C. C. Crittenden, Secretary of the North Carolina Historical Commission, of Raleigh; Mr. S. A. Ashe of Raleigh; Mr. R. H. Haynes of the Harvard College Library; Miss Laura E. Hanson of the American Philosophical Society Library; Judge Alvin T. Embrey of Fredericksburg; Mr. Cecil M. P. Cross, the former First Secretary of the

United States Embassy in France; Miss Beatrix Carey Davenport of Washington; Mrs. R. T. Newcombe of Raleigh; Mrs. Vivian Minor Fleming of Fredericksburg; Mrs. Savage Babbitt of Washington; and Marshall Hopkins Gould of Boston.

For nearly three quarters of a century the United States Naval Institute has been the Navy's forum "For the advancement of professional, literary, and scientific knowledge in the Navy." It seems particularly fitting that a service organization with headquarters always at the United States Naval Academy, where the body of Jones rests, should publish a biography of him. I deeply feel the honor to have the Board of Control of the Naval Institute publish this biography.

I reserve to mention last several persons to whom I owe such gratitude that I prefer to imply rather than express it. All of them read the manuscript. I hasten to add, however, that the limitations of the book are of course chargeable to me alone. Mr. William Bell Clark of Evanston, Illinois, the author of biographies of the naval officers John Barry and Lambert Wickes, criticized the historical and naval background of the Revolution in particular and provided me with important data and suggestions in general. Captain Dudley W. Knox, U.S.N. (Ret.), author and Officer-in-Charge of the Naval Records and Library of the Navy Department, offered invaluable suggestions and corrections especially as to characterization of associates of Jones, phases of seamanship and naval tactics, and details of nautical terminology. Captain H. A. Baldridge, U.S.N. (Ret.), Curator of the Museum of the United States Naval Academy, contributed with unflagging zeal to make the book the more accurate and apt from both general and specialized points of view. I note in particular his generosity in preparing the charts and providing the illustrations from the Museum and other acknowledged sources, and his early interest in recommending the manuscript to the attention of the United States Naval Institute. My brothers, Messrs. Keith and Joseph Lorenz, made various suggestions which largely aided me in the undertaking. Mr. John L. Senior of Roxbury, Connecticut, inspired my special gratitude, as I explain in the Dedication, and the least I can do is to honor it with his name.

LINCOLN LORENZ

Hyattsville, Maryland, December 1, 1942.

Past and Present

Who can surprise well must conquer.
> Jones to the American Commissioners to France; Nantes, February 10, 1778.

When an enemy thinks a design against him improbable, he can always be surprised and attacked with advantage. It is true, I must run great risk; but no gallant action was ever performed without danger.
> Jones to the Marine Committee; L'Orient, February 22, 1778.

I wish to have no connection with any ship that does not sail fast; for I intend to go in harm's way.
> Jones to M. de Chaumont; Brest, November 16, 1778.

The situation of America is new in the annals of mankind; her affairs cry haste, and speed must answer them. Trifles, therefore, ought to be wholly disregarded, as being in the old vulgar proverb "penny wise, pound foolish."
> Jones to Robert Morris; Newport, R.I., October 17, 1776.

In time of peace it is necessary to prepare, and be always prepared for war by sea.
> Jones to the U. S. Minister of Marine at the close of the War; Philadelphia, September 22, 1782.

America must become the first marine power in the world.
> Jones to Robert Morris of the Marine Committee, Philadelphia; Nantes, December 11, 1777.

I have not drawn my sword in our glorious cause for hire . . . I hoisted with my own hands the flag of freedom the first time it was displayed on board the Alfred in the Delaware, and I have attended it ever since with veneration on the ocean.
> Jones to the President of the Continental Congress; The Texel, December 7, 1779.

*An honorable peace is and always was my first wish! I can take
no delight in the effusion of human blood; but, if this war should
continue, I wish to have the most active part in it.*
> Jones to Gouverneur Morris; Portsmouth, N.H., September 2, 1782.

*I can never renounce the glorious title of a citizen of the United
States.*
> Jones to Jefferson; Copenhagen, April 8, 1788.

*I can in no situation, however remote I am, be easy while the
liberties of America seem to me to be in danger.*
> Jones to Jefferson; The *Vladimir,* before Oczakow, September 9, 1788.

I saw that I must conquer or die. For me there was no retreat.
> Jones' *Journal of the Campaign in the Liman;* St. Petersburg, 1789.

*I am not ill pleased that you can discover a species of inflexi-
bility in my nature. . . . If I cannot rise by even and direct dealing,
I will not rise at all.*
> Jones to Jonathan Williams; Brest, November 5, 1778.

The first duty of a gentleman is to respect his own character.
> Jones' *Journal of the Campaign in the Liman;* St. Petersburg, 1789.

I have always regarded war as the scourge of the human race.
> Jones to Madame Le Mair d'Altigny; Amsterdam, February 8, 1790.

*The English nation may hate me, but I will force them to esteem
me too.*
> Jones to Madame la présidente d'Ormoy; L'Orient, October 16, 1780.

*I consider this officer [Jones] as the principal hope of our future
efforts on the ocean.*
> Jefferson to William Carmichael; Paris, August 12, 1788.

*The fame of the brave outlives him; his portion is immortality.
What more flattering homage could we pay to the manes of Paul
Jones than to swear on his tomb to live or to die free?*
> Address by Paul Henri Marron at Jones' funeral; Paris, July 20, 1792.

I have not yet begun to fight.
> Jones to Captain Pearson; The *Bonhomme Richard,* off Flamborough
> Head, September 23, 1779.

Contents

PART 3
THE AMERICAN NAVAL LEADER IN WAR ABROAD

PART 4
VICISSITUDES, PERSONAL AND PROFESSIONAL, IN PARIS AND L'ORIENT

PART 5

TRIUMPHS, HONORS, AND LEADERSHIP IN THE UNITED STATES

PART 6

PUBLIC MISSIONS AND PRIVATE INTERESTS IN FRANCE AND DENMARK; THE RUSSIAN APPOINTMENT

Contents

APPENDICES

Charts and Illustrations

(The United States Naval Academy Museum owns the subjects illustrated
except in instances of separate acknowledgment.)

Part 1

The Sailor of Scotland, the West Indies, and Colonial America

◇◇

Chapter I

A Scottish Birthright of Liberty and the Sea

T HE PASSION for freedom and action which marked both the childhood environment and the heredity of John Paul Jones had its image in an expanse of the ocean surging only a quarter mile from the cottage of his birth in Scotland. This small, one-story dwelling of his parents on the estate of a laird in Kirkcud-brightshire lay on a promontory swept by the freshening winds and the swift tidal currents of the Solway Firth. From earliest memories the voices of the sea reverberated in his ears; and the vista of its waters, varying in tinge with the skies and flecked with the sails of vessels as they plied their routes along the coast, gleamed before his eyes even more magnetically.

But the allurement from the headland site of his home in the parish of Kirkbean was less arresting than the panorama from Criffel, the mountain of granite rising eighteen hundred feet only a few miles away. Towards the rugged coast in the nearer distance, this historic landmark opened to view the hills and valleys of an idyllic scene, which characteristically aided some years later to transform the stonecutter Allan Cunningham into the widely known poet. Towards the horizon in the farther distance, this granite height lengthened its outlook upon the majestic expanse of the Solway, the sapphire cliffs and the paled mountains of northern England, and even the remote pathways of the sea, in-viting the gazer to the ocean and the west.

As a child, John Paul—Jones' original name—proceeded not only like others of his age to sail miniature frigates on the inlets neighboring his home, but also like a commodore apart to thunder his imitative commands from an overhanging rock to his fancied captains and fleet. The little haven of Carsethorn Bay, below the nearby mouth of the Nith River and scarcely more than a mile from his doorstep, had its special fascination. Here he scrutinized the large ships at close range as they often sought shelter from storms and as they unloaded cargoes for Dumfries on the upper shores of the river. Here he clambered aboard the strange merchantmen, listened to the vernacular of the sailors, and treasured the tales of distant lands, especially America.

The Highland and Lowland blood of his parents, with its familiar Celtic and uncommon Gaelic strains, was as richly varied as this gentle and rugged region, picturesque, sweeping, and dramatic, which surrounded his birthplace.

His mother, Jean McDuff, was the daughter of a farmer from the thirteenth-century parish of New Abbey, neighboring Kirkbean and bordering the estuary of the Nith above its junction with the Solway. Some members of her race had lived in the district of Kirkbean for an immemorial period;[1] others, it was told, had come from Argyllshire in the west and from the north.[2] She was a Celtic daughter of Caledonia whose blood in the veins of her offspring pulsated with the characteristic fervor of the adventurous Highland clans. She also transmitted her inheritance of a time-honored tradition of the sea bred at the Solway's shores and inborn from Norse migrants to Galloway with the bold instincts of their Viking ancestors.

The family of her husband, John Paul, Sr., was from Fife on the eastern coast, and in this region they had lived the independence of yeomen. But the father of this elder Paul had moved across the Firth of Forth to Leith, near which he had kept what was known as a garden, a combination of a wayside inn and a small market for produce which he raised. His business, according to contemporary views, was a step forward in social prestige, for taverns however unpretentious were almost the only resource of the younger members of landed families when they felt constrained to enter trade. John Paul, Sr., and also his brother George learned in turn the vocation of gardening, but they likewise refined upon it by further study of horticulture. And as young men, both migrated southward to the county of Kirkcudbright.[3]

The father of John Paul had in his Lowland blood the distinctive traits of the regions in which he was born and trained. These qualities combined, according to one of the ablest historians of his country, "an extraordinary mixture of intellectual subtlety and keen practical common sense, of indomitable perseverance and obstinate adherence to old ways, of restless independence and innate respect for authority, of stolid reserve and susceptibility to the stirrings of romance and poetry . . . poverty was at once a hardening experience and an unfailing impulse."[4] Less the historian than the literary artist, Ruskin added in reference to an area including these districts: "All the highest intellectual and moral qualities of Scotland were developed in a well-defined territory of the Lowlands." And he attributed to it "more import in the true world's history than all the lovely countries of the South except only Palestine."[5] But "the Scottish nation," a third historical commentator did not fail to note, "was to the last degree proud and intractable, steeped in the traditions of centuries of independence."[6] Such characteristics indicate, from the side of John Paul, Sr. alone, the potential versatility of his son.

In Kirkbean, shortly after his marriage, the father had become the gardener of Arbigland, the estate of the laird William Craik, whose ancestor of the same name had purchased it about 1690 from the Earl of Southesk.[7] Living here in the stone cottage slightly west of the laird's home, he proved his skill as a landscape gardener by the picturesque design of the grounds, to which magnificent trees of his planting contributed for a century and a half. The genial surroundings throve the more under his practiced hands because he had in Mr. Craik both a kindly master and an inventive agriculturist of nation-wide reputation. In America the laird's scientific talents and human sympathies were to reappear in his natural son, James Craik, the future eminent surgeon and devoted friend of Washington. Such an environment offered also to the youthful John Paul the more gentle, refining influences of nature and affection which he was disposed to cherish, however much they might be obscured by early manifestations of an active, enterprising, and indeed martial temper.

The military and political history of the Lowlands, as well as the modern more warlike reputation of the Highlands, confirmed these dynamic attributes in a child who combined both strains to leaven each other. The Lowlands home of John Paul in Galloway, which comprised Kirkcudbright and Wigtown, was a centre of traditional liberty. From the distant period when the native Gaels had here overthrown Roman sovereignty almost as soon as it was established, this region had fought with relentless perseverance and repeated success for its independence. As distinct as Cornwall was from the rest of England, Galloway, which by name means stranger Gaels, remained proudly itself amid the shires of Scotland. The burnished weapons in the hands of its warriors as they flashed from the rifted clouds of history could not fail to strike the eyes of the liberty-nurtured Scots boy from Kirkcudbright.

His political inheritance was the independent spirit of Britain, south as well as north of the Tweed River and the Cheviot Hills, during her countless years of strife for freedom beginning with the Roman invasion in 55 B.C. But the hostility between the Scotch and English, which reached a climax at the rout of Prince Charles Edward of the Stuarts at Culloden in 1746, rankled in his heart. This epochal defeat was only one year before his birth and only a few before the time that his childhood began to implant deep resentment in its consciousness for the stern penalties which befell the Jacobites after the attempt to seize the throne of Britain. With indelible impressions of British liberty on the one hand and of Scottish nationalism on the other, he was destined to evidence, in his later-adopted America instead of his native Scotland, the freedom made memorable both before and after by warriors like Wallace and Bruce, by literary geniuses like Scott, Carlyle, and Burns, by leaders in religion like Knox and the Covenanters, and by the fierce communal patriotism of the Border ballads.

The intimate family circumstances during Jones' early development were such as to speed him on the militant course towards which he was impelled. They probably had greater force even than those which led illegitimate James Craik to migrate to America. In contrast with the vast reach of sea and mountain that surrounded him, the narrow sphere inside the doorstep of the home destiny was to fight the harder, he must have considered himself of the boy John Paul was the more restricted. An underdog, whose even in childhood as he began to weigh his environment. He lived in a roughhewn stone cottage poor and mean, his father was a servant rather than an employer, he had both a senior brother and two older sisters. Born July 6, 1747, he was the fourth child.[8] William the eldest, Elizabeth born in 1739, and Janet in 1741 preceded him; Mary Ann born in 1749 and two children who died in infancy followed. William was to leave home and emigrate to the West Indies and the American Continent so that any disadvantages John may have felt on the score of an older brother gave place in time to a promising link across the Atlantic. Yet the circumstances were contracted enough. Certainly any possible belief in his youth of the illegitimate birth with which he has been charged[9] was unnecessary as an additional factor to turn his steps as well as hopes to the distance.

Whatever he thought himself, the circumstances of his birth, including the year, have been a question on many tongues. The first sources and the manner of growth of these suspicions provided the basis for their unusual nature and wide publicity. They found their inspiration and coloring chiefly in the assumed authority of such contemporaries as were motivated by ribald jest, false patriotism, and melodramatic chapbooks. Even accounts supported by personal association written by American seamen and petty officers blended the record of their experiences with private malice, sheer gossip, and the grotesquery of sailors' yarns. But later the whisperings flourished even with the knowing nods of some distant relatives of Jones; and the charges of illegitimacy, including the claim that Jones believed them, have gained wide and respected consideration. These reports told that the Earl of Selkirk, or George Paul the brother of John Paul, Sr., or even possibly one of the Dukes of Queensbury was in fact the father of John Paul Jones.

As the scope of the boy grew with his years, his first ventures from home followed in altogether reasonable sequence to his recognized parentage and the environment which it afforded. He undoubtedly visited, perhaps in vessels from the Carsethorn, some of the larger harbors, including Kirkcudbright Bay, which was at this time both the best known port of his own shire and one of the more important of Scotland. It has been said that his very first employment at sea was for a short period in a collier engaged in nearby coastwise trade; such a vessel undoubtedly had Kirkcud-bright and possibly Whitehaven as ports of call. Initial voyages, if not continuous service, in these localities may well account for a probable visit as a stranger to St. Mary's Isle, on Kirkcudbright Bay as it is, and in part for the chimerical traditions of his parentage that arose in its setting. It was at St. Mary's that his uncle George Paul had been employed earlier, that the fourth Earl of Selkirk acquired an inheritance later, and that the Duke of Queens-bury possibly visited some of his distant relatives who owned the estate.[10] Such occasional travels may indicate also wider association among owners of merchant ships than would ordinarily have fallen even to an aggressive youth in his early teens during a period when boys commonly shipped before the mast.

With the bent of his formative years set for a career aboard ships, he was apparently persuasive but deferential in following his wishes. He did not run off for a life of adventure, but had the approval and encouragement of his parents to leave home as his brother had done before him in a period when migration was rife. It is possible that he had also the advice, even the aid, of the employer and friend of his father, William Craik, for he later assured him, "I shall take no step whatever without your knowledge and approbation."[11] So at the age of twelve he closed his books in the small but highly respectable parish school of Kirkbean, and set forth to shape essentially in his own fashion an education as well as a career.

In thus completing the prelude of his childhood, he looked to his sturdy self-dependence. Whether a chance meeting with the Duke of Queensbury was fact or fiction, his early boyhood gave no evidence of initial opportunity at the hands of such a benefactor. Nor did he instinctively turn to George Paul or with higher hopes to Lord Selkirk in search of the prospects which private or public suspicions of their paternity might have induced. Nor, either early or late, did he betray with meaningful irony a rebellious nature, and feel indifference towards a mother and hate for a father. Least of all, in particular during his maturer years, did he turn to cynicism. John Paul had an assertive, dramatic talent, and later quoted and even acted his Shakspere, his limited formal education notwithstanding, but it does not seem that he felt impelled like the illegitimate Edmund in *King Lear* to soliloquize bitterly:

> Why bastard? Wherefore base?

It remains, on the contrary, that the liberty-loving nature of his recognized parents, descended from ancient free-born ancestors and stamped in increasing proportions of intimacy with the manifold qualities of Scotland, the Highlands, the Lowlands, Kirkcudbright, Kirkbean, and Arbigland, was the ultimate heritage of John Paul Jones. And all the diversified forces radiating from the scene of his home to compass points of sea and sky, moor and mountain, gave it direction. His birth and early breeding had progressively fixed his course to sail the Atlantic. He now embarked to live after the manner in which the poet Cunningham of his neighborhood was to sing from his own vantage heights of Criffel and from his own shores of Kirkbean:

> A wet sheet and a flowing sea—
> A wind that follows fast,
> And fills the white and rustling sail,
> And bends the gallant mast—
> And bends the gallant mast, my boys,
> While, like the eagle free,
> Away the good ship flies, and leaves
> Old England on the lea.
>
> There's tempest in yon hornéd moon,
> And lightning in yon cloud;
> And hark the music, mariners!
> The wind is piping loud—
> The wind is piping loud, my boys,
> The lightning flashing free;
> While the hollow bark our palace is,
> Our heritage the sea.

◇◇◇

Chapter II

Shipboy to America, Master to Scotland

B OUND FOR America, John Paul on his initial Atlantic passage looked with a stout boyish heart to the west and the future. He had crossed the Solway to Whitehaven, the town in which his foot probably first touched English soil and his hand undoubtedly first signed an indenture. In the service of John Younger, a merchant engaged in American trade, who also was a member of the Board of Trustees of the Town and Harbor of Whitehaven, he had an opportunity to make the voyage in the *Friendship* of this port, under the command of Captain Benson, to the shores of the Rappahannock in Virginia. The destination was near Fredericksburg, the adopted home of his brother.

When the *Friendship* weighed anchor at daybreak as the sun reddened over the nearby Cumbrian Mountains, Paul to be sure eagerly explored the vessel and energetically turned to his tasks. The harbor, the decks, the rigging, the science of navigation—all of them comprised his intuitive study. However much occupied as an apprentice, he had spare moments to take a favorite station high in the tops and catch glimpses of the receding landscapes.

With the last vision of the rugged Kirkcudbright coast, he must have felt the hardness of his poor and obscure condition along with all that he cherished of Scottish loyalty and love. As the greenish-blue cliffs of St. Bees Head blended with the aquamarine of the sea, he must also have thought of England less in terms of the Lowlands', especially the Border's, traditional hostility than of gratitude for the bridge that Britain afforded him from Cumberland to Virginia. And although his sailor's instinct already may have prompted him to impress upon his memory the outlines of navigable waters of harbor and channel during this first White-haven passage, he cannot have had even a distant premonition of his own pilotage of the course on the memorable occasion that was to mark his last return to the port.

On the day that the *Friendship* arrived at the Rappahannock and sailed up its broad waters, youthful John Paul fastened his eyes upon the novelty and felt the lure of colonial Virginia. He hastened to his brother in Fredericksburg, an early gateway to the West and a centre in Virginia from which the spirit of the Revolution was to spring. In the light of his more mature years and his future deeds, Paul's words in description of the Colonies, "my favorite country from the age of thirteen when I first saw it,"[1] were

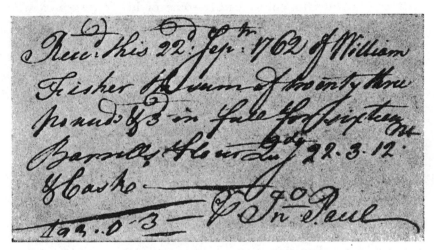

SIGNATURE "Jɴ PAUL" AT AGE FIFTEEN AT
FREDERICKSBURG, VA., 1762

to assume a meaning written in fire and blood. Assuredly America in 1760, with its plasticity for youth and its freedom for individualism, appealed in particular to one of his nature. It was an aboriginal country suited to an adventurous spirit athirst for a pioneer's opportunity and action.

At this colonial period Paul passed a considerable part of the next few years at Fredericksburg in the intervals at port between voyages and perhaps during a leave of absence. He had the opportunity while residing at such times in the home of his brother

William both to gain an early knowledge of the town and its environs and to pursue zealously his reading of books in navigation even to the extent, in his own words, of habitual "midnight study."[2] On occasion he may have aided his brother, who had become a tailor with select customers and a merchant of other pursuits, by delivering clothes and rendering further mercantile assistance. But there is no indication, either on his brother's part or his own, that such duties were congenial to him during these formative years.

In the early democracy of Virginia, such services may have widened the friendships of his youth among the influential persons to whom his brother's business led him. Through William he naturally learned to know readily some of his countrymen who like his brother had come to Fredericksburg. Their number had increased considerably since Culloden had led sympathizers in addition to followers of the Jacobite cause to leave Scotland through compulsion as well as choice. By his own initiative he doubtlessly laid the foundation of acquaintances with merchants and shipowners of nearby counties when his voyages brought him to ports in Virginia and possibly in North Carolina.

But the growing bond with America broke abruptly. After a span of years he learned at the end of one of his passages from Fredericksburg that Mr. Younger found it necessary to close his business as a merchant trader. His employer seems, according to the unusual resignation in 1766 of his trusteeship at Whitehaven, to have become involved in financial difficulties. Accordingly, John Paul had his indentures returned to him. Thus at the home port of Whitehaven he found himself free to choose his course again.

Now he resolved to satisfy a wish which had probably been born when his mimic ships had scudded in the inlets of the Solway. He would enter, if possible, the British Navy. Cannon and all the accoutrements of battle at sea were without doubt already familiar to him.. Merchantmen frequently went armed to the teeth or resorted to convoy for protection not only against buccaneers and pirates, but against privateers of hostile nations and indeed of any countries that happened to roam the seas for easy prey when the greed of ship toward ship on the seas was commonly not unlike the cannibalism of fish toward fish below them. The privateers of

France were to be sure a special source of danger to Britain until the Peace of Paris in 1763. But the marauders without commissions from any government, whose nests were in the West Indies and on the shores of the Mediterranean, knew no truce. Under such pressing need for the self-defense of merchant vessels, he already had thorough knowledge of armament as well as navigation, and, what is more, full recognition of the cruel avarice that largely reigned over the ocean and often changed its aspect in his youthful eyes from romance to tragedy.

The Seven Years' War was only recently ended. It had humbled France more than any other in her recent history, typified as the conditions of peace were by suffering an English governor on her own shores at Dunkirk. Contrastingly, the British flag flew in highest triumph in frigate and ship of the line. Now Paul saw them at Whitehaven, formerly he had espied them in distant waters from the masthead of the *Friendship,* and in the glamour of childhood he had imagined them. His knowledge followed in the footsteps of his interest. "I had made," he was to explain, "the art of war at sea in some degree my study, and been fond of a navy, from my boyish days up."[3] In the circumstances, his self-confidence and resourcefulness were to avail him. Perhaps it was the good will of the Duke of Queensbury which led to an appointment as acting midshipman in the British Navy; possibly it was the influence of Mr. Craik, Mr. Younger, or Captain Benson. It is more to be presumed that his sheer arresting personality and intelligence early manifested themselves and attracted favorable notice so as to be the chief factors in his engagement. These qualities, combined with recommendations of those who could speak of him, would seem to explain his "intimacy with many officers of note in the British Navy,"[4] even if his words be exaggerated in view of his youth at the time of his supposed relations with them. Whatever the avenues of his service, Jones later gave assurance that he "had sailed before this [the American] Revolution in armed ships and frigates."[5]

His term upon a British man-of-war proved neither long nor happy. He had come aboard, in the sailors' vernacular, through the hawse hole rather than the cabin window. He found that the British Navy was almost as autocratic as the French, which required as a feudal tradition that an officer should inherit the blood of four generations of the nobility. Such appointments and promotions as escaped the English artistocratic families could not hope to elude the grasp of political hirelings. If the Navy was still flushed with the spirit of the British lion that had won the French wars, it was soon to become decadent as well as privileged under the rule of Jemmy Twitcher, the sobriquet of Sandwich the Lord Admiral. Of his administration it was said: "The man who studies the Court Calendar will be sorry to see interest so generally take place of long service and real merit. He will find lieutenants of long standing in the Navy set aside for boys, who cannot have the least comparative claims for their pretensions."

Youthful Paul was not disposed by nature to hide his light under a bushel. With speed in decision along with proverbial Scottish pride and poverty sensitive to offense, he did not apparently remain long in a British frigate after perceiving that "family interest had more influence than personal merit."[6] Perhaps he already felt a sting which was to lead him so far in self-assurance as to refer to "that insolent and faithless nation."

He had been disillusioned like many another sailor to find that the prejudice and intrigue behind the curtain of a navy contrasted strangely with the panoply and patriotism on the stage before it. The idealistic Britisher turned practical Scotchman. The poor apprentice in a merchant trader, the ignored acting midshipman in a man-of-war, determined to blunt his squeamish scruples and become a rich officer in a slave ship. So at Whitehaven again, with need at his elbow, he accepted an appointment as third mate in a slaver named—loyal to sovereign and renegade to man—the *King George*. After some service in this vessel, in 1766 he obtained at the age of only nineteen the post of chief mate in a brigantine of Kingston, Jamaica, engaged in the same commerce and likewise cryptically christened the *Two Friends*. Advanced as was his position, lucrative as was his employment, he soon abandoned the nefarious traffic after the arrival of the vessel on one occasion at Kingston as he witnessed and was required to be a party to the cruelty of shipping human cargoes of slaves. He could bear no longer his cumulative distaste.

Today no virtue at all attaches to the condemnation of Negro slavery; in 1768 the man who not only opposed it in principle but refused in practice to stain his hands with the lucre born of its human affliction stood apart from his contemporaries. Fallen among traffickers in a pursuit that had the one doubtful merit of popular acceptance, Paul still in his minority gave proof of an independent, just spirit. Poor, he turned away from the lure of large profits; rugged himself, he was keenly sensitive to suffering of others; restricted by his own birth, he was the more alive regardless of color to the violated liberty of human beings. The trade of many a respected merchant from colonial Massachusetts to Georgia in America and the enactments of many an imposing parliament and cabinet in England were less humane but more obligated.

Even after the Declaration of Independence made slavery an anachronism in theory and success in the war left America free to deal as she wished with a traffic fostered and persisted in by England, the avarice it had engendered and the economic institutions it had established were already ominous. Although Massachusetts was foremost in shaking off the curse by her new constitution in 1783, other states even in New England persisted in the commerce of slaves. As late as 1788 Franklin, in behalf of the Pennsylvania Society for Promoting the Abolition of Slavery, wrote to John Langdon, the Governor of New Hampshire: "The Society have heard with regret that a considerable part of the slaves who have been sold in the Southern states since the establishment of the Peace have been imported in vessels fitted out in the state over which your Excellency presides."[7] The subtlety of Franklin was not put greatly to task in reminding the former private and public ship-builder of the Revolution of his duty, not to speak of his patriotism.

Set against such a background of social compromise, Paul early stood the more apart. His pen witnessed in curious fashion that apparently the cause of the Negro became to him one of the conditions of liberty. In writing a fellow-officer early in the Revolution, he requested him "to put the enclosed into the hands of the celebrated Phillis the African Favorite of the Muse and of Apollo—should she reply, I hope you will be the bearer."[8] What but one of his own first poetic attempts, an ode very likely to the freedom of man black as well as white, would he have sent to the Negro poetess, Phyllis Wheatley, who had been kidnapped in Africa and brought to Boston at the age of eight years, wrote her initial verses at thirteen "To the University of Cambridge in New England," and later received acclaim for her surprising talents in London as well as in Boston. And what the amateur verses to her by the naval officer, undoubtedly more sincere than artistic, may have failed to express, he was already vowed at the time of his letter to write in a more professional hand with his sword.

Stranded in Jamaica after ending his connection with the *Two Friends,* he accepted a type of employment which may seem in one of his vocation even stranger than verse writing. Perhaps the dramatic realities of a life at sea and its opportunities for contemplation, in addition to the distinctive Scotch heritage of John Paul, leavened in his case the romance commonly ingrained in the heart of the sailor, which has expressed itself perforce in the memorable patriotic epigrams of many a famed naval commander and even in the less impassioned but characteristic phrases of minor officers and ordinary seamen. Paul shared traits of those who respond to the lure of the sea, but his complex character also revealed others individual to him. His schooling, short as it had proved, and his private reading, restricted as his professional interests had compelled it to be, combined with his dramatic fervor to equip him with an ear for literary style and a corresponding taste for distinguished sentiments. Although the Scotch pastoral James Thomson was his professed favorite poet, dynamic Shakspere served by word and phrase to ornament many a letter of his prime. Therefore it is not surprising to find him, when his purse was thin and opportunity knocked, an actor in Jamaica.

Here in a troupe which toured the West Indies under the management of John Moody of Shaksperian fame, his first rôle was that of the younger Bevil in the *Conscious Lovers* by Richard Steele.[9] But the part that he must have felt best fitted for his maturing talents was on a scale which the enterprise of Mr. Moody even with his Shakspere repertoire could not hope to provide. It was the immediate drama of life rather than its representation, and its setting was the seas born of nature rather than a stage fashioned by man.

Adventure is to be sure proverbially to the adventurous. With the sea calling him again, Paul stepped at a favorable occasion from the boards of the theatre to the gangplank of a ship. When the *John*, a brigantine at Tobago, slipped her cables in 1768 for her home port, Kirkcudbright, he stood on her deck, a passenger to the same destination.

Early in the voyage Captain MacAdam and the first mate of the *John* died of fever. Their sudden loss was characteristic of the ravages of malaria in tropical countries before the common use of quinine and before the crusade against the anopheles mosquito a century and a half later. The passenger was recognized as the most capable mariner remaining in the ship, and it was he who brought her safely to port to the keeping of her owners, Currie, Beck, and Company, merchants of Kirkcudbright.

"A warrior is always ready,"[10] is a sentiment he was to express and already practiced. In recognition of his resourceful abilities, Paul received the appointment as master and supercargo of the *John* at the age of twenty-one. Bound for America, he had sailed nine years earlier as a boy in the forecastle; to his native Scotland he had now returned as a captain on the quarter-deck.

◇◇

Chapter III

Mungo Maxwell and "Paul Jones"

In Memory
of
John Paul Senior who died at
Arbigland the 24 October 1767
Universealy Esteemed

———

Erected by John Paul Juneor

S o READS the inscription in the ancient churchyard of Kirkbean Church on the tombstone of Paul's father,[1] who was no longer alive at his son's return to hear the good fortune of his captaincy of the *John.* The spelling on the memorial may have indicated the illiteracy of a stone mason rather than the mistakes of Paul, whose proficiency in composition, in any event, improved with years almost beyond belief. As to the avowal of the relationship before the eyes of all who cared to read, it signified that the son both particularly prized the good name of his father and felt no backwardness in bearing witness to his own parentage. Granted that the words of commemoration were not conspicuous for modesty, they were those of a bereaved young son and therefore are scarcely open to criticism on this score. If, however, he thought himself the son of the Earl of Selkirk or of George Paul, or felt mortified because of his humble birth, it is further revealing as to his parentage that he scarcely would have professed such filial regard towards his commonly accepted father and even less likely would have inscribed here in stone the name "John Paul, Juneor."

His ship was tugging at her anchor in the harbor of Kirkcud-

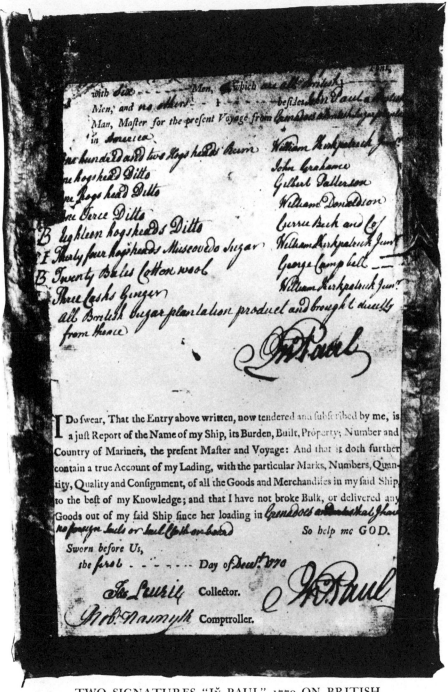

with Six - - - - - Men, which are all British
Men, and no others - - - besides John Paul a British
Man, Master for the present Voyage from Grenada admeasuring
in America

one hundred and two Hogsheads Rum   William Kirkpatrick Jun.
one hogshead Ditto   John Grahame
one hogshead Ditto   Gilbert Patterson
one Terce Ditto   William Donaldson
B Eighteen hogsheads Ditto   Currie Beck and Co
F Thirty four hogsheads Muscovado Sugar William Kirkpatrick Jun.
B Twenty Bales Cotton wool   George Campbell
Three Casks Ginger   William Kirkpatrick Jun.
all British Sugar plantation product and brought directly
from thence

I Do swear, That the Entry above written, now tendered and subscribed by me, is
a just Report of the Name of my Ship, its Burden, Built, Property, Number and
Country of Mariners, the present Master and Voyage: And that it doth further
contain a true Account of my Lading, with the particular Marks, Numbers, Quantity, Quality and Consignment, of all the Goods and Merchandises in my said Ship,
to the best of my Knowledge; and that I have not broke Bulk, or delivered any
Goods out of my said Ship since her loading in Grenada and intending that I have
no foreign sails or sail cloth on board   So help me GOD.

Sworn before Us,
   the first - - - - - - - Day of Decer. 1770
         Jas Laurie Collector.   Jn Paul
         Robt Nasmyth Comptroller.

TWO SIGNATURES "Jñ PAUL" 1770 ON BRITISH
CUSTOMS DECLARATION
Courtesy of John L. Senior

bright. It now devolved mainly upon him to provide for his mother and sisters. So need, enthusiasm for a first command, and the spur of greater freedom as well as responsibility after his father's death combined with his natural energy when he began his duties aboard the *John*. He completed one voyage to the West Indies with despatch and success as both navigator and merchant, and in April, 1770 arrived the second time at Rockley Bay in Tobago. Both his prosperity and repute—the latter already more important to him than the former—were auspicious.

Like the acorn fallen in the field as the potential oak, the life of a young man of exceptional capacity may thrive or decline by reason of a mere incident, and yet the effects of that occurrence often proceed more from character than circumstance. Such imponderables were now to beset the path of John Paul. It happened that the carpenter of his ship, Mungo Maxwell, whose home like his own was in Kirkcudbrightshire, showed himself negligent, incapable, and lazy. Paul had the cat-o'-nine-tails applied to the carpenter's bare back. He might have whipped another member of the crew for somewhat similar reasons in lieu of the provocation by Maxwell. There were undoubtedly additional shiftless seamen not to the taste of a spirited John Paul. Maxwell smarted from the punishment in mind as well as body. And the captain in a calmer moment felt somewhat regretful, but at the same time considered the correction as a routine act of discipline taken in his stride as he speeded on with his activities aboard the *John*.

The marks of several stripes upon his shoulders as evidence, Maxwell appealed for justice to the Court of Vice-Admiralty in Tobago. Judge Surrogate James Simpson examined his wounds and heard Paul in defense. He took no action because of his opinion that the punishment was both slight and warranted by the provocation. The carpenter then left the ship to accept employment on another at the same port, a Barcelona packet bound for Antigua, under the command of James Eastment.[2] And for the present Maxwell passed from the sphere of his former captain and shipmates.

Preparations for the return of the *John* continued apace, although Paul suffered several malarial attacks in the summer heat of the tropics and heard disquieting rumors of his employers' intention to dissolve partnership and discontinue their trade in the West Indies. As his activity had already demonstrated, it was not the nature of the captain to be unready. He regretted that the information had not come more in season to have enabled him with the aid of business acquaintances in St. George's, Granada, to act beforehand and possibly to secure the command of a larger ship, the *Betsy* of London. Paul wrote Mr. Craik concerning the situation; in particular he assured him religiously "it is a maxim with me to do my best, and leave the rest to Providence," and begged the laird of Arbigland "to supply my mother, should she want anything, as I well know your readiness."[3]

In contrast with this modest communication, strange reports reached the laird's ears as they began to thicken in coming from Tobago to Kirkcudbright and Arbigland. Unhappy rumors penetrated even within the walls of the cottage of Paul's mother and sisters. Six months had passed and the *John* had not yet returned from Tobago; but it was whispered among seamen from other vessels that Maxwell had died and that the cruelty of Paul was responsible for his fate. Local gossip was the greater because Mungo happened to be the son of Robert Maxwell, a native of nearby Clonyards, who in his grief made a petition to the Vice-Admiral of Scotland, William Earl of March and Ruglen, and to his deputy, John Goldie, in the jurisdiction of Galloway. The accusation was stern enough, whatever the accuracy of the seamen who provided his vague information: "On board the said vessel, he [Mungo Maxwell] was most unmercifully, by the said John Paul, with a cudgel or baton, beat, bled, and bruised, and wounded upon his back and other parts of his body, and of which wounds and bruises he soon afterwards died on board the Barcelona packet of London, then in the West Indies, and lying near to the place where the said other vessel was. That the informer cannot learn the particular time or place when and where his said son received the aforesaid wounds, nor the particular time or place when and where he died, but he is well satisfied that the men and other sailors on board the said brigantine, upon examination before your lordships, will clear up the matter. . . ."[4]

The warrant for the arrest of Paul, which was served upon him soon after his return in the *John* early in November, 1770 to Kirk-

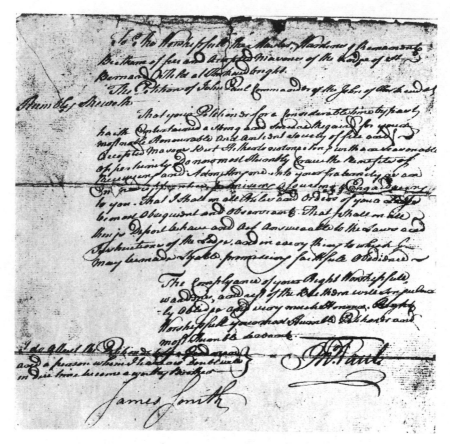

SIGNATURE "J.ᴺ PAUL OF APPLICATION TO JOIN
MASONIC LODGE 1770

*One of the four known extant signatures of John Paul Jones before he adopted
the name of "Jones." Courtesy of John L. Senior, who owns the original letter
written on board the ship "John."*

cudbright, contrasted disagreeably with his first captain's papers when he had sailed in her two years previously from the same port. He was taken shortly to the stout Tolbooth of Kirkcudbright and imprisoned without bail. His confidence was apparent in a petition presented November 15, within a few days after the warrant had been issued, in which he stated: "There is not the least evidence or presumption that Mungo Maxwell died of any abuse received from the petitioner, nor was there any proof brought of his being actually dead." He asked to be liberated on bail to stand trial for the alleged crime; and his request was granted upon the consent of Maxwell's father on the condition that he should appear in answer to any indictment in Scotland within six months under the penalty of "one thousand merks Scots."[5] The gloom of the Tolbooth shadowed him as he hastened to the *John* and his employment with her cargo.

Perhaps it was more than a coincidence that within twelve days of his release he presented a petition of a very different character— a petition for admission to membership in the Masonic Lodge of St. Bernard, Kirkcudbright. The friend who attested it was James Smith, presumably the brother of the junior member of the ship merchants firm of Hewes & Smith of Edenton, North Carolina, an American connection of future importance to him. He was duly admitted to the first and second degrees. As Jones received the second degree on February 1, 1771 and attended at least one subsequent meeting as late as April 9 of this year, it is almost certain that he was admitted likewise to the third degree.[6] Although the popularity of the Masons was great and the occasion in general opportune, Mungo Maxwell may have been the immediate motive for his affiliation in view of a possible emergency. The Masonic records of his membership have the significant notation "Paul Jones entered."[7] While these words were conceivably of a later date, the Maxwell episode links itself also with what bears possible explanation as the first tentative change of John Paul to Paul Jones.

At the outlook of a possible trial for murder, his loyalty reached a crossways whose turning would tend to lead him away from all his Scottish associations. He was quick to take offense. He had by nature a fervent desire for the esteem of men, but it changed to bitterness at a deeply resented accusation. The suspicion, even the lack of confidence, that required of him both bail and his availability for a possible court summons within a half year was little to his taste for independence and honor. He was later to express himself characteristically: "I will not accept the half-confidence of any man living." So he chafed like a restless lion.

In the meantime, as had been expected, Currie, Beck, and Company dissolved partnership, and the *John* was sold. The firm gave him a testimonial on April 1, 1771 that "he approved himself every way qualified both as a navigator and supercargo" and that "all accounts between him and the owners are amicably settled." The association of the Master Mason with the Kirkcudbright lodge seemed to end after April 9, for the time of his possible trial was soon to lapse, the recommendations from his former employers were in his hands, and his speedy departure for new enterprise urged him. He was not disposed, however, to accept tamely the challenge to his good name and to leave it smutched behind him. "I staked my honor, life, and fortune," he wrote to his mother and sisters, "for six long months on the verdict of a British jury, notwithstanding I was sensible of the general prejudices which ran against me; but, after all, none of my accusers had the courage to confront me. Yet I am willing to convince the world, if reason and facts will do it, that they have had no foundation for their harsh treatment."[8]

Although it may be remarked that his bond, not his free will, was surety for the hazard of a trial, biased as it might have been, he took pains when this hazard had passed to enforce his word by deed. He sailed soon from Scotland to the West Indies both to see his former business friends and to secure evidence that the death of Maxwell was not due to him. At Tobago he received an affidavit sworn before William Young, the Lieutenant Governor, and prepared by James Simpson, the former Judge Advocate of the Vice-Admiralty, before whom the carpenter had made his charges, that the latter had "dismissed the complaint as frivolous . . . understood [Maxwell] died afterwards on board of a different vessel on her passage to some of the Leeward Islands . . . in the most solemn manner declares and believes [the charge] to be, in his judgment, without any just foundation, so far as it relates to the stripes . . .

which this deponent very particularly examined."⁹ Although both Simpson and Young seemed to know well the former captain of the *John,* it is improbable that they colored the testimonial appreciably if at all in his favor for this reason.

One affidavit did not satisfy his sensitiveness. Upon the return from the West Indies, both business interests and further vindication of his name brought him in September, 1772 directly to London as they had taken him to the islands. Here a few months later he secured a second testimonial, sworn before the mayor of London, from James Eastment, the master in whose vessel Maxwell had died. This captain averred that Maxwell in the capacity of a carpenter had "acted as such in every respect in perfect health for some days after he came on board . . . the Barcelona packet, after which he was taken ill of a fever and lowness of spirits," and that "he . . . verily believes his death was occasioned by a fever or lowness of spirits, as aforesaid, and not by or through any other cause or causes whatever."¹⁰ There was no basis for questioning the good faith of this testimony.

"You will see," Paul Jones again informed his mother and sisters, "with how little reason my life has been thirsted after, and, which is much dearer to me, my honor, by maliciously loading my fair character with obloquy and vile aspersions." Certainly he had found himself in an unhappy as well as a dangerous situation which the evidence had failed to warrant. It remains true that he was a young commander, probably more often severe than gentle, more often efficient than considerate. Yet the safety and discipline of a ship naturally required by reason of its special isolation and danger a mastery foreign to a society of men on shore. The customs of the sea bred distance between captain and crew to insure authority, and the stern admiralty laws attested to the imminent peril of lesser offenses as well as of mutiny. So it is understandable that, when an occasion for discipline arose, he may have been prone to err on the side of justice tempered more by strict duty than humaneness.

Armed with the two documents to establish his innocence beyond question, he sent a certified copy of one of them, possibly of both, to Mr. Craik, whose "nice feelings," he further wrote his relatives at Arbigland, "will not perhaps be otherwise satisfied.

His ungracious conduct to me before I left Scotland I have not yet been able to get the better of." The laird seemed to have some doubts at first concerning the conduct in Tobago of the ambitious son of his deceased gardener, and this attitude tended to alienate Jones the more from his home ties. He apparently sent testimonials to others whose good opinion he still valued. He was doubly alert to his reputation because it had been impeached, like those who, once bitten by an adder, are always fearful of its sting. "Every person of feeling," he confided, "must think meanly of adding to the load of the afflicted. It is true I bore it with seeming unconcern, but Heaven can witness for me that I suffered the more on that account. But enough of this."[11]

He turned with renewed initiative and vigor to commerce. For a short period his route lay between ports in England and the nearby Isle of Man. As this island had often been linked with the tradition of smugglers from the shores of the Solway, notably from their hidden craggy caverns of Kirkcudbrightshire, it was rumored that Jones engaged in illegal traffic very much in the manner of Scott's later picture in *Guy Mannering* of the brigand Dick Hatteraick along the Galloway coast. The unsubstantial basis of the report was the more obvious because the first entry of licensed goods from English ports to the Isle of Man after its annexation to Britain appeared significantly to his honor under his own name in the custom house books in Douglas the capital. Apart from these records, it is improbable psychologically that a man who had just taken great pains to prove his innocence of one crime and to all appearances prized his character as well as reputation most highly should have exposed himself deliberately and immediately to charges of another.

In command of the *Betsy* of London, which his resources had enabled him to obtain approximately at the end of 1772,[12] he chose to reëstablish his trade in the West Indies as an independent merchant, now that the curtain of Maxwell's death and of the proof of his own innocence had fallen. Strangely and fatefully, during the second voyage of the *Betsy*, as in the second of the *John*, and at the same port of Rockley Bay in Tobago, the curtain of a parallel and an even more serious scene was now to rise.

◇◇◇

Chapter IV

The Mutineer and "John Paul Jones"

S WORD IN HAND, Paul Jones came to a sudden stop on the quarter-deck of the *Betsy* when in stepping backward his heel touched an open hatchway. However resourceful his mind and deft his movement, not a second remained to enter his cabin, shunning as he did an imminent encounter. As the body of a mutinous ring-leader lunged forward with the descending overhead swing of his bludgeon, the sword which the master of the merchantman held fixed for defense ran him through. The major climax of Jones' twenty-six years, close on the traces of the minor crisis involving Mungo Maxwell, was at hand.[1]

Jones in the prime of his young manhood had countered the infuriated attack of a towering ruffian whom he described as of strength even "three times his own." Immediately he was conscious of future evil report more than of present peril. He visualized his unremitting labors from the age of twelve for an honored name and a distinguished career about to sink deeper than before in the darkness of calumny.

Now from the deck the cowed former accomplices and well-wishers of the dead mutineer lying prone in the gangway looked upon the scene. Most of the crew who were well disposed towards Jones happened to be either ashore or below in their hammocks because of illness with fever of the tropics. The first mate only recently advanced to his present office had fraternized with the hostile sailors in his designs upon the command. The second mate on whose justice the captain could have counted was sick along with the seamen. The testimony before a court from such a rout, he knew, would be prejudiced by the drunkenness, theft, and wanton neglect of duty of which they had been guilty only in degree less than their ringleader. And he needed no prompting to realize that the second charge of murder would flame into the greater passion because of suppressed rage of the first.

With all his self-assurance, he had some scruples as to his treatment of the crew. "His all depended on despatch," he said, but in zeal for his own interests he may have overlooked somewhat the interests of others. He had invested all his available funds in a large return cargo and expected to settle his accounts after realizing upon it. The mutineer in his passion had charged that the postponement of wages was fourteen months, which in any event did not apply to himself, for he and others had signed the muster roll at Tobago only since the last passage from London.[2] But it was true that Jones had been in command of the *Betsy* more than a year and that a number of the crew had been with him for that period, approximately from October, 1772 to December, 1773.[3] Whatever discretion the men's agreements may have allowed the captain, he apparently had deferred to pay some of the early enlisted sailors longer than was either considerate or just.

Otherwise there was less reason for repentance. He had provided food, clothing, and quarters for the seamen as competently as his means and the accommodations of the ship afforded. He had been less strict and more considerate in discipline of the crew of the *Betsy* than of the *John*. He had even been mild towards the rebellious sailor until the latter charged at him with a weapon. Although he felt that in truth his hand was not accountable for the blood upon his quarter-deck, the death of the mutineer on the heels of the death of Maxwell left him with deeply troubled thoughts.

Jones left the *Betsy* to hasten to his friends in Tobago. He offered himself freely as a prisoner to a justice of the peace. As the case came within the jurisdiction of the admiralty courts and no admiralty commission was then at the island, the justice stated that he need not surrender himself until one was convened. His previous supporters, James Simpson the former Judge Surrogate who had given him in Tobago his affidavit concerning Maxwell, and William Young the Lieutenant Governor before whom it had been sworn, concurred in the opinion that he should absent himself pending the next session of a commission. All his friends, in fact, urged that for the present he should leave the country. They saddled his horse and insisted that he ride.[4] Probably he was not averse to be persuaded.

In the emergency he placed his business affairs in the hands of associates in Tobago, principally in those of an agent named Ferguson of Orange Valley.[5] He had already persevered so well in his rise from obscure poverty as to have accumulated a balance of £909 in conection with the *Betsy*, £281 in an account with a London merchant, Robert Young, and other assets in Tobago and elsewhere.[6] With confidence in the availability of these resources as his needs and wishes would determine, he set forth with only £50.

Although "that great misfortune of my life"[7] had just happened, which he characterized in these terms however much the mortal sword-thrust had been accidental and in self-defense, the outlook even in the haste of departure was not unpromising. His visions were a land, career, and name—all new. His instinct told him that the new would afford greater liberty to shape his future in an original pattern. Again his destination was America, for which he felt himself best fitted. He would return there not as boy but man, not softened by success but steeled by adversity.

Yet he considered choosing in this pioneer land a vocation nearer to his heart, as he then believed, than his present calling. He was at the first of several psychological periods when repugnance for savage aspects of commerce and of war on the ocean escaped his lips. Distaste for the sea, induced by his harsh experiences and by nostalgia conventionally assumed by the sailor for life ashore, was apparently not the sole influence in his seemingly strange plan. "It had been my intention from the time of my misfortune," he later revealed, "to quit the sea service altogether, and, after standing trial, to purchase some small tracts of land on the Continent . . . I had settled my future plan of retirement in 'calm contemplation and poetic ease.' "[8] The man who already appeared of dynamic personality, a spring poised for action, expressed his transient mood of sentiment and philosophic living in soft accents reminiscent of Thomson, his pastoral Scotch favorite poet. The words harked back to memories of his youth in the romantic as well as stern parish of Kirkbean and indeed in all of picturesque Scotland which he had known. And they came warm from the son of both an imaginative Celtic mother and of an artistically inclined father who had revealed in his chosen vocation as gardener an aesthetic along with a practical intimacy with nature.

A different name seemed fitting, if the transformation was to be complete, along with a new career and country. The first emergency must have suggested the thought, as the records of the Masonic Lodge of St. Bernard possibly indicated; this second and more threatening predicament was to lead him to act fully upon it. Now that anonymity became expedient until the trial, it was the more desirable particularly in another land. The change, which he himself probably suggested, became in fact the recommendation of his supporters in Tobago: "It was the advice of my friends . . . that I should retire incognito to the Continent of America, and remain there until an admiralty commission should arrive in the island, and then return."[9]

Thus his plans determined even as to hidden identity, he galloped off on a horse to a rendezvous on the shores of Tobago in order to embark from there or from the neighboring larger islands of Trinidad or Granada for America. Disguised, it is presumed, in appearance as well as in name before he took ship, approximately at the close of 1773 John Paul of Arbigland and possibly Paul Jones of the Masonic Lodge of Kirkcudbright became John Paul Jones of history.

Chapter V

✧✧

The "Pirate" from Tobago to America

ACTOR AS the former captain of the *Betsy* had been, his talent and experience enhanced his address in the new rôle during his planned interlude as the self-styled John Paul Jones. If at any time so far in his life he justified the epithet of pirate, it may have been paradoxically at this juncture when his design perhaps prompted him to assume the part as an opportune cloak for his disguised identity.

Sailors of later years under the command of Jones, especially those prone to dislike his discipline, who rehearsed versions of the story of his cat-o'-nine-tails as the indirect cause in one man's death and of his ready sword as the direct instrument in another's, had a fanciful structure about which to spin new fanciful yarns.[1] "Are you a pirate, sir," was a question which the seafaring man several centuries ago accepted not as an aspersion but a simple inquiry concerning his business. Even late in the eighteenth century the practices at sea rendered the term more common and less opprobrious than today. What with the nests of marauders from the West Indies, the buccaneers along the American mainland, and the anonymity which Jones adopted at this time according to his later declared "incog," suspicious conjecture has been rife. The word "pirate" has proved especially pleasing to romance when masked with truth to disguise fiction. It had attraction also as an echo of the hate which Jones was to arouse as a formidable adversary.

According to such preconceptions against him, he must have hastened from the scene of the second charge against the honor of his name only to enter immediately and advisedly upon another fraught with greater reflection upon his character. The circumstances indeed may have lent themselves readily to erroneous interpretation. His resolve once fixed to leave Tobago for America, he was not the man to tarry or to be lacking in expedients. He sailed probably on one of the first vessels at hand. If the ship did not proceed directly for a port of his choice, a circuitous route may have proved convenient to cover his traces; if she was small and nondescript, the obscurity may have aided to avoid persons who knew him. For similar reasons he may have preferred not an English but a Spanish or other foreign vessel which hailed from Tortuga, Jamaica, or other islands of the Indies in a period when privateers ravaging the enemy in war and pirate craft preying indiscriminately at all times were less distinguishable in principle than they might seem. Once aboard, he was an experienced sailor adaptable to emergencies.

It is likely that he found himself on a ship none too reputable, perhaps a privateer, perhaps even a corsair. In this craft, apparently, he gained ascendancy over the crew and visited Martha's Vineyard, off the mainland of Massachusetts. A ready acquaintance at the small settlement was the native Thomas Chase, who subsequently became a sailor with him.[2] Jones wished here to provide decent burial for an officer, his predecessor in command, who had been killed in an encounter with a British vessel near Long Island, and he happened to enlist the services of Chase as an amateur carpenter to fashion a coffin. For a few days the inhabitants satisfied their curiosity in regard to the bronzed, hardy young captain, his motley crew, and his strange vessel. In turn the visitors, however surprising their appearance, roamed ashore without giving offense. When the sailors were again aboard, except one or two who had already found future wives, Jones pointed the head of his ship seaward.

To credit more concerning a rakish *Black Buccaneer,* "a set of Spanish and Portuguese desperadoes," and a retreat at Corunna, Spain, not to consider flagrant contradictions of known facts of earlier and later occurrence, is to lend an ear to the gossiping and possibly unscrupulous tongues of three or four none too intelligent seamen who may have sailed at one time or another with Jones. It is to hear them, also, not through the corrective medium of Thomas Chase, but with the ready acceptance of his grandson more than fifty years later, who naïvely confessed as to his hearsay information: "I have never been able to get hold of anything that appears to me so consistent and reasonable."[3]

Whatever the ship in which Jones sailed to America, to all appearances he arrived, as he had planned, in secrecy. She had served his purpose, black as her paint and rakish as her lines may have been. If he had raised his hand as a buccaneer even for a short period, where, first of all, was his booty for immediate comfortable living, not to mention his treasure for positive opulence in the tradition of Captain Kidd and his pieces of eight? The fifty pounds with which he had left Tobago were to dwindle more and more. His penury was not only a price of his successful disguise but also evidence of his honesty. In addition to these circumstances, his abandonment of the slave trade, his reputation which he had been at great pains to sustain after the Maxwell charges, his affirmation to relatives in fullest confidence that he valued his honor dearer than his life, and his self-respect which was implicit in his words and already proved the best witness to his character—all contradicted the ruthlessness of the pirate.

Chapter VI

Incognito in America

WHEN JONES stepped on American soil, he entered upon a further scene in the rôle of his disguised identity. His counselors had recommended that he should not only "retire incog" from Tobago but also "remain incog" on the Continent.[1] Still he may have expected to find a few staunch friends in the adopted country to whom he could divulge his situation and upon whom he could depend not to make it public. With his past traces obscured in a foreign land, his concern must have been less to avoid the citizens of Fredericksburg and of other towns who knew him than to maintain his secret. So now after the approximate fourteen months of his command of the *Betsy* and perhaps an additional month of his circuitous passage from Tobago to his American destination, he returned first, for at least a short, retired, and perhaps somewhat disguised visit, to his familiar surroundings in Virginia, particularly in Fredericksburg, at the close of 1773 or the beginning of 1774 upon the outset of his new career.[2]

His reasonable initial purpose was to learn of if not to see his brother. He must have found William mortally ill, or, as is more likely, already in his grave. Tradition tells that his brother died towards the end of 1773;[3] his sandstone slab in St. George's Protestant Episcopal Church in Fredericksburg records "Wm. Paul, 1774." It is possible that the date at the grave may coincide with the year in which Jones returned to Fredericksburg and in which, according to the words marking the restoration in 1930, he "first set in place" the stone, rather than with the actual year of William's death. The original sandstone and in addition the probate of a will late in 1774 are more reliable for corroboration of the time of his brother's death as well as of Jones' reappearance than both tradition and its uncertain basis in the memory of an eye-witness. Judge

Francis T. Brooke of St. Julien, near Fredericksburg, wrote somewhat vaguely more than fifty years later: "All I remember of John
Paul Jones I had from my brother [Dr. Laurence Brooke] who was
surgeon of the *Bon Homme Richard* the whole of his celebrated
cruise. I think I remember when very young to have seen him in
the year 1773. I was at school in Fredericksburg and his brother
William Paul was a Scotch tailor who made my clothes. On his
death John came to Fredericksburg to administer on his property.
I think I saw him in the shop when I went for my clothes. . . . I
do not think he remained long in Fredericksburg. The next year I
think he was employed in the Navy."[4]

However blurred as to time and circumstance, this glimpse of
Jones at one of the properties of his deceased brother, probably
the shop and house at Main (or Caroline) and Prussia streets, of
which the site if not the original structure still remains today, gives
credence, along with the gravestone and tradition, that he made
bold to return without delay to Fredericksburg. The immediate
reason for his coming must have remained unknown to all except
a chosen few. And the coincidence of William's death lent color in
the minds of citizens to his sudden presence, as the mists of recollection indicate. He obviously was not disposed to disillusion them
in regard to the pressing circumstances of his re-entry on American
soil.

According to the will of his brother, which had been executed
on March 22, 1772,[5] Jones' arrival was neither expected nor necessary. William Paul had bequeathed his estate of "lots and houses
in this town" and of other property to his youngest "beloved sister
Mary Young (*née* Paul) and her two eldest children."[6] Nowhere
within the instrument did he even mention his younger brother.
This omission was presumably no special slight in his case, for
William had likewise made no bequest to either his two other
sisters or his mother. At the same time, neither the provisions of
the will, nor the property, nor the name William Paul retained at
his death, nor any family record gave any basis whatever for the
future report that either he or Jones himself received a heritage
from a William Jones or a Cadwallader Jones in Virginia and
adopted his surname as a condition for becoming his heir.[7]

In the administration of the estate of William Paul, apparently the unannounced advent of Jones caused complications. The will was not probated until December 16, 1774,[8] seemingly an extended date following the testator's death. The two executors named in the instrument renounced the office for some unspecified reason; in their place one of the witnesses to the will, John Atkinson, received the appointment as administrator. It may be true that Jones was responsible for the change in executors, that he acted by proxy, and that his name failed to appear upon the document only because of his incognito.

No financial benefit, however, accrued to Jones for the present. The personal property was seemingly small as judged by Atkinson's bond of five hundred pounds; the real property must have required time for sale and settlement, and the ports of Virginia already may have become closed before the proceeds proved available for transmission to Scotland. Whatever the reasons, the nature of the administration remained obscure. The Court of Spottsylvania County has no record of the settlement of the estate.[9] And the mother and sisters of Jones in Scotland, including the married sister Mary named in the will, continued seemingly unaware of its terms. Even fifty years later Jones' niece, Miss Janette Taylor (the daughter of Janet his second and favorite sister), who particularly cherished her uncle's name and provided the material for his early responsible biographies, believed that William Paul died intestate, his brother was his heir at law, and he recovered about ten thousand dollars from what she termed "the wreck" of William's fortune.[10]

Ultimately, all the proceeds from "the wreck," it is fairly certain, came into Jones' hands. With these funds presumably in mind, truth more than pride prompted some of his assertions several years later apropos of disinterested motives for his services in the war. "I stepped forth," he wrote on one occasion, ". . . not in search of riches, whereof, I thank God, I inherit a sufficiency";[11] and "My fortune is liberal enough," he wrote on another, "having no wife and children . . ."[12] But neither some of his friends in America who must have known of the will nor his relatives in Scotland who were unaware of it entertained any sentiments which were not to his honor. Although he had other means at this subsequent period of avowal of financial independence, his special professions of duty and love towards relatives pointed to conscientious dictates to fulfill honorably a self-appointed trusteeship as well as to follow the natural promptings of a son and brother.

With his incognito still not set wholly aside, early in the war he was to send several small amounts, although they happened to miscarry, by indirect means to Arbigland;[13] it had been his endeavor, as he wrote to no less important a confidant than Franklin, "to watch over the happiness of my poor relations *unseen*." Likewise at this stage he was to make a will, which, according to his testimony, "will evince that I have not been unmindful of the duties which I owe to nature."[14] In a more noteworthy instance, when precariously occupied in the Revolution, he was to charge a friend at Tobago, in words dictated by love rather than obligation, to oversee his provision for his parent: "As I hope my dear mother is still alive, I must inform you that I wish my property in Tobago, or in England, after paying my just debts, to be applied for her support. Your own feelings, my dear sir, make it unnecessary for me to use argument to prevail with you on this tender point . . . she has several orphan grandchildren to provide for."[15]

Thus his filial thoughtfulness, his sole presence in America as the kin of William Paul, the hazards of communication before as well as after the ports had closed, and perhaps the arbitrary nature of his brother's will—all these considerations weighed in the balance in favor of the discretion which Jones apparently exercised as a self-appointed trustee. His habitual assurance may well explain the readiness to act in this capacity. His wishes were, indeed, to provide suitably for his relatives, even from funds of his own as well as from those of his brother; but he also was not averse to doing so, in a manner somewhat reminiscent of his connection with the *Betsy* crew, with regard first to his own interests and ambitions.

Unfortunately for Jones, in sharp contrast with his comparative affluence when the proceeds from his brother's estate and from some of his own past business enterprises came into his hands several years after this arrival in America at Fredericksburg, was his unexpected privation for a long period beginning with his flight from Tobago with only fifty pounds. Under his disadvantages of both secrecy and scant funds, Ferguson, his agent in Tobago, and even Robert Young and Thomas McCall, his merchant associates in London, proceeded unscrupulously to betray his trust. Of these supposed friends in England, he was to write: "I pity their little souls who could be capable of taking such mean advantages of my situation after having inspired me with full confidence."[16] Of the faithless deputy in the West Indies, he was to say: "He left me in exile for twenty months, a prey to melancholy and want, and withheld my property, without writing a word in excuse of his conduct."[17]

Adrift in such fashion, Jones saw many months pass—eighteen before the ports closed and the possibility of trial by an admiralty court came to an end, twenty while the fifty pounds and any other emergency resources vanished. Obscure, he became the more appreciative of a supporting hand. To understand his future part in the Revolution is not to fail to consider his pledge of fidelity to opportune benefactors in America—a pledge which the twenty months impressed cumulatively upon his sympathies.

During these protracted months, both the circumspection and the interests of Jones undoubtedly prompted his departure from Fredericksburg soon after the completion of his immediate affairs connected with his brother. Even his limited stay, however, must have confirmed the attraction for Virginia that he had felt almost fifteen years earlier upon coming to her shores as an apprentice in the *Friendship*. Now the liberty-loving atmosphere began to assume an incomparably more dynamic, militant quality.

Influences were close at hand. Washington had lived his boyhood on the Ferry Farm, which lay picturesquely in view on a hill above the Rappahannock, less than half a mile from William Paul's house. Six generals of the Revolution were to come from Fredericksburg. Jefferson, Henry, Monroe, and Marshall would soon be familiar faces in the environs. Many patriots of national reputation, including Washington, belonged to the local Masonic lodge, organized possibly as early as 1735, certainly by 1752; and it is understood that Jones, now a Master Mason, attended on occasion.[18] Fredericksburg was indeed a centre of the spirit of the Revolution even in such a distinctive American colony as Virginia.

The time and place were ripe to enlist not only Jones' patriotism but also his affection. He probably renewed and established friendships in nearby counties of Virginia both during and following his stay in Fredericksburg. His incognito naturally led him to less populous places. Likewise his previously mentioned resolves concerning retirement in "calm contemplation and poetic ease" must have drawn him away from the town.

In neighboring Hanover County lived his amiable friend, Dr. John K. Read, the nephew of Franklin's wife Deborah, whose rustic mood harmonized during this period with his own. Possibly their acquaintance had begun somewhere in Scotland, if not in Virginia, when Read, like all students of medicine in colonial times, went abroad for his training, presumably to Edinburgh. Possibly, too, they met through Masonic affiliations, for the order was then fully as flourishing in Virginia as abroad and drew to its membership almost all persons of repute. The bond between them became close; Jones confided to his friend the secret of the mutineer's death, the circumstances in which his financial agents had abandoned him, and even his more personal family concerns. He impressed Read at this time and later so far that his friend attributed to him "a nice sentiment of honor and the sure though slow reward of merit."[19]

Jones inspired, in fact, the affection along with the respect of this cultivated man. The supposedly hardened sailor lived a contemplative rural interlude that mirrored qualities of the heritage from his forbears and his Scotland. "I was inexpressibly pleased," Read wrote in retrospect, "at the receipt of your last. . . . Shall I tell you I had my fear that my friend had forgot me—but those fears were momentary and gave place to other feelings when I reflected on the many sentimental hours which (solitarily enough) passed between us at the *Grove.* I never missed an opportunity of inquiring after you. . . ."[20] The *Grove,* it is presumed, was the not uncommon name of Read's home, which he probably occupied alone in 1774 between the death of his first and his marriage to his second wife.[21] These circumstances of Read together with the recent experiences of Jones may particularly explain that their mood disposed them to hours described as sentimental and solitary.

Their attitude, however, although possibly in step with the tradition of sensibility late in the eighteenth century, was by no means one of softness. Read's action probably bespoke his mind; he shortly married a second time. Jones was now or soon to be in love, and chose characteristically as high as his heart moved him. Not far from the residence of Read was the home of young Dorothea Dandridge, who by both her mother and her father was descended from eminent British nobility. For her he felt, so far as is known, the first passion of his manhood. And he must have suffused it with his philosophic dream of a home among the hills and rivers of Virginia and with a tenderness and fire prophetic of his spirit. But his still-shadowed name, his obscure background, and his actual need, along with the cumulative rumblings of war, set in movement an opposing tide of emotions which impelled him to bide his time. And, to all appearances, with wisdom in silence.

Whatever ambitions he may have entertained for making his vision real, after the romantic fashion of a strong and reticent soldier-lover returning with glory if not also fortune, were to end several years later when Read informed him from a distance of three thousand miles: "You tell me you are under some expectation of purchasing a Virginia estate; but some more agreeable idea will, I fear, call you off and deprive us of you. Miss Dandridge is no more—that is, she a few months ago gave herself into the arms of Governor [Patrick] Henry."[22]

◇◇◇

Chapter VII

Joseph Hewes—Willie and Allen Jones

NOT THE passion of love but the sentiment of gratitude linked with honor—"gratitude for unmerited favors received from America before that Continent declared itself to be independent of Britain, and at the time of that declaration"[1]—now was to impel Jones particularly to his future course as one of the first of America's citizens and warriors. Although the estate of his brother, the camaraderie with Read, and the allure of Dorothea Dandridge determined in the main the regions of his sojourn in Virginia, the close friendship with James Smith, his Masonic sponsor at Kirkcudbright, probably led his steps also to Edenton, North Carolina. It was North Carolina which happened to be a special haven of Jacobite followers of Prince Charles Edward after their emigration from Scotland.

In this State, undoubtedly the James Smith in question was the former "son of fortune"[2] whom Jones compared with himself, a fellow master of merchant ships subject to the many accidents of trading at sea, whose brother happened to be Robert Smith, the junior member, as previously indicated, of Hewes & Smith, ship merchants in Edenton and owners of a branch business in Philadelphia. Their vessels were known in many ports, especially in those of the West Indies. James had proved a trustworthy friend at his hour of need after the Mungo Maxwell charges;[3] now in a second less immediate but more dangerous emergency, he must have sought him again. Whether or not he found him is uncertain. He did meet Robert, however, at this time or another, in Edenton or possibly later in Philadelphia;[4] and he soon made the acquaintance of Joseph Hewes, the senior member of the firm, at the seaport on Albemarle Sound.

"Edenton," it has been said, "might well have been styled the granary of the province . . . within its limits and in its immediate vicinity there was, in proportion to its population, a greater number of men eminent for ability, virtue, and erudition than in any other part of America."[5] Yet amid such competitive quality, Hewes was "the patron and the greatest honor of it."[6] He achieved success as a merchant and won honor as a statesman. But if self-sacrifice appears to best advantage on the battlefield, he was fitted to win renown as a soldier. In addition to special amenities attributed to him, Hewes evinced a public devotion which repeatedly won him the election first to the Assembly of North Carolina and later to the Continental Congress.

In the interim of Jones' incognito, late in 1774 or early in 1775 in the South, rather than subsequently at the seat of the Continental Congress in Philadelphia, he confided to Hewes as he had already imparted to Read his situation in America. He must have told him much now, as he told him even more later upon referring to "all the former misfortunes of my life."[7] Egocentric as Jones may have been in the difficulties that beset his ambitions, he already evinced devotion to men and principles, and it was the ardor of such feelings which was destined to transform his strong sense of personal interest into the highest public service. In his zeal to rise, his means revealed ever-increasing discrimination, as already evidenced by his successive steps from shipboy on the *Friendship* to progressive rank in the British Navy, the slave traffic, and the merchant trade. When Hewes saw a potential warrior like Jones, the patriot must have recognized him almost immediately for what he was. And now that the one was benignant, the other grateful, and both were destined to be equally ardent at the growing challenge to liberty, a prospect of service in a Continental Navy began to unfold.

Perhaps, but less likely, it grew also under other influences. As the friendships of Hewes were extensive, he knew, of course, the two Jones brothers of North Carolina, Willie of Halifax County and Allen of Northampton.[8] In recognizing that their homes were reasonably near Edenton, it is possible that Hewes introduced John Paul Jones to them, or that he met them independently.

They were among the wealthiest men of the province, outstanding in social prestige, and important as politicians and statesmen. An old tradition associates the newcomer to America with one or both of them;[9] it tells in variant form and nature that he not only knew them but passed a period at their estates, that he not only enjoyed their hospitality in his obscure and almost penniless situation but owed to them his appointment in the American Navy, that he not only received through them his commission and a sum of money but adopted their name in token of his gratitude and with the vow to honor it.

Traditions often acquire embellishments which distort but do not invalidate their partial or basic truth; so it becomes the more difficult to view them with justice. The charges concerning Mungo Maxwell, however, may have been the occasion for the first change of John Paul to Paul Jones as recorded in the books of the St. Bernard Lodge possibly long before he is supposed to have met Willie or Allen Jones and adopted a new name in America.[10] And certainly the death of the mutineer was the occasion for the second, if not also the first, change from John Paul to Paul Jones and John Paul Jones in accordance with his declared incognito upon leaving Tobago and choosing a tentative home on the Continent.[11] Thus the pseudonym *Jones* had a distinctive cause for adoption, it reasonably assumed this particular form because of the special anonymity which the popular name *Jones* like *Smith* promoted, and it fulfilled an immediate as well as general purpose after his flight to America for secret communication with his agents and others in Tobago. None of these rational motives had any apparent connection in incident, time, or place with the brothers Willie and Allen.

On the contrary, the circumstances under which Willie Jones is supposed to have extended his hospitality to the wanderer from Tobago are in almost every case difficult to reconcile. The estate in Halifax County on which "the Grove" was erected and at which Willie Jones is said to have received him belonged as late as 1776 to his future father-in-law Joseph Montford, and he became its owner only after his marriage to Montford's daughter Mary following her father's death.[12] It is inconceivable, therefore, that "the many sentimental hours which (solitarily enough) passed between us at 'the Grove,' " according to Read in reference to John Paul Jones and himself, could have occurred in 1776 or later, instead of in 1774 or 1775 when the newcomer to America was last known to be in Fredericksburg, presumably elsewhere in Virginia, and possibly in North Carolina.

It is most unlikely, also, that "the Grove" in question was not Read's own home in Hanover County, Virginia, within a reasonable distance from Fredericksburg.[13] Otherwise, by implication, he as well as his comrade journeyed coincidentally to the residence of a host as far away as Halifax County in North Carolina; and there, as a reward for their pains, the master, the mistress, and the other guests had such views of hospitality and courtesy as to permit them to pass their time "solitarily enough." If, on the other hand, the visit is supposed to have occurred at the bachelor home of Willie Jones, or at the estate of the father of Mary Montford before her marriage in 1776 and the construction of a mansion with the popular name of "the Grove" on its acres, or at the residence of Allen Jones in Northampton County—in any of these views, the tradition of a visit, unsupported by consistent particulars, assumes the form of variable reminiscence combining some possible truth with other certain fiction.

The claim that John Paul Jones owed his first commission in the American Navy to Willie and Allen is even less substantiated than his reputed sojourn at their homes. Influential as the North Carolina brothers were, it appears that in comparison with Joseph Hewes they had little opportunity or reason at this period to aid the future naval officer. Neither was, like Hewes, a shipowner and merchant who could best appreciate Jones' talents and had many connections naval as well as commercial. Neither was to be, like Hewes, a member of the First and Second Continental congresses and of the early Naval Committee of seven, which had direct knowledge and authority regarding the Continental Navy appointments. Neither, it appears, has, like Hewes, left behind him a moderate but eloquent number of letters from Jones to attest an intimate association with his first services in the newly organized navy. Even the copy of the Houdon bust of the Revolutionary officer which was subsequently offered to the North Carolina Legislature seemed to be tacit confirmatory witness to his naval appointment through Hewes rather than other citizens of the State.

The tradition concerning the generosity of the brothers Willie and Allen towards John Paul Jones remains intangible. Unless some subtle reason weighed with the stranger in America, circumstances deny that his name, good will, or naval preferment was particularly associated with them. His boldness might have prompted him to seek their influence, and his personality might have led him to the society of their houses, even if obstacles rendered the approach difficult. But strange indeed is the absence of any written word either between them and the future naval officer or even contemporaneously among their friends—there exists a pin as a possible memento[14]—to establish a credible relationship. The doubt is the greater because Jones was very articulate in expressions of gratitude whenever they were due as well as whenever they served his interests. One motive, somewhat ironical, may possibly remain for both thankfulness and reticence by him in this particular case—the willingness if not the positive effort to curtain as much as possible from history the actual unhappy reason for the change from Paul to Jones by the ready expedient of a false scent, the coincidence of his adoption of the popular name *Jones* and of the possession of this family name by Willie and Allen.

It is rather to be remembered that if Jones wished to adopt as a tribute the surname of the man whose beneficence in the period of his incognito gave him his greatest opportunity, there seems little doubt that he would have chosen that of Hewes. The new citizen and future naval officer of America was to write him in simple sincerity: "You have laid me under the most singular obligations, and you are indeed the angel of my happiness, since to your friendship I owe my present enjoyments as well as my future prospects. I will not attempt to thank you by letter, but endeavor to prove by my conduct that your friendship and good opinion are not misplaced."[15] In other instances he was to declare to a confidant "the great obligation I owe to Mr. Hewes"[16] and to assure Hewes himself of "a heart that esteems you with perfect gratitude."[17]

Part 2

The American Lieutenant, Captain, and Squadron
Commander in War at Home

◇◇◇

First Lieutenant in the Continental Navy

AFTER HEWES had returned to Philadelphia as a member of the Second Continental Congress, Jones also travelled northward in the summer of 1775 to the executive seat of America. England closed the ports of the Colonies in July of this year, and thereby locked the door, at least for the period of the Revolution, against his intended return to Tobago for trial by an admiralty commission. "I had waited," he himself described, "that event eighteen months before swords were drawn and the ports of the Continent were shut."[1] The Continental Army under Washington became a reality at Cambridge early in the summer; Jones was now one of the first to offer his services at the prospect of a Continental Navy. "I had not then heard the doctrine of independence even in a whisper and . . . I could have no views of protection from a new government,"[2] the volunteer claimed in evidence of his disinterested patriotism.

Scrupulously he avowed still further so as to dispel any suspicion of an ordinary refugee from justice hiding under a pseudonym and seeking escape in the turmoil of war: "As I adhered to my first resolution of returning to the West Indies to stand trial, and to settle my affairs there as soon as peace should be restored to the Continent, it was the advice of my friends that I should, till that wished event might be brought about, remain incognito."[3] Such were his confidences to Benjamin Franklin at a later date as well as to John K. Read at this time in explanation of his conduct following the mortal thrust of his sword in self-defense against the ruffian mutineer of the *Betsy*. They implied his reasons for open adoption of the name John Paul Jones when he came to Philadelphia and sought to enlist in the cause of America as one of her first patriots.

It may be said of Jones as an individual, with due qualification as to time and place, essentially what John Adams remarked concerning the Colonies: "The Revolution was in the minds and hearts of the people . . . to be traced back for two hundred years, and sought in the history of the country from the first plantation in America."[4] All indeed were ultimately Britons, those born and bred in England or in Scotland or in America. Therefore when some of these citizens attempted to subjugate others among them, they inevitably invited civil war by reason of an effort to force upon their kin chains which their own memorable struggles from a day even more distant than Magna Charta had broken.

Tory England in the time of George III, proud as an empire following the burning humiliation of France at the Peace of Paris in 1763, became unmindful of her traditions of freedom, and her sons in the Colonies happened to be the victims of her forgetfulness. Although Jones was born a Scot, not an American, it remains that Scotland's love and struggle for liberty was more time-honored than America's by hundreds of years and that this particular son of Caledonia had been inured to circumstances even sterner than those of the typical frontiersman. As a child he had seen the widespread desolation and death in Scotland that followed in the train of the crushing defeat at Culloden, and as a young man he had come upon its traces even among refugees in the Colonies. Culloden was, to be sure, a decisive battle in the English conquest of the land of his birth; therefore it served as an added strong reason for his support of America. His intermittent sojourns in the New World from the age of thirteen,[5] especially his residence in the Colonies during the years 1774 and 1775, had made him particularly alive to its virgin contrast with the Old World and heightened the more his inherited sympathies, boldness, and decision.

When Jones arrived at Philadelphia from the South, he had been imbued with the passionate spirit of resistance that her colonies had already shown. His thoughts and his language as well as his future deeds sprang at first essentially from the environs of Fredericksburg and indeed the whole South. In Virginia, Jefferson

had recently penned the State resolutions with their earnest appeal
to "the even-handed justice of that Being who doth no wrong,"
and Henry had delivered his ringing challenge of "liberty or
death." In North Carolina, Hewes and his fellow-delegates to the
Second Continental Congress were empowered to present the
Mecklenburg County Resolves of May, 1775 which proclaimed
actual independence, but they refrained from doing so formally
because they thought that the times were not ripe for their acceptance. In South Carolina, Gadsden repeatedly and fearlessly
exhorted the colonists to maintain their rights. In every colony
resistance to the royal governors led to bitterness and conflict more
and more crucial. Even before Virginia's special grievance at the
burning of Norfolk, Lord Dunmore had been an object of particular hate, and Jones was later to write of his "perfidy and ingratitude." The newcomer in Philadelphia heard the accounts of ever-
increasing conflict in New England, especially in Massachusetts.
His naval background made him particularly mindful of operations by sea, beginning with such hostilities as the devastation of
Falmouth (Portland) by the British and the burning of the *Gaspee*
and the capture of the *Margaretta*, English revenue vessels, by the
Americans.

To understand the enlistment of Jones in the cause of America
is to appreciate his humaneness as well as intrepidity. Retaliation
for cruelties of war and redemption of prisoners were among his
first and most zealous objects. Falmouth in ashes in October, 1775
and its roofless men, women, and children exposed to the rigors
of a Maine winter had stirred him as much as the most indignant
members of Congress. And that the destruction was not irresponsible but expressed a fixed policy appeared in the later concurrence
of George III in any plan of "distressing America, . . . recommending that the rebels should be annoyed by sudden and unexpected
attacks of their seaboard towns during the winter."[6] The fact remains, however, that before the British burned the town, the inhabitants had first prevented them from loading a ship with
timber and, following this hostility, had refused to surrender their
arms and ammunition.

How unfortunate but characteristic that the fraternity between
Englishmen and Americans once broken was to result, like the di-

vision between Americans of the North and South in the Civil War, in greater cruelty than most conflicts between unrelated peoples. Even Franklin, whose words were usually well-weighed, prepared at this early period a letter intended for the Englishman Mr. Strahan: "You are a member of Parliament, and one of that majority which has doomed my country to destruction. You have begun to burn our towns and murder our people. Look upon your hands! They are stained with the blood of your relations! You and I were long friends; you are now my enemy and I am yours."[7] It is not surprising, then, that Jones the sailor, certainly of more impetuous blood than Franklin the statesman, philosopher, and scientist, should in those impassioned times have volunteered his services and even later contemplated "to teach the enemy humanity by some exemplary stroke of retaliation."

A generous but more personal motive than the spirit of freedom and humanity which he identified with America also influenced him. His love of admiration, related to a deep sense of gratitude, sought the applause especially of those towards whom he felt respect and obligation. He was partly disposed to fight just for the sake of his private loyalties. John Paul was a name still clouded; John Paul Jones was another almost unknown. Equally unfortunate from a practical point of view in his obscure new situation in America, he was nearly penniless because his unscrupulous agent in Tobago had taken advantage of his adopted rôle to withhold remittances from his property. His chivalric declaration to a confidant, Stuart Mawey in Tobago, was in character: "After an unprofitable suspense of twenty months (having subsisted on fifty pounds only during that time), when my hopes of relief were entirely cut off, and there remained no possibility of my receiving wherewithal to subsist upon from my effects in your island, or in England, I at last had recourse to strangers for that aid and comfort which was denied me by those friends whom I had entrusted with my all. The good offices which are rendered to persons in their extreme need ought to make deep impressions on grateful minds; in my case I feel the truth of that sentiment, and am bound by gratitude as well as honour, to follow the fortunes of my late benefactors."[8] "Gratitude as well as honor," then, was the banner under which he volunteered to step aboard a Continental frigate.

Evidently at Philadelphia in the autumn of 1775, about twenty months, as he said, after his arrival in America, these strangers had opportunely proved his benefactors. Possibly one was James Read who had the office of signing Continental currency; he was the father of Dr. Read, whose recent comradeship with Jones impelled him to write three intimate letters from Virginia to his friend in Pennsylvania, regardless of no replies, from the time of Jones' departure in the summer until October 13.[9] Probably another disposed to aid him was Jefferson, who served as Read's intermediary for one of his messages.[10] A third may have been James Smith, the sailing master of Philadelphia whom Jones knew, presumably his Masonic friend and the brother of Robert Smith, the partner of Hewes.[11] And certainly a fourth was Hewes himself.

As a member of the Second Continental Congress and one of its ablest authorities on ships and commerce, Hewes "the patron and greatest honor"[12] of Edenton kept Jones well in mind. The memory of John Adams must have been at fault many years later—he himself termed it a sieve in his old age—in his reference to Hewes as one of the last instead of the very first to advocate drastic action for independence.[13] Although a statesman, the North Carolina delegate was ardent to be a soldier, and wrote as early as July, 1775 to his noted fellow townsman Samuel Johnston: "I consider myself now over head and ears in what the Ministry calls rebellion. I feel no compunction for the part I have taken nor for the number of our enemies lately slain at the battle of Bunker Hill. I wish to be in the camp before Boston, though I fear I shall not be able to get there till next campaign." Apart from his essential services in Congress, he declared further: "We ought to bring ourselves to such a temper of mind as to stand unmoved at the bursting of an earthquake. . . . I have furnished myself with a good musket and bayonet, and when I can no longer be useful in council, I hope I shall be willing to take the field." Not many members of Congress, John Adams included, who were physically fit to be soldiers, not to consider those of Hewes' frailty, expressed equal eagerness to adopt this course.

It was Hewes likewise who had, as he confessed, "the weight of North Carolina on my shoulders within a day or two of three months" preceding the Declaration of Independence. "I have sat some days from six in the morning till five or six in the afternoon without eating or drinking."[14] Along with their common interest in ships and the sea, the potential warrior in Hewes must have recognized the fighter in Jones.

The very first measures towards creating a Continental Navy were practically beyond the direct province of Congress as well as Hewes. When Washington organized his heterogeneous army at Cambridge in the summer and fall of 1775, the lack of powder, ordnance, and equipment in general was most acute. It had been one of the first precautions of the mother country to render the Colonies dependent upon her for military stores, and of powder in particular there were neither immediate supplies nor adequate technical skill and facilities for its manufacture. "It is not in the pages of history, perhaps," Washington wrote to Congress in January, 1776, "to furnish a case like ours. To maintain a post within musket shot of the enemy, for six months together, without powder . . . is more probably than ever was attempted."[15]

In such dire need, the Commander in Chief undertook his earliest naval enterprises upon his own initiative. As early as August 4, 1775 he requested Governor Cooke of Rhode Island to send an armed ship of the colony to "Bermuda where there is a very considerable magazine of powder in a remote part of the island and the inhabitants are well-disposed." On September 2 he himself began to fit out and commission "armed vessels with the design to pick up some of their storeships and transports." In this manner, with the approval of Congress, which still had no ships, he applied to Massachusetts for two armed vessels for the purpose of intercepting several brigs laden with military supplies; they had sailed from England bound for Quebec and were expected at the Gulf of St. Lawrence. The ensuing enterprise under the command of Captain Nicholas Broughton of Massachusetts missed the brigs, but Washington quickly organized other expeditions manned by sailor-trained volunteers of his army to cruise in Massachusetts Bay. He did not scruple in his desperate need to commission privateers as well as to employ vessels of the separate colonies and of the Continental Government. He confided in October to his brother John, "I have fitted out and am fitting out several privateers and I have no doubt of making captures of several of their transports."[16] "In answer to your in-

quiries respecting armed vessels," he informed in November
Richard Henry Lee of the Congressional Naval Committee, "there
are none of any tolerable force belonging to this Government. I
know of but two of any kind, these very small. At the Continental
expense I have fitted out six . . . these vessels are all manned by
officers and soldiers."[17]

At the head of "Washington's fleet" was John Manley of the
Lee and the *Hancock,* a fisherman from Marblehead in Massachusetts, whose famed achievements included the capture of the
Nancy containing military supplies both valuable and opportune,
a cannon christened the *Congress* and placed on Cambridge Common which was "the noblest piece of ordnance ever landed in
America," and many important letters divulging British military
plans. During the early period of naval operations he had the
admiration of Washington as well as his native colony. "You no
doubt have heard of Captain Manley," read a published account
from Beverly, Massachusetts, "who goes in a privateer out of this
harbor; because his name is famous, and as many towns contend
for the honour of his birth as did for that of Homer's."[18]

While Manley's exploits were heralded, Jones still bided his
time in Philadelphia. Congress had at first greater scruples to
adopt measures of offense than defense, and to resort to a navy
than an army. Strange as the distinction appeared, to England an
American soldier was a rebel, but a sailor was a pirate. Nevertheless the principles arrived at by reason, the feeling stirred by actual
warfare, and the resourcefulness awakened by necessity were destined to overcome the hesitancy of the American leaders. Reconciliation with Britain had become a phantom. Washington urged
his dire needs. The Rhode Island Assembly, representing a colony
especially exposed by sea, instructed its delegates to propose a
national navy. Falmouth soon excited definite plans for reprisal.
John Adams with characteristic boldness was among the first to
move the Continental Congress to action. On October 5, 1775 it
appointed a committee of three consisting of him, John Langdon
of New Hampshire, and Silas Deane of Connecticut to propose
a plan for intercepting British ships with stores. The committee
quickly reported the next day, and Congress decided on October
13 to fit out two armed vessels; a new committee to estimate the

expense was Deane, Langdon, and, in place of Adams, Christopher Gadsden of South Carolina. When Congress received their report on October 30, it directed that two more vessels should be prepared for sea and that this Naval Committee, as it was termed, should have four additional members—Richard Henry Lee of Virginia, Stephen Hopkins of Rhode Island, Adams, and Hewes. These members received authority to spend $100,000 to equip the four ships.

"The first beginning of our Navy," recalled Jones, "was, as navies now rank, so singularly small that I am of opinion it has no precedent in history."[19] As no regular war vessels proved available, the four ships purchased, renovated, and armed with guns of varying size were former merchantmen. The two larger, the *Alfred* of thirty guns, previously the *Black Prince,* and the *Columbus* of twenty-eight, previously the *Sally,* seemed staunch but crank and slow. The two smaller, the *Andrew Doria* of sixteen guns and the *Cabot* of fourteen, were brigantines. To these were added soon the sloop *Providence* of twelve guns, formerly the *Katy* owned by the future Commodore of the fleet, and shortly afterwards three smaller sloops and schooners, the *Hornet, Wasp,* and *Fly.*

Like the limited armament, the commissions were severely restricted. Of the small number, it is surprising to note the grounds on which the Naval Committee must have made its first appointments, announced on December 22, 1775. One may suspect that there was method in the conviviality, if not the madness, of old Stephen Hopkins, the Governor of Rhode Island many times as well as the Chairman of the Committee. Surely he must have smiled to himself when he wrote to his brother Esek that *they* had pitched upon him to be Commodore.[20] And he could not have failed to note how even astute John Adams was charmed and rendered unsuspicious by his wine and poetry, although it remains true that the member from Massachusetts may have had also his political reasons for succumbing to the lure. "The pleasantest part of the labors from 1774 to 1778," wrote Adams in reminiscence, "was in the Committee on Naval Affairs. Mr. Lee and Mr. Gadsden were sensible men and very cheerful, but Governor Hopkins of Rhode Island, about seventy years of age, kept us all

MARINE COMMITTEE'S LETTER OF NOVEMBER 27, 1775,
TO DUDLEY SALTONSTALL

Presented by John L. Senior. (Saltonstall was appointed a Captain and Jones was appointed the senior of the First Lieutenants. Both were ordered to the flagship of Esek Hopkins. . . . Three of the signers—Hopkins, Adams and Hewes—were to be signers of the Declaration of Independence more than seven months later.)

alive. . . . His custom was to drink nothing all day until eight in the evening, then his beverage was Jamaica spirits and water. . . . Hopkins never drank to excess, but all he drank was immediately not only converted into wit, sense, knowledge, and good humor, but inspired us all with similar qualities."[21]

Intimately connected with the Commodore of the fleet, Esek Hopkins, brother of the bibulous Stephen who blended politics and poetry, were John B. Hopkins, the Captain of the *Cabot,* and Abraham Whipple, the Captain of the *Columbus,* the former a son and the latter a relative of Esek. The command of the flagship *Alfred* fell to Dudley Saltonstall, a brother-in-law of Deane, a member of the Committee, and that of the *Providence,* which became available at a late moment, to Captain Hazard. Four of these officers were from Rhode Island, and the fifth from Connecticut. As an obvious sop for the powers in Pennsylvania, the captaincy of the *Andrew Doria* was reserved for Nicholas Biddle of Philadelphia.

There were also three grades of lieutenants. Foremost on the list of the first lieutenants was John Paul Jones, assigned to the *Alfred* after having refused the captaincy of the *Providence* for reasons of inexperience in navigating a sloop and of greater opportunities for training and service in the flagship. Certainly he did not have Adams to thank for his commission. "I was gone home by leave of Congress," wrote the Massachusetts member as if to explain what might not have occurred in the event of his presence, "but I presume . . . Jones was appointed by this Committee."[22] That Hewes had been responsible for the choice of Jones is evident from the number and warmth of his assurances of gratitude which have already been indicated. He was to declare further to his benefactor: "I now as always acknowledge my debt to you more than to any other person." Kinship and intimacy with appointees apart, their achievements will reveal whether Stephen Hopkins and John Adams were as wise in judgment and as disinterested in patriotism as the North Carolinian who gave Jones his opportunity.

Hardihood, at least, most of the officers of the first Continental fleet seemed to possess. The Declaration of Independence was still a vague uncertainty, and some of those who refused commissions, according to Jones, stated that they did "not choose to be hanged."

Others, "some respectable gentlemen," he recalled caustically, "accepted the appointments of captain and lieutenant of a provincial vessel for the protection of the river, after our fleet had sailed from it; and on board of which they had refused to embark, though I pretend not to know their reason."[23] In 1775 the American naval force was too insignificant for comparison with that of the British on the North American coast, and even in 1776 its vessels were less than one-third and its guns only one-fourth of the enemy's in American waters. It was only after considerable hesitation that Congress had the courage to direct and a small number of officers and sailors had the audacity to undertake the initial naval offensive. "Was it proof of madness in the first corps of sea officers," asked Jones, "to have at so critical a period launched out on the ocean with only two armed merchant ships, two armed brigantines, and one armed sloop, to make war against such a power as Great Britain?"[24]

The personnel of the Continental Navy, if not of the fleet at this time, was soon to be limited by still other factors. Within a few months the Continental Congress authorized commissions for privateers and letters of marque, of which the former were outfitted to capture enemy commerce and the latter to carry cargo primarily but also to take prizes if they desired. Privateering was safer than service in the Navy because its prey was almost exclusively merchantmen. Privateering was more lucrative, very much like wartime profiteering, because most of the booty fell to the civilian owners, officers, and crews. Privateering was more personal and parasitic because its enterprise depended chiefly upon self-interest, and its full crews desperately depleted the ranks of the Continental ships. Yet the institution of the privateer and the letter of marque was in vogue in England more than a century before the Revolution. The career of Captain Kidd, whose privateer fitted out and owned by English nobility turned and become notorious as a pirate ship, offered only an exaggerated instance of the kinship of the one to the other in an age when the sea called particularly to the adventurous, irresponsible spirit of the buccaneer.

The maritime heritage of the Colonists from the best sea-trained nations of Europe and their pioneer commercial experience along the vast American coastlines and waterways, as well as their common use of privateers in conjunction with England during the four wars with France earlier in the eighteenth century, were chiefly the background of the American seamen who now swarmed upon privately owned armed vessels as the Revolution became a reality. Because of the immediate need of war supplies and the absence of full, centralized authority, Congress enacted naval laws which authorized the owners and crews of privateers to retain for themselves the whole value of captured merchant and supply vessels but limited the officers and men of Continental ships to one-third the value of similar vessels and one-half the value of ships of war. They reserved the remainder for the Government. The vicious circle which the system promoted of lessened federal income, fewer Continental ships, and ever-decreasing sailors to man them made the popularity and selfishness of the privately owned vessels the more glaring. It was not surprising under the circumstances that some of the most noted of the early naval officers, including Hopkins, Barry, Manley, Truxtun, and Barney, served at one time or another on privateers or letters of marque. But as the purpose of this second class of vessels was often the same as that of ordinary merchantmen, the disposition of an officer rather than the ship in which he sailed was the better criterion as to his principles.

Jones, nevertheless, stands apart. Pirate as he has been named more than any other officer of the Revolution, he appears characteristically at the opening of the door of naval operations, not as the master of a privateer, a letter of marque, or any other vessel of questionable nature, but as the first lieutenant in the *Alfred* of the Continental Navy.

Chapter IX

Flag Officer, Pilot, and Strategist of the New Providence Cruise

I HOISTED with my own hands the flag of freedom the first time it was displayed on board the *Alfred* in the Delaware; and I have attended it ever since with veneration on the ocean," Jones affirmed.[1] The flag-raising occurred on December 3, 1775,[2] one day after James Wharton, a Philadelphia merchant, charged to the account of the *Alfred* the following: 49 yards of broad and 52½ yards of narrow bunting and the services of Margaret Manny a milliner for preparing an ensign.[3] It was the new Continental flag provided by these means which Jones hoisted in the presence of Commodore Hopkins and other officers of the fleet in the river and amid the acclaim of thousands of citizens crowded along the shore.[4]

This ensign, described on the occasion as "a Union Flag with thirteen stripes in the field emblematical of the Thirteen United Colonies," as "the Continental Flag," and as "English colors but more striped," still retained in its canton the British Union, the crosses of St. George and St. Andrew, but newly combined with it a pattern of thirteen red and white lines.[5] Sometime after January 13, not until the squadron was already on its passage down the Delaware, Gadsden as a member of the Naval Committee forwarded to Hopkins the personal standard of the Commander in Chief, the well-known yellow flag with a coiled serpent and the words "Don't Tread on Me."[6] As for the *Alfred's* flag which Jones himself notably hoisted on December 3, no other officer seems to have had such a distinction.

Washington hoisted apparently a similar flag, the Grand Union, for the first time almost a month later, January 2, 1776, on Prospect Hill at the siege of Boston.[7] The first Continental vessels commanded by Manley and others used standards of the separate colonies and personal ensigns such as the Pine Tree and Rattlesnake flags. The final American flag with the stars as well as the stripes was not adopted unofficially by the people until the Declaration of Independence and officially by Congress until June 14, 1777. Therefore it appears that Jones first displayed on an important occasion of either the Continental Army or the Navy the initial flag which bore a pronounced resemblance in design and symbolic meaning to the present Stars and Stripes. "Though this was but a slight circumstance," he recalled with sentiment regarding his connection with the standard, "yet I feel for its honor more than I think I should have done if it had not happened."[8]

The informal appointment of the officers who were present at the flag ceremonial was followed by the formal award of commissions. The first lieutenancy of Jones was of December 7, 1775,[9] and the confirmation by Congress of all the commissions occurred December 22. The officers of the *Alfred* happened to be the first appointed; and in the absence of Captain Saltonstall, who did not appear until one or two days before the fleet sailed from Philadelphia, Jones was the Continental officer initially in charge of fitting out and manning the fleet, subject to the orders of the Commodore. It was the intention, in fact, of Hopkins, until the final arrival of Saltonstall, to give him the captaincy of the flagship.[10]

Under his direction as the acting officer in command, the merchantman *Black Prince* became the ship of war *Alfred* of considerable staunchness and efficiency. Partly owned by Robert Morris and captained for two transatlantic voyages by John Barry, who while still a civilian took a part in the equipment of her and soon himself became an officer of the Continental Navy, she was armed with twenty nine-pounders on the lower deck and from two to ten smaller guns on the upper, painted with conspicuous yellow stripes, and adorned with a figurehead such as was in vogue. "I formed an exercise," wrote Jones, "and trained the men so well to the great guns in the *Alfred* that they went through the motions of broadsides and rounds as exactly as soldiers generally perform the manual exercise."[11] The enlistment of sailors and a special guard to prevent desertions were other preliminary tasks which he supervised shortly before the harbors began to swarm with privateers. Among his fellow officers of the fleet, we see him at the age of twenty-eight, in the prime of his physical if not his mental capacities and with his arresting energies as the supplement to his limited experience. He was beginning to reveal, as pictured subsequently by an astute observer, "the boldness which is produced by madness, the bravery which is the effect of animal spirits, and the courage which is the result of reflection."[12]

In command of the *Columbus,* approximately of twenty guns, painted completely black with the exception of her white bottom, devoid of the usual figurehead, Captain Abraham Whipple had already given proof of his activity and patriotism. It had been he, it was understood, who in 1772 had led the Americans attired like Indians and armed with stones as well as muskets at the capture and burning of the British revenue vessel *Gaspee* in Narragansett Bay. The Colonists had justified the act on the ground of unjustified interference with the coast trade, and Whipple as the American leader had replied to a British threat of arrest and execution: "Always catch a man before you hang him." He likewise had inspired sufficient confidence to receive an important commission in 1775 to seek powder supplies from the friendly people of Bermuda.

A captain at twenty-seven years, Nicholas Biddle gave promise of greater mental resources and even physical courage than Whipple. From boyhood he had adopted the navy, sailing under the British flag as a midshipman at the prospect of war between England and Spain in 1770 and shipping before the mast in an expedition to the region of the North Pole under Commodore Phipps. At the outbreak of the Revolution, he was one of the very few Americans in the British Navy who returned to the homeland for service. He early showed his leadership by a single-handed recapture of two deserters from his vessel, regardless of their levelled muskets which had cowed a squad of his men. Not less conspicuous was his humane consideration for sailors with smallpox; he even relinquished to them his cabin and cot and slept in the hold with the ordinary seamen.

Aside from Dudley Saltonstall of the *Alfred,* "the sleepy gentleman" as Jones characterized him, and John B. Hopkins of the *Cabot,* the son of the Commodore, the measure of whose fitness as captains will appear later, there remained Esek Hopkins himself. "The Admiral," as General Knox, Washington's aide-de-camp described him, "is an antiquated figure. He brought to my mind Van Tromp, the famous Dutch Admiral. Although antiquated in figure, he is shrewd and sensible. I, who you think only a little enthusiastic, should have taken him for an angel, only he swore now and then."[13] Neither his quaintness at the age of fifty-seven nor his swearing among hardened New England privateersmen would seem to be very material as to his abilities. According to a Newbern, North Carolina, newspaper correspondent, he was "a most experienced and venerable sea-captain."

His long record both as a captain of merchantmen and as a commander of privateers in the English wars with France testified considerably to his training as a mariner and to his experience in minor naval operations. It gave no evidence, however, of a capacity for major naval warfare or of a distinction in personality which might have justified singling him out as the head of the Navy in any way comparable with the choice of Washington as the Commander in Chief of the Army. An appointment based on political pressure and compromise between the North and South, especially New England and Virginia, it was to bear ironic political fruit in the fortunes of war.

Speed and opportune resource were particularly important for the strategy of the squadron while the naval forces of Britain on the American coast were still small and scattered. "The situation of America is new in the annals of mankind; her affairs cry haste, and speed must answer them," urged Jones at the outset.[14] Powder had continued to be an imminent need since Washington had first felt acutely the lack of it. In November, Congress had learned at a secret session that there was "a large quantity of powder on the island of [New] Providence" and ordered that the Naval Committee should take measures to obtain this precious supply. The depredations by British ships along the Atlantic, notably by the squadron under Lord Dunmore after he had been forced to flee from Virginia, particularly aroused Congress to resolution and despatch for an enterprise by sea. Hastily as the merchantmen had been converted into vessels of war, equipped with scant naval stores aboard, and manned with sailors who cast an envious eye upon the prospective privateers, the chief officers of the fleet were severely handicapped from the outset.

Captain Saltonstall appeared only a day or two before the ships sailed to take command of the *Alfred* conveniently outfitted by Jones and others. Hopkins had arrived in Philadelphia before the Grand Union Flag was raised on December 3, 1775, and he weighed anchor for the cruise early in the afternoon of January 4 amid the cheers of a second multitude along the shores of the Delaware. He had to anchor at nightfall of the same day at "ye Pierse at Liberty Island."

Here, as the Log of the *Andrew Doria* explained, "much ice in ye river" detained the ships until the 17th; then they ran down to Reedy Island and became blocked a second time in its grip until February 11, 1776. The squadron waited off the Delaware capes almost another week, during which two small vessels, the *Hornet* and the *Wasp*, following a third, the *Fly*, joined the enterprise. It is very probable that the delays were largely unavoidable in view of the temporary absence of some of the officers and the last-minute arrival of supplies, as well as the obstruction of the floating ice. Hopkins himself wrote to the Marine Committee on January 27 that the river was "still froze so much that the pilots will not undertake to carry us from here."[15] As late as February 9, a report from Newbern, North Carolina, said, "Unhappily for us, the ice in the river Delaware as yet obstructs the passage down." But according to Jones' declaration, not at this period but considerably later, "Mr. Hopkins displayed neither zeal nor talents upon this occasion, and lost so much time that his squadron was frozen in the Delaware."

The orders which Hopkins had received on January 5, 1776 are significant:

". . . you are instructed with the utmost diligence to proceed with the said fleet to sea, and if the winds and weather will possibly admit of it to proceed directly for Chesapeake Bay in Virginia. . . . If you should be so fortunate as to execute this business successfully in Virginia, you are then to proceed immediately to the southward and make yourself master of such forces as the enemy may have both in North and South Carolina in such manner as you may think most prudent from the intelligence you shall receive. . . .

"Having completed your business in the Carolinas, you are without delay to proceed northward directly to Rhode Island, and attack, take, and destroy all the enemy's naval force you may find there. . . .

"Notwithstanding these particular orders, which it is hoped you will be able to execute, if bad winds or stormy weather, or any unforeseen accident or disaster disable you to do so, you are then to follow such courses as your best judgment shall suggest to you as most useful to the American cause. . . ."[16]

The Commodore received in addition separate letters from Christopher Gadsden, one of the members of the Marine Committee, who urged him to come to the Carolinas. The orders to attack the British ships successively off the coasts of Virginia, the Carolinas, and Rhode Island were a large assignment, especially in view of their number, force, and tried crews, as compared with his merchantmen converted into ships of war and the inexperience of his officers and men.

Finally the squadron put to sea from Cape Henlopen with a smart northeast wind which shortly became a gale. The frail *Hornet* and *Fly,* among the last to join the expedition, soon became separated from it; they collided and seriously damaged each other in the storm. The former, disabled, was driven down the coast as far as South Carolina and succeeded in reaching port after many weeks, while the latter managed to make repairs and was to rejoin the squadron off Abaco, one of the Bahama Islands, the rendezvous appointed for such an emergency.

Hopkins must have realized that it was late to search out the enemy, that he was at a disadvantage for attacking the British in their chosen places of security and in stormy weather, and above all that they were too formidable for him. Even an epidemic of smallpox had broken out among the seamen so as to weaken the effectiveness of his crews.

In the light of these circumstances and the provision in his orders for the use of his "best judgment," it seems a reasonable decision that he chose to avoid the wintry, storm-ridden American

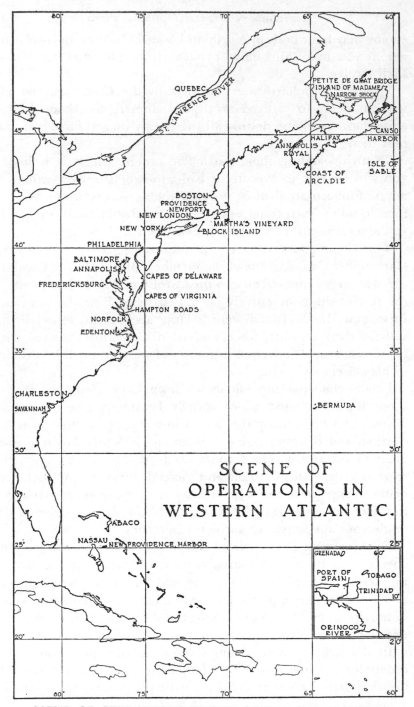

SCENE OF OPERATIONS IN THE WESTERN ATLANTIC

capes and to sail directly with his ships to the rendezvous off the southern shore of Abaco for an alternative object.

This second purpose was to cruise in the warmer region of the Bahama Islands in search of military stores, particularly gunpowder and ordnance. Even as early as July, 1775 General Gage had sent the ship of war *Falcon* with two transports to New Providence in order to carry its war supplies to a place of safety after he had received "certain intelligence . . . of the intention of the rebels in North America to seize them."[17] But in the absence of Governor Browne on this occasion, the civil authorities and the people disregarded the precautionary measure of Gage, holding that they would defend the stores in an emergency. Whether or not there was connivance by any of the inhabitants, the American squadron arrived off the shores of New Providence at a time when "the Company of the Fourteenth Regiment was removed from hence, and the *Savage* sloop of war recalled from this station."[18]

Hopkins now had his opportunity for strategy. Fortifications of nature by land and sea had made New Providence a haven for Spanish pirates and buccaneers from the early history of exploration in the Western Hemisphere, and this Colony retained much of its primitive lawlessness even under later English rule. Nassau its guardian town, set on a high hill sloping to the water's edge and encircled by the sunlit blue of the tropic seas, was protected in front by a long narrow island and on either side by defenses: Fort Nassau on the west which ships of larger draught could approach, and Fort Montague on the east which vessels of smaller size only might hope to reach. The sudden, adventurous appearance of the American squadron in this idyllic setting with its lurid traditions of the Spanish Main seemed more fiction-like than factual.

Hopkins' plan was to land a party of marines and sailors near Fort Nassau, to storm the citadel in a surprise attack, and then to advance upon Fort Montague. Its execution failed for the simple reason that the ships approached the bar by day instead of night; cannon fired the signal of alarm upon sight of the fleet even though the troops hid below decks, and so the advantage of an unexpected assault vanished.[19] Jones urged in the ensuing conference of Hopkins with his officers that the attack should be delivered first upon

Fort Montague because the distance from the point of disembarkation of the troops to the fort was shorter and offered better terrain, and that, in view of the shallower waters on the east side of the harbor, the fleet should anchor in Hanover Sound under a key three leagues distant and the soldiers should proceed from that base in two captured schooners under the protection of the *Providence* and *Wasp*. In answer to the final objection of the Commodore that he would not entrust the fleet to the two captured pilots in order to reach the key, Jones, confident in his earlier experience in Caribbean waters, took his post in the fore-topmast crosstrees of the *Alfred* in company with the two navigators and saw the squadron safely moored in the Sound.[20]

To make the attack itself, two hundred marines under Captain Nicholas and fifty sailors under Lieutenant Weaver who was well acquainted with the island sailed from the anchorage and landed below Fort Montague. The garrison, most of which had been called to the western fort at the first appearance of the fleet, was the more unprepared to meet the assault upon the eastern. Against the bold advance of the Continental marines, apparently the first action in their distinguished history, the enemy directed no fire at the landing and in fact made little resistance to the capture of Fort Montague. Part of the militia was marching back at this time from the other citadel; but their total number was decidedly less than the Americans, their ordnance was defective, and their shot and accessory stores were wanting. So the Continental flag waved overnight from the ramparts of the fort without hindrance.[21]

The next morning Captain Nicholas and his men marched westward towards the town and Fort Nassau. An aide of Governor Montfort Browne met these troops on their way to inform them that the garrison would offer no resistance and that this second fort was at their command. At the arsenal they took possession of a large number of guns and mortars, a variety of stores, and a supply of gunpowder. The previous night, however, the Governor had availed himself of the daring of a loyal merchant, Captain William Chambers, who cast overboard his cargo of lumber, loaded his vessel with 162 large barrels of gunpowder, and at two a.m. sailed through the unguarded eastern channel for St. Augustine to deliver them in safety to Governor Tonyn.[22]

Nicholas was apparently censurable in failing to anticipate the removal of the powder by proceeding from the one to the other fort on the same instead of the next day, especially since the military supplies were obviously not at Fort Montague. As Hopkins' responsibility was greater, he was seemingly even more at fault in neglecting both to instruct his officer to make no delay unless unavoidable and to guard with his ships the eastern as well as the western entrance.

Otherwise the enterprise was not the less creditable because the British had left New Providence almost defenseless by the removal of both a company of regulars and a sloop of war, and the Americans had availed themselves of their opportunity. What the capture lost in valor it gained as an expression of good will towards America by British colonists in the Bahama Islands. Anger may have distorted but did not wholly belie this message from George Germain to Governor Browne: "There can be little doubt from the whole behavior of the generality of the inhabitants of the Bahamas that the rebels were invited to undertake the enterprise they formed against those Islands, and the refusal of the President and Council to deliver the ordnance and stores to General Gage's order was evidently in consequence of a plan they had concerted with the rebels for putting them into their hands."[23] Governor Browne and Captain Chambers at least had given proof enough of their British loyalty by spiriting away 162 barrels of powder, and Hopkins retaliated so far as to take the Governor and several others aboard the *Alfred* as hostages. He soon sailed with the captured military supplies, which included seventy-one cannon, fifteen brass mortars, and twenty-four casks of gunpowder remaining from the precious supply that lack of prevision had lost in part.

The strategy and daring of Jones the first lieutenant, in spite of the limited opportunities which his rank afforded, were conspicuous. Although Hopkins had chosen the sensible expedition to New Providence instead of the hazardous challenge to Lord Dunmore and his marauding ships, not to consider the other British squadrons, it was Jones who had retrieved the error of the Commodore's first plan to attack Fort Nassau instead of Fort Montague. It was he also who had made possible the second successful attempt by shouldering responsibility for the whole fleet as its emergency pilot.

◇◇◇

Chapter X

In Command of the Flagship's Guns Against the *Glasgow*

WHEN THE squadron set sail on March 17, 1776, for the return passage northward from New Providence, a sudden new test of the abilities of the officers was in store. Arriving the 5th of the following month off Block Island, Hopkins captured the tender *Hawke* and the bomb brig *Bolton* belonging to Captain Wallace of the British Navy, whose small fleet with its base at Newport had been making raids off the coast of Rhode Island. The following morning at one a.m. Captain Biddle's *Andrew Doria* spied a strange sail to the southeast against the black horizon and signaled the *Alfred* accordingly.[1] An hour later she was distinguishable as a ship of force. Hopkins must have surmised that she was hostile and other ships might be in the offing, for the Americans were now near the British rendezvous and the captured small vessels evidently had sailed ahead to reconnoitre.

Certainly in the event of a battle between the American and British ships, the occasion was not propitious for the former. The crews as well as the officers were untried. Smallpox had broken out among the men. The ships, as converted merchantmen, had proved dull sailers, and had become the duller laden as they now were with heavy cannon and other stores. A considerable number of the best seamen and two of the officers had been detailed to man the captured vessels.[2] And, what was more diverting than creditable to the discipline maintained by the Commodore and some of his associates, at least a score of the sailors "had got too much liquor out of the prizes to be fit for duty."[3]

It was fortunate under these circumstances that the one sail described by Biddle did not prove the forerunner of others. When Hopkins suspected that the vessel was strong but alone, he and his captains cleared ship for action in a smooth sea with a light wind from the northwest. At the same time the stranger hauled up her mainsail and boldly kept standing on towards the Commodore's squadron. Especially in view of the unexpectedness of the encounter and the difficulties of manœuvre at night with untried officers and men, Hopkins made no attempt to change the order of sailing. It happened that at two-thirty a.m. the little *Cabot* of only fourteen guns first came within range of the unknown ship.

Each signaled and failed of course to answer satisfactorily the other. Then both hailed and boldly announced their identity. The *Cabot* also signaled the enemy's presence to the other ships of the American squadron, particularly the *Alfred* and *Columbus*. The adversary proved to be indeed the English ship *Glasgow* of twenty guns under Captain Tyringham Howe commissioned to carry despatches from both General Howe and Vice Admiral Shuldham to southern ports. With only the *Hawke* and *Bolton* ahead on scouting service, she had just tacked from her course toward Newport in order to investigate the unknown vessels sighted to windward, although other ships of the British squadron had informed her that they were turning back to await some of their delayed consorts.[4]

Immediately after the challenges and replies, the *Cabot* opened fire with a well-aimed broadside and with hand grenades from her tops. Almost simultaneously the *Glasgow* flamed with her heavier cannonade. The brig soon found herself in a duel too severe for her size and armament, drew ahead, and lay on the enemy's bow. She had already suffered a considerable number of casualties among her officers and men, including her captain.

Then the *Alfred* came into action and exchanged heavy broadsides with the Englishman whenever her position enabled Jones to bring his battery to bear. Unfortunately a lucky shot from the *Glasgow* carried away the *Alfred's* wheel rope and blocks, and she broached to and was raked several times before the relieving tackles brought her under control in the emergency.[5] The duties of Jones as first lieutenant were connected in no way with the manœuvres of the ship, but exclusively with the lower main battery, and he directed a cannonade with such skill, regardless of indifferent gunners, against the masts and rigging of the *Glasgow* as to threaten to make her unmanageable.[6] His tactics accorded with the practice of the French Navy; those of the British, which they characteristically adopted against the *Alfred,* were to direct most of their shot against the adversary's hull, especially between wind and water, in the endeavor to sink her. In this duel the *Glasgow* suffered the greater damage, and her situation appeared so desperate that the clerk entrusted with her bag of despatches weighted it and flung the letters overboard.[7]

But the *Alfred* received little support from other members of the squadron. The *Cabot* had suffered for her bravado. Biddle in the *Andrew Doria* fired with considerable effectiveness at close range, although his aid was the less because, first, he had to tack to avoid fouling the *Cabot* when the latter sheered off and, secondly, he was compelled to fall away when the *Alfred* herself became unmanageable and suffered considerable damage.[8] Whipple of the *Columbus,* although in command of the only Continental ship comparable with the *Alfred,* arrived late in position to engage because of difficulties which he claimed were beyond his control, and even then his broadsides while crossing the stern and the lee quarter of the *Glasgow* were high and did inconsiderable harm to ship and men. Even worse, Hazard in the *Providence* poured a fitful and ineffective fire at long range.

At daybreak, after a duel of almost three hours, the beaten enemy crowded on all sail and bore away in retreat to Newport. She soon signaled for assistance from the rest of the British fleet, while the Americans followed on her quarters with a very warm fire. Superior speed and mobility, however, enabled her to show her heels despite the great damage to her rigging and spars. "Away came the poor *Glasgow,*" according to an observer on shore, "under all the sail she could set, yelping from the mouths of her cannon like a broken-legged dog, as a signal of her being sadly wounded."[9] Finally she approached so close to Newport that Hopkins signalled at six-thirty a.m. to abandon the chase and haul by the wind to join the squadron's prizes. He feared not without reason at this unpropitious time to be decoyed under the guns of the formidable, newly fitted fleet of Captain Wallace, including the *Rose, Swan,* and *Nautilus,* which, in fact, was working out of the harbor early in the morning in answer to the volleys of alarm.[10] And so the Commodore and his captains, with the *Bolton,* but not the *Hawke* which had been recaptured, and with the supplies from New Providence intact, shaped their course for New London and brought to a successful end the first Continental Navy cruise.

The repercussions were now to begin. The public was extravagant first in applause and then in condemnation. The reports acclaimed the severe treatment which the *Glasgow* had suffered as a signal victory until the realization that the guns of the American squadron were more than three times the equivalent of the enemy's. It was soon maintained also, without due recognition of the special circumstances, that the Commodore had committed a double tactical error: first, he had permitted the *Cabot* instead of the *Alfred* to begin the engagement, and, secondly, he had failed to align his ships in advance with the *Columbus* as his first and near auxiliary.[11] Members of Congress, especially those from the South, resented what they chose to consider as Hopkins' disobedience to his primary instructions to search out the ships of Dunmore and retaliate for his depredations along the Southern coast. Finally, valuable as were the naval stores brought from the Bahamas, the loss of the major part of the gunpowder obscured considerably the achievements of the cruise.

Demands arose for an investigation. One group in Congress wished an accounting from Hopkins, and another defended him. Some Southern members, especially "that polite speaker Middleton"[12] whose eloquence, we are sarcastically told, entertained the members for the greater part of two days, were his chief accusers; New Englanders, especially John Adams, were his advocates. A court-martial, especially of Whipple, who bluntly asked for it himself, took place in Providence. Later Congress directed the Marine Committee "to inform Commodore Hopkins, Captain Saltonstall, and Captain Whipple of the complaints lodged against them, and order them immediately to repair to Philadelphia."[13] The hearings took place, not without forethought, after Jones had found occasion to be in the city, and they were postponed at least in one instance to have him testify as the chief witness.[14]

"The night we fell in with the Glasgow man-of-war," asserted Whipple in his defense, "two of my lieutenants were on board the two prizes we had taken, and fourteen of my best seamen." He maintained that the *Columbus* was to leeward and in the wake of the *Alfred* so that the wind was deadened and prevented him from taking a more active part against the enemy. "If I did not do my duty," he explained, "it proceeded not from cowardice but from lack of judgment." There is no question as to his courage and loyalty. Perhaps he had shown himself inexpert in failing to gain a favorable position under adverse circumstances in an encounter lasting three hours. He won an acquittal, and among his defenders was Jones.

Hazard, however, came to trial on the charge of cowardice and suffered a summary dismissal. As to Saltonstall, he seems to have escaped behind the shield of Hopkins his superior and Jones his subordinate officers in the *Alfred*.

Congress finally passed a resolution of censure against Hopkins on the unwise if not mistaken ground that "during his cruise to the southward he did not pay due regard to the tenor of his instructions."[15] But it neither published the details nor removed him from his command. For the present he remained intrenched as commodore. "I cannot think of it with patience," wrote John Jay; "nothing but more than ladylike delicacy could have prevailed on your august body to secrete the sentence they passed upon that petty genius."

Jones and Biddle alone of all the officers completed the cruise not only without blemish but with unqualified merit. The strategy, courage, and adeptness of the First Lieutenant of the *Alfred* at New Providence as well as his efficiency against the *Glasgow* augured well for his future. When the captaincy of the *Providence* became vacant again shortly after the return from the enterprise, Jones confidently accepted the command of the sloop from Hopkins, who even before the proceedings in Philadelphia had appreciated and rewarded his services past and potential. On May 10, 1776, he first became a Continental captain.[16]

◇◇◇

Chapter XI

Captain Jones: The *Providence* Cruise

WITH THE NEW commission written informally by Commodore Hopkins on the back of the old one as first lieutenant, Captain Jones of the *Providence* now had greater scope for his fertility of mind and energy of body. However great his love of freedom from supervision, he had bided his time by refusing previously the command of either the *Providence* or the *Fly;* as the first lieutenant of the *Alfred,* he had taught more than learned and, comparing himself with fellow-officers, was now confirmed in his self-confidence. Even so his zeal for improvement as a naval officer was so great that only an immediate reason prompted him to leave the *Alfred*—Saltonstall, who was not only "sleepy" but also "ill-natured and narrowminded," who suspected his loyalty to America, who had tried to withhold from him a copy of the *Alfred's* log-book prepared by the facile pen of the former first lieutenant himself.[1]

Jones resented especially what he ascribed to an absence of refinement of character in Saltonstall. "I now reflect with pleasure," he confided to Hewes, "that I had philosophy sufficient to avoid quarreling with him and that I even obtained his blessings at parting. May he too soon become of an affable, even disposition, and may he too find pleasure in communicating happiness around him."[2] The gardener's son knew his own temperament none too well in attributing to himself an "even disposition" unless it had very recently developed in repentance for his troubles in Tobago, and he had not yet unlearned patronage and self-praise from the pinnacle of his acquired gentility. Still the intimate words to his warmest friend were honest in intent and reveal what Jones wished to be if not what he altogether was.

Such gentility on which Jones prided himself as a man happily softened in no way his will as a warrior. From the beginning of his command of the *Providence,* he evinced the free exercise of his maturing talents—his circumspection, his courage, his naval acumen. It is understandable also, particularly in view of notorious partisanship and influence in the appointment and promotion of officers, that the same whole-heartedness with which he was prepared to fight for America should move him to urge zealously what he considered justice in his future rank in the navy.

After the fleet had anchored first at New London and then at Providence, he executed with safety and despatch his initial orders to carry in his vessel to New York about one hundred soldiers whom Washington had loaned to Hopkins for a special purpose. Other services which he performed with the *Providence* as a convoy were likewise without loss, although British ships were at every point off Rhode Island and New York. He showed his wariness as well as bravery by making attempt after attempt but refraining from a foolhardy dash to accompany the *Fly* laden with stores as far westward as Fisher's Island. There were more important tasks at hand. He outwitted and outsailed the British frigate *Cerberus* of thirty-two guns during his escort of vessels carrying heavy artillery from Rhode Island to New York. He adroitly thwarted her further by effecting the escape of a San Domingo merchantman with naval stores consigned to the Colonies. This ship, later purchased by Congress, became the *Hampden.* Finally, he convoyed a coal fleet from Boston to Philadelphia, where his arrival on August 1, 1776 at the Delaware capes was without loss after eluding ships of war under Lord Howe bound from England and Canada for New York.

Then at the seat of the Government, Jones looked to authority other than that of Hopkins for both orders and rank. In Philadelphia he could expect to see Hewes and some of the other members of the Marine Committee, one from each colony, which had succeeded the Naval Committee after Congress had authorized on the preceding December 14 the building of thirteen frigates. John Hancock, President of Congress, had become head of the Committee, and an influential member was Robert Morris. Jones wished, not unnaturally, to command one of the new ships; but he had well-founded fears that all the commissions would shortly be apportioned in an arbitrary, political manner rather than based on the merits and seniority of the officers. Further, the captain of the *Fly*, the command of which he had earlier refused, questioned his seniority in rank, and Hopkins had referred the matter to Congress. Even before Jones had known of Hewes' coming to the capital, he had written without backwardness to him: "I should esteem myself happy in being sent for to Philadelphia to act under the more immediate direction of Congress, especially in one of the new ships."[3]

This request came indirectly to the receptive ears of Hancock and Morris as well as directly to those of Hewes. Jones had shown and expressed respect and even loyal regard for Hopkins, but his own powers must have made him aware that his chief lacked the aggressive personality essential for the emergencies of war. In the absence of such a leader, he was the more ready to turn to higher authority. The Commodore had done nothing since the return of the fleet to inspire confidence; in fact, his continued inaction was ominous, granted the sickness of many of his sailors and the entice-ment of others by the privateers. Morris had written to Silas Deane: "Commodore Hopkins has fallen short of expectations, and his fleet, which might have performed most signal service under an active, vigilant man, has been most useless. He remains with the *Alfred* at Rhode Island, and the rest are gone and going on separate cruises."[4]

While Hopkins lost prestige in the eyes of the Marine Commit-tee, Jones came the more to its notice. The President of Congress and several other members of the Committee signed on August 6 an order, practically *carte blanche,* directing him in the *Providence* "to proceed immediately on a cruise against our enemies."[5] Two days later Hancock confirmed his captaincy of May 10, 1776, by a new commission,[6] the first issued after the Declaration of Independ-ence with Congressional sanction. Although Hewes was apparently the advocate and Hancock the official authority, Morris proved the power upon whom the new enterprise depended. "I forget not," Jones wrote him respectfully after putting to sea, "the singular obligation I owe to Mr. Morris."[7] At the same time possibly his sympathetic and loyal instincts more than his judgment and candor prompted these consoling words to Hopkins: "I know you will not suspect me of flattery when I affirm that I have not experienced a more sincere pleasure for a long past than the account I have had of your having gained your cause at Philadelphia in spite of party. Your late trouble will tend to your future advantage. . . . "[8]

Fast and trim, the *Providence* with twelve four-pounders and seventy men, which Jones preferred to the larger but slower *Hampden* offered by Congress, cleared the Delaware capes on August 21, bound upon the first independent cruise of her captain. Sailing eastward at first in the vicinity of Bermuda, as the committee had suggested subject to his own choice, he took three prizes and met an enemy which tried the mettle of both his ship and skill. Upon sight of five sail, one of which seemed a large East Indiaman or a Jamaica three-decker, the officers of the *Providence* were urgent to investigate—apparently against the wishes of Jones himself, who averred that it was necessary to command by persuasion at this stage of the war—and found themselves almost within cannon shot of an English frigate of twenty-six guns. The *Providence* at once veered from her course, and tried, close-hauled, to escape on the wind and in a heavy cross sea, while the *Solebay,* as she proved to be, turned in pursuit and without showing colors opened an occasional fire. When Jones displayed his American ensign in defiance of such a practice, the frigate fired a gun to leeward in token of amity; but the ruse was apparent to him.

A tense chase of four hours ensued, at the end of which the enemy was within musket shot, and the sloop was doomed if she continued to lose distance or if her pursuer rounded to and delivered a well-directed broadside. But the Captain of the *Providence* had carefully prepared for this contingency, and now acted with decision. He knew that his little sloop sailed best not close-hauled but free. So having edged unnoticeably, little by little, on the lee bow of the *Solebay,* suddenly he put his helm up, set his steering sails and all his light canvas, and bore away across the forefoot of the enemy—to leeward dead before the wind. The dexterity and unexpectedness of the manœuvre were such that, before the frigate could counter, Jones, as he himself described, "was almost out of reach of grape and soon after out of reach of cannon shot. Our 'hairbreadth escape' and the saucy manner of making it must have mortified him not a little."[9]

Now in southern latitudes, the *Providence* kept a sharp lookout for prizes during several weeks until her wood and water began to run short; she then squared away to the north for some port of Nova Scotia or Cape Breton Island with the prospect of replenishing her supplies and destroying the English shipping in that region. In a severe gale, Jones found it necessary to remove all his guns from the exposed deck of the sloop and to stow them and all movable equipment in the hold. After the storm had cleared and the *Providence* sailed between Sable Island and Nova Scotia, a second English ship, the *Milford,* threatened another encounter. "I had hove to," related Jones with ridicule, "to give my people an opportunity of taking fish, when the frigate came in sight directly to windward, and was so good natured as to save me the trouble of chasing him, by bearing down, the instant he discovered us. When he came within cannon shot, I made sail to try his speed. Quartering and finding that I had the advantage, I shortened sail to give him a wild goose chase, and tempt him to throw away powder and shot. Accordingly a curious mock engagement was maintained between us, for eight hours, until night, with her sable curtains, put an end to this famous exploit of English knight-errantry.

"He excited my contempt so much by his continued firing, at more than twice the proper distance, that when he rounded to, to give his broadside, I ordered my marine officer to return the salute with only a single musket."[10]

With his crew in high good humor at the sport, Jones turned his attention to the British fishery in the Bay of Canso and the nearby harbors of the Island of Madame. One night he reconnoitred off the port of the town of Canso, the next day anchored and secured his needed supply of wood and water, and the night following burned one English schooner, sank another, and made a prize of a third.

From Canso the *Providence* sailed to Madame, at which nine vessels of varying tonnage, he had learned, were in its two harbors.

So Jones dispatched two boats, well manned and armed, to attack them separately and simultaneously, while he himself "kept off and on with the sloop, to keep them in awe at both places." The surprise, indeed the panic, was so great that the surrender was without bloodshed regardless of the vastly superior numbers of the three hundred fishermen, whom Jones persuaded so far as to have them fit out and rig the ships he wanted as prizes on condition that he left them several to return to their homes across the seas. Unfortunately a gale soon arose, destroying several ships and endangering the *Providence* and the other prizes by delay on the enemy's coast.

With regret that his diminished and ill-clad crew, the stormy and cold weather, and the battered sloop did not permit a further raid upon the large fishing fleet near Louisburg, Jones shaped his course homeward and arrived on October 7, 1776 safely at port in Rhode Island. In less than seven weeks he had manned and sent in eight prizes, and burnt and sunk an equal number; and in the destruction of the fisheries at Canso and Madame, tempered as it was by considerable scruples in war, he had sought to give warning to Britain of the retaliation to which new Falmouths and Norfolks would inevitably lead. As for his escape in the little sloop from two powerful frigates, especially the *Solebay* fast as well as formidable, it presaged the day when a ship would serve him not to flee but to fight.

‹‹◊◊◊››

Chapter XII

Superseded

J ONES WAS now to suffer on October 10, 1776, three days after his return, what would prove to be one of the most unexpected as well as greatest wounds to his professional standing, if not to his honor, in the course of his life. It was not the less because he remained at present seemingly unaware of it. He had just given rein for the first time to some of his talents as an officer in command, and he panted to be off on a second cruise. In the absence of further orders awaiting him from Congress, his purpose was to refit the *Providence* expeditiously, cruise off Sandy Hook, and then return to Philadelphia. But Hopkins had other plans for him; and Jones, who saw an opportunity for further action which required speed as essential to success, centered his immediate thoughts upon service not rank. For some time he was not to learn what had taken place at Philadelphia in the sessions of Congress on this important date, and no one probably dared to inform him. It touched the Captain too closely.

To understand the surprise in store for Jones is to appreciate fully the personal favoritism, the local and state pride, the political prejudices and intrigues which were potent factors in the choice and preferment of naval and military officers. In the Army, like the Navy, machinations at the expense of talents helped to undermine, as is well known, the loyalty of the morally-weak Arnold and aimed even at the overthrow of Washington. Along with their virtues, the characteristic jealousy of the cousins Samuel and John Adams and of the brothers Richard Henry and Arthur Lee towards those whom abilities and even genius raised to power took form in the alignment, with internal divisions, of the state rights against the national party and found a most mischievous expression in the Conway Cabal, the plot to supplant Washington by Gates. Samuel

Adams began in effect to engineer it, notwithstanding his denial of such a purpose, perhaps earlier than January 9, 1777, when he wrote to John Adams: "You have seen the power with which General Washington is vested for a limited time. Congress is very attentive to the northern army. . . . General Gates is here. How shall we make him the head of that Army?"[1] Ramifications of such jaundiced influence were to extend to the diplomatic as well as the military and naval services and attack even Franklin as unscrupulously as Washington. Of course other men in positions of less power had the weaker means to escape the toils.

Congress in October, 1776, almost on the eve of its flight to Baltimore, had visibly begun to decline in character. It was not the Congress of 1774 or of 1775. On the one hand is the early picture by John Adams of a body of men of heroic stature; on the other is a later one by Dr. Benjamin Rush, who was "surprised to observe how little of the spirit of that instrument [the Declaration of Independence] actuated many of the members."[2]

Various deficiencies arose, traceable to the public as well as to Congress and emphasized in many of Jones' future recommendations for naval reforms of administration and morale. "Little attention," commented the French Minister Gérard de Rayneval, "had been paid to the talents that are requisite for the enormous labor which every branch of the administration demands. . . . In some departments there is not a member who is familiar with their details. If one member happens to be more conspicuous than another on account of his intelligence, private jealousy and the principle of anticipating personal ascendancy throw him in the background. A competent merchant on the Committee of Commerce is transferred to that of Foreign Affairs. . . . There are many colonels and generals in Congress, but none are employed on the war committees."

The envoy's criticism of the public is even more fundamentally severe than of Congress: "A selfish and calculating spirit is widespread in this land, and although I can well see that limits are put to its extension, there is no condemnation of the sentiment. Mercantile cupidity forms, perhaps, one of the distinctive traits of the American, especially of the Northern people, and it will undoubtedly exercise an important influence upon the future destiny of the Republic." These censures accord only too well with those of De Ségur, later a French volunteer in the Revolution, besides one of Jones' staunchest friends in a crucial hour. He feared "luxury and corruption" in the train of "excessive opulence" in America, a prevision which has the greater weight in the light of another forecast. "Is not that difference which is observable between the manners and situation of the North and the South," asked De Ségur, "calculated, in fact, to create an apprehension for the future of a political separation?"[3] The opinions of De Rayneval and De Ségur may be prejudiced as well as objective from their foreign point of view, but they accord certainly, apropos of the Continental Navy, with the greed of privateers and the bias in appointment of officers.

As party discords, personal and state jealousies, and material gain were too often the chief forces behind the emblems of liberty and philanthropy, it is not surprising that Chairman Stephen Hopkins of Rhode Island had used his influence with a New England majority on the Naval Committee to appoint his brother as commodore and other New Englanders, chiefly from Rhode Island, as captains of the initial fleet. It is true at least that Rhode Island, the first Colony to advocate a Continental Navy, assumed leadership and was in so far entitled to honors as well as responsibilities.

The judgment of Congress in delegating power in the Navy continued, with the expansion of the department, to be partial and misguided. "You would be surprised to hear," Hewes informed Jones the following May, "what a vast number of applications are continually making for officers of the new frigates, especially the command. The strong recommendations from those provinces where any frigates are building have great weight."[4] The apportionment provided for the construction of four vessels in Pennsylvania, two each in New York, Rhode Island, and Massachusetts, and one each in New Hampshire, Connecticut, and Maryland; but for none in North Carolina, to which Jones could look for favorable consideration. Congress lent itself to still additional local influence when a resolution of April 17, 1776 provided; "The nomination or appointment of captains or commanders of Continental vessels shall not establish rank, which is to be settled before commissions are granted." This provision, ambiguous in word if not in intention as to men who had already received commissions, promoted the ranking of officers not on the customary basis of proved services and seniority but of arbitrary appointment.

When candidates received commissions for most of the new frigates, Jones was busily employed in convoy service with his little sloop the *Providence;* and when the definitive rank of all the captains was established on October 10, 1776, he was at sea on his first memorable cruise in the same vessel. Hewes happened to be absent in North Carolina, Morris still knew him little, and Hancock had even less knowledge of him. In contrast with his situation, members of Congress were not at all behindhand in promoting the interests of friends and relatives, and many officers themselves were in Philadelphia. John Manley journeyed from Boston and remained all summer at the seat of the Government to make certain of receiving what he considered his due; and although others travelled less far, at least nine naval captains, apart from lesser officers, came to the town at this opportune period.[5] The time was the more propitious for them because the pressure of business rendered Congress the less deliberate while the increasing British threat to capture Philadelphia hastened the members to fly to Baltimore. Therefore the circumstances attendant upon the establishment of naval rank on October 10 were not likely to promote consideration for the merits of Jones.

This naval list of captains—no officers of higher rank appear in it—had second in order Captain Manley, whose pressure upon Congress, as well as his seniority and services, appears to have had its reward. His standing was initially third, but a threat to resign succeeded in raising it one step.[6] The appointee by Washington in the summer of 1775 as captain and on January 1, 1776 as commodore of a little fleet,[7] he was the first officer to receive a commission from a source of national authority and to make important captures of powder, cannon, and medicines. He received also the handsome reward of commanding the *Hancock* of thirty-two guns, one of the first frigates to slip down the ways.

Following in seniority were the officers of Hopkins' fleet, who fared in various wise. Biddle was fifth, and became captain of the *Randolph,* likewise of thirty-two guns. As he had served capably

after as well as during the New Providence expedition and belonged to a family of political as well as social importance in Pennsylvania, he fulfilled too many requirements to be slighted. Saltonstall ranked directly above him, fourth, and gained the command of the *Trumbull* of twenty-eight guns; his only qualification
was the earlier appointment as captain of the *Alfred,* for which his
fitness had not been evident—but he was the brother-in-law of Silas
Deane. Whipple and the younger Hopkins were respectively
twelfth with the command of the *Providence* (not the sloop but
the frigate) of twenty-eight guns, and thirteenth with the command
of the *Warren* of thirty-two guns; neither why they were so low
in standing if Saltonstall was so high, nor why they were so high
if Jones was very considerably lower, is explainable except on
the score of considerations other than proved abilities. Even two
former lieutenants of the New Providence cruise, Hoysted Hacker,
sixteenth in rank and newly appointed captain of the *Hampden,*
and Isaiah Robinson, seventeenth and captain of the *Andrew
Doria,* junior to Jones previously were senior to him now.

Next to Manley and the officers of Hopkins' fleet in length of
Continental service were John Barry, seventh, whose frigate was
the *Effingham* of twenty-eight guns, and Lambert Wickes, eleventh,
whose command was not a frigate but the ship *Reprisal* of sixteen
guns. Barry had already shown abilities as the merchant captain of
the *Black Prince,* renamed the *Alfred,* upon her conversion into
a ship of war, aided greatly in the equipment of Hopkins' vessels,
and, after his appointment on March 14, 1776 to the command of
the brig *Lexington* of sixteen small guns, patrolled the lower
Delaware with conspicuous success. Although he knew Robert
Morris well, part owner of the *Alfred* when she had been a merchantman, Barry was worthy of even higher rank, regardless of
their business association. Wickes had fought with honor against
a British sloop of war off the coast of Martinique, showed an aptitude for diplomatic negotiation, and inspired such confidence in
his courage and discretion as to be chosen for the secret mission
of carrying Franklin to France.[8] He, too, knew Morris; but although his standing was not low, his ship as well as his rank even
at this period scarcely did him justice.

Among others who gained high station, but who had been in the service of individual states, not the Continental Government, or in no government naval service at all, were Hector McNeill, Thomas Thompson, Thomas Reed, and James Nicholson. Mc-Neill, who had acquired experience in the British Navy and had strong recommendations from Massachusetts, ranked third and received the command of the frigate *Boston* of twenty-four guns; he had the good opinion of Jones, which may indicate further that his precedence over many others was based on superior capacities.[9] Thompson, sixth, the captain of the *Raleigh* of thirty-two guns, was of less certain merit. Jones prophetically called him "that dull inactive genius more fit to be a ship carpenter than a captain."[10] Nevertheless, the political influence behind Thompson might have been greater than it was; William Whipple, a New Hampshire member of the Marine Committee who happened to be absent from its sessions, stated: "Thompson is sixth on the list. Had I been here, I certainly would have had him higher; however, considering the train after him, I think it pretty well."[11] As for Thomas Read, eighth, captain of the *Washington* of thirty-two guns, and formerly in command of the *Montgomery*, a ship of Pennsylvania, which he had directed with little promise, his rank was obviously the result of strong backing in Congress.

The most shameless case of political influence was that of James Nicholson, who was placed at the head of the list of captains. He had performed some minor services on the Chesapeake below Baltimore in the Maryland state navy, and received the appointment to the *Virginia* of twenty-eight guns. If Richard Henry Lee, both a leader in Congress and a member of its Marine Committee, and S. Purviance, Jr., Chairman of the Committee of Baltimore, could have gained even a commodoreship for Nicholson, to all appearances they would have done so. "Nicholson may be assured," wrote the one to the other shortly before the list appeared, "that in settling the rank of the captains his merit will not be forgotten. It is not probable that the frigates will sail in fleets for some time; and therefore it is likely that no higher appointment than that of captain will soon take place."[12] Lee, a political ally of Samuel and John Adams, must have made a suitable compromise with them for a Southern appointment to balance several Northern commissions otherwise inexplicable. So he found it possible to write further to Purviance: "I have the pleasure to acquaint you that in ranking the captains of our Continental ships, the Congress have placed Captain Nicholson at the head, he being the first captain."[13]

After Manley the early appointee of Washington, after these various captains and lieutenants of Hopkins' fleet, after Barry and Wickes whose first commissions followed those of Hopkins' officers, after additional captains whose initial Continental appointments were still later by several months, after officers among them who either had refused to enter the Continental service at the beginning because, by their own confession, they "did not choose to be hanged" or had chosen commissions from the provinces for guarding coastal rivers as safer—after all of them, without drawing comparisons in services as well as in seniority, stood John Paul Jones, linked still with the little sloop *Providence* of twelve small guns and in rank eighteenth.

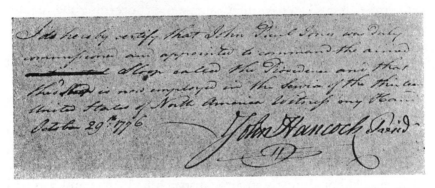

CERTIFICATE SIGNED BY JOHN HANCOCK, PRESIDENT OF
THE CONTINENTAL CONGRESS

Courtesy of the New York Historical Society (Naval History Section), New York City, which owns the original.

Chapter XIII

◇◇

Commander of the *Alfred-Hampden-Providence* Enterprise

IT IS IRONIC that precisely during this period when Congress in Philadelphia degraded Jones without his knowledge to the rank of eighteenth captain, Hopkins in Rhode Island offered him the command of the *Alfred, Hampden,* and *Providence* for a second cruise. Jones had told the Commodore concerning the further contemplated raids which his limited resources with the small sloop alone had rendered impracticable. And the Commodore independently had learned of a hundred American prisoners at forced labor in the coal mines of Cape Breton. Hopkins was not averse at this time to directing another enterprise which gave great promise under so proved a warrior as Jones.

At the same time the relations of the Commodore with the authorities in Philadelphia were of increasing seriousness. He as well as the *Alfred* had remained in port since returning from the Bahamas, although dispatch after dispatch had come and was still coming for a cruise, especially along the coast of Virginia and the Carolinas.[1] He seems to have followed, rather, his own wishes and those of his friend Governor Trumbull for various enterprises under his captains with single vessels or small squadrons.[2] When his ships as a unit were accordingly not available, Hopkins assured the Marine Committee in suave terms: "I am glad to have your orders for an expedition to the southward, that I may have it in my power to convince the gentlemen in every state that I have nothing at heart but the common cause."[3]

All the motives of the Commodore were not yet clear in giving Jones the command of three ships for a second northern enterprise against the coal fleet off Cape Breton and the fishery of Newfoundland. The recent letter of sympathy from the Captain concerning the trials of the Commodore marked a climax of good will between them. To Jones, however, neither the ultimate purpose of Hopkins nor his supersedure at the hands of the Marine Committee seemed of present moment. The expedition was his object, and the haste of circumstances whetted the haste of his nature.

Essential for success of his pending service was arrival at his cruising ground before the coal and fishery fleets were gone for the winter season and before the northern ports were icebound. It was already mid-October, and the ever-increasing dearth of seamen, one of the reasons for the failure of Hopkins to sail with his whole fleet, now also delayed and sorely troubled Jones. The *Providence*, thanks to his precautions, still retained most of her crew, but the *Alfred* had only about thirty men and the *Hampden* none.[4] If the Continental ships were so fortunate as to enlist a few sailors, the privateers inveigled most of them away even when a month's wages were paid in advance. Neither Congress nor the colonial legislatures took measures to thwart the monopoly of seamen which these privately owned vessels gained by their appeal to avarice and by their other unscrupulous enticements.

The situation was the worse because the first naval regulations of November 25, 1775 permitted the privateers, as already noted, to retain the whole value of their booty, but apportioned to the Continental ships only one-third the proceeds from captured merchantmen and one-half from captured war vessels, and designated the remaining shares for the Government. Jones strenuously objected to this policy as "penny wise and pound foolish." Both his immediate predicament and his purpose to aid in improving and building the naval system accounted apparently for an early and wiser provision. When scarcely beyond Delaware Bay on September 4 during his previous cruise, he had already sent Morris the first of his series of suggestions, introducing them in these terms: "As the regulations of the Navy are of the utmost consequence, you will not think it presumption if with the utmost diffidence I venture to communicate to you such hints as in my judgment will promote its honor and good government."[5] Now while striving to man his ships, he urged him to effect a change by which sailors on Continental vessels would receive as much as on privateers, and would continue their service not for a single cruise or for a year but for the term of the war. His advice must have had influence, for scarcely more than two months after the date of his letter new naval regulations of October 30, 1776 provided that Continental crews should receive one half the value of merchant vessels and all the proceeds from ships of war which they captured.

The Colonies employed fifteen thousand sailors in the merchant service before the Revolution; and they had almost sixty thousand men in the privately owned ships licensed by the Government, apart from many others in vessels registered by the separate colonies, in the course of the war. Not without reason, then, Jones urged expediency, condemned the owners of the privateers even more than their sailors and officers, and lamented: "It is to the last degree distressing to contemplate the state and establishment of our Navy. The common class of mankind are actuated by no nobler principle than that of self-interest."[6]

In the meantime Jones and, to some extent, Hopkins took the emergency in their own hands. Appeals to Congress to break the monopoly upon sailors exercised by privateers were in vain; traditions of independent enterprise were so inbred in the Colonial mind that it resented in most cases discipline even in war. "We are too well acquainted," stated the naval authorities, "with the infamous methods taken to man private ships to the prejudice of the public and wish it were in our power to prevent it. Our only remedy at present is to take the course of law." Hopkins himself applied to the General Assembly of Rhode Island for an embargo upon privateers until the Continental fleet was manned, but failed to have it passed by a margin of two votes. He attributed the defeat to "a number of the members being deeply concerned in privateering," and added in his report to the Marine Committee: "I wish I had your orders giving me leave, whenever I found any man on board the privateers, not only to take him out, but all the rest of the men. That might make them more cautious of taking the men out of the service of the States."[7]

What the greed of owners of privateers may have lacked among the vices, the mutinous temper of sailors seems fully to have supplied. Even Washington had lost patience with the seamen who manned his little fleet: "The plague, trouble, and vexation I have had with the crews of all the armed vessels is inexpressible. I do believe there is not on earth a more disorderly set."[8]

So Jones with much ado and with as great speed as possible managed to increase the *Alfred's* nucleus of thirty seamen to a skeleton crew of one hundred and forty, and provided a meagre number for the *Hampden* from some of his sailors of the *Providence,* which the lack of man-power determined him to leave behind. His next care was to prevent privateers from enticing them away faster than they had enlisted. Upon receiving on October 22, 1776 his final orders for the expedition, he was fully determined to follow his own wishes as well as various suggestions and instructions of Hopkins to discipline any privateers discoverable on his course by removing from them both deserters from the Continental Navy and other sailors for good measure.

Despite his haste to sail opportunely, Jones had to contend not only with the difficulties of signing crews and the belatedness of Hopkins, but also with the alleged inefficiency of Hoysted Hacker, who was in command of the *Hampden.* At last, on October 27, Jones and Hacker weighed anchor and shortly rounded the Rhode Island coast only to have the captain of the *Hampden* reveal his want of skill as a navigator by running his ship upon a ledge of rocks. As the keel suffered injury, both captains put back to Newport. And now Jones wrote a letter to Hopkins at Providence which seems to have marked the parting of the ways between them; yet the first overt flare must have had its ultimate origin in mutual antagonism born of greater familiarity between two diverse natures. The accident meant new delay, and patience was not Jones' greatest virtue, especially when an expedition demanded dispatch and his blood surged for action.

So his message may have expressed unjust accusations against his chief as well as just ones against Hacker. Hopkins possibly disliked the information more than its tone, but Jones was not to blame for the information. The Commodore's reply did not apparently convey all that he thought: "I received your disagreeable letter, and you are hereby directed to go immediately to Newport with the *Alfred;* and if the *Hampden* will not do for the cruise, Captain Hacker and the whole of the *Hampden's* crew are to take the *Providence* in her room, and follow the former directions. If I can, I will be at Newport tomorrow."[9] There was possibly more form than meaning either open or veiled in the last words which Hopkins used almost habitually in writing to his officers: "I am your friend."

Ever less timely as it became for the cruise, Jones accepted the suggestion for the transfer, and set out again early on November 2, 1776 with the *Alfred* and *Providence.* Following his course to round Cape Cod, he decided in a light wind to pass through the shoals and so discovered a privateer, the *Eagle,* under a certain Captain Field in Tarpawling Cove near Nantucket. Even in his haste it was not his intention to ignore the desertion of sailors. He sent an officer to examine the *Eagle,* who found two men belonging to Hopkins' fleet and two others of the Rhode Island Brigade concealed in such remote parts of the vessel that it was necessary to break a bulkhead to ferret them out. These and twenty others Jones took aboard the *Alfred,* and then crowded sail for Nova Scotia.[10]

The friendship which he cherished warmest is evident in the consignment of his first important capture of the expedition, the *Active,* taken off Cape Breton on November 12, to Robert Smith, who was a prize agent at Edenton, North Carolina, as well as the brother of his comrade James and the partner of Joseph Hewes.[11] Neither any agent in New England nearer at hand, nor Hopkins through whom he might have acted, nor any other but Hewes, of whom he wrote Morris, "There is no man whom I respect more than him," prompted this indication of his affection as well as regard. Jones was the more justified in following any wishes of his own not contrary to directions of the Marine Committee because this body informed Hopkins that he was not to share in any prizes of the *Providence* after she had passed under the Committee's orders the preceding August 6.[12] Presumably the same principle was to apply to other ships of the fleet which he did not actually command himself. As for the *Active,* the prize master whom Jones placed aboard brought her, with a perversity too characteristic, not to Edenton but to Dartmouth, where a relative of his own was prize agent. Although Jones' purpose was thwarted, his message of gratitude remains; "I am happy," he wrote in the *Alfred* for transmission to Robert Smith, "in this opportunity of acknowledging the great obligation I owe to Mr. Hewes."[13]

Near Louisburg, close by the scene of his previous captures and on a traffic lane for ships from Britain to Canada, he took on the same day his most valuable merchant prize, the *Mellish*. She was a large armed vessel which carried ten thousand complete uniforms for the armies of Generals Carleton and Burgoyne and had on board two marine officers and an army captain with a company of soldiers. The cargo was so precious that he cautioned his prize master, if separated from him, to seek the nearest port in the United States, and to avoid the enemy's cruising vessels off Block Island by sailing through Nantucket Shoals. And in a letter entrusted to him for Hancock as President of the Marine Committee, he stated: "The loss of the *Mellish* will distress the enemy more than can be easily imagined, as the clothing on board of her is the last intended to be sent out for Canada this season, and all that has preceded it is already taken. The situation of Burgoyne's army must soon become insupportable. I will not lose sight of a prize of such importance but will sink her rather than suffer her to fall again into their hands."[14]

At this point, with a valuable prize to be guarded, severer weather to be endured on a northern coast in winter, and a bold descent to be made ashore, Hacker in the *Providence* was as fearful as he had previously proved incompetent. His officers and seamen also were more fit for privateers than Continental ships; they had no stomach to suffer cold and privations in the achievement of a bold exploit. "Should we meet with a severe gale," wrote about ten subscribers to a round robin addressed to Hacker, "it is our opinions both pumps will not keep her free unless we scudded. We have a quarter part of our hands sick and the prizes we have taken will still reduce our number, as they are of great value. Should you think proper to continue further to the northward, we are ready and willing to do everything in our power for the good of the expedition, but we are of opinion it will too much endanger the vessel."[15] The views of Hacker were evidently more timid than those of the subscribers, for he presented the petition to Jones and soon afterwards slipped away for Rhode Island under cover of the night. So the commander of the *Alfred* found himself alone in the enemy's waters.

Jones then made a raid upon the coast of Nova Scotia, burning a laden transport inshore and several oil warehouses of the fisheries. He captured in the fog four ships of a fleet convoyed by the frigate *Flora.* He took also a staunch Liverpool letter of marque of sixteen guns. He found it impossible, however, to achieve his most cherished object, the rescue of the one hundred American prisoners in the coal pits near Cape Breton, because of ice-bound harbors. Thanks especially to the delays occasioned by Hacker and the privateering interests, his championship of the cause of captured seamen suffered this initial defeat, but indicates at the same time the humaneness that was to offset the destructive forces to which the policies of war impelled him.

The depletion of the small crew of the *Alfred* to man the prizes coincident with the numerous prisoners from them, the convoy of the valuable captures, and the ebb of supplies determined Jones at last to make for an American port. On the edge of St. George's Bank, however, a challenge lay before him. It was the *Milford* again, the slow frigate mocked on the previous cruise, which he recognized to windward in the distance late in the afternoon. Unready at the closing scene of the expedition and deserted by the *Providence,* he was not in a suitable state to fight; yet convoying his prizes, among which was the *Mellish,* he refused to flee.

A ruse was the remaining alternative. He estimated on the basis of his former trial of the *Milford's* sailing that she could not come up before the night of the short winter day so as to compel an immediate issue. In the meantime the *Alfred* and the captured letter of marque, now commanded by Lieutenant Saunders, took positions between the approaching enemy and the rest of his prizes, and he ordered the latter to crowd sail all night on the track they then held without regard for his further signals and his lanterns. It was understood that, if he should not be with them the next morning, the prizes were to make the best of their way to a home port.

As the *Milford* gradually overhauled the *Alfred* and her slow convoy, they calmly held to their course in the deepening darkness.

At midnight the *Alfred* with the letter of marque tacked, and she carried a top light, to all appearances as a beacon for her prizes but in fact as a decoy for the English frigate. The prizes, as directed, farther from the enemy than the *Alfred,* continued their separate course unseen and at daybreak had disappeared over the horizon. When the beacon increasingly paled and was removed, the *Alfred* and the letter of marque only were visible to the *Milford* still in pursuit.

Now more free to attack or to run, Jones was determined, poorly provided as he was for battle, to satisfy himself fully as to the strength of the enemy. He could see only her bow, for she was beyond gunfire range on his lee quarter; he therefore ordered Lieutenant Saunders in the letter of marque, which "held a better wind than the *Alfred,* to drop slowly astern, until he could discover by a view of the enemy's side whether she was of superior or inferior force, and to make a signal accordingly."[16] During the manœuvres which followed, Jones was able to see the *Milford's* side fairly open, and his estimate of her battery determined him not to fight in his present condition unless necessary. His greater skill in seamanship, as well as squally weather which presaged a storm, soon enabled him to do as he chose. But to his great surprise, the letter of marque, either recaptured by mutiny of her English crew or foolishly or traitorously commanded by Saunders, "bore down on the *Milford,* made the signal of her inferior force, ran under her lee, and was taken!"[17]

Again alone in the *Alfred,* Jones bore away a second time for home, and he stood in to the harbor of Boston in mid-December with only two days' water and provisions remaining. Here he learned that all the prizes of his convoy had reached port safely, including the *Mellish.* "This news," he wrote concerning the transport with her ten thousand uniforms, "reached the army in the critical minute before General Washington recrossed the Delaware and turned the tables upon the enemy."[18] So the second enterprise under the command of Jones concluded with the threat and foil of the *Milford,* which emphasized the truth that the limitations of the cruise were due chiefly to others and the successes to himself. Still the opportunity had come from the Commodore.

◇◇

Chapter XIV

Jones, Not Hopkins or Manley, Leader of the American Navy

THE ZEST OF Jones for an active and constructive part in the Revolution, which his two expeditions had sharpened, made him now in Boston the less tolerant of the ineffective administration of Hopkins. He had brought in the *Alfred* from his prizes one hundred and fifty British prisoners for the purpose of exchange for Americans, notwithstanding his abandoned plan to free those compatriots in the Canadian coal pits; but he did not believe that his proper function was to be a "jailkeeper" for as long as a month. As he had already proved that the sufferings of American prisoners awakened more compassion in him than in any of his fellow naval officers, he resented criticism of his considerateness towards one of his English prisoners in the case of a moving personal appeal by the captive's wife and children. With such incidents, the opening estrangement between Jones and Hopkins signalized by the "disagreeable letter" was destined to grow quickly. Former intimacy and present separation at the distance between Boston, which was now freed from the British, and Providence, which was becoming more and more blockaded, served to increase it.

Hopkins still failed to curb the privateers and to man his fleet, although his efforts were at times positive enough. He did not stir to escape from encircled Providence to reopened Boston. He undertook no further expedition himself, although his flagship was now the new thirty-two gun frigate *Warren* and the Marine Committee continued to send him orders particularly to end Dunmore's ravages along the Southern coast.[1] But while claiming to serve the Government without pay, he insisted upon receiving one-twentieth of the proceeds from all prizes taken by the fleet, and possibly his most important if not initial secret grievance against Jones was that his Captain acted himself and urged the hand of the Marine Committee to withhold from him this source of gain.

The blunt manner of Hopkins, far more than his essential principles, left its sting and provoked enemies. As Commodore, he maintained little discipline, not to speak of inspiring morale, among such officers and seamen as he was able to secure. They were without doubt callous enough, but his practice of condemning the Marine Committee openly, of forfeiting respect by indiscriminate oaths, and of shutting his eyes to libertine habits of his sailors was not calculated to increase their number or their efficiency. A Providence minister who remonstrated concerning the morals of the Navy may well have been a righteous meddler, but the reply of Hopkins, telling as it was, reflects his characteristic tendency to deplore his means instead of assuming both the responsibility and authority of his position: "As to your complaints of the morals of the people belonging to the Navy, I am now to let you know that I did not enter into the Navy as a divine, and that I am not qualified to act or give directions in that matter; the Congress whom I serve made provisions for a chaplain to perform that necessary duty, but to my mortification I have not been able to get a single man to act in that character . . . if none can be procured, I cannot but condole with you the depravity of the times."[2]

No spiritual leader in a general sense, no aggressive naval fighter, no masterly executive, he was to fail America in failing Jones,[3] although it is true enough that the Captain was too uncompromising, efficient, and ambitious to be a good subordinate. The Commodore had talked of exemplary punishment of the privateers, and the Captain had acted drastically in the case of the *Eagle*.[4] As the principle involved was of moment to the Continental ships in general as well as to the fleet, Jones was the more surprised to learn from Hopkins almost immediately upon his return to Boston that the owner of the *Eagle* had brought a suit for £10,000 against him. Both his orders and the issue itself made the cause, in fact the legal action, Hopkins' own. But he chose to act lamely. He made a counterclaim against the privateer for taking men from his fleet. He sent the Marine Committee a letter of excuse.[5] And he prevaricated about his instructions in a report which came to Jones.[6]

When the Captain found that the Commodore set aside explicit responsibility as his superior officer, he wrote his attorney Tillinghast: "Your kindness in taking up my action claims my most grateful thanks. In consequence of some insinuations which I have heard, I must request you to put the question to Admiral Hopkins whether he means to disavow the express orders which he gave me repeatedly at Newport respecting the matter or whether he is determined to justify my conduct—yes or no—that I may take my measures accordingly. . . ."[7] The decisive character of Jones was foreign to Hopkins. The one demanded justification for his act, the other offered excuses for it.

"You have his orders in writing," Tillinghast reported as to Hopkins' answer, "which if that will justify your conduct, it's well; if not, he's ready and willing to do anything in his power to assist and serve you."[8] Jones read between these lines that the Commodore avoided the issue, and he mistrusted him the more upon the arrival of further communications. He learned from his commander, who remained non-committal, that seven new suits were pending against him by the owners of privateers in behalf of the deserters taken aboard the *Alfred*. He received the ironic assurance that he would be "safe" if he came from Boston to Providence aboard the *Warren*.

While the outcome of the *Eagle* suit was still pending, Jones' own bold devotion shines in these words: "Be the consequence what it will, I glory in having been the first who has broke through the shameful abuses which have been too long practiced upon the Navy by mercenaries whose governing principle has been that of self-interest."[9] The final judgment of the court, which nonsuited the action against him, was vindication of the justice and honor of his course.

From Providence to Boston soon came a message of the Commodore that Captain Olney was to take command of the *Cabot* and Captain Hinman of the *Alfred*. Hopkins assumed responsibility for the first order and referred to Congress for the second. Congress, according to Robert Morris, had provided the less for Jones because they "never doubted that your active genius would find useful employment for the ship under your command, as you were so near the Commodore and could go clothed with his authority."[10] The excuse for having given Jones neither suitable rank—he was still unaware of his official standing—nor a new frigate was weak, and the confidence in continued good will of the Commodore was unduly optimistic. As the clash developed, other officers gained command of the better ships of the fleet, and Jones had the advice of Hopkins to return to the *Providence.* Although no additional ones of consequence remained, the Commodore then offered "any other vessel that is in my power to give you."

Now that Jones' two successful cruises had won for him so little as to have the jealousy of Hopkins as well as the manœuvres of Congress shackle his opportunities for further services, he turned the greater attention to his rank. First he expressed himself to his most intimate supporter Hewes "with a freedom becoming an honest man" and pictured with his pen some of the officers who were his colleagues in Boston while Hopkins in Providence compelled him to mark time.

As to Hoysted Hacker, the Captain of the *Providence,* who had given him "the slip in the night" during his recent cruise, he declared: "If such doings are permitted, the Navy will never rise above contempt. The aforesaid noble captain doth not understand the first case of plain trigonometry, yet it is averred that he had the honor and that his abilities have enabled him to command a passage boat between Rhode Island and Providence long before the war began."[11]

But Jones reserved his special sarcasm for John Manley, whom Washington had independently appointed "Commodore of our little squadron" in the course of earlier operations. Born in England and formerly employed in a minor post in her Navy, Manley was now the commander of the *Hancock* of thirty-two guns at Boston in reward for his recent successes; but his reputation was to fall almost as much as it had risen under the circumstances of his later loss of this frigate to the enemy and his resulting controversy with Captain McNeill of the *Boston* of twenty-eight guns, who described him as "ignorant, obstinate, overbearing, and tyrannical beyond description." Perhaps in the light of this future history,

Jones' acidulous judgment upon Manley, sharpened by proximity to him and by professional respect and personal friendship for McNeill, was not particularly amiss, the early services of the criticized officer and his appointment by Washington notwithstanding:

"There is a fellow who calls himself a Commodore, and who keeps us at an awful distance by wearing an English broad pendant. He had lately the honor of being a stick officer, vulgarly called boatswain's mate in an English man-of-war, and was duly qualified for that high station, if fame says true, as appears by his deigning to read English.

"Besides among many evident proofs of his abilities as post captain that might be enumerated, this notable one may perhaps be sufficient—for it seems that in his absence he directs his first lieutenant to take orders from the boatswain. Nay 'tis said that on certain occasions he takes the speaking trumpet out of the lieutenant's hand on the quarter-deck and delivers it on the forecastle to the boatswain. To be very serious that such despicable characters should have obtained commissions as commodores in a navy is truly astonishing, and would pass for romance with me unless I had been convinced by my senses of the sad reality. I could easily enumerate many other characters as truly original as commission officers, but it gives me extreme pain to be under the necessity of attacking private characters. It is, however, some consolation, indeed a great one, that this depravity is not universal. . . . I need not therefore name this great man, this *Commodore;* though I will if called upon, and in the meantime aver that he is altogether unfit to command a frigate of thirty-two guns."[12]

The self-respect of Jones soon prompted a more direct plea to the Marine Committee, in which the ripening genius of the naval officer began to show itself in the maturing style of the man. The tone sets him apart from his fellow-officers. His honor, in effect his rank, was by his avowal dearer to him than his life, but he exercised the restraint to open his appeal to the Committee against supersedure at the hands of Hopkins with a deferential statement concerning his seniority:

"As I am unconscious of any neglect of duty, or misconduct, since my appointment at the first as eldest lieutenant of the Navy, I cannot suppose that you can have intended to set me aside, in favor of any man who did not at that time bear a captain's commission, unless indeed that man, by exerting his superior abilities, has rendered or can render more important services to America. Those who stepped forth at the first, in ships altogether unfit for war, were generally considered as frantic rather than wise men; for it must be remembered that almost everything then made against them." To emphasize his performance, he took occasion to contrast it inferentially with that of Hopkins, Saltonstall, and other captains: "And although the success in the affair with the *Glasgow* was not equal to what it might have been, yet the blame ought not to be general. The principal or principals in command alone are culpable."[13] This implication against Hopkins is scarcely reconcilable with the earlier congratulation of him "for having gained [his] cause at Philadelphia in spite of party." It reflects the extent of the two officers' growing antagonism; it reflects more significantly Jones' present assertive frankness concerning the Commodore and towards the Marine Committee.

In addition to seniority and services, qualities of a gentleman were a further criterion which he suggested to the Committee for its choice and preferment of officers. Although the Captain implied too obviously that he himself met such requirements and that others did not, his standards and capacities tended to counterbalance his self-sufficiency: "There were, it is true, divers persons, from misrepresentation, put into commission at the beginning, without fit qualification, and perhaps the number may have been increased by later appointments; but it follows not that the gentleman or man of merit should be neglected or overlooked on their account. None other than a gentleman, as well as a seaman both in theory and practice, is qualified to support the character of a commission officer in the Navy; nor is any man fit to command a ship of war who is not also capable of communicating his ideas on paper in language that becomes his rank."[14] It is not unlikely that these later words impressed members of the Marine Committee in a period when scholarly attainments in a naval officer were rare.

Jones set himself still further apart. He bared his motives, the springs of his patriotism, which reveal him as more courageous than politic. He stated to an American body of men on whom he was dependent for promotion that his spirit as an officer in the war embraced but also transcended the cause of America. It was the first but not the last occasion on which he took more of an international than a national stand: "When I entered into the service, I was not actuated by motives of self-interest. I stepped forth as a free citizen of the world, in defense of the violated rights of mankind, and not in search of riches, whereof, I thank God, I inherit a sufficiency; but I should prove my degeneracy were I not in the highest degree tenacious of my rank and seniority. As a gentleman, I can yield this point up only to persons of superior abilities and superior merit; and under such persons it would be my highest ambition to learn."[15] Although the dignity of mankind and internationalism were more popular philosophies then than recently and even today, however much related to the individualism and democracy of the Revolution which have again become primary living issues, it was characteristic of the man to address himself so freely to members of Congress whose sentiments were somewhat strictly American.

At this time the spirit of America as a nation, as compared with the principles for which America fought, had crystallized less, of course, than after the adoption of the Constitution. His declaration, therefore, had less meaning than it might appear to assume, especially in the light of his future words and acts as a most ardent citizen of the United States.

The final quality of an officer which Jones pictured almost unconsciously but superbly is not love of mankind, gentlemanly attributes, service, or seniority—but character. Character inspired him with the courage and truthfulness to say: "As the base-minded only are capable of inconsistencies, you will not blame my free soul, which can never stoop where I cannot also esteem."[16] Idealistic in one breath and practical in the next, he returned to his objectives: the rank to which he considered himself entitled and the future service for which he hoped under the direction of the Marine Committee—not Hopkins.

This individualistic letter concerning naval officers as they should be, reached the Marine Committee the same day that another also from Jones' pen came to Morris concerning Hopkins as he apparently was. "When you look over the enclosed memorandum," he stated, "which I took down from the mouth of my late prize master (Mr. Vesey), you will, perhaps, think the account more extraordinary than even the noted affair with the *Glasgow*. I am not yet sufficiently informed to risk my opinion." The English frigate *Diamond* ran aground below Providence; for thirty hours, according to reports, she had no assistance from enemy ships. Hopkins went in the sloop *Providence* to try to destroy her, but his measures were so dilatory and inexpert, in the course of which he allowed himself to be marooned on a sandbar and brought to bear few guns, that she finally escaped.[17] As the Commodore himself recounted that the frigate was on a flat *almost* under cover of a fifty-gun ship and that he thought the possibility of capture or destruction of *no moment*,[18] it would seem that his own words as well as those of the accusers reflect upon him. There were, nevertheless, certain contingencies of which it was difficult to judge, and Jones himself did not later "risk [his] opinion."

It was less the Captain's own degradation in rank at the hands of Hopkins than the impotence of the Navy that impelled him to present to Morris a more detailed account of this Commodore appointed by Congress, apart from the other chosen by Washington. "The Navy," he lamented, "is in a wretched condition. It wants a man of abilities at its head who could bring on a purgation and distinguish between the abilities of a gentleman and those of a mere sailor or boatswain's mate. . . ." His initial indignation at the *Eagle* episode swept him on to language justified in the sailor but somewhat jarring in his superior rôle: "A man who has the meanness of soul to deny his word is a despicable being indeed. He sinks beneath the condition of the poorest reptile that crawls on the earth. And it is not uncharitable to suspect him as being capable of any baseness whatever."[19] Hopkins prevaricated, but to attribute to him a more culpable act at this time seems unwarranted. Jones is to be admired for his uncompromising strength. In the heat of his feelings against the Commodore, who stood directly in the path of his naval duties and ambitions, it can scarcely be said, however, that he was charitable.

He felt at every turn the lack of organization in the Navy, and attributed it to the incapacity of the Commodore and his chief captains. In Boston he tried to coöperate with some of these officers to formulate constructive rules and regulations, but desisted as he explained with grim humor: "We have had sundry meetings here for this purpose without being able to effect anything. And as this is a natural consequence where the understanding is contracted, I have determined that if I subscribe to nonsense, it shall be nonsense of my own, not that of others."

Having been delayed week after week in guarding and exchanging his prisoners aboard the *Alfred,* supervising the sale of prizes and the payment of prize money and wages, enlisting seamen again, and refitting the ship, he recommended that such duties not connected with active service at sea should be delegated to carefully chosen commissioners of dockyards and of other departments. He objected especially to a prize system which permitted inactive officers, Hopkins among others, to share in prize money along with the actual captors. He reiterated the urgency of longer terms of enlistment for seamen and of stern punishment for deserters in order to insure full crews and proper discipline. His opinion of Hopkins was evident in a final indirect reference: "I shall only add at present that the Navy would be far better without a head than with a bad one."[20]

Chapter XV

◇◇

Jones, Commodore in Authority, Obstructed by Hopkins

THE CONTENTS in every instance have been very acceptable, always entertaining, and in many parts useful. These letters I have from time to time communicated to the members of the Marine Committee, all of whom express their satisfaction with your conduct."[1] So Robert Morris, genial as well as astute, informed Jones concerning his reports of the two cruises, his recommendations for the Navy, and his criticisms of Hopkins. Discreetly he made no reference to his rank as eighteenth captain, which he and others among his more conscientious colleagues must now have recognized as unwise as well as prejudiced.

Morris almost alone was now conducting not only naval affairs but practically all Continental executive duties after Congress, near the close of 1776, in fear of British occupation of Philadelphia had fled to Baltimore in haste and repented there at leisure. "If you wish to please your friends, come soon to us," Benjamin Harrison characteristically wrote him from Baltimore, "but if you desire to keep out of the damnedest hole in the world come not here."[2] The financier-patriot was of too hardy metal to find necessary the warning to avoid the quagmires of Baltimore so as to persist singlehandedly in performing most of the work of the whole Congress. And at the present opportunity he both served Jones and brought him to the attention of Hancock, President of Congress and titular head of the Marine Committee. From both men, the one in Philadelphia and the other in Baltimore, expressions of respect and admiration grew with the deeds and apt, sincere words of the Captain.

As early as December 16, 1776 Morris had forwarded to Hancock several letters addressed to the Marine Committee, "especially a very pleasing one from Capt. Jones"[3] which related his expedition in the *Providence;* on the following January 16 he transmitted another containing the account of the cruise in the *Alfred,* and remarked that Jones was "a fine fellow and should be kept employed" and that he would "suggest expeditions to him and let him choose."[4] From Hancock in turn came words of similar approval and warmth: "I admire the spirited conduct of little Jones; pray push him out again. I know he does not love to be idle; and I am as certain you wish him to be constantly active. He is a fine fellow and he shall meet with every notice of mine; and I am confident you will join me."[5]

Praises from Hewes, in addition to those from Morris and Hancock, were the less during this period because he found it necessary to be absent a great deal from the councils of Congress in view of frail health and public duties in Edenton. But further commendations, characteristically founded not on personal favor but the capacities of Jones, were evident in a reply of Morris to John Wendell, a wealthy New Englander particularly disposed to exploit friendships: "I have long been very sensible of Captain Jones' merit as an officer, which alone was a sufficient inducement for me to take him by the hand in all things that with propriety I could."[6]

At this juncture the Marine Committee was to realize that Hopkins neither could man and equip his vessels for a cruise nor would undertake to go to sea himself. It still deferred so far to him on January 21, 1777 as to issue from Baltimore the following instructions: "You are hereby directed to fit for sea the Continental frigates *Warren* and *Providence* with all possible expedition, and order them to proceed forthwith to cruise against the enemy's ships of war that are now interrupting the commerce of the United States from the harbor of Newport to the Capes of Virginia."[7] Whatever sectional or other unfriendly spirit might have colored these particular orders, it was reasonable to expect, difficulties notwithstanding, the two new frigates under his command to be of active service.

The Commodore now failed once too often to execute his orders. His next were in a different tone and by a different hand; Morris informed him on February 5, 1777: "By consent of the Honorable Congress, I have this day given instruction to John Paul Jones, Esq., commander of the *Alfred,* to take upon him the conduct of an expedition wherein he will require the assistance of the *Columbus, Cabot, Hampden,* and sloop *Providence,* and you will please to order the commanders to join him and put themselves under his command. I flatter myself with having your utmost exertions to get these vessels well and expeditiously manned and completely fitted that they may sail as soon as possible."[8]

True to their avowed purpose, Morris and Hancock had turned resolutely to Jones. With the approval of the Marine Committee, Morris also sent the Captain a long letter as appreciative as surprising which empowered him to command the five ships mentioned in the orders to Hopkins.[9] The bold and ingenious vice-president of the Committee suggested daring expeditions particularly to the island of Saint Christopher, to the northern coast of Jamaica, and to Pensacola, but permitted him freedom to follow his own suggestions for a cruise to the coast of Africa. The purpose, as both agreed, was less to capture supplies and destroy British vessels than to decentralize the efforts of the British Navy so as to divert it especially from the American coast and ports. "Destroying their settlements, spreading alarms, showing and keeping up a spirit of enterprise that will oblige them to defend their extensive possessions at all points," in the words of Morris, "is of infinitely more consequence to the United States than all the plunder that can be taken." Jones received his official instructions, sent on February 5 from Philadelphia, on the following 18th at Boston; but Hopkins, whose instructions had been sent on the same date as Jones' and doubtlessly had arrived at Providence a few days sooner than his, was still to show his hand.

To all appearances, after receipt of his directions from Morris, the Commodore once more ignored the Marine Committee and tried to thwart Jones when on February 16 he sent him word: "You are hereby authorized to enlist as many men as you think sufficient to man the sloop *Providence,* as soon as possible, in order to go out on a cruise."[10] Having pretended to be unaware of the appointment from Philadelphia, Hopkins next affected to disbelieve it after Jones requested his coöperation on the basis of his own instructions received in Boston on February 18. He seems likewise to have authorized the *Hampden* to depart subsequent to the information that had reached him. And he ordered Captain Olney of the *Cabot* to cruise for six weeks even after his own admission that he had received Morris' instructions.[11]

"When I placed a confidence in you," Jones wrote to Hopkins on February 28 in a third request for the ships, "I did not think you capable of prevarication. . . . However, waiving everything of a private nature, the best way is to coöperate cheerfully together that the public service may be forwarded, and that scorn may yet forbear to point her finger at a fleet under your command."[12] To these terms of mingled contempt and conciliation, the one expressing the Captain's personal feelings and the other his zeal for America, the Commodore replied: "I rec'd yours of —— express and do absolutely think that it is impracticable to get those vessels fitted or manned for your proposed expedition and shall acquaint the Honorable Marine Board with my reasons."[13]

The true reasons he wisely forbore to mention. He veiled these personal motives behind an incoherent appeal to Hancock for a court-martial to try Jones, but set aside the responsibility to summon it himself. His only tangible accusations were that the Captain of the *Alfred* had refused to pay the wages of sailors unless they made him their agent and that he had failed to aid Lieutenant Saunders in his engagement with the *Milford*. As to the first charge, punishment for desertions, need for re-enlistments, and generosity of the Captain in paying wages from his own pocket seem amply to have warranted his stand; as to the second, it has already appeared that Saunders had been both foolhardy and disobedient according to the most generous interpretation, and that Jones simply had refrained from being equally foolhardy. Hopkins contradicted himself in this case as in others. Only a few days later he generously confessed to William Ellery of the Marine Committee: "I believe that most of the success Captain Jones has had is owing to his valour and good conduct."[14]

Such occasional frank admissions reveal the better aspects of Hopkins' character. But they indicate also that some of his hostile acts were the less expected. He had invited the Captain aboard the *Warren* at a time ominously close to the suggestion to Hancock for a court-martial. He had assured Hancock as well as his own brother that, in view of his age and the difficult problems that beset the Continental Navy, patriotism prompted him to be ready, even glad, to step aside in favor of a younger, more capable commander. When the Marine Committee through the courageous hand of Morris had acted to give Jones his chance as Commodore, Hopkins ignored Morris and wrote insipidly to Hancock. He went further and even tried to tarnish the reputation of the successful Captain by insinuations that he had stolen a hoard of gold from the *Mellish*. Jones answered with his characteristic thoroughness by testimony of the prize agents.

But the curtain was now descending upon Hopkins' dominance as Commodore. It was not necessary for the rival Captain to refute him further; members of Congress and other officers of the fleet opposed him with reason as well as prejudice. Perhaps it was the irony of justice that the immediate occasion for the end of his rule was in part the unscrupulous enmity of owners of privateers who found it comparatively easy to conduct a lobby even at that time through their connection with members of Congress associated with them in their profits. As the Commodore had tried with fearless patriotism to curb these hostile persons who outfitted privateers, but had given Jones half-hearted support when he drastically retaliated upon them, it seems the more fateful retribution that these sons of avarice should have conducted a successful cabal against him. Whatever their secret part in the proceedings, the charges impeaching the personal character of Hopkins to a greater extent than his professional reputation were both unusual and drastic.

John Grannis and nine other members of Hopkins' ship the *Warren* presented a petition to the Marine Committee; others followed their example.[15] The statement of John Reed the chaplain—the Commodore had finally secured a minister with questionable results—was more temperate and possibly more trustworthy than the words of the officers and crew: "He allows himself in anger in common conversation to take the name of God in vain; he is remarkably addicted to profane swearing. In this respect as well as in many other respects he sets his officers and men a most irreligious and impious example. . . . In this part of America, people are afraid of him. They are jealous of him, and he is an effectual obstacle to the fleet's being properly manned."[16] The testimony of another in less restrained language accused him of "ridiculing virtue" and of being the cause for the enlistment of few sailors in the *Warren* as "people are afraid to engage in the fleet through fear of their being turned over to this ship." A third bore witness that he characterized the Continental Congress as "a pack of damned rascals, the best of them mere lawyers' clerks, who knew nothing of their business." A fourth averred to the investigating committee: "When the frigates were at Newport before the British occupation of that place, more than a hundred men who were discharged from the Army, most of them seamen, were willing to come on board the ships and assist them to Boston or any other place to the eastward in order that they might be manned, but Commodore Hopkins utterly refused." Several of those who had signed the petition against him, including John Reed the chaplain, later made contrary statements in his favor and admitted that they had been influenced "by some gentlemen of the town [Providence]."[17]

Whether prejudiced or impartial, whether primary or secondary, the testimony against Hopkins was too much in accord with his temperament to turn Congress from its views—it was in accord with his disregard of some of the orders from the Marine Committee, his skeleton crews for the fleet, his sacrifice of public service to personal jealousy in relation to Jones. As members of Congress, furthermore, had not shown themselves particularly wise in such orders to Hopkins as those on the occasion of the New Providence cruise and as their censure of him after this enterprise had seemed to be even less well-considered, they may have felt the more keenly the alleged aspersions by the Commodore that "the best of them were lawyers' clerks who knew nothing of their business." Hopkins first received a suspension from his command and later, in January, 1778, a dismissal from service in the Navy.

It is not evident that anyone defended Hopkins at the time of his suspension as resolutely as John Adams had done after the New Providence cruise. On the occasion of the earlier trial, his New

England advocate had declared: "It appeared to me that the Commodore was pursued and persecuted by that anti-New England spirit which haunted Congress in many other of their. proceedings. I saw nothing in the conduct of Hopkins which indicated corruption or want of integrity. Experience and skill might have been deficient in several particulars; but where could we find greater experience or skill? I knew of none to be found."[18] Adams related further: "When the trial was over, Mr. Ellery of Newport came to me and said, 'You have made the old man your friend for life; he will hear of your defense of him and he never forgets a kindness.' More than twenty years afterwards, the old gentleman hobbled on his crutches to the inn in Providence, at fourscore years of age, one half of him dead in consequence of a paralytic stroke, with his eyes overflowing with tears, to express his gratitude to me."[19]

In the course of the proceedings leading to the suspension of the Commodore, Jones left the *Alfred* in Boston with Hinman, her newly appointed captain, and set forth to lay his situation before the Marine Committee in Philadelphia.

Chapter XVI

Independent Command
of the *Ranger*

GREATER FREEDOM for enterprise promised soon to open before Jones and to provide the stage for more spectacular exploits natural to his daring initiative. Even before his coming to Philadelphia, the Marine Committee took steps to make amends, at least in part, for disregard of its orders by the Commodore. As early as March 25, 1777 a resolution of Congress provided that Jones should have his preference among three ships which were to be purchased "until better provision [could] be made for him." In the interval, however, between the despatch of these orders and their arrival in Boston, where the vessels were to be bought from the Colony of Massachusetts, he appeared in person.

Now that Congress, its panic past and its powers resumed, had returned from Baltimore to the Continental capital, Morris was able to limit his activity to his more particular duties. Hewes had lost his re-election for the current year in spite of sterling services,[1] and so for the present his direct influence in naval matters was absent. Although the administration of the Navy devolved more upon Morris than upon any other member of the Marine Committee, Hancock as head of this body as well as of Congress was most in authority. His opinion of the Captain continued to be highly favorable, but neither his character nor his political associations were of such independence as to withstand freely the influences of sectionalism and other prejudice. He had to reconcile such powerful advocates for favored officers as John Adams, who was to consider Jones and Barry "those emigrant foreigners of the South,"[2] and as Richard Henry Lee, who had gained for Nicholson the highest rank in the list of October 10 of the preceding year.

JOHN PAUL JONES' COMMISSION AS CAPTAIN, OCTOBER 10, 1776

Presented by John L. Senior and now in the Crypt of the Naval Academy Chapel near the dies of the gold medal,

Hancock and his colleagues of the Marine Committee were as diplomatic as possible in trying to weather the storm that they feared might break from the deep-charged feelings of Jones when he was finally to learn the details of his low official standing. They informed him of course concerning the orders, already on their way to Boston, to provide a ship for him. They availed themselves of his broad professional knowledge, and later were to adopt in many respects his further recommendations for the improvement of the Navy, especially as to the administration of dockyards, the appointment of commissioners under a board of admiralty, and the examination and training of naval officers.[3]

At length, before Jones' return to Boston at the close of April, 1777, Hancock undertook to apprize him indirectly of his standing. The frankness of the sailor appears in a better light than the subtlety of the statesman, according to the former's account: "He requested me to show him the captain's commission [of August 8, 1776] he had given me the year before. I did so. He then desired me to leave it with him a day or two, till he could find a leisure moment to fill up a new commission. I made no difficulty. When I waited on him the day before my departure, to my great surprise he put into my hands a commission dated the 10th day of October, 1776, and numbered *eighteen* on the margin. I told him that was not what I expected, and requested my former commission. He turned over various papers on the table, and at last told me he was sorry to have lost or mislaid it. I shall here make no remark on such conduct in a President of Congress. Perhaps it needs none.

"He paid me many compliments on the services I had performed in vessels of little force, and assured me no officer stood higher in the opinion of Congress than I; a proof of which, he said, was my late appointment to the command of *secret* expeditions, with five sail and men proportioned, against St. Kitts, Pensacola, Augustine, etc. That the table of naval rank that had been adopted the 10th of October, 1776, had been drawn up in a hurry, and without well knowing the different merits and qualifications of the officers; but it was the intention of Congress to render impartial justice, and always to honour, promote, and reward merit. And, as to myself, that I might depend on receiving a very agreeable appointment soon after my return to Boston; and, until I was perfectly satisfied respecting my rank, I should have a separate command."[4]

Unbecoming as the subterfuge of Hancock appears, his explanation of the circumstances under which Jones received his standing from Congress is the more reasonable in view of the stress of political forces which the President undoubtedly had to reconcile. His assurances were generous and convincing enough to make the Captain feel that the wound, however great, would at least be healed. And it is notably to the credit of Jones, in contrast with other officers, that, strenuously as he was to exert himself to remedy the apparent reflection upon his professional honor and the setback to his opportunities for the greater enterprise, he neither entertained the thought of resigning his commission nor even was disposed to sulk in his services. The injustice was, on the contrary, a flint to strike the more burning ardor in his ambitious patriotism.

The gratitude also that he felt towards Hewes for his first appointment as a lieutenant had turned equally towards Morris for his command, although unrealized, of Hopkins' fleet. So his human warmth, along with his new resolution, prompted these words to Hewes expressive of his expansive appreciation: "I confess in the overflowing of my heart that the command of the important expedition which was allotted to me by Mr. Morris last winter far exceeded my expectation. I am also deeply sensible of the distinctions and preference which I have since that time experienced from Congress and from the Marine and Secret Committees; and I attribute the mistake in the line of rank not to intention but to your absence, and to the partial recommendations which were then exhibited."[5]

Heartened by the prospect of a new enterprise and by many assurances, Jones was back in Boston early in May, 1777, scarcely a month after he had journeyed to Philadelphia. Before the purchase of the ship for him authorized by Congress, he received on May 9 further orders which provided for his command of the French ship *Amphitrite* at Portsmouth with the view of proceeding to France and securing there, by direction of the Marine Committee to the American commissioners in Paris, a formidable frigate under construction in Holland armed with thirty-six eighteen-pounders on one deck.

The *Amphitrite* of twenty guns had arrived with a valuable cargo of military stores from Roderique Hortalez & Company, the strange Paris mercantile house financed chiefly by France and in some measure by Spain behind the screen of its founder and executive, Beaumarchais. It was he who with hidden political aims in relation to England on the one hand and America on the other carried on in commerce a seeming quixotic comedy. His purpose in this case was not less definite than his ridicule of the Old Regime in France by means of his memorable plays.

The mysterious generosity of Beaumarchais as to payment for his stores in terms of tobacco or fish sent "to the French cape" was one reason which led members of Congress to believe that America need not pay at all and indeed that not only the cargo of the *Amphitrite* but the *Amphitrite* herself was at America's disposal. As to the latter, if not the former assumption, the commander of the ship disillusioned them quickly and decisively. When Jones came aboard to assume the captaincy, the Frenchman took occasion to state that he would accept him only as a passenger; when the misconceived if not high-handed orders of Congress became evident to the American, his only course was quietly to step ashore and await further instructions.

Although Jones then proposed that his prize ship the *Mellish* should be fitted for war, Congress shortly set aside this suggestion at his own instance and decided in favor of the Continental sloop of war *Ranger* of eighteen six-pounders. Colonel Langdon, the shipbuilder of New Hampshire, who was completing her in Portsmouth, had recommended him for the command.

Congress passed the resolution for his appointment on June 14, 1777, the same date on which it provided "that the flag of the United States be thirteen stripes, alternate red and white; that the union be thirteen stars, white on a blue field, representing a new constellation." The first raising of the Grand Union flag in a Continental ship had linked itself with his name and the *Alfred,* and one of the first appearances of the Stars and Stripes was probably aboard the *Ranger.* The circumstances which associated him with the Continental flag in the second instance as in the first may well have heightened intuitively the zeal with which he was soon to enforce its command of the greater respect among Americans abroad, among allies and neutrals, and most of all among the British.

As to the *Ranger*, the Marine Committee now gave Jones even more liberal instructions than when it had decided upon his passage to Europe in the *Amphitrite*. "We shall not limit you," his orders provided, "to any particular cruising station, but leave you at large to search for yourself where the greatest chance of success presents." Jones, original as he was, prized most highly such confidence in his judgment and resourcefulness, and it was his ambition to be worthy of the freedom afforded him.

He planned, nevertheless, to follow in part the instructions which he had received when the enterprise across the Atlantic in the *Amphitrite* had been contemplated. Abroad he could look forward to the command of the *Indienne*, under construction at Amsterdam for America, "as a reward for his zeal, and the important services he had performed in vessels of little force." "We hope," the Marine Committee urged upon the American Commissioners on May 9, "you may not delay this business one moment, but purchase, in such port or place in Europe as it can be done with most convenience and despatch, a fine fast-sailing frigate or larger ship . . . you must make it a point not to disappoint Captain Jones' wishes and expectations on this occasion."[6]

The Committee was less generous in providing that Langdon, the builder, and William Whipple, one of its members from New Hampshire, as well as Jones should appoint the officers of the *Ranger*. So again the selections were in important instances more on the basis of influence than abilities. Thomas Simpson, the first lieutenant, who was a brother-in-law of Langdon[7] and a relative both of Hancock and of John Wendell, the wealthy and widely connected resident of Portsmouth,[8] had never sailed in a ship of war. Other officers possessed scarcely more experience. Wendell's fulsome eulogy of Simpson for the favor of the Commissioners in Paris may well illustrate the basis of his appointment: "A gentleman of most distinguished character as an officer and one whose abilities are known to be very great and universally respected amongst us. His promotion will be generally accepted of by every friend to America."[9] Perhaps somewhat flattered and deceived himself for a period by the professions of Wendell, Jones also accepted his young and untrained son as a volunteer, who hoped at the instance of his father to become at an early opportunity a third lieutenant.[10] To such officers and even men whose names were so applauded but whose acts would later reveal them, the Captain reconciled himself for the present on the ground of policy rather than judgment.

Enlistment of sailors, the more arduous task, depended upon his own exertions, which were prompt and resourceful. While the prospect of sailing in the *Amphitrite* had pended, he had wasted no time in directing a warrant officer John Dobie to engage "prime seamen" and to set before them the prospect of service in a frigate in foreign waters. Shortly after the *Ranger* was assigned to him but before the receipt of instructions for manning the ship, he sent another officer named Charrier to enlist sailors in New Bedford, Salem, Marblehead, and Providence. He later detailed for recruiting service in these and other ports Elijah Hall his second lieutenant, Samuel Wallingsford and Matthew Parke his lieutenant and captain of marines respectively, and Simpson his first lieutenant. In Providence occurred a last hostile act of Hopkins and his son, who thwarted the efforts of his officers to secure sailors at this port.

The enlistment of an adequate crew was so great a task that Jones even made urgent appeals to the New Hampshire legislature with the result that he was empowered "to enlist from the matross companies in the Batteries in the Piscataqua Harbour a number of men not exceeding twenty."[11] "The *Ranger* is getting ready with all possible despatch," Whipple reported to Congress on July 21; he stated again about five weeks later, "Captain Jones tells me he has more than one hundred men on his roll, and he has a fair prospect of filling up his complement in a few days."[12] "Since the establishment of our Navy," the Captain with marked enthusiasm assured one of his recruiting officers, "no persons in it have had so good, so fair a prospect of success."

To hasten enlistments, Jones also availed himself of incentives which Congress had provided with the understanding that sailors would continue in the service for periods ranging from one to three years. Accordingly he furnished his officers with handbills which advertised that able-bodied seamen would receive an advance of forty and landsmen of twenty dollars and that their relatives at home would likewise be beneficiaries of certain allotments. As the sailors objected to long enlistments, Jones found it necessary to modify the terms and took precautions against possible dangers. "When the ship's company signed the Entry Book in America," he subsequently explained, "I was resolved, should I meet with any misfortune which might oblige me to put in to the southward, not to leave it in their power to desert the *Ranger* as another set of men had done the *Randolph* when she was demasted and put into Charleston; therefore I gave Mr. Simpson, who had charge of overseeing that subscription, a slip of paper whereon was written these words to be inserted opposite each man's name under the terms of entry: 'Twelve months and while absent from the Eastern States,' or 'For the cruise and while absent from the Eastern States.' This I desired him to read and explain to each of them."[13] In the light of future serious difficulties with the crew concerning the period of their service, these precautions seem to indicate no sharp practice at the time of their enlistment; undoubtedly there were illiteracy among the sailors and possibly negligence on the part of Simpson.

Apart from politic considerations in the case of some of his officers and men, Jones adopted a bold, uncompromising attitude in his preparations as Captain of the *Ranger*. He came into conflict particularly with Langdon, although indebted to him for a recommendation to command the ship. According to the orders of September 6 from the Marine Committee, he was "to make immediate application to the proper persons to get [his] vessel victualled and fitted for sea."[14] Probably Langdon was disposed to interfere in the equipment of the ship on the ground that he was her builder just as he had had a hand in the appointment of her officers as provided by Congress. Jones resented an assumption of authority in the one case the more perhaps because he foresaw the incapacity of his politically appointed officers in the other. The Captain's sensitive pride in addition to his independent leadership was evident in the remonstrances to the shipbuilder. "Congress have been pleased," he stated on September 11, "to authorize me to 'equip, officer, and man the *Ranger* as well and as soon as possible.' Of course no person has a right to contradict any necessary order which I have given or may give for that salutary purpose. My orders will always speak for themselves, and I am accountable to Congress alone for their propriety."

A day before the *Ranger* sailed on October 31, 1777, his objections became more specific: "It gives me much concern and I have been particularly unhappy in thinking that you have assumed to yourself a command and authority over me. . . . In the line of my conduct I am sure I have not exceeded, but on the contrary kept far within the letter as well as spirit of my orders. . . . I thank you, sir, for all civilities shown or intended. . . . I lament that there should be the least misunderstanding between us; your refusing to pay my order is perhaps the first instance of the kind that hath happened in our navy, it is the first draft of mine that ever was dishonored.

"I am now going to sea with thirty gallons of rum only for sea stores, yet that article may be purchased, many other articles—a boatswain's call among others could have been purchased—but are wanting.

"I should have taken no notice of this had I not been informed that you have reflected on the detention of the ship—the concerned know how indefatigable I have been, how indefatigable every officer of mine hath been in the outfit, notwithstanding the many obstacles. . . . And though you once told me that you knew as well as I how to equip, govern, or fight a ship of war, that is a point which it is not your province nor mine to determine. . . ."[15]

Jones made it his province on the same day, however, to resent the odious professional comparison by the despatch of a message concerning Langdon to John Brown, the Secretary of the Marine Committee: "Instead of meeting with the necessary assistance of the agent, he thinks himself my master, and he, who was bred in a shop and hath been but a voyage or two at sea under a nurse, had once the assurance to tell me that he knew as well as myself how to fit out, govern, and fight a ship of war!" And as to the inadequate supply of rum for his crew, Jones also declared, "This alone was enough to cause a mutiny."[16]

Notwithstanding what may have been exaggerated emphasis upon liquor and boatswains' calls under conditions of pinched Continental resources, it does seem as if Langdon, the alleged nurse-bred sailor, overstepped his authority as primarily an agent, whose office was to supply the equipment that the Captain required in accordance with his instructions from Congress rather than to exercise his own discretion in fitting out the ship. Patriotic as Langdon was, his advancement of Simpson to the post of first officer, his riches from the building of privateers, his tolerance of slavery in the state of which he later became governor, and his shifting politics may well indicate that he steered close by the wind of his own advantage and that in Jones he met a man who refused to trim his own sails to please him. Yet the Captain was too much of an artist in his judgment of a ship and too liberal by nature to be very sensible of expenditures; and this occasion proved to be neither the last nor the most important on which his bills for public expenditures were dishonored. The future promised, too, sharper conflict with Langdon.

What galled Jones most, as his own words confessed, was the aspersion cast upon him because of the delay in sailing. "When I took this command the middle of last month," he himself sent word on August 30 to the Commissioners abroad, "the *Ranger* was entirely unrigged, the mast yards and hull alone remained, warlike and other stores were wanting. These and other difficulties, although they appeared almost insuperable at first, are now in great measure overcome. . . . I hope to have the *Ranger* equipped, manned, and at sea in a shorter space of time than any ship has yet been fitted in the service. I hope to sail within ten days."[17]

He was finally ready not ten days but almost two months later. Undue optimism might have influenced his judgment. Although the ship was manned in good time because of his foresight, he himself soon told of unusual difficulties in securing sails and other equipment. Likewise "a heavy gale from the N. E.," involving the cessation of work and the repair of damage, might readily have delayed preparations for a considerable period. His fervent wish also to avoid any connections abroad with American officers who were his superiors in rank was conceivably a secret influence in his plans, especially since he waited until the *Raleigh* and *Alfred* had weighed anchor for L'Orient before applying to enlist a few men from the garrison in Portsmouth. It should be remembered, too, that a source of interference with professional duties concerning which Jones seemed particularly disposed to remain silent, whatever the facts might have been, was the women who often inter-

ested him. This Captain, whose armor as a devoted naval officer
was to prove weakest in his susceptibility to female attractions and,
on occasion, blandishments, might have deceived himself into
thinking or at least saying that preparations and storms occasioned
this delay, even if it was due partly to reasons of sentiment. His
words were to be somewhat similar and even less convincing under
conditions in the future fraught with important military consequences. In the present instance, he came to know Miss Wendell,
who was the daughter of the relative of Hancock and Langdon,
and "other agreeable ladies of [his] acquaintance in Portsmouth."
But in any event he awoke not the less resolutely to his stern purposes of war.

Perhaps such interests at Portsmouth as well as inadequate ship
supplies gave occasion for the pretty tradition that the patriotic
young women of this town, the more patriotic as the result of the
gallantry and courtship of the Captain, fashioned their best petticoats into sails and a flag for the *Ranger*. This romantic story is
probably fanciful. "With all my industry," Jones made known to
the Marine Committee on October 31, "I could not get a single
suit of sails completed until the 20th current. Since that time, the
winds and weather have laid me under the necessity of continuing
in port. At this time it blows a very heavy gale from the N.E. The
ship with difficulty rides it out, with yards and topmast struck, and
whole cables ahead. When it clears up, I expect the wind from the
N.W. and shall not fail to embrace it, although I have not now a
spare sail, nor materials to make one. Some of those I have are
made of *Hessings* (a coarse thin stuff)."[18]

Therefore it seems likely that neither the romantic young ladies
of Portsmouth sacrificed their silken petticoats nor the hard-headed
Langdon exerted himself to provide less poetic but more serviceable naval raiment; but that Jones himself managed to furnish
such poor sails as his crew bent to the yards of the *Ranger*.

His ship equipped at last, he looked the more impatiently for
favorable weather because of the Continental despatches which he
might be the first to deliver to the Commissioners abroad, "the joy-
ful and important news of Burgoyne's surrender." Before the departure, private as well as public duties had his attention. He
prepared a will in favor of his relatives, chiefly his mother, in Scot-

land, and asked Hewes and Morris to be his executors. At the threshold of most active warlike exploits, he turned his glance to future idyllic retirement, his previously avowed purpose upon fleeing from Tobago. For this intention which had slumbered, he asked Hewes to offer his opinion concerning a farm which Major Frazer, now a volunteer on board his ship, recommended. "He hath given me a description," Jones wrote to Hewes, "so truly Elysian to a small estate on the Mattapony, Virginia, that I wish to become the purchaser. . . ."

Finally, at the prospect of absence from America for an indefinite period, he reiterated to Hewes, to Morris, to the Marine Committee, and even to the Commissioners in Europe the injustice of his rank and the urgent need of its amendment. He feared particularly that, once abroad, another American commander higher than himself in naval standing might give him orders. Captain Thompson of the *Raleigh* was his specific dread; this officer, according to Jones, "may be a good carpenter, [but] is by no means conversant in an enterprise, or in the art of war."[19] To reinforce the assurances from Congress of an independent ship, the Captain of the *Ranger* avowed: "I am determined never to draw my sword under the command of any man who was not in the Navy as early as myself, unless he has merited a preference by his superior services and abilities." Truly he meant his prayer to Morris, "Guard me against such connections, which would be far worse than death."[20]

On November 1, 1777, Jones slipped the moorings of the *Ranger* at Portsmouth and got under way to race across the Atlantic and begin the enterprises of which his cruises in the *Providence* and *Alfred* had been token. He kept closely to his course and crowded on all sail in order to deliver as soon as possible his despatches regarding Burgoyne's surrender. He turned aside, however, so far as to take two prizes, brigantines with fruit bound from Malaga to London, and to try off Ushant to detach some merchantmen from a strong convoy to which they clung so closely as to elude him. Notwithstanding two days lost in this attempt and considerable rough weather, he reached Nantes on December 2, only shortly after the arrival at another French port of a swift packet bearing the emissary John Loring Austin, who was the first to bring to the Commissioners news of Burgoyne.

From Nantes Jones sent shortly to Whipple, the member of the Marine Committee who had first brought him information of his appointment to the *Ranger,* some details of the passage, revealing his buoyant spirits, his dynamic discipline of the crew, and his zeal betokening gratitude. "I had passed the Western Islands," he recounted, "before a sail appeared within our horizon from the mast-head; but this halcyon season was then interrupted, and changed into continued alarms night and day till the *Ranger* cast anchor here . . . this afforded me excellent opportunities of exercising the officers and men especially in the night, and it is with much pleasure that I assure you their behavior was to my entire satisfaction. . . .

"My particular thanks are due to you, sir, as one of the four members of that honorable committee to whose generous intention and approbation I more immediately owe this great and unsolicited obligation, but I hope for opportunities of proving by my conduct the deep sense I entertain of that favor."[21]

A poetical outburst conformable with the traditional style of the times but also with his sincere interest in a pastoral life on the Mattapony came likewise from his pen at the close of the voyage. It was to Wendell, the influential New Englander who still continued his friend, that he wrote: "The *Ranger* was wafted by the pinions of the gentlest and most friendly gales along the surface of the blue profound of Neptune, and not the swelling bosom of a friend's or even an enemy's sail appeared within our placid horizon until after we had passed the everlasting mountains of the sea (called Azores) whose tops are in the clouds, and whose foundations are in the center."[22] He admitted in a humorous vein his uncertainty whether such poetical language would be understood. The style, ornate as it is, seems certainly creditable to a sailor, especially as he was none too serious as to the literary merits; and it clearly reveals his sanguine, almost gay, spirits at entering the new theatre of war.

He was serious enough, serious as only one of his depth of ambition and sensitiveness could be, in still another communication. To Morris he spoke from his heart: "When I have the honor of hearing from the Commissioners, I will return my thanks to the Secret Committee, but what form of thanks shall I render to you? Words are wanting here! I am utterly at a loss, nor know I where or how to begin. The obligations I owe to you are so many, so important, and were so unexpected, that I must be ungrateful indeed did I not feel more than I can express. . . . I feel by a prophetic impulse in my breast that I shall either manifest a grateful sense of your friendship by my conduct in life, or by meeting my death in support of the great cause. . . ."[23]

Part 3

The American Naval Leader in War Abroad

◇◇◇

Chapter XVII

The Diplomatic and Naval Setting in France

IN THE European setting Jones was to find cumulative stimulus to his natural ardor. Whatever new restrictions in this sphere might prejudice his judgment and enterprise, he now was removed three thousand miles from America, entrusted with a separate command, and freed from the last trace of Hopkins' domination. His gratitude, which had first expressed itself in deed as well as word to Hewes, was now ambitious to do honor not only to Morris and the Marine Committee in America but also to Franklin in France. His devotion to liberty, for which he professed an international as well as a national idealism, was to arouse him to the highest pitch upon learning closer at hand of the sufferings in England, instigated particularly by George III himself, among American prisoners taken at sea. His proximity to the British coasts was to impel him to take advantage of the special opportunity for daring raids of retaliatory and strategic importance. His association with French admirals, ministers, citizens, and even the King himself was to stimulate heart and brain at the same time that it was to strengthen his devotion to America. All these influences were to lead him to the climax of his career as a fighter.

The time of Jones' arrival at Nantes was propitious for the cause of America. It was not important that John Loring Austin happened to be able to precede him in bringing to Paris the dramatic news of Burgoyne's surrender to the eager ears of the French Ministry as well as of Franklin and his fellow Commissioners Silas Deane and Arthur Lee. The American success was to effect a decisive improvement in the prospects of the Revolution abroad in addition to those at home. But, paradoxically, it would complicate and render less as well as more favorable the circumstances of Jones' part in the struggle.

First, the Declaration of Independence and, secondly, the victory at Saratoga swung France from a policy of cautious lukewarmness and secret aid to the prospect of an open alliance. Upon this diplomatic objective, which began with subterfuge on the part of France to cloak her attitude towards the United States and bade fair to result in an entente between them, naturally depended the reception in French ports of American ships of war. In the development from neutrality to intervention, the *Ranger* herself proceeded to influence the hidden as well as the open naval practice of France.

Jones was to be sure not the first American naval officer, although the most outstanding, to step ashore on French soil since the opening of hostilities. Lambert Wickes, Gustavus Conyngham, Henry Johnson, and Samuel Nicholson, the brother of James, had preceded him. They had suffered unpredictable treatment depending upon changeful winds of diplomacy at ports chosen to refit, purchase stores, and sell prizes.

Wickes, who had brought Franklin to France in his snug fast ship the *Reprisal* of eighteen six-pounders and who later was at the head of a small squadron composed of his own vessel and Johnson's *Lexington* and Nicholson's *Dolphin,* found himself alternately welcome and unwelcome at French harbors. On occasion he received instructions from the American Commissioner to anchor "somewhere in the offing" and to sell his prizes surreptitiously. He proved an unhappy but brave pawn in the political manœuvering among Franklin, Vergennes the French Foreign Minister, and Stormont the English Ambassador in Paris. He came, in fact, within a hairbreadth of precipitating an open breach at an early date between England and France, which was of course what Franklin and America wished.

Even more spectacular, if less important politically, was Conyngham, the captor of the English packet *Prince of Orange* from Harwich and a victim of the enemy's prison cruelties. As typical of his strange adventures, France made him a hostage in token of her good faith towards England and released him in connivance with American emissaries in token of her sympathies towards the United States. This disingenuousness in the case of a dangerous naval officer could not promote gentle treatment when he again became a prisoner in Britain.

Such countenance as naval officers from the United States received in France was implicit in the measure of encouragement given to American commissioners in Paris and agents at commercial ports. It reflected a French policy long-planned and watchfully executed. Yet despite the prevision of Choiseul the Foreign Minister under Louis XV, the astuteness of Vergenness his successor in the reign of Louis XVI, the confidence of Beaumarchais the public commercial agent in the guise of a private merchant, and the distaste of Louis XVI for an offensive war against Britain, the march of events shaped itself by accident as much as by design. Humbled as France had been by the Peace of Paris in 1763 and cynical as Europe had become in the latter part of the eighteenth century concerning the political morality of nation towards nation, the Government assumed a difficult as well as disingenuous rôle to restore the balance of power upset by her conqueror. On the one hand the Ministry rendered aid in hidden forms to America and on the other hand professed friendship towards Britain. Of course French philosophers, writers, patriots, and others, in the democratic trend that was to lead the country even so far as her own Revolution, had an enthusiasm for the principles of the infant Republic fighting for existence. So while the *Ranger* lay at Nantes, France still continued her Beaumarchais-inspired precarious policy towards the belligerents, America was urgent for a treaty of alliance, and Britain without illusions as to the duplicity practiced upon her remonstrated repeatedly and drastically. These circumstances were not such as to dispose the country of Jones' birth to look with favor upon his prospective part as an instrument of her open and curtained adversaries.

An indirect repercussion was quick to reach Jones. He had been at Nantes only a few days when the promise which had lent wings to his passage to Europe suffered disappointment. The *Indienne,* planned as a frigate of outstanding armament and original design, was not to be his, according to reports of naval and commercial agents in Nantes, especially Jonathan Williams a nephew of Franklin, Thomas Morris a half brother of Robert, and John Ross a Scotch business agent from Philadelphia. Like the first merchant vessels laden with war supplies which had come to the Colonies from the contriving, mysterious hand of Beaumarchais, alias Roderique Hortalez & Company, this ship under construction at Amsterdam had been shrouded in uncertainty.

Whether through the activities of spies in the pay of England, or the indiscretions of American officials, or, as is more likely, through both avenues, Britain had learned that the *Indienne* was intended for the United States. Almost a month before Jones' arrival in the French port, Wentworth, the chief English intermediary for espionage, informed the Earl of Suffolk: "The Court of France have bought the ship building at Amsterdam by Boux for Deane and Franklin, and are going to build many frigates on the same plan. . . ."[1] Of course the publicity discouraged and delayed the intentions of France. It prompted Holland even more to remain aloof from any involvement with the United States, particularly since she was bound to Britain by the Treaty of Utrecht of 1678, however much some of her diverse parties disliked the alliance. America accepted of necessity the sudden turn of circumstances.

Jones, too, bowed before his sudden frustration with more composure and grace than might have been expected of him. His attitude evinced that, if satisfied in principle, he could reconcile himself to a deep-seated personal loss. "I understand," he explained in his first report from Europe to the Marine Committee, "that the Commissioners had provided for me one of the finest frigates that ever was built, calculated for thirty guns on one deck, and capable of carrying thirty-six pounders, but were under the necessity of giving her up on account of some difficulties which they met with at Court. Perhaps the news of our late successes may now put that Court in a better humor. But my unfeigned thanks are equally due for the intention as for the act."[2]

Acquiescence was to turn to resentment after he soon gained further information. Trifling with him, as he believed, by ministers of France assumed a different light. "I can bear the disappointment with philosophy," he wrote again to the Marine Committee. "Yet I confess I was rather hurt when at Paris I understood that the new frigate at Amsterdam had never been intended for me, before my appearance, but for the constructor."[3]

Pending instructions from the Commissioners at the French capital, Jones realized that for the present he might have to content himself with the *Ranger;* so in his eagerness for action in European seas, he set about with care and expedition to prepare her for a cruise. The Captain had been more optimistic about the sloop before than after crossing the Atlantic. He may have permitted his enthusiasm to color his judgment as to the exceptional qualities which alone could satisfy him but which had failed to materialize. She was crank and slow, and she warranted no comparison in armament with a ship like the *Indienne.* To improve her trim and increase her speed, he shortened the lower masts, shifted the mainmast further aft, added ballast, and careened the bottom. The changes were so various and adept that his undiscriminating officers and men began to grumble.

When a request reached him on December 17, 1777 to visit the Commissioners, Jones delayed a short period longer before proceeding to Paris because, as he replied to them, "I wish to leave the *Ranger* in such a situation as to expect to find her nearly ready for sea on my return, as I think it will be for the interest of the service that I should then proceed with her alone unless an additional force can be very soon procured." In Europe as in America he was zealous not only to sail but also to make the best use of the means at hand.

Approximately at the beginning of 1778, Jones arrived in Paris and proceeded to Passy, the nearby suburb in which Franklin had taken residence in a commodious home more pleasing to his taste for rustic surroundings and more suitable to the private needs of diplomacy than apartments in the city. Among the numerous company which thronged the American headquarters, the Captain shortly met the two other Commissioners, Silas Deane, who occupied apartments adjoining Franklin's, and Arthur Lee, who lived elsewhere; Ralph Izard, who had been appointed Minister to the Grand Duke of Tuscany; Edward Bancroft, the enemy's spy who served at the same time as a confidential agent of Franklin; and Le Ray de Chaumont, the owner of this estate named the Hôtel Valentinois at which Franklin and Deane lived in the smaller wing and his own family in the larger. Although a rent-free provision for the Americans proceeded to all appearances from sheer hospitality of the Frenchman, it was presumably, like the services of

Beaumarchais, at the instance and with the responsibility of the Court. At Passy there also came and went, drawn especially by Franklin, soldiers of fortune, political adventurers, spies, stranded sailors, and curious travellers as well as diplomats, bankers, commercial agents, scientists, and philosophers. Saratoga, too, had raised the prestige of the United States, and so the center of American authority in Europe was the more astir.

However multifarious Franklin's duties and interests and however extensive his knowledge of men, he must have looked forward to meeting Jones with both unusual curiosity and pleasure. The Commissioners had already received several letters from the Captain, in addition to those from the Marine Committee, which introduced him as an uncommon officer. They were expressive of a personality both deferential and bold, embodying his self-styled "candor and ingenuity" and above all his impassioned patriotism. Significantly in the first communication from Nantes he had affirmed: "The singular honor which Congress have done me by their generous acknowledgment of my past services has inspired me with sentiments of gratitude which I shall carry with me to the grave; and if a life of services devoted to America can be made instrumental in securing its independence, I shall regard the continuance of such approbation as an honor far superior to what kings can bestow."[4] It is unlikely that the liberty-loving Doctor overlooked this profession. Jones' vow of self-sacrifice as a naval officer at the age of thirty-one was not less sincere, apart from his passion for glory, than Franklin's as a diplomat at the age of seventy, "Perhaps the best use such an old fellow can be put to is to make a martyr of him."

Although the fortunes of the Captain were to lead to dealings with all these men, his sojourn at Passy on this first occasion was expeditious. He panted to set out on his initial European enterprise, certainly with the *Indienne* if possible but without her if necessary. He now knew that the French were equivocal, the Dutch fearful, and the Americans devoid of authority as to the disposition of the frigate. She was, moreover, not yet equipped. So turning again resolutely to his plans for the *Ranger,* he received from the Commissioners an order directing Jonathan Williams at Nantes to advance him five hundred louis d'ors; he also carried with him an announcement for encouraging his officers and crew. That Jones found it expedient to avail himself of such a message to his men is a signal indication of their indifferent morale as well as of his initiative and original plans. "Whereas we understand," Franklin, Deane, and Lee had written accordingly on January 15, 1778, "that Captain Jones has in view to strike a stroke upon the enemy that may be greatly to their damage, but in its nature not probably profitable to his ship's company, unless some reward be received from the Congress adequate to the service done, and we being of opinion that rewards in such cases are not only necessary for encouragement, but are really acts of justice, do hereby promise that in case of the good and gallant behavior of the people under his command and their punctual obedience to orders so as to obtain success in the undertaking so far as depends on them, we will warmly recommend them to the Congress for a generous gratification proportioned to their merit." Surely, if such material inducements were necessary, the crew on the one hand were more fitted for a privateer than a ship of war and on the other hand must have been fearful that Jones would lead them into the lion's mouth.

Final orders from Paris shortly arrived. Although the *Indienne* was definitely not to be his for the present, the instructions permitted him freedom to follow his own judgment untrammeled by any officer equal or superior in rank. The confidence reposed in the Captain was apparent: "As it is not in our power to procure you such a ship as you expected, we advise you, after equipping the *Ranger* in the best manner for the cruise you propose, that you proceed with her in the way you shall judge best for distressing the enemies of the United States, by sea or otherwise, consistent with the laws of war, and the terms of your commission. . . . We rely on your ability as well as your zeal to serve the United States, and therefore do not give you particular instructions as to your operations." It is well to note this early message in view of the epithets of pirate and corsair soon to be applied to Jones' name and to reverberate a century and a half after his deeds. The three official representatives from America confidentially knew the general nature of his plans, including operations "by sea or otherwise," and Franklin, a benefactor of mankind, was the first to affix his signature to the orders.

Particular wishes of the Commissioners were manifest in advice concerning ports to which Jones was to send prizes and return himself. They suggested as their first choice that he should direct captured vessels to points in Spain; as their second choice, to points in France. Along with this purpose to incite England against Spain as well as France, they desired to avoid antagonizing France and Spain against the United States. "If you make an attempt on the coast of Great Britain," they added, "we advise you not to return immediately into the ports of France, unless forced by stress of weather or the pursuit of the enemy . . . we must caution you against giving any cause of complaint to the subjects of France and Spain or of other neutral powers."[5] In other words, continuing the policy begun previously by the cruises of Conyngham and Wickes, the Commissioners undertook to comply with neutral laws as far as expediency dictated; and for this object they desired Jones to be a diplomat as well as a sailor. This politically directed end to gain allies with the aid of naval officers was consistent with European politics of the age, promoted by the encouragement of France, and calculated not to involve neutral nations against their wishes.

Aside from these recommendations acceptable to the three Commissioners, Lee withheld his signature from the designation by Franklin and Deane of Gourlade & Moylan, American merchants at Nantes, as agents for the sale of Jones' prospective prizes. The difference in opinion among them was in itself of little immediate concern to the Captain; it was prophetic, however, of the train of obstacles which Lee was to try to set in the path of his future career.

Lee's assigned reason for objection to Gourlade & Moylan was unsatisfactory services;[6] his real reason lay in the interests of his brother William and his special hostility to Deane. "You know," William Lee objected to Deane, "that I was appointed by the Secret Committee, in conjunction with Mr. Thomas Morris, as commercial agent for the affairs of America in France." Thomas Morris had entered upon these duties at the port of Nantes but had proved himself grossly negligent. At the time of his own appointment, William Lee still had been an alderman in London as well as a British subject. He had learned of it unofficially in England from Deane, but after his delayed arrival in France failed to receive for many months an expected confirmation from Congress. Lee charged that Deane advised him to remain for the present in Paris; Deane contended that he urged Lee to proceed at once to Nantes. Pending further authority from America and during the immediate need for a responsible person to transact naval and special commercial business, Deane with the approval of Franklin appointed Jonathan Williams, not less efficient than honest, as naval agent at Nantes.

Whether or not this office infringed upon the commercial agency and was within the jurisdiction of the two Commissioners under the particular circumstances, the Lees began to raise objections. William Lee soon received a further appointment from Congress, particularly through the influence of his brother Richard Henry, as Minister to the Courts of Prussia and Vienna; and his inability to straddle the agency and the diplomatic post at the same time contributed to clamors from him against Deane and Franklin.[7] There were to be echoes from Arthur in Paris, re-echoes from Richard Henry in Philadelphia, and further reverberations from the cousins Samuel and John Adams in the councils at Independence Hall. These voices, in the person of well-meaning but choleric John Adams, were even to recross the ocean. Against this crescendo, Jay later spoke calmly and characteristically in opposition, referring to the "family compact," by which he meant that four brothers of the Lee family held two seats in Congress, four foreign missions, the French commercial agency, and a London aldermanship under Wilkes.[8] He failed to mention also the son of Richard Henry in the commercial affairs at Nantes under a foreign incumbent appointed by William Lee.[9] It is not to minimize the bad judgment, rascality, and even traitorous leanings of Deane, which more than offset his early helpful services, to indicate the partisanship of the Adamses and the self-seeking of the Lees. The contentiousness serves rather to introduce the vengeful spirit of Arthur Lee as affecting Jones because of his good will towards men like Williams and Franklin.

While these animosities were developing, the surrender of Burgoyne added the final impetus to swing France decisively on the side of the United States. Thanks to Franklin as the American Commissioner who had long and carefully prepared the ground, Vergennes now considered the time ripe for the treaties which the

Doctor urged. Vergennes had played his card, by material and moral aid to the United States, now to see Britain so deeply involved with America that she could not withdraw except by surrender of independence to her; Franklin, whose turn it was to play his, offered to guarantee to the Foreign Minister that America would not compromise with England and leave her free to retaliate upon France if the latter would enter into an open alliance with the United States.[10] In the face of these developments, there were, on the one hand, the earlier opposition of Louis XVI, warnings of Turgot, and fears of Maurepas that secret aid would lead to war, and, on the other hand, the assurances of Beaumarchais that such a result need not follow. There was, too, the positive hostility of Spain, the ally of France, towards the republicanism of America as well as towards the colonial rise of Britain so that Grimaldi her Minister characteristically expressed to Vergennes the sentiments of his nation, "Surely it suits us that the revolt of these people be kept up, and we ought to desire that they and the English exhaust themselves reciprocally."

Notwithstanding these considerations, France took on February 6, 1778 the decisive step of a twofold pact with America. The open treaty of amity and commerce was to insure the United States greater aid to wage the war; the secret treaty of conditional and defensive alliance was to protect France against a separate peace. The three Commissioners, Lee and Deane along with Franklin, signed the documents. It was long believed that indiscretion if not disloyalty among them obstructed the diplomacy of the Doctor. As to Lee, however, the unmasking of Edward Bancroft the spy (nearly a century later) has proved that this guileful secretary of Franklin manœuvered to turn suspicion from himself when the Virginia Commissioner suffered the accusation of informing Lord Shelburne: "If England wants to prevent closer ties between France and the United States, she must not delay." As to Deane, the correspondence of another spy George Lupton with British officials and the tenor of subsequent revelations concerning the American Commissioner compel belief that he made the statement attributed to him half a year before the treaty: "It is a pity that Great Britain does not bring about a reconciliation with the Colonies and jointly make war against France."[11]

Only four days after the formal alliance, Jones wrote from Nantes a letter to the Commissioners in Paris which revealed that the scope of his strategy as a naval officer was even then worthy of comparison with the genius of Franklin as a diplomat. His timely initiative appeared the greater because he seemingly was still unaware of the treaty and remained circumscribed in the limited sphere of preparing for an expedition in the *Ranger*. By the arrival of newspapers in a vessel from America, he had just learned the position of Lord Howe's fleet in the Delaware. His special knowledge of the harbor at Philadelphia and the strength of the enemy's ships led him to conceive a plan for an attack as bold as unexpected. He despatched it at once, in care of Deane, for the Commissioners:

"Were any Continental marine power in Europe disposed to avail itself of the present situation of affairs in America, and willing to deserve our friendship, a single blow well directed would now do the needful. Ten or twelve sail of the line with frigates well equipped and provided would give a good account of the fleet under Lord Howe, for as that force would be superior to any one of Howe's divisions, the strongest one being taken—the victorious squadron might sail in quest of the next in strength and reach it before advice. . . .

"However extravagant this calculation may appear on a slight view, it will not be found so in reality. Had Lord Howe or any commander in the enemy's fleet an idea or expectation of such a visit, it is certain that the attempt would be folly and madness, but as our enemies ride in perfect security, that security would prove their ruin and insure our success. Who can surprise well must conquer."[12]

Deane accepted the plan as his own; he proposed it to Louis XVI, who later rewarded him with a royal picture in miniature, diamond-encased.[13] As for executing such an expedition in any way comparable to the speed with which Jones had urged it, there were several obstacles. France was the more hesitant to begin offensive warfare against Britain because Holland felt bound by an English treaty to aid her ally in such an event. There were also more controlling difficulties in the way of speedy sailing, although fleets had assembled at Toulon and Brest. Few French naval or civil officers had Jones' special aptitude for ready action. De Sartine in particular had been a capable commissioner of police, but he was yet to prove his fitness as the Minister of Marine. And fewer recognized in this instance the force of Jones' intuitive strategy: "Who can surprise well must conquer." Time was to demonstrate the wisdom of both his advice and example.

The honor along with the triumph of America was paramount in the mind of the Captain. The first to unfurl the Grand Union flag of the fleet on the Delaware, he was now to be the first on a ship of war of the United States to receive a salute from France in recognition of American independence and to have its confirmation by the Minister of Marine and the King. Although Captain Daniel McNeil in the *General Mifflin* had previously reported a salute from the French Admiral du Chaffault, it received no government approval.[14] And although the *Andrew Doria* flying the Grand Union flag saluted in November, 1776 the fort at St. Eustatius in the West Indies with thirteen guns and received eleven in return, the Netherlands temporarily recalled and disavowed the act by De Graaf, the governor of this Dutch islet, from which the United States secretly received war supplies. Even more a matter of form than significance was a still earlier salute in October of the same year from the Danish fort at St. Croix to an American schooner;[15] later Denmark was to show herself so sympathetic towards England as to return to her several of Jones' prizes which entered the supposedly neutral port of Bergen, then under Danish rule.

The recognition which the Captain gained in behalf of the United States was the more distinctive because he did his best to receive as large a number of guns as possible in return for his own salute, and because he also seized his opportunity to suggest the exchange of courtesies before the Franco-American alliance was public knowledge as well as to have it meet with government approval. He took pains likewise to emphasize the ceremony by having it occur on three distinct occasions. To the Marine Committee in Philadelphia, to Williams in Nantes, to Deane in Paris, his active pen sent versions of the honor. The account to Deane, which came into the hands of English spies, perhaps intentionally, was of February 26 from Quiberon Bay:

"I imagine that you have already been informed of the mutual

FIRST RECOGNITION OF THE AMERICAN FLAG BY A FOREIGN GOVERNMENT

In Quiberon Bay, February 14, 1778. The salute of John Paul Jones in the "Ranger" is returned by a French Squadron. No. 8 of a set of Edward Moran's "Thirteen Historical Marine Paintings" (oil). Presented by Paul E. Sutro.

salute in this bay for the first time between the flag of liberty and that of France. Here are the details; those which you have received are not perhaps exact.

"The vessel *Independence* accepted my convoy from Nantes here; I arrived on the 13th and immediately despatched my long boat to find out whether the Admiral would return my salute. He sent reply that he would return it, as being that of the senior officer of the American Continent, at present in Europe, with the same salute that he was authorized to give an admiral of Holland or any republic, that is, four guns less. I hesitated, for I had asked shot for shot; so I cast anchor at the entrance of the bay, at a little distance from the French fleet.

"But seeing from some private information I received on the 14th that he had really spoken the truth, I accepted his offer the more readily as after all it was a recognition of our independence. The wind being contrary, and rather violent, it was only after sunset that the *Ranger* could approach near enough to salute La Motte Picquet with thirteen guns; he returned it with nine. However I did not allow the *Independence* to salute him until the next morning, when I sent word to the Admiral that I wished to pass through his squadron, and to salute him again by daylight. He was singularly flattered by this and again returned my salute with nine guns.

"The officers of this squadron are extremely well-bred and polite. They all visited my vessel the *Ranger* and expressed the greatest satisfaction with it, saying it is a perfect jewel. When we visited their vessels, they received us with every sign of pleasure and consideration, and saluted us with a *feu de joie*. . . ."[16]

At Brest, several weeks later, Jones received his third salute. It was from Admiral d'Orvilliers, the head of the French fleet at this station, who quickly became his cordial friend.[17]

During the course of these honors for the Stars and Stripes at Quiberon Bay and Brest, the Captain employed the *Ranger* in several preliminary pursuits. He convoyed a number of American vessels off the French coast. He planned a dangerous, secret venture with the *Ranger* in disguise near Cammaret, but abandoned it when his purpose mysteriously became known to the enemy. For this undertaking D'Orvilliers had generously offered him a French commission to insure his safety in the event of capture by a superior force; he replied that it was neither his right nor his inclination to set aside the American commission in his keeping.[18] He also tested further the sailing qualities of his ship with the result that the hold received fifteen tons of lead as additional ballast to improve the trim.

As for his officers and crew, difficulties were brewing. Prize money was so much in their minds that the officers objected to retaining on the roll of the ship the Captain of Marines Matthew Parke, the only man aboard commissioned by Jones himself. They insisted on the letter of the regulation of Congress which did not provide for such an officer on vessels of less than twenty guns; as the *Ranger* was of eighteen, it was not their intention to share prize money with him. And the crew became restive with the passing of the months when their enlistments promised of necessity to be not for a year but the period of absence from America. They particularly resented the precaution by Jones to have stated the terms in the entry book containing their signatures.

Regardless of mutinous indications, Jones sought before leaving Brest to strengthen bridges behind him not for retreat but future onset. In a letter characteristically compounded of bluffness and deference, he wrote for the first time to De Sartine. His two chief topics were the *Indienne* and the British fleet in America. As for the latter, he reiterated his advice for an attack, late as it was now becoming: "I am, sir, convinced that the capture of Lord Howe's light ships and frigates in America, and the destruction of the enemy's fishery in Newfoundland, which might easily be effected this summer, would effectually destroy the sinews of their Marine." As for the former, he called to his attention: "I am destined by Congress to command a frigate of very large construction lately built at Amsterdam; and as political reasons made it necessary for that frigate to become French property, I am now induced to hope that on her arrival in France she will again become the property of America and of course be put under my command. . . .

"The Admiral d'Orvilliers has, I doubt not, communicated a project of mine. I am, sir, ambitious of being employed in active and enterprising services; but my ship is too small a force and does not sail as fast as I could wish. If I am successful, I will return to France, and hope for your countenance and protection."

The plea to De Sartine was basically more in the interest of America than of himself. Jones' ambition was not in conflict with his loyalty, although D'Orvilliers had offered to procure him an appointment as Captain in the Navy of France for a project in America, apart from the commission for the planned special enterprise off Cammaret. He refused at this time to entertain the thought of such divided allegiance. Just recently in a letter to the Marine Committee he had conveyed anew his attachment and gratitude: "I want words to express my sense of the reasons which you have given for showing me such preference when I find among them mention made of my *zeal* and *signal services* which it is the intention of Congress to *reward*. I can only say that I beg of you gentlemen to assure Congress it shall be the ambition of my life to merit the continuance of their approbation, which I shall always esteem as the greatest honor and the most ample *reward*."[19]

After loss of time in preliminaries which only keyed Jones the more to his resolution, he was ready to put his avowals to new proof. "I have in contemplation," he confided to Williams, "several enterprises of some importance. . . . When an enemy thinks a design against him improbable, he can always he surprised and attacked with advantage. It is true I must run great risk; but no gallant action was ever performed without danger. Therefore, though I cannot insure success, I will endeavor to deserve it."[20]

With such a spirit of her Captain, the *Ranger* sailed on April 9, 1778 from Brest, but she found it necessary to turn back because of stormy head winds which prevented her from weathering Ushant. The next day, however, she rounded the island and set her course boldly for the west coasts of England and Scotland, flying a Dutch pendant and an English Jack at the main topgallant masthead for disguise.

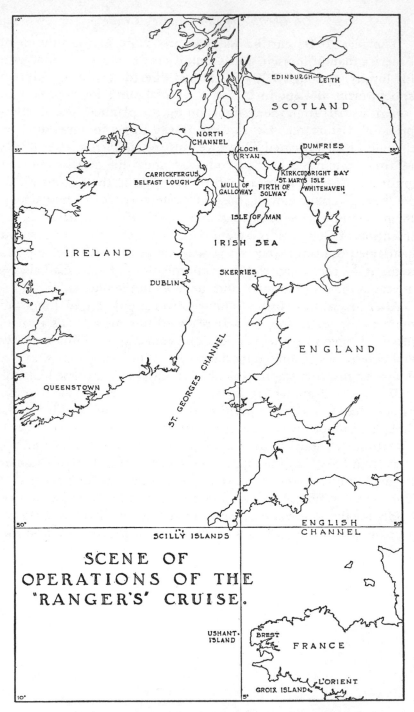

SCENE OF OPERATIONS OF THE *RANGER'S* CRUISE

Chapter XVIII

<><><><><><><><><><><><><><><><><><><><><><><><><><><><><><><><><><><><><><><><><><>

The Incursion to Burn the
Shipping at Whitehaven

A s the bows of the *Ranger* ploughed the seas northward towards
St. George's Channel, the secret plans of Jones took form.
"My first object," he affirmed, "was to secure an exchange of
American prisoners in Europe, and my second to put an end to
burnings in America by making one good fire in England of
shipping."[1] These aims, of which in execution the latter was to
precede the former, expressed on the whole the resentment of the
American public as well as his own convictions. The Declaration
of Independence itself listed among the grievances against George
III: "He has plundered our seas, ravaged our coasts, burned our
towns, and destroyed the lives of our people." Yet these charges
applied, it should be remembered, to the mode of warfare after,
rather than before, hostilities on both sides had begun.

At the advent of Jones abroad, the measures of Britain by land
had been limited to so-called civilized warfare; but those by sea
and on seacoast had become especially severe. He in particular felt
bitterly what seemed to him the measure of the wrongs. They happened on or were otherwise associated with his element the sea.
And while the *Ranger* now neared the coast lines familiar to his
youth, they evoked in his memory all the circumstances which had
alienated him from England, beginning with traditions of penalties in Scotland for the final Jacobite rebellion in 1745, just two
years before his birth, and ending with personal misfortunes at
Tobago.

"I resolved," he said, "to make the greatest efforts . . . to bring
to an end the barbarous ravages to which the English turned in
America, bringing in their train fire to its homes and destruction

to its property, even to entire towns. I had received no order at all to avenge these injuries, and I had not at all communicated my plans for this object to the American Commissioners at Paris." It should be recognized, however, that resistance in some cases had been by American civilians. And it should be recalled also that on his cruises in the *Providence* and in the *Alfred* he had already retaliated on the Canadian coast by the destruction of warehouses in addition to shipping and that even poor fishermen, despite his considerateness, had suffered at his hands far from their homes.

Strong in his convictions of public wrongs, which dominated over his private sentiments and which made him fearless even with a crew bordering on mutiny, the Captain prepared to act with secrecy, swiftness, concentration upon exemplary projects, and the special advantage of his familiarity with British coasts. So pursuing his northward route, he took as a preliminary, to the special satisfaction of his seamen, a valuable ship the *Lord Chatham,* which he ordered with a prize crew to Brest. With promising weather and favorable winds, he stood over towards evening of April 18, 1778 from the Isle of Man, well-known to him from his years as a trader, to make "a descent at Whitehaven." Whitehaven, then, was to be the scene of his initial enterprise in Europe—Whitehaven from which he had first sailed as a boy of twelve.

In a British merchantman he had left this English port near his birthplace across the Solway as dawn and early youth began to unfold before him seas, continents, and wide activities of men; in an American sloop of war he now approached it twenty years later as nightfall blotted out his boyhood associations and smouldering torches focussed his thoughts upon his predetermined purpose and its immediate execution. He planned to burn the shipping at the wharves of Whitehaven.

By ten p.m. the *Ranger* was off the harbor, the pulling boats were ready to be lowered for rowing ashore, and Jones had managed to enlist from his sullen crew a party of thirty volunteers. "But before eleven," as he related, "the wind greatly increased and shifted, so as to blow directly upon the shore; the sea increased, of course, and it became impossible to effect a landing. This obliged me to carry all possible sail so as to clear the land, and to await a more favorable opportunity."[2]

Biding his time, Jones met the fast revenue vessel *Hussar*, while the *Ranger* was in disguise as a merchantman. He requested a pilot in order to approach the nearer. At the refusal of the vessel, according to Captain Gurley her commander, "in an instant the ports were knocked open, the decks were filled with men and a tier of guns was run out, several volleys of small arms were then fired into the *Hussar*, and such of the great guns as could be brought to bear on her. The *Hussar* tacked several times, keeping as much as possible on the ship's quarter, until they got out of reach of her guns."[3] Although this encounter sent the *Hussar* scurrying to spread the alarm from port to port, Jones remained unruffled. He then sank several small craft chiefly to prevent further reports regarding an American ship in nearby waters, and took the crews aboard as prisoners, although it was not his desire to encumber himself more than necessary at this early stage of his extensive designs. He also entertained a project against ten or twelve merchant ships at anchor in nearby Loch Ryan in Scotland but abandoned it because of an adverse wind.

The beginning of a second important enterprise occurred the next day, the 21st, near Carrickfergus, off Belfast Lough, which was to culminate later in the cruise in a battle with the British sloop of war *Drake*. But in the meantime, the plan for a descent upon Whitehaven, interrupted by contrary seas and winds, now became promising again. After a gale had obliged Jones to take shelter under the south shore of Scotland, "The 22nd introduced fair weather," he recounted, "though the three kingdoms were, as far as the eye could reach, covered with snow. I now resolved once more to attempt Whitehaven."[4]

Again he called for volunteers.. The first and second lieutenants, Simpson and Hall, demoralized the sailors instead of setting them an example. These officers declared to Jones that they were poor and that their object was gain, not honor; and they feigned illness at the hour of action.[5] The Captain then announced that he would lead the enterprise. Among those who stepped forward was a young man of twenty-two, enrolled in the ship's books as David Smith, whose willing, even eager, attitude contrasted strangely with that of his shipmates and might have justified more suspicion than praise of his motives.[6] Another was Edward Meyer, a lieutenant of the

Swedish Army who, planning to secure a commission in America, had engaged temporarily to serve aboard the *Ranger*. The lieutenant of marines, Wallingsford, and a midshipman, Benjamin Hill, agreed to take part in the expedition. Of the pair of boats which were to make their way ashore, Jones entrusted the supervision of one of them to Wallingsford and Hill, and he himself, with Meyer as an aide, assumed command of the other. In each were two lanterns and a plentiful supply of flint and tinder and of pine faggots and torches. Every sailor had his pistol and cutlass.

Before they embarked in the boats, according to Smith, "in the night Jones explained his design fully to his men, and exhorted them to stand by him; that he would be the first who landed and the last who left the shore; that he hoped to destroy all the ships in the harbor, and to set fire to the town; that if success attended the undertaking, as he fully expected, the honor would be great to himself, which was all he desired; to money he resigned all pretensions to his men."[7]

In the course of the preparations, during which Jones was his own pilot in the Solway Firth, the wind became very light so that the *Ranger* did not approach in proper time as near Whitehaven as he had hoped. And after the Captain and his volunteers had embarked in the boats at midnight, both the opposing tide and the considerable distance to the shore, imperfectly estimated in the darkness, made the rowing an unexpectedly arduous and long task. "When we reached the outer pier," Jones related, "the day began to dawn; I would not, however, abandon my enterprise, but despatched one boat under the direction of Mr. Hill and Lieutenant Wallingsford, with the necessary combustibles to set fire to the shipping on the north side of the harbor, while I went with the other party to attempt the south side."[8]

The deeds of Jones himself and even those of his party while under his eyes promised success, but the conduct of these same men when unobserved by him and that of the group under Wallingsford and Hill seemed destined to turn them to failure. "We took the fort by storm," he described; "lacking ladders, we had to climb it by mounting upon the shoulders of our largest and strongest men, and entered it in this manner through the embrasures. I commanded this operation, and I was also the first who entered the fort. The morning was cold, and the sentinels had retired to the guard-room; they were not expecting such a hostile visit. No blood at all was shed in securing their post; we spiked thirty-six cannon of the fort and battery, and I advanced at length to the southern part of the harbor to burn all the ships there when, to my great astonishment, I saw that the boat sent to the northern part had returned without having accomplished anything. Those who had gone in it pretended to have been frightened by certain noises which they had heard, but I told them that these noises existed only in their imagination."[9]

This failure even of Jones' volunteers—not to consider the rest of his officers and crew—to prove their worthiness at the initial test revealed their disaffection. They proceeded to offer the excuse that not only noises confused them but also that their candles had burnt out at the moment it was intended to set the shipping afire. At the time of these excuses, Jones' party as well as the other stated that their candles also had become extinguished. The specious coincidence added to the improbability that either group lacked lights except so far as they conspired to have none. The loss of time and the state of mind of Wallingsford's men in going to an alehouse render their explanation the more implausible. Meyer, the aide in Jones' boat, had found that his companions wished to enlist his help in obstructing the expedition in every way. To extinguish the lights and attribute the absence of them to accident was the readiest means for their design.

Jones harbored a traitor as well as enemies. David Smith of the ship's enlistment roll was in truth David Freeman of Irish birth who had engaged to serve in the *Ranger* for the purpose of avoiding imprisonment in America as a British soldier and of escaping to his native country. At the first moment that his steps had been unobserved by the other members of his boat, he had run from the wharf to nearby streets, shouting and knocking at doors, to arouse the inhabitants so as to prevent the impending conflagration. He stated in the closing words of his testimony before the civil authorities, to which he certified by his mark because of illiteracy: "The said Freeman made his escape from the boat he was in as soon as it was possible, alarmed the town, and delivered himself up to a man in the streets unarmed, having thrown his arms away soon after his escape.

his

David   X   Freeman."[10]

mark

In ignorance of the traitor and in spite of the two treacherous parties, the Captain persevered. His own will and arm almost alone served him. "The day too came on apace, yet I would by no means retreat while any hopes of success remained," was his characteristic determination. "Having again placed sentinels, a light was obtained at a house disjoined from the town [a watchhouse on the quay] and a fire was kindled in the steerage of a large ship [the *Thomson*], which was surrounded by at least an hundred and fifty others, chiefly from two to four hundred tons burthen, and lying side by side, aground, unsurrounded by the water.

"There were, besides, from seventy to a hundred large ships in the north arm of the harbor, aground, clear of the water, and divided from the rest only by a stone pier of a ship's height. I should have kindled fires in other places if the time had permitted. As it did not, our care was to prevent the one kindled from being easily extinguished. After some search a barrel of tar was found, and poured into the flames, which now ascended from all the hatchways."[11]

The retirement of Jones from the scene was undaunted, although traitors, enemies, and the elements alone prevailed against him to the extent that the shipping was saved. "As it was almost eight o'clock in the morning, and as the inhabitants came running by thousands, I was not able to delay longer my retreat, which I made in very good order. When all my people had re-embarked, I still remained for some minutes upon the outside mole to observe at my leisure the terror, panic, and stupidity of the inhabitants, who in numbers of at least ten thousand remained motionless like statues or ran hither and thither like madmen to reach the hills on the other side of the town. The retirement had already carried my boats some distance from the shore when the English dared to draw nearer from their fort; finding the cannon spiked there, they brought some pieces taken from vessels and fired upon my boats. I answered their salute with several swivel guns which I had placed in the stern of my barge."[12] His intrepidity becomes amazing when it is realized that he made his solitary stand in the face of his sailors' plot to row off without him, particularly if he tarried longer than they thought safe for themselves; and that their perfidy did not reach such lengths only because of the opposition of Meyer and his own dominating personality.[13]

Psychologically the victory was Jones'; morally also it was his, if it is true that the possible burning of the town in addition to the shipping had been more of a threat than an imminent danger. The effect of his strategy upon British morale was particularly in his thought: "What was done . . . is sufficient to show that not all their boasted navy can protect their own coasts; and that the scenes of distress which they have occasioned in America may be soon brought home to their own door."[14]

Jones' final reflections concerning the descent significantly revealed his humane instincts, however inconsistent they might have seemed with the conflagration that had been his purpose. "One of my people was missing," he remarked, "and must, I fear, have fallen into the enemy's hands after our departure. I was pleased that in this business we neither killed nor wounded any person." The merit of the Captain was not the less because his compassion unwittingly concerned itself in part with a traitor like Freeman. And in view of his special regard for human life, provided of course honor did not call for its sacrifice, he presumably believed that the fire would not spread from the ships at the wharves to the houses of the town, and that even if it did the loss would be in terms of property, not lives.

Relative to the destruction of shipping alone, he gave the United States his best services as an officer and satisfied his conscience even as a man born in Scotland. The naval policy of America, except to the extent that she had the aid of French ships of war, was almost exclusively to harry the commerce of Britain so as to divert in many directions the enemy's vastly superior strength at sea, which she could not hope to meet on equal terms. Hence her encouragement, first, of privateers, which glutted their greed in roaming off the American coast; secondly, of Continental ships, which confined their efforts more to merchant than war vessels and also generally restricted them to nearby American waters; and, thirdly, of other government-commissioned ships, conspicuously those of Wickes and Conyngham, which more aggressively made their captures in British seas. Broader in scope, superior in strategy, bolder in act, Jones at the first opportunity conducted his operations on a more original and telling plan. He had less in mind the capture of prizes and the private gain sought by his crews in taking ships singly and in small groups than the destruction of shipping to the advantage of America by burning large numbers of vessels at their ports or capturing large merchant fleets on their established routes.

In pursuit of such a purpose at Whitehaven, the initiative of Jones was not inconsistent with his earlier instructions from the Marine Committee in America, particularly from Morris, or with those later from the Commissioners in Paris, particularly from Franklin. It has had the admiration of a naval strategist like Admiral Mahan, who remarked: "Let a single ship of war, commerce-destroyer, meet twenty or thirty merchant ships at sea, he can take but a few; the rest scatter and escape. . . . Corner the same squadron in port, and neither difficulty, as a rule exists. Moreover, Jones' plan contemplated destruction, not capture; injury to the enemy, not prize money primarily.

"This expresses decisively the career that Jones, throughout the Revolutionary War, proposed to follow—to pursue the enemy, not in occasional merchant ships, but where great interests were concentrated and inadequately protected; and to do so not with a single ship, seeking to snatch a hasty morsel, but with a squadron capable of deliberately insuring the destruction of the enemy rather than its own profit. Such a conception places its author far above the level of the mere prize-seeker, as well in loftiness of purpose as in breadth of view."[15]

Even granted that the man should sacrifice nothing to the officer, it remains to ask whether Jones lost prestige on the one hand in gaining it on the other. Professionally, the choice of Whitehaven had special advantages: he knew the nearby waters and could be his own pilot, he was acquainted with the forts and walls and could lead the assault and spike the guns, he was aware of the exposure of the ships at low tide so as to render feasible an extensive fire, he understood the psychology of the inhabitants at this period and could count upon the success of a sudden attack. As for his selection of this scene, according to James Fenimore Cooper, both moralist and naval expert, "in a military point of view, he would have been censurable for neglecting [it] under the circumstances."[16]

Privately, there was little to weigh against the preponderant professional considerations. Whitehaven was in England, not in his native Scotland, and he still remembered the persecution after the Jacobite defeat in 1746. Whitehaven was his port of departure for America at the age of twelve, but never his home; it recalled the cruel slave ships in which he had embarked, the British Royal Navy in which he had found no chance for promotion, the Mungo Maxwell episode with the seaport rumors which none had had the courage to bring before a court of law. His relatives were in Arbigland, thirty miles across the Solway; his friends, such few as may have remained with the passing of years, were in Kirkcudbright where he had received his first command, the *John,* and had become a Mason, and in London where he had acquired business associates. He felt no abiding personal bond with Whitehaven and was too devoted an American officer to sacrifice both reason and duty to false sentiment. The only flaw seemed to be that he offered an excuse for his own act of war, concerning which an excuse was scarcely necessary, by exaggerated emphasis upon the cruelty of the enemy's attacks on the coast of America at towns like Falmouth and Norfolk.

Despite wind and tide, two boats filled with recalcitrant officers and men, and a traitor for full measure, Jones gave Britain a memorable experience. In the face of the obstacles, the tenacity of his valor was prophetic. It had its keynote in his words at the most discouraging moment on the shores of Whitehaven when dawn had arrived and his two parties had both failed to set fire to the ships and permitted their lantern lights to become extinguished: "I would by no means retreat while any hopes of success remained."

Chapter XIX

◇◇

The Raid at St. Mary's Isle; the Silver Plate

Now WHILE the British continued unprepared and bewildered was the time Jones chose to strike again in fulfillment of his twofold resolve to succor American prisoners as well as to retaliate upon enemy seaports. No sooner did he, both pilot and captain in the Solway Firth, step from his barge to the deck of the *Ranger* than the ship bore away for St. Mary's Isle and Kirkcudbright, within less than two hours' sail from Whitehaven. When the sun still had not reached its meridian, the *Ranger* was off the Scottish coast, hove to at the Little Ross and its lighthouse guarding the entrance of Kirkcudbright Bay, and Jones with a party of only twelve including two officers set out by boat for peninsular St. Mary's.[1]

As they neared the estate of the Earl of Selkirk, the Captain expedited his plan to carry the earl away as a hostage for the American seamen suffering and dying within the walls of Mill and Forton prisons. The undertaking was sudden and strange, but scarcely more so than the descent at Whitehaven; and both were natural to his bold originality. Little did Jones dream of the web of romantic fabrication which would interweave his personal with his public history as the result of his startling choice of the Earl of Selkirk for this object and his unconventional ardor in subsequently explaining himself and his act by a letter to the earl's wife.

Jones had set himself the duty to free American naval prisoners as part of the larger purpose to maintain rights of the United States by sea. Even in his early cruise with the *Alfred,* he had shown his zeal in behalf of the captives at the coal pits of Cape Breton. The cruelties suffered by Americans taken from war vessels had been known at home by the nearby accounts from the notorious prison ships anchored in the waters neighboring New York.[2] They probably had been the more familiar to him by reason of his knowledge of the Commissary of Naval Prisons, David Sproat, a former Scotch countryman from Kirkcudbright. They had met his eyes in the emaciated appearance of seamen who had gained their freedom in America.

On the Continent, they came to his ears more recently in the tales of those who had escaped to France from under or over the walls of the prisons in England. They had manifold confirmation for him by Franklin, who remonstrated with his British friend Sir Grey Cooper concerning "the miserable situation and hard treatment of my countrymen at Portsmouth and Plymouth."[3] The Doctor also informed Lord Stormont, the English Ambassador at Paris: "The United States are not unacquainted with the barbarous treatment their people receive when they have the misfortune of being your prisoners in Europe." And he had the satisfaction to be rewarded for his pains by a reply consistent with the reported treatment of the prisoners: "The King's Ambassador receives no applications from rebels, unless they come to implore His Majesty's mercy."[4] Still the terms of the answer were scarcely more harsh than those of the demand, and so Franklin the philosopher had considerable reason to digest his own provocation.

How ingrained the convictions of Jones concerning Britain's naval war had become and how justified he felt in acting upon them have already been evident only in part by his incursion at Whitehaven. The sufferings of seamen were to him even a more urgent reason for retaliation. In his own case the spirit of such hostility towards Americans was to live for generations in the epithet *pirate*. This term, in fact, was not reserved for him alone. "In the month of February, 1776 the Parliament of England," Jones took occasion to remember, "had authorized George III to consider and to treat all Americans taken at sea who were armed as traitors, pirates, and felons."

"This circumstance more than any other," he added, "rendered me the avowed enemy of Great Britain. Never before had history furnished us the example of a people arrogant enough to assume sovereignty with such deliberate cruelty. . . . From the beginning of the war in America, the exchange of prisoners in the army had taken place between General Washington and the English generals. In spite of all her pride, Great Britain had been obliged to agree to this arrangement and to consider as prisoners of war all the Americans who were captured in military service. To be captured, armed against her, upon her assumed empire of the ocean was an irretrievable crime . . . fear alone prevented England during this war from giving the world for the second time the unhappy spectacle of the horrors which desolated Scotland in 1745. . . . Justly indignant at the barbarous treatment which these Americans suffered, I resolved to make the greatest efforts to succor them."[5]

It is true that in the heat of his sympathies Jones ignored certain qualifying circumstances. In the United States at least, the prisoners had themselves largely to blame. They happened to be Americans taken chiefly from privateers, not from Continental ships of war. When English officials offered to return them for British soldiers, Washington refused, explaining that "the arrangement would give the enemy a very considerable reinforcement . . . while the exchanged American prisoners, being captured while employed in private enterprises, would return to their homes."[6] The privateersmen, moreover, sometimes did not trouble themselves to take English prisoners during their self-centered operations; so for this second reason, too, their sufferings when captured were in part the reward of selfishness.[7]

Jones chose to forget that the failure of some Continental ships as well as some privateers to take prisoners had caused him to exclaim—not without Shaksperian quotations—as vehemently against the commanders of both classes of vessels as he expressed himself against the British: "Were this base conduct practiced by those licensed robbers alone, 'I should have found within my soul one drop of patience' but to find individuals in our Navy affected with the same foul contagion racks me with distressing passions, and covers me with shame! One instance during many may be sufficient; the redoubtable Manley went near the entrance of St. Johns and disdaining advantages made the enemy a present of eighty seamen at once. Such conduct on our part at a time when our cruel enemies are enforcing an act of their Parliament . . . is a wonder 'passing strange' and will be deemed romance by future ages."[8]

These conditions of exchange and hardship of prisoners in America did not apply to an equal degree to those in Europe. And as to those in America, it is necessary to look no further than to the prison camps of both the North and the South during the American Civil War to find charges of cruelties scarcely less than those which he made against the British, three thousand miles from their base of supplies in England.

In the light of his passionate sentiments, Jones was now to exercise forbearance as conspicuous as his design was bold. While the *Ranger* hovered off the shore with a British flag at her masthead and in disguise as a merchantman, the party arrived in the barge at St. Mary's Isle and turned towards the residence of the Earl of Selkirk. The peaceful and picturesque Isle with its removed coast line, secluded heavily-wooded paths, and unguarded mansion house seemed a strange choice for this utterly unexpected raid from America. When the Captain and his small party of officers and men, chosen with perhaps one or two exceptions from the larger number which had gone ashore with him at Whitehaven, met some of the inhabitants along their route, they announced themselves as English sailors in search of men for impressment; and so the report quickly spread and caused able-bodied persons of the estate and surroundings to scamper away in hiding.[9] They asked what vessels and sailors were in the nearby harbor of Kirkcudbright in order to lend the more plausibility to the ruse and to govern later movements. In answer, however, to his essential inquiry concerning the Earl of Selkirk, Jones learned that he was not at home but in London. As the Captain felt after this information that he had no further purpose at St. Mary's Isle, he turned away with his men to retrace his steps to the sands where their guarded boat lay waiting for them.[10]

One of his officers expressed his discontent and stopped in remonstrance. It was represented to Jones—officers and men of the *Ranger* characteristically chose to argue instead of to obey—"that in America no delicacy was shown by the English, who took away all sorts of movable property, setting fire not only to towns and to the houses of the rich, without distinction, but not even sparing the wretched milch cows of the poor and helpless at the approach of inclement weather. . . ."[11] The Captain was in a quandary; to accede to their demands would have been to degrade war to brigandage and his special championship of prisoners to common lust for booty; to deny sternly their demands would have been to incite the greater spirit of insubordination in the face of his own knowledge of English severities on American coasts and in disregard for the volunteer service, however lukewarm, at White-haven and St. Mary's Isle.

Jones had barely a moment as he walked to consider the best policy, and in that moment determined to permit them to demand the silver plate at the home of Lord Selkirk; he realized the avarice and niggardliness of his crew, preferred to divert them from more serious depredations, and recognized that his object was to sway the men not only to obey but to fight in battle. He charged the officers, however, to enter the house themselves without any of the seamen, to injure nothing within it, to accord Lady Selkirk "the utmost respect," and to accept the plate tendered without search or further insistence. At the same time his hidden purpose was later to buy the plate and return it. After final orders to execute the plan with despatch and to post several sentinels along the route, he decided to await their return under the towering trees near his boat at the shore. "The tenderness of his heart," according to a report of natives who saw and later identified the Captain, "would not allow him to come to the house."[12]

The consternation of the inmates, consisting at the time of the Countess of Selkirk, her son, a relative Miss Eliot, a friend Mrs. Wood and her three mature daughters, and the servants, was so great at the arrival of the party, although the professed intention to impress seamen had been reported to them, that accounts of the number varied from fifteen to forty.[13] While the sailors remained on guard at the doors, the two officers entered the house. Lady Selkirk, who was one of the few to be outwardly composed, came down to the parlor to them. The elder officer shortly explained that they were Americans from a ship of war whose purpose had been to take the earl as a hostage for the redemption of prisoners and whose present object was to secure the plate. "Of the two officers," the countess described, "one was a civil young man in a green uniform. . . . He came to the house in a blue greatcoat. He was but second. The principal one was in blue, [wore] no uniform, and seemed by nature very disagreeable . . . had a vile blackguard look, still kept civil as well he might, but I should suspect might have been rough enough had he met with provocation." In demanding the plate, he said, "Produce it directly. We are masters of this house and everything in it. It is needless to resist."

"I am very sensible of that," Lady Selkirk replied. She related further: "I called Daniel [the butler], told him what was wanted, ordered him to get it, and followed him to the pantry. . . . I found Daniel filling one of the maids' aprons with whatever he could lift first to hide it. I made him lay it down again, resolving not to dispute or deny it to them, by which means they very deliberately called for sacks to put everything up. . . . Upon the whole, I must say they behaved civilly. The men on the outside of the house were each armed with a musket and bayonet, two large pistols and a hanger. The doors were opened. None of them offered to come in, nor asked for anything. . . . But if no accident had ensued, I now see some plate might have been saved by leaving it to the servants, for they went nowhere below but to the pantry, did not look sharp about them, and looked alarmed when they saw the bewildered crowd at the door of it."[14]

The countess half-rued her quixotic honesty but at the same time tendered each of the officers a glass of wine. If the report is to be believed, she even intimated a wish, in view of the moderation of Jones' orders and the observance of them by his men, to go to the shore, a mile distant, for the purpose of inviting him to dinner.[15] The officers were nevertheless in such haste that, although accepting the wine, they did not compare the inventory, which their victim, turned hostess, asked them to sign as a receipt, with the contents of the bags; later a considerable discrepancy was evident to them.

"They appeared," wrote her son, "in consternation most of the time. . . . The commanding officer seemed not to be able to write or read; so he gave the inventory of the plate to the other, and bade him write a receipt to it when asked to do so by my mother. Williamford [Wallingsford], the name of the under officer, took a pen and wrote, *this is to cert* . . . then found fault with the pen, and said it was no matter, for everybody would soon know they had been there. . . . They were in all about half an hour on land. The ship set sail as soon as the boat put off. They said they intended to come to Kirkcudbright; so the people were sadly alarmed, and brought some cannon from a ship and about thirty muskets to the point of the Isle."[16]

This parting threat probably came from the lips of the senior officer, who also had boasted of the complete destruction of the ships at Whitehaven and had been modestly corrected by Wallingsford.[17] Superior in rank to this lieutenant of marines, he must have been not Hill the midshipman, who had volunteered for the earlier raid, but Hall the second or Simpson the first lieutenant. A son-in-law of Hall claimed the doubtful distinction for his relative, but the part seems consistent with the character of either officer in view of the uncomplimentary description of him by the countess, his proclivities for booty, and the likelihood that he who had refused to engage in the expedition to Whitehaven would be most disposed to misrepresent and boast about it.

As for designs upon Kirkcudbright, Jones had no intention to fritter away time and energy; he laid comprehensive plans now as before, however much they had miscarried at Whitehaven and St. Mary's Isle. But thanks to his boat crew, especially the officers, and the silver plate as their booty rather than his own object to take the Earl of Selkirk as a hostage, he left in his wake a rising tide of rumors about him heightened by the winds of local gossip and of national resentment at his future naval achievements. Particularly while Jones continued his cruise, the mystified and almost frenzied excitement of little St. Mary's Isle and of adjoining Kirkcudbright spent itself in coloring the reputation of the former nearby inhabitant.

Letter followed letter from the nearest postoffice. The Countess of Selkirk herself, later somewhat less composed and more resentful, credulously recounted some of the reports with their tangled mesh of truth and falsehood. "At going off they said," the countess wrote her husband, "that they belonged to the *Ranger* frigate, Captain Paul Jones, Esq., commander. . . . It was immediately known that this Paul Jones is one John Paul, born at Arbigland, who once commanded a Kirkcudbright vessel belonging to Mr.

Muir and others, a great villain as ever was born, guilty of many crimes and several murders by ill usage, was tried and condemned for one, escaped and followed a piratical life till he engaged with the Americans. He seems to delight in that still, as robbing a house is below the dignity of the States of America. The sailors at the door told that their Captain . . . knew my lord (whose name and the name of the place those in the house pretended ignorance of), had a great opinion of him, and for that reason had given orders that no more should be done."[18]

In the course of several weeks, as residents of the district made current new disclosures based on slight foundations, Lady Selkirk sent.to her sister a further account which was both more detailed and, in some respects, more distorted: "I omitted mentioning to you respecting our privateer that the Captain was born on the coast betwixt [sic] and Dumfries, was bound apprentice to the sea service at Whitehaven, commanded some years a Kirkcudbright vessel that sailed to the West Indies, during that time was guilty of several shocking bad things with respect to the treatment of men on board amounting to their deaths. For one he was tried, but for want of sufficient evidence was either acquitted or the prosecution dropped. On another occasion he killed a man in a sort of duel, but I believe it was understood an unfair stab. What sort of a trial he stood for that I do not know, but upon that or some other occasion he did not choose to come home, and went and offered his services to the Congress, got command of a ship, took a considerable prize, cheated the Congress in their share of it, and was turned off. He afterwards got command of a privateer, this same *Ranger,* and I think is likely to recover credit with the Congress he had lost and be a great hero. He is acknowledged to be very clever, but was always very passionate and of no principles. The attempt to burn Whitehaven, the place he was bred as a boy, represents him in a very bad light. As to the expedition here, I know not what to say if, as some say, it was to ascertain his power of landing on the British coast. The attempt at Whitehaven made that clear. For my own [part] I did believe that . . . having a few hours to spare he wished for a little private booty."[19]

These letters with their confusion of facts reveal less the beliefs to which one person was prone than the ill-founded opinions of many others of the surrounding towns and countryside; from them, in turn, provincial errors were to span the ocean. Yet they disclose, although in distorted form, not only the punishment meted to the carpenter Mungo Maxwell, which coincidentally preceded his fatal illness, but also the struggle with the mutineer, which resulted directly in the death of the latter and the sailing of Jones for America—ostensible secrets, especially the second episode, locked with sorrow in the Captain's heart and divulged by him only to his most confidential friends.

In contrast with these two communications from Lady Selkirk, a third letter from her to Mr. Craik of Arbigland, formerly the employer of Jones' father and a patron of Jones himself, contains statements in corroboration of the facts of the Captain's birthplace and parentage, with which the laird was undoubtedly familiar; but it becomes typically misleading in regard to other matters which he probably could judge with less authority. "They [the American officers] told me," the countess explained to him, "that they were of the *Ranger* frigate, belonging to the States of America, commanded by Captain Paul Jones, Esquire, whom I understand you know better than me, being John Paul, who they say was born in your ground, and is a gardener's son of yours. Afterwards he had the command of a trading vessel in this place, and is understood to have deserved the gallows oftener than once. It seems it is known this is the name he takes, and he was seen in the Isle, though the tenderness of his heart, they said, would not allow him to come to the house. . . ."[20]

"The tenderness of his heart," this description, already remarked, of Jones—the leader at Whitehaven and the laggard at St. Mary's—which Lady Selkirk heard the inhabitants express regardless of their hostility to him, testified with eloquence that seizure of the silver plate was not at all to his liking. "The tenderness of his heart," this phrase was paradoxical applied to a fighter like Jones as if to illustrate the maxim that the bravest are the tenderest; yet the countess and the natives came to feel its truth, although it was not to be expected of the officers and men to unmask themselves so far as to confess that they, not their commander, were really responsible for the pillage of her plate. "The tenderness of his heart," this meaning lay at the core of the chivalric letter that Jones soon wrote to Lady Selkirk, by which he must have removed her illusion of his personal interest in the robbery. The greater understanding with which she necessarily saw him in relation to the attack upon her home, accompanied as it was by a decorum not common to pillagers as the result of his strict injunctions, must also have revealed to her new rays amid those shadows upon his reputation which rumors had spread and she herself had been prone to believe and blacken.

This long, anomalous letter which Jones wrote to the countess laid bare many facets of his complex character. Composed aboard the *Ranger* after the departure from St. Mary's Isle, amid the stress of a crew disposed to mutiny and of a battle fought against the enemy, he did not post it until the end of the cruise. The spirit and meaning, however, belonged particularly to the immediate circumstances. The letter mirrored the Captain who fought bloody engagements but strove in behalf of prisoners and peace; who championed America but professed to a subject of Britain an international philanthropy; who was chivalric towards women but planned the capture of a woman's husband as a hostage; who wrote on this occasion in a manner more inflated than that of most of the Fathers of the Revolution concerning his devotion to liberty and his zeal for mankind but confessed his sacrifice of "the softer affections of the heart" and of his "prospects of domestic happiness." Yet the inconsistencies are more external than basic. Although Jones admittedly fought better than he wrote, his pen, destined to mature, was generally skillful enough at this period even without allowance for his limited formal schooling. In this special instance the strain of his enterprises and his susceptibility when women were concerned, as well as an attempt possibly to surpass himself, did not improve either his style or his sentiments.

"It cannot be too much lamented," he began in this recital to the Countess of Selkirk, "that in the profession of arms, the officer of fine feelings and sensibility should be under the necessity of winking at any action of persons under his command which his heart cannot approve; but the reflection is doubly severe when he finds himself obliged in appearance to countenance such action by his authority.

"This hard case was mine, when, on the 23rd of April last I

landed on St. Mary's Isle. Knowing Lord Selkirk's interest with his King, and esteeming *as I do* his private character, I wished to make him the happy instrument of alleviating the horrors of hopeless captivity, when the brave are overpowered and made prisoners of war.

"It was perhaps fortunate for you, madam, that he was from home, for it was my intention to have taken him on board the *Ranger,* and to have detained him until, thro' his means, a general and fair exchange of prisoners as well in Europe as in America had been effected."

After, in addition, an explanation of his dilemma incident to the seizure of the silver plate and an account of later happenings of the cruise, he continued: "Tho' I have drawn my sword in the present generous struggle for the rights of men, yet I am not in arms as an American, nor am I in pursuit of riches. My fortune is liberal enough, having no wife nor family, and having lived long enough to know that riches cannot insure happiness. I profess myself a citizen of the world, totally unfettered by the little mean distinctions of climate or of country, which diminish the benevolence of the heart and set bounds to philanthropy. Before this war began, I had, at an early time of life, withdrawn from the sea service, in favor of 'calm contemplation and poetic ease.' I have sacrificed not only my favourite scheme of life, but *the softer affections of the heart,* and my prospects of domestic happiness, and I am ready to sacrifice my life also with cheerfulness, if that forfeiture could restore peace and good will among mankind.

"As the feelings of your gentle bosom cannot but be congenial with mine, let me entreat you, madam, to use your soft persuasive arts with your husband, to endeavor to stop this cruel and destructive war, in which Britain never can succeed. Heaven can never countenance the barbarous and unmanly practices of the Britons in America, which savages would blush at, and which, if not discontinued, will soon be retaliated in Britain by a justly enraged people. . . .

"I hope this cruel contest will soon be closed; but, should it continue, I wage no war with the fair. I acknowledge their power, and bend before it with profound submission; let not, therefore, the amiable Countess of Selkirk regard me as an enemy. I am ambitious of her esteem and friendship, and would do anything consistent with my duty to merit it.

"The honor of a line from your hand, in answer to this will lay me under a very singular obligation; and if I can render you any acceptable service in France or elsewhere, I hope you see into my character so far as to command me without the least grain of reserve.

"I wish to know exactly the behavior of my people, as I determine to punish them if they have exceeded their liberty."[21]

Despite the gallantry of this enigmatic letter to the countess, which was probably only less surprising to her than the raid itself, she did not undertake a reply. Her pen had been ready enough before, but the Earl of Selkirk had returned home and assumed it now. His long, deliberate answer complemented the less considered conclusions by his wife regarding Jones and offset the letter from Jones himself. It helped more indirectly than directly to unfold the character of the Captain, the public motives of his raid, and such relation as they bore to his past personal life:

"The letter you wrote to Lady Selkirk . . . came to hand t'other day. . . . It was matter of surprise both to my wife and to me, as no apology was expected. . . .

"Your lamenting the necessity of these things in the profession of arms, and of being obliged to gratify your officers by permitting them to go to my house, and carry off some plate, and your expressing the great sensibility of your feelings at what your heart can not approve, are things which we, who have no knowledge of you, nor your character but by report, can form no proper judgment of, but must leave to your own conscience, and to the Almighty Judge of the real motives of all actions. . . .

"I own I do not understand how a man of *sensibility to fine feelings* could reconcile this to what his heart approved, especially as the carrying me off could have no possible effect for the purpose you mention, which you say was, 'knowing my interest with the King, your intention was to detain me, until through my means, a general and fair exchange of prisoners, as well in Europe as in America, had been effected.' Now, sir, nothing can be more erroneous than these ideas, for I have no interest whatever with the King. . . . With regard to the King's Ministers, I neither have nor can have any interest with them, as I have generally disapproved of most of their measures, and in particular of almost their whole conduct in the unhappy and ill-judged American war. . . . How then would it have been possible for such a man to effect a general exchange of prisoners when so many men of great power and influence in both houses of Parliament have not been able to bring it about? . . . had your attempt succeeded, its only effect would have been to distress a family that never injured any person, and whose wishes have certainly been very friendly to the Constitutions and just liberties of America.

"You exclaim on the barbarities committed in America, and say they will be retaliated in Britain if not discontinued. I have always been extremely sorry at the accounts of these things, no man can be a greater enemy to all ungenerous inhumanities in war than I am. God knows best which side began these things, and which has most to account for, but it is certainly the general opinion in Britain that the Americans began the unusual and cruel practice complained of, and first against their own countrymen who adhered to the British Government.

"In your letter you profess yourself a citizen of the world, and that you have drawn your sword in support of the rights of man, yet you say you are not in arms as an American nor in pursuit of riches. If you are not in arms as an American, I do not understand in what character you act, and unless you have an American commission, I doubt the laws of war and of nations would not be very favorable to you as a citizen of the world, which however ought to be a very honorable character, and you will do well to endeavor to act up to the humanity and honour of it. Consider then, sir, the impropriety and danger to the common interests and happiness of society in your departing from the established and usual practice of modern war. . . .

"It was certainly fortunate both for Lady Selkirk and me, that I was from home, and it was also fortunate for you, sir, that your officers and men behaved well, for had any of my family suffered outrage, murder, or violence, no quarter of the globe should have secured you, nor even some of those under whose commission you act, from my vengeance. But, sir, I am happy that their welfare enables me to inform you that the orders you mention in your letter were punctually obeyed by your two officers and men, who in every respect behaved as well as could be expected on such an occasion. . . .

"What you mention is certainly so, that some of the plate was left, but that was contrary to Lady Selkirk's intention and to her orders, but happened partly by accident, confusion, and hurry, and partly by the improper inclinations of some servants. . . .

"Your genteel offer, sir, of returning the plate is very polite, but at the same time neither Lady Selkirk nor I can think of accepting of it, as you must purchase it you say for that purpose, but if your delicacy makes you unwilling to keep that share of its value which as Captain you are entitled to, without purchasing, I would in that case wish that part to be given to those private men who were on the party, as an encouragement for their good behaviour. You, sir, are entitled to what is more honorable, viz: the praise of having your men under good discipline, which on all occasions I take care to make known. . . .

"Though your letter is wrote like a man who means well, and who wishes to be considered a man of honour, yet some people in this country who say they know you (tho' I do not think it certain you are the person they mean) laugh at your saying you are not in pursuit of riches, and at your intention of taking me for the purpose of a general exchange of prisoners. They say your design must have been a ransom, and that your offer of returning the plate is only a snare, to put me off my guard. But as I chanced to be entirely ignorant of you and your character, till your enterprise on the 23rd of April, I have therefore nothing certain to judge by but your behaviour, then and since, and as that has, in so far as regarded my family, been genteel, and though your intention of taking me was certainly absurd, yet as it was so from mistake I therefore will not allow myself to think with those people, that a man who professes honorable sentiments, and is acting under an honorable commission for what he thinks is supporting the rights of mankind, would for the sake of a pitiful ransom degrade himself to the low and vile character of a Barbary pirate, which would be the case if these people were right in the opinion they give, but I chuse to judge more favourably of you."[22]

In this understanding and kindly spirit Selkirk wrote to Jones.

In a manner somewhat less independent of public opinion, he communicated with Lord Le Despencer, his friend the Postmaster General, whom he requested to transmit the letter, as he believed it would be withheld at London if sent by ordinary post. "He is such an odd fellow," the earl explained, "by what I hear of him, (for we were perfectly unacquainted with him till his landing at my house) that it is not easy to know how to write to him nor yet very proper to neglect answering him . . . he seems to be an enthusiast, absurd and ignorant of the springs and moves of our affairs, and as such I would wish to convince him that he had no business to meddle with me; but if he is the man whom the people here believe him to be, he is both a dangerous and worthless fellow by all accounts I can hear of him. He is said to . . . have committed no less than three murders, and that in absconding from the West Indies after the last one, he fled to America, and so commenced heroic vindicator of the rights of mankind and officer of fine feelings. I have made my letter to him intolerably long, but I could not well help it, unless I had given him a very short answer, which might have made him burn my house at his next trip to these coasts; but we should give the devil his due, he certainly, be he who he will, behaved well at my house, notwithstanding that some plate was taken away. His letter was so long and so absurd that it has forced me to be very diffuse also and perhaps as absurd, to think of arguing with the captain of a privateer."[23]

Lord Le Despencer refused his request. "I cannot help doubting, in the situation I am in," he stated, "the propriety of my forwarding a letter to such a rascal and rebel as this Jones." So the reply of the Earl of Selkirk, which would have been congenial to the Captain, never reached his hands, but the import of the correspondence by both of them remains.

Was the plan to take the earl as a hostage cruel? Was it ill-judged? The war aroused the bitter passions of divided allegiance and kindred; it was waged chiefly in a rude, pioneer land unrestrained by traditions. Whatever the depredations by England on the American coast and whatever her treatment of prisoners taken at sea, there were many Britons like Selkirk who were of the opinion that the cruelties began with the Americans, that the exchange of sailors was a zealous object of influential statesmen in Parliament such as Burke and Shelburne,[24] and that even the policies of the King and Ministry were censurable. Jones was disposed to ignore the force of these points of view by Britons themselves as well as such considerations as restrained Washington from returning captured English soldiers for American privateersmen.

Yet to end a public wrong, however difficult it was to determine its measure amid the blindness and inhumanity of war itself, the Captain undertook to inflict only a minor, private one. Although the earl was clearly not a wise choice through whom to effect an exchange of prisoners, Jones' presence in nearby waters and his acquaintance with the coast, the tides, and the location of the estate invited the enterprise and rendered it the more feasible. Likewise the Earl of Selkirk's humaneness and sympathy towards America made him potentially an able advocate of her cause.[25] But certainly the Captain's ignorance of the political bearing of his plan, which stood in utter contrast with his mastery of seamanship and naval warfare, remained a flaw in his strategy.

Larger inferences regarding the life of Jones derive from the letters of the earl, the one to Le Despencer as well as the other to his intended captor. They make the more obvious that both the Earl and Countess of Selkirk had previously known nothing of Jones. There was, consequently, no intimate personal reason, based on any association acknowledged by them, for their visitor to have considered himself either before or after this period—as has sometimes been held and here been earlier denied—an illegitimate son of the earl. They make evident also that the widespread evil reports of his early career from the lips of unthinking and prejudiced persons were to a man of independent and deliberate judgment like the Earl of Selkirk at variance with both the letter to the countess and the civility of the officers and men under his direction. They lead further to the conclusion that, limited as were the means of Selkirk for arriving at a just estimate of Jones and unconsidered as seemed in his view the choice of himself, without political influence, as an intended hostage, at this time he looked upon his correspondent neither as a naval genius nor even as a highly talented commander but rather as "an exotic character" and "the captain of a privateer."

In fact few Americans and fewer Englishmen then fathomed Jones' passionate dedication to the honor of America and to his love of glory as the reward for eminent services. These two impulses beat in his heart with prodigal fire. His word, as the event would prove characteristically to the Earl and Countess of Selkirk, was his bond for the return of the silver plate. His resolution to redeem the American prisoners was typically also his certificate for its performance or his death in the endeavor. Scarcely had he failed at St. Mary's Isle in his plan on a minor scale before he swiftly set his course in the *Ranger* to achieve it on a major, tempered by defeat to new resources of skill and to fiery martial valor.

Chapter XX

The *Ranger* Captures the *Drake*

BEFORE A WORD had been penned regarding the alarm at St. Mary's Isle, the inhabitants had seen the *Ranger* square her yards and disappear under a crowd of canvas to the westward in the direction of Belfast Lough. She was again in search of the British ship of war *Drake,* which had been in the roadstead of Carrickfergus.

Jones had made his initial attempt to attack this vessel of twenty guns on April 21, 1778—after the first approach to Whitehaven but before the raid at this port as well as at the Isle. Cruising off Belfast Lough, he had seen her at anchor and learned her identity from a vessel with fishermen captured earlier in nearby waters; and these prisoners then served him opportunely as pilots. He had stood off and on about an hour and then had put about to take the ship at anchor. When the wind blew fresh and the crew showed unwillingness to sail into the harbor, however, he had deferred his plan to capture the *Drake* until midnight and prepared to execute it less by force than stratagem.[1]

The Captain had taken the precaution to make no warlike appearance off the Lough. The *Ranger* had been in her frequent disguise as a merchantman, even with a Dutch pendant and an English Jack at the main topgallant masthead.[2] Her ports had been closed to hide the guns with their lighted matches ready for instant battle; her anchor, grapplings, and helm had been in readiness for a manœuvre to be executed with speed and precision; her men had been at quarters, some ready to spring to the deck by the guns and tackles, others to the tops with their grenades and muskets, and still others to battle stations most favorable for boarding or repelling boarders. Cleared for action, flying only her topsails and jibs, guided by the fishermen whose lives would have been the forfeit of treachery, she had slipped into the road under cover of night and confidently approached as if to take her berth next to the *Drake*. Jones had planned not only to lay the enemy athwart hawse so as to have the advantage of raking her at the outset of the engagement without fear of broadsides in return but also to maintain this position by means of anchor and grapplings so as to keep her at his mercy until she surrendered.[3]

The high wind had required the more skill in timing the manœuvre. The boatswain's mate whose task it had been to let go the anchor at the moment of the signal had drunk too much grog. In the darkness he had failed to execute the order at the instant of the Captain's command; consequently the ship had brought to upon the enemy's quarter at the distance of half a cable's length. Instead of having the *Drake* in the hoped-for disadvantageous position, Jones had found himself in imminent peril.

Calmly, quietly, speedily he had set about to make his escape, deeming it wiser to try again under more favorable circumstances than to make the best of his sudden predicament. He had cut his cable, which was likely to give the enemy the impression of having snubbed and parted in the night during the movements of some clumsy merchantman. He then had beat out of the Lough, barely escaping the lighthouse on the lee side as the gale heightened. The weather had become, in fact, so stormy that it had been impossible to return for a second attempt before daybreak; the *Ranger* had found it necessary even to take shelter under the south shore of Scotland. In the meantime the crew of the *Drake* had recovered the anchor and cable of the mysterious stranger.

Following this adventure and the recounted interlude of the second passage to Whitehaven and of the descent at St. Mary's Isle, the *Ranger* at the return to Belfast Lough early on the morning of April 24 was prepared again to encounter the *Drake*. To Jones' great satisfaction she was still in the road by Carrickfergus. On this occasion he determined, regardless of renewed opposition of his crew, to challenge her by daylight. If she refused to venture from her anchorage, as first appeared probable in the morning, it was his bold purpose to encounter her in the Lough.

In the meantime the rebellious spirit of Jones' officers and men rose to mutiny.[4] At Whitehaven the faithfulness of the volunteer Edward Meyer had alone saved him from being abandoned by his boats and left single-handed on the shore to the fury of the assembled thousands.[5] Off the Lough, several of the lieutenants were in open opposition at the prospect of a grim battle with a British sloop of war. They objected the more strongly to the bold purpose of Jones again to attack the enemy at her haven when she still showed no positive intention of leaving the road. They reiterated that they were poor and that their object from the beginning had been profit, not honor. The susceptible crew became infected so much with the virus of their avarice and fear that leaders among them plotted to place their Captain in fetters or hurl him into the sea and then to return to America under the command of Simpson.[6] Only Jones' ready action at threatened danger saved his life and prevented the *Ranger* from shamelessly showing her heels to the *Drake*. "The mutiny," he related, "almost reduced me to the necessity of putting some of them to death."[7] At this crisis Jones faced hostile Americans on his own deck scarcely less formidable than the enemy on a British ship of war, such as none had ever conquered in the memory of his time on the open seas, much less in narrow home waters within sight of the three British kingdoms.

The vicious mood of the officers and crew of the *Ranger* was still brewing when at noon the intentions of the *Drake* seemed to change as she loosed her sails and sent a boat to reconnoitre the strange ship off the road. The British barge came nearer, but the suppressed hostility aboard the *Ranger* towards her Captain continued to be tense. There were, to be sure, reasons for fear. During four days the presence of the foreign ship in local waters had been bruited by land and sea as an American viking. Express despatches from Whitehaven had arrived the preceding night at Belfast and Carrickfergus describing the raid and warning these ports of further possible incursions. And after the *Drake* had recovered the lost anchor and cut cable, Carrickfergus saw the more reason for suspicion.

The enemy's boat strangely continued to approach as if in confident disregard of the alarms and of the presence of the *Ranger*, which a British officer scrutinized through his spyglass. Jones' surly crew at quarters looked on with increasing wonder. Herd-like they had conspired to overthrow their Captain, and herd-like they now marveled at the promise of his cunning against the scout. "It tickled their caprice," explained Jones, "and soothed them again into good humor."[8]

This craft drew even closer. Now by day the *Ranger* hid her identity more carefully than she had done at night. Again Jones had disguised her as a merchantman, masked her batteries, and sent her sailors below decks. He flew the British flag pending the moment of battle. And unerringly he kept the stern of the *Ranger* directly towards the bow of the approaching boat; as often as the latter altered her course so as to have the side of the former, starboard or port, exposed to her view, he accordingly shifted the helm so that only the stern or at most either quarter was open. At length the British officer with his five sailors approached so near in his barge as to be under the guns and muskets of the *Ranger*. He came aboard and to his consternation found himself a prisoner and his boat a prize. The crew had watched the capture with enchantment, hailed it as an omen of victory, and was electrified with the will to fight.[9]

Shortly several guns boomed from the *Drake* as a signal of recall to her tender, but the only answer was silence. Then she herself weighed anchor, and with a very moderate wind and against the tide worked out slowly from Belfast Lough. Pleasure vessels, too, curious and confident, put out from Carrickfergus astern her, and the smoke of alarm fires rose on all sides in the background. The *Ranger*, with courses up and maintopsail to the mast, awaited her adversary by clewing down several times. But after the *Drake* had weathered the lighthouse point, Jones determined not to permit her to come within hail until he had led her almost to the middle of the North Channel between Ireland and Scotland for more freedom of manœuvre in hostile waters and for prevention of her possible flight.

At the imminence of battle, the *Drake* had behind her the morale of British traditions of long unbroken mastery on the seas. In contrast the *Ranger* possessed no prestige worthy of the name except in so far as America was kin, like a poor relation, to Britain and her Navy. The crew of Burdon the British Captain consisted of approximately 175 officers and men, including at least a score of last-minute volunteers from Belfast and the vicinity, among whom was Lieutenant Dobbs, on leave from a ship of the line, serving in the emergency as second in command.[10] The personnel under Jones was considerably less in number, 123, and unquestionably less reliable, whatever spirit the men had just given promise of in the special circumstances.

As for armament, the *Drake* had twenty four-pounders and the *Ranger* eighteen six-pounders; but as the calibre of Jones' cannon was in fact less than the theoretical size, the advantage in this respect of the American ship over her adversary became comparatively little. Therefore it would seem that the superiority in man power of the British compensated the superiority in guns of the Americans so that neither side had an important preponderance tangibly. Intangibly, however, the morale of the enemy prided itself upon an historic background incomparably more promising and conducive to confidence. Victory or defeat was apparently to rest chiefly upon the somewhat imponderable human qualities of valor in leader and follower, training, equipment in so far as the means reveal the efficiency of the man, and tactical and strategic skill.

Measuring the strength of the *Drake* as the *Ranger* kept to windward, Jones finally led her late in the afternoon to the middle of the Channel within pistol shot of his ship. The *Drake* hoisted her English colors and the *Ranger* at the same instant displayed her Stars and Stripes. The formalities began to bore Jones when the enemy soon afterwards hailed, demanding to know the name of her opponent. The *Ranger* had been in sight in the offing since sunrise, her Captain had taken the British boat which was to be seen in tow and had caused the pleasure craft to put back in fear, he had learned from the officer sent to reconnoitre that reports of his exploits were rife along the coasts and that his anchor and cable had been recovered, and finally he had raised the American flag to disclose his identity. Slightly impatient, somewhat jocose, and even more crafty, perhaps, so as to afford the *Ranger* an opportunity to manœuvre a precious extra moment while the attention of Captain Burdon was occupied with his lengthy rejoinder, Jones directed his master to announce: "This is the American Continental ship *Ranger;* we are waiting for you, and desire that you come on; the sun is now little more than an hour from setting, it is therefore time to begin."[11]

The weather gage which Jones had been careful to gain and hold, and possibly, too, the extra second in distracting the attention of the *Drake,* enabled him to order the helm up in time to cross the bow of the enemy so as to deliver the first broadside. He must have veered sharply again both to avoid losing his position to windward and to escape a raking by the *Drake* as she attempted in turn to pass across his stern. In this manœuvre the *Ranger* did not receive a shot.[12] "The battle," as Jones related, "was warm, close, and obstinate. It lasted an hour and four minutes, when the enemy called for quarters; her fore and main-topsail yards being both cut away, and down on the cap; the top-gallant yard and mizzen-gaff both hanging up and down along the mast; the second ensign which they had hoisted shot away, and hanging on the quarter gallery in the water; the jib shot away; her sails and rigging entirely cut to pieces; her masts and yards all wounded, and her hull also very much galled. I lost only Lieutenant Wallingsford and one seaman, John Dougall, killed, and six wounded. . . . The loss of the enemy . . . was in killed and wounded forty-two men. The Captain and lieutenant were among the wounded; the former, having received a musket ball in the head the minute before they called for quarters, lived and was sensible some time after my people boarded the prize. The lieutenant survived two days. They were buried with the honors due to their rank and with the respect due to their memory."[13]

In contrast with this report by Jones the officer, succinct and matter of fact, is another account by Jones the man, philosophical and poetical: . . . "the awful pomp and dreadful carnage of a sea engagement, both affording ample subject for the pencil, as well as melancholy reflection to the contemplative mind. Humanity starts back from such scenes of horror, and cannot sufficiently execrate the vile promoters of this detestable war.

> 'For *they,* 'twas *they* unsheathed the ruthless blade,
> And Heaven shall ask the havoc it has made.'

". . . the gallant Captain of the *Drake* fell . . . the amiable lieutenant lay mortally wounded . . . a melancholy demonstration of the uncertainty of human prospects, and of the sad reverse of fortune which an hour can produce."[14]

The engagement was not only without parallel as the first victory of an American Continental vessel over an English ship of war; it also stood in marked contrast with most European encounters among frigates and ships of the line, especially in the case of fleets, during the first three-quarters of the eighteenth century when they had narrowed almost invariably to formal tactical manœuvres and cannon duels at comparatively long ranges with minor, indecisive results. Obviously Jones neither followed inflexible rules of naval warfare nor feared to fight at close quarters. He had refused to open the battle until the *Drake* had come within pistol shot. He had concentrated his gunfire more upon the spars and sails than upon the hull of the *Drake* and so had succeeded in rendering her unmanageable and at the mercy of his broadsides. As part of his object in bringing her within pistol shot, he had made greater use than was the custom of muskets and grenades in the hands of marines and sailors stationed in the tops to sweep the exposed decks. Finally, he had been in position to board the enemy in the event that expediency dictated this resource. Jones had struck adroitly and hard, weighing contingencies and seizing opportunities in the endeavor, according to his own expressed resolution, if not to insure success at least to deserve it.

And he had deserved it. The naval tradition of Britain seemingly would not have availed her regardless of whatever disadvantages beset the *Drake*. Captain Burdon may have been ill as well as overconfident, his lieutenant and boatswain recently deceased and no officers appointed in their places, his inferior powder and other stores provided by a profiteering commissary, his ship unfortunately rendered unmanageable, and his volunteer first lieutenant wounded early in the engagement.[15] Although the flagrant corruption that began to infect the Royal Navy under the ill-famed regime of Lord Sandwich is to be recognized, unreadiness, poor means, and bad luck are proverbial, and were not wanting in this notable instance, as the excuse for the defeated in the face of the promptitude, efficiency, and opportunism respectively of the victorious.

At this the highest pitch of his resolution during the cruise, Jones was practically invincible. The wide margin of his victory demonstrated in itself his powers in reserve. The marred initial plans to attack the *Drake* by day or night, the two unsatisfactory undertakings at Whitehaven, the humiliating as well as unsuccessful enterprise at St. Mary's Isle, and the increasingly obstructive and vicious behavior of the *Ranger's* men from the first episode with the *Drake* at the beginning of the cruise almost to the very moment of the ultimate conflict with her—all had moved the heart and mind of the Captain to a cumulative fixity of will as set as the coils of a tense spring for the final dramatic moment of action. Even the gallant behavior of the sailors at the crisis had been the sheer result of his magnetic personality. Jones alone was the imponderable human factor that had won the battle.

Chapter XXI

◇◇

The Ships Reach Brest

Now THE TASK was quickly to repair both sloops of war for sailing, especially the *Drake,* and safely to return to France in spite of the pursuit that would follow the reports speeding from nearby coasts. When Jones offered to Simpson the undertaking to prepare the prize for service in the course of the mild night, the officer argued with the backwardness natural to him that the shattered condition of the ship rendered it impossible of performance within the given time. The Captain than assigned the duty to Hall the second lieutenant, who with the aid of forty men had the *Drake* in trim to proceed in company with the *Ranger* by daybreak.

Jones planned to sail boldly southward through St. George's Channel, in which the enemy would be the more likely to search for him; but with the shifting of the wind, he determined to pass by the north and round the west coast of Ireland. This route brought him on the evening after the engagement once more off Belfast Lough. "It was now time," as he described and as local British accounts largely corroborated, "to release the honest fishermen, whom I took up here on the 21st, and as the poor fellows had lost their boat, she having sunk in the late stormy weather, I was happy in having it in my power to give them the necessary sum to purchase everything new which they had lost. I gave them also a good boat [a tender belonging to the *Drake*] to transport themselves ashore; and sent with them two infirm men, on whom I bestowed the last guineas [seventeen] in my possession, to defray their travelling expenses to their proper home in Dublin. They took one of the *Drake's* sails, which would sufficiently explain what had happened. . . . The grateful fishermen were in raptures, and expressed their joy in three huzzas as they passed the *Ranger's* quarter."[1]

The reward was unquestionable, but it appears upon examination less disinterested than the words "honest fishermen" suggest. Honest to Jones as noncombatant prisoners who served him as informists and pilots in the taking of the *Drake,* they ironically showed themselves unfaithful to their country. Although their aid may have been due more to fear than choice, his deed, regardless of his disingenuous phrase, shines with warmth of compassion amid the sombre and bloody background of war.

Although Hall, not Simpson, had repaired the *Drake* and although the insubordination of the latter had incited the crew to mutiny on the morning of the conflict, Jones continued to exercise almost unbelievable restraint towards this officer chosen and supported by fellow New Englanders, principally his brother-in-law Langdon and his other relatives Wendell and Hancock.[2] "Without any prelude," as the Captain described, "Mr. Simpson came hastily and publicly upon the quarter-deck and addressed himself to me in terms and manner which amounted to downright challenge. . . . I would not, however, lay hold of this, but on the contrary after the engagement, having him express a wish for a sword, I presented him with the sword of the late brave Captain Burdon as the most valuable gift in my possession."[3]

To crown evil with good, he had also placed Simpson in charge of the prize. He took the precaution, however, to issue to him in writing the following explicit orders: "You are hereby appointed commander of our prize, the English ship of war *Drake.* You are to keep company with me, and to pay punctual attention to the signals delivered herewith for your government. You are to superintend the navigation and defense of the ship under your command and to support me, as much as possible, should we fall in with and engage any of the enemy's ships. The honor of our flag is much concerned in the preservation of this prize; therefore keep close by me and she shall not be given tamely up. You are to take your station on the *Ranger's* starboard quarter, at or about the distance of a cable's length. Should bad weather or any accident separate you from the *Ranger,* you are to make the best of your way to France, and I recommend the port of Brest to your preference."[4] Regardless of these specific orders, the conduct of Simpson in the past gave little promise of his fulfillment of them—that the *Drake* was to accompany and coöperate with the *Ranger* and that only in the event of storm or accident which might separate the ships was Simpson to pursue his course to port alone.

The two ships arrived on May 5, 1778 within fifteen leagues of Ushant off the French coast, although the winds had been contrary in the mouth of the North Channel and the *Drake* was necessarily slower than the *Ranger* because of the greater damage she had suffered. Jones became hopeful of additional prizes when his position was favorable for intercepting vessels, especially those which rounded their course from the English Channel to St. George's Channel. With a favorable wind and the distance inconsiderable for Brest so as to insure the safety of his own ships, he saw at dawn a sail to leeward and decided to run down to her. He now ordered that the *Drake* should cast off the hawser, for his own ship had taken her in tow on the preceding day; Simpson accordingly cut the line. Jones likewise gave orders to the sailing-master of the *Ranger* to wear ship and give chase, and the officer accordingly hailed Simpson to inform him of these intentions and to direct him to make sail—to make sail, as the order meant and the navigator who received it understood, in company with Jones.[5]

Immediately the *Drake* set a course of her own. She was almost out of sight when Jones spoke the chase after an hour and ten minutes. "In the course of the day," wrote the Captain, "many large ships appeared, steering into the Channel, but the extraordinary evolutions of the *Drake* made it impossible for me to avail myself of these favorable circumstances." Simpson persisted in his disregard of orders throughout the night in spite of signals and apparent recognition of the *Ranger* in pursuit. "I gave chase to a sail," Jones wrote further, "which appeared bearing S.S.W. the next morning at a great distance. The chase discovered no intention to speak with the *Ranger;* she was, however, at length brought to, and proved to be the *Drake.* I immediately put Lieutenant Simpson under suspension and arrest for disobedience of my orders dated the 26 ult. . . ."

In fact, even after the *Ranger* had come up with the *Drake,* Jones seemed disposed to bear patiently with Simpson. But when the Captain directed him to haul more easterly, and the lieutenant, in the hearing of both crews, replied to ask whether he thought they were far enough to the south of Ushant, he ordered the *Drake* to heave to and sent a boat with Lieutenant Hall aboard to assume command.[6] Jones may have chosen his course with the view of taking prizes, or of sailing through the Four Passage to Brest; whatever his reasons, the public remonstrance of Simpson from the quarterdeck of one ship to the quarterdeck of the other was in character with the example of insubordination that he had set the crew.

He had, of course, his ready excuses for the evolutions of the *Drake*. Yet, apart from the violation of written orders to keep close by the *Ranger*, even Elijah Hall, David Cullam the sailing-master, and Ezra Green the surgeon, friends and fellow-officers of Simpson as they were to describe themselves in a petition to authority higher than Jones, admitted that he had not followed the orders given him when the Captain's ship had hailed. They palliated his conduct, however, on the ground that he had not disobeyed but misunderstood and that contrary to practice no signals had been given.[7] The prize crew under Simpson aboard the *Drake*, overzealous in his defense, in another affidavit averred that his orders had been to make the best of his way to Brest,[8] a contradiction of the admission of his friends, Hall, Cullam, and Green aboard the *Ranger*, who were in the position not only of hearing the instructions from the deck of their own ship but also of knowing them positively because Cullam the sailing-master had himself hailed the *Drake*.

Aside from the invalid claim of Simpson that "every person on the ship's deck, American and prisoners," including himself, had understood his orders were to proceed to Brest, his further plea that the *Drake* soon fell in with a brig under her lee, which caused him to make all the sail he could to escape her, failed to explain why he did not keep company with the *Ranger* from the moment the hawser was cut.[9] It divulged rather what he had sought to hide off the dangerous frequented waters of the English Channel and what had been, along with his avarice, his leading instinct earlier in the cruise—his fear. It was easier for Simpson to infect the crew and other officers, such as they were, with this emotion than for Jones to inspire them, except momentarily, with his bravery; for this reason especially, as birds of a feather, they flocked about the lieutenant and supported him. Almost without exception they had enlisted in the spirit of privateersmen, and remained privateersmen in their hearts.

The crew and officers as a body were indeed the worst that the Captain so far had aboard his ships in the course of his naval career. In comparing them with the men of the *Providence* and *Alfred,* Jones stated, for instance, that if the personnel of these earlier commands had been with him at Whitehaven, two or three hundred vessels would have been burnt to ashes.[10] Of Simpson in particular, whose appointment as first lieutenant was attributable to patronage and politics, he felt constrained later to write to the Commissioners: "I have faithfully supported and fought the dignified cause of human nature ever since the American banners first waved on the Delaware and on the ocean. This I did when that man did not call himself a Republican, but left the Continent and served its enemies. And this I did when that man appeared dastardly backward and did not support me. . . ." The records spoke eloquently enough in his behalf, but he also offered as a witness concerning events off Carrickfergus as well as Whitehaven his friend Edward Meyer, the Swedish lieutenant, "who having been with me as a volunteer can and will I am persuaded represent to you the conduct of the officers and men towards me both before I left Brest and afterwards in the Irish Channel as well as my conduct towards them."[11]

In spite of the craven and disloyal officers and men who had tried to thwart Jones in almost every endeavor, the *Ranger* with her prize arrived at Brest on May 8, 1778, to mark a memorable end to the cruise. When the *Drake* came in view, the conquered British flag blazoned the signal achievement of the American Captain. A fifth climactic enterprise had resulted in palpable victory after four brave attempts.

Britain awoke to realization of the impunity, daring, and potential retaliation with which an American officer first stepped on her shores. She armed her towns with feverish haste, raised her marine insurance rates to unprecedented levels, and particularly underwent a psychological shock the more severe in its suddenness. The agitation at Whitehaven was typical in the main of the state of mind at many British seacoast towns; the foundation of truth appeared beneath the structure of humorous exaggeration in an English journal: "The people of Whitehaven, it is thought, can never recover from their fright; two-thirds of the people are bordering on insanity; the remainder on idiotism; the defence of the harbor is left to the care of the old women, who declare that had they been called into power earlier, they would have preserved the town with their mopsticks, and cut off the retreat of the rebels.

"We hear that Dr. ——, with about a dozen half-starved Scotch physicians from Glasgow and Edinburgh, is shortly to go to Whitehaven to restore the inhabitants to their senses; but should those gentlemen not succeed, it is determined that a Scotch architect be employed to build them a madhouse."[12]

Along with the more intangible effects, Britain suffered at the hands of an American officer both the initial defeat of a ship of war, even in her home waters, and the capture of almost two hundred prisoners from her and merchant vessels during the cruise. He compelled the King and his Ministry to bethink themselves, as they had refused sometimes to do previously upon the petition of American authorities, of treating American naval prisoners with greater consideration and of making exchanges. Still, if Washington saw fit in America not to make certain exchanges which he believed would redound to the advantage of the British, the British were not less justified in their reluctance to make exchanges in Europe which they had reason to think would be to the advantage of the United States. Apart from this view, Jones had achieved at the very doors of the enemy, all difficulties notwithstanding, the two primary objects of his first expedition abroad.

◇◇◇

Chapter XXII

The Meshes of Politics

THE *Ranger* and the *Drake* flying the flag of the United States, with "the English colors inverted under the American stars" of the prize, hove to and rode at anchor in the road of Brest as if in disregard of further questions of French neutrality, although they were obviously ships of war. Jones had previously entered Nantes with the *Ranger* in the peaceful guise of a merchantman, instructed as he had been to make no warlike appearance. Conyngham and Wickes before him had been harried both to leave French ports expeditiously with their ships as well as to bring none of their prizes into them. The Treaty of Utrecht signed in 1713 and reaffirmed subsequently declared that ships of any power at war with England or France must not enter their ports for the purchase of supplies and for the sale of prizes, and that in the event of refuge from storms they must sail elsewhere as soon as possible. Notwithstanding the restrictions of this pact and the new provocation of Jones' presence in British eyes, he was again in Brest and assumed a more conspicuous rôle.

It was promising for the accommodation of the Captain that between his first and second arrivals at harbors of France the disguised breach of neutrality had become practically overt. Britain secured information of it from hidden sources as well as from open activities in France. Spies like Joseph Hynson, "an honest rascal" as a British agent termed him, who escaped by trickery with a bag of the Commissioners' despatches of six months for Congress entrusted to Folger, the Captain of an American merchant vessel; double spies like Bancroft, who was adept in making a bargain for his services with bidders on both sides and turning state secrets to his advantage for speculations in the stock market; and dupes of spies like Franklin and Lee—all of them had contributed wittingly or unwittingly to cause the Franco-American negotiations, notably the commercial and defensive alliances, to be known in England even before signatures were affixed and months before official reports reached the United States. The intricate activities of spies, especially those of Bancroft, were still to evolve.

After the pacts of February 6, 1778,[1] by which France openly recognized America as a belligerent and secretly arranged that neither should enter into a separate peace with England, her so-called neutrality became more and more a transparent mask. She soon was disposed to recognize officially the exchange of salutes between Jones and her Admirals. On March 16 Lord Stormont left Paris, and the Marquis de Noailles, the French Ambassador, likewise returned from London. On April 13 Count d'Estaing with twelve ships of the line and five frigates finally sailed from Toulon on the expedition against Lord Howe in the Delaware, which Jones had urged as early as February 10.[2] Only an actual combat, in either Europe or America, was still necessary as the equivalent of a declaration of war.

The King of France had yielded only after persuasion to the aggressive policies of Vergennes and Beaumarchais and remained reluctant to precipitate bloodshed. The Ministry hesitated the more to strike the first blow in order to have further time for naval preparations and to afford the Netherlands no pretext for adhering to her treaties with England, rather than joining with France, on the ground of an offensive war waged against an ally.

At this period of indecision, Jones turned to refit the *Ranger* and *Drake,* arrange for the sale of his prizes, provide for his prisoners and wounded men, and plan a new, more important enterprise. For coöperation in the performance of these tasks, no Continental agent, naval or commercial, authorized by the Commissioners in Paris, was at hand in Brest, although they had been aware of his purpose to return to this port. The Captain set about his undertakings alone. His prisoners were his first thought now just as the captives in Mill and Forton Prisons had been the first object of his expedition. To insure an exchange he prepared for quick and drastic action.

First, on the day of his arrival, he sent the memorable letter to

Lady Selkirk, which was directed unsealed in care of the British Postmaster General so that the Ministers and even the King might possibly read his challenge to England's treatment of American naval prisoners. Next, he lost no time in visiting Admiral d'Orvilliers on board his flagship for counsel as to the men taken on his cruise and in writing to the Commissioners as to his immediate resolution concerning them. "I have brought in," he explained in the haste of his first day ashore, "nearly two hundred prisoners, and as Comte d'Orvilliers is apprehensive that, as war with England is not yet declared, they may perhaps be given up without exchange, I have resolved to equip the *Drake* with all possible expedition at Cammaret and to send the prisoners in her to America; so fully am I convinced of the bad policy of releasing prisoners, especially seamen, without an exchange that I am determined never to do it while there remains an alternative. I should not, however, have taken a resolution of such importance without consulting you, had not Comte d'Orvilliers told me that the return of a letter from the Minister might perhaps put it out of my power, and therefore recommended me that I should lose no time.

"Notwithstanding this, you will perhaps find it expedient to effect an exchange of these prisoners in Europe, and should the Minister agree to hold them avowedly as prisoners of war, you will of course inform me thereof per express so as to reach me if possible before the departure of the *Drake*."[3]

Again the efforts of Jones in behalf of American prisoners, as contrasted with those of other captains, stand apart for his self-reliance. Wickes, to his conspicuous credit, had brought to the shores of France on a single occasion one hundred English prisoners, but they had gained their freedom because it was understood that America could not keep them confined in France. In fact, he, Conyngham, Johnson, and Nicholson had taken half a thousand captives, but the Commissioners had considered it wise and necessary to release them. "I have above five hundred other paroles," stated Franklin, "solemnly given in writing, by which the Englishmen promised either to send our people in exchange, or to surrender themselves to me in France, not one of which has been re-

garded, so little faith and honor remain in that corrupted nation."[4]
Jones took the matter of his prisoners largely in his own hands; he
negotiated with French officials, he spurred the American Commissioners, he prepared as a last resort to act independently if
loss of his captives threatened.

The Captain deliberated further before receiving any advice
from Paris; it was hazardous to send the prisoners to America in
the hastily-equipped *Drake* and with an unreliable skeleton crew
from the *Ranger*. He therefore awaited developments. When the
Commissioners finally replied, they allayed some of his fears by
the assurance of having received considerable encouragement from
England to expect an exchange in Europe. Soon this prospect developed so far that Calais was named as the place for the transfer.

But difficulties arose again from another quarter. De Sartine, the
French Minister of Marine, made the objection to both the Commissioners and D'Orvilliers that to permit the prisoners to land
temporarily on French soil would constitute a breach of neutrality,
which France could not allow. Pending more definite action by England and more favorable orders from France, Jones kept the prisoners first on board the *Drake* and later aboard another prize, the
Patience, in the road of Brest. As for the instructions of the Commissioners to keep them "securely confined," the Captain found
it fitting to explain: "I could have no dependence on the officers
and marines of the *Ranger* because they had suffered the prisoners
to escape at Nantes which were taken on the passage from America.
Therefore on my arrival from the Irish Channel the 9th of May,
I applied to my friend Comte d'Orvilliers, who immediately furnished a guard of twelve soldiers with officers. . . ."[5] He had to
intervene even to insure the delivery of whatever petitions the
English prisoners addressed to the Commissioners and through
them to British authorities for their exchange. He discovered that
one professed friend and agent Riou was, by his own confession,
a scoundrel; and he finally arranged to have Father John, the
chaplain of D'Orvilliers, as their intermediary. But even after the
issue of neutrality had passed, the little *Patience,* fittingly named,
waited long with her crowded prisoners for the exchange of Englishmen and Americans as she rode at anchor in the rough waters

of the Brest road and Jones of necessity turned to other pressing tasks.

His crew as well as his prisoners required food, clothing, and medical attention; both officers and men clamored for half their wages, which it had been agreed to pay them in France; they looked impatiently for their prize money and bounties; and the *Ranger* as well as the *Drake* needed to be refitted extensively. The Captain had become involved in a dispute with Langdon concerning expenditures when the *Ranger* was still at Portsmouth, and he now found himself with larger needs and corresponding self-assurance at the threshold of a greater controversy regarding funds. Although the Marine Committee in Philadelphia had intended and even expressly stated that Jones should receive from the proper agents at European ports such stores as he might need, it clearly reserved at the same time to the Commissioners in Paris the right to oversee his expenditures, especially since they were to pay for them, as well as to govern at their discretion his naval operations.

The independence and liberality of Jones without doubt promoted difficulties. A special agreement, approved by the secretary of the Marine Committee, which the Captain had made to increase enlistments for the *Ranger,* rendered him personally responsible to the crew for prompt payment of their wages; unfortunately, Lee alone among the Commissioners was aware of this understanding.[6] He had already received, according to a remonstrance from the Commissioners to De Sartine, 100,000 livres for the needs of his ship. Before the cruise, Lee himself had signed an authorization to Williams as agent to permit the Captain to draw 500 louis d'ors, about 12,000 livres. Likewise before the enterprise, Bersolle a commissary had made drafts upon the bankers of the Commissioners for payment of supplies, although neither he nor Jones sent them statements to verify the expenditures. The refusal of the Commissioners to accept these bills was a warning which the Captain either had not known or had failed to heed in preoccupation with his imminent sailing.

Now for a week after his return, Jones found no Continental deputy at hand to supply his many needs. Williams, the early appointee as naval agent by Deane with the approval of Franklin, had become uncertain whether he retained authority. William Lee, the appointee by Congress as commercial agent, had finally delegated his office to Schweighauser, a Swiss merchant at Nantes, with whom he shared, Deane claimed, the commissions of five per cent, more than twice as much as Williams had charged, and with whom he also placed the young son of his own brother Richard as a clerk or partner. In the course of the week Jones received a letter from Schweighauser, of whom he had known nothing; the contents and tone of his message and the absence of any word from the Commissioners confirming his representations as the official Continental agent were sufficient to cause Jones not to reply. This agent evinced a disposition, according to the Captain, "to sell [his] prizes at a distance," and took no steps to provide for his prisoners, his crew, and his ships. In this situation, although the letter of credit for 500 louis d'or was still in his hands, he signed on May 16 a draft upon the Commissioners in favor of Bersolle for 24,000 livres. His purpose, he informed them, was to distribute this amount among the brave officers and men to whom he owed his late success.

The assigned reason, however well-intentioned, was neither exact nor valid, although Lee knew of his special obligation to the crew. Jones had not taken the trouble, occupied as he was, to inform the Commissioners, prior to the draft, concerning the cruise in detail, particularly the prizes in addition to the *Drake,* which concerned them financially. He had in a manner flouted their deputy Schweighauser. On a previous occasion he had invited a warning as to protested bills. In the present instance the Commissioners, as they informed him, were "under the disagreeable necessity of refusing payment" of his draft.

Jones had reckoned without Arthur Lee and the new Commissioner John Adams, of whom the latter had recently arrived to assume the vacated place of Deane. This untrustworthy envoy in France had been recalled in appearance to render a report to Congress concerning American affairs abroad, but in reality to answer the charges and to make way for the power of the Lees in Europe and the Lees in concert with the Adamses, especially Samuel Adams, in America. Their alliance had begun with reciprocal favoritism when Samuel Adams had appointed Arthur Lee as the agent for Massachusetts in London, conditional upon resignation of the office by Franklin. Its political coils, as will later appear more fully, extended to Franklin as well as Deane. The hostility against the Doctor was to meet the defense of staunch patriots in Congress, including new members in 1778, who refused to bend to the will of intrigue. Richard Henry Lee, characterized by Gérard, the French Ambassador to the United States, as having Puritanic manners, Presbyterian staidness, and ruthless ambition and dissimulation like Orientals,[7] came to lament to his brother Francis: "It has, however, been resolved not to recall Dr. Franklin and so far the party have failed, because the plan was to recall them all to make room."[8]

"To make room?" Naturally, with the compliance of brother towards brother, for the ambitions of Arthur Lee to become the dominating European representative of the United States, the centre in Paris of all American proceedings. Likewise for the security of William Lee to retain, in addition to other lucrative appointments, all the American commercial and naval agencies in the ports of France. Franklin and Deane had aggravatingly obstructed these fraternal-inspired objectives.

The limitations of Deane do not palliate the wrongs to which his enemies lent themselves. Even Jones had well-founded grievances against this Commissioner. It had been typical of Deane to assume to himself the credit and to gain the gratitude of Louis XVI for the plan to capture Howe's fleet, which the Captain had transmitted through him to the French Government.[9] It had been also typical of Deane to recommend to Congress the French naval officer, Landais, a future evil genius of Jones, as "a skilful seaman, of long experience in every part of the world, of good judgment, and of a most unsuspicious honor and probity."[10] Granted his vanity, indiscretion, and self-seeking, granted even his early political vacillation[11] as well as his later disloyalty under the stress of poverty and calumny,[12] this ex-Commissioner had rendered untiring services for America in France before the arrival of Franklin and in company with him when the emergency was grave. And at his recall he had written in anticipation to Congress concerning the Lees in Europe with a truth that was particularly uncomfortable to them: "I am ignorant of what kind of complaint the two brothers here will prefer against me. I know they are implacable and indefatigable. Whatever these complaints may be, I pray I may not be condemned unheard. I cannot live with these men, or do business with them, nor can I find the man in the world who can. . . ."[13]

Franklin let his services, present as well as past, speak for him in Philadelphia, and he customarily answered the presumption of Arthur Lee by silence in Paris. When he did reply, however, between the departure of Deane and the arrival of Adams, during which the arrogance of Lee became particularly offensive, his words were the more telling: "You ask me why I act so inconsistently with my duty to the public? This is a heavy charge, sir, which I have not deserved. But it is to the public that I am accountable, and not to you. I have been a servant to many publics, through a long life. . . . There is not a single instance of my even being accused before of acting contrary to their interest or duty. I shall account to the Congress, when called upon, for this my terrible offence of being silent to you about Mr. Deane's and Mr. Gérard's departure.

"It is true that I have omitted answering some of your letters, particularly your angry ones, in which you with very majesterial airs schooled and documented me as if I had been one of your domestics. I saw in the strongest light the importance of our living in decent civility towards each other, while our great affairs were depending here. I saw your jealous, suspicious, malignant, and quarrelsome temper, which was daily manifesting itself against Mr. Deane and almost every other person you had any concern with. I, therefore, passed your affronts in silence, did not answer, and burnt your angry letters, and received you when I next saw you, with the same civility, as if you had never wrote them. Perhaps I may still pursue the same conduct, and not send you this . . . of all things, I hate altercation."[14]

Even Jones now found himself involved in one of the feuds which followed from the Paris-Philadelphia bond of the Lees and Adamses, although his purpose as a naval officer was to refrain severely from meddling with political concerns. Previously, of the three Commissioners, Franklin and Deane had coöperated in the main in public affairs, particularly in negotiations with France, which regarded the former as the most responsible American emissary; therefore the antagonism of Lee had been the less material. With the replacement of Deane by John Adams as one of the Commissioners, Lee gained on most questions an ally who, appointed largely through the influence of his brother Richard, was disposed at this irascible period of his career to conspicuous vanity, egotism, and rage, he himself confessed, like the lion in its excess rather than its power.[15] As Lee and Adams now had two votes against the single voice of Franklin, they could employ this dominance to settle to their satisfaction the controversy regarding the business agents Schweighauser and Williams. This source of assumed grievance on the part of Lee in behalf of his brother William against Deane had aroused his enmity scarcely less than exclusion from the recalled Commissioner's commercial dealings with Beaumarchais. The opportunity was at hand to strike indirectly at Franklin through the medium of Jones.

With impetuousness on his own part and with persuasion on the part of Lee, Adams had scarcely arrived in Paris and assumed his duties before he prepared on May 25, 1778 a letter to Jones informing him that his draft had been dishonored because he had not made application to Schweighauser as the official agent and because the Commissioners had no authority to dispense public funds for the purposes indicated to them. The first two signatures were those of Lee and Adams; the third was Franklin's set far apart from the others as if unconsciously to express his protest.[16]

Adams wrote also to Williams, canceling his appointment; to Schweighauser, confirming his office as agent for all transactions, naval as well as commercial, at the ports of France; and finally to De Sartine, requesting American disposition of the prizes taken by Jones and disclaiming responsibility of the Commissioners for his draft. Along with Lee and Adams, Franklin added his signature likewise to the additional communications. "By these letters, the die was cast," related Adams in reminiscence, "and one great scene of controversy closed for the present. I . . . produced them to my colleagues as soon as I could get them together. I was doubtful whether Mr. Franklin would sign them, but when he saw that Mr. Lee and I would sign them without him if he refused, with his habitual wisdom he very composedly put his signature to them all. . . ."[17] Adams had gained a victory pleasing to his *amour-propre,* but the possible loss to America, involving both the best services of her most important naval officer in France and the jeopardy of some of her merchant ships at sea, did not enter into his accounting.

When Jones first received notice of the refusal of his draft, which came to him before receipt of Adams' letter, he wrote on May 27 to the Commissioners in terms revealing greater regard for the honor of the United States than can be attributed in this instance to Adams and Lee: "Three posts have already arrived here from Paris since Comte d'Orvilliers showed me the answer which he received from the Minister to the letter which enclosed mine to you. Yet you remain silent. M. Bersolle has this moment informed me of the fate of my bills; the more extraordinary, as I have not yet made use of your letters of credit of the 10th of January last, whereby I then seemed entitled to call for half the amount of my last draft, and I did not expect to be thought extravagant, when, on the 16th current, I doubled that demand. Could this indignity be kept secret I should disregard it; and, though it is already public in Brest, and in the fleet, as it affects only my private credit I will not complain. I cannot, however, be silent when I find the public credit involved in the same disgrace. I conceive this might have been prevented. To make me completely wretched, Monsieur Bersolle has told me that he now stops his hand not only of the necessary articles to refit the ship, but also of the *daily provisions.* I know not where to find tomorrow's dinner for the great number of mouths that depend on me for food. Are then the Continental ships of war to depend on the sale of their prizes for a daily dinner for their men? 'Publish it not in Gath.'

"My officers, as well as men, want clothes, and the prizes are precluded from being sold before further orders arrive from the Minister. I will ask you, gentlemen, if I have deserved all this? Whoever calls himself an American ought to be protected here."[18]

As for Schweighauser, Jones answered, after receipt of the letter framed by Adams, with reasonableness: "When you determined to change the Continental agent, I wish you had sent that information in a letter to meet me here on my arrival, as I had advised you of my intention to return to Brest. All disagreeable altercation might then have been avoided. My situation is not now mended by your last, the gentleman you mention being at Nantes, and no person appearing in his behalf at Brest." Apart from exposure of Adams' pretext on the score of the agent, Jones pointed to the practical circumstances under which the Commissioners had shown so little judgment and faith as not to support him. In one breath, at the outset, he was conciliatory: "I frankly ask your pardon for the undue liberty I took the 16th ult. when I ventured to sign a draft upon you for the purpose of supplying the people under my command with necessary clothing, etc., and I promise you never to be guilty of the like offense again." In the next breath, impelled by his convictions and his courage in maintaining them, he asserted in justification: "I hope you do not, however, mean to impute to me a desire to receive 'presents of the public money'; or even to touch a dollar of it, for any private purpose of my own. On the contrary, I need not now assert, that I stepped forth at the beginning from nobler motives. My accounts before I left America testify that I am more than fifteen hundred pounds in advance of the public service, exclusive of any concern with the *Ranger;* and as for wages, I never received any. . . . The rules whereby Congress have been pleased to command me to regulate my conduct in the Navy, authorize me to issue my warrant to the agent, etc., and I humbly conceive that it is his province to furnish me with an estimate of the amount of expenses. . . .

"A space of sixteen months is now elapsed since Congress thought of me, and placed under my command *seven times* my present force, leaving me at full liberty how and where to apply it. And if I am not now capable of supporting the internal government of a single sloop of war, I wish that some person more deserving had my place, and I in America to answer for my misconduct. I have 'well considered,' and yet I shall persist in justifying the steps I have taken. . . ."[19]

In the verbal duel between the sailor and the diplomat, the spirit in which the former, however bluff and nettled at control, served the cause of America was more effective armed even with the mere pen than the punctilio of the latter employing a special weapon of his profession.

It was for Lee that Jones reserved a greater rebuff than for Adams when the Commissioner later accused him of a want of due respect. In terms blunt yet civil, distant yet dignified, the principles of the Captain revealed the more openly by contrast the unscrupulousness of the envoy: "Neither Dr. Franklin nor Mr. Adams was acquainted with my engagement to the crew; but Mr. Lee, who had been better informed, concurred to dishonour my draft and left me with two hundred prisoners, a number of sick and wounded, an almost naked crew, and a ship after a severe engagement, in want of stores and provisions, from the 9th of May till the 13th of June, destitute of any public support; yet I found means to cure my wounded, feed my people, refit my ship, and guard my prisoners.

"The dishonor that had been done me was known through the French fleet and elsewhere; yet though I was the first that had appeared at Brest and obtained from France the honors due the American flag, I made no public complaints, and only expressed my concern by letter to the commissioners at the disgraceful wound which the public credit had suffered through me. And now I beg leave to ask Mr. Lee if I have deserved such treatment?

". . . Mr. Amiel [Jones' future secretary] has told me that you objected to my receiving copies of some papers that concern me, because you thought I had not made a respectful application. A copy of it is enclosed, which though not in form of humble petition, I believe it will be difficult to construe into disrespect. True respect can never be extorted; and I will say of myself,

> The tribute of respect to greatness due,
> Not the bribed sycophant more freely pays."[20]

Even Franklin did not unmask Lee with greater freedom and pointedness; and so it becomes the more understandable that, despite the separate spheres of diplomat and naval officer, the Virginian was to conspire for revenge against Jones scarcely less than against the Doctor.

During the emergency at Brest, Jones had been obliged to secure advances on his personal credit from Admiral d'Orvilliers, the

Duke de Chartres who commanded part of the Admiral's fleet, and the Intendant at Brest, all of whom were stationed at the port. The sale of his prizes to satisfy urgent needs was protracted because of French intervention and the controversy and delay among the Commissioners regarding an authorized agent as well as because of the agent himself. Finally the Commissioners arranged to provide food for the prisoners and the crew and repairs for the *Ranger,* but they assumed no responsibility for wages and clothes of the sailors and for refitting the *Drake,* in conformity with the letter rather than the spirit of American regulations for ships in foreign ports.

Schweighauser remained at Nantes. He made no reasonable effort to relieve the necessities of the *Ranger's* men. He disregarded his explicit duty to take proper care of the prizes, to advertise suitably in advance the public sale, and to effect it in a reasonable period. He was not an American, and, despite pressing American needs, gave evidence of no loyal interests except his own. And in furtherance of his unscrupulous selfishness, he even served apparently like a spy as the means for furnishing his nephew Dobrée with information as to the sailing of American merchantmen, and thereby enabled him the better to employ privateers from Jersey to prey upon them.[21] Surely it was unwise to have chosen this Swiss in preference to many an American in Europe, including on the one hand honest and efficient Williams and on the other several capable Scotch Americans, who as a people were anathema to all the Lee brothers. Thus first fruits matured and others were in growth, while in Paris Adams remained vain and Lee vitriolic.

Franklin, in contrast, with broad understanding and sympathies, however hampered by his associates and disposed to economize by nature and by reason of very limited American funds, afforded the Captain at this time his chief moral and material encouragement. He was able to visualize his position. He took occasion to write in private enthusiastically to Jones after learning in detail the achievements of the cruise; his words largely counteracted those activities of Lee and Adams which had already borne results. The Doctor could appreciate the underlying merit in the narrative of the landing at St. Mary's Isle addressed to the Countess of Selkirk, overlook some oddities of style, and generously say, "It is a gallant letter, and must give her ladyship a high and just opinion of your gallantry and nobleness of mind." He could also echo Jones' indignation and even generalize perhaps too freely concerning a report in English newspapers that the descent upon Whitehaven had been a mere mercenary undertaking: "The dirty insinuation you mention is of a piece with many others from the same quarter, the natural production of base minds, who, feeling no other motive in their own breasts but sordid self-interest, imagine no other motive can exist in others. . . ."

There was promise, too, that tangible aid would follow his remark: "I congratulate you most cordially on your late success and wish for a continuance and increase of the honor you have acquired." Without Franklin, probably the beginning of the Captain's career in Europe would have been the prelude to its speedy ending.

◇◇

Chapter XXIII

A Malicious Lieutenant and a Homesick Crew

THE HOPE OF Jones was that the cruise of the *Ranger,* reinforcing the earlier instructions of Congress for his Captaincy of the *Indienne,* would now at last be a steppingstone to a more important command. Instead, a train of misfortunes threatened him from a new quarter after the dishonored draft. His discipline over the officers and men, his command of the *Ranger,* his reputation, even his future career became endangered. The crew, in the main unintelligent as well as greedy, insisted like Shylock upon the fulfillment of their bond, for which they looked to Jones, not to Adams or Lee. They clamored also for a speedy return to America, for which they looked likewise to the Captain, not to the terms of their enlistment. And Simpson, nursing the grievances of the guilty, seized the opportunity to foment further the unstable, susceptible passions of the men in hostility to Jones and in favor of himself.

At first, after the return to Brest, the Captain was considerate, even lenient, towards his recalcitrant officer. Under arrest in the *Drake,* he had ample, comfortable quarters and liberty to walk the deck. But repaying favor by injury as was his habit, Simpson made such use of his constant intercourse with the crew that when Jones stepped on board "they became so insolent as to refuse duty and go . . . below repeatedly before the Captain's face."[1] He was then removed, with the advice of D'Orvilliers and with the view of using the *Drake* to transport the prisoners to America, to a ship the *Admiral,* in which the French confined even officers of high standing. Here his comforts were similar to those which he had enjoyed in the *Drake;* nevertheless his behavior was again so extravagant that D'Orvilliers on his own initiative ordered him to the prison of the port, at which Jones "paid his expenses out of his own pocket."

Directly upon the return of the *Ranger* and *Drake,* Simpson had appealed over the authority of Jones to the Commissioners. Adams and Lee were disposed to intercede for him, although in this case, even more than in that of the draft, the exercise of their political prerogatives involved the danger of trespassing upon the province of internal naval administration. Adams, who betrayed his prejudice against Jones so far as to refer to him in particular even many years later as one of "those emigrant foreigners of the South,"[2] had already revealed his favoritism towards his familiars from New England. There were, for example, Stephen Hopkins, towards whom his memories of Jamaica rum warmed his heart; Esek Hopkins, for whom his early zealous defense in a poor cause was tantamount to accusation of Jones as the later chief adversary of the Commodore; John Langdon, upon whom he looked as his first Northern well-wisher for his appointment as one of the three envoys to France. At the same time, Lee, whose brother Richard had arbitrarily placed Samuel Nicholson at the head of the Continental captains in America, was coöperatively disposed not to permit Jones to rise from his formal rank of almost last at home to preëminent standing in Europe.

To these advocates and to Franklin, Simpson had presented from his warped point of view the circumstances already recounted which had led to his arrest. He now offered, typically, to support his perversions of the truth, recommendations partial to him without disclosing the reason for the partiality: "I beg leave to refer your honors to a letter wrote you by John Langdon, Esq. of Portsmouth, which was to be delivered by me. . . . The character Mr. Langdon has been pleased to give me in that letter you are acquainted with. I only desire your permission to observe that Mr. Langdon has been fully acquainted with my behavior in every station that I have acted, from my childhood, to the period of this writing, being both natives of Portsmouth."[3] The lieutenant withheld the simple but pertinent fact, necessary to judge the fitness of his appointment as the first lieutenant of the *Ranger* and to weigh the justice of the eulogistic recommendation, that by marriage to

Mrs. Martha Barrell, the second by both him and her, he was a brother-in-law of John Langdon.[4]

Apparently in the light of such generous references, the Commissioners, upon the initiative of Lee, undertook at an early occasion to warn Jones: "As the consequences of an arrest in foreign countries is extremely troublesome, they should be well considered before they are made."

Simpson now pursued his guileful course on land not unlike his traitorous evolutions as prizemaster of the *Drake* in the English Channel. Only as an officer under arrest, his malice had grown doubly venomous as he had walked the deck of the *Drake* and whispered his hatred into the ears of the men. The dishonored draft signed by Jones was timely and apt for his purposes. Adams and Lee thereby confirmed the distrust of the Captain which the lieutenant had instilled in the minds of the sailors and which now turned to conviction and hate. The Commissioners, the crew reasoned—if mob-like they retained a few grains of reason to temper their rage—had repudiated Jones; they also, who had the promises of their Captain on the one hand counterbalanced by neither clothes, nor wages, nor bounties, nor prize money, nor immediate prospects of returning to America on the other, should repudiate him. And in dethroning the Captain they exalted the lieutenant, their champion, in whose name they were now committed to perjure themselves.

Petition after petition came from the officers and crew to the Commissioners immediately after it became known in Brest that they would not receive the 24,000 livres which Jones had solicited particularly for them. Ironically they complained in favor of Simpson, who had urged them to cowardice and treachery, and against Jones, who had tried to serve them; ironically they appealed not only to Franklin but also to Adams and Lee, the very instruments who in thwarting the Captain and in supporting the lieutenant had occasioned their distress. As the faithless letters arrived from all ranks, Lee and Adams must perforce have read in them at least a glimmer of their own faithlessness.

The accounts of Hall, Cullam, and Green of the *Ranger*[5] and of the prize crew in the *Drake*[6] were so inconsistent and revealed such special pleading, as has already been observed, that they afforded no justification for Simpson's manœuvres in the Channel. A separate detailed complaint by Hall the second lieutenant[7] in regard to events from the sailing at Portsmouth to the current situation at Brest practically defeated itself. He stated, for instance, that Jones had "promised them half their wages in France, which he has not done," and that "the crew are much in want of clothing"—circumstances for which the Commissioners themselves could best answer. He averred that the Captain had been "seven months from America and not two of them at sea, the most of our time being spent in cutting our masts and yards, and altering sails to little or no purpose"—a situation which, largely in the light of the *Ranger's* initial poor trim and slowness and of Jones' standards for his ship's speed and efficiency for battle, analogous to an artist's constant striving for an ideal, was essentially true and the more admirable as judged by his achievements. Again he maintained: "All the people are dissatisfied with Captain Jones, which is the sole cause of the disorder on board the ship"—a general charge which, as "the sole cause," does not seem consistent with unsubstantiated particular ones and with the writing of the petition immediately after the 24,000 livres were lost to the officers and men.

A letter from the petty and warrant officers included an accusation that, if true, was especially serious in its implications: "We were informed that Captain Jones was a man of honor, which to our sorrow we are obliged to declare from our own experience is quite the reverse, his government arbitrary, his temper and treatment insufferable, for the most trivial matters threatening to shoot the person or persons whom he in sallies of passion calls ignorant or disobedient."[8] Whoever may have colored this portrait and whatever may have been the measure of fidelity to the subject, the provocations that the crew had occasioned Jones for many months were apparently greater than those which had tried to the utmost the patience of Washington upon fitting out his privateers in the first year of the war,[9] and which likewise had caused a hardy and humane commander like Wickes actually to suffer a mutiny of his unpaid sailors.[10] "My treatment of officers and men in the *Ranger*," confided Jones to Ross, a mercantile agent of Robert Morris, "has been strictly consistent with the laws of hospitality and humanity; I am ready to justify every measure which I have adopted toward them, though some of them were measures I could have wished to avoid."[11]

"The Jovial Tars," as seventy-seven men of Jones' crew styled themselves, honored the Commissioners with the most artless as well as graphic record of the alleged wrongs which they and Simpson suffered. Ornamented as the accusations of the lieutenant were by the picturesque style of these tars, jovial apparently in spite of supposed misfortunes, their charges are consistent with the less buoyant but not more authentic recitals in his behalf by penmen of greater scholarship; "That your Petitioners regard & love For their Country, & dutey to there ancient forr Fathers, have most of them left there wives & Familey Cruized the wide Atalantick, in the most dangerous places, greatley Damadgeing and distressing our enemys, and all the Satisfaction & recompence we receive for our Labour, are Vain and Flattering Promises. . . .

"That the greates number of them entered in the Service particulrely upon Mr. Simpsons our first leitenants account knowing him to be a Gentleman of honour worthey & capable of his Officeships, and who is now confined inocentley, *as we think,* in a Lousey, Dirtey, french Goal."[12]

"Inocentley, *as we think*" is a phrase which with its underscoring sets apart the "Jovial Tars" on an intellectual plane of their own for reserved, deliberate judgment such as their betters, not only the other petitioners but also Adams and Lee, might well have emulated in this case. For at the distance of Paris the Commissioners wrote concerning Simpson to Jones with less apparent knowledge but with more positiveness: "We are constrained to say that his confinement in a prison on shore appears to us to carry in it a degree of severity which can not be justified by reason or law. We therefore desire you would release Mr. Simpson from his imprisonment and permit him to go at large upon his parole to Nantes, there to take his passage to America . . . in order to take his trial by a court martial."[13] It is likely, in further contrast, that if the "Jovial Tars" had not been under the influence of Simpson and other disaffected officers, they would have evinced not only suspended judgment but also loyalty towards Jones.

Chapter XXIV

Jones Loses the *Ranger* and Wins Only Promises

WHILE ADAMS and Lee interceded for Simpson but were less disposed to coöperate in meeting the financial obligations of the naval force, Franklin as well as Jones kept his eyes upon their object—not dissension among Americans but war against the British. This concentration of purpose of the diplomat and officer, regardless of vexations and obstacles, was a quality of their common genius. "My roses are not without thorns," Jones explained privately concerning the *Ranger* cruise to Franklin, the one Commissioner in whom he retained confidence; the impediments in fact spurred him to strive the more energetically for a better ship and a tolerable crew. At last the *Indienne* in Holland, according to reports, was equipped for service. The Duke de Chartres as well as Admiral d'Orvilliers was fully disposed to recommend him to the King for the command; he felt sure that other influential men in Brest would likewise lend their support; and he begged Franklin to bear in mind the purpose of Congress to provide the ship for him.

But with or without the *Indienne,* the Captain proposed many new enterprises against the larger towns and the more important shipping on the coasts of Britain and against valuable merchant fleets under convoy, especially the Baltic, West India, and Hudson Bay ships. He wished to continue the object of harrying the coasts, and he advised as of particular strategy the aim to cut off Britain's food supplies. A few frigates engaged in special enterprises, he suggested, offered greater prospects than a large squadron with the object of ordinary combat. Regardless of his hope for an undertaking on an important scale, regardless of his confession that the *Ranger* was crank, slow, and of trifling force, he expressed to

Franklin his complete readiness to adopt the latter's suggestion
for a cruise against the Jersey privateers, which did "a great deal
of mischief by intercepting our supplies"—not unlikely in part the
predatory Jersey vessels of the too well-informed Dobrée, nephew
of Schweighauser. At the same time he took occasion to state
certain indispensable compromises essential for success with the
backward crew of the *Ranger:* "great views of interest," protection
by the French flag in the English Channel against enemies of
superior force, and the removal of such officers as were "dangerously ill" with "homesickness" as contagious as smallpox.[1]

This disillusioning description of the morale among the officers
and men must have stimulated Franklin's renewed efforts to secure
for Jones a better crew as well as a superior ship. He wrote him
further twice in private, once tentatively and once in confirmation,
that it was now determined to place the *Indienne* under his command, and he requested him to answer also in private. "The other
Commissioners," he explained, "are not acquainted with this
proposition as yet; and you see by the nature of it that it is necessary to be kept a secret till we have got the vessel here, for fear of
difficulties in Holland, and interception; you will, therefore, direct
your answer to me alone. It being desired that the affair should
rest between you and me, perhaps it may be best for you to take
a trip up here to concert matters."[2] The French Ministry as well
as Franklin had reasons for preferring at this time not to divulge
the arrangement to Adams and Lee.

The Commissioner planned, in keeping with the *Indienne,* a
crew to be composed of Americans in exchange for the British prisoners at Brest and of such French seamen as would be necessary
to fill the ship's complement. In appreciation of Jones' poor
opinion of the men aboard the *Ranger,* he also suggested: "If by
this means you can get a good new crew, I think it would be best
that you are quite free of the old; for a mixture might introduce
the infection of that sickness you complain of. But this may be
left to your discretion." The recognition by Franklin of Jones'
achievements and promise indicated that, if the power lay in the
hands of the Commissioner, the Captain was on the road to become
an admiral: "The project of giving you the command of the ship

pleases me the more as it is a probable opening to the higher preferment you so justly merit."[3]

Before Jones, on the wings of these expectations, speeded to Paris, where he could hope at the same time to present more effectively to the Commissioners the needs of his men, prisoners, and ships at Brest, he awaited assurances at least from Schweighauser, who continued in Nantes, concerning suitable attention to the duties of agent during his absence. It remained to act upon the request of the Commissioners for the parole of Simpson, which he was the more disposed to grant for several reasons: his own uncertain future connection with the *Ranger,* the difficulty of summoning in France a court-martial of nine American captains and lieutenants as required by the naval regulations, and his buoyancy at the prospects before him.

The same day, June 10, 1778, that Franklin sent his second letter confirming the decision as to the *Indienne,* Simpson found himself freed from confinement in Brest upon signing his parole: "I, Lieutenant Thomas Simpson . . . now under suspension and arrest for disobedience of written orders from Captain John Paul Jones, do hereby promise on my parole of honor, that being at my particular request released from my present arrest, I will consider myself as under suspension until I am called upon to meet Captain Jones face to face before a court martial, unless Captain Jones should in the meantime release me also from this parole."[4]

These duties performed, Jones came to Passy. In the light of the instructions he shortly received, the motives of Franklin and De Sartine, the French Minister of Marine, for secrecy relative to the *Indienne* were only too well-founded. Surely the two other American Commissioners would have been entrusted with the information if the only reasons were to avoid offending Holland in her neutrality and to prevent England from defeating the transfer of the ship from the Texel to a French port. Whether Lee and Adams suspected the plan or actually learned it in due time, the Captain suddenly received on June 16 instructions "forthwith [to] make preparations with all possible dispatch for a voyage to America."[5] Obviously in the *Ranger.* Franklin signed the order along with his colleagues, apparently in compliance with their insistent purpose. The insubordination of Simpson and the "homesickness" of the crew may have been minor reasons; the major object pointed to the elimination of Jones from any connection with the *Indienne* at the very time she had been promised to him. It seemed to indicate a disposition of Lee and Adams to sacrifice in time of war the services of a brave officer for their personal ends. And it was contrary to the urgent recommendations regarding Jones from the Marine Committee to the Commissioners.

At the eleventh hour, other unexpected circumstances further complicated the disposal of the *Indienne* and rendered uncertain both the ship that the Captain was to command and the sphere, America or Europe, of his future operations. On the one hand, the frigate in Holland would not be completely equipped for three months at least, according to the unreliable report brought from Amsterdam by Prince Nassau Siegen, an intriguing condottiere of whom more will appear hereafter. On the other hand, only one day after Jones had received his orders to return in the *Ranger,* the first actual warfare between France and England occurred, an indecisive engagement off Ushant between the frigates *La Belle Poule* and the *Arethusa.*[6] From that time the two traditional enemies were in open conflict; no further occasion remained for secret instead of open assistance to America. The action between the two ships of war hastened final preparations for a combat on a vast scale; the large French fleet of ships of the line and frigates under D'Orvilliers and Chartres at Brest prepared to meet that of the English under Keppel. And the other French fleet under Count d'Estaing, which Jones had advised on February 10 to blockade and capture Lord Howe in the Delaware, had finally sailed from Toulon on April 13, almost two months before the engagement between the frigates off Ushant, so that reports of this further act of hostility were soon due to come from America to England. Although the French would wait long before they boasted a naval success, whether on a small or large scale, like Jones' in taking the *Drake,* active war between the two European countries more than any other factor deprived him, at least for the present, of the long-cherished *Indienne.*

Now the earnest injunction from Congress to its deputies to provide Jones with a ship of force under his separate command had been twice defeated. He had come to Europe in accordance

with the plan of Morris, the executive officer of the Marine Committee, to give larger scope to his abilities and to make amends
for the politics which had deprived him of his just naval rank and
for the jealousy of Hopkins which had lost him the American
fleet. Again he faced a highly important crossways of his career.
One direction led to America and the distant hope of receiving an
appointment to a newly built frigate; the other to his continuance
in France and reliance upon further promises. He chose the latter,
pregnant with suffering as well as achievement not possible for
him to foretell.

Notwithstanding the changed situation in France, on July 5, 1778
De Sartine made a request in writing to the Commissioners which he
had in effect made earlier in person to Jones: "As I find myself,
sirs, in a situation to have need of Captain Jones for a special
expedition, I should like to have him remain here. If you see no
inconvenience in any way to this arrangement, you will confer a
favor upon me to leave him to my disposition." Consistent with this
request, Jones placed in the hands of the Commissioners approximately at the same time a letter occasioned, it seems, by the
British spies who swarmed in Paris and penetrated even Passy:
"The Minister told me his plan, but demanded my parole of honor
not to reveal it to any person whatsoever. I am not therefore at
liberty to communicate it even to you. . . .

"I can however assure you that what has been communicated to
me is perfectly consistent with my duty as an American officer, with
the interests of the United States, and with the most disinterested
friendship on the part of France."[7] It is to the credit of all the
Commissioners, especially in view of the earlier orders for his return to America, that they gracefully acquiesced: "We readily consent that he should be at Your Excellency's disposition; and shall
be happy if his services may be in any respect useful to the designs
Your Excellency may have in contemplation."[8]

It may be assumed that Jones gladly accepted, if he did not
actually propose, his parole of secrecy. His awareness of espionage
in behalf of the British when he first had disguised the *Ranger* off
Quiberon for a strategic enterprise, as well as his habitual canniness, availed him on this occasion against spies, even against Bancroft, who as a secretary of Franklin became, to the Captain's

danger, practically his own bosom friend. And if Franklin in concert with De Sartine had found it wise, as the event had proved,
not to impart the plans for the *Indienne* to Adams and Lee, so
Jones, now likewise in concert with the French Minister, probably
followed his intuition upon withholding details from all the Commissioners.

At the same time the Captain hoped to retain the *Ranger* in
France as an auxiliary in the enterprise contemplated by De Sartine. He represented to the Commissioners that it had been the
intention of Congress to have the sloop of war continue under his
direction and be commanded by a lieutenant. His view seemed the
more reasonable in the situation which released the United States
from the expense of providing him with another ship. The pretensions of Simpson to the command, which to the prejudice of
discipline he had urged upon the crew from the beginning of the
passage to Europe, were typical of his arrogance. Certainly there
was no basis for them in the orders of the Marine Committee;
possibly Langdon and Wendell, his interested eulogists, who had
no authority in the matter, put this bee in the bonnet of their
relative. Wendell, it is recalled, had written of him to Franklin
as "a gentleman of a most distinguished character as an officer
and one whose abilities are known to be very great and universally
respected amongst us. His promotion will be generally accepted of
by every friend to America."[9] With disregard for Simpson's plotting, Jones undertook to propitiate the crew, exercise forbearance
towards the lieutenant, and persuade the Commissioners that his
purpose was just and feasible.

From Passy the Captain sent to the officers and men of the *Ranger* an optimistic message respecting the sale of their prizes and
the payment of their wages. Not less welcome was the prospect he
held before them of their return to America. "I shall soon be able,"
he concluded, in terms of promise which might prove beyond his
powers of fulfillment, "to convince every person under my command that I take particular pleasure to make them rich and
happy." And to the Commissioners he stated his present views concerning Simpson and the ship: "As the French Ministry has now
in contemplation plans which promise honor to the American
flag, the *Ranger* might be useful to assist in carrying them into

execution. Lieutenant Simpson has certainly behaved amiss; yet I can forgive as well as resent; and upon his making a proper concession, I will, with your approbation, not only forgive the past but leave him the command of the *Ranger*."[10] Conciliatory as the Captain was, if the Commissioners accepted his proposals, he would not only retain control of the ship even though Simpson should return as her lieutenant, but, equally important to him, "a proper concession" from Simpson would be tantamount to the moral satisfaction of an apology.

These proposals were to the taste neither of Adams and Lee nor of Simpson. Possibly Franklin too was confirmed in the opinion, partly by the accounts from Jones himself, that the crew of the *Ranger* was incorrigible, and that the only recourse lay in the return of the men to America, for which they persistently clamored. In justifying themselves, the men reiterated their claim of ignorance concerning the written stipulation in the ship's books that the term of enlistment was not for a year but "for the cruise and while absent from the Eastern States."[11] It was characteristic of Jones not to retreat from his objectives in spite of the turbulent, faithless crew. But Lee, who considered him as well as his men at fault and wrote more in malice than ignorance to Congress that the Commissioners had done all in their power "to bring him and his officers into order, but hitherto in vain";[12] Adams, who almost invariably at this time stood by his Virginia colleague; and Franklin, who in youth had learned to stoop so as to escape many a hard thump—all determined to follow the easier course of having the *Ranger* sail for home. It remained to decide who should command her. If Adams and Lee would not accede to the wishes of Jones, neither would he accede to theirs. Simpson under parole did not promote a solution to their conflicting purposes.

Whether or not Jones would continue in control of the *Ranger*, he had ample reason to expect a French command under the American flag. The confidence with which he looked forward to having a frigate, possibly a small squadron, led him to make inquiries concerning a suitable chaplain. Although the American naval laws provided for such noncombatants in the case of commands of sufficient size, the qualifications which he looked for were very considerable. In view of the blunt captains and rough crews at sea, they appeared actually fastidious. Whatever were the tastes of his men, Jones specified unusual accomplishments: "I should wish him to be a man of reading and letters, who understands, speaks, and writes the French and English with elegance and propriety. For political reasons, it would be well if he were a clergyman of the Protestant profession, whose sanctity of manners and happy natural principles would diffuse unanimity and cheerfulness through the ship; and if to these essentials were added the talent of writing fast, and in fair characters, such a man would necessarily be worthy the highest confidence, and might, therefore, assure himself of a place at my table, the regulations whereof should be entirely under his direction."[13] These delicate perceptions seem strangely at variance with the fighter embroiled in blood. And they indicate that the chaplain, in addition to promoting a congenial, if not spiritual atmosphere, was to serve the condescending Captain in the practical capacity of an interpreter and secretary. Certainly his large correspondence attested to the need.

His letters, which already stood foremost in both quality and quantity among those of naval officers of the Revolution, reflected the scope of his acquaintances and friendships, social as well as professional, as they increased during his sojourn in Paris. He met a large and varied circle in the course of his frequent visits to Franklin at Passy. Here he also came face to face and discussed his affairs with the two other Commissioners. Adams, at Franklin's invitation, had accepted as his abode in the Hôtel Valentinois the apartments vacated by Deane, but had taken the precaution to receive assurances from De Chaumont that the attractive accommodations were not chargeable to the United States; and Lee, uninvited to live in the same residence, continued to dwell in a mansion at the nearby suburb, Chaillot—with a mistress, according to Wentworth, the English intermediary for Bancroft's spying—and came to Passy for the consultations with his colleagues.

During this second and longer stay than his first, Jones became more intimately acquainted with Bancroft, who insinuated himself increasingly in his confidence, as he had done in Franklin's and Deane's. With rare, professional duplicity, this confidential agent availed himself of the trust inspired by his earlier patriotic writings and past familiarity with these two men to furnish Britain with a large store of information, especially diplomatic and naval. He was able to conceal his treason the more ingeniously because through him the Commissioners sent and received letters in their correspondence with some of those liberal English statesmen who were almost as much opposed to their country's policies as Americans themselves.

Bancroft now lived, spy as he was, seemingly absorbed in "good eating and drinking,"[14] under the same roof with Franklin. He had recently become more chary and circumspect in betraying American secrets to his friend and fellow-conspirator Wentworth because a good coup in the market by means of his advance knowledge of the Franco-American Alliance had for the present glutted his avarice. Besides, the cumulative suspicions of Lee, of Vergennes, and even of Franklin, who affirmed that "such information must spring from a source very near them."[15] made him particularly apprehensive of discovery. But he had the artifice to divert distrust from himself to others by specious insinuations, as well as the cunning to hide his own course by resort to invisible white ink for his letters and to dark nights, isolated places, and strange contrivances of bottles, pegs, cards, and strings for transmitting them.[16]

Among the French at Passy, Jones formed also a close association with De Chaumont and his wife, who, it is recalled, lived in the more pretentious part of the mansion which also amply accommodated Franklin and Adams. De Chaumont interested the Captain as a French merchant and seeming public official of large associations in business and at Court who ostensibly on his own account had shipped large supplies of clothing and ammunition to America and was disposed to render further aid. The wife of De Chaumont appeared to be the first French woman who fanned a flare of sentiment in Jones' heart, which was in conflict with his wish for steady devotion of his services to the Revolution but less obviously at variance with his recognition of obligation to her husband. This happening had potential secret significance in the professional relations of the two men.

Beyond this sphere of Franklin, Jones enterprisingly developed connections at Versailles and Paris. The most important of these were with the Duke and Duchess de Chartres.[17] Having known the

Duke at Brest, he had taken letters from him to his mansion the Palais Royal and to Versailles. The amiable and generous Duchess received him with such sympathy for his patriotic and brave enterprises, associated as her family was with French royalty and the French Navy, that Jones was exceedingly grateful. Her kindly attention emboldened him to entertain the thought of asking her influence in the event of professional urgency,[18] and gave rise at the same time to the unfounded romantic tradition that he promised to return to lay a frigate at her feet.[19]

While these concerns, directly or indirectly connected with a new command, occupied Jones, the Commissioners determined to choose Musco Livingston, an American lieutenant who happened to be in Paris, for the captaincy of the *Ranger* and the return passage to America. He had made a short cruise from Bordeaux as his base, but was now not in active service on the plea of poor health; neither seniority nor achievement was his to justify the promotion. As Jones had by no means forgotten the injustice in rank which he himself had suffered and which had not yet been corrected, he objected to the appointment as unfair to many officers in the United States.[20] The disagreeable alternative open to the Captain was to release Simpson from his parole and have him command the *Ranger*. In this dilemma, he chose the latter course, designating further motives: "I . . . offered to relinquish the claims of justice to the softer voice of mercy and forgiveness, in favor of a man subject like myself to human frailties, but more especially in favor of his wife and family, that the innocent might not suffer through the guilty."[21] It is probable that Jones had met Mrs. Simpson in Portsmouth, the home of his lieutenant, before the sailing of the ship, and of course he knew his relatives Langdon and Wendell.

The Captain, governed less by justice than generosity and expecting justice if not generosity in return, signed away his rights in a statement welcome to Adams and Lee: "When I took Lieutenant Simpson's parole, I did not expect to have been long absent from America. But as circumstances have now rendered the time of my return less certain, I am willing to let the dispute between us drop forever by giving up that parole which will enable him to command the *Ranger*. I bear no malice; and if I have done him an injury, this will be making him all the present satisfaction in my power. If on the contrary he has injured me, I will trust to himself for an acknowledgment."[22] In this second offer to release Simpson from his parole, Jones made no stipulation as in the first either for "a proper concession" on the part of the lieutenant or for the continuance of the *Ranger* abroad. It gave the Commissioners, stated Captain Whipple, who now happened to be in Europe in command of the frigate *Providence,* "the greatest satisfaction in affording them an opportunity to reinstate Lieutenant Simpson." It provided Simpson an occasion to assure them with his customary self-approbation that "their appointment affords the greatest satisfaction to officers and men." It induced Jones to ponder whether he had chosen a fitting instance for the practice of his own Christian precept: "Every lesser virtue may pass away, but charity comes from Heaven and is immortal."[23]

The Commissioners failed to show the courtesy and ignored the moral obligation to have Simpson request and receive the release from his parole not at their hands but at those of Jones who had given it; they chose to interpret the overture according to the letter instead of the spirit. Of course the lieutenant himself made no acknowledgment of wrongdoing. On the contrary, as he had done again and again and as the Captain had every reason to expect, he returned evil for good. He was not only mean-spirited in accepting a generous act and repaying it by ingratitude, but also venomous in broadcasting false reports, especially in Brest among the French as well as the Americans, concerning his too merciful commander. But Jones in Paris was unaware for the present of the aspersions cast upon his name.

On the day following this charity and before Simpson could use his new-found freedom to spread calumny abroad, the Captain with active service ever in mind pressed De Sartine for performance of his promise. He had tentatively relinquished command of the *Ranger,* he was cutting himself off from a command in America, and he had reason to suspect the sincerity of the Minister of the Marine. The American officer had brought to his attention a number of strategic enterprises, but none so far had materialized. The delay, if not loss, of the *Indienne,* too, was still in regretful memory: "Had your first plan taken effect, the most pleasing prospect of success would have been before me."

Then the Minister's offer of the *Epervier,* which was represented
as a vessel of very large dimensions but upon investigation proved
to be "a small brigantine" and "a very dull sailer," must have
aroused his positive resentment, however much he disguised it
beneath his expressions of appreciation and his terms alternatively
modest and assertive as to the recognition previously accorded him
in America: "I am bound in honor to communicate faithfully to
Congress the generous offer which the King now makes of lending
the *Epervier* in the meantime to be employed under my command
under the flag of America. . . . I have now under my command a
ship bound to America. On my arrival there, from the former
confidence of Congress, I have reason to expect an immediate removal into one of their best ships. I have reason to expect the chief
command of the first squadron destined for an expedition, having
in my possession several similar appointments; and when Congress
sees fit to appoint admirals, I have assurance that my name will not
be forgot. These are flattering prospects to a man who has drawn
his sword only upon principles of philanthropy, and in support of
the dignity of human nature. But as I prefer a solid to a shining
reputation, a useful to a splendid command, I hold myself ready,
with the approbation of the commissioners, to be governed by you
in any measure that may tend to distress the common enemy."[24]
At this early skirmish with the Minister, his tone and meaning
were by no means reserved. Still they had provocation and even
warrant in the presumption to have offered him as a bounty less
than he already had as a right.

Pending availability of the *Indienne,* Jones continued to wait
for several weeks at Passy as patiently as he could in expectation of
a suitable command to be provided by the French Government.
De Sartine had made his promise, and the Captain had made his
decision not to return to America. At length the Minister agreed
to adopt one of the naval operations which the officer had particularly urged. This enterprise was to capture the Baltic merchant
fleet of one hundred sail at anchor, protected by only a single ship
of war and removed from possible reinforcements, at a time and
place off the British coast concerning which the Captain had secret
information. Three frigates at Brest, one of which he was to command in person, and three cutters at St. Malo were to unite and

constitute his small squadron. According to an alternative plan not his own, it was proposed to offer him an armament of cutters and other small vessels for the object of alarming the coasts of England and checking the Jersey privateers. These understandings clearly made, Jones had two matters still to dispatch before setting forth speedily for L'Orient en route to Brest.

The crew of the *Ranger* and he were apparently about to pursue their separate courses. His last opportunity to serve them had come, and he embraced it. He had already done his best to hasten the sale of the prizes and to arrange for the payments from other sources due them. Now, notwithstanding the evil light in which their petitions to the Commissioners had represented him, particularly in regard to Simpson, he looked kindly upon the men in general as misguided by the lieutenant and sought to reward definitely those of whom he could speak with any praise at all.

Before his departure, therefore, he persuaded Franklin to prepare a statement, which also received Adams' approval, requesting the favor of Congress towards the volunteers who had accompanied him at the raid on the English coast. He sent it to the Marine Committee with remarks of his own: "It was my intention from the beginning to beseech you also to recommend the men who landed with me at Whitehaven to the bounty of Congress. The service being unprecedented in latter wars accounts for the extreme difficulty which I found prevailing with the handful of men who at last reluctantly undertook it. The men, however, have in my judgment well merited a reward, and bestowing it liberally on so few would, I hope, have a happy effect in prompting others to attempt still greater enterprises. . . ."[25] In these terms, especially with recognition of the backward spirit of the *Ranger* crew in general, are manifest both the thoughtfulness and leadership of the Captain.

In his expectation to command immediately a small squadron abroad, as a final act at Passy he took the liberty to address Washington across the seas. Remarking that the scene of naval war was in process of change from America to Europe and that his continuance in France was at the request of the Minster of the Marine, he continued: "I will not intrude upon Your Excellency's time even by attempting to pay you the respect which you so justly command. The intention of this letter is only to beg your acceptance of two epaulettes with which it is accompanied, and which my friend Mr. Williams of Nantes has undertaken to forward. I expected to have had the honor of delivering this little present into your own hands; but not having that satisfaction, if in the meantime I can render you any acceptable services in France, I hope you will command me without reserve."[26]

Very likely Jones would not have written this letter if he had anticipated his mortification upon arrival in L'Orient and Brest. As for the armament at L'Orient, "speed and force though both requisite, were both wanting," he described. "Happily for me this . . . failed, and I was thereby saved from a dreadful prospect of ruin and dishonor." As for the ships supposedly at Brest, neither the frigate intended as his flagship nor the other vessels designated for his direction awaited him. Before he left Passy, in fact, De Sartine had issued orders that the frigate in question should be bestowed upon a French officer and that the squadron should sail at once on the expedition.[27] D'Orvilliers at Brest had the duty of giving the ship without delay to one of his own lieutenants and of making apologies to Jones. It was finally represented to him that the rules of the French Marine and the protests of French aspirants had necessitated the changed arrangements. In the meantime De Sartine had availed himself of the secret information which the Captain had provided; and the Captain, fully disposed to serve the common cause by counsel as well as action, tried to put a favorable construction upon this behavior of the Minister.

At Brest, Jones found himself without any command; the *Ranger* as well as the French squadrons were in other hands. In this port he had received the respect of a French salute of nine guns to the American flag, the acclaim of his victory over the *Drake,* and during his intimacy with D'Orvilliers "uncommon attention" and even "the honors due to an admiral." His present situation, in contrast, grew even more humiliating when he became aware of the reports circulated by Simpson, who had been in command of the *Ranger* since July 27 by order of the Commissioners. As they had invested him with the ship on the one hand and had required no apology for release from his parole on the other, the lieutenant waxed the more boastful at the expense of his Captain.

Aboard the *Ranger,* through the French fleet, and ashore he took pains to state that Jones had been discharged from the service, that now he had his command with a captain's commission, that the parole had been annulled not by grace of the displaced officer but by orders from Passy.

To make matters worse, the Commissioners not only had been pleased to reinstate Simpson and had released him from the parole given to Jones, not to them, but they wrote the lieutenant in a manner to give indeed the impression that the Captain "had quit the Continental Service." The tenor of Franklin's attitude toward Jones excluded him from a willing part in these proceedings; they must have lain at the door of Adams and Lee, and of the former less than the latter.

When the extent of the impudence of Simpson and the favor of the Commissioners in his behalf became fully evident to Jones after five days in Brest, he addressed to Passy an impassioned plea, recounting the history of his lieutenant who early in the war "left the Continent and served its enemies";[28] requesting again that they assure themselves of the truth of his charges against Simpson and the crew by the testimony of Edward Meyer, the Swedish volunteer formerly of the *Ranger* and now resident in Paris; insisting especially, regardless of their former opposition, that they should authorize a trial. "That these reports prevail," he avowed, "is not an idle conjecture, but a melancholy fact. Therefore I beseech you, I conjure you, I demand of you to afford me redress—redress by a court martial, to form which we have now . . . a sufficient number of officers in France."[29]

Within a few days the American frigates *Providence* and *Boston,* which had been at Nantes, came as expected to Brest. At once Jones sent a second request for a naval investigation to the senior officer, Captain Abraham Whipple of the *Providence,* under whom the Commissioners had directed that Simpson should assume command of the *Ranger.* Abraham Whipple—not William Whipple the earlier associate of Jones and Langdon at Portsmouth—was, it is recalled, the former Captain of the *Columbus* and the intimate of Commodore Hopkins, who had been tried but acquitted for his failure properly to aid the *Alfred* during the engagement with the *Glasgow.* As the friend of Hopkins, whose arch-defender had been

Adams, he was also the friend of this Commissioner. Whatever the extent of the bond between these New Englanders, Whipple was ill-disposed towards Jones' purpose. He maintained that one of the officers, Hinman, declined to sit because of a pending investigation of his own conduct, and he freely volunteered his personal judgment that the case was closed by the Captain's letter offering to release the lieutenant from his parole and by the Commissioners' action.[30] After Whipple had forwarded his reply on August 19, the *Providence* and *Boston,* with the *Ranger* accompanying them, prepared to sail without delay for America.[31]

Immediately Jones rejoined, the speed of his retort corresponding with the indignation and sharpness of his phrases directed at both Simpson and Whipple: "The base-minded only are capable of receiving an obligation from the hand that has injured them. The base-minded only are capable of receiving an obligation without acknowledging it in terms of gratitude. And let me tell you, sir, that the parole in question, which you have taken so much and such elaborate pains to explain is by no means the less binding because it was lately offered to be given up. Why was not that offer then nor since accepted? It was not from the Commissioners that the parole was taken—of course they have no power to take it out of my hands—nor can even Congress themselves render it void. . . .

"It was not your particular province, my dear sir, to enter singly into the merits of the case—my request not having been for the favor of your private judgment and decision, but for your summoning a court martial, which I have an unquestioned right to demand. . . .

"I remember a time when you were not yourself prejudged by me as one of your peers, far less had I the presumption to do it as an individual out of doors."[32]

This rebuke was on a moral plane above the conception and beyond the answer of Whipple as well as Simpson. Prudently, after it was received, the ships moved on August 20 further down the Brest Road to a station about four leagues from the port. The officers were now the more anxious to sail at once because of the fear that Jones might receive in the meantime a favorable response from the Commissioners requiring Whipple to summon a court-martial despite his efforts to avoid it.

But little did the crew of the *Ranger* either understand or like the precipitate proceedings, regardless of their former praises of Simpson now in command, for they still had not received their prize money, thanks to Schweighauser, nor their wages and bounties, thanks to Lee and Adams. Half naked and penniless as the sailors were, the officers tried to propitiate them. The ships put topsails aback and hove to in the road, the men received eight or nine crowns each at this pause before sailing, and a few scant hours were at their disposal to go to Brest for spending the pittance as they saw fit.

All in haste, on the morning of the next day, August 21, 1778, the *Ranger* in company with her consorts weighed anchor for America and ran out from the road with sails squared in a lively breeze.[33] The crew had been dragged away. As the shores with the prizes won with their blood faded from view and disillusionment concerning Simpson dawned upon them, "they kept below, refusing duty and imprecating general curses on the public service, the public agents, and all concerned."[34]

A week after Jones had sent from Brest to Paris his demand to the Commissioners for a court-martial, they acceded to his wishes on condition that the proper number of officers should be available and that Simpson should retain his command pending the decision.[35] But as approximately nine days, including two for transit of the reply, elapsed after the Captain had requested the trial, the order did not reach him until about August 24—three days after the *Ranger* had sailed.[36] Apparently the Commissioners knew that it would arrive too late, for they had given instructions regarding Simpson and the *Ranger* to Whipple; and therefore the consent may have been finally forthcoming only because they were well aware that it could not now take effect.

In America, Simpson retained command of the *Ranger,* for the generosity of Jones, under disadvantageous circumstances of place and time, caused him later to set aside the Commissioners' order for a court-martial and to refrain from public exposure of the lieutenant's perfidy. But to crown injustice with injustice, the lieutenant became acting Captain if not Captain under the patronage apparently of some of those who had initially appointed him, and he was the commander of the *Ranger* in operations conducted in company with Whipple of the *Providence*. During his captaincy, the destruction of the vessel, along with other ships of an American squadron, as an alternative preferable to capture by the British at the siege of Charleston in May, 1780, was as commonplace as her cruise under Jones had been notable.

It was symbolic of Simpson's character and naval career, more than of some other officers for whom Continental ships were not available, that his last command was the *Alexander*, a privateer. Of such vessels authority speaks in the judgment of William Whipple, who, as a member of the Marine Committee and as one of the two associates of Jones in appointing the officers of the *Ranger* at Portsmouth, knew, among others, Langdon an owner of privateers and Simpson a commander of them: "I agree . . . that the privateers have much distressed the trade of our enemies, but had there been no privateers, is it not probable there would have been a much larger number of public ships than has been fitted out, which might have distressed the enemy nearly as much and furnished these states with necessaries on much better terms than they have been supplied . . . it is now attended with the most pernicious consequences. No kind of business can so effectually introduce luxury, extravagance, and every kind of dissipation that tend to the destruction of the morals of the people. Those who are actually engaged in it soon lose every idea of right and wrong, and for want of an opportunity of gratifying their insatiable avarice with the property of the enemies of their country, will, without the least compunction, seize that of her friends."[37]

Whatever the light of Jones' conscience, it did not serve to disperse the gloom of his situation at Brest. With the *Ranger* gone and the fleet of D'Orvilliers standing out in the road preparatory to a second cruise, all that remained for him ashore was increasing realization of Simpson's unrefuted aspersions spread abroad by land and sea. To support the common opinion of his loss in prestige was the present deprivation from all his expected commands. More repugnant than the wound to his reputation in France was another that might follow in America. Most galling of all was inaction for want of a frigate as the war became more grim and as every fibre of his being grew vibrant to fight with the greater valor. So keyed for martial deeds and so condemned to utter idleness, he expressed a trend of his thoughts to insinuating Bancroft, who as a spy may well have subtly made a suggestion to occasion Jones' words and could not have been averse to divert the Captain's keen eyes from himself, a traitor, to a pretty French face. "I need not now tell you," remarked the solitary warrior, "that if I had a mistress here, I have time enough on my hands to show her attention."[38]

◇◇

Chapter XXV

Fighting for Another Command: The *Bonhomme Richard*

Not BANCROFT alone was to have brought home to him that Jones utterly refused to be drawn from his long-fixed purpose to bear as active and honorable a part in the Revolution as was within his human power. De Sartine and De Chaumont practicing their stratagems on the one hand and in a sense even Franklin and Louis XVI preoccupied with affairs of state on the other were to realize that here was a man whom they could not ignore without reflection upon themselves. Particularly now that the *Ranger* and Simpson were gone, Jones set his mind as resolutely as a bulldog fastens his teeth upon one thought—a ship that could both sail and fight. "This suspense," he avowed, "is hell itself."[1]

More than ever before his challenge resolved itself into a battle not at sea but on land, not against the obstruction of officers and crew but of ministers and intermediaries. Since the day that the *Ranger* had anchored at Nantes, the earlier difficulties which Lee and Adams had provoked were the prelude to the series of disappointments which De Sartine had now occasioned. First, the exaggerated obstacles in the way of investing him with the command of the *Indienne;* secondly, the inferiority and disposal of the vessels which he had examined at L'Orient; thirdly, the false hopes with which he had been encouraged for the ships at Brest—these circumstances introduced him to difficulties in Europe conspicuously more complex than those he had experienced at the hands of Hopkins in America.

His next frustration was especially bitter. Before D'Orvilliers had sailed from Brest with his fleet for his first engagement with Keppel's, Jones had requested permission from De Sartine to accompany the French Admiral for the practical study of large-scale naval tactics and strategy. The petition had not been granted. Again, before D'Orvilliers weighed anchor for his second cruise, Jones finding himself at Brest without any of the commands that had been promised him, considered this occasion particularly opportune to go with the Admiral and applied for permission from the Minister. From August 10, 1778 when the Captain had returned to the port until August 17 when the fleet sailed, he was frequently aboard the flagship *Bretagne* with D'Orvilliers, dined at his table, and received his assurances of personal welcome for the cruise. But no official permission arrived from Paris. When the fleet had already left the road, he continued to hope for passage in the first ship which was to join it. But still no word came. In a final effort he sought to secure an authorization from the Admiral himself so as to present it to the superintendent at Brest, who demanded express permission from either De Sartine or D'Orvilliers. "I ardently wish," he concluded in his appeal conveyed to the Admiral, "to attend you with my eyes, even to the pinnacle of fame, and to learn from so great and good a general, how I may hereafter ascend the slippery precipices, beyond which the edifice is erected."[2]

At this late occasion, D'Orvilliers seems not to have had the opportunity to invite him. Neither early nor late did De Sartine forward an order which reached Jones or the public authorities at Brest; it is barely possible that a message miscarried. And when the Minister insinuated that Jones had lost his opportunity by a sojourn at L'Orient, the assumption was obviously mistaken, for the Captain had devoted only three days to his trip from Paris to Brest via L'Orient, and had arrived more than a fortnight before the fleet was beyond communication with the port. "I am unable," remarked Jones, "to draw any agreeable conclusion. All I can do in the present moment is to suspend my judgment."

Apart from the consistency of this incident with the three earlier disappointments due to De Sartine and the increasing scepticism which it provoked, the cruise itself might well have been only an occasion for the Captain to teach almost as much as to learn. The manœuvres of ships of the line and frigates in fleets continued during this period to be governed by formal rules; the line abreast was used in bearing down upon an enemy and the line ahead with heavy broadside was employed as the formation in fighting. The long evolution of this practice resulted in rigid adherence to it so that battles had come to lack flexibility, daring, and decisiveness. Rodney and later Nelson were among the first British admirals whose genius modified such principles of naval warfare to the historic loss of their foes across the Channel.

In attacks upon convoys as well as upon ships of war, the French seem at this time to have lacked freedom in naval tactics. "It is here reported," Jones was led to comment, "that the Jamaica fleet of seventy sail, under convoy of the *Portland* and four frigates, passed in sight of the Brest fleet, and got clear, because Comte D'Orvilliers would not break his line to give chase. I wish to disbelieve this account, because I had written to him that such a fleet was expected."[3]

This traditional fear to break the formal line of ships, in combination with other tactical mistakes at the engagement between the French and British fleets, may have had also an indirect effect upon the fortunes of Jones. It shadowed somewhat the reputation of D'Orvilliers and eclipsed that of the Duke de Chartres, in command of part of his fleet. The encounter was scarcely more than one of manœuvre. "Whether it was owing to the winds, or to the faults of the commanders themselves, the two fleets appeared rather to shun than to seek each other." The investigation of the conduct of the French strategists indicated especially that De Chartres had either disobeyed the signals of his senior officer, or failed to observe them in due time, or conformed to the faulty manœuvers of captains in the line of ships ahead of his own. Royal connections had resulted in a command greater than his naval experience and talents seem to have warranted, and his naval career came practically to an end. De Chartres, as one of the first who had shown a cordial interest in the enterprises of Jones, was likewise one of the first to whom he appealed in his present situation; but in view of the Duke's own mounting troubles, the Captain understood a meaningful silence as his answer.

To many another Jones now turned. Curiously, although now lacking a ship, he had a secretary, Lieutenant Amiel, who was master of both French and English. Perhaps De Sartine with Gallic humor and irony had a part in providing him with the one in lieu of the other. In any event, the Captain employed his energies the more in dictating letters for translation into French, which he read with ease but wrote with some difficulty at this period. The communications of Jones, however, were eminently not an end but a means. Within a few weeks after finding himself solitary, with Amiel alone, at Brest, he set forth his situation regarding a command to De Nassau-Siegen, Ross, De Chaumont, and Franklin as well as to De Sartine.

Towards De Nassau-Siegen, who had reported the delay of the *Indienne,* he was at this time credulously confiding: "If the ship that was at first proposed, cannot with certainty be got ready for sea next month, you, my Prince, can obtain another. . . ." The Prince justified his faith so far as not to reply, although with less reason than De Chartres. To Ross, whose pessimism deepened his own resentment at neglect from the Commissioners, he gave assurance at a tart moment of placing "no dependence in the men in power" since his bill had been protested.

To De Chaumont, who had largely gained his good will by a compliant manner, he voiced his remonstrance in varied strains: "I am actually considered here as a poor victim who has been sacrificed to some base underhand intrigue of party. I would not wish my worst enemy to be in such a situation—all is mystery and wonder to everyone as well as to myself so that I blush to appear in public. The connection was not at the beginning of my seeking: and if I was an object worthy of notice in June I am not less so now in September. My desire of fame is infinite; but I am not an adventurer of fortune. . . . And I must not, and will not, so far forget my own honor and what I owe to my friends and to America as to remain inactive."[4] This ending sounded a rather lofty key for the ear of De Chaumont, who in the last analysis was a practical business man; and it may also have reminded him of the correspondent's gallant attentions to his wife.

Franklin was too absorbed with affairs of diplomacy and too circumspect to wish to embroil himself in the growing breach between the Captain and the Minister. Yet at Passy he had promised to answer all the letters from Jones, and at the latter's departure had shown him affectionate interest. One communication shortly followed another from Brest to Passy. In addition came various letters for transmission, subject to Franklin's approval, to persons in authority. The Commissioner enlisted his grandson, William Temple Franklin, and his agent, Bancroft, to handle the increasing volume of manuscript. "This is the nice moment," Jones had urged before the sailing of the French fleet," when I ought either to be in search of marine knowledge with Count d'Orvilliers, or in search of honor in attempting some private enterprise." After Franklin counselled patience, he replied, "I have need of some of your philosophy"; but his patience endured only so long as to lead him to propose almost in the same breath, "I have seen the *Fox* mounting 24 guns (taken formerly by the *Hancock* and *Boston*) and would accept that ship, attended by the *Alert,* unless something better is immediately bestowed. I shall, with this command, expect unlimited orders."

Nor did Jones refrain from sending De Sartine what he termed an "explicit letter," recapitulating his cumulative disappointments, asserting with greater emphasis than in the account to De Chaumont his motives of patriotism, philanthropy, and honor, and requesting above all a decision: "I do not wish to interfere with the harmony of the French marine; but if I am still thought worthy of your attention, I shall hope for a separate command, with liberal orders. If, on the contrary, you have no further occasion for my services, I have then only to ask the *Alert,* and a few seamen, with permission to return in that small vessel to America before winter."[5] Jones appreciated more than the United States Commissioners, Franklin excepted, the vast importance of the varied aid of France in prosecuting the war; he was conciliatory because of gratitude towards a nation, not want of spirit towards a man. But De Sartine, who apparently did not recognize the strength behind the tempered words, proceeded, as he had toyed with the Captain so far, to toy with him further.

It was humiliating to Jones to contemplate a premature return to America, leaving behind him the evil reports circulated by Simpson in Europe and seemingly corroborated by his deprivation from all expected commands. It was painful to look forward to facing the Marine Committee and begging a ship after having informed the members of his continuance abroad at the particular request of the Court of France. He might have sacrificed his feelings to this degree, strengthened as he was by his forceful convictions concerning himself and by his grim determination to serve America in spite of personal cost. But his forbearance gave place to militancy when De Sartine continued his game, probably not without the greater malice because the Captain had fearlessly and plainly exposed his deceptions to many eyes.

To the chain of disappointments, the Minister added another link by his refusal of the comparatively modest request for the *Fox*. But the climax was the sardonic jocosity with which he now proposed to send the Captain back to America. He informed the Commissioners that it might be possible to provide a small French vessel but that it would be necessary to furnish an American crew. As the last act of his little play, he signified to D'Orvilliers his intention to send Jones home in *"une bonne voiture."*[6] When the Captain learned from the Admiral concerning such jesting solicitude in his behalf, his deference turned to challenge. "This is absolutely adding insult to injury," he protested to the Duke de la Rochefoucauld, one of his sincerest friends at Passy, "and it is the proposition of a man whose veracity I have not experienced in former cases. . . . The Minister, to my infinite mortification, after possessing himself of my schemes and ideas has treated me like a child five times successively, by leading me on from great to little, and from little to less." And he concluded not without justice and dignity: "M. de Sartine may think as he pleases, but Congress will not thank him for having thus treated an officer who has always been honoured with their favour and friendship."[7]

At this juncture, De Chaumont, who acted in behalf of De Sartine, assumed further his artful rôle. He sought on the one hand to propitiate Jones by assuring him that the Minister had sworn "by the Styx" and had promised "très positivement" that he should have a ship. The suave business man offered him on the other hand a privateer. For this mercenary proposal, the Captain framed a rebuff to De Chaumont which fitted the better because it sought to put a generous construction upon what to all appearances was a calculating attempt to prostitute his patriotism to money: "I believe your proposition respecting your ship *Union* to be very disinterested; as such it claims my warmest thanks. But I am not my own master; and as a servant of the Imperial Republic of America, honored with the friendship and favor of Congress, I cannot, from my own authority or inclination, serve either myself or even my best friends, in any private line whatever; unless where the honor and interest of America is the premier object."[8] De Chaumont must have smiled; and he prepared to change his tack.

Jones had more uncompromising terms in reserve upon referring to De Sartine: "I have already lost near five months of my time, the best season of the year, and such opportunities of serving my country, and *acquiring honor, as I cannot again expect this year* . . . he will make a direct written apology to me, suitable to the injury which I have sustained; otherwise in vindication of my sacred honor, painful as it will be, I must publish in the gazettes of Europe the conduct he has held towards me."[9]

Matters had come to such a pass that even Franklin must have considered it wiser for Jones to return to the United States. He suggested to Amiel, who was an American, the advisability of leaving France because of better prospects of employment at home. Upon hearing of this counsel, Jones, now the fighter who knew no retreat, expressed his passionate alarm and resolution: "But if I am included in your advice to Mr. Amiel—perish the thought. It is impossible. Had it been possible for me to anticipate half of the heartache and sorrow that I have experienced since my return to Brest, I would have expired on the rack rather than have undergone as lingering and ignominious a torment; and I would now lay down my life rather than return to America before my honor is made perfectly whole."[10]

His deeply felt convictions lent him the greater courage, and the force of his courage spurred him to audacity; at the same time his audacity had the counterpoise of deliberation. Disregarding counts, dukes, and princes as well as ministers, he addressed a letter to the King himself. In a second letter, he petitioned the Duchess of Chartres to deliver it personally, but in a third he requested Franklin, to whom he submitted the two others, to forward them subject to his discretion. His powers of persuasion were as apt and original as his choice of persons upon whom to employ them was bold. To Franklin he professed the feelings of "veneration and affection of a son who ardently wishes to render himself worthy of [his] regard." To the Duchess he made his entreaty with grace as well as courage, assuring her that he would be "supremely happy to succeed through the influence of so amiable a princess and so powerful an advocate," and avowing with the fitness not unbecoming a professed frank sailor "the artless simplicity of [his] heart."[11] To the King he addressed himself with confidence and freedom as well as with austere respect in recounting the circumstances of his present inactivity in France. "As your Majesty," he ended his petition, "by espousing the cause of America has become 'the protector of the Rights of Human Nature,' I am persuaded that you will not disregard my situation nor suffer me to remain any longer in this insupportable disgrace."

The appeal to Louis XVI over the heads of French Ministers and American Commissioners may well have had a greater indirect influence than these statesmen were disposed to permit to become public. It seems more than a coincidence that the three letters were dated October 19, 1778, and that William Temple Franklin, in the capacity of his grandfather's secretary, informed Jones on October 21, very shortly after the letters must have arrived, concerning "the Minister's final intention" by a postscript which may have craftily simulated rather than have been a real afterthought. This "final intention," according to the elder Franklin's advice, removed the occasion for sending the petitions, although he made known his readiness to forward them upon a further request. De Sartine must have preferred not to have his treatment of Jones appear bluntly before the eyes of the King, and Franklin may have considered it diplomatic to avoid unnecessary publicity in such a Franco-American altercation. Presumably the letter, along with the influence of De la Rochefoucauld and others, spurred the Commissioner to urge a ship for Jones and the Minister to offer new positive assurances. Presumably, too, it explained why De Chaumont informed the Captain only a few days later, October 28, that he had received orders from the Minister to procure a vessel for him and why he requested information concerning any at French ports that might be suitable. Most of all, it served final notice upon those who were responsible for his remaining in France that in a matter so vitally interwoven with his career in the Revolution his life meant less to him than his honor, and diplomats however artful regarded him lightly at their peril.

The resolution which had emboldened an appeal even to the highest authority in France received encouragement from another source not the less highly regarded because it came from distant shores. America appreciated him. And the more recognition he received, the more he characteristically strove to merit it and win the greater recognition. Thomas Bell, an American Captain, had arrived in port and told of the acclaim with which the cruise of the *Ranger* had been received in the United States. The manner in which Jones acknowledged the praises demonstrated that, however much he loved glory, he prized it with modesty, discrimination, and gratitude: "Your account of the particular affection towards me of Mr. Morris, Mr. Hewes, and other worthy characters affords me the truest pleasure. I would far rather have the esteem and friendship of a few such men than the empty applause of millions, who possess less liberal souls—yet I confess to you that my vanity is greatly flattered by your account of the generous public approbation of my past services. And I pledge myself to that generous public that it shall be my first care and my heart's supremest wish to merit the continuance of its approbation. . . ."[12]

He also indulged himself in thoughts not associated with his profession at this moment of comparative cheer. As a lover, he had so far proved himself a good sailor; his bantering style towards Bell testified that he recognized this truth: "I am sorry and much disappointed by not hearing from Young, who said so much about his wife's friend, my fair mistress. By his silence I fear I have a rival who by opportunity and importunity may make great and dangerous advances towards the heart before I can arrive to raise the siege."[13] He brought Young himself to task: "And now, sir, I have an account to settle with you. What can you say for yourself. You, who said so much about Mrs. Young's friend, the fair Miss *xxxx*. You have sinned. And must prove your repentance by amendment; else I will never trust you again with affairs of importance. I had more dependence on Mrs. Young than on her husband from the beginning. . . . But if rigid duty and stern honor did not command

my further stay on this side of the Atlantic, I should hope to succeed better by personal application than by proxy. Present my best
compliments to Mrs. Young."[14]

This interlude of light comedy had scarcely occupied a free hour
before Jones set aside further sentiment in favor of "rigid duty and
stern honor." De Sartine, not surprisingly, was slow in redeeming
his latest assurances; but as it now was impolitic to tender the Captain nothing, he seems to have decided to offer him, through his
intermediary De Chaumont, only a sop. The merchant having
proposed a privateer, now recommended an inferior sloop, although only a short period had elapsed since he had agreed that
Jones was justified in refusing an inconsiderable command. "I
would rather be shot ashore," Jones remonstrated to him, "than
be sent to sea in such things as the armed prizes I have described."
To Williams he expressed himself more plainly regarding De
Chaumont and his sloop: "To this I sent my absolute refusal; I
could not do less . . . and I can find no reason why I should hold
my honor at so cheap a rate. He knows that I mean to go in harm's
way. Why, then, should he give me up to a prospect of certain ruin,
for what less could I expect were I to proceed in ships that can
neither sail nor fight?"[15] De Chaumont himself could have answered best, but his later deeds may suffice to answer for him.

In the meantime Jones and others whom he enlisted in his task
investigated many ships at many ports. As France had become increasingly involved in the war, her naval officers were most tenacious in reserving for themselves all the available commands in
the royal marine. It was maintained in addition that to detach
ships from the King's yard for a foreign officer was contrary to
established rules. Jones pointed, however, to the repeated promises
that had been made to him, and to the generosity of the United
States by the choice of a French captain for the command of one of
its best frigates the *Alliance* and by the engagement of a considerable number of French military officers for her Army. "The noble-
minded Congress," he urged, "know not the little mean distinctions of climate or place of nativity"—a sentiment which, although
it served his special purpose, had valid application to his situation.
Yet he became convinced that it would prove impossible to obtain
one of the best government frigates; so his attention turned the

more to vessels of private ownership for conversion into ships of war.

Among those who searched in his behalf for a suitable ship was James Moylan, still engaged, with his partner Gourlade, as a commercial agent in L'Orient. At this port, he recommended, among other vessels, an East India merchantman for sale, built in 1766, of 900 tons, and of 74 foot keel. "If that ship," replied Jones from Brest, "is known to *sail fast* and is in condition to carry the metal you mention, I believe she must be ours. . . ." Although he had in mind also superior ships, such as the *Turgot* which had recently been sold and the *Beaumont* which was daily expected from America, and resolved to "search out of this kingdom or build" if necessary, his choice reverted to the *Duras* as directly available and moderate in price. Yet despite De Sartine's many encouragements regarding an immediate purchase, Jones had no authority to act even now. His course was so restricted in his relations with the French marine that he actually felt uncertain of his liberty to go to L'Orient. To Franklin he gave assurances of a guarantee, secured by his own property, for the payment of the wages of the seamen who signed for his next cruise, because he was determined not to permit past memories, notably his troubles with the crew of the *Ranger,* to weigh against his present plans. To De Chaumont as the direct agent, he sent message after message while further suspense during the imminent uncertainty of gaining or losing the particular ship continued to the point of being unbearable.

On one day, he exhorted him: "The next season for enterprises approaches apace; I conjure you by heaven, my dear friend, not to leave me lose it like the last one."[16] On another, he apologized that he had taken "this step" of coming to L'Orient to judge himself concerning the *Duras*. On a third, he gave a detailed account of her and begged a favorable decision, concluding with the assurances that "the frame is now thought very good," that she "bears a good character for sailing and working," and that "I am inclined to believe these reports since I freely give it to you as my opinion that the *Duras* is the only ship now for sale in France that will answer our purpose." Neither *caveat emptor* served as a warning, nor "answer our purpose" could be considered as an encomium—but Jones was desperate.

Seven times the Captain wrote De Chaumont concerning the Minister's declared purpose from the day when he had received the offer of the inconsiderable sloop until December 16, 1778, when he forwarded a summary message.[17] Not one response had come. Bernier, the owner of the *Duras,* set ten days as the term that his ship would continue to be available for purchase. "If this letter," Jones then informed De Chaumont, "does not produce me an immediate and satisfactory answer, it shall be the last forfeiture of my discretion on this trifling and fruitless business.

"My reluctant eyes will then be opened and I shall be convinced, however great the mortification, that under the mask of friendship I have been betrayed and sacrificed with premeditation and in the abuse of confidence from the very beginning."[18] Still no response came from De Chaumont or De Sartine or Franklin.

His health suffered, for even the most robust constitution could not well withstand the stress of a temperament as vibrant as his. He was unable to sleep, and it became impossible for him to devote himself to the professional studies which were constantly a part of his routine. As the sharpest wound to his nature, self-respecting and independent to the degree that he was one of the first defenders of American liberty, it irked him intolerably to petition, especially to petition those towards whom he could no longer feel esteem. "I can say," he declared, "from my own sad experience,

> Were I to curse the man I hate,
> Attendance and dependence be his fate."[19]

The ten days of grace for the purchase of the ship were slipping by, and the owner had in prospect another buyer. "I am for the first time in my life," Jones affirmed in an appeal to Bancroft, "in a disposition to doubt almost all the world . . . nothing is done. . . . I begin to see through the mist."[20] "A few days," he declared to Williams, who happened to be at Passy with Franklin, "must convince me whether I have or have not had to do with honest men." Doubtful of men, possibly he was the more confiding to women. He added a message for delivery at Passy, which revealed not just courtesy and gallantry but apparent attachment to the wife of the one person with whom his professional relations were now closest: "Tell Madame de Chaumont that I shall ever retain the most grateful remembrance of her friendship and hospitality. I would have written to her often, but unhappily am not able to express myself in French in language that would do justice to my sentiments [perhaps his Franco-American secretary was not a suitable intermediary for them], and my mind has been so perplexed that I have not been able to study."[21] While the Captain sent this unconsidered communication fraught with possible hidden dangers, only a few days still remained for the purchase of the *Duras*.

"I could have written to you by every post," he admitted to an intimate friend at Brest, Father Mehegan, chaplain of D'Orvillier's fleet, who had expressed concern at his silence; "but this would have been giving you some token of existence merely—not of *life*." At this juncture the ten days actually elapsed.

Jones secured a short additional term of grace. At last on January 2, 1779, De Chaumont sent his approval and indicated that the King had made provision for the purchase. The bargain, however, was not yet definitely concluded. Within a few days it seemed, in fact, that the acquisition of the ship was nearer to being cancelled than consummated. Franklin himself had business dealings with De Chaumont in which an agreement was no sooner arrived at than his neighbor at Passy proposed such a succession of changes as would render the original understanding null.[22] Now this man of business adopted a somewhat similar course—a course which reminded Jones of De Sartine's propensity for leading his hopes from great to little and from little to less.

The ninth month was passing since the Minister had repaid the courtesy of Jones and, in his professional capacity, of the United States with repeated, flagrant disrespect if not positive dishonor. The Captain, who had exercised more patience than less active and outspoken men would have been capable of, decided to set aside his pen, hasten to Versailles and Passy, and face De Sartine and De Chaumont. He wished also to see Franklin, from whom he had received no direct word for months. The advice indeed of Franklin himself came to his mind, the saying of the fraternally disposed Richard in his almanac: "If you would have your business done, come yourself; if not, send."

De Sartine received Jones with complaisance. He must have deemed it wise to do so, mindful of further intercession by Franklin, the prestige of the captain in America and France notwith-

standing intrigue against him at home and abroad, the magnetic
personality of the officer himself in his presence, and the petition
to the King. The Minister carried his ostensible good will so far
as to press upon him the acceptance of the *Maréchal de Broglio,* a
fine ship of sixty-four guns which was for sale, but he refused because in the absence of permission to enlist French seamen it did
not seem possible to find a sufficient number of volunteers for her.
De Sartine then effected at length the purchase of the *Duras,* and
confirmed it in writing. The expedition was to be under the
American flag; the armament at the cost of France; the crew
composed of volunteers, not sailors in the French service; the plans
of the cruise at the sole discretion of the Captain—*carte blanche.*
As close to his heart as the wish for a ship that could both sail fast
and fight was the provision allowing him freedom to determine his
own strategy and to adhere to his own judgment.

M. Garnier, who had been the French chargé d'affaires in England, handed Jones this communication from De Sartine, which at
last sealed the bestowal of the *Duras* by the King of France. The
Captain's pleasure was so great, his present gratitude was so much
stronger than his past resentment, and his recognition of the importance of French good will rendered him so tactful that his
reply to the Minister would have been worthy of better diplomats
than several of those whom America had sent to Paris: "It shall be
my duty to represent in the strongest terms to Congress the generous and voluntary resolution which their great ally, the protector of the rights of human nature, and the best of kings, has
taken to promote the honor of their flag, and I beseech you to
assure His Majesty that my heart is impressed with the deepest
sense of the obligation which I owe his condescending favor and
good opinion and which it shall be my highest ambition to merit,
by rendering every service in my power to the common cause. I
cannot insure success, but I will endeavor to deserve it."[23]

The strain of grandiloquence may be allowed the grateful sailor
in his diplomatic warmth; his warmth in its simplicity is more
apparent in his incidental tribute to Franklin: "Your having permitted me to alter the name of the ship has given me a pleasing
opportunity of paying a well-merited compliment to a great and
good man to whom I am under obligations and who honors me

with his friendship."[24] In honor of the Commissioner and the counsel in his almanac, the *Duras* was to be the *Bon Homme Richard,* variantly in the French idiom today the *Bonhomme Richard*—the brotherly disposed rather than simply the good Franklin.

The Minister of the Marine had delegated to Garnier the duty to coöperate with the Captain in effecting the plans and providing for the needs of the cruise. This choice was propitious for Jones, who represented him as a man of "large vision and sound judgment." It seemed especially promising in the light of nine months of increasing torturous suspense as an unconsidered chessman in the politics of De Sartine and as an even more precarious pawn for the devious motives of De Chaumont.

Chapter XXVI

Franklin and Others in a New Background

A SQUADRON of four or five sail as auxiliary to the *Bonhomme Richard*, several fireships, five hundred chosen troops in addition to the naval complement of sailors and marines, and an enterprise of outstanding boldness and originality under the untrammeled, sole command of Jones—these were the brilliant prospects before the Captain which began to assume form at Paris and Passy in counsel with Garnier, with the approval of De Sartine, and with the coöperation of Franklin. But they had scarcely begun to perfect them before this association ended upon the expectancy of Garnier to receive the appointment as successor to Gérard de Rayneval, the French Minister to the United States. "It is a misfortune," Jones recognized, "which I am not able to lament too much, to have been deprived forthright of the aid of a man of such great abilities."[1] And in his place stepped De Chaumont.

"An intermediary between the Government and the Commissioners," a grandson of De Chaumont described the host of Franklin at the Hôtel Valentinois in Passy. De Chaumont's services reveal him in the light of a minor and less versatile Beaumarchais whose apparent beneficence was to a greater extent as a subordinate agent of France and a venturesome private merchant than as a philanthropist and a patriot in devotion to America.[2] In so far as his generous impulses were concerned, they seem to have been due chiefly to Franklin, not to the United States, and it was to Franklin's testimonial that he owes the most favorable interpretation of his part in American history as "the first in France who gave us credit, and before the Court showed us any countenance trusted us with two thousand barrels of gunpowder and from time to time afterwards exerted himself to furnish Congress with supplies of various kinds."

Although Jones at Passy was socially intimate with the family of De Chaumont as well as professionally connected with De Chaumont himself, the difficult course of events which had finally resulted in the purchase of the *Duras* was not a promising prelude to further relations between them. What outwardly may have suggested a more successful association but covertly tended towards less sincerity was the increasing warmth between Jones and Madame de Chaumont. With a disarming frankness he had appealed for the advancement of his naval plans to the Duchess in addition to the Duke of Chartres; in a more personal manner he thought perhaps to influence De Chaumont favorably through the persuasion of his wife. Especially as the result of preoccupation with his ambitions, he may have overlooked the possible existence of dislike, if not jealousy, in the mind of the husband.

The concentration of Jones at this time upon his new enterprise was in fact so all-absorbing that for this reason, besides his disposition to be both courteous and sincere, there remains scant basis for suspecting important purposes in his heart alien to his professional ambitions. He was in great haste to leave Passy for French seaports to prepare his armament. Only a few matters of business and honor associated especially with his past in the *Ranger* seemed still to require his particular attention before departure.

More than ten months had elapsed since he had received no answer to his conscientious and "gallant" letter to the Countess of Selkirk even regarding the silver plate, which it remained his determination to return. The generous reply of the earl, who undoubtedly appreciated his escape from assuming the sudden rôle as a hostage for American prisoners, had lain at the London post-office a number of months before it had finally been returned to him by Le Despencer. The Postmaster General had refused to employ either the public mails or his personal authority in any association with Jones "the pirate." Now at Passy the Captain met William Alexander, an acquaintance of Franklin and in turn a friend of Selkirk, who undertook to be an intermediary regarding the plate. Apropos of prisoners, more important than the plate, associated with the *Ranger,* Jones also urged Franklin to make new efforts to effect the exchange of the remaining British captives taken in the *Drake*—some had escaped through careless supervision by Schweighauser—for Americans in England. He hoped that they might both terminate their misery in Forton and Portsmouth prisons and also be available for volunteer service in his approaching enterprise.

And last, for the protection of his honor, which to suspicious persons the episode of the *Ranger* and Simpson had called into question, he secured a letter from Franklin and Adams—probably the signature of Lee was neither desired nor tendered—certifying to the actual circumstances. In private life as in war Jones was not averse to arming himself for contingencies; hence this certificate: "As your separation from the *Ranger* and the appointment of Lieutenant Simpson to the command of her will be liable to misinterpretation by persons who are unacquainted with the real cause of those facts, we hereby certify that your leaving the *Ranger* was by our consent, at the express request of His Excellency Monsieur de Sartine, who informed us that he had occasion to employ you in some public service; that Lieutenant Simpson was appointed to the command of the *Ranger* with your consent, after having consented to release him from an arrest under which you had put him.

"That your leaving the *Ranger* in our opinion ought not and cannot be an injury to your rank or character in the service of the United States; and that your commission in their Navy continues in full force."[3] It was not the least evidence of Jones' generosity that he refrained from bringing any future charges against Simpson; nor was it an unworthy mark of his self-respect that he kept the letter as an answer to any possible maligners in both France and America.

Strangely coincident with this finale to Simpson and the *Ranger* was the prelude to Landais and the *Alliance*. Landais, the former French officer who had been discharged because of his quarrelsome and insubordinate conduct from the naval service of his country and had gone to the United States in September, 1777, had contrived to secure from Congress the Captaincy of the finest American frigate, which had just been built at Salisbury and outfitted at Newburyport in Massachusetts. He had also made extravagant stipulations regarding advances and a salary, to which those who appointed him acceded. In fact, he had gained abroad the tolerance of Franklin as well as the favor of Deane,[4] deceived the Marine Committee concerning his questionable reputation as well as abilities, profited by the countermoves of factions in Congress, and turned to his interest the wish of America to pay a compliment to France both by naming the ship in commemoration of the recent treaty with her new ally and by giving the command to one of her supposedly honored officers. Adventurers like Landais in the Navy and Du Coudray and his corps in the Army of the United States moved Washington to exclaim: "Our officers think it extremely hard after they have toiled in this service . . . to have strangers put over them whose merit probably is not equal to their own, but whose effrontery will take no denial." The effrontery of Landais was already unquestionable, and it boded ill as to his other traits.

The first voyage of the *Alliance* under his command from America to France, with Lafayette on leave of absence as his special passenger, foreshadowed the difficulties which he was to create abroad, particularly in conflict with Jones. In the absence of a sufficient number of Americans for the crew, Landais had enlisted about eighty British prisoners, taken from the British ship of war *Somerset* wrecked off the New England coast, who planned a bold and savage mutiny for the capture of the frigate and the disposal of the officers and the remaining seamen. The cruelty of the plot, which was discovered at the eleventh hour through the loyalty of an American whose Irish accent had led to his acceptance as a Briton and as one of the conspirators, indicated at the same time that Landais had been particularly offensive to the mutineers. In revenge they had intended to set him adrift, heavily chained, in a boat without food, water, oars, or sails.[5] His temperament became manifest in relations with faithful Americans as well as rebellious Englishmen. He had quarreled with his three lieutenants, his captain of marines, and his master. The *Alliance* had scarcely hove to in the road of Brest before one of the officers Stephen Hills and five others dispatched an appeal to Franklin reminiscent in part of Esek Hopkins and his boatswain: ". . . there is not that harmony subsisting between Captain Landais and ourselves that we wish for sincerely . . . where the captain is more intimate with the purser and makes him a greater confidant than his principal officers very little happiness can be found."[6] Lafayette likewise made known Landais' hostile disposition upon his arrival at Passy with despatches for Franklin from Congress, which informed the Commissioner that he had been appointed the Minister Plenipotentiary to France.

That Franklin, without Adams and Lee, was now the chief American authority in Europe with whom Jones in the future would take counsel and from whom he would receive instructions concerning the *Bonhomme Richard* brought pleasure and promise to the Captain, who had already hastened to the seaports for volunteers, cannon, and ship supplies. The refusal of his draft and the evils in its wake had been evidence enough that Adams was lukewarm and Lee was hostile to his original character and independent objectives. In relation to Franklin, he could expect as both man and officer a mutual bond of understanding, regard, and even affection. Despite an occasional expression of impatience which escaped him in the stress of his dynamic nature compelled to inactivity and in forgetfulness of the Minister's gout and many diplomatic concerns, there was scarcely an American in France who appreciated the qualities of Franklin more wholeheartedly than Jones.

The prestige of Franklin both abroad and at home had been great as a Commissioner and was destined to become even greater as the Minister Plenipotentiary. It continued to grow notwithstanding Lee and Adams and others who were prone to be his detractors, notwithstanding also such serious but unrecognized mistakes as his choice of Bancroft for his secretary and such less far-reaching errors as were later to increase the difficulties of Jones. His comprehensive personality was versatile, humanistic, and venerable; his character, which ran the gamut of the ideal and the real, identified him with nature in its largest sense. As an idealist, he was disarming and won confidence and loyalty; as a realist, he was circumspect in essentials and turned craft and deceit against themselves in favor of his own honesty. Such qualities of the man and the minister fitted him to be the chief American diplomat of the Revolution, especially in France which was more appreciative than other nations of his human traits and of the democracy of the newly-risen country that he incomparably exemplified. He had the good will of Vergennes and Louis XVI as best testified by the loans of 26,000,000 livres (5,000,000 gold dollars at that time) which his efforts won, and he had the adoration of the French people as similarly witnessed by reproductions of his portraits on almost every conceivable article and by the use of his name for countless "hats, canes, snuff boxes, everything."

Although it was more difficult to be a hero, much less a prophet, in his own country, the appointment of Franklin as sole Minister made clear that his advocates in the United States as well as in France were sufficiently emphatic and strong to gain a victory in his behalf over his enemies. The accusations against him, ranging widely in kind and degree, even linking his name with the protracted bitter controversy that raged about Deane in Congress and in the press, comprised almost all the seven deadly sins. Of Americans in Europe, Arthur Lee, who had a mistress in Paris,[7] accused Franklin of various evils including libertinism;[8] John Adams, whose greatest failings were rooted in conceit, charged him with vanity;[9] William Lee, who held at one time three public offices, British as well as American, complained of his avarice;[10] Ralph Izard, who grasped at public funds without rendering the services for which he had been appointed but presumed to meddle with affairs for which he had received no commission, spread reports of his dishonesty.[11]

Of Americans in the United States, Samuel Adams, whose partisanship was vindictive at home, pharisaically condemned "a faction on the other side of the Atlantic" attributed largely to the pride of Franklin; and Richard Henry Lee not only tried in the interests of his brothers Arthur and William to displace Franklin in France but also wished, after the failure of "the party . . . to make room,"[12] to eliminate him altogether from the political scene. "How long must the dignity, honor, and interest of the United States be sacrificed to the bad passions of that old man under the idea of his being a philosopher?" exclaimed Richard Henry Lee to Samuel Adams in the exasperation of his intrigue. "If this man must be retained in the public service with all his imperfections on his head, let him be sent to some court, *causa honoris,* where he can do neither good nor harm—the Emperor's for instance or her of all the Russias. . . ."[13] Since Richard was so considerate as to wish to render Franklin incapable of good as well as harm in the affairs of the nation, not to speak of his aim at banishing him from the political arena, it is only just to conclude that this one of the family trio in public office had the welfare of the United States considerably less in mind than an unobstructed stage for the ambitions of the Lees.

Despite the direct attacks upon Franklin and his indirect inclusion in the storm of charges and countercharges between Arthur Lee and Deane, he had received the appointment by Congress as the sole, trusted intermediary between America and France. So he assumed his enlarged duties. Now that one Minister had superseded three Commissioners, Adams found himself summarily removed from his office and Lee retained only the dubious position of Commissioner to Spain. The former had recognized and honorably proposed that the tripartite arrangement should be changed; but the latter, who had recommended himself for the post in Paris, felt revenge smouldering within him. He bided his time for covert plotting against Franklin, recognizing as possible pawns in Europe Landais and De Chaumont on the one hand and Jones on the other. The more unswerving the loyalty of the Captain of the *Bonhomme Richard* to Franklin, the more unscrupulous was Lee to consider him an instrument for his purposes when opportunity would serve.

Especially during this period the letters of the Captain became more confiding and those of the Minister more familiar. This spirit was manifest in an interlude both humorous and serious. About a fortnight after Jones had returned from Passy to L'Orient, Franklin sent him a communication of which the postscript was to the Captain of vastly greater meaning than the main message. The message explained, concerning the complexities which the silver plate involved, that Alexander reported the readiness of Selkirk to accept it from Congress but not from an individual—Jones by implication.[14] The postscript, to Franklin merely the reference to a mystery as he termed it, a little joke with which he had amused himself in a moment of relaxation, was to Jones an all-important hint as to the turning point of his life, the long-past killing of the mutineer at Tobago. However accidental, it had engrossed his mind and now prompted him to a significant revelation. He forwarded the account to Franklin on March 6, 1779 in the form of a narrative, impersonal as well as poignant, which outwardly hid the identity of the actor.[15]

In a separate letter he explained himself more fully and added that Hewes, Morris, and several others were already aware of this crucial happening of his past. His confidence now extended not only to Franklin but also, strangely, to Bancroft: "In short, however checkered my fortune may have been, I feel no sentiment in my breast that can ever make me wish to conceal any event of my life from persons of candor and ingenuity—therefore you are at perfect liberty to communicate my story to whom you think proper, and particularly to Doctor Bancroft." The honesty which impelled him to lay bare his conscience dictated also, perhaps with a measure of judicious flattery, a tribute to the Minister: "In the fullness of my heart I congratulate you on your well-merited appointment, and I trust you will believe me that I do now and ever shall rejoice in every circumstance that tends to the honor or happiness of a great and good man, who has taught me as well as his country to regard him with the veneration and affection which proceeds directly from the heart, and that is due only to the best of friends."[16]

Although taken aback by the unexpected dramatic disclosures in Jones' narrative and accompanying letter, which his joking allusion to a mystery had served to reveal, Franklin artfully soothed any qualms that the Captain may have felt anew concerning his past history. Perhaps the better to offset Jones' downright seriousness and at the same time to indulge himself as a story-teller, he sent from Passy an explanation reminiscent of Franklin the knowing journalist:

"I have looked over the copy of my letter to you of February 24, [1779], not being able to imagine what part of it could have given you the idea that I hinted at an affair I never knew. Not finding anything in the letter, I suppose it must have been the postscript, of which I have no copy and which I know now that you could not understand. . . .

"The story I alluded to is this: L'Abbe Rochon had just been telling me and Madame de Chaumont that the old gardener and his wife had complained to the curate of your having attacked her in the garden about seven o'clock the evening before your departure, and attempted to ravish her, relating all the circumstances, some of which are not fit for me to write. The serious part of it was that three of her sons were determined to kill you, if you had not gone off; the rest occasioned some laughing; for the old woman being one of the grossest, coarsest, dirtiest, and ugliest that we may find in a thousand, Madame de Chaumont said it gave a high idea of the strength of appetite and courage of the Americans.

"A day or two after I learned that it was the *femme de chambre* of Mademoiselle de Chaumont who had disguised herself in a suit, I think, of your clothes, to divert herself under that masquerade, as is customary the last evening of carnival; and that meeting the old woman in the garden, she took it into her head to try her chastity, which it seems was found proof."

His allusion to the mystery that had been in his own mind now explained, he turned to the meaning that Jones' confession had given it: "As to the unhappy affair of which you gave me an account, there is no doubt but that the facts being as you state them, the person must have been acquitted if he had been tried, it being merely *se defendendo*." Finally, not with the past but the future in view, he added heartily, "I wish you all imaginable success in your present undertaking."

For all the concentration of Jones upon equipping the *Bonhomme Richard,* other incidents which had their source in Passy also interrupted somewhat the singleness of his purpose. Ill-advisedly he had recently linked Bancroft with Franklin as a possible confidant regarding his own private life; unhappily he now came to Bancroft's aid in dispelling suspicions of activities as a government spy. Bancroft, the Massachusetts apprentice, who as a boy had run off to sea and carried with him some property of his master; who had written a novel, *The History of Sir Charles Wentworth,* vilifying Christianity; who was "a meddler in the stocks and frequently went into the alley and into the deepest and darkest retirements and recesses of the brokers and jobbers"; who sent by William Carmichael, alias Mr. Bolton,[17] hidden messages in white ink to Samuel Wharton, the American engaged in London as a speculator and as a lobbyist for the acquisition of vast lands by the Grand Ohio Company—Bancroft, this insinuating secretary of Franklin and Deane and counterplotting agent of Wentworth and other Englishmen,[18] now tricked, of all persons, even Jones to render a disservice to America by coming to his defense.

It happened that while the Captain was at Nantes, among other ports, engaged in the varied occupations preparatory to his cruise that he heard Musco Livingston, who had been considered for the command of the *Ranger,* make the accusation that Bancroft had prostituted his public trust to private profit. Livingston appealed, in fact, to Jones to aid in proving the validity of his claim. The lieutenant placed in the hands of the senior officer his affidavit linking Samuel Wharton with Bancroft: "I do certify that I was shown a letter in London dated 27 January last [1778] which I was told was written by Doctor Bancroft to Mr. Wharton, informing him, that he might depend upon it, he had it from the very best authority that the treaty with the Court of France was to be signed on the 5th or 6th of February and desiring him to make his speculations accordingly. . . . I do also certify that I have seen Doctor Bancroft's handwriting on other occasions, and that I believe the above-mentioned letter to have been written by him."[19] At the same time, Wharton acknowledged in the presence of Jones that he had received a letter from Bancroft on the subject alluded to in the certificate.[20]

There seemed little more necessary to prove that the speculations of Wharton as well as Bancroft were of greater concern to them than the duty to guard their country's secrets at a crucial stage of the war. But to all appearances Wharton showed himself in this instance scarcely less skilful at subterfuge than Bancroft. Confronted by Livingston, who had Jones as a witness, he declared his readiness to "make oath that he never had received any letter or information whatsoever from Doctor Bancroft respecting the subject of the certificate until after the publication of the treaty between France and America."[21]

As the message was dated as early as January 27, ten days before the signing of the treaty, it was neither the fault of Bancroft if it required a longer period in transit from Paris to London, nor the fault of Wharton if he was unable to profit by it opportunely.

The intent of the one as the sender and of the other as the recipient remains the same. And when it is recalled that Bancroft boasted of having transmitted to London information in regard to this treaty only forty-two hours after the signatures were affixed to the document, the veracity of Wharton becomes the more doubtful.

The unscrupulousness of the letter in the first instance and the subterfuge of Wharton's excuse in the second seem to take color from the guile of Bancroft in a third. He evaded the issue by stating that no other charge had appeared against him in America—an assertion which no one but the accused certified. He caused Livingston to become uncertain of the evidence of his own eyes through the artifice of Wharton. He diverted suspicion, as already indicated, from himself to Arthur Lee, making it appear that the latter gave advance notice of the treaty to Lord Shelburne for the purpose of stock jobbing. And it is to be regretted that he led Jones so far by the nose as to adopt the rôle of a misguided peacemaker, who in writing to Livingston strangled the evidence at its source: "Doctor Bancroft has actually received letters from America which inform him that your certificate was the only thing that appeared in America against him. As this was in your opinion very doubtful, and as you thought proper to communicate the subject of your dispute to me, I think it a duty which I owe to your confidence to set you thus far right, and I wish it were in my power to remove every misunderstanding that may unhappily exist between any of the subjects of the United States."[22]

The initial factor in disarming Jones' suspicions was of course the office of Bancroft as a confidential secretary of Franklin, who as his employer was in the last analysis most responsible. The Captain was undoubtedly impressed, too, like many others, by the intelligence and ostensible patriotism of the writings of the spy, who in addition to his more pretentious works was the author of articles and pamphlets in defense of the American cause. He may have felt also the attractions of Bancroft's personality; his smile, according to Mrs. John Adams, who had no mean powers as a physiognomist to supplement her woman's intuition, was of "vast advantage to his features, enlightening them and dispelling the scowl that appeared upon his brow." Certainly Jones, and another very much like him, Lafayette, came to feel almost a brotherly regard for Bancroft—during this period. Jones was undoubtedly drawn to him most of all as a substitute for correspondence with Franklin and as a means for eliciting information in regard to British merchant fleets and ships of war.

For all the genius of Bancroft in double-dealing, scarcely any American or Frenchman was as sharply on his guard against spies, and probably curbed as much the operations of this particular spy, as Jones. Naturally he was somewhat blinded, along with Deane and Franklin, Lafayette and Vergennes, by the British intelligence which Bancroft furnished to the Americans as a cloak for the American secrets which the agent conveyed to the Britons. Yet from the time when the Captain complained shortly after arrival in Europe that his strategic plans with the *Ranger* off Quiberon Bay were "in every broker's mouth," his experience as well as his instinct for secrecy induced him more and more to breathe no unnecessary words concerning his enterprises. Only Arthur and William Lee, who in their habits of suspicion attacked almost everyone and so singled out Bancroft, bear comparison with him for wariness against the enemy. Notwithstanding the readiness of Franklin to supply the liberals in England with such information of American affairs as suited his purpose, it is to the credit of the Lees that William, for instance, wrote of him to Richard Henry as "perpetually surrounded by persons to whom his papers are exposed . . . and whom everybody but himself takes to be spies of our enemies."[23] But, ironically, Arthur Lee was not careful enough during his residence in Berlin to escape the purloining of official letters by the British Minister Elliot; he employed for a period as his secretary the spy Major Thornton who had posed as a compassionate friend of American prisoners in England; and he was from time to time the dupe of other enemy agents.

Offset against this background of espionage, Jones bent every effort, as the equipment for the *Bonhomme Richard* continued apace, to observe the strictest secrecy for his cruise. If persons besides Bancroft, and indeed if even Bancroft, learned of some of his objectives, the fault was scarcely his own. He gave every man his ear but few his voice. When he persisted in his purpose to restore the silver plate, feeling himself "above the idea of receiving any profit from such a pillage" despite Franklin's advice to trouble himself no further, his guardedness against Alexander, who had corresponded with Selkirk, testified to his awareness of danger. Whether or not Alexander tried to serve Britain as well as the earl, the circumspection which Jones both expressed and exercised was characteristic: "He has frequently, by appearing to disclose his own plans in some measure, endeavored to fish out mine . . . this I know, that let them place around me as many spies as they please, as I have no confidants near me, and as I do not keep my intentions by me in writing, they cannot betray my counsel; I may yet appear in a quarter of the globe which they little imagine."[24] In fact, what with spying by the enemy on the one hand and with indiscretion, bad faith, and jealousy of some supposed friends and allies on the other, he already had need of every precaution and resource to prevent the cruise of the *Bonhomme Richard* from ending in disaster.

Before the shadows of Landais and De Chaumont were to lengthen across Jones' enterprise, Lafayette, chafing for brilliant action in Europe comparable with his earlier service in America, cast a gleam of promise upon it. Knowing firsthand, too, the acute financial needs of Washington with his army and learning newly from Franklin the stringent lack of essential funds, the adopted American patriot entertained the prospect of making a bold descent upon England and possibly of exacting a heavy ransom. Franklin, the military as well as diplomatic strategist, strengthened if he did not implant the purpose in his mind: "It is certain that the coasts of England and Scotland are extremely open and defenceless; there are also many rich towns near the sea, which four or five thousand men, landing unexpectedly might easily surprise and destroy, or exact from them a heavy contribution. . . ." He named, among others, Bristol, Bath, Whitehaven, and Liverpool, and suggested a coöperative enterprise under a sailor along with a soldier: "Much will depend on a prudent and brave sea commànder who knows the coasts and on a leader of the troops who has the affair at heart. . . . On the whole it may be encouraging to reflect on the many instances of history which prove that in war attempts thought to be impossible do often for that reason become possible and practicable because nobody expects them. . . ."[25] Naturally both

Franklin and Lafayette thought at once of Jones as precisely fitted by his record and his present plans to be the sea commander with whom to execute the undertaking, similar to the raids by the commandos of the present World War.

The Captain received a sudden summons to Passy. There the proposition of an enlarged enterprise in conjunction with Lafayette had his hearty approval. The addition of the *Alliance* under Landais to his squadron was also under immediate consideration. He had allowed himself little time to take breath in coming, and he now allowed himself even less in leaving to act upon the plans so far as they had been concerted.

"The Marquis de La Fayette will be with you soon," Franklin assured him on April 27, 1779, shortly after his return to L'Orient. "It has been observed that joined expeditions of land and sea forces often miscarry through jealousies and misunderstandings between the officers of the different corps. This must happen where there are little minds, actuated more by personal views of profit or honor to themselves than by the warm and sincere desire of good to their country. Knowing you both as I do, and your just manner of thinking on these occasions, I am confident nothing of the kind can happen between you. . . . I look upon this expedition as an introduction only to greater trusts and more extensive commands.

"As this is understood to be an American expedition, under the Congress commission and colors, the Marquis, who is a major general in that service, has of course the step in rank, and he must have command of the land forces, which are committed by the King to his care; but the command of the ships will be entirely in you, in which I am persuaded that whatever authority his rank might in strictness give him, he will not have the least desire to interfere with you. There is honor enough to be got for both of you if the expedition is conducted with a prudent unanimity."[26]

Every likelihood pointed to harmony between Jones and Lafayette because their intrepidity as men and their principles as patriots were almost identical. "The love of the public cause," Lafayette wrote his fellow officer on the same day that Franklin tactfully urged coöperation between them, "made me happy to take it [this command]; and as this motive is the only one which conducts all my private and public actions, I am sure I'll find in you the same zeal, and we shall do as much, and more than any others would perform in the same situation. Be certain, my dear sir, that I'll be happy to divide with you whatever share of glory may await us, and that my esteem and affection for you is truly felt and will last forever."

At once Jones replied to these welcome missives. To his younger brother in arms he expressed himself with a faithfulness and humility that might have been due an older: "So flattering and affectionate a proof of your esteem and friendship has made an impression on my mind that will attend me while I live. This I hope to prove by more than words. Where men of fine feelings are concerned, there is seldom misunderstanding; and I am sure I should do violence to my sensibility if I were capable of giving you a moment's pain by any part of my conduct. Therefore, without any apology, I shall expect you to point out my errors when we are together alone with perfect freedom, and I think I dare promise you your reproof shall not be lost."

To his astute venerable counselor at Passy, he conveyed even more deeply-stirred feelings: "Your liberal and noble-minded instructions would make a coward brave. You have called up every sentiment of public virtue in my breast, and it shall be my pride and ambition, in strict pursuit of your instructions, to deserve success.

"Be assured that very few prospects could afford me so true a satisfaction as that of rendering some acceptable service to the common cause, and at the same time relieving from captivity (by furnishing the means of exchange) our unfortunate fellow subjects from the hands of the enemy."[27] This present solicitude for American prisoners indicated that the Captain who had succored many during his command of the *Alfred* and of the *Ranger* would not be less their champion during his command of the *Bonhomme Richard*.

After having waited ten months for a ship and passed several additional months without effective coöperation in providing her with cannon, seamen, and supplies, Jones' hopes rose and his devotedness deepened. Yet almost at once new impediments, some obvious and others hidden, some immediate and others in abeyance, began to develop. In one notable instance Lafayette interceded in his behalf with the speed of youth and genius and with the influence of wealth and name. He sought to remove the official obstructions and delays in providing dependable armament for the *Richard*. He discovered that De Chaumont not only was involved in equipping the ship but also was aware through De Sartine of some of the secret plans which Jones had framed with Garnier. De Chaumont had become, therefore, "a half confidant, the most dangerous of all things because it gives information without binding to secrecy." As Lafayette fully recognized the need of breathing no unnecessary words concerning details of the enterprise, his premonition told him that they might come to the notice of the enemy through an indiscretion of De Chaumont. So he unhesitatingly unfolded the dangerous situation in an appeal to Vergennes.

Whatever difficulties threatened from the direction of De Chaumont, others loomed from the direction of Landais. It had been intended to have the *Alliance* return shortly to America with a convoy under her protection and John Adams as a passenger. But after consideration, Franklin sent Landais instructions to proceed from Nantes where the *Alliance* then was to L'Orient where the *Bonhomme Richard* squadron was being outfitted. A number of factors led to this decision: a French frigate which was soon to sail would afford accommodations for Adams, most of the merchantmen had already weighed anchor, De Sartine expressed the wish to have the *Alliance* join the *Richard,* Franklin believed her speed would aid in taking prizes and capturing prisoners for exchange, and Jones himself thought she might strengthen his hand.

In further orders to Landais, significantly, perhaps, after the earlier ones to sail to L'Orient when no mention of Jones had appeared, the Minister stated expressly: "You are to join Captain Jones, put yourself under his command as your senior officer, proceed with him on the cruise he is about to make, and obey his orders until your return to France."[28] As Landais was prone to misinterpret Franklin to suit his own purposes, building his guile upon an infirm understanding of English, it was well that these terms were specific. In following these orders at least, he brought the *Alliance* in due time to L'Orient.

Now from a third direction, the one which had been especially

promising in contrast with the two others which remained ominous, came an unhappy message. On the eve that Jones expected
Lafayette from Paris, he learned that his fellow patriot was not to
undertake the cruise with him. Political and military reasons, it
seemed, determined the change in plans. Spain had entered into a
new alliance with France, declared war against England, and was
to join her ally in a projected "grand invasion" with sea and land
forces. Although Lafayette now received orders for service under
the King, he was undoubtedly the more disposed to comply because of prospects for action on a large scale in making a descent
with troops on the English coast. And the King and Court could
not have been averse to the opportunity to divert the somewhat
unamenable young nobleman from the enterprise with Jones in
view of its audacious and unprecedented indications.

Lafayette himself informed Jones that he was to take command
of the King's regiment at Jaints—a commission which appears
prosaic for a soldier of his temperament and was clearly to serve
just an immediate purpose. He also assured him: "Nothing could
please me more than the pleasure of having again something of
the kind to undertake with such an officer as Captain Jones. That
occasion I shall ever wish for, and I will, I hope, find it before the
end of this war." Whatever comfort lay in these words of personal
and professional fidelity, the unexpected severance of Lafayette's
coöperation was a keen disappointment to the Captain at L'Orient.

Lafayette now, like Garnier earlier, was lost to him. De Sartine's
support had depended principally upon theirs. Even Franklin
came to interest himself less upon the withdrawal of these men
and upon his recognition that France and Frenchmen bore the
expense of the ships and armament. All of them receded into the
background. Franklin, to whom Jones had opened his heart, and
Lafayette, of whom he had made a particular exception in gladly
adopting the plan of a joint command, now left him to face his
obstacles essentially alone. With the passing of Lafayette's support,
passed also the project of laying under contribution Liverpool, the
second city of England; with the fading of other special assistance,
faded likewise a project "even more important." But whatever his
means might be, Jones set his will to give a memorable account of
himself singlehanded.

◇◇

Chapter XXVII

Preparation of the Squadron; De Chaumont and Landais

JONES BECAME in a sense even less than singlehanded in view of the part that De Chaumont and Landais began to assume as the scene of preparations now changed in the main from Passy and Versailles, at which the policy and equipment of the squadron were determined, to L'Orient and other ports, at which the plans were being put into effect. The men supposed to coöperate with him had their counterpart in his ships. And if the armament, as well as the *Bonhomme Richard* herself and the other vessels of the squadron, was not exactly a gift horse, some resemblances seemed marked. The unavailing travels which Jones made in trying to procure suitable cannon, not to consider the limitations in the way of enlisting a dependable crew, were of a piece with the ships supposedly under his command and with his commissary and his officer next in rank.

The problem to equip the *Richard* with dependable cannon involved special difficulties. Whether none of the proper calibre were quickly available in the King's arsenals or they were reserved exclusively for the King's own ships, Jones at first had to look elsewhere. His initial purpose was to mount only one large battery of eighteen-pounders as the most fitting and formidable armament for his vessel. Although he hastened from one town to another, among which were Nantes, Bordeaux, and Angoulême as well as L'Orient, to find guns which might reasonably serve, all his efforts were unavailing. The pressure upon him to accept discarded, nondescript cannon was strong. "I think you are extremely right," Lafayette had agreed with him when their joint enterprise had been contemplated, "in refusing such guns as would expose your reputation, the lives of your men, and even the honor of your flag. . . ." Finally Jones succeeded in arranging to have them cast at the King's foundries at Angoulême, and urged the greatest despatch. But the pace of the manufacturers was as slow as that of Jones in his preparations of the *Richard* was speedy, so that the prospect of new guns gave place to the compromise of accepting a battery of twenty-eight secondhand, indifferent twelve-pounders for the main deck, six old-fashioned long eighteen-pounders for the lower gun-deck in which the number of ports cut made it possible to fire all of them on either side, and eight nine-pounders for the quarter-deck, forecastle, and gangways.[1] On the basis of later accounts, however, there were not these forty-two but only forty guns.[2] Upon De Chaumont as the deputy of De Sartine depended the means at the disposal of Jones, and he exercised his authority to no better advantage than to compel the Captain in the limited time available to resort to such inferior, nondescript cannon.

The selection of capable seamen and qualified officers was even more important than the guns and occasioned greater obstacles. It was not permitted to enroll sailors from the French marine for the *Richard*. Jones was limited, therefore, to such American volunteers as he could enlist and to such seamen and civilians of other nationalities as he might discover suitable for his purpose. He found himself compelled to search the ports for sailors not less than for cannon. On March 6 he reported to Franklin that thirty-three seamen from Brest had just joined him, that "volunteers for soldiers enlisted daily to serve for three years or during the war," and that he hoped "soon to have a full set of brave and deserving men for officers."

His hopes, however, as had happened before, were more sanguine than his prospects warranted. The Americans whom he was able to find as late as the close of March were chiefly a few straggling escaped prisoners from England. No cartel of American seamen had arrived in exchange for British prisoners in France, notably those whom Jones had taken in the *Drake,* regardless of many protests from Franklin and many assurances in turn from

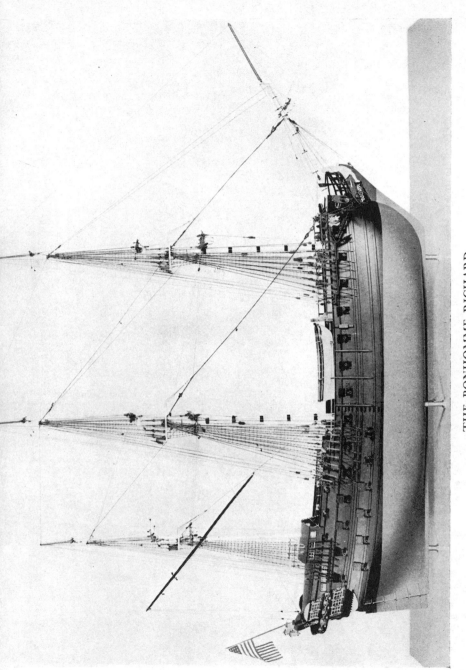

THE BONHOMME RICHARD

Scale model recently acquired by the Naval Academy Museum. Royal yards with sails could be sent aloft when required. The ship was also equipped to carry studding sails.

authorities in England. The American Minister stated plainly on March 21, 1779 to Hartley his English correspondent: "It is now evident that the delays have been of design to give more opportunity of reducing the men by promises and hardships to seek their liberty in engaging against their country."[3] He added, probably not without thought of the enemy's prison ships off New York, that the lot of the British prisoners in a small vessel in the road of Brest was unfortunately not free from severe suffering. His remonstrance seems finally to have been effective, for the first cartel of Americans came to French shores in April. On the eleventh of this month Jones directed Amiel, who was still with him, to join Matthew Mease, his newly-engaged purser, to enlist available Americans at Paimbœuf and to bring them to L'Orient. In urgent need of sailors as he was, the Captain disingenuously expressed the hope that the number to enroll would be the greater upon learning that he was about to sail for America. That he made some misstatements of this kind one of his midshipmen Nathaniel Fanning also later attested. Despite such misrepresentation, he did not engage above a maximum of thirty men.

Another source for seamen was likewise not very fruitful. Although necessity caused him to resort to raw French peasants, to English prisoners prone to mutiny, and to mere boys, he sought to choose with due discrimination. As to the lack of such care on the part of one of his officers, he remonstrated: "Mr. Thompson has a day or two ago sent a set of dirty beings here escorted by two French officers at a very great expense. Two-thirds of the creatures who came as American volunteers were rejected as unfit for anything . . . the rest were English prisoners whose names I actually blotted out of the list before his face and expressly forbade him to forward because they had . . . in my absence . . . enlisted to serve in a privateer."[4] As for English volunteers, whatever the apparent faithfulness of their pledge, he later explained to De Sartine: "I did not at the beginning advise it as a prudent measure to take on board so great a proportion of English seamen. But M. de Chaumont can inform you that *he* thought it expedient, and that it would be attended with no risk, after the embarkation of the troops under the orders of the Marquis de la Fayette. When that expedition was laid aside, and I was forbidden to enlist French seamen, I had no means to replace the English, and they remained on board from necessity, not from choice."

In addition to a small company of Americans, he had at the end of April a miscellaneous group of volunteers of many nationalities. "The crew," he averred, "was so ungovernable that I found the sole expedient by which I could control them was to divide them into two parties and to place one knave under the eye and guard of the other."[5]

His choice of officers was equally circumscribed by the small number available, although his standards of loyalty and efficiency were not only high but even severe. He may have had just grounds for dislike of Musco Livingston, his informer concerning Bancroft, possibly because the lieutenant had left a ship on the score of impaired health; but certainly his attitude, however ambitious, appears aloof toward him: "I have not yet made out any arrangement of officers . . . it will perhaps be difficult for me to please everyone, as everyone seems to want to be *first*. . . . I mean to give a preference to seniority except where merit or abilities determine me otherwise . . . I do not choose to order or even to invite any man to put himself under my command. I wish for none but volunteers who with all their hearts are determined to go with me anywhere and everywhere in pursuit of honor, and who having the happiness to bear commissions under the flag of freedom are far too proud to consider themselves as *servants by the year* or merely as sons of interest. . . ."[6] Livingston apparently had made conditions to which Jones was not receptive, and his name was not to appear upon the rolls of the *Bonhomme Richard*.

The Captain's standards caused him, for example, to reprimand Amiel, whom he accused of trifling with "the rules of order and discipline which Congress have established . . . and given me power and authority to put into execution."[7] Such views likewise must have prompted Jones first to accept Richard Dale as his master's mate and later to assign him as first lieutenant—Dale who had gone to sea like himself at twelve, had been twice in English prisons and had twice escaped, and had served on several ships of war including the *Lexington,* one of Lambert Wickes' adventurous squadron of three. The zeal and faithfulness of Dale must have more than compensated for his bad spelling at this period when

The DELEGATES of the UNITED STATES of New-Hampshire, Massachusetts-Bay, Rhode-Island, Connecticut, New-York, New-Jersey, Pennsylvania, Delaware, Maryland, Virginia, North-Carolina, South-Carolina, and Georgia, TO

Richard Dale Gentleman.

WE, repofing efpecial Truft and Confidence in your Patriotifm, Valour, Conduct and Fidelity, DO, by thefe Prefents, conftitute and appoint you to be *Lieutenant in the Navy* ———————— of the United States of North-America, fitted out for the Defence of American Liberty, and for repelling every hoftile Invafion thereof. You are therefore carefully and diligently to difcharge the Duty of *Lieutenant* by doing and performing all manner of Things thereunto belonging. And we do ftrictly charge and require all Officers, Marines and Seamen under your Command, to be obedient to your Orders as *Lieutenant.* - - And you are to obferve and follow fuch Orders and Directions from Time to Time, as you fhall receive from this or a future Congrefs of the United States, or Committee of Congrefs for that Purpofe appointed, or Commander in Chief for the Time being of the Navy of the United States, or any other your fuperior Officer, according to the Rules and Difcipline of War, the Ufage of the Sea, and the Inftructions herewith given you, in Purfuance of the Truft repofed in you. This Commiffion to continue in Force until revoked by this or a future Congrefs.

DATED at *Pafsy in France the 10th day of June 1779.*

By Order of the CONGRESS,

Jolin Hancock

PRESIDENT.

ATTEST. *Cha Thompson*

RICHARD DALE'S COMMISSION AS LIEUTENANT, JUNE 10, 1779

On the same form as Jones' Commission and probably signed in blank and forwarded to Benjamin Franklin at Paris to fill in. Courtesy of Edward C. Dale, who owns the original.

Jones sent him to Brest to assume charge of a small vessel and to sail "with all possible dispatch to L'Orient." His eloquent reply from Brest, however untutored, was expressive of his worth as the first officer of the *Bonhomme Richard:* "Sir: I shall make all haste imaginable to git everything ready to com round, I should have been every glad to had things in radiness to com round amidiatly but as they was not I hope you will not think hard of me for it would give me a great deal of satisfaction to pleas you if lay in my power—Humble servant, Richard Dale."[8]

The spirit of Dale, radiating from the personality of Jones, had its parallel, however variant in kind and degree, in the spirit of the *Bonhomme Richard's* marines. Although heterogeneous with the exception of a body of Frenchmen and free as most of them were from any ties with America, they developed unusual morale and prepared to serve in a special stratagem. At this juncture, Adams, for instance, who was waiting at L'Orient to sail for America, described both them and the commander: "Walked out to see Jones' marines, dressed in the English uniform, red and white; a number of very active and clever sergeants and corporals are employed to teach them the exercise, and manœuvres, and marches, etc. . . . This is the most ambitious and intriguing officer in the American Navy. Jones has art and secrecy, and aspires very high. You see the character of the man in his uniform, and that of his officers and marines, variant from the uniforms established by Congress—golden buttonholes for himself, two epaulettes—marines in red and white, instead of green. Eccentricities and irregularities are to be expected from him. They are in his character, they are visible in his eyes. His voice is soft and still and small; his eye has keenness and wildness and softness in it."[9] Little as Adams liked Jones, his judgment was sharp in gauging both the Captain and his contemplated exploits amid the haste in outfitting the *Richard.*

The *Alliance,* new and trim, riding at anchor near the old and reconstructed *Bonhomme Richard* with her antiquated high poop, fittingly had an effective armament of thirty-six twelve- and nine-pounders, but she presented a contrast very much less in her favor as to crew and Captain. She had few marines, whether in English or American uniform, who were in training for a special enterprise. She lacked them, to all appearances, not only because her

Captain failed to possess Jones' initiative but also because, as Lafayette had stated, there was fear of "disputes between the land officers and Landais." Otherwise, apart from a greater number of Americans and Frenchmen—her English mutineers had largely been removed—the sailors of the *Alliance* did not differ materially from those of the *Richard*. But second-rate as were the officers, Dale excepted, available for Jones, they were not in a state of constant disagreement with their commander as were those of the *Alliance* with Landais. "I am sorry for and ashamed of the dissensions on board the *Alliance*," Franklin admitted to Jones. At this stage of the embroilments, Landais sought the intercession of his senior Captain in these terms of his limited English: "I persist beging of you for a court of inquiry or a court martial as you will think proper for to juges between my officers, viz. (the three lieutenants of the ship, the Captain of Marines, and the master of the ship) and me." Only a few days later two of the officers aboard the *Alliance* informed Franklin with finality that they were obliged to resign their positions because of the manner in which Landais exercised his command of the ship, although Jones had tried in vain to influence him to act reasonably.

Jones asked for information and advice from Adams, who still had his quarters aboard the *Alliance*, assuring him that he was determined to preserve order and discipline where he commanded, but wished to reprove with moderation and never to punish while there remained a good alternative. It is still to be seen how Landais repaid his forbearance. Adams, who was disposed to favor Landais in view of his bond with the Lees and Samuel Adams, chiefly responsible for the Frenchman's appointment,[10] and perhaps also in view of his objection to Franklin's orders that the *Alliance* should not return directly to America, confided less to Jones than to his diary. "Landais," he wrote, "is jealous of everything, jealous of everybody, of all his officers, all his passengers; he knows not how to treat his officers, nor his passengers, nor anybody else. Silence, reserve, and a forbidding air will never gain . . . our Americans. There is in this man an inactivity and an indecision that will ruin him; he is bewildered—an absent bewildered man, an embarrassed mind. . . ."[11] In this portrait of Landais as well as the earlier one of Jones, Adams painted with an unwilling but honest hand; and it remains, in the words of Hamlet, to look here upon this picture and on this.

In addition to the *Alliance,* three smaller French vessels under American commissions were to form a part of Jones' little squadron led by the *Bonhomme Richard,* as planned in the middle of May when Lafayette had still expected to command the land forces. They also rode at anchor in the harbor of L'Orient: the *Pallas* a war-converted merchantman of thirty to thirty-two guns under Captain Cottineau, the *Cerf* a cutter of eighteen guns under Captain Varage, and the *Vengeance* a tender of twelve guns under Captain Ricot.[12] Of the three, only the *Cerf* was efficient and fast. Their equipment, including alterations to quarter soldiers, had continued day and night for several weeks in anticipation of Lafayette's arrival, particularly to have them serve, along with the *Richard,* in part as transports for the Marquis and his four or five hundred troops. Notwithstanding the absence of the military force as well as its commander, the ships remained at L'Orient awaiting only the final plans to be completed by Jones in concert with the French authorities and Franklin.

After Lafayette had withdrawn at the close of May, 1779, the hand of De Sartine as well as of De Chaumont became the more dominant. For a preliminary cruise, they directed Jones to employ the squadron to convoy a number of merchantmen to several French ports, to put to flight the pirate ships which operated in the Bay of Biscay, and to cruise for prizes. The commander prepared to obey his instructions with alacrity, although the service did not call for the talents which he was eager to exercise and the fertile plans which he had spun in his brain, particularly at this time when Count d'Orvilliers was soon to be in the English Channel with a combined French and Spanish fleet of sixty-six ships and his own enterprise, therefore, promised to be the more opportune. Yet his own cruise could remain in abeyance for a short period. What became ominous were the manner and substance of his instructions from De Chaumont, apparently supported by De Sartine.

An early indication occurred when De Chaumont recommended that Franklin should go to L'Orient to remove the contentions among the officers of the *Alliance* and the *Bonhomme Richard;* as for himself, he was "tired enough of trying to reconcile these Americans and supply their numerous wants." When the time approached for sailing, he addressed Jones on June 10, 1779 in a series of formal instructions such as: "M. de Chaumont informs . . . Mr. Jones that he will have papers to sign before his departure for the sundry articles which the King has furnished to his ship; therefore M. de Chaumont earnestly entreats Mr. Jones not to neglect it, considering the immense expense which the vessels in the port have occasioned to the King."[13] The outlay was the heavier because Lafayette and his troops had been expected; yet Jones complained that De Chaumont had refused even to supply manacles for the prisoners he might take. Notwithstanding the disbursements, very considerable as they may have been, which the King had agreed to defray, these orders from De Chaumont were only the introduction to others more stringent.

At this hour, the irony of Jones' intimate friendship with Madame de Chaumont, offset by his wavering distrust of her husband, almost reached its height. He expressed the greater warmth for her just as his relations with him were to assume positive coldness and hostility. He was gallant, he hungered as a sailor for affection and as a patriot for understanding, he was about to embark and felt a duty to bid farewell, he may have reasoned mistakenly again that she would advance his professional objects. Thus he wrote her on June 13, 1779 in a strain somewhat enigmatically both reserved and free: "Although my pen has hitherto been silent, yet my thoughts have done ample justice to the affectionate friendship of Madame de Chaumont. . . . As I have been so long under involuntary silence, you have a just right to expect me to say something that can make atonement in this letter, and I ardently wish not to disappoint you. I feel, however, that I never had more to say, nor less power to express myself. . . . To support the cause of human nature, I sacrifice all the soft emotions of the heart, at a time too when love is my duty. But my soul's supreme ambition is to merit the partial praises of my friends, which I have not yet done by my services. . . ."[14] To the mature married Frenchwoman the missive must have been pleasing but naïve; to her husband who must have known the attitude which the letter reflected, if he did not see the letter itself, his French subtlety not improbably made him feel uneasiness and even danger in the Captain's bold naïveté.

De Chaumont, moreover, remained a business man of a particular stamp. There was nothing in De Sartine's past behavior towards Jones to justify believing that he was averse to a strict commercial basis for the squadron upon his choice of De Chaumont to fulfill his ill-defined office as intermediary of the Court, commissary, or speculator in privateers. When the letter from Jones to Madame de Chaumont was still in transit, another of June 14 was on its way from her husband to Jones which suddenly revealed him to the Captain in a part altogether unfriendly and unauthorized: "The situation of the officers who have accepted commissions from Congress to join the armament of the ship *Bonhomme Richard,* which you command, may be in contradiction with the interests of their own ships; this induces me to request you to enter into an engagement with me that you shall not require from the said vessels any services but such as will be conformable with the orders which those officers shall have, that in no case you shall require any changes to be made in the formation of their crews, which, as well as the vessels themselves and their armaments, shall be entirely at the disposition of the commandants of the said vessels, who shall be answerable to those who have armed them. I also beg you to agree that all the prizes which shall be made be addressed to such consignees as I shall point out for the preservation of the interests of all concerned."[15]

Was Jones to be in command of the squadron only in name? Were the ships to sail not under the sovereignty of America but of France or even of a French individual as privateers? Were the American regulations concerning prizes taken under the American flag to be displaced in favor of the special orders of De Chaumont, who was an agent or merely a commissary designated by the French Minister of Marine? These were some of the questions which chafed the commander of the *Bonhomme Richard,* who had suffered ten long months before the flattering promises of the French Court had materialized to the extent of his receiving a thirteen-year-old merchantman to be converted into a ship of war and who now, after four additional months of feverish preparation, saw his authority over the nondescript little squadron completely compromised. He had persevered so far, and he determined to persevere further—his object was not to wrangle with De Chaumont as it had been not to quarrel with others, but to fight for America.

◇◇

Chapter XXVIII

The Preliminary Cruise;
Further Preparations;
the Concordat

SUSTAINED BY his desperate resolution in the face of progressively limited means and authority, Jones sailed from Groix off L'Orient on June 19, 1779 with the *Bonhomme Richard* and the four accompanying vessels to fulfill his preliminary diverse missions. Almost at once Landais gave token of insubordinate behavior among some of the Captains, which De Chaumont's instructions had already encouraged. A pretext for controversy instead of an occasion for coöperation occurred at midnight of the first day at sea when the *Richard* collided with the *Alliance*. "Just as the starboard watch was going on deck . . . and we were lying with our topsails back to the masts," according to a sailor aboard the latter ship, "Captain Jones came down before the wind and ran us down upon our starboard quarter, carrying away our mizzenmast and doing us much damage and himself more by springing his bowsprit, carrying away his head and cutwater; but fortunately no one was killed on board either of the ships."[1]

At the time of the accident Jones was in his cabin so that he had no direct connection with it. Landais, however, came on deck of the *Alliance* while the collision impended, and saw the *Bonhomme Richard* approaching and heard shouts from her bowsprit and forecastle, which he fearfully interpreted not as a warning but as a mutiny of her British sailors. He then ran below in search of his pistols for self-protection. If not in error at failing immediately to do what he could to avoid or lessen the consequent damages of the impending collision despite the absence of signals from the flagship when the *Richard's* watch officer certainly was remiss in station-keeping, Landais had shown himself irresponsible as well as cowardly by abandoning his command at the moment of peril and decision.

Later, by sentence of a court-martial at L'Orient, Robert Robinson, the first lieutenant of the *Richard,* who had been in charge of her watch when the accident occurred, was adjudged "guilty of negligence of duty." The court, which Jones had called for the trial of Robinson and which he reprimanded for the comparative mildness of its sentence upon his own lieutenant, cast a gratuitous reflection upon the Captain himself for entrusting a watch to an officer whom it described as unworthy of such confidence. Jones, in turn, severely informed the members of the court, who favored Landais, of the express purpose for which he had convened them and of his complete readiness, if warrantable, to submit his own conduct to public inquiry.

In the meantime the squadron proceeded without further mishap to complete effectively the services on which the ships had entered; but Jones suffered another disappointment which had even more serious implications to him than the collision. The *Bonhomme Richard* was conspicuously slow. His first experience of her poor sailing qualities occurred on the return passage when three ships of war appeared to windward. "They bore down in a line abreast for some time; but seeing we were prepared to receive them, they hauled their wind, and by carrying a press of sail got clear, in spite of our utmost endeavors to bring them to action."[2]

The second occasion of her slowness occurred under more discouraging circumstances. The *Bonhomme Richard* was alone; she had given her consorts a rendezvous but had failed to find them. Two British ships of war appeared in the offing and bore down. "Hove about and stood from them," recorded the log book, "to get in readiness for action; then hove mizzen-topsail to the mast, down all staysails and up mizzen sail. Then they hove about and stood from us. Immediately we tacked ship and stood after them.

"After which they wore ship and stood for us. Captain Jones, *gentleman-like,* called all his officers and consulted them, whether they were willing to see them. They all said 'Yes.' Made sail after them, but they being better sailers than we, got from us. At 1 a.m. tacked ship."

Presumably the clerk's term *gentleman-like* was sincere and not intended as flattery for the eyes of the Captain. Apart from this entry, the martial spirit of his officers and also of his crew pleased Jones; but as for his ship, he himself related that the enemy "fled with precipitation and to my mortification outsailed the *Bon Homme Richard* and got clear."[3] Repeatedly, from the time that de Sartine had made proffers of vessels to him in a descending scale of little to less, Jones had vowed that he would accept nothing that sailed slow. The *Bonhomme Richard* now had revealed herself as the slowest ship of the squadron, not excepting the *Pallas,* which was a decidedly poor sailer.

Jones had scarcely returned to L'Orient to consider such improvements in the trim of his ship as might be possible and to ascertain exactly and repair the damage of the recent collision to Landais' as well as his own command, before he received further instructions from De Chaumont which provided for an almost revolutionary change in the plans of his delayed expedition. They referred chiefly to cruising after privateers and merchantmen, emphasizing characteristically the commercial purposes of De Chaumont as contrasted with the military objectives of Jones. They also directed him in detail to send prizes to certain ports at which De Chaumont had business correspondents, regardless of expediencies of war and of American naval laws. They rigidly limited the period of the expedition to August 15, 1779. But in designating that the cruise should end at the Texel in Holland, they served a justifiable diplomatic purpose, however dangerous this port might prove for the squadron. At the instigation of De Chaumont, the orders had, too, the signature of Franklin. "As the Court is at the chief expense," the Doctor stated, "I think they have the best right to direct."[4]

On grounds of both truth and expediency, Jones did not submit with tameness. Regardless of what Franklin may have thought, these and other orders were inconsistent with the terms by which the King had placed the *Bonhomme Richard* under his command according to the express statements on February 4 of De Sartine, his Minister: "You will set sail without waiting for ulterior orders;

and you will determine yourself the course you are to take." They were inconsistent also with the spirit of his authorization from the same source "to hoist the flag of the United States."[5] They contradicted the American marine regulations for prizes, notwithstanding the American Minister's acquiescence to De Chaumont's representations that the King wished them to be at his disposition. "By this order contrary to the laws of the American flag," as Jones did not fear to explain, "Mr. Franklin trespassed beyond the limits of the authority which Congress had delegated to him."[6]

The orders were also unwise because Jones the naval officer knew better than De Chaumont the businessman and Franklin the diplomat the services for which the squadron, especially the *Bonhomme Richard,* was best fitted. That his ship was slow stared him in the face. At the same time that De Chaumont stressed the purpose of capturing privateers, Jones sorrowfully explained to Franklin: "I cannot help observing that our ships are very unfit to cruise after privateers. We can get sight of them it is true, but that is all, for we are unable to overtake them."[7] The ships, furthermore, had been renovated and equipped according to earlier plans to serve especially for the transport of troops intended for a coast invasion. Consequently the trim of the *Richard* in particular was the poorer. Jones had retained her upper deck and her high poop and bulwarks, had built a roundhouse at the foot of the mizzenmast, and in the absence of one open battery of thirty eighteen-pounders, originally planned, had resorted to guns of variant size on her two covered and her upper decks. Expediency as well as good faith dictated that Jones should be permitted to use his untrammeled judgment.

The entire success of the expedition, in fact, after the King had bestowed the *Bonhomme Richard* hinged upon such a course. Garnier had given Jones *carte blanche* as consistent with the conditions transmitted by De Sartine from the King. Lafayette had elected to accompany him in conformity with a special understanding of harmoniously sharing this freedom between them. And Franklin had been the intermediary who had promoted such independent discretionary powers on their part and confirmed them by the tenor of his recommendations. Franklin indeed, with express reference to an incursion from the ships, had stirred Jones' enthusiasm the more by urging the capture of prisoners for redemption of Americans. He also counseled moderation towards British captives on the part of the Captain's own men "lest the more than barbarous usage by the English in many places towards the Americans should occasion a retaliation and imitation of what ought rather to be detested and avoided for the sake of humanity and for the honor of our country." Finally he cautioned Jones to exercise his own generous feelings in demanding ransoms "although the English have wantonly burnt many defenseless towns in America."[8]

These instructions from Franklin, regardless of the subsequent withdrawal of the Marquis and his troops, were strangely unlike those from De Chaumont which he had later approved. And it is to be noted that the American Minister was not averse to putting his best foot forward when he later received a letter from Congress by James Lovell in behalf of the Committee of Foreign Affairs in which it was urged: "Will no one under a commission from the United States retaliate on the coasts of England for the burning of our beautiful Fairfield?" He replied in agreement, "The late provocations by the burning of Fairfield and other towns, added to the preceding, have at length demolished all my moderation, and were such another expedition (as that of Jones) to be concerted, I think so much of that disposition would not appear in the instructions." He also enclosed the orders given when Lafayette had planned his part in the expedition; but it is not apparent that Franklin likewise sent the other orders which contradicted them in effect and had been calculated to tie Jones' hands.

Chaumont, and probably De Sartine behind him, to direct the

Yet the commander of the squadron was too assertive of his rights and Franklin was too reasonable and canny to permit De operations altogether to please themselves. Regardless of discouraging words from the American Minister that what was once determined in the councils could not be changed, especially because of the stress of business, Jones represented to him that his last orders would limit greater possibilities, such as "to intercept commerce of larger consequence, to make descents and alarm the enemy in the north, and to effect a considerable diversion in favor of the Count d'Orvilliers, who was in the Channel with sixty-six ships of the line and who it was expected would destroy Plymouth or Portsmouth or perhaps both of them."[9] His arguments appealed to the commercial interests of De Chaumont as well as to the strategic instincts of Franklin. Consequently the American diplomat again gave him more liberal orders, apart from the control of prizes and the stipulation that the cruise should terminate by October 1, 1779 at the Texel. He hinted, as a bait for Jones, that the purpose in entering the port in Holland was, according to his understanding, to have the Captain take command there of the long-sought *Indienne*. Presumably both he and the French authorities who prompted him knew better.

The coincident uncertain relations with De Chaumont and De Chaumont's wife were strangely brewing a new and greater conflict. Jones seemed unable to refrain from writing Madame de Chaumont, and De Chaumont seemed unable to refrain from meddling with the internal affairs of the squadron. During the repairs and the other final preparations aboard the ships, the Captain sent her a note on July 22: "I am very sorry to hear . . . that Madame de Chaumont had been unwell and *unable it is feared to mend her pen.* I cannot suppose her to have been unwilling to bestow on me the favor of a letter; and I know that leisure always attends the happy abodes of Passy."[10]

A few days later De Chaumont impressed upon De Sartine the proclivities toward mutiny of Jones' crew, notwithstanding his own previous insistence upon enlisting a large number of English prisoners. He not only criticized the commander as incapable of maintaining discipline in the *Bonhomme Richard* but also secured the French Minister's recommendation that Franklin should instruct Landais to cruise alone until October 1. At the same time he undertook a second trip himself to L'Orient with the purpose ostensibly of securing a better crew but actually, as Jones maintained and as circumstances indicated, to incite cabals and to disrupt in general his authority and plans.

Only the caution of Franklin in providing that a separate cruise of the *Alliance* should be contingent upon an enforced delay of the *Richard* and the speed of Jones in improving the personnel of his ship by the enlistment of Americans who had just arrived on French soil in a cartel of one hundred and nineteen men prevented

De Chaumont from effecting his purpose to have Landais sail separately.[11] Yet his success in this particular might have proved, as will later appear, a godsend in disguise.

Considerably before the arrival of De Chaumont, the Captain had sent to Nantes on July 28 his second and third lieutenants, Henry and Cutting Lunt, with instructions to enlist all of the released prisoners who were "able and willing to serve America." Presumably he wished to make a good bargain, if not merely to prevent imposition, by informing Gourlade & Moylan, the commercial agents who were disposed to act as brokers, that he wished to find one hundred men to serve "at a cheap rate" and that he was unable to offer more than the established regulations of Congress allowed. Simultaneously he directed Cutting Lunt to extend to the sailors the same encouragement and conditions that had been given the men enlisted from the earlier cartel and to inform them of the opportunity to "enrich themselves." Prize money rather than wages was presumably the lure.

One of the Americans from this cartel, Nathaniel Fanning who received an appointment as acting midshipman in the *Bonhomme Richard,* maintained that Jones represented to him, as he apparently had already represented to others, that the ship was preparing to sail directly for America. Fanning's assertion seems credible, although his record of experiences as a member of Jones' crews during eighteen months is alternately true and false, colored as it appears by his prejudices, vanity, and sensationalism. In this instance, Jones wanted quickly a better crew to give the lie to De Chaumont's calumnies as well as to strengthen the morale of his ship. He had, therefore, the more reason to exhibit the patience and interest in enlisting sailors which Fanning probably noted in his own case as well as in that of a shipmate: "I have seen him walk to and fro upon the quay in L'Orient for hours together with a single seaman in order to persuade him to sign the ship's articles."[12] It is not to be gainsaid, however, that the chronic difficulties in enlisting sailors and the contentiousness and avarice which governed many of them caused him on occasion to counter with cunning and even with half truths. There may well be considerable foundation for Fanning's further opinion: "His smoothness of tongue and flattery to seamen when he wanted them was persuasive, and in [this regard] he excelled every other man I ever was acquainted with." Yet, if he lied at need, he did so apparently less for himself than for America.

A moderate number of the American prisoners of this second cartel enlisted in the *Bonhomme Richard's* crew. Cutting Lunt brought most of them from Nantes to L'Orient with despatch, if not "without losing an hour" as his Captain had ordered. A fortnight earlier about one hundred and thirty seamen of Portuguese and other nationalities had arrived in port in the French *Epervier* and a second vessel, of whom a considerable proportion also joined Jones. Chiefly from this source he acquired a crew of many nationalities, including larger groups of Portuguese and Swedish sailors, and of smaller groups of others, Irish, Scotch, Norwegian, Swiss, Italian, Bengal, and Indian. The French marines under Colonel de Chamillard and Lieutenant Colonel Weibert also increased the number.

Officers, too, from the Irish regiment of marine artillery of the Comte de Walsh-Serrant were a spirited reinforcement. "Your reputation, sir," wrote Walsh-Serrant, "is such in my regiment that Mr. O'Kelly, sub-lieutenant of grenadiers, wishes to join his two comrades Messrs. Stack and McCarthy to serve under your orders. . . ."[13] Unlike volunteer officers of this type, a certain Buisson de Basseville stipulated first that he should have a commission as captain, two hundred livres in French money per month, and three months' salary in advance. In a summary reply Jones informed him that he was not the commander of a privateer, could make no bargains with individuals, and had neither the power nor inclination to recommend to Congress nor advance himself any persons except such as distinguished themselves by their courage and conduct under his command.

Thus the Captain had as his final crew approximately seventy-five Americans, of whom almost twenty-five, however, were boys; about fifty Englishmen winnowed from almost three times as many; about thirty Portuguese; and a sort of foreign legion of almost one hundred, including Irishmen and Scotchmen, who must have contributed a babel of tongues. In addition were the marines, chiefly French. "I have the satisfaction to assure Your Excellency," he then informed De Sartine in a laconic but courteous style, "that this second journey of M. de Chaumont was altogether unnecessary. . . . My crew now in this ship consists of three hundred and eighty officers, men, and boys, inclusive of one hundred and thirty-seven marine soldiers."[14] No pretext remained, incidentally, for the *Alliance* to sail alone.

Jones came to desire also an additional vessel to join his squadron to render feasible one of his secret enterprises. He planned to capture in the course of his cruise the Jamaica merchant fleet, which was to sail homeward, according to his information, protected by a ship of fifty guns and two strong frigates. Franklin seems to have assented to adding the *Monsieur,* 40 guns, and the *Granville,* 14 guns, both privateers, to his squadron, so as to insure a more suitable force against the enemy. The danger which Jones felt, nevertheless, in associating himself with such vessels was in no way counteracted by De Chaumont, who busied himself enough otherwise in the organization of the squadron. If it was not possible to change their character from privateers to government ships, at least some informal mode of control was expedient. "The commissary," according to Jones, "did not wish to consider taking from them any bond for their honorable behavior. This stand created the impression that the squadron belonged neither to Congress nor to France, but to the outfitters of the ships with whom the deputy and Dr. Franklin were associated."[15] Such suspicions upon the whole squadron as a band of privateers masquerading under the American flag and Continental commissions were not calculated to enhance the morale of the crews and their confidence in its commander.

The last and most wounding thrust which De Chaumont was to aim at Jones before the sailing of the squadron remained in reserve. It was true at least that the Captain had wanted the privateers; De Chaumont had let him have them on the worst terms. The suspicions they awakened were after all only suspicions. Now Jones had De Chaumont to thank for a direct, brazen attempt to undermine his authority and prestige. And scarcely less harmful than his own purpose as an apparent enemy were his indiscreet if not malicious intentions in making indiscriminate confidants of the Captain's secret plans.

An essential for success in strategic operations is secrecy. For

Jones whose purposes more than those of any other naval officer of his time were contingent upon surprise, boldness, and speed, secrecy almost approximated success. Not without reason he suspected that the loquacity of De Chaumont was a subtle if unexpressed basis in part for Lafayette's final determination not to undertake the cruise with him. Not without reason he objected as again and again De Chaumont communicated all he surmised as well as all he knew concerning his cruise both to the other captains of the squadron and even to persons not associated with it. His remonstrances were especially to Franklin, Lafayette, De Sartine, and—Bancroft. If Bancroft, as well as De Chaumont, caused Jones to be on tenterhooks—there is no evidence that the spy acted such a part against him at this period and little that he did so as any time—at least betrayal by the one could not have been as pervasive as by the other. Although the commander of the squadron may not have known of all the efforts to victimize him, he took practically every precaution. He had assured Franklin during his suspicions of Alexander that no word spoken or written concerning his purposes would come from him. Now at the point of departure, he informed Lafayette that, if their joint enterprise had taken place, after sailing he would have imparted to him a new plan one hour and would have executed it the next. Whatever such circumspection might avail, it could at best not wholly counteract the injury which De Chaumont's confidences, especially to the other captains, threatened to his leadership.

This obstruction was precisely a part of De Chaumont's larger purpose. His goal was to deprive Jones of his power or even to displace him. To break the discipline of the senior commander over his junior captains as well as over his other officers and his crew was the lever which this commissary chose to employ. He had already set it in position just before the preliminary cruise by his letter of June 14, which had been for Jones' eyes alone. Now he timed the operation of it on the eve of the crucial final sailing by means of his concordat,[16] which was for the eyes of all the captains and for the ears of all others among whom the influence might spread from officers to boys. His first object was to uproot subordination. And De Chaumont could not have had an accomplice more apt than Landais.

The concordat required Jones to subscribe to arbitrary restrictions and to suffer public stigma. One provision gave the separate ships independence and therefore promoted insubordination: ". . . it has been agreed that such armed vessels, whether French or American, may be associated therewith [the squadron] by common consent." A second provision gave the French agent special control over the prize money: "It has been agreed that M. le Ray de Chaumont be requested not to give up the part of the prizes coming to all the crews, and to each individual of said squadron, but to their order, and to be responsible for the same in his own and proper name." Above all, a third provision gave him the authority to superintend the prizes themselves and even to make it appear that the cruise was not under the flag of the United States but an enterprise of privateers which he personally had oufitted: "Considering the necessity there is of preserving the interests of each individual, the prizes that shall be taken shall be remitted to the orders of Monsieur Le Ray de Chaumont . . . who has furnished the expenses of the armament of the said squadron." As the commissary craftily demanded the signature of Jones on the eve of the squadron's departure from Groix, there remained no opportunity for appeal or delay. It was too late for remonstrance to Franklin, De Sartine, or possibly the King. It was inexpedient to postpone sailing in view of Jones' carefully timed plans for the interception of British merchant fleets and for coördinating his minor cruise with the major operations of the French-Spanish armada in the English Channel.

If Jones refused to sign the concordat, De Chaumont threatened that he would exercise the authority, which he maintained had been delegated to him, to dispossess the Captain from his command.[17] If Jones affixed his name, De Chaumont as well as he knew that his authority would be precarious and his self-esteem would suffer. On the one hand the Captain saw the vision of honor, for which he had slaved and sacrificed for a whole year all other considerations, including his health, in imminent danger of being shattered at its very threshold. On the other hand he recognized standing in the way of his duty to himself and to his country an enemy motivated, like many others earlier in his experience, by some of the common vices of man, and he wisely compromised so that his strength might avail in fighting for a cause worthy of him. Yet he might not have permitted the name of John Paul Jones to appear on the concordat if the moment had been less unfavorable. "At any other time and in all other circumstances," he declared, "I should have rejected these conditions with disdain; I saw the danger which I ran, but having announced in America that I had remained in Europe because the Court of France had wished me to do so in order to take command of secret expeditions, I took the resolution to expose myself to every peril."[18]

It was not a vain resolution. His motive lay in the freedom of America and in the dedication of his name to the cause of that freedom. It was his fixed purpose by his own daring choice "to go into harm's way." It became also his fixed purpose regardless of cumulative obstacles to persevere in his determination. Not to recall the tribulations of his earlier life in America, one difficulty had been only a stepping-stone to another since his arrival in Europe. In obstruction at every turn, Simpson had given place to De Sartine, and De Sartine to De Chaumont; Garnier and Lafayette had strengthened his arm only to leave it bound; even Franklin, who particularly wished him well, was more discreet than zealous in his steady endeavor not to commit himself to the disadvantage of his French connections. Jones owed to these men his present circumstances. The slow and literally rotten ship, the cast-off cannon and the desperate crew, the buccaneering privateersmen and the malicious Landais, above all the irresponsibility of the squadron to which he himself had just set the seal of his forced signature in the concordat—these manifold and fundamental weaknesses of the means at his command served as a gauge to his indomitable steadfastness of heart and mind at the approaching greatest climax of his life. Yet the spirit of one man pitted against almost all the forces of the six ships which were to begin the cruise with the *Bonhomme Richard* seemed doomed to defeat.

◇◇

Chapter XXIX

From Groix to Flamborough Head: Frustration

AT FOUR A.M. [Jones was writing letters at midnight] called all hands and got under way from the Isle of Groix," the officer who kept the log of the *Bonhomme Richard* recorded on August 14, 1779.[1] Thus in the twilight before dawn, with the rising sun as the only spy of the secret movements, the squadron of seven ships made sail, as the commander had ordered, after having run down five days earlier from L'Orient. An eighth vessel from America, the *General Mifflin,* had been invited to join them but refused. Although the *Alliance* was in her station, Landais had schemed unsuccessfully to weigh anchor separately—if not earlier during the changes in the crew of the *Bonhomme Richard,* then later following his contentious investigation as to a small prize ship which had sunk at her moorings.[2]

Jones had given written instructions upon arrival at Groix to each of the accompanying captains to pay careful attention to every signal and to all orders; he cautioned them to avoid losing company with the squadron and to proceed in emergency to the places indicated in the sealed letters of rendezvous. But in contradiction to these reasonable terms of authority together with responsibility of the commander, four of the captains had signed the concordat practically as his colleagues and the two remaining captains of the privateers had not subscribed even to such a document to control in any way their conduct at sea.[3] In view of the potential conflict between his unstable means at hand for the cruise and his iron resolve fixed by long, mounting tribulations, it is not surprising that Jones later confessed: "I did not sleep three hours in the twenty-four from L'Orient to the Texel." And if the cruise should

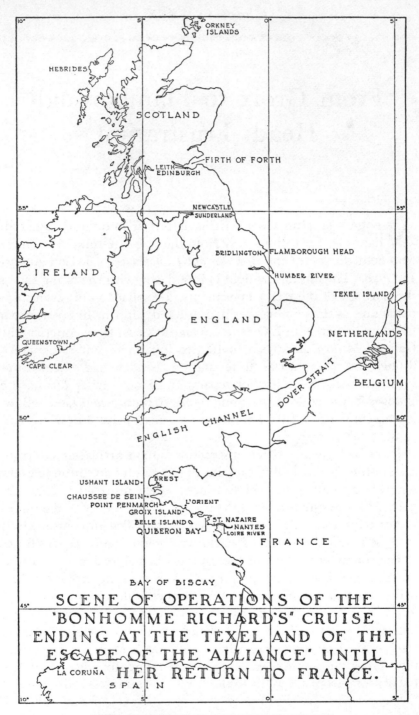

THE BONHOMME RICHARD'S CRUISE

end in defeat, he set out early enough to fight for victory.

The *Monsieur* gave early evidence of avarice and discord in the squadron at the capture of the first prize. Although the *Bonhomme Richard* directed the taking of the *Verwagting* in behalf of the fleet, the privateer presumed to consider the vessel her own; her Captain plundered the stores in the night and wrote orders and sent aboard a prize crew. Jones promptly thwarted such high-handed measures. Discomfited, the *Monsieur* lagged astern and then slipped away to return to France. Her one merit was first to return to the *Richard* some signal flags and pennants. She had detained the squadron twenty-four hours—"the result," Jones commented, "of being concerned with privateers, where good faith and honor are generally strangers." Notwithstanding this delay and the pursuit and capture of other prizes, they sighted Cape Clear and the southwestern coast of Ireland on the 23rd, and Jones looked forward to the first of his more important, strategic undertakings.

Landais, however, now began to show his hand, encouraged to act at sea as he had not dared ashore. He betrayed cowardice and resented Jones' cognizance of it upon his failure to execute an order to learn the identity of a large sail, which proved to be not a fifty-gun ship as he had contended but a valuable merchantman. He resented the commander's refusal to permit him in search of prizes to approach the rocky shores of the Skallocks and Blaskets of which he knew nothing. He also had the assurance of the ignorant to condemn his superior officer on the mistaken ground that a serious misadventure was the result of imprudence in sending boats to capture a prize.

It happened that, in a calm and near dangerous coastal waters, Jones had dispatched his barge ahead to tow the *Bonhomme Richard* after her helm had proved unable to swing her free from the sweep of the tide. The barge's crew, chiefly Englishmen, who had towed the ship, finding the occasion opportune to desert, cut the tow line, decamped with the barge, and fled to the nearby shore. Cutting Lunt, the third lieutenant, with a number of sailors and marines, lowered and manned another of the ship's boats and pursued them without the Captain's orders; he ventured too far, a fog soon arose, and signal guns from the *Bonhomme Richard* brought no recall. At this time Landais came aboard and sought to ridicule Jones, however mistaken the Frenchman was and stubbornly remained as to the intended purpose of the barge. Along with his perverse error, he added disrespect and impertinence to a degree which only the testimony of Colonel Weibert and other witnesses and the forbearance of Jones himself make credible.

Already accustomed to ignoring the words and actions of Landais as much as he might in the interests of the cruise, Jones remained near the coast in hope of the return of Lunt and his party of twenty of the best seamen. When he sent the *Cerf* to reconnoitre, this vessel was maladroit enough to hoist English colors and fire upon the boat of the third lieutenant at the very time he approached her. In the opinion that he had mistaken her identity, Lunt fled to the shore, landed, and terminated his second capture by death in an English prison. The *Cerf* now crowned her blunder by the well-nigh treasonable act of secretly following the *Monsieur* to France.

Not to be outdone by the *Monsieur* and *Cerf*, the *Granville*, which had just captured a prize calculated to satisfy her cravings, also set her course homeward to feast without restraint upon her prey. Perhaps Jones had reason for his faith when he next sent the *Vengeance* twice in search of both Lunt and the *Cerf;* she returned but had learned of neither. His own repeated signals by gun and flag for three days were equally without result. The period which the ships had passed on this coast during these efforts now led Landais to threaten that he would leave Jones if they remained longer. To be sure the alarm of their presence must have spread widely and their danger increased hour by hour. At this stage, the *Bonhomme Richard* seemed fated to cruise with only the *Pallas* and *Vengeance*.

The ferment created on the coasts of Britain, which had not forgotten the cruise of the *Ranger*, had indeed begun. The purposes of the commander were to divert attention from Count d'Orvilliers' great fleet, retaliate in a humane but monitory manner for English depredations in America, and achieve some brilliant exploit which would be sufficiently memorable both to depress the morale of England and to raise that of America. Panic spread almost like a conflagration as dispatch after dispatch arriving by land

and sea brought exaggerated accounts of Jones' force and plans. The expectancy of his coming, attributable probably to some of his English sailors if not to De Chaumont, had started at least as early as the past August when an English officer, one of his prisoners taken in the *Drake,* sent a report to England of preparations for his expedition.[4]

Now his presence was a reality. The seven men from the barge who had landed and escaped at Ballinskellix in the County of Kerry brought information of the squadron to a coast officer, through whom it was relayed from Tralee to Cork and from Cork to London.[5] The accounts told of "a large quantity of combustibles" aboard the ships, of four prizes already taken, of a score of additional men who had gone ashore in pursuit of the seven, of the ships in full view and "the country in an uproar," and of the intention of Jones to "scour the coasts and burn as many places as he could."[6] Reports from Dublin and Workingham, likewise transmitted to London newspapers, added ominously that he had a force of two thousand sailors and marines; others from Valencia sent warning by express of "the critical situation of our coast."[7] Still other messages from Cork reported that his appearance on this coast had "so increased the fears of the people that they considered an invasion as inevitable," and that "the drift of this adventurer was to intercept fleets bound to or from this port." A somewhat less black account of Jones, apparently almost incredible to the person who wrote it, described that he had landed a number of men for the purpose of securing provisions and fresh water; and that the sailors had carried off some sheep and oxen, for which the Captain "bountifully paid the owners . . . without committing any sort of hostility on the inhabitants."[8]

Beset by the apprehensive countermoves of the British on the one hand and the fears and vehement objections of Landais on the other, Jones weighed his situation. He was loath to abandon Lunt and his men near hostile shores without strenuous attempts to succor them. The continued absence of the *Cerf* was inexplicable, although he had some hopes that this vessel would rescue the party and reappear with them at a later rendezvous. But his most serious reason for prolonging his watch along this region of the Irish coast, which he could not sufficiently impress upon the captains in their anxiety, was that he lay in wait at the same time for a fleet of West Indiamen bound for the nearby port of Limerick.

As with characteristic enterprise he had gained secret information of their expected arrival at the Shannon, it was his resolve to stand off and on in this latitude a fortnight if necessary to intercept them. He was prepared likewise to avail himself of his strategic position for the capture of other vessels either homeward or outward bound. Thus by one adroit stroke he would inflict greater injury and win richer prizes than his squadron might achieve through ordinary means in the course of a long cruise. Landais' response, impudent as well as ironic, was that he considered himself the only officer under an American Government commission in contrast with the others who, he alleged, were in command of French corsairs.[9] He asserted as his right and declared as his intention the independent pursuit of his own wishes.

The onset of stormy weather on the evening of August 26, rendering unlikely any immediate developments at the station off Limerick, seems to have been the final factor which induced the commander to set his course northward rather than to lose the *Alliance*. Still the *Richard* carried a very moderate sail both with the view of possibly turning back and of avoiding separation of the ships as the gale and the thick weather increased. Although Jones hoisted pennants at the mizzen peak and fired a gun every quarter hour during almost two watches in the night, the lookout sighted neither the *Alliance* nor the *Pallas* in the morning. The *Vengeance* soon reappeared. The *Pallas* having broken her tiller had lost company. But the *Alliance* had vanished for reasons best known to her Captain. The faint last hope of taking the eight Indiamen was gone, and the disappointment of Jones did not prove the less when he soon learned that they arrived off the Shannon only three days after his squadron had passed from sight of its shores.[10] In the meantime, after further unavailing signals the *Bonhomme Richard* bore away for the north of Scotland in the region of Cape Wrath, the next rendezvous.

Off the cape at daybreak of September 1, 1779, Jones looked for his consorts. Sighting one sail to windward, the Captain gave chase; soon he observed two others to leeward which later proved to be the *Alliance* with a prize. The *Bonhomme Richard* brought to at noon the windward vessel, the letter of marque *Union* bound from London to Quebec with valuable naval stores, but lost the enemy's public dispatches because the *Alliance* in following very imprudently hoisted the American flag at the same time that English colors were flying on board Jones' ship. Landais was so modest as to expiate his error by impudence. As Jones preferred not to weaken more than necessary his already depleted crew, he was disposed to have the *Alliance* man the capture. Then Landais peremptorily stated that, if his sailors did so, he would permit "neither boat nor persons from the *Bonhomme Richard* to go near the prize." "Ridiculous as this appeared to me, I yielded to it for the sake of peace," the Captain who expected to give, not receive, instructions remarked in explanation of his exemplary forbearance. Nor did Jones fail in this instance, concerned as he characteristically was to hold prisoners for purposes of exchange, to receive those from the prize on his own ship. An unhappy fate was in store for the valuable *Union* and a second capture the *Betsy,* both with orders from Landais, in accordance with the advice of De Chaumont, that they should proceed to prize agents at Bergen in Norway.

Degree by degree the conduct of Landais now revealed his blatant mischievousness. The power at sea in the *Alliance* which had been entrusted to his hands threatened increasing dangers. His arrogance in regard to the *Union* had scarcely vented itself before he ignored signals to give chase to another sail on the same day and to speak with the *Bonhomme Richard* during the next morning. Hope of concerted effort revived faintly when a ship discovered at dawn of September 2 proved to be the previously disabled *Pallas.* But as if to disrupt any possible coöperation, the *Alliance* disappeared again until the 5th.

On the evening of that day, Jones signalled all the captains to come aboard the *Bonhomme Richard* for the purpose of determining future plans. Cottineau and Ricot obeyed, Landais did not. The commander then sent messages to the *Alliance* in one instance by his capable purser Mease, and in another by Cottineau and De Chamillard as well as Mease. "In vain," recounted the purser, "did those gentlemen represent to him the absolute necessity there was for his joining in consultation with his brother officers; that the good of the service demanded his compliance, as an enterprise of some moment was to be deliberated on; but alas! in vain did they waste an hour or more in arguments to this end— in vain did they attempt to persuade him—in vain did they entreat him—in vain did they tell him what he had to dread from the consequences of his obstinately refusing to obey the orders of his commanding officer. Instead of paying polite attention to the advice given him, he, on the contrary, not only disregarded it, but gave himself the liberty to speak of Captain Jones in terms highly disrespectful and insolent, and said he would see him on shore, when they must kill one or the other, etc."[11] The written reply of Landais to a third summons indicated that he was not less obstinate than malicious: "I shall not go on board the *Bonhomme Richard,* as I told you in my last letter; you know the reason why; for which this is my answer." What words or deeds Jones had reserved for him did not materialize at this stage of the cruise when fleeting time and little achievement impelled the commander to rivet his eyes with the greater fixity upon objectives. And once more the *Alliance* vanished.

Continued gales and contrary winds prevented sight of the coast line until September 13; finally the Cheviot Hills in the southeast of Scotland became visible. Jones had vainly hoped to find the *Cerf* at the third rendezvous after having left the second; but only the *Pallas* and *Vengeance* were still in company with him. Now he formed a plan for an enterprise on Scotland's east coast comparable in daring with the descent of the Ranger's boats upon Whitehaven, but larger in scope than this earlier incursion. It was his purpose to execute a sudden, opportune raid upon Leith and possibly also Edinburgh a mile beyond; he was to demand a large ransom, and, in case of refusal of his terms, the practice of Britain in burning towns would provide the basis for his threat, if not the example for his retaliation.

The audacity of the undertaking was not without advisement on the part of the commander. Both prisoners in the *Bonhomme Richard* and public papers which he had taken from prizes informed him that Edinburgh and Leith were practically defenceless. He learned also that they had only an armed ship of twenty guns and two or three cutters at anchor in the road of Leith.[12] He had artfully secured pilots for almost the whole length of the British coast, especially for the Firth of Forth,[13] among whom was Andrew Robertson, master of a small vessel from the nearby town of Kirk-caldy; the subsequent services as well as tears of this navigator were to impel Jones, notwithstanding American regulations, to return his ship under the transparent guise of a ransom and to free the man. He planned, finally, to succeed by stratagem as well as skill and speed.

If the *Bonhomme Richard* had been on a cruise independently, once the object was determined and the preparations were com-pleted, Jones would have made the firstlings of his heart the firstlings of his hand. But when wind and tide served on the 15th, the *Pallas* and *Vengeance* had seen fit to chase for prizes so that the *Richard* had to follow practically from one to seven P.M. to speak them, and her commander was obliged to use his best powers of persuasion from seven to eleven to win the coöperation of Cap-tains Cottineau and Ricot.[14]

Apparently their reluctance was the greater because of common reports that the ships would be obliged to pass within range of formidable guns of Edinburgh Castle, described by Fanning, the midshipman, as composed of two awe-inspiring "tiers of twenty-four and forty-eight pounders." "They made many objections and difficulties to the project," Jones recounted. "At last, however, they appeared to think better of the design after I had assured them that I hoped to raise a contribution of 200,000 pounds sterling on Leith, and that there was no battery of cannon there to oppose our landing. So much time, however, was unavoidably spent in pointed remarks and sage deliberation that night, that the wind became contrary in the morning."

Regardless of this adverse change in the wind, the three ships with two recent prizes, tacking and wearing again and again, con-tinued to work to windward up the firth for Leith. Jones got up a hawser for a spring on the cable, prepared to hoist out the launch and other boats in which six swivel guns were mounted, dressed himself along with some of his officers and crew in the red British uniform, and distributed similar clothing to the *Pallas* and *Ven-geance* in order to screen the squadron's identity and convey the impression of large numbers of troops. This disguise promised so well as to induce a town official, who was under the delusion that the ships were British and in search of Jones, to send a shore boat to the *Bonhomme Richard* with the purpose of requesting powder and shot to prepare against his squadron reported in these waters. Jones himself graciously expressed his regret that he had no shot of suitable size but tendered a keg of powder with his compliments. And with his usual presence of mind, he retained the chief messenger to supplement the local information and the professional skill of his other pilots.[15]

At 4:30 a.m. of September 17, the ships had beat as far as Inchkeith, the island which shelters the road from the sea, almost within cannon shot of Leith. The *Bonhomme Richard* lowered her boats and secured them astern. A quota of one hundred and forty marines to be commanded by Colonel Chamillard took their stations in them. The officer himself had received final instructions from Jones: to demand an indemnity of £100,000, one half in cash and one half to be secured by six hostages, and to allow thirty minutes for acceptance or rejection of the terms. In the letter which De Chamillard was to hand to the provost of Leith or in his absence to the chief magistrate, Jones stated, after reference to the Colonel as the commander of the vanguard of his troops: "I do not wish to distress the poor inhabitants; my intention is only to demand your contribution towards the reimbursement which Britain owes to the much injured citizens of America. Savages would blush at the unmanly violation and rapacity that has marked the tracks of British tyranny in America. . . .

"Leith and its port now lie at our mercy, and did not the plea of humanity stay the hand of just retaliation, I should, *without advertisement,* lay it in ashes. Before I proceed to that stern duty as an officer, my duty *as a man* induces me to propose to you, by the means of a reasonable ransom, to prevent such a scene of horror and distress."[16] With signals arranged for support of the marines by the ships in the event of refusal or danger, and with precautions in the terms of capitulation for the safety of the squadron in case of delay by adverse winds in departing from the firth, the project was at the point of execution. Then a squall struck the *Bonhomme Richard* as Chamillard and Dale, of whom the latter was to command the nautical part of the debarkation, were about to get in their boats with Jones' final words in their ears.

The squall became a gale. The marines and sailors in the boats came on board again. The ships clewed up sails. Now a pinnace which Jones had sent to reconnoitre returned with the information that a sail in the offing was an English cutter which had been watching the movements of the squadron all morning. Still the *Bonhomme Richard* handed all sails but the mizzen staysail and hove to. When the gale continued on the morning of the 18th, Jones hoisted aboard all the ship's boats. He learned that during the dark night the swift English cutter had continued her investigation, boarding one of the prizes and carrying off a member of the English crew.[17] To cap the warnings which had reached the shore, the gale became so severe and contrary that one of the prizes sank and her crew was saved with difficulty. It compelled the ships to bear away and drove them from the firth. As the mind of Jones was not less flexible than resolute, he recognized plainly that the loss of surprise and speed meant the loss of his prospects of success against the potential strength of Leith and Edinburgh.

The delay, in fact, between the conception of the plan and its execution, during which the ships had been sighted for several days off the coast and even in the firth, aroused the nearby towns to unprecedented excitement and to such feverish preparations for defense as their unready means enabled them to make. At Kirkcaldy in particular, only ten miles from Leith across the Firth of Forth and only one or two miles from the guns of the squadron when the ships were off Inchkeith and stood in close to the northern shore,[18] the consternation was colored by Scotch humor and heightened in time by tradition. This town on the Fifeshire littoral, the birthplace of legendary wizards like Michael Scott, attracted its inhabitants to the shoreline in throngs of thousands as they beheld Jones' ships beat against a strong headwind and as their fears were confirmed by news that the brig *Friendship,* belonging to a Kirkcaldy shipowner, had been taken by the squadron. According to embellished local reports, the town had as its sole defense two dozen firelocks of which many were antiquated, a few pistols, and a half dozen hangars and cutlasses. But what this material strength of the natives lacked, their spiritual power allegedly availed in the person of the Reverend Mr. Shirra. Instead of officiating at services in his church, he opportunely convened his larger impromptu congregation at the beach. They saw the storm from the southwest drive the ships from the firth and heard—to the extent that they were disposed to listen—the eccentric minister succeed by passionate prayers in his homely Scottish dialect, and so with God's help, as he modestly admitted, in "raising the wind."[19] Tradition apart, Kirkcaldy had been dismayed as well as defenseless.

Leith and Edinburgh were more prepared but scarcely less apprehensive than Kirkcaldy after they had received their first warnings. The alarm of lengthened hours had afforded the latter as well as the former the opportunity to provide emergency resistance. Edinburgh, as Jones himself well knew, is only a mile from Leith and always quartered a number of troops. Yet this unsucccessful approach to the gates of English cities left its indelible impression. Even from Edinburgh, at five o'clock of the 16th the ships had been visible "with the naked eye, standing up the firth."

In retrospect, Walter Scott told in person a fellow novelist, James Fenimore Cooper, the extraordinary turmoil and preparations which the squadron had occasioned in his native town; and he wrote to another author, Maria Edgeworth, a stirring account of a transformation in military preparedness from three companies of soldiers to five thousand men with complete appointments.[20] "Jones and his myrmidons," described another Edinburgh citizen, "frightened the people more than Charley did in the late rebellion. Everyone was for securing his effects by hiding them; the three banks had all their money packed up and ready to be sent off. . . ."[21]

At nearby Dunbar, off the entrance of the firth, an inhabitant pictured the scene which Jones left behind him: "The most mcmorable occurrence which I was witness to in 1779 was the appearance of Paul Jones off our town . . . where, with a squadron of five vessels, he continued for some days, keeping us all on the alert and in alarm, by day and by night, with our batteries thrown up at all points and our homes crowded with soldiers. This was the stirring time of war with us. . . ."[22]

Retribution, capture of commerce, and dispersal of the enemy's strength were part of Jones' purpose, in which his achievements were greater than he was currently aware. Still what would have

been success to another seemed almost failure to him. In one respect, however, his accomplishments availed less than he had
reason to believe at this time because of an event beyond his control. D'Orvilliers' vast fleet had abandoned battle against the English ships as well as intended raids upon Portsmouth and Plymouth, in favor of which Jones had already diverted attention and
decentralized considerable military and naval power.

With the failure at Leith to be added to the earlier disappointments at Limerick, with the *Alliance* gone and the captains of
the *Pallas* and *Vengeance* apprehensive, the unshaken purpose and
ready resource of the commander turned opportunely to a third
project as the *Bonhomme Richard* with her two consorts stood out
to sea and bore southward. At noon of September 19 they were only
three leagues off the harbor of the Tyne, with the shipping of
South Shields and Tynemouth in full view and with Newcastle-
on-the-Tyne only a short distance upstream.[23] Jones had long ago
recommended as a strategic undertaking the destruction of the
winter coal supply for London at its source in Newcastle. Now
wind and tide were again promising, now he had just taken several
prizes, including a sloop with building timber, which could afford
special means for a striking enterprise, now he needed only to
have Cottineau and Ricot second him. Undoubtedly this project,
which he urged upon Cottineau as "highly honorable though not
profitable," was to burn the shipping at the mouth of the Tyne, if
not a short distance up the river at Newcastle. He himself—not
Garnier—had provided the fireships originally promised to him.

This hazardous proposal had little appeal to the Captain of the
Pallas. There was even no lure as at Leith of possibly reaping a
golden reward for the danger. Cottineau remonstrated, moreover,
that their present situation was perilous, that the enemy would
send a superior force against them, and that, if Jones obstinately
continued on the coast of England two days longer, they would all
be taken. "As I afterward understood," recounted the commander,
"he told M. de Chamillard that, unless I joined them the next day,
both the *Pallas* and *Vengeance* would leave that coast."

While his consorts continued southward to minimize the danger
of pursuit by the enemy and to shape their course towards the
Texel, the *Bonhomme Richard* hove to for the repair of her

maintopmast, which had been damaged. Alone, Jones entertained thoughts of executing the raid independently. His officers ardently supported him. But hesitating and deciding negatively, he made sail along the shore also to the southward. "Nothing prevented me," he admitted, "from pursuing my design but the reproach that would have been cast upon my character *as a man of prudence* had the enterprise miscarried. It would have been said, 'Was he not forewarned by Captain Cottineau and others?' "[24]

Admiral Mahan has made this admission the basis of a judgment which fails to take reasonably into account the determining circumstances. He has used Jones' words as an occasion for moralizing in regard to the highest duty of an officer: "The subordination of public enterprises to considerations of personal consequences, even to reputation, is a declension from the noblest standard in a public man. Not life only, but personal credit, is to be freely risked for the attainments of public ends."[25] Nothing can be said against this pronouncement in itself. But much should be said against its application to Jones in apparent disregard for a larger situation if not in misunderstanding of it.

The question involved, according to the statement by Jones as well as the only charge which Mahan ventured clearly to found upon it, is not fear of death—an accusation readily refuted—but fear for his reputation. Now to determine whether his name before the world was a greater force with the commander of the *Bonhomme Richard* than public ends even on this one occasion, it is necessary to judge initially whether Jones had the authority and the means to make his choice—whether they went hand in hand, as Mahan implicitly assumed, with the responsibility. What basis is there for the assumption? Uncompromising support by De Sartine? By De Chaumont? Even by Franklin? In the terms of the concordat? In the character of Landais? Of the captains of the *Monsieur,* the *Granville,* and the *Cerf?* And now of the captains of the *Pallas* and *Vengeance? Carte blanche,* which Jones had repeatedly both begged and demanded, had been denied him.

The duty of Jones as an officer of America fighting for her liberties became truly the greatest passion of its existence, for which he was prepared in the crisis at hand to sacrifice all things on the altar of his integrity. "The reproach that would have been cast upon my character as a man of prudence," the Captain of the *Bonhomme Richard* had said and Mahan has condemned. Prudence? If ever a martyr of religion on the rack of torture made a so-called confession one day and retracted it the next even with the flames licking at his feet, so Jones with the halter of the concordat constantly at his neck submitted bitterly to it on a number of occasions and then flung it aside with a fury that testified to his challenge to man and God in the name of his country.

◇◇

Chapter XXX

The Battle of the *Bonhomme Richard* and the *Serapis*

OFF FLAMBOROUGH HEAD the last rendezvous, on September 23, 1779, only eight days before the cruise was to end at the Texel, Jones felt that his career in the Revolution, in fact his life, lay in the balance. On this momentous occasion he was resolved to abide by his own bold judgment. Neither Landais nor Cottineau, neither De Chaumont nor De Sartine nor Franklin, neither an old and slow ship nor nondescript cannon and seamen, neither wind nor tide nor night, in short no impediment direct or indirect, against which the last resources of his brain and the last breath of his life might avail, would snatch from him the valorous victory on which his existence was set like adamant.

The Baltic fleet was this last object, the merchantmen which more than any other vessels provided Britain with the sinews of war. To capture or destroy them would cripple the sources for equipment of the English Navy for many months and so give France and Spain a naval superiority for operations in British and American waters, including even the attack of strongholds like Gibraltar.[1] And if the fleet itself should escape, there remained the ships of war that convoyed it; victory over them would raise the morale of America now practically without any warships at all in the proportion that it humbled the assumed invincibility of Britain.

The *Pallas* and *Vengeance* were in company with Jones at his final cruising ground. The services they could render might prove valuable, but the time was past to compromise, even to lose an hour, at any backwardness on their part. He looked for the *Cerf* only to confirm his suspicions of her treachery. He sighted again

PATON'S CONTEMPORARY OIL PAINTING OF THE *BONHOMME RICHARD–SERAPIS* BATTLE

Famous painting of the engagement by Sir Richard Paton. Presented by Christian A. Zabriskie.

the *Alliance* on her fantastic wanderings. When the *Bonhomme Richard* had been returning to Flamborough during the preceding night, after a reconnaissance southward off the Humber, at which a convoy had put back in fear, Jones had signalled two sail in the darkness and received only partial recognition. In doubt, he had called his crew to quarters at two a.m. only to discover at dawn that they were the *Alliance* and *Pallas*.[2] Thanks to this characteristic coöperation of his consorts, Jones and his men had been primed for battle during the whole night before the day on which their fighting would not be just anticipation.

Now Jones lay in watch for the Baltic fleet, for which his expectancy hour by hour was confirmed by prisoners and pilots. In turn, like Leith, Edinburgh, Sunderland, and other towns northward, the neighboring coast was in alarm. From Scarborough above and Hull below came urgent warnings of his presence on the coast. Vessels crowded on September 21 into the harbor of nearby Bridlington to such a degree that "a great number could only find security in being chained to each other on the outside of the piers."[3] Ashore, "two companies of the Northumberland militia, then quartered in the town, were called to arms by beat of drum after midnight, and the inhabitants, armed with such weapons as could be readily procured, proceeded to muster at the quay, while a number of the more opulent were making preparations for sending their families into the interior. Business was now at a stand, and the attention of all was directed to the expected invasion."[4] Early in the afternoon of September 23, a concourse of the inhabitants at Flamborough Head beheld in suspense the large Baltic fleet unguardedly crowding sail from the north on one side of the cape and the American ships patrolling the waters on the other side hidden from view of the fast-approaching merchantmen.

While the *Bonhomme Richard* had early assumed her station south of the head so as to take by surprise the vessels as they rounded the promontory on their course from the Baltic to London, the *Pallas* was somewhat northward, and the *Alliance* continued to follow her own perverse devices. Ever watchful for the fleet, Jones with Cottineau was at the same time chasing several prizes. As a number of captures were in prospect for the afternoon, he sent his pilot boat, armed, with Henry Lunt his second lieutenant, brother of Cutting Lunt, and a group of sailors and marines to take a brigantine.

Within an hour, at two p.m., the commander spied, circling the head, some of the foremost of a fleet of forty-one sail and in company with them two ships of war which, he learned from his informants in the *Bonhomme Richard,* were the *Serapis* of fifty and the *Countess of Scarborough* of twenty-two guns. These vessels comprised the Baltic fleet and its naval escort. After Jones had made propositions to capture the ships of the Baltic trade route a year and a half earlier and had planned his present cruise with the intention of making them his final and greatest objective, he saw his opportunity to challenge them about to be realized at last.

Immediately the *Richard* recalled the pilot boat and hoisted a signal for a general chase. Her crew set steering sails, trimming them fore and aft, and swayed up the yards to square royals and set studding sails (stuns'ls). Although at eleven o'clock the magistrates of Scarborough had already conveyed to the *Serapis* by dispatch boat their alarm at the presence of a flying squadron, with the result that Captain Pearson had both made a signal for the merchantmen to bear down under his lee and repeated it with two guns, the convoy had ignored the warnings. Now, with the strange ships in sight and to windward sweeping towards them, the merchant vessels tacked, let fly their topgallant sheets, and fired guns in distress.

Landais with his swift frigate might have been able to circumvent the flight of many of the merchantmen. The *Bonhomme Richard* herself crowded every possible sail in pursuit and "made the signal for the line of battle, to which the *Alliance* showed no attention." At the same time the *Serapis* stood out to sea for the better protection of her convoy and signaled to the *Countess of Scarborough,* which was inshore for the same purpose, to join her. Even if the two British ships of war were not able to thwart him in this manner, it was unlikely that Jones could cut off a considerable number of the merchantmen with his own vessel; at the beginning of the pursuit he had less than two leagues from shore in which to overtake them, the light breeze from south-southwest was only somewhat favorable, and to approach within range of the batteries of Scarborough Castle towards which they flew would have been folly. The first aim of Pearson was the safety of his convoy; the first purpose of Jones, with such consorts as he had, was the more immediate and wise as well as more dramatic capture not of the merchantmen but the ships of war.

In the dusk shortly before six p.m. the *Bonhomme Richard* with the *Pallas* and *Vengeance* in line of battle astern was still bearing down upon the enemy. Although the *Serapis* and *Countess of Scarborough* now tacked in order to keep their station better between their convoy and the American ships, they unmistakably stood in for the coast. And as the twilight deepened into autumn early darkness, just before the moon was to rise, they trimmed their yards under a full press of sail for shore and the protecting guns of Scarborough Castle. Jones was not to let them elude him at this stage. Without his night-glass, the manœuvre would have defeated his watchfulness until too late; with it, he altered his course to port six points early enough to prevent the British ships from escape to their haven.[5] The *Pallas,* however, misinterpreted with hasty judgment the change of course of the *Bonhomme Richard* towards the coast as an indication that the English seamen among her crew had mutinied, gained command of the ship, and made wildly for land. As a precaution, Cottineau hauled his wind and stood out to sea; Landais, now as well as before, lay to with topsails aback, safe and far to windward. A trial of Jones' resolution had impended; if he had wavered, he would have failed; if he had acted only when seconded by his consorts, the ships of war as well as the convoy would have escaped him. "I was obliged," he stated, "to run every risk and to bring the enemy to action with the *Bonhomme Richard* alone.[6]

Even before the American ship bore away northwestward and the British westward, the drums had already beat to quarters aboard both of them. The nearer they approached each other, the more the officers and crews at their stations in both frigates strained to judge the power of their adversaries. Not only the strength of each side but also the estimate of it for comparison in the minds of the combatants was destined to affect the conflict. The Americans had dared to challenge the generally-accepted supremacy of British ships of war of large armament. They recognized that the odds of naval force as well as of experience and tradition were against them when they visualized nearer and nearer the possibilities of victory or defeat, honor and prize money or suffering and imprisonment, life or death. "From the commencement to the termination of the action," recalled Lieutenant Dale, "there was not a man on board the *Bon Homme Richard* ignorant of the superiority of the *Serapis* both in weight of metal and in the qualities of the crews."

Pearson commanded a copper-sheathed frigate, launched only four months earlier at Deptford and constructed on the most approved principles of British shipbuilding. The *Serapis* had on her lower and main decks twenty eighteen-pounders and twenty nine-pounders respectively and on her quarter-deck and forecastle ten six-pounders; her broadside, therefore, was three hundred pounds of metal. The *Bonhomme Richard,* on the other hand, had guns already described (six eighteens, twenty-eight twelves, and eight nines) which were intended to throw a broadside of two hundred and fifty-eight or three hundred and twelve pounds of metal, according to the use of only three or all six of her eighteen-pounders at one time on either her port or starboard broadside. As the ship had these forty-two guns on the preliminary cruise, but possibly only forty on the present occasion, her broadside may have been somewhat less. In addition to the danger in employing any of the six eighteen-pounders except in a smooth sea because of the closeness of their improvised ports to the waterline, the twelve-pounders of the Americans were proportionally less powerful than the large battery of eighteen-pounders of the British, regardless of the comparative totals in weight of metal. Thus in contrast with Jones' ship, the *Serapis* was new and copper-sheathed, had speed consistent with her compact design and prime condition, and presented a more dependable and powerful armament.

The crew and officers of the *Serapis* promised even greater superiority in numbers and abilities. In addition to her complement of three hundred and twenty men, all Britons of common traditions with the exception of fifteen Lascars, she had taken aboard in Denmark some English sailors en route from the West Indies to a home port, and so had increased her crew to more than four hundred.[7] Her three lieutenants, Wright, Stanhope, and Shuckburgh, were worthy officers; and Pearson himself, who had entered the British Navy at fourteen, had served a long and honorable apprenticeship, distinguishing himself under Kempenfelt in a hurricane before his first command. Now the total personnel on board the *Bonhomme Richard* was only three hundred and twenty-two.[8] She had early lost off the Irish coast the deserters in the barge and Third Lieutenant Cutting Lunt with his sailors and marines in pursuit of them; Second Lieutenant Henry Lunt with his boat crew had been recalled but was still absent; and a considerable number of minor officers and sailors had received the assignment as prize crews of captured vessels. Along with the weaknesses and dangers of her depleted crew, including boys, Englishmen, and natives of many neutral countries, arose the necessity of appointing midshipmen and inexperienced volunteers to important duties.

Jones apart, the advantage between the *Bonhomme Richard* and the *Serapis* lay decisively with the British. As auxiliaries, the *Pallas* of thirty-two eight-pounders had greater potential strength than the *Countess of Scarborough* of twenty-two six-pounders. The enemy saw of course as other prospective opponents the *Vengeance* with her twelve three-pounders as well as the swift and well-equipped *Alliance*. As a psychological and potential factor to the British, the *Alliance* especially might have importance; as a direct asset or liability to her consorts, she was incalculable except in so far as the behavior of Landais had already been perverse, insubordinate, and dastardly.

Jones, the ostensible commander of the American squadron as well as the Captain of the *Bonhomme Richard* remained the most intangible but promising influence. However much one or more of his consorts might fail him, he was destined otherwise to reap what he had sown from the day when he had become a sailor boy at the age of twelve until the hour when the quality of his training, preparations, and leadership was to have its greatest trial beginning with the moment that now impended.

While the full moon in the east rose over an ocean calm at evening, illuminating the sea as well as the sky and casting a radiance over the tracks of the American vessels, and while Flamborough Head less than a league away thronged with awed spectators, the *Bonhomme Richard* bore down first upon the enemy's ships, keeping head on so as to hide her identity and guns the better until she and the *Serapis* were within pistol shot of each other.[9] When she came to on the port bow of the British ship[10] shortly after seven p.m., her crew had been at quarters more than an hour in all the pent expectancy of a battle such as the daring and adroitness of Jones had just presaged.

Even then as if in anticipation of the thunder of warfare about to be loosed, the peacefulness of the moonlit scene induced the greater hush of premonition among seamen as well as officers of both ships. The tense minutes inspired thoughts that flashed and emotions that pulsed of deeper revelation than those habitual to the crew. If the occasion stirred even the crude sailor, it aroused in Jones the deepest awareness of his resolve to redeem in full the obscurity and shadow of his early life, the renunciation of love and wealth which he could appreciate more than most of those who grasped them, and the genius of his talents as an officer and a patriot in the cause of America.

Only in poise for action came this fleeting moment of intuitions. Jones was prepared for the first as well as the last stroke. And awaiting the signal of his officers, who in turn were awaiting his orders, were the crew at their stations. Whatever thoughts nostalgic as well as warlike the expectant moment prompted among them aboard the *Bonhomme Richard,* the topmen held fixed in their hands the grenades of their wicker baskets, the marines kept their fingers lightly on the triggers of their muskets, and the gunners surveyed at arms' reach their matches, powder horns, rammers, shot, cartridges, and other accoutrements.

"What ship is that?" broke the vibrant stillness as a hoarse, stern voice hailed from the *Serapis,* although Pearson could scarcely have had any remaining doubts as to his antagonist.

"I can't hear what you say" and *"The Princess Royal"* were replies calculated to gain time which came from an officer of the *Bonhomme Richard.*[11] To Jones words were now superfluous except to the extent that he wished a final moment for a manœuvre of his ship after having brought the enemy to bay. The *Richard* was now to windward on the port bow of the *Serapis* as the former still stood northwestward and the latter westward. Pearson sharply hailed a second time and received a second indefinite answer; he then threatened in a third demand to fire unless he immediately had a reply to his satisfaction.[12] The muzzles of the two tiers of guns on the starboard side of the *Bonhomme Richard* bristled through their opened ports, the matches had been lit, and the trains of powder had been laid. Dale and Weibert were giving final commands to the gun crews of the twelve-pounders on the main deck, and a master gunner under their direction similarly had charge of a detail of sixty men for the eighteen-pounders on the lower gun-deck. Momentarily Dale waited and watched for a signal from Jones.

With the ships abreast as they then sailed on parallel courses, now Jones gave his signal to Dale. Now the starboard twelves and eighteens flamed and thundered from the American ship. Instantaneously, having already seen the lighted ports of her adversary as she steadied on the parallel course to deliver her broadside, the *Serapis* fired the port guns of her main and upper deck batteries.

Perhaps only then realizing that she had a stronger opponent than previously expected, the *Serapis* opened the ports and ran out also the guns of her lower deck, visible by the lanterns, and trained upon the *Richard* the belching fire of her eighteen pounders. Broadside followed broadside as the two ships levelled their guns with converging fire and swept the exposed decks of each other. The shot from the *Serapis* began to take particular effect against the running rigging and the hull between wind and water, and that from the *Bonhomme Richard* against the masts and the standing and the running rigging. The American ship also suffered at her stern some of the broadsides from the *Countess of Scarborough* as neither the *Pallas* nor the *Alliance* had so far closed upon this second British adversary.[13]

Thus early in the action, Jones had to fight not only against the superior armament and manœuvering qualities of the *Serapis* and the support of her consort but also against a grave and almost fatal accident. Two of the six eighteen-pounders of the *Richard*—only three were used as the other three were mounted in the port battery—burst at the first broadside, and they killed or wounded or totally unstrung all their gun crews and other men who had been nearby. Since it became necessary to abandon the remaining eighteen-pounders, the Captain lost his six largest guns as well as a considerable number of his crew before the battle had fairly begun.

In the face of this misfortune, Jones turned to a bold decision.

The *Bonhomme Richard* had been unable at the opening of the battle to improve her first position so as to rake the *Serapis* from bow to stern. "As I had to deal with an enemy of *greatly superior force*," Jones described, "I was under the necessity of closing with him to prevent the advantage which he had over me in point of manœuvre." His object now was to board the *Serapis* and carry her by close fighting. The more feasible plan was directly to try to board her from the sides at several places rather than to attempt to lay her athwart hawse, rake her, and then board by the narrow bow.

In the meantime, however, Pearson seized his chance, although the extent to which his seamanship availed is uncertain. Neither he, Jones, Dale, nor any other reasonably reliable authority has seen fit to commit himself very far. Perhaps Pearson claimed less than his due in seamanship because he should have gained a greater advantage. Probably Jones did not see occasion for expounding in detail what he considered attributable not to him but to his ship. Clearly Dale, loyal to his Captain as he was, described all that he thought proper and more, it seems, than he knew accurately, for his observation must have been obstructed in the course of his duties on the lower and main decks. If the admissions of Dale and Jones, if the account of Fanning the midshipman, and if the charges of Cottineau in anger against his superior are to be recognized, the *Serapis* gained several times a favorable position "in spite of my best endeavors," as Jones said, "to prevent it."[14]

The extent of the advantages is conjectural. It is possible that the *Serapis* lay upon the starboard quarter of the American ship and raked her. It is improbable that the *Serapis* also was able to pass to windward and fire a volley upon her port side. The closed ports of the British ship's starboard lower battery late in the battle make the more implausible the view that she passed to windward of the *Richard* at an earlier time, notwithstanding the alleged explanation that this battery was not used when the opportunity presented itself or that the ports, although opened, were subsequently shut to prevent boarding. It is particularly difficult to believe that, if the slow *Richard* lost the weather gage at this period, she could have regained it subsequently from the fast *Serapis*. Testimony of officers and men from both the *Richard* and *Pallas* further implied that the *Serapis* was never on the port side of Jones' ship.

Jones was doing his utmost in sailing the *Richard,* whatever the extent of Pearson's successful manœuvres at this early stage. He could not outsail Pearson; he had to outwit him. The *Richard* backed her topsails and dropped upon the *Serapis'* quarter within pistol shot; she then filled again and went ahead. Jones put his helm aweather in order that the *Richard* might run the *Serapis* on board at a favorable position, but he succeeded only in running the bows of the *Richard* into the stern of the *Serapis* on her weather quarter.[15]

The purpose was excellent, but the result was questionable. If Jones succeeded in eliminating the superiority of the *Serapis* in sailing as a governing factor of the battle, he could hope to fight on incalculably better terms. Yet the *Richard* had not been able to close with the enemy at a place of vantage for either her guns or her boarders. Almost in line with one another as the ships now were, the one as well as the other could not bring her broadsides to bear; and with the inability of the guns to prepare the way, and only a narrow space to be defended against the onrush of a line of bold men who might try to storm the decks of the enemy, boarding too offered no prospect of success. Boarders were indeed ready, marines with muskets and grenades, sailors with pikes and cutlasses, crouching in the bow of the *Richard,* and awaiting the order to leap upon the stern of the *Serapis;* but the time was not ripe and Jones withheld the command. In this indecisive situation, the *Bonhomme Richard* shortly backed her topsails and dropped clear. Before she sheered off, the enemy, according to Dale, hailed, "Has your ship struck?"[16] Even if Jones heard, he apparently did not deign at this time to reply.

"Has your ship struck?" The question was already warranted. The *Serapis* had proved her ability to outsail the *Richard,* to fire her heavier weight of metal into the starboard side and possibly the quarter of her adversary, to render futile an attempt to bring her to close fighting. Jones knew likewise, although Pearson was ignorant at least in part of the circumstances, that two of his eighteen-pounders had burst and the others had been abandoned, with the loss of most of the men on the lower gun-deck; that even his main battery of twelve-pounders was now broken, silenced, and abandoned; that sundry eighteen-pound shot had struck below the water line and occasioned an ominous leaking; and finally that some of the braces had been shot away so as to render the *Richard* less manageable than before. As if the advantage of the *Serapis* were not enough, the *Countess of Scarborough* continued to fire her broadsides upon the stern of the *Richard,* contributing to kill most of the marines who had been stationed with Chamillard on the poop and driving the few survivors to shelter.

When Pearson now saw the *Richard* astern the *Serapis* and to windward, he laid his topsails aback to get square with her again so as to avoid being raked. No sooner did Jones observe the beginning of this manœuvre than he set sail after sail and trimmed his yards to a fresh gust of wind so that he again drew ahead. At the same time he put his helm aweather to make a supreme effort to lay his ship athwart the enemy's hawse and at the same time to grapple her.[17]

It was perilously late and imperative after battling an hour to prove that Jones' eloquent silence as his reply to the challenge for surrender was not braggart but brave, not vain but symbolic of victory. None was more alive to the crisis than the commander of the *Richard,* calm and determined and resourceful as he remained. "In this unhappy extremity," as he himself described his situation, "I had recourse to the dangerous expedient of hurling grapnels upon the *Serapis.*"[18] Synchronous with the moment that the *Richard,* according to his purpose, was to lay athwart the enemy's bow, chosen sailors stationed at vantage points of the outer yards were to cast their grapnels into the rigging of the enemy and help to draw her to his own ship. Regardless of the braces shot away, the slowness with which the *Richard* responded to her sails and helm, and the incalculable movement of the enemy astern, Jones managed by his speed in thought and skill in seamanship to bring the starboard side of the *Richard* alongside the *Serapis,* not amidships nearly abreast the mainmast as he would have preferred but somewhat farther aft, so that the jibboom of the enemy became entangled in his starboard shrouds near the mizzenmast and over the poop of his ship.[19]

"Well done, my brave lads, we have got her now," cried Jones.

He ordered additional grappling irons to be thrown aboard the *Serapis* to hold her fast, although the enemy cut them away almost as quickly as they were flung. He commanded the boarders to be ready to rush upon her decks at strategic points, although British sailors already lay in wait to receive them at the first step. Jones quickly grasping the situation, shouted to the sailing master to get a hawser, and pending the delay in finding one, himself made the lines that hung from the enemy's bowsprit secure to the mizzen-mast of the *Bonhomme Richard*. When Stacey finally returned with the hawser, and the Captain and he were passing this additional heavy line around the bowsprit and mizzenmast, difficulty in the task prompted the sailing master to swear. At such a moment, Jones chose to temper his feelings with humor: "Mr. Stacey, it is no time for swearing now, you may by the next moment be in eternity; but let us do our duty."[20]

In a desperate effort to free the *Serapis*, Pearson now let go his port anchor, hoping that the wind and tide would break the entanglement.[21] The expedient, however, failed; instead of separating the ships riding to the *Serapis'* anchor, the light southwesterly wind and the northerly tidal current swung the *Serapis*, with her jibboom as a pivot until it broke, to a parallel position with respect to the *Richard,* so that the ships lay starboard broadside to starboard broadside, with the bow and stern of the one opposite respectively the stern and bow of the other. The grapple became fixed when the fluke of the *Serapis'* spare anchor hooked the starboard quarter of the *Richard,* accidentally according to Pearson. The yards were now completely entangled, the muzzles of the guns of the enemies touched one another, and the rammers were projected from the gun ports of one ship into those of the second in order to load. Even the closed starboard lower ports of the *Serapis* now had to be blown away to make room for running out her eighteen-pounders.

Against the fire that recommenced at such close quarters from the nine- and eighteen-pounders of the starboard batteries of the *Serapis,* the *Richard* now had few guns for counterattack. Mease the purser, who had taken charge of the nine-pounders in view of the scarcity of officers, was now dangerously wounded and under the care of Dr. Brooke in the cockpit. The Captain saw two nine-pounders still available on the quarter-deck; he found likewise two others on the port side which it was his purpose to carry into position. For one he was able to rally a few men to set it in place, but for the second even so little help was not at hand amid the tumult and confusion. Jones himself now took charge of the operation of the three guns, although Mease with a bandaged head returned later to help him. He supervised two which were well served with scattering grape and canister shot against the musketry and decks of the *Serapis,* and personally directed the fire of the third with penetrative double-headed shot against her yellow-painted mainmast.[22] Yet these special efforts seemed inconsiderable as compared with the incessant furious fire of the enemy's lower starboard battery in particular, which was beating in one side of the *Bonhomme Richard* and blowing out the other from the mainmast to the stern, cutting off the rudder entirely from its frame, almost severing the transoms, and driving many of the men to the forecastle.

Another resource, however, for which Jones had carefully planned and trained his officers and crew and given them final instructions as the battle had commenced was the skilful bombardment by the details assigned to the large platform-like tops of the *Richard.* Especially the marines, who were to have shown their valor and skill in the descent upon Leith, now had their opportunity. A score armed with their muskets under the command of Chamillard on the exposed poop had scarcely begun their sharpshooting before they themselves had been mown down by a raking fire. In the hidden shelter of the tops of the *Richard,* the prospects were better. The Irish volunteer Lieutenant Stack with Midshipman Fanning as an aide and a party of eighteen, chiefly marines, chose their places amid the rigging and sails in the maintop; Midshipman Coram with twelve in the foretop; and another midshipman with ten in the mizzentop. Jones had instructed them first to clear the corresponding tops of the *Serapis* and then to direct their efforts upon her open main and quarter-decks so as to gain by this sequence the greater ultimate advantage. They succeeded so well as in many instances to pass along the interlocked yards into the tops of the *Serapis* and to gain possession of them. In fact the fusillade from their grenades, muskets, pistols, swivels, and other weap-

ELLIOTT'S CONTEMPORARY OIL PAINTING OF THE *SERAPIS–BONHOMME RICHARD* BATTLE

By Lieutenant William Elliott, Royal Navy. Presented by "The Friends of the United States Navy."
Exhibited in the Royal Academy in 1789.

ons was on so large a scale and so effective as to set an example of a
mode of naval fighting which had long been insufficiently regarded
since the prominence gained by cannon, and was newly to be
emulated with notable success in history. The most striking parallel
was to occur in the famous duel between the *Victory* and the *Redoubtable* in the battles of Nelson.

This desperate countermove against the chaos of broken timbers
and guns wrought by the enemy's eighteen-pounders had scarcely
gained impetus before a new threat arose not less sudden and even
more dangerous than the earlier bursting of the *Richard's* two
eighteen-pounders. With a stealth suitable to the subdued light of
the moon, it proceeded from Landais. The *Alliance* moving un-
certainly to and fro under her topsails had been to windward
of the *Countess of Scarborough* when the British vessel raked the
Bonhomme Richard, but she had done nothing to prevent her; she
had also stood off when the *Pallas* closed with the *Countess of
Scarborough;* now she moved along the unengaged side of her
consort, and when crossing the bow of the *Richard* and the stern
of the *Serapis* discharged her broadside upon them. Excitable,
cowardly, and half-mad as Landais had already seemed on less
momentous occasions, he must have been especially excitable and
cowardly and almost wholly mad now. He used crossbar and grape
shot which scattered and struck both vessels indiscriminately; he
fired beyond the range of muskets to avoid the possibility of
furious retaliation from the *Richard;* and he ignored the warning
of some of his own officers that his guns bore upon the wrong ship
and the refusal of others to obey his commands.

"The *Alliance* rakes us," "The *Alliance* is manned with Englishmen and firing upon us," "The *Alliance* has wounded Mr. Caswell
the master's mate with several men,"[23] rose the cry as her volleys
swept especially the forecastle, to which many had already gone to
seek shelter from the *Serapis'* guns. As this firing occurred more
than an hour after the battle had begun, there was no possibility,
Jones averred in his indignation, that Landais himself mistook the
one ship for the other; the moon had already risen high enough to
cast bright beams upon the distinguishing black hull and the high
poop of the *Richard,* which contrasted with the yellow sides and the
low stern of the *Serapis.* It seems almost unbelievable, however,

that the quarrelsome temper and the mounting hate which Landais had manifested towards Jones earlier in the cruise now took the form of utter treachery against the allied ship.

Nevertheless Jones took pains not to afford the slightest subterfuge for a recurrence of such a broadside from the *Alliance* against the *Richard* behind the mere curtain, as it seemed to him, of a volley against the *Serapis*. He hoisted the signal of recognition, three large lanterns with proper wax candles in them, all well lighted, in a horizontal line over the bow, quarter, and waist of his ship. Ominously Landais approached again, after the *Pallas* in an hour's fight had captured the *Countess of Scarborough,* which had scarcely been a match for the stronger ship, and after Cottineau had offered the *Alliance* the choice of taking possession of his prize or of aiding Jones. This time the *Alliance* tacked, gained the wind, and ran down to leeward towards the *Richard* in a more uncertain course than previously. When now seen on the port quarter of the *Richard,* Landais fired with the same strange perversity that he had shown before as if believing that his target was only the bow of the *Serapis,* not at all the stern of the *Richard.*[24] A hundred voices exclaimed to the *Alliance* that she was firing upon the *Richard.* As she passed along the port beam, Lieutenant Stack in the maintop had difficulty in preventing his men from firing upon her in turn. "I beg you will not sink us," he entreated her.[25]

Amid the chorus of outcries, Midshipman Linthwaite at Jones' direction hailed her with the order to lay the enemy on board. In fear that she might not have heard, Midshipman Coram, also at his direction, hailed her with the same order. They asked whether she had understood. "Ay, ay" was the reply; "ay, ay" came a second time. The *Alliance* now turned across the bow of the *Richard* at a safe distance from the Americans as well as the British, and again cannonaded them with grape and canister shot that scattered widely, once more injuring her consort perhaps more than the enemy, especially because of the earlier retreat of the men of the *Richard* to her forecastle in the new line of fire, as contrasted with the refuge of the crew of the *Serapis* under her sheltered lower deck. "I then had not the least doubt of his intention to sink us," Stack affirmed, "and should have fired on the *Alliance* in preference to the *Serapis* but that the maintopsail and other sails concealed her from us. . . . In my opinion there was not a soul on board the *Bonhomme Richard* who did not believe that M. Landais knew us before he fired. . . ."[26]

Like a buzzard awaiting its prey when dead, Landais now stood off at a point of safety, fearful as well as disinclined even then to approach the disengaged side of the *Serapis,* largely spent as her men were after long fighting. He thought it no harm, according to his own cynical remark, if the *Richard* struck, for the opportunity would then be his both to retake her and to take the *Serapis.*[27] Still this statement should perhaps be discounted as typical of his braggadocio.

An opportunity to capture both ships seemed close to realization. The water in the hold of the *Richard* was rising dangerously. Officers and midshipmen were to claim that this desperate situation followed after the broadsides from the *Alliance,* especially from shots that had struck their mark on the port quarter and bow between wind and water. At the same time they were to imply that the cannonade from the *Serapis* had been exclusively against the *Richard's* starboard side. At least two considerations cast doubt upon the view that the assaults by Landais marked the period that the water in the *Richard* first became a serious threat. Inasmuch as the *Alliance* used shot which scattered, her volleys when compared with those from the eighteen-pounders of the *Serapis* could scarcely have been penetrating enough to cause the flood to mount higher and higher. In fact, a master carpenter was to attribute the chief danger of foundering not to damage on either the starboard or port side but to the shattered bottom.[28]

Fire became a danger as great as water. The *Richard* was the more vulnerable because her dry old timbers had a plentiful supply of pitch, tar, and oakum. As the variety of weapons set the torch, flames burst forth from time to time in almost all sections of both ships, often approaching the powder magazines, and frequently spreading from the rigging of one vessel to that of the other. Men left their stations to combat the fire. They used half their clothes to smother it, and they resorted to every other available means, including tubs of water close at hand, to control this insidious and watchful enemy. "We were on fire," reported Pearson, describing the condition of his adversary as well as the *Serapis,* "not less than ten or twelve times in different parts of the ship, and it was with the greatest difficulty and exertion imaginable at times that we were able to get it extinguished."[29]

While the fire gained, the water rose, the *Serapis'* guns continued to splinter, mangle, and blast the *Richard* into fragments, and the *Alliance* lay to windward ready to swoop down at the favorable final moment, some of the officers of Jones urged him to surrender. They were officers, as their commander described them, "of whose courage and good sense I entertain a high opinion." "For God's sake, Captain, strike," cried one of them, the lieutenant of marines, who found him almost exhausted with fatigue and pouring with sweat as he sat down for a moment on a broken timber. Jones glanced at him, paused a moment, and leaping up said, "No, I will sink, I will never strike."[30]

Whether or not the commander still meant what he said came to an almost immediate test. Only a minute later he was to learn how close at hand seemed the alternatives of sinking or striking. A shot had just carried away one of the four pumps of the *Richard* so that water in the hold gained the faster upon the three which remained. The carpenter now seized with panic told the master gunner that he feared the ship would sink; both had slight wounds which helped to unnerve them. The master gunner flew with the report to the master-at-arms, and they concluded that she already was sinking. At the same time someone told the gunner that Jones and Dale had been killed. Under the impression of being the officer next in command, he ran precipitately aft upon the poop to haul down the American flag, and indeed would have succeeded before anyone could have prevented him if a cannonball had not previously swept away the ensign staff with the colors.[31] Fortunately thwarted in attempting one means of surrender, he turned to another: he now called to the *Serapis* for quarters.

"Do you ask for quarters? Do you ask for quarters?" loudly responded Pearson above the roar of battle with more eagerness than he wished to reveal, for he himself had been at the point of surrender. Until this stage Jones was unaware of what had transpired among the carpenter, gunner, and master-at-arms, occupied as he had been with the guns upon the quarter-deck. Pearson called specifically to the Captain of the ship; otherwise the three sub-

ENGRAVED PORTRAIT OF JOHN PAUL JONES AFTER THE DRAWING
BY C. J. NOTTÉ

*Engraved by Carl Guttenberg. Courtesy of John L. Senior who owns the original copper
plate engraved at Paris circa 1782 (?)*

ordinate officers might have assumed the authority to assure him of surrender.[32]

Now, and not till now, Jones replied, "No, sir, I will not—we have had but a small fight as yet."[33] According to his words taken not from tongue but pen, he declared, "I don't dream of surrender, but am determined to make you strike."[34] But Dale's version of his answer is the most pithy and renowned: "I have not yet begun to fight." The Captain emphasized these terms, as described in a report which must have reflected truthfully his mood if not his act, by hurling at the head of the gunner his two pistols, one of which struck the mark and felled him at the foot of the gangway ladder.[35]

In the wake of the example of fear, cowardice, and even treachery which the three men set for the crew, arose a danger that threatened to cross the very threshold of certain defeat. While the gunner had run aft to strike the colors, the master-at-arms, whose duty it was to guard the prisoners, opened the hatchways, without the knowledge and against the repeated injunctions of Jones. Thus he let loose several hundred prisoners, and they were now free to rush wildly upon the decks. Thanks to De Chaumont, who had refused to provide fetters or hand-irons, as well as to the master-at-arms, nothing prevented them from stampeding the crew of the *Richard*, leaping through the portholes to the *Serapis*, swinging from the decks of the one ship to the other, and ending the combat, as Jones himself said, by killing him or hurling him into the sea.[36]

Nothing prevented them, to be sure, except the presence of mind of Jones, with the aid of Dale, who took advantage of their sudden fright at the fear of sinking, which was impressed upon them before they had time to get their bearings, so as to set them to work at the pumps and otherwise to diminish the flood in the hold. Still one of the prisoners, the captain of a twenty-gun ship which had recently been taken, was alert enough at the moment of liberation to pass through the ports to the *Serapis*. He informed Pearson "that if he would hold out only a little while longer, the ship alongside would either strike or sink, and that all the prisoners had been released to save their lives."[37]

The spur to fight for victory which was now almost within his grasp, along with the sting of Jones' replies to the question whether he had asked for quarter, impelled Pearson to summon his last resources with the fury of both vengeance and despair. First he rallied his boarders, who leaped with pistol, pike, and cutlass upon the deck of the *Richard* only to retreat at seeing, or more likely at the fearful impression of seeing, a superior number armed and lying under cover who were prepared to challenge them. Then he sent his men below to open a concentrated fire from the two batteries. The volleys blazed now almost unimpeded through the farther as well as nearer side of the American ship and found their ultimate mark in the sea, although, if the guns had been more depressed to blow out her bottom, probably the sinking would have been soon achieved. Only an old stanchion remained here and there to uphold the poop and prevent it from falling in upon the magazine. The rudder was completely cut and broken. Even the tops, in which the groups of marines and sailors remained, had most of the supporting shrouds shot away, and only preventer stoppers kept the tops from crashing down.

It was for these topmen, it seemed, that Jones had reserved a special honor as he overcame danger after danger. They had early not only driven the enemy topmen from their places but also cleared the exposed decks of the *Serapis* again and again so that scarcely a Briton dared to appear upon them. The maintop especially, in which Stack commanded and Fanning helped him, rendered valiant service. From this top a Scotch sailor, probably William Hamilton, "on his own initiative," as Jones described, "took with him a lighted match and a basket of grenades, and advanced along the mainyard of the *Bonhomme Richard* until he was directly over the decks of the enemy. As the flames of the decks, bulwarks, and shrouds blended with the gleam of the moon, he saw everything which happened upon the adversary's ship. Thus on each occasion that he descried two or three persons gathered together, he let a grenade fall among them; he had the presence of mind also to throw several down the hatchways, and one of them set afire a cartridge of an eighteen pounder. . . ."[38] The flames ran aft from cartridge to cartridge, which the powder-monkeys had brought from the magazines, and caused an explosion which put out of action five starboard guns and killed or wounded or shattered the nerves of a large number of men. "Many," Dale saw from the *Richard's* ports, "stood with only the collars of their shirts upon their bodies."[39] Others, among whom was First Lieutenant Stanhope, jumped overboard in order to extinguish the flames of their clothes.[40]

The mettle of Pearson as the adversary of Jones shone in his continuance of the battle with even greater instead of subdued intensity long after this reverse. But at length the *Serapis'* riddled mainmast tottered. Her gunfire, too, appeared to lessen. Her Captain saw the *Alliance* still hover in expectation, and he naturally feared possible injury to his ship from her in addition to the *Richard.*

The fire from Jones' three remaining nine-pounders continued even more resolute and the effect of the one he personally directed upon the mainmast more telling. The steadfast topmen still seconded his guns with muskets and grenades. As the enemy's mainmast threatened to fall, the *Serapis* called at last for quarter, and Jones hailed that she should strike her colors. Dale saw Pearson lower with his own hand the flag, which had been nailed to the mast, after apparently none of his available officers was willing to venture aloft on this duty under the watchful eyes of the *Richard's* topmen. The mainmast was reeling. It only remained to signalize the victory further by Pearson's surrender of his sword to Jones after three and one half hours of desperate battle.

In the lull of the surrender, there must now have echoed in the ears of some of the *Bonhomme Richard* officers and men, as if it passed again between the two ships and drifted across the still moonlit waters, the immortal reply of Jones, which had aroused their hearts to beat with sustained and passionate rhythm: "I have not yet begun to fight."

◇◇

Chapter XXXI

Fire and Flood; British Pursuit and Retrospect

U PON FINDING that the flag of the *Serapis* had been struck, I
went to Captain Jones," recounted Dale, "and asked whether
I might board the *Serapis,* to which he consented; and, jumping
upon the gunwale, seized the main-brace pennant, and swung
myself upon her quarter-deck. Midshipman Mayrant followed with
a party of men, and was immediately run through the thigh with
a boarding-pike by some of the enemy stationed in the waist, who
were not informed of the surrender of their ship. I found Captain
Pearson standing on the leeward side of the quarter-deck, and,
addressing myself to him, said, 'Sir, I have orders to send you on
board the ship alongside.'

"The first lieutenant of the *Serapis,* coming up at this moment,
inquired of Captain Pearson whether the ship alongside had struck
to him. To which I replied, 'No, sir, the contrary; he has struck to
us.'

"The lieutenant renewing his inquiry, 'Have you struck, sir?'
was answered, 'Yes, I have.'

"The lieutenant replied, 'I have nothing more to say'; and was
about to return below, when I informed him he must accompany
Captain Pearson on board the ship alongside."[1]

Dale refused the request of Lieutenant Stanhope to go below
for his ostensible purpose of silencing the lower deck guns because
of doubt whether the officer might not madly renew the battle regardless of the surrender by Pearson. While several guns discharged
again from the *Serapis* before further orders ended all firing, the
American officer took care to have Stanhope as well as Pearson
pass to the deck of the *Bonhomme Richard.*

Pearson, it has been said, stepped on board without need of

bridge or boat and "delivered his sword to Captain Jones, who returned it to him because he had bravely used it."[2] It is difficult to believe the report that the former arrogantly stated, "I cannot, sir, but feel much mortification at the idea of surrendering my sword to a man who has fought me with a rope around his neck." It is even less credible that the latter meekly replied, apart from the question as to the return of the sword at this time, "You have fought gallantly, sir, and I hope your king will give you a better ship."[3] Jones was generous in victory, as he had shown himself, for instance, by his kindness towards English prisoners of the *Alfred* at the entreaty of their wives and by his modest words at the death of Captain Burdon of the *Drake,* but none would have been quicker to resent a scornful allusion as to a traitor and pirate by a meaningful silence if not a summary act. Indeed, it is practically certain that he did not return this sword until a later occasion, and it is most likely that he would not have restored the token of his triumph at all if his courtesy had met with such rudeness.

The battle done, Jones directed Dale to cut loose the lashings and follow him with the *Serapis.* The faithful lieutenant learned for the first time of a wound in his leg, of which the excitement of the struggle had kept him unaware, when he jumped in surprise from his seat of a moment on the binnacle of the British ship as she failed to respond to helm and sails. Dale had not known that she was at anchor; he now ordered the cable to be cut, and pending care of his wound placed the *Serapis* in command of Henry Lunt, who had reappeared for the first time since his departure hours earlier in the armed pilot boat.

The second lieutenant had reached the *Vengeance,* which was to windward, when the battle already raged, and received from Ricot the signalled orders to return to the *Richard;* but in Lunt's own terms, "It being night, I thought it not prudent to go alongside in time of action." Although to board from the unengaged side was difficult as well as not prudent under the special circumstances, Lunt's conduct seems strangely at variance with the hazards of those who had been in the struggle. Ricot, too, gained the doubtful honor of prudence, for he had stood off beyond gunshot; yet it had been difficult for him to help with his small vessel. Landais had made prudence one of his cowardly attributes. Cottineau had added merit to his own prudence by the capture and possession of the *Countess of Scarborough*.

Whatever her precarious future might be, the *Richard* now in victory broke the deadly embrace with the *Serapis*. As the American ship led, the British followed, having her mainmast and also her mizzen-topmast finally fall overboard. Yet in a physical sense, as contrasted with the human spirit that governed her, the *Richard* rather than the *Serapis* appeared the defeated vessel. She was "mangled," according to Jones' own picture, "beyond my power of description, and a person must have been an eye-witness to form a just idea of the tremendous scene of carnage, wreck, and ruin which everywhere appeared."

The condition of the ship supports unofficial accounts of the loss of life, which was presumably so lamentable that Jones abstained from recording it. Pearson himself stated, "She [the *Richard*] had three hundred and six men killed and wounded in the action; our loss in the *Serapis* was also very great." This estimate of the casualties on the American vessel was almost certainly an exaggeration, for in case it were true scarcely two score of her officers and men in the battle would have remained uninjured. Yet the number mentioned by Fanning, grossly unreliable as he may be in this instance, was almost the same—three hundred and two. Without question the human toll on both sides was fearful. In view of such sacrifice, the valor of Jones in fighting to the last extremity had a proper counterpoise in the pity and repulsion that came from his heart: "Humanity cannot but recoil from the prospect of such finished horror, and lament that war should be capable of producing such fatal consequences." And among these consequences still to be combatted were, as he said with truth as well as perhaps with vanity, "two enemies . . . far more formidable than the British . . . fire and water."[4]

The fire aboard the *Richard* was the more immediate if not the more dangerous enemy. It repeatedly burst forth anew in various parts of the ship, in particular when the wind rose even to a moderate degree, and finally made its way to the magazine, within a few inches of the powder. Some sailors broke its wooden partition from the inner side and flooded the smouldering timbers with water; others carried the powder upon the deck, from which they were prepared in the last extremity to throw it overboard. The crew fought the flames throughout the night, and it was only at ten o'clock the next morning that they had extinguished the last embers.

The water, six to seven feet deep in the hold, was more ominous. After the *Richard* hoisted signals of distress, officers and men came to aid quickly from the *Pallas* and *Vengeance* and tardily from the *Alliance*. Jones pressed into service the carpenters from both the *Serapis* and his consorts. Details from these ships aided the crew of the *Richard* in working the pumps throughout the night and continuing the next day as they did their utmost to stem the leaks particularly on the port side between wind and water and under water. As the log grimly recorded, they tried to raise the water-line and also "assisted in heaving the lower deck guns overboard and the dead men, etc."[5] Despite efforts which rose from zealous to frantic and despite Jones' most ardent wish to save the *Richard,* the carpenters, Cottineau, and other officers were convinced by five o'clock of the afternoon following the battle that it would be impossible to keep her afloat long enough to reach a port if the moderate wind then prevailing increased appreciably.

When Jones returned at seven p.m. to the *Richard* after a visit to the *Serapis,* he found that the water in the hold was still rising regardless of the utmost energies of the carpenters and of the men at the pumps. He now ordered that the prisoners, the wounded, and a few indispensable articles should be taken to the other ships. At ten p.m. he directed further that officers and men who did not belong to the *Richard* should abandon the pumps and return to their own vessels; and at four a.m. as the water rose almost to the lower deck the crew of the *Richard* also abandoned them. Throughout the second night, especially during the latter part of it, the pilot boat and the other small craft of the squadron carried the wounded men from the foundering ship to her consorts and to the *Serapis.* Pearson later spread a report concerning the *Richard,* even more unreliable than his estimate of her casualties, that she "sank with a great number of her wounded people on board her."[6] His sincerity must be doubted in some matters touching his galled pride. It had scarcely been possible for him to judge inasmuch as he had left the American ship in Jones' company at two p.m. on the day before she was to founder. Characteristic of his further misstatements was the declaration that the *Countess of Scarborough* fought the *Pallas* for two hours, although other accounts mention only one. Cottineau also was later to charge that Jones had left wounded seamen in his ship, but as this accusation was one of many poorly supported which he made only in a sudden blast of anger, it deserves even less credence than Pearson's.

By ten o'clock of the second morning after the engagement, everyone had left the *Bonhomme Richard*. In addition to the wounded sailors and the prisoners, the crew had brought away only the signal flags; most of the personal effects of the Captain, which he valued at fifty thousand livres, nearly all his papers, and the clothes and bedding of the officers and men remained aboard.

Only half an hour later, Jones in the *Serapis* ordered Fanning with three men to return to the ship in order to secure certain papers, which he represented as priceless, even at the risk of his life. The midshipman, however, had not made his way beyond hail when the Captain cautioned him not to incur any danger. At his arrival alongside the *Richard,* Fanning found her "lying nearly head to the wind, with her topsails aback, and the water running in and out at her lower deck ports."[7] Realizing that she was at the point of sinking, he and his men pulled away a short distance from her to escape the suction. At this close range, they saw the *Richard* as "she fetched a heavy pitch into a sea and a heavy roll, and disappeared instantaneously."[8] At the distance of a mile in the *Serapis,* Jones watched her as she sank with the stern and mizzenmast uppermost and with the colors flying. "A little after ten," he recorded, "I saw with inexpressible grief the last glimpse of the *Bonhomme Richard*."[9]

After this epilogue, literally testifying that he had stepped from defeat to victory, the new commander of the *Serapis* had as his next object the safety of his ships and his prisoners. As for the merchantmen which had fled to refuge, fog, in addition to the state of the *Richard,* had rendered it impossible for him to pursue them the morning after the battle; Cottineau also had been fully occupied; and Ricot and Landais had seen fit not to seize whatever opportunity still remained. Now on the second morning after the action, the squadron without loss of time left the scene at which it had continued almost thirty-six hours and stood off about twelve leagues from Flamborough Head. Although the *Serapis* was by no means in a sailing condition, the new station hid the ships from further view along the British coast.[10] There they lay to for a night in making urgent repairs, and shaped their course north-northeast the next morning as they continued to refit.

Jones pressed his *Serapis* crew in particular to hasten their work in order to be prepared as soon as possible for any emergency against the undoubted pursuit by British frigates and ships of the line. Amid his new immediate concerns, he did not neglect to put the master-at-arms in leg-irons for releasing the prisoners on the night of the engagement. On September 27 his men stepped the mizzen topmast and renewed its rigging, and on the 28th they stepped a jury mainmast. Finally on the night of the 29th the *Serapis* changed course; she hoisted five lanterns at the mizzen peak and fired a gun as a signal for the squadron to heave to in stays and stand to the westward. But within twelve hours they wore ship and stood to the eastward again.[11] Contrary winds helped to make the route uncertain, and the opposition of Jones' fellow-captains even in the present circumstances rendered it even more so.

Aside from his captains and the winds, there was method in the madness of Jones as he tossed to and fro for ten days in the North Sea. Strong British forces were at his heels. Eight of the enemy ships appeared in sight of Scarborough Castle on the morning of September 26 after he had left the scene less than twenty-four hours.[12] A ship of the line and three frigates were already cruising to intercept him at the strategic position off Yarmouth under the reasonable impression that he would sail southerly for one of the nearest havens in the Netherlands or France. When Jones foiling them bore away north-northeast, one part of a squadron in pursuit concluded that he was bound for a port in Norway, and according to reports was "within three hours' sail of him, and going under a pressed sail." When he hauled westward, a second part of this squadron received orders "to take in water and provisions, and sail immediately for the Irish Channel . . . in case he should be gone north about." When he finally veered eastward, a third squadron, "eleven sail of men-of-war, were in full chase." The ships followed his courses in every possible direction only to lose them: "Paul Jones resembles a Jack O'Lantern to mislead our mariners and terrify our coasts. He is no sooner seen than lost. Hey! Presto! Like

Mungo in the farce—'Mungo here, Mungo there, and Mungo everywhere!' "[13]

While the British ships, "always a day or two too late," as critics of the Admiralty said, were trying to catch up with Jones, the newspapers showed themselves less sluggish in the easier task of calumniating the unaccountable sailor who now excited national curiosity as well as alarm. One account, which purported to be based on the authority of seven British seamen who had escaped ashore after the battle, aimed to depict his desperation: "In the engagement between the *Serapis* and Paul Jones [Jones, it is noted, personified the *Bonhomme Richard,* but the *Serapis* remained only the *Serapis*], his vessel was so disabled that the Captain of the *Serapis* called out to Jones to strike, else he would sink him. To which the latter replied that he might if he could; for whenever the Devil was ready to take him, he would rather obey his summons than strike to anyone."

Another report, supposedly on the same authority, painted him as the fabled pirate, having at the same time a fictitious nephew as one of his officers: "During the engagement Paul Jones (who was dressed in a short jacket and long trousers with about twelve charged pistols slung in a belt round his middle, and a cutlass in his hand) shot seven of his men for deserting from their quarters; and to his nephew, whom he thought a little dastardly, he said that damn his eyes he would not blow his brains out, but he would pepper his shins, and actually had the barbarity to shoot at the lad's legs, who is a lieutenant in his ship."[14]

Still another accredited report from London raked up a fantastic story concerning his early life, based on the Maxwell episode, and incidentally revealed the contemporary embers of contention between the English and the Scotch: "This new American commodore and terror of the Irish Seas is by birth a Scotchman, and is said never to have disgraced his country in one single instance of being too nice and delicate in the means of promoting his interests. . . . There was on board his ship a carpenter put in by his owners, a man of integrity and knowledge of his business. With him Paul could never agree. . . .

"As the carpenter was, on one of the hot days of summer, lying fast asleep upon the deck, Paul anointed his hair pretty plentifully with turpentine, after which he laid a train of gunpowder at some distance, which setting fire to the carpenter, he instantly bounded up and, in the confusion which must appear to a man wakened out of his sleep under such alarming circumstances, jumped overboard and was never more heard of.

"Some of the sailors, however, observing this horrid action, lodged examinations against him on his arrival in Scotland; but Paul, being good at manœuvering, so contrived it that on his trial no evidence appeared, and he was of course acquitted."[15]

After due allowance of course for newspaper sensationalism even in the England of that day, it remains that penny pamphlets and current epithets supported a similar view of Jones, which was just becoming widespread. With contrasting sincerity and truth, however, the focus of publicity began also to turn from Jones to self-criticism; ironically the conduct of the so-called pirate was a mirror through which the British recognized the more clearly the limitations of their own. Bold, independent, and decisive as Jones was, he had followed Franklin's instructions as well as his own instincts to shun as much as possible the cruelties of war, and his restraint in the light of his special opportunities was to arouse appreciation as well as wonder. However much the journalists condemned him because he had wounded British pride, they condemned their own political and naval authorities even more:

"Some people are surprised why Paul Jones and his squadron have not burned the towns on the Northern coast which he has visited. True, he had it in his power; but they ought not to be surprised at it. Paul Jones is a pirate indeed, a plunderer, but he is not a barbarian; he does not hold his commission from the Administration of Britain, and therefore he has no order to ravage and lay waste its dwellings of the innocent. Perhaps, indeed, as soon as the reports of Sir George Collier's conduct have reached him, he will think it his duty to retaliate upon us; and since neither the laws of war nor the dictates of humanity can restrain us from going into all the extremes of bloodshed, he will try what the force of retaliation can effect. Good God! what fools and madmen are those who venture to destroy the towns of the Americans in so lawless a manner."[16]

These sentiments express an attitude towards the Revolution

by a large part of the British public as well as by many of the statesmen too often forgotten in view of the controlling influence of the King and his followers in Parliament. Many also recognized truly enough that the information of the burning of Fairfield and other American towns, in addition to the earlier cruelties, had fortunately reached Europe since Jones had set forth on his cruise and Franklin had given him final suggestions: "What will be the consequences of burning Fairfield and Norwalk? Paul Jones has done no mischief yet; but had he known of the burning of these towns, is it not probable he would have burned Leith and Hull? They were as completely at his mercy. When this burning business comes to be retaliated upon our own coasts, we shall then see the Ministers' scribblers expatiating upon the cruelty of it, of its being contrary to the rules of war, etc., and those public prints, which are paid and bribed by public money . . . will be the foremost to publish those complaints. . . .

"By the examination of the four men belonging to one of Paul Jones's squadron before the Mayor and Magistrates of Hull, it appears that Jones's orders were not to burn any houses or towns. What an example of honor and greatness does America thus show us! While our troops are running about from town to town on their coast, and burning everything with a wanton, wicked, and deliberate barbarity, Dr. Franklin gives no orders to retaliate. He is above it. And there was a time when an English Minister would have disdained to make war in so villainous a mode. It is a disgrace to the nation. But notwithstanding the moderation hitherto shown by the Americans upon our own coast, it is to be feared that moderation will cease in a little time."[17]

This prophecy was to materialize in thought if not in deed within a few short weeks. Franklin very soon assured the President of Congress, it will be recalled, that his temperate purpose was at an end and "were such another expedition to be concerted, I think so much of that disposition would not appear in the instructions."[18] A few days later Jones himself wrote Lafayette: "The late brutalities of the Britons in America fill me with horror and indignation. They forget that they are men; and I believe nothing will bring them to their senses but the most exemplary retaliation."[19]

While Jones helped to bring the British to a realization of their cruelties in America, he indirectly brought home to them also the treatment which some even then accorded the Scotch. The slur which they cast upon him as a Scotchman as well as a pirate was symptomatic of a more inclusive point of view. Exaggerated as this antagonism was in an ultra-Whig like Horace Walpole, a measure of it among the populace is traceable from his extreme words: "France has a right to humble us. The true English who are in America have behaved like Englishmen, without any Scot alloy. The victories of France will be over Scots. Dr. Franklin's triumph has been over a Scot Ambassador (Stormont)."

Scotland reciprocated in part the unfriendliness, especially of the House of Hanover, even at this late stage of her historic struggle against England. In the instance at hand, the terms of her advocate were probably the milder because they were also the more discreet: "The people in Scotland have shown their loyalty by raising men and money, and supporting government; yet they are not to be trusted with arms. This is the continuation of that wretched, narrow-minded system of policy which has lost us America. . . . The renegade Paul Jones has been on our coast for five weeks taking our ships, yet no force has been sent against him. Seeing therefore that we cannot hope for any assistance from the wisdom and vigor of His Majesty's confidential servants, it seems to be the general opinion in Dumfries that we should take up arms . . . for surely we have a right to defend ourselves, our families, and our properties."[20] But the English themselves were soon to be the spokesmen against their country's political and naval administrations, as they had already been against the cruelties in America. And once more Jones was to provide the occasion.

These British criticisms, plain-spoken and emphatic, remained largely in abeyance pending the outcome of the prospects of capturing Jones. Uncertainty continued for ten days—uncertainty for both the pursued and the pursuers. Again Jones' captains rather than the enemy squadrons stood in the way of his fearless purpose, which was to sail for a port of his choice regardless of the danger at his back. He now had over five hundred prisoners, whom it was his hope to land safely in France to insure their exchange for Americans—a primary object of his fighting. As De Chaumont, however, had fully informed Landais and Cottineau that the cruise was to end at the Texel, they set sail for this destination regardless of the commander's signals, probably in fear of the British as well as in challenge to his orders.

It remained for Jones, with the *Serapis* to windward of her consorts, to sail after them or to choose a course of his own. In this situation he most probably would have made for Dunkirk to land the prisoners and then would have proceeded to the Texel, if these men had not been apportioned to the *Pallas* and the *Countess of Scarborough* as well as to his own ship. The last opportunity to effect his purpose ended at two p.m. on October 3, 1779 when the coast of Holland, near the Texel, lay in sight five leagues distant, the pursuing British ships remained unseen, and the "fresh gales and large tumbling swell" were still favorable for Dunkirk.[21] Jones, however, who had a distaste for private dissension as great as his keenness in a public cause, found it expedient not to lead but to follow. At six a.m. the next morning the squadron stood inshore, and at noon all the ships came to anchor in the Texel Road.

It was not surprising that the last act of his fellow-captains at the close of the cruise should be consistent with their obstructions from the beginning, and that it should contribute to involve him at a neutral port of Holland in new, diplomatic difficulties with the Dutch on the one hand and the British on the other. It was certain also that the British lion would roar the louder upon the discovery that again the ships in pursuit had been "a day or two too late." Notwithstanding difficulties and dangers from many quarters, Jones was pledge in the new emergency that the *Bonhomme Richard* had not borne the American flag in vain.

◇◇

Chapter XXXII

"The Pirate Paul Jones" at the Texel

T HE PIRATE Paul Jones"[1]—this was the epithet which began to pass current as the *Serapis* and her consorts, flying the American flag, stood up towards the historic Texel. So some of the British were to name the victor, some of the Dutch were to consider him, some of the French were to try to make him, even some of the American officers and citizens were to represent him to his crews.[2]

The Commodore—others now justly accorded him this title on the practical basis of his leadership of the squadron—entered the roadstead with serious premonitions, regardless of the orders of Franklin and De Sartine, regardless too of the intimation that he was to assume command of the *Indienne* in Holland. But as the security of his many prisoners was now his first concern, with his prisoners he was determined to take his stand. At least for the present he bowed without question before the diplomacy of France and America, which had as ultimate purposes recognition of the United States by the Netherlands, trade agreements, and loans. It was prophetic of his uncertain welcome by the Dutch that three days elapsed before he passed from the outer to the inner road of the Texel; at last on October 6 the squadron moored ship.[3]

Jones had scarcely entered the neutral port before he looked forward to his departure. Difficulties, however, arising from his shattered *Serapis* and his wounded prisoners, prearranged instructions awaiting him from Franklin and De Sartine, and the possibility of a safe and peaceful exchange in Holland of his prisoners for Americans led to complications and delay. His arrival became at once a matter of serious concern to the neutral Dutch Government; it aroused the English and French Ambassadors at The Hague to speedy action; it echoed straightway in London and Paris; it became a matter of international political interest as to the relations between Holland and Britain; it even foreshadowed the Armed Neutrality sponsored by Russia, which for a period was to be of outstanding importance to Europe.[4]

Sir Joseph Yorke, the British Ambassador at The Hague, was alert at once to all the possible implications in the sudden appearance of the squadron. As soon as the news had come from the Helder to The Hague, he "waited on the Prince of Orange [the hereditary executive of the State] and the Dutch Ministers to inquire what conduct they intended to hold upon the occasion."[5] Forthwith the Ambassador reported to the Home Office: "The Prince of Orange told me that he had sent immediate orders to take no notice of the American flag if produced, and that he hoped they would be able to oblige their ships with their prizes to go out to sea again immediately. I represented to the Prince that our treaties would require more than that if reclaimed, and that I was apprehensive it was a plan formed to embroil the States with Great Britain. . . ."

Following his visit, Yorke presented a memorial to the Dutch Parliament, the States General usually addressed officially as High Mightinesses, in which he demanded the surrender to his Government of the ships, officers, and crews of the squadron. And he referred to the commander as "a certain Paul Jones, a subject of the King, who according to treaties and the laws of war can only be considered as a rebel and a pirate."

While the British Ambassador was urgent and even unscrupulous, Holland proceeded with deliberation. Her conflicting interests and loyalties rendered difficult a decisive policy. The Prince of Orange was allied to England by blood and sympathies. The States General, the assemblies of the seventeen provinces which constituted the Dutch Republic, and the people as a whole resented the political and commercial supervision which Britain had imposed upon them by century-old treaties and by new restrictions incident to the American Revolution. As a maritime nation, the Netherlands in general and the merchants of Amsterdam in particular strained under this control to a special degree as her stronger ally stood in the way of large war profits from trade with the United States.

A treaty of 1674 between the commercial rivals recognized the principle of free ships free goods, and excluded naval stores and shipbuilding timber from the category of contraband, but a second treaty of 1678 committed the Netherlands to assist Britain with stipulated forces in the event of war. At the outbreak of the conflict in America, Holland sought to avail herself of the privileges of the former and inclined to consider as outworn the obligations of the latter. Yet the States General, at the instance of the British Ambassador, issued a proclamation in March, 1775, renewed at later periods, which undertook to prohibit the export of goods by indirect as well as direct means to the British Colonies. Even the sincere purpose of a party in the Dutch Government availed little as opposed to the commercial zeal of the traders who in many instances also held political office. Consequently a large clandestine traffic sprang up with America by the circuitous route of French ports and of the Dutch islets of St. Eustatius and Curaçao in the Caribbean.[6]

The Amsterdammers saw an opportunity to challenge the colonial trade monopoly of their rival, and were by no means disposed to lose the golden profits. While the British Ambassador at The Hague presented the objections of his Government, the Dutch merchants carried on their trade. Yorke reported in April, 1776 that eighty-five thousand pounds of gunpowder, which were certainly destined for America, had been shipped from Amsterdam to ports in France. He succeeded in having one Dutch governor of St. Eustatius who was favorably disposed towards the United States replaced by another only to find that the second facilitated the war commerce even more than the first. This new Governor, Johannes de Graaf, also exchanged a salute in November, 1776 with the *Andrew Doria,* the American brigantine which had been one of Hopkins' Continental squadron; but he later affirmed, obviously to propitiate the British, that the recognition had been in courtesy to a vessel which he had thought was a merchantman, not a ship of war. Although Britain knew better than to believe his specious excuse, she had weightier problems requiring her attention, as war with America had already led also to war with France, and threatened to involve her likewise with Holland and Spain.

The eagerness of the Dutch merchants for trade with the United States was further evident in an unofficial commercial agreement drawn the preceding year by William Lee and by Jean de Neufville, the merchant who collaborated in preparing this document at the instance of Van Berckel, the Grand Pensionary of Amsterdam. De Neufville was also the agent who supplied Jones' present needs for his ships, and Van Berckel was the subsequent author, with Dumas the Dutch confidential representative of America as the witness, of a highly laudatory certificate concerning the naval and political aspects of his stay at the Texel. Tentative as the commercial treaty of De Neufville and Lee had been, the circumstance that the English later secured a copy of it at sea, among papers thrown overboard but retrieved belonging to Henry Laurens, the newly appointed Commissioner of the United States to Holland, was to arouse special suspicions regarding Dutch aid and sympathies for America. For the present, however, Jones was their concern. Whatever the trade interests of the Netherlands and whatever the associations and good wishes of a small party in the old republic with the struggle of the people in the new, the States General as well as the Prince of Orange had been decisively opposed to recognition of America when the advent of the unexpected ships brought them face to face with the issue.

Now the personality of Jones and his victory over the *Serapis*, as well as the embroilment in which his presence threatened to involve Holland with Britain, focussed attention upon the Texel. The American Commodore acted even more speedily than the British diplomat at The Hague. Upon his arrival in the outer road on October 3, he had already prepared and he immediately dispatched a long letter to Franklin which described the battle and his impending situation.[7] On October 5, before the *Serapis* was at her final anchorage in the roadstead, he had also informed the Duke de la Vauguyon, the French Ambassador at The Hague, concerning his preparation of both the *Countess of Scarborough* and the *Vengeance* to transport the prisoners at once to Dunkirk in the event that a reliable arrangement for their exchange seemed improbable. He informed him likewise concerning the need of "great and immediate assistance" in order to execute the special instructions from Franklin which had been waiting for him at the Texel in the hands of Dumas. For him to depart before the end of the month, he made clear, "the *Serapis* must be entirely new masted and rigged; nothing being left above deck that is capable of sustaining a passage of any length in the approaching season. She wants also sails, rigging, boats, and provision. . . ."

Jones saw in present difficulties a further result of earlier and a further cause of later complications like those of the fabled nail for want of which the loss extended from the horse's shoe to the kingdom. If he had been properly seconded by his consorts, the squadron would have been fit for quick, decisive action such as now would become more and more difficult as the British ships had time to gather outside the port to await him. To crown error with error, if De Chaumont had not informed the captains—Jones himself had not definitely known—concerning a special purpose which their coming to the Texel was to serve, the complications, great as they already were, would not at least have threatened to become greater.

The sealed orders which Dumas gave the Commodore entrusted to him the highly important task of convoying from the Texel to Brest about one hundred Dutch vessels laden with war materials and shipbuilding timber consigned to France and apparently intended for the United States. To his amazement at both the knowledge and unreserve of his captains, Jones heard them openly discuss this commission for the squadron as soon as they had arrived in Holland.[8] Notice of it also appeared shortly in the local newspapers.

Ironically the instructions from Franklin contained the caution "to keep his intention of convoying these vessels as secret as possible." The suspicions of Jones as to the main if not the only sources through which this project became public had final warrant in a report of the British Ambassador. "One of the chief of Jones' squadron said that their intention in coming here was with a view of convoying the Dutch store ships, and it was part of the plan when they set out to touch at the Texel."[9] Without question the enemy ships of war thickened in the offing at the prospect of so sweet a morsel as one hundred merchant vessels, to say nothing of Jones and his squadron.

The Commodore foresaw clearly the dangerous possibilities, and informed the French Ministers of the probable necessity to abandon the plan when the British had not yet found sufficient time thoroughly to whet their appetite. The lack of secrecy was akin to the lack of subordination which had prevailed throughout the cruise. In his detailed letter to Franklin concerning the battle, he had already spoken boldly of De Chaumont and his concordat and of Landais. With the new problems at the Texel in mind, he had stated prophetically as well as boldly his need of independent authority and his insistence upon it: "In short, while my life remains, if I have any capacity to render good and acceptable services to the common cause, no man will step forth with greater cheerfulness and alacrity than myself, but I am not made to be dishonored, nor can I accept the *half confidence* of any man living; of course I cannot, consistent with my honor and a prospect of success, undertake future expeditions except when the object and destination are communicated to me alone and to no other person in the marine line. In cases where troops are embarked, a like confidence is due alone to their commander in chief. On no other condition will I ever undertake the chief command of a private expedition; and when I do not command in chief, I have no desire to be in the secret."[10] This remonstrance is to be sure not conspicuously modest; but in view of his forbearance as well as his difficulties of the immediate past, present, and future, it scarcely does more than frankly assert what he knew was essential to success in such daring undertakings as only his genius could both plan and execute. His attitude also accorded with fundamental military principles.

It was still incumbent upon Jones to deal expeditiously with Landais because of the new mischief which he might threaten in addition to the old which was scored against him. A court-martial was not in order because of the small number of qualified American officers available. Pending resort to other summary action, Jones had written Franklin: "His conduct has been base and unpardonable. . . . Either Captain Landais or myself is highly criminal, and one or the other must be punished. I forbear to take any steps with him until I have the advice and approbation of Your Excellency. I have been advised by all the officers of the squadron to put M. Landais under arrest; but as I have postponed it so long, I will bear with him a little longer until the return of my express." Further provocations by Landais quickly followed. Upon arriving at the Texel, he had stated to his officers that if Jones should hoist a broad pennant he would display another "to vex him." Ashore, he boasted that the victory over the *Serapis* was due to his own merit. "He proposes," Jones described, "after gadding about in this city (Amsterdam), to figure away at The Hague. He continues to affect an entire independence of my control, and has given in here an extraordinary demand for supplies of every kind."

Now that the cruise had ended, Landais was to Jones only a vicious subordinate whom he wished to thrust aside with as little internal strife and publicity as possible. Yet in contrast with the distinguished powers which the Commodore habitually brought to bear against the national enemy, he seemed disposed to adopt an indecisive if not too-forgiving attitude towards an unregenerate personal antagonist, as exemplified previously in the case of Simpson as well as at present in that of Landais. Of course Jones expected scarcely any trouble in the future from the Frenchman. The Commodore had reason to look for coöperation from the civil authorities of America and France in dealing further with him, and he now faced a problem of more immediate and particular importance.

His precarious situation in the Texel threatened the flag which he had not lowered although the *Richard* had been sinking almost under his feet. It involved the security of his prisoners. It concerned a subterfuge of diplomacy for which his principles as an American naval officer and patriot had not prepared him. The Duke de la Vauguyon seems to have insinuated that it might prove expedient to replace the American by the French flag aboard his ships. Jones did not delay in communicating his concern to Franklin: "His Excellency . . . I understand makes propositions respecting certain commissions. Whatever you may find consonant with the good of the common cause and with the high respect which I shall ever entertain for freedom's flag will always meet with my earnest and full attention, and especially while in pursuit of the object for which Congress thought proper to send me to

France; but I can accept of no honor that can call in question my ardent attachment to the American cause and to the dignity of its flag or that can give the least offense to America. . . ."[11] Whoever might try to compromise Jones' honor had here his warning.

At least for a short period the cloud which had just distantly threatened to darken over his service in the American Navy was not in evidence; on the contrary his glory as an officer of the United States came to shine with new lustre for his magnificent victory. Probably his greatest satisfaction came from the carefully weighed words of the man in whose honor he had named the *Richard:* "For some days after the arrival of your express," wrote Franklin in his hearty first reply, "scarce anything was talked of at Paris and Versailles but your cool conduct and persevering bravery during that terrible conflict. You may believe that the impression on my mind was not less strong than that of others, but I do not choose to say in a letter to yourself all I think on such an occasion."[12] And for eyes other than those of the Commodore he also stated: "Few actions at sea have demonstrated such steady, cool, determined bravery as that of Jones in taking the *Serapis.*"[13]

There was acclaim close at hand when the refitting of his ships by De Neufville and conferences with La Vauguyon and Dumas brought him ashore to the Helder, to Amsterdam, and to The Hague. His attitude towards public applause contributed to reveal the worthiness of his motives by reason of the modesty and discrimination with which he received it. He allowed himself only a few days for business at Amsterdam and The Hague, and refused almost all social invitations.

Even English accounts of his visits were in some instances favorable. One transmitted from Amsterdam on October 8 related: "Captain Paul Jones arrived here yesterday and at two o'clock appeared on 'change'; the crowd of persons assembled together to see him was astonishing, and it was with the utmost difficulty he could afterwards pass to the house of the gentleman with whom he was to dine."[14] Another described him: "He is a very different man from what he is generally represented; good sense, a genteel address, and a very good, though small person. Great Britain will find him a man capable of giving her a great deal of trouble."[15]

A third included a more definite statement of his reception and appearance: "The French agent and the Americans paid him such a volley of compliments, and such homage, as he could only answer with a bow; he was dressed in the American uniform, with a Scotch bonnet edged with gold; is of a middling stature, stern countenance, and swarthy complexion."[16] Even a Dutch sailor's song, *Hier Komt Paul Jones Aan*, testified to the extent to which he won the popular imagination.

In general, however, a British sense of fairness found itself overwhelmed in Holland by a hue and cry led by Sir Joseph Yorke himself, which reverberated resoundingly in England. Not content with publicly and privately calumniating Jones as a pirate, he even entertained the plot of seizing him on some pretext. "A thought struck me yesterday upon hearing that Paul Jones was come to Amsterdam," he wrote on October 8 to London, "that if I could arrest him I might help myself by puzzling others, and I dispatched a friend on purpose to attempt it, but the high bailiff Mr. Dedel said without proofs and affidavits of robberies or demands of money (all of which we had not at hand) it was not in his power, as the affair would immediately become a political one; I was obliged then to give up that scent to my great regret."[17] Almost equally absurd and arrogant were the threats of a Dutch merchant who accosted Jones in Amsterdam with the demand for the return of his ship which had been retaken by the squadron from a British privateer as a lawful prize. Not to be outdone by fact, English prints, newspapers, and pamphlets turned newly to fiction. Characteristic of their extravagance was an account of Jones, apparently not content with booty as a pirate, in the new guise of a highwayman on the byways of London.

Offset against this mounting resentment at the escape in addition to the victory of Jones was a candor which sometimes tempered it in varying degree. In such cases only the Englishman's patriotism and his understandable view of Jones as a renegade to Britain prevented complete honesty with himself: "Merit loses half its lustre in a man who is supposed to be engaged in a bad cause, his bravery is said to flow from despair, and his bold perseverance is termed perverse obstinacy. This is verified in Paul Jones, whose late gallant behaviour would have been extolled to the skies, if his bravery had been exerted in our service, but as he fought against us, we cannot find in our hearts to allow him any merit at all. Justice, however, requires that while we execrate the principles of him who fights against his country, we should not rob him of those merits which we see him possess as a man, in a very eminent degree."[18] At least from this point of view of Jones the man, America herself could scarcely praise her naval officer with greater appreciation.

With complete honesty the British began to condemn in uncompromising terms their own political and naval administrators. At the same time some critics linked Jones with them as a disloyal subject when they turned to invective replete with bitter sarcasm and irony. The denunciation of Lord Sandwich (Jemmy Twitcher) and his Navy in connection with Jones was in fact not new; it had begun during the cruise of the *Ranger* and was only reaching a climax. During the earlier invasion of the coasts, the public had asked whether there were sails for even three ships of the line and whether the emergency was a suitable time, indeed "the very hour for amusing His Majesty with *fresh water spectacles and puppet show naumachia.*"[19] Now a Vice Admiral said concerning the First Lord of the Admiralty as to pursuit of the "pirate": "I do not wish too much to irritate the feelings of the people. But it is my duty to inform them that while the pirate was ravaging our coasts and filling even St. James with terror and apprehension, more than forty frigates were lying idle in port or employed to no national advantage. And with what wisdom or prospect of success was the detachment selected which was at last sent against him? A few frigates sheathed with copper, a foul sixty-four-gun ship (*Jupiter*) that was notoriously a heavy sailer. . . ."[20]

The sarcasm of a journalist was more biting as well as picturesque than the plain facts related by the Admiral. He ascribed to Jones a letter of appreciation, dated October 9, to Jemmy Twitcher:

"I should think myself the most ungrateful of all men living were I not to take the earliest opportunity of expressing the great obligation I lie under to your Lordship in permitting me, for so long a time, to seize, plunder, and carry off the vessels of the merchants, in the British and Irish seas, as I am perfectly sensible, my Lord, I could not have done so, but by your Lordship's kind permission . . . a familiarity of principles, lives, and circumstances generally begets mutual affection between men; and there appears to be a very strong and striking likeness between your Lordship's principles, life, and circumstances, when compared with my own. . . .

"Your Lordship and I do, both of us, heartily despise all the musty rules of religion; your Lordship and I do, both of us, love a bottle and a wench . . . you and I, my Lord, have both of us the command of fleets; you and I, my Lord, have both of us plundered the British nation, and are thereby become opulent; you and I, my Lord, are both of us hated and dreaded by the people of England . . . I . . . flatter myself with the hope of paying your Lordship another visit in the British seas before the winter is over. . . ."[21]

Irony took the place of sarcasm in condemning Jones along with three of the most powerful politicians of the British Government. *Paul Jones: A Song* opened in a characteristic vein:

Of heroes and statesmen, I'll just mention four
That cannot be matched if we trace the world o'er;
For none of such fame ever slept o'er the stones,
As Germain, Jem Twitcher, Lord North, and Paul Jones.[22]

Silence was the eloquent reply of the Commodore to the aspersions which, even from some supposed friends as well as proclaimed foes, thickened about him in proportion to the growth of his fame. Still a Dutch self-styled "old and tried friend" of America as well as admirer of Jones, M. Vander Capellan, elicited sufficient information concerning his life to stand forth as his major champion in Holland. He had learned something of the battle with the *Serapis* from De Neufville and sought a more intimate account such as only the Commodore could present: "I long to hear directly from yourself an authentic and circumstanced one, containing all the particulars of a sea fight rather to be found in the books of a former century than in our present age on the ocean. What emboldens me, moreover, to ask you the favor of such an account is that I have the mortification to see a despicable party spirit endeavoring to deprive you of a praise which even your antagonist, the commander of the *Serapis,* if he be as just as he seems valorous, will not deny you."

Jones' private words, at the instance of Capellan, were not less emphatic than his public silence: "I hope you will be convinced that in the British prints I have been censured unjustly. I was, indeed, born in Britain, but I do not inherit the degenerate spirit of that fallen nation, which I at once lament and despise. It is far beneath me to reply to their hireling invectives. They are strangers to the inward approbation that greatly animates and rewards the man who draws his sword only in support of the dignity of freedom."

Then followed his memorable remark, already noted in connection with his initial arrival in Virginia as a boy: "America has been the country of my fond election from the age of thirteen, when I first saw it." And likewise his comment upon the flag of the *Alfred:* "I had the honor to hoist, with my own hands, the flag of freedom the first time that it was displayed on the Delaware, and I have attended it with veneration ever since on the ocean. . . ."[23]

In the course of further inquiry, Capellan asked several intimate questions with the generous motive, to all appearances, of disproving discreditable rumors concerning the Commodore's life as well as a current belief that he was "a rough, unpolished sailor . . . a man of little understanding and no morals and sensibility." Jones furnished his advocate with various letters which were convincing enough that all the aspersions were false. He included among them the communication to the Countess of Selkirk, of which he refused publication because her consent was not at hand; and he mentioned concerning her husband, as has been suggested previously in connection with his parentage, that he "never had any obligation to Lord Selkirk, except for his good opinion, nor does he know me or mine except by character." The self-respect and candor of the replies were in themselves the seal of his sincerity and honor.

A citizen of Britain as well as one of Holland stood forth as a defender of Jones at this period when the breath of vilification, partly offset by the candor of English self-criticism, swept hot about him. This Englishman knew the Commodore intimately; he was

Thomas Scott, a merchant of London, with whom Jones had had business relations long ago as a trader at Tobago. He now fully revealed that the persons in whose hands the former merchant captain had left his affairs upon departure from the West Indies for America, Young, McCall, and Ferguson in particular, had not only defrauded him but also abused his personal name in England. As for his reputation in the war, "numbers in this kingdom entertain a very extraordinary opinion of you. Carried away with the torrent of popular clamor, they don't allow themselves time to reflect whether your conduct merits the censure it receives or not. Your plea [?] would weigh with the impartial and it would, I think, be doing you the highest injustice not to insert it in the papers. . . ."[24]

Jones felt with too deep conviction merely to speak to the popular ear. Privately, however, he again gave witness to the forces which motivated him. In one message concerning more personal affairs, he assured Scott, "The good opinion which you entertain of me, as a man of 'feeling for the distressed,' affords me the most rational and sincere pleasure. I acknowledge the great obligation that I owe to your attachment. . . . I have thought myself particularly fortunate in never having met with the ships of my former friends. . . ."[25]

In another message concerning more public matters, he stated as his conscience prompted: "If 'the torrent of popular clamor' had been in my favor in England, it would have been no proof of my having done my duty in the service of America. I should be very glad, though now an enemy, to merit the good opinion of the good men in England by my conduct in the war, which I pledge myself to you shall . . . mark me as a man of honor and principle; not serving America from pique or ill nature towards England nor from views of profit to myself, but acting from the noblest of all principles, gratitude for unmerited favors received from America before that Continent declared itself independent of Britain and at the time of that declaration. . . .

"You are exceedingly kind in wishing to remove the prejudice which Britons have imbibed against me. I have too modest an opinion of my writings to think they merit the public attention; and whatever the people of Britain may think of me, I must console myself with the hope that the rest of the world will do justice to my character and—remember it with affection when I am no more."[26] The words seem to have come honestly as well as eloquently from his heart, except to the extent that he probably deemed it unkind to express to an English friend, as he often avowed to others, the influence of the mode of British warfare upon his point of view.

Characteristically the Commodore gave such close attention to matters affecting his honor in correspondence with persons whose good opinion he valued. They received a due share of his time in the midst of pressing concerns which put his judgment and principles to new tests. In fact seldom in his life were passiveness and compromise more easy and resolution that squared with his sense of honor more difficult than in the circumstances which were now rising before him.

But the full stress of his situation was still to materialize. Yorke as well as Jones was anxious to have the wounded prisoners sent ashore for better quarters and care than were possible aboard the ships; the Ambassador sought, however, to have them pass from the control of the Commodore. Such a surrender was, of course, unthinkable to him. Temporarily the States General appeased both the one and the other by its readiness to coöperate as far as humane consideration for the captive officers and men was concerned.

At this juncture, Pearson as the prisoner of highest rank complained to Jones that he was not treated with due consideration and courtesy, and urged dispatch for his own release and that of all others confined with him. The American found the occasion opportune to remind the Briton of a presuming attitude taken by Yorke which had rendered premature any present measures for an exchange of captives. He called his attention also to the sufferings in English prisons of Conyngham, the Continental Captain, who himself described hunger which tempted the eating of dogs, cats, and stray bones; and quarters with a cold plank as his bed and a stone as his pillow. According to Conyngham, his tale, if the hardened rocks could hear, "would melt them asunder." "I know not," Jones replied to Pearson, "what difference of respect is due to 'rank' between your service and ours; I suppose, however, the difference must be thought very great in England, since I am informed that Captain Conyngham, of equal denomination, who bears a senior rank in the service of America than yours in the service of England, is now confined in Plymouth in a dungeon and in fetters."[27]

With practical results rather than verbal duels in mind, Jones requested him to intercede in behalf of Conyngham, calling his attention to retaliation contemplated by Congress as well as suggesting retaliation at the instance of Franklin and himself. Likewise he made an agreement with him for the greater security of the wounded British prisoners who might be landed to further their recovery. A formal reply of the States General to Yorke soon followed. In accordance with the Government's views, it confirmed the privilege of landing prisoners by Jones. It emphasized at the same time, however, a strict neutrality by reference to the placard of 1756, which provided for emergency aid only to ships in distress; and it emphasized that Holland took sides in the issue at hand with neither Britain nor America.

Jones had gained in a sense a victory—for the present. He possessed the good will of Captain Reimersma, the commandant in the Texel road, who sought to serve him. He could look forward to a respite which might permit his departure when conditions were favorable. He was able to provide suitably for his prisoners and to maintain so far in a neutral port the rights of the United States as a belligerent. He informed Bancroft with great satisfaction: "In spite of Sir Joseph, the flag of freedom is highly respected at the Texel. I had yesterday the honor to receive authority by the unanimous resolution of the States General and by an order of the Prince of Orange to land as many prisoners as a I please, to place sentinels to guard them in the fort on the Texel, to haul up the drawbridge of that fort, and to take them away again from thence whenever I think proper, and dispose of them afterwards as though they had never been landed. Huzza, America!" Whether deserved or not, the privilege to garrison a fort in a neutral country, even for the sake of prisoners, was unique in diplomatic history. It was progressively the warrior of the United States, as contrasted with the citizen of the world, who cried, "Huzza, America!"

◇◇

Chapter XXXIII

An Interim of Personalities

THE FAVORABLE turn of affairs afforded Jones a few days' respite. He employed it chiefly for correspondence, excusing himself in one instance for possible remissness on the ground that "the ticklish and uncertain situation of the politics of this country, as affecting the flag of America, has hitherto so occupied my attention that I have found little leisure to write."

Feelings which had been subordinated to stern action since his sailing from L'Orient now found an opportunity for verbal expression. He communicated especially with De Chaumont, his wife, and his son; with Bancroft as just indicated and with Lafayette; and with Franklin in relation particularly to Landais. In fact, his letters at this period became surprisingly voluminous in view of his precarious outlook and concurrent activities.

De Chaumont continued prominently in his mind. Franklin had written in a postscript of his congratulatory letter: "I am sorry for your misunderstanding with M. de Chaumont, who has a great regard for you." Jones must have asked himself whether the statement was well-informed and sincere or merely politic. De Chaumont himself had addressed him in a spirit of high compliment which possessed an uncertain ring. One of the first statements from his pen had revealed that his thoughts were especially upon the merchantmen which had evaded the squadron. Another seemed to protest too much his satisfaction that the Commodore had escaped death: "What regrets would have been ours if the flames had blown up both the victor and vanquished!" Jones had already expressed openly to De Chaumont his conviction of the lack of subordination and secrecy due to him: "I wish to act a candid part towards all men, and, therefore, wish you to have a copy of that letter [to Franklin] that you may see my sentiments respecting the 'concordat,' which you imposed upon me in the moment of my departure from Groix. What could have inspired you with such sentiments of distrust towards me, after the ocular proofs of hospitality which I so long experienced in your house . . . exceeds my mental faculties to comprehend. . . ."[1]

In the light of this straightforwardness, his next letter to De Chaumont appears at first glance to indicate an impulsive if not hypocritical attitude under the influence of compliments. Upon consideration, however, it reflects the personal kindness and forbearance which repeatedly characterized him for the sake of human relationships in the one case and of public interests in the other. And when occasions for action matured, all his being turned uncompromisingly and relentlessly from personal sympathies to professional acumen and zeal for his country's welfare. Under divided influences, he stated in propitiation, feeling perhaps that a bad agent and commissary was better than no agent and commissary at all: "It shall be my pride to acknowledge everywhere how much I owe to the attentions of France, and to the personal friendship of M. de Chaumont, for furnishing me with the means of giving liberty to all the American prisoners now in Europe; for that is the greatest triumph which a good man can boast, and is therefore a thousand times more flattering to me than victory."[2] Unfortunately he was to find that both the means and the end were far from being accomplished facts.

"I ardently wish," he added, "for future opportunities to render real services to our common cause. . . ." At the same time he did not fail to impress in detail upon him the perfidy of Landais and the assertion by the French Captain that it had been the intention of the commissary at L'Orient to change the command of the *Bonhomme Richard*. Although generosity impelled Jones to apologize for his previous frank words to De Chaumont, De Chaumont failed to apologize to him for his own sinister designs.

The spirit of conciliation led the Commodore so far as to write in terms of explanation and good will to De Chaumont's son. He conveyed also his appreciation of the services aboard the *Richard* of a volunteer whom the young man had recommended, the youthful Baptiste Trevallier, who had used his coat when a sailor called for a wad in loading one of the guns and his shirt dipped in water for smothering flames when they burst forth near the magazine.

Once more Jones ventured to communicate with Mme. de Chaumont, although he had not heard from her since his phrases had been tinged with an emotion that must have contributed to her silence. "The concordat . . . he imposed on me at the moment of my departure from L'Orient," his pen expressed plainly, "was the most humiliating paper that ever a friend forced upon the commander of a squadron, and even my success has not wiped off the dishonor of my having signed it!"[3] As for his mode of address to the lady herself, time, silence, and perhaps his unhappy relations with her husband taught him to change the key from his first ardor to his present courtesy. He mentioned discreetly "the polite attention and friendship of the amiable family at Passy, which I beseech you to believe I shall ever remember with sentiments of the most lively esteem and affection." Mme. de Chaumont's only recorded words in reply are few but meaningful; she confessed that the concordat was to her a "conjuring book."[4]

While Jones exchanged expressions of good will with his former intimate friends at Passy, De Chaumont coincidently showed an interest in Landais as a foil to him. He sent to Franklin a letter and a memoir which he stated might prove of use to the Captain of the *Alliance,* whose reputation suffered from the accounts in the gazettes. It was also with his advice that Franklin decided not to have a court-martial try Landais, but to conduct an investigation in private.

The Minister in studied words summoned Landais to Paris: "I am sorry to find that there are charges against you for disobedience to orders, and also that the Ministry here think the great loss among the King's subjects, viz. the French volunteers on board the *Bonhomme Richard,* was owing to your not coming up sooner to her assistance, as it is supposed you might have done. M. de Sartine has in consequence written to me that it is expected I should cause an immediate inquiry to be made into your conduct.

"A court-martial is the regular way, if you choose it. But as that may occasion a long discussion, and be in many respects at this time inconvenient to the service, I have (with the advice too of your

friend M. de Chaumont) thought it better to give you an opportunity of justifying yourself both to the Ministry and to me by
coming directly to Paris, which I do hereby accordingly desire or
to use a stronger expression (as you may think such necessary to
justify your leaving your ship) I do require that you render
yourself here as soon as possible. I need not advise you to bring
with you such papers and testimonies as you may think proper for
your justification, and will only add that you may be sure of
finding in me every disposition to do that justice to your character which it shall appear to merit."[5]

In a different vein Franklin informed Jones on the same day
concerning these proceedings: I know not whether he will obey
my orders, nor what the Ministry will do with him if he comes, but
I suspect that they may by some of their concise operations save
the trouble of a court-martial. It will be well, however, for you
to furnish me with what you may judge proper to support the
charges against him, that I may be able to give a just and clear
account of the affair to Congress.

"In the meantime it will be necessary, if he should refuse to
come, that you should put him under arrest, and in that case, as
well as if he comes, that you should either appoint some person
to command his ship, or take it upon yourself; for I know of no
person to recommend to you as fit for that station."

Landais prepared to obey the summons from Franklin. He
prefaced his departure by a quarrel with Cottineau, who had both
testified against him in favor of Jones and had refused to support
the fabric of false evidence which he sought to weave with the
aid of some of the *Alliance* officers. After Cottineau, it appears,
suffered a serious wound from the sword of the challenger, Landais
had not the least reason to expect a testimonial of any kind from
him, although he still had the temerity to try to exact a statement in
his favor. Then in fear at his delay, he wrote disingenuously to
Franklin: "I . . . would have complied with your order . . . immediately . . . had I not been detained on board one day to over-
haul my papers, and when I came on shore thinking I wanted but
half an hour . . . to have a certificate from under the hand of
M. Cottineau . . . I found him so ill that he was neither to be
spoken to or to be seen. I have ever since been waiting for a

moment of relief, but it is not yet come. I do not know what to do."[6]

With his habitual insolence, he finally determined to follow the challenge to Cottineau by another to Jones, who promptly sent persons to arrest him. When this intention came to Landais' ears, it sped him on his way to Paris, with jealousy, revenge, and semi-madness as his companions. And for want of a better officer aboard the *Alliance,* Jones appointed Lieutenant Degge as her temporary commander.

Unable as Jones was to confront Landais at the investigation to be made in Paris, he prepared an overwhelming array of evidence against him. It took the form of twenty-five articles attested to by number according to the specific knowledge of each of the twenty-one officers and midshipmen who affixed their names to the document. It had also ten separate detailed testimonials by some of them. The names included officers not only of the *Bonhomme Richard* but also of the *Pallas, Vengeance,* and *Alliance,* including Captains Cottineau and Ricot of their respective ships and Captain of Marines Parke, Lieutenant Degge, and several minor officers of the *Alliance.* The charges were a history of the misdeeds of Landais from the preliminary cruise to the arrival at the Texel.[7]

In confidence Ricot expressed in epitome to Jones his judgment concerning the subject of these accusations: "Landais is a madman from whom there is everything to fear." Cottineau also bore witness to his choleric temper that bordered upon insanity. But after the Captain of the *Pallas* came to learn of Jones' letter to Franklin in which the account of the attempt upon Leith and other remarks impressed him as immodest and unjust, his favor turned to extreme resentment towards its author. He then charged Jones with incapacity as the chief officer of the squadron, responsibility for loss of the merchant vessels, and inhumanity towards his wounded men.[8] The last part of this accusation, it is recalled, has already appeared in respect to prejudiced and unwitnessed assertions by Pearson, and so it loses rather than gains support from the British Captain. Cottineau's diatribe tends to reveal that Jones was often self-centered; but the condemnation wants credence in proportion to its spleen and its inconsistency with earlier views.

Jones delayed somewhat in forwarding his testimony because La Vauguyon had advised against sending it by ordinary post, and he himself remained uncertain when Landais left Amsterdam for Paris. He had refrained from arresting the Frenchman in good season, from dueling with him, even from taking command of the *Alliance*. It now seemingly rested with Franklin to deal with the incorrigible officer.

In contrast with the contentions as well as dangers which Landais and De Chaumont had provoked, a buoyancy inherent in his nature and stimulated by an idealistic personality somewhat similar to his own pulsed in his veins and took form in his phrases when Lafayette was his correspondent. The lure and love felt for the sea which bespeak the poet, regardless of all disillusioning realities and practical obstacles, forced themselves at least to a word of expression, hidden as emotion was beneath banter: "I am very much concerned and ashamed to understand that my 'numbers' that you received from L'Orient were so ill-composed. It is proof that their ladyships the muses, however condescending they may be on the banks of the Helicon, will not dispense their favors to the sons of Neptune, especially while they are

> By bounding billows and rude winds that blow
> Alternate tossed in air or sunk to sands below."[9]

As the forte of Jones was deeds rather than song, however, he conveyed in prose to better purpose the poetical quality which inspired him as a warrior. This he did implicitly and frankly when, in retracting certain minor criticisms of Cottineau and Ricot and giving them due credit, he added: "I must speak plainly my opinions since you desire it. I do not think that the desire of glory was the uppermost sentiment in the breast of any captain under my command at the time we left L'Orient."[10] Although an implication concerning himself was evident under the circumstances of Lafayette's inquiry, the dominant motives of Jones, in which his love of honor sprang essentially from his devotion as an American, distinguished him none the less highly.

◇◇◇

Chapter XXXIV

The Three-Fold Pressure by Holland, France, and Britain

THE ABEYANCE of difficulties in the neutral port had scarcely allowed the Commodore a few days for concerns reverting to his cruise before he became aware of a new serious turn in his immediate situation. Sir Joseph Yorke had continued to be unremitting in his bold efforts to have Holland deal summarily with Jones and his squadron. As the Prince of Orange was partial to England, Yorke represented especially to him that the Netherlands was being "duped by the intrigues of France"; he alleged that the French Ambassador had not officially recognized Jones, that the States of Holland had not acknowledged the American Congress, and that therefore "nothing seemed to [him] so easy as to turn the intrigue back upon them."[1]

Yorke took upon himself also to communicate to the Prince "some particulars of the conduct of Jones, which could not but offend him." His opprobrium toward the commander as well as his political charges was even more apparent in his second memorial of October 29, 1779 to the States General than in his first address to them. He inveighed in such terms: ". . . that these ships and their crews may be stopped and delivered up, which the pirate Paul Jones of Scotland, who is a rebel subject and a criminal of the State, has taken . . . the placards even of your High Mightinesses authorize, according to the custom of admiralties, to treat all those as pirates whose letters are found to be illegal, for want of being granted by a sovereign power.

"The quality of Paul Jones, and all the circumstances of the affair, are too notorious for your High Mightinesses to be ignorant of them. The eyes of all Europe are fixed upon your resolution. . . ."[2]

Some of the political arguments of Yorke, notably those regarding the placard of 1756, departed from truth almost as much as the epithets which he directed in hate at Jones. Yet they succeeded so far as to lead at once to new concern and action on the part of Holland in fear of international repercussions. Only a few days after the Ambassador's memorial, on November 4 the commandant of the Texel road had a letter from the Prince of Orange, on the basis of which "he questioned me," Jones reported to Vauguyon, "very closely whether I had a French commission." His insistence that the squadron should depart forthwith, even while the refitting had not been completed, prompted the Commodore to retort that, "as there are eight of the enemy's ships lying in wait for me at the south entrance and four more at the north entrance of the port, I [am] unable to fight more than three times my force. . . ."[3] In place of Captain Riemersma, Vice-Admiral Reynst assumed command in the road on November 6 with thirteen ships of the line. He was opposed politically to America as much as Captain Riemersma had shown himself favorable towards her, and proceeded to act immediately in accordance with the orders of the Prince. He pressed Jones further to make the utmost despatch for sailing, and sought to restrain him from sending his prisoners in advance to a French port. He insinuated also that his entry had been not by hazard but design and that "it was not much in rule to bear and make use of two commissions"—remarks to be placed at the door not of the Commodore but the diplomats behind him.

Jones recognized well enough the toils of the British and the Dutch which were closing about him, and he turned the more resolutely to his purpose of leaving the Texel with his ships, his prisoners, and his honor as an American officer and as a man. He now had a premonition, too, of a third source of danger, French diplomacy, however well or ill intended; the earlier hints from La Vauguyon of the possible expediency of changing the American for the French flag might become more in the nature of a command. He therefore considered the feasibility of embarking most of his prisoners on board the *Countess of Scarborough* and the *Vengeance* and of "sending them out by the first spurt of wind that will permit them to sail."⁴ He expedited his preparations as much as possible in the face of various adverse circumstances: weather which prevented the Dutch carpenters from performing more than a day's work in a week; a distance of twenty-six leagues at the Texel from the source of water and other supplies at Amsterdam; bread that was "literally speaking, rotten"; the continued absence of clothes and bedding for the sailors of the *Bonhomme Richard;* discontent of the seamen without a farthing of wages and with fears for the loss of their prizes from the British ships in the offing.

Even France in addition to Holland and Britain was now to force Jones' back to the wall. Nor did the United States, in the person of the Minister Plenipotentiary, particularly help him. De Sartine transmitted orders for the squadron to Franklin, and Franklin gave his general consent when the Minister of Marine forwarded them likewise to Ambassador de la Vauguyon. The dangers besetting the ships had come fully to their notice, and De Sartine determined upon the safe if not the more courageous course for preventing the capture of them, however distasteful his procedure was to be to the Commodore. The Frenchman stated on November 6, 1779 in a brief note to the American Minister: "Circumstances require that the expedition of the squadron, under the orders of Mr. Jones, should terminate at the Texel. It seems indispensable to give a new destination to the different ships which compose it. You are at liberty, sir, to dispose of the American frigate, the *Alliance,* according to the views you may entertain in relation to the service of the United States. . . ."⁵

Franklin reserved judgment as to provision for the English prisoners. They were as important to him as to Jones. He had earlier remarked upon learning of their arrival at the Texel: "I am uneasy about your prisoners (504 in number). I wish they were safe in France. You will then have completed the glorious work of giving liberty to all the Americans that have so long languished for it in the British prisons, for there are not so many there as you have now taken."⁶

Doubts thickened about Jones on this score as well as others. On November 12 La Vauguyon, having heard from De Sartine, instructed the commander not to sail before further notice; on the same day Reynst was insistent that he depart with the first fair wind. On November 17 the States of Holland, acting upon the more recent petition of Yorke, reiterated their strict neutrality and decided by a plurality of votes to press and if necessary to force him to put to sea with the utmost expedition, although some of the deputies, including those from Amsterdam, emphatically opposed the drastic resolutions as unconstitutional. This further development induced La Vauguyon to require that the *Pallas* and *Vengeance* should at once raise the French flag and to urge the necessity of having the prizes and the prisoners appear at the same time under French colors.

After learning these orders from Dumas, Jones sped from the Texel to Amsterdam to consult with La Vauguyon. He had already refused suggestions to command the squadron under a French commission. Instructions from De Sartine and Franklin now ostensibly left open questions only as to the prisoners, the prizes, and the *Alliance*. When the Commodore had previously considered entrusting his prisoners to La Vauguyon, with the purpose of exchanging them for Frenchmen held in Britain and with the further view of exchanging other English prisoners held by France for Americans, the French Ambassador had given Franklin such assurances, supported by De Sartine and Vergennes, as to induce him to agree to this arrangement. The danger of otherwise losing the prisoners to the enemy cruisers lying in wait was a factor in this decision.

After deliberation for thirteen hours, Jones now conformed to this understanding primarily because of the special promises of Vauguyon. Then to facilitate it, he deferred to the wishes of the French Ministry even more than Franklin expressly required. In his reliance upon the good offices of the Ambassador to insure the interests of his crews in their prizes, in addition to effecting an exchange of prisoners, he agreed to have the French flag raised aboard the *Serapis* and *Countess of Scarborough* so as to provide suitable means for transporting all the captive Englishmen. The selfishness of De Chaumont, who exercised pressure upon the

Ministry, was the chief influence, he afterwards believed, in effecting this surrender of his prizes. Yet for one of his hardihood there was more renunciation than necessity in his act, as he later indicated: "It may here be remarked that I made on this occasion a greater sacrifice in the eyes of all Europe than any other officer in the Revolution. I sacrificed that military pride which prevents an officer in a neutral port from depriving himself of his prizes and his prisoners which have cost him so dear; it is known that the prizes belong, according to the laws of the American flag, exclusively to those who make them."[7]

In vain was the sacrifice, which is measurable by the paramount importance to Jones of the prisoners, for whose sake the Stars and Stripes were to be lowered in a neutral port by the hand that had refused to strike them aboard a beaten, sinking ship. The later disappointment of Franklin and Jones indicates by contrast the hope which moved them at this earlier time. From one point of view inculpating Britain, the Minister was to write to Congress: "I did expect to have had all the prisoners taken by the squadron to exchange for Americans in consideration of my having lent the *Alliance,* and Captain Pearson engaged, in behalf of the British Government, by written agreement, that those set on shore in Holland should be considered prisoners of war to the United States. . . . But the English Government afterward refused, very unjustly, to give any Americans in exchange for English that had not been taken by Americans. . . ." From another point of view inculpating France, the Commodore was to address De Castries, the subsequent successor to De Sartine, concerning these prisoners: "If I had not been assured that Mr. Franklin had made an infallible arrangement with the Courts of France and England for their immediate redemption, nothing but a superior force should have wrested them out of my hands, until they had been actually exchanged for the unhappy Americans in England."[8] And he was to express his resentment even more plainly to a still later French Minister: "Would you suppose, sir, that my prisoners, six hundred in number, were treacherously taken out of my hands in the Texel, with two of my prizes. . . ."

These future passionate words reverberated with the emotion that Jones felt at the Texel for the honor of the American flag as well as the redemption of the prisoners. "Nothing but a superior force should have wrested them out of my hands"—he was now to put the spirit of this assertion in particular to the proof. In happy ignorance of what would actually ensue after the concessions in regard to the prisoners and prizes, he and Franklin had reserved at least the *Alliance* and her flag. Jones could be trusted not to cast discredit upon them even in his increasingly trying situation.

He hastened back from his conferences with La Vauguyon, arriving at night on November 18 and giving orders at once for the transfer from the *Serapis* to the *Alliance*.[9] Turning to work immediately until midnight, the crew carried a great amount of supplies from the one ship to the other during the next three days. All the officers and men formerly of the *Bonhomme Richard,* exclusive of the French volunteers, went aboard the *Alliance* to join the Americans already on the ship. All the British prisoners in the *Alliance,* with the exception of some of the sick and wounded, transferred finally to the other vessels. And while Cottineau hoisted the French colors in the *Serapis,* Jones kept the American flag flying in the *Alliance.*

In many respects Jones did not relish his new position. His major motive, he said, "was to preserve the honor of the American flag in the worst of times. In any other light it was a most disagreeable and mortifying change." He had transferred from the command of a squadron to that of a frigate. He smarted at the rather summary manner in which his connection with France had ended, and resented it the more because "the connection was not at the beginning of [his] seeking." He knew, too, that notwithstanding the instructions of Franklin for taking upon himself the Captaincy of the *Alliance* and the ignoble behavior of her former commander, which rendered his dismissal imperative, Landais and other enemies would insinuate that he had usurped the ship. In fact, he himself spoke of "a delicacy" which had restrained him from coming on board the *Alliance* since the departure of Landais.

As a substitute, too, for the *Serapis,* which was his symbol of victory, his and his men's possession by right of both war and law, and his witness of order, wholesomeness, and general efficiency aboard ship, the *Alliance* was in contrast, thanks of course to Landais, in a worse condition than any other frigate Jones had ever seen. Rats ruled and epidemics raged. The ship was so insanitary that the *Bonhomme Richard's* surgeon, Dr. Brooke, sought to terminate his connection with the American Navy on the score of his own health, and perhaps the somewhat disingenuous persuasions of Jones for continuing his services had some justification because of the particular need of so able a physician. Suffice it to say further that the *Alliance* did not have one good sail and possessed only one anchor, and that because of Landais' queer arrangement of her ballast and the size of her topmasts, yards, and rigging, she was "very crank—plunged very deep in a head sea, and could neither sail nor work as a frigate." There remained time, moreover, for providing only the most immediate needs.

Even so much time seemed, in fact, scarcely available. Before the Dutch resolutions of November 17, Vice-Admiral Reynst had been insistent enough; after them, clothed with the full official authority that they gave him, he grew domineering. He was taken aback temporarily when his aide, Captain Van Overmeer, came aboard the *Serapis* just subsequent to the change in officers and crews and reiterated the orders of his superior only to learn that the ship was now under a French command. As Holland was very desirous of maintaining good relations with France and as privileges to her antagonized the British very much less than consideration shown to the United States and her "pirate," the *Serapis* and the other ships now under the French flag enjoyed renewed hospitality.

The jeopardy of the *Alliance* increased. Regardless of unfavorable winds, regardless of final preparations, regardless in a measure even of the lack of suitable pilots, Reynst threatened and gave substance to his menaces by the close presence of his thirteen ships of the line. As Yorke had won in part a diplomatic victory, it was now in order to try to push it home. With all the vessels of the squadron, except the *Alliance,* in refuge under French colors, the attention of both the Dutch and the British focussed upon the lone ship at bay. Synchronous with the persistent bullying of Reynst within the port and the continual guard of twelve ships of the enemy outside it, the British Admiralty had immediate information to expect the American frigate, and Lord Sandwich on this occasion at least roused himself from his lethargy. "For God's sake," he urged Captain Francis Reynolds on November 23, "get to sea instantly in consequence of the orders you have received. If you can take Paul Jones, you will be as high in the estimation of the public as if you had beat the combined fleets. The whole of this business depends on dispatch; therefore not a moment is to be lost on any consideration. . . ."

If Jones did not know all the traps set for the *Alliance*, he was unruffled enough not to permit increased pressure, however authoritative, to impel him to hasty, ill-advised action. Fanning relates that Vice-Admiral Reynst refrained from sending his barge daily to threaten the Commodore after the latter stated that if they were at sea, the Americans with the *Alliance* and the Hollanders with a sixty-four gun ship, there would be a speedy end to the insults offered to him.[10] Dumas, whose account is of course more dependable than Fanning's, tells of repeated fulminations. Under such provocation Dumas himself in one instance discomfited the Admiral's officer sent to hasten the *Alliance:* "I made him confess with a loud voice, in presence of our crew and of his own rowers, that he required an impossibility; a declaration which I made the pilot sign afterwards. Then he let us alone during ten days."

Although fixed in the determination not to be hurried, Jones was equally resolute not to let slip the first favorable opportunity for escape. Beginning with November 29, the *Alliance* was almost daily prepared to escape, waiting for a favorable shift of the wind. Repeatedly the crew hoisted sails only to reef them, swayed up yards and topmasts and struck them again, even unmoored ship and got all clear for going to sea and then came to anchor once more.[11] In this detestable harbor, as Jones described it, the late autumn and early winter became stormy, and the winds which were prevailingly west and south proved unsuitable for the strategy of his contemplated dash for freedom.

At the final prospect of departure, the American officers and crew, especially those formerly of the *Bonhomme Richard,* had reasons for dissatisfaction perhaps even greater than Jones. He had gained at least public acclaim as well as suffered detraction; they in their modest sphere had little more than such approval as their consciences afforded them. Even the *Serapis* won with wounds and death, their legal American capture, passed before their eyes and with unforseeable results into French hands. Although Jones had done his best to safeguard their rights by promises from La Vauguyon and understandings with Franklin, he could only pass on these unsubstantial assurances to them. They were likewise almost naked and without wages as well as prize money. "My people on board here, both officers and men," the Commodore informed Franklin, "having lost their clothes with the *Bonhomme Richard* are in great want of everything. I am afraid to say a word of this to M. de Chaumont after the unmerited reproaches he has made me on the same account."

Apropos of the need of the men from both ships and an effort to propitiate them, the *Alliance* log on November 28 stated without remark: "Mr. Blodgett [the purser] paid the people one ducat each as part of wages." But Fanning has provided a commentary which may well be galley news in part but is obviously true at least as far as the amount received by the sailors is concerned and fairly acceptable as to their probable resentment: "We were informed that there was a large sum of money sent on board of our ship from the American agent at Amsterdam [Dumas] . . . but when it came to be divided the officers received only about five ducats apiece . . . and the sailors—one ducat each (not far from half a guinea). We were all very much disappointed, but particularly the sailors, some of whom, as soon as they had received each a ducat, in a fit of rage threw [it] as far as they could from the ship into the sea. . . ."[12] A further vague report that the amount remitted from Amsterdam was large and that the Commodore reserved most of it for himself seems in particular to have originated in the galley or near the scuttle-butt.

However mindful Jones sought to be of his crew and however occupied he was by the impending flight of the *Alliance* while she lay "barricaded," as he described, by two of the Dutch ships of the line to insure her speedy departure, his thoughts already turned to further enterprises, to the ending of his connection with the French Court, and to the hoped-for new beginning of his services under the direction of Congress. He felt afresh his ardor for the United States as his feet paced the deck of an American ship in fact as well as name and his eyes met aloft the American flag, despite the hostility of the Dutch and English and the diplomacy of the French.

With such feelings and under such circumstances, he wrote home both to Morris and to Huntington the President of Congress. Although the former, as Captain Thomas Bell had informed him more than a year earlier at L'Orient, "had left the Marine and everything is going to the devil as fast as it can," Jones previously had sent the Philadelphian an account of the *Bonhomme Richard* cruise and now did not forget his friendship and influence. "I am persuaded," he explained on this occasion frankly and boldly to Morris, "you will observe with pleasure that my connection with a court is at an end, and that my prospect of returning to America approaches. The great seem to wish only to be concerned with tools, who dare not speak or write truth. I am not sorry that my connection with them is at an end. In the course of that connection I ran ten chances of ruin and dishonor for one of reputation; and all the honors or profit that France could bestow should not tempt me again to undertake the same service with an armament equally ill-composed, and with powers equally limited. . . . When the prisoners we have taken are safely lodged in France, I shall have no further business in Europe . . . and I shall hope hereafter to be usefully employed under the immediate direction of Congress."[13]

To Huntington, with the notice of Congress in mind, he addressed himself with less familiarity but more obvious feeling. He recalled his services at the instance of Hancock, the former President, in presenting the outlines of his ideas on a navy system, which had led to the establishment shortly afterwards of the Navy Board at Boston and to various enactments corresponding closely with his suggestions. More particularly he retold with vibrant words the springs of his patriotism for America and indicated with effectiveness his hopes of a suitable future opportunity to serve her: "I have not drawn my sword in our glorious cause for hire, but in support of the dignity of human nature and in obedience to the genuine and divine feelings of philanthropy! I hoisted with my own hands the flag of freedom the first time it was displayed on board the *Alfred* in the Delaware, and I have attended it ever since with veneration on the ocean. I claimed and obtained its first salute from that of France, before our independence was otherwise announced in that kingdom; and no man can wish more ardently to support its rising glory than myself.

"I have never asked, and I have now to ask no other favor from Congress than the continuance of that good opinion which has in time past made me so happy, and so greatly overpaid my endeavors to do my duty."[14]

Precisely at this time when Jones with his isolated little company of Americans aboard a *bona fide* American ship felt the spirit of devotion and sacrifice to his chosen country at the highest key, the French Court chose to tender him its greatest provocation. This ignominy, which he thrust aside without hesitation, seemed the more premeditated on the part of the Ministry because it was analogous to previous treatment at Brest by De Sartine, when he had led him on "from great to little, and from little to less." Earlier Jones had refused to consider a commission in the French Navy as commander of the squadron for the better security of the prisoners, the prizes, and the other ships with which he had entered the Texel; now with the interests of France served in these respects, but with other ill-defined motives of expediency, the Ministry on December 13, 1779 proffered him a letter of marque and desired him also to affirm falsely to the Dutch authorities and in contradiction to his recent assertions to them that he had earlier possessed a French commission lost with his other papers on the *Bonhomme Richard.* It invited him, in short, to slink away like a coward from the Texel, to the dishonor of an American frigate and her flag, and in the guise of a privateersman.

"The proposition," as Jones has recorded, "was given me in writing . . . by the Chevalier de Lironcourt [the French commissary of marine at Amsterdam] to induce me to say and sign a falsehood." It was to these words that he flatly refused to affix his signature: "Commodore Paul Jones announces to Vice-Admiral Reynst that, although as an American he has used only his commission of the United States, it was not the less true that he had one from France, which was lost . . . and of which the document addressed to him [the Vice-Admiral] is a copy. Commodore Paul Jones will make this same declaration in his handwriting and will sign it if perhaps the Vice-Admiral should set this requirement."[15]

De Lironcourt acted by no means unofficially; La Vauguyon the Ambassador was not less concerned as an agent of the Court. The extent to which the Ministry was disposed to have Jones serve as a cat's-paw appeared not only in the untruth and in the kind of commission offered to him but also in the freedom with which it presumed to speak in his name. "I was informed by the Prince of Orange," Yorke wrote to Lord Stormont on December 14, "that the French Ambassador had just declared to the pensionary that Paul Jones had a commission from His Most Christian Majesty, and had been honored with it even before he sailed from L'Orient. This is the more striking because the man has twice given it under his hand that he had no other than a Congress commission. . . . I am told the Pensionary desired to have a copy of the commission which the French Ambassador promised him, but the next morning called again to excuse himself, as he said upon reflection he did not think he was authorized to give a copy."[16] Whatever measure of excuse there may be for the Ministry must lie in a wish to propitiate the Netherlands and to avoid being an obvious accessory to her further involvement with Britain.

Jones had the courage of a martyr to freedom; he scorned the weakness of a victim to subterfuges of diplomacy. On the same day that De Lironcourt offered the letter of marque and placed before him the untruthful certificate for his signature, he expressed his sentiments to La Vauguyon fearlessly and brilliantly: "Perhaps there are many men in the world who would esteem as an honor the commission that I have this day refused. My rank from the beginning knew no superior in the marine of America; how then must I be humbled were I to accept a letter of marque! I should, my lord, esteem myself inexcusable were I to accept even a commission of equal or superior denomination to that I bear, unless I were previously authorized by Congress, or some other competent authority in Europe. And I must tell you that on my arrival at Brest from the Irish Channel, Count d'Orvilliers offered to procure for me from Court a commission of 'Capitaine de Vaisseau,' which I did not accept for the same reason, although the war between France and England was not then begun, and of course the commission of France would have protected me from an enemy of superior force.

"It is a matter of the highest astonishment to me that, after so many compliments and fair professions, the Court should offer the present insult to my understanding, and suppose me capable of disgracing my present commission. I confess that I never merited all the praise bestowed on my past conduct, but I also feel that I have far less merited such a reward. Where profession and practice are so opposite, I am no longer weak enough to form a wrong conclusion. They may think as they please of me; but where I cannot continue my esteem, praise or censure from any man is to me a matter of indifference. . . .

"It gives me the more pain, my lord, to write this letter because the Court has enjoined you to prepare what would destroy my peace of mind and my future veracity in the opinion of the world.

"When, *with the consent of Court* and by order of the American Ambassador I gave American commissions to French officers, I did not fill up those commissions to command privateers, nor even for a rank *equal* to that of their commissions in the marine of France. They were promoted to rank *far superior,* and why? . . . from the respect which I believed America would wish to show for the service of France.

"While I remained eight months seemingly forgot by the Court at Brest, many commissions, such as that in question, were offered to me; and I believe (when I am in pursuit of *plunder*) I can still obtain such an one without application to Court."[17]

Jones, an American as he referred to himself in further words of his remonstrance, had scarcely done greater honor to America by his victory over the *Serapis* than he now did to both his country and himself by this declaration of the values by which he weighed his character, name, and services: his "peace of mind," his "future veracity in the opinion of the world," and concretely and finally his scorn for "the pursuit of *plunder*." The best commentary upon his sentiments are the words which came quickly and fierily from his pen for the eyes of fellow-Americans in France. To Franklin he wrote on the same day as to La Vauguyon, enclosing a copy of the statement just made to the French Ambassador: ". . . I am persuaded that it could never be your intention or wish that I should be made the tool of any great R—— whatsoever, or that the commission of America should be overlaid by the dirty piece of parchment which I have this day rejected! They have played upon my good humor too long already, but the spell is at last dissolved. They would play me off with the assurance of the personal and particular esteem of the King to induce me to do what would render me contemptible even in the eyes of my own servants! Accustomed to speak untruths themselves, they would also have me give under my hand that I am a liar and a scoundrel. . . ."

As for his approaching dash from the Texel, the scant regard for his honor only fortified his decision to run the gauntlet of English squadrons awaiting him. "The ship is well-manned," he concluded, "and shall not be given away."[18]

Within two days he voiced his resentment not less pointedly to other Americans, Gourlade & Moylan at L'Orient and Jonathan Williams at Nantes. To the former, he spoke of "the professions of a Court to which I have so long been a dupe," and of his disillusionment: "Lately, however, they have offered such an insult to my understanding as has fairly opened my eyes and enabled me to discover truth from falsehood. The spell is broken and I am again master of myself. . . ."[19]

To the latter of these correspondents, with whom he was even more free than with the former, he confided: "Before this time I suppose you have heard of the strange behavior towards me of the Court? Having shown them that the enemies' coasts are vulnerable as well as their two-decked ships of war, they now feel bold enough to assume the white flag. They insult my understanding. They invite me to disgrace the Stars of America and overlay its commission by a dirty piece of parchment! They are mistaken. The Stars of freedom are but rising here. . . .

"They are not rich enough to buy 'the pirate Paul Jones'!"[20]

However emphatically Jones had refused a commission from the French and disclaimed to the Dutch any service except under the American flag, La Vauguyon had already propagated the report that the *Alliance* was under the direction of the ally of the United States. The statements made by the Ambassador in conflict with those by Jones offered Yorke an opportunity for arousing widespread ridicule. He published in the newspapers his reply to an English woman concerning his purported efforts to secure the release of her husband who had been in the *Bonhomme Richard-Serapis* battle and was now a prisoner. He explained particularly for the benefit of the public: "As the people who took him are sometimes French and sometimes rebels, as it suits their convenience, that renders the affair more difficult than it would be if they allowed themselves to be French."[21]

The new uncertainty in regard to the standing of the ship came of course to the ears of Vice-Admiral Reynst, who lost no time in trying to resolve the question. The Vice-Admiral sent a request to Jones to come aboard his ship; it is not unlikely that Reynst and Yorke had concerted a little plot to make the Commodore prisoner in case he avowed again that he had an American commission only, for the English Ambassador certainly tried more than once to effect his arrest. In any case, Jones not unwisely refrained from accepting the invitation for a visit. The Vice-Admiral next wrote to ask expressly whether he was to consider the *Alliance* as a French or an American ship and to warn that, if she was the latter, her commander should "omit no occasion of departing." Jones replied that the American flag was the only one which he was authorized to raise and that he would sail just as soon as the pilot would undertake to conduct the ship to sea.

As if he had not difficulties enough, the pilots presented an added obstacle. Their wives as well as their own perversity and drunkenness occasioned precarious negotiations with women in addition to men. Jones had scarcely entered the Texel before he had requested Dumas to try to secure a number of pilots for the various ports along the coast in anticipation of an early departure. But the agent seems to have been able to fulfill this mission very poorly. On December 15 John de Neufville informed the Commodore with rueful humor as well as in uncertain English: "We have nothing left but to acquaint you ourselves that the Ladie Pilotes are afraid you will carry their husbands off. If they were it themselves, and some handsome ones, they should not be so afraid perhaps.

"But the matter is too serious to railly upon. . . ."[22]

Jones found it necessary not only to give assurances that his pilot would return in safety but also to content himself with one who was temperamental, addicted to drink, and otherwise unreliable for a ship waiting only for a favorable wind. Possibly these limitations rendered a "ladie pilote" less solicitous for her husband. In any event, Jones was able to reply to De Neufville on December 17: "I have this day received authority from the Vice-Admiral to detain the pilot on board. I fancy he will stay without compulsion. He makes difficulties only when he is drunk, which is always in bad weather. Of course I should not be sorry to change him for a better subject."[23]

Before the pilot was sober and the wind blew from the desired quarter, both De Lironcourt and La Vauguyon sought to placate Jones even if they now had little expectation of influencing his action. De Lironcourt offered assurances that the letters Reynst had sent the Commodore were further evidence that the use of the French flag would "give great pleasure," but he refrained from additional urging except to maintain that the commission concerning which Jones "imagined a thousand ill-natured motives" was intended for the good of the common cause and only for a transient object.

La Vauguyon argued vaguely but more subtly that the Ministers of the King had no intention to cause him "the least disagreeable feelings." He sent him "honorable testimonials of the esteem of His Majesty." He aimed at what was one of the weakest points in the Commodore's armor by promises of personal efforts to procure him "the means to increase still more the glory" that he had already won. He probed him at a still more vulnerable place by implying that any personal sacrifice was for the sake of the common cause of France and America—a consideration of the same purport and almost in the same words as that which De Lironcourt had shrewdly advanced.

Jones softened, but did not deceive himself. His heart was too warm to remain hostile under even very considerable provocations, but his mind was too penetrating and his convictions were too honorable not to distinguish the true from the false and not to offset the generosity of his affections by clear-eyed recognition of confirmed injustice. In a reply that held to the issue in the face of diplomatic blandishments, he candidly asked the Ambassador whether the treatment which he had experienced at Brest, exclusive of that at the Texel, justified further connection with the French Ministry, and also whether recent reproaches by De Lironcourt as to the expense at which France had been to give him reputation, in preference to twenty captains of the Royal Navy better qualified than he, was not insult added to injury.

"I may add here," said Jones, "that with a force so ill composed and with powers so limited I ran ten chances of ruin and dishonor to one of gaining reputation; and had not the plea of humanity in favor of the unfortunate Americans in English dungeons superseded all consideration of self, I faithfully assure you, my lord, that I would not have proceeded under such circumstances from Groix." The late provocations impelled him to make clear that the *Bonhomme Richard* cruise redounded very little to the credit of the French Ministry. He spoke plainly and impressively: ". . . the mind is free and can be bound only by kind treatment."[24] The fire through which his spirit had gone strengthened him to be sufficiently wary as well as honorable not to sign away his reputation in history as the most brilliant officer of the American Continental Navy in order to subscribe himself a French privateer. This victory as a man and an American patriot was a fitting complement to his glory as an American fighter. The calumny which was to hound him more than a hundred years and which was to be the more persistent because it had less reason in his case than in that of a score of other officers lost on this occasion the handle that it would dearly have wished to gain for pronouncing him a pirate.

Chapter XXXV

◇◇

The Dash of the *Alliance* in Triumph of the American Flag

However notable Jones' remonstrance and however ungracious the French offer were, it still remained to demonstrate at this late hour that he had not scorned compromise only to prove himself foolhardy. The Dutch fleet continued to press the *Alliance* from within and the English squadrons to await her from without, north and south of the harbor and elsewhere at strategic points. Since November 28, 1779 when many of the sailors had hurled their single ducats into the sea and November 29 when, as the log told, they "cleared hawse and got all ready to get under sail," the winds had been favorable, easterly or northeasterly, only twice, and had shifted before the *Alliance* could get under way.

On Christmas day the wind hauled to the eastward again, and Jones unmoored ship. On December 26th, thanks to the drunken pilot who had her ride by a single anchor and to a clumsy Dutch merchantman, the frigate got foul of this vessel but escaped injury. At four a.m. on December 27 a fresh easterly wind was blowing and Jones determined to make his dash. Soon the crew hove up the small bower anchor, at nine they "got a spring on the sheet cable from the starboard quarter to cant the ship, at ten cut the cable and got under way with several Dutch men-of-war and a number of merchantmen, at eleven got clear of the bay and hove to for a boat to take out the pilot."[1]

Possibly the influence of the Dutch and French well-wishers of Jones and the regard of Holland for protection by a neutral within her waters, if not a final desire to expedite the departure, afforded him the company of several ships of war until he cleared the bar of the Texel.[2] Then, after fulfilling his promise to lower the pilot for his return, he bore away. There were forty-two British war vessels at various times on the lookout for him, patrolling almost the length of the British Isles; and all of them must have been mindful of the declaration of Lord Sandwich that if they took Paul Jones they would be as high in the estimation of the public as if they had beat the combined fleets.

Now it was necessary for Jones to prove his strategy and seamanship. Characteristically he chose a course bold, well-judged, and unexpected. Instead of flying before the wind in the North Sea, where he could have room, the Commodore turned in the opposite direction towards the Strait of Dover and the English Channel, where he would obviously be at close quarters with the enemy. And instead of choosing a south wind which would have seen him well started upon such a flight, he embraced one from the east which might have afforded the weather gage to British ships in wait off the Dutch and French coasts. Nevertheless, on the first day at sea, the Commodore sent a short, confident message to Dumas by the returning pilot: "I am here, my philosopher, with a good wind at east, and under my best American colors—so far you have your wish. What may be the event of this critical moment I know not. I am not, however, without good hopes."[3]

Dale described the course adopted by Jones as a daring experiment which succeeded perfectly because it was altogether unlooked for.[4] When the *Alliance* left the security of the Texel, she hugged the shoals by the Flemish shore and gained a point to windward of the British ships stationed in blockade off the road. Then as the crew set topsails, steering sails, and staysails, and let out reef after reef, she squared away towards the open sea in preparation for her run through the Strait of Dover and the English Channel. When the frigate approached the Strait at dawn of December 28, the fresh easterly breezes emboldened the Commodore to pass to windward within sight of the Downs and several British ships of war.[5] If the wind had suddenly veered and occasioned extreme danger, Dunkirk probably would have been within reach as a port of refuge. On next day, with the breeze hauling east-southeast, Jones steered not less hardily to windward along the southern coast of England and within view of the Isle of Wight and the fleet at Portsmouth. The log relates laconically: "At 10 do. all hands to quarters—up all hammocks—exercise the cannon."[6] It will be recalled that he had assured Franklin two weeks earlier apropos of his determination to sail under the American flag, "The ship is well manned and shall not be given away." One hundred to one were the constant chances of a very serious encounter with the enemy, according to Jones; yet this degree of danger apparently applied to a typical commander, not to him.

On New Year's Day he had escaped beyond the English Channel and the net of the enemy. Now there was a three-fold reason for his exhilaration: this latest triumph over the British, the signal recognition by the Dutch of neutral rights for the United States, and the uncompromising honor of the American flag and his own name regardless of the dipomatic purposes of the French. He celebrated the event in a manner which foretold a quality of his nature long subject to the stern discipline of his martial career; it gave token of his ardent susceptibility to the attraction of women, which under favoring circumstances might challenge his zeal in war more decisively than when he had known Dorothea Dandridge in Virginia.

In the present instance, however, he did not take too seriously either himself or his correspondent, the poetic daughter of the learned Dumas. He had met her in the course of his connections with her father. She had written some eulogistic verses in praise of his achievements, subscribing herself the *Virgin Muse,* and she also had planned a festival in his honor on the occasion of one of his visits to The Hague. Jones had worries enough at the Texel without distractions of gallantry and the writing of verses; yet he had promised, although "a son of Neptune," to answer her poem by another "in some leisure moment." Now that the *Alliance* was safe off Ushant and the day was New Year's, he shared his mood of triumph by some lines to the young woman, adding a warning note to her parent: "To show you that I am entirely disposed to obey you, I have enclosed *un petit badinage* for the Virgin Muse. But if I don't find critical mercy, you shall not take me in so a second time. . . ."[7]

The apology for the verses, judged by their intrinsic merits and in relation to the approved poetic diction and the formal rhythm of their period, was in the main unnecessary. It was the more unnecessary in view of "the purgatory," as he expressed it, through which he had just gone at the Texel, apart from the meagre opportunities of his life for the development of the art of poetry. Not only politeness or bias in his favor led Dumas to reply that his daughter would "preciously guard the Commodore's charming verses":

> Were I, Paul Jones, dear maid, "the king of sea,"
> I find such merit in thy virgin song,
> A coral crown with bays I'd give to thee,
> A car which on the waves should smoothly glide along;
> The nereids all about thy side should wait,
> And gladly sing in triumph of thy state
> "Vivat, vivat, the happy virgin muse!
> Of liberty the friend, who tyrant power pursues!"
>
> Or happier lot! were fair Columbia free
> From British tyranny—and youth still mine,
> I'd tell a tender tale to one like thee
> With artless looks and breast as pure as thine.
> If she approved my flame, distrust apart,
> Like faithful turtles we'd have but one heart;
> Together then we'd tune the silver lyre,
> As love or sacred freedom should our lays inspire.
>
> But since, alas! the rage of war prevails,
> And cruel Britons desolate our land,
> For freedom still I spread my willing sails,
> My unsheathed sword my injured country shall command.
> Go on, bright maid! the muses all attend
> Genius like thine, and wish to be its friend.
> Trust me, although conveyed through this poor shift,
> My New Year's thoughts are grateful for thy gift.[8]

Practically no other American naval officer of the Revolution wrote prose with the accuracy, much less with the impassioned grace of which Jones was capable; and his metrical talent, however uncultivated, set him altogether apart. These rhythmic lines to Mlle. Dumas have sentiment supported by conviction, and war for which he still renounced a gentler mode of life rose spontaneously as his theme:

> "For freedom still I spread my willing sails."

As the sails of his frigate on new missions now filled before the winds of the Atlantic, the services Jones had just rendered were further to fructify. In addition to his more intangible patriotic and moral victories, his honest as well as brave course of action at the Texel in the service of America was to aid concretely in leading to the alignment of Holland as an ally of the United States and France and to loans of vital aid in the last years of the war. Indeed, of the published grievances in the proclamation of December 20, 1780 by Britain to Holland, in the name of the King, the initial definite charge is: "In direct and open violation of treaty, they suffered an American pirate to remain several weeks in one of their ports, and even permitted a part of his crew to mount guard in a fort in the Texel."[9] The privilege, without precedent in diplomatic annals, which Jones had won to garrison a stronghold in a neutral nation, even for watching over his prisoners, undoubtedly merited conspicuous mention in a declaration of war. The valor and devotion of Jones as an American, in the light of all the circumstances, were not the less admirable.

Part 4

Vicissitudes, Personal and Professional,
in Paris and L'Orient

Chapter XXXVI

The *Alliance* Returns to France; the Prize Money Crisis

THE PASSION for new achievement rose in Jones' veins at the free opportunity before him with a strong frigate and a large crew at his command, although the one was badly in need of refitting and the other was increasingly discontented. As for himself, he ignored the strain from his high tension of many months. He sought to allay the impatience of most of his officers and men to return directly to L'Orient for the purpose of receiving their wages and realizing upon their prizes. He steered the *Alliance,* however crank she was, in the direction of the Spanish coast in the hope of meeting English ships of war as well as merchantmen off Cape Finisterre. At the approach of a severe storm and with immediate needs of his ship and crew in mind, however, he came to anchor on January 16, 1780 in the harbor of Corunna.[1]

In port the dissatisfaction of the seamen again became manifest. Jones' sympathy was strong, but his Spartan nature and his ambition outran it. "All the people," the log stated on January 19, "refused doing duty until they got some part of the money due them." Their commander was evidently persuasive, for the log continued the next day: "The people were satisfied by the Captain so as to appear cheerfully to duty."[2] They naturally looked for some reasonable material recompense after their hardships. The *Bonhomme Richard* crew was still without sufficient clothing and other necessities, important even in the shelter of a haven and doubly important during exposure at sea. The original *Alliance* personnel, particularly the officers, had a record of dissensions and mutiny, heightened by the evil influences of Landais; nor did the scorn and hostility which the *Richard* men bluntly manifested towards them improve their dispositions.

When the *Alliance*, therefore, got under way on January 28 in company with a French frigate *La Sensible* bound for Brest, but bound herself on a short cruise, many reasons contributed to the discord which prevailed. So it was the less surprising that the officers objected after Jones informed them of his intention to look for enemy ships during about two weeks before returning to L'Orient. "Well then," he said to them, according to Fanning, who in this instance may be relied upon for embellishment, "I mean to cruise as long as I please. I do not want your advice; neither did I send for you to comply with your denial, but only by way of paying you a compliment, which is more than you deserve by your opposition. Go to your duty, each one of you and let me hear no more grumbling." The suspicion arises that, even if the Commodore had originally given assurances of sailing directly from the Texel to L'Orient in order to hearten his crew, the *Alliance* portion of the combined officers and men was in haste for the return through fear of a second *Bonhomme Richard-Serapis* battle.

Although the frigate now had very much the aspect of a British ship of war, Jones himself wearing an English uniform and his marines appearing in outfits found on board the *Serapis,* the strategy as well as the opportunism of the commander seemed unavailing in the course of a short cruise to the westward of Cape Finisterre. They met few ships. The crew was ill-disposed to search for merchantmen, much less to fight. And when Jones happened upon the *Livingston,* an American merchant vessel bound for France, he decided that it was his duty to take her under convoy. Both ships came to anchor at Groix on February 10, but because of adverse winds did not run into the harbor of L'Orient until February 19, when they moored at the King's wharf.[3] In an early account to Franklin. Jones mentioned the state of his health in explanation of his arrival at L'Orient before the *Alliance* had proceeded from Groix. It was one of the few occasions so far in his life on which he thought fit to consider or refer to the subject: "From my late fatigues my health is rather impaired; and being also, when we anchored, almost blind with sore eyes, I the next evening came up here at the desire of my friends. I have found some benefit from the change of air; otherwise I could not now have seen to write."[4]

In France again, Jones faced new situations which were to require more of his diplomatic than professional qualities. He wished to counteract some mistaken impressions which had arisen at the Texel from his blunt independence towards the French Ministry. He planned to refit the *Alliance* at once and to urge the acquisition of other vessels, notably the *Serapis,* for the service of America. He determined to exert his efforts as well as to fulfill his pledges in behalf of his officers and men for their wages and prize money.

The Commodore had scarcely returned to French soil before clarifying his views of the nation which had made possible the *Bonhomme Richard* cruise. He drew a distinction between the repeated difficulties which the French Ministry had caused him, having especially in mind De Sartine and his agent De Chaumont in Paris and to a lesser degree Le Vauguyon and De Lironcourt at The Hague, as compared with the gratitude and good will which the King and the French people had inspired in his heart. He tried also not to have his professional resentment affect his personal friendships. If his differentiations were somewhat overdrawn, his provocations had been great and only the rarest perseverance and the highest respect for himself and for the honor of America had saved him from compromises with far-reaching implications.

Not surprisingly his remonstrances from Brest as well as the Texel had stirred considerable questioning. He hastened to explain himself especially to Lafayette and La Vauguyon. The reply in particular to his brother-in-arms is memorable: ". . . here follows my political profession. I am a citizen of the world, totally unfettered by the little mean distinctions of country or of climate, which diminish or set bounds to the benevolence of the heart. Impelled by principles of gratitude and philanthropy, I drew my sword at the beginning of the American Revolution, and when France so nobly espoused that great cause, no individual felt the obligation with truer gratitude than myself. When the Court of France soon after invited me to remain for a time in Europe, I considered myself as highly honored by the application that was made to the American Commissioners. Since that time I have been at every instant, and I still am, ready to do my utmost for the good of the common cause of France and America. As an American officer and as a man, I affectionately love and respect the character and nation of France, and hope the alliance with America may last forever. I owe the greatest obligation to the generous praises of the French nation on my past conduct, and shall be happy to merit future favor. I greatly love and esteem His Most Christian Majesty as the great ally of America, the best of kings, and the amiable friend and 'protector of the rights of human nature'; therefore he has very few of his own subjects who would bleed in his present cause with greater freedom than myself, and none who are more disinterested. At the same time I lament the calamities of war, and wish above all things for an honorable, happy, and lasting peace. . . ."[5]

The professions toward the King were not amiss in view of his direct indebtedness to him and in the light of comparison with the regard which Franklin, democratic as he was, characteristically showed toward the French sovereign when remonstrating to Congress at John Adams' brusque thanklessness on the ground that France entered the war not for America's sake but her own. Nor was it to his discredit that, having views of international conçiliation in mind, in this instance as well as in his early, propitiating letter to the Countess of Selkirk, he characterized himself as a citizen not simply of the United States but of the world.

In contrast with these distant principles, an immediate activity was the completion of the repairs for the *Alliance*, which he had been able only to begin at the Texel. The ignorance and sloth which had governed the frigate under the command of Landais rendered the task of refitting her great in itself, and it proved the greater because of the exceptionally advanced standards of Jones in the art of shipbuilding.

On February 22 the Commodore returned on board from L'Orient and gave orders to unrig the ship. More than a week earlier he had communicated to Franklin her condition and needs. He had become partly aware of them at the Texel, but it was only after the passage to Spain that all her injuries and sailing defects were apparent to him. The repairs which he had in mind were so extensive that the Minister, who knew from earlier experience his liberality and expertness as far as ships were concerned, alternately entreated and ordered him to economize. "As for refitting your ship at the expense of this Court," he said, "I must acquaint you that there is not the least probability of obtaining it, and therefore I cannot ask it. I hear too much already of the extraordinary expense you made in Holland to think of proposing an addition to it, especially as you seem to impute the damage she has sustained more to Captain Landais' negligence than to accidents of the cruise. The whole expense will therefore fall on me, and I am ill provided to bear it, having so many unexpected calls upon me from all quarters. I therefore beg you would have mercy on me, put me to as little charge as possible, and take nothing you can possibly do without. As to sheathing it with copper, it is totally out of the question . . . let me repeat it, for God's sake be sparing, unless you mean to make me a bankrupt, or have your drafts dishonored, for want of money in my hands to pay them."

Although Franklin might threaten as well as beg, Jones was apparently confident that he would not deliberately dishonor his draft, as Lee and Adams had done after the cruise in the *Ranger*. With good intentions he replied, "I feel your reasons for urging frugality, and as I have not hitherto been among the most extravagant servants of America, so you may depend on it, my regard for you will make me particularly nice in my present situation."[6]

He was not conspicuously scrupulous in fulfilling his assurances. Yet the bad seamanship and the general inefficiency of Landais on the one hand and his own sense of naval perfection on the other are considerable excuses for him. The log supported the Commodore's long recital of conditions as he discovered them aboard the *Alliance;* it stated, for example, ". . . found one of the cables we got in Holland eat in several places by the ratts as much as 20 yards off."[7] In addition to the improvements made in haste at the Texel, Jones now repaired the cutwater; shortened the bowsprit and made its line less horizontal; completely changed the position of the ballast, which, as he said, "Captain Landais [had] extended along the ceiling from stern-post to the stem, an idea that I believe he may without vanity call his own"; diminished the size of topmasts, yards, and rigging so as to give the masts better support and to improve in general the trim of the ship; renovated the storerooms, gangways, and hatches; lengthened the distance between the mainmast and the mizzenmast. "After my arrival at L'Orient," he later explained to the Board of Admiralty," the essential repairs were finished early in April by the crew of the ship and four or five American carpenters hired . . . to assist ours. The materials of the old arrangement did not fall much short of finishing the new. Judges have allowed that, when the business was finished, everything about that frigate was perfect. I know not what was the amount of the disbursements." He failed to add that Franklin undoubtedly knew only too well.

The elaborate remodeling of the *Alliance* was, of course, to profit the United States more than Jones, even if he expected to remain long her commander. Similarly his repeated recommendations to Franklin for the purchase of the *Serapis* were not as personally interested as they may first appear. It was the natural wish of the *Bonhomme Richard* crew as well as of Jones that she should become the property of America rather than pass into the hands of some speculator. Especially as the *Serapis* had been safely convoyed to L'Orient and the *Countess of Scarborough* to Dunkirk by Dutch ships, and as the former was now moored at a wharf near the *Alliance,* proximity encouraged a further desire for Continental possession.

The frigate belonged wholly to the captors by the prize laws of the United States, but a public sale, which was the custom, would undoubtedly see her sold at a sacrifice. For reasons of economy in addition to sentiment, Jones had early urged that the American Minister should make the purchase: "It is the best ship I ever saw of the kind and would cost the Continent less than any frigate that has yet been under our flag."[8] Although repeated similar recommendations evoked no response, he had lately added with candor, "I wish she could be made the property of America." The reply of Franklin, harried as he was in bearing the financial burdens of the United States, explained simply that he had neither money nor orders to buy the ship.

It is true that while the Commodore considered the *Serapis* primarily as a potential American ship of war, the sailors, especially the *Alliance* contingent, viewed it in the main as one of their assets to be converted as soon as possible into prize money. Increasingly, now that they were in L'Orient, the men asked that expectations and promises of wages as well as prize money be converted into cash. If the rebellious officers and men originally of the *Alliance* were the more insistent, those of the *Bonhomme Richard* were the more needy. Therefore delay, let alone nonpayment, was to court mutiny, to which American sailors had been very prone in European waters since the time that Lambert Wickes in his *Reprisal* had brought Franklin to France as a Commissioner. In fact, the naval laws of the United States had not provided for payment of wages in foreign ports.

Jones was thoroughly alive to the situation because of past as well as present experience. He desired to satisfy the officers and seamen with the more expedition in order to have them sail willingly to America as soon as the *Alliance* was refitted and the arms and ammunition for America, which Franklin had in part already provided for early transportation, were stowed on board. The approximate time at which the ship expected to weigh anchor seemed to Franklin sufficiently near on February 19 to warrant his request of passage to the United States for several Americans, John Ross and Samuel Wharton who were welcome enough to Jones, and Lee and Izard who were very much less acceptable. But he replied in the affirmative with an ironic implication in his hospitality, which could not have been lost upon the Minister: "I will pay the most cheerful regard to the accommodation of the four gentlemen that you mention as passengers. I hope they will agree together, and I shall be happy in showing them attentions." The plans for the return were proceeding apace when Franklin informed the President of Congress on March 4 that Landais no longer commanded the *Alliance* and that Jones would "carry her home, unless he should be persuaded to enter another service, which, however, I think is not likely; although he has gained immense reputation all over Europe for his bravery."⁹

This renown of the Commodore failed, nevertheless, to dazzle the crew so as to render them less mindful of the money that they expected. As the time for sailing home distantly approached, they became the more insistent. They cared little for explanations. They made their sentiments manifest to Jones, and he in turn appealed especially to Franklin. Only a few days after the return to L'Orient he had expressed his hopes that the wages of the *Bonhomme Richard* men in particular would be remitted at once, and soon afterwards he had plainly stated, "Unless the prize money is paid, my throat will assuredly be cut."[10]

The difficulties in the way of settlement, especially of prize money, had been complicated by the outfitting of the squadron at the ostensible expense of the King and more particularly by the deputyship of De Chaumont, not excluding his concordat, to which Jones ironically referred as the agent's means to keep him honest. By the terms, in fact, of this document which the Commodore had resented bitterly on the score of the insubordination it promoted, he was scarcely responsible in any financial way to his crew, for Gourlade & Moylan and in turn De Chaumont became the agents for the receipts from their prizes and for disbursement of them. However zealously Jones might act in behalf of his men despite these agreements, he later took occasion to state not only that De Chaumont had usurped authority but also that Franklin had been misled by him to disregard the American laws governing the prizes. "The commissary," he explained, "persuaded Mr. Franklin that the intention of the King was to place the prizes at his disposition [the commissary's], and the American Minister gave him in consequence an order to this effect. By this order contrary to the laws of the American flag, Mr. Franklin exceeded the bounds of the authority which Congress had conferred upon him."[11]

It is certain that Franklin had permitted De Chaumont to give instructions to the squadron regarding prizes as the representative of the Court, although the right of the Frenchman to have assumed such control was increasingly questionable. The squadron had been commissioned as Continental ships; but the funds for their purchase, equipment, and upkeep presented a financial maze in which De Chaumont to all appearances had some commercial interest with the Ministry and was very intent upon advancing it by means of his indefinite position on the border between commissary and secret agent. Jones had felt unquestionably that his power was curtailed after Franklin had informed him in acquiescence to De Chaumont's financial arrangements: ". . . as the Court is at the chief expense, I think they have the best right to direct."[12]

As a sequel, the Commodore had subscribed under grim necessity to the express provision in the concordat that the prizes taken "shall be remitted to the order of Monsieur La Ray de Chaumont . . . who has furnished the expenses of the armament of the said squadron." This provision and its reason were in contradiction to the sovereignty of the American flag, to the Continental commissions for all the officers of the ships exclusive of those aboard the two privateers, to the *Bonhomme Richard* conceived as a tribute from the King to America in the person of her commander, to the references by De Chaumont himself as well as Franklin and De Sartine to the squadron as bestowed by the French Government, and to the assertion of Jones before the American Board of Admiralty that "the expense of the armament was paid by the Court of France."[13]

But perhaps the future would remedy the past. Franklin had been very much occupied with other concerns upon his old shoulders, and had been unable to examine the marine affairs with the care which he otherwise would have taken. He may have been prone also to be compliant with De Chaumont, either through his benevolence or his profitable habit of harmony with the French King and Ministry. And De Chaumont having been so scrupulous in guarding the interests of the officers and men against Jones might now be expected to be equally zealous in serving them himself.

Apart from the wages of the crew for which the Court appeared to have assumed responsibility, at least for the period of the cruise, there was the prize money from the proceeds of eight of the fifteen ships taken by the squadron, including the *Serapis* and *Countess of Scarborough*, for which the seamen impatiently awaited an accounting. Of the others, several had been sunk or burnt; one had gone astray; and the two valuable letters of marque taken off the coast of Scotland, which Landais, as Jones remarked, "took upon himself, *even under my nose* and without my knowledge to order . . . to Bergen in Norway," had been returned to Britain through the offices of the Danish Government. Now the time approached for De Chaumont to reveal his hand as the agent, whether self-assumed or appointed, for the eight safely arrived prizes, in view of his own express stipulation in the concordat, which he had taken such pains to have Jones sign and which he had signed himself.

De Chaumont inauspiciously did nothing towards appeasing the sailors for a month after the return of the *Alliance* to L'Orient, although Franklin had already tried to serve them. "I wish the prize money due to your people," the Minister assured Jones on March 18, "could be paid before you go. I have spoken often about it." He informed him, too, of his understanding that the ships of war were to be valued and then sold to the King, an arrangement which, whether for better or worse, was contrary to the American naval laws providing for public sale and had been concluded without the knowledge of Jones and his men. Finally, in view of possible delays, he offered to advance to them 24,000 livres, for which they were to be accountable. "I do this," he explained, "to prevent, as far as in me lies, the bad effect of any uneasiness among them; for I suppose that regularly all payments to seamen should be made at home."[14] The crew, as will appear, emphatically differed with him in believing that they should be made in Europe. Franklin was the more concerned about satisfying the sailors because he wished to have the *Alliance,* carrying a full, valuable cargo, sail if possible early in April at the same time that a convoy of French ships planned to weigh anchor.

A surge of wrath swept a portion of the crew when Jones was in doubt whether the 24,000 livres should be divided among the original *Alliance* as well as the *Bonhomme Richard* men, particularly in view of the special needs of the latter. Franklin replied that the sum was intended for both crews, and promised his efforts to secure the prize money for the *Serapis* and *Countess of Scarborough.* He had experienced enough contention, however, as a peacemaker among the crew, De Chaumont, and Jones, aside from Landais, to state at the same time his wish "to have nothing more to do with ships." He expressed this view also to Congress, urging his manifold other duties and his ignorance of maritime affairs as sufficient reasons; subsequent replies from Philadelphia only complimented him for the high character of his past services and weighed him down with new ones.[15]

At last De Chaumont seemed to act, prodded apparently by Franklin as well as Jones. For on April 1, the day following the previous statements to the Commodore, Franklin informed him that De Chaumont had instructed a French banker at L'Orient, De Montplaisir, to advance 100,000 livres for the Americans of the *Alliance* and *Bonhomme Richard* pending the payment of their prize money. Jones had no sooner received this information than he begged De Montplaisir to be as speedy as possible in paying these funds because his men had "neither money nor clothing." The banker answered that it was not possible for him to provide them, explaining that De Chaumont had told one story to Jones, a different one to Williams at Nantes, and another at variance with both to Franklin.[16] At once Jones made a further remonstrance to the American Minister, who had been disposed to find excuses for De Chaumont: "I fear that you will now find that M. C— has imposed upon you by promising what he has no intention to perform. He has given no means of advancing money here—and if the people remain much longer dissatisfied, I tremble and let him tremble too for the consequence!"[17]

While the sailors looked unswervingly for the payment of their money, Franklin at Passy, the passengers at L'Orient, consignors and consignees in general of the stores aboard the *Alliance* awaited her sailing. Jones standing between them had an urgent duty to the latter group, but also a more pressing obligation to the former. Although his responsibility to the crew was moral not legal, such words as "I tremble and let him tremble too," which never would pass his lips in battle, indicate the mounting dangers to which his eyes were open as long as the men remained unpaid. The blunt sailors did not need De Chaumont's business subtlety to recognize as well as he obviously did, now that most of the prize funds from the merchant vessels were already in his hands and those from the two ships of war would soon be realized, that the new delays and uncertainties promised to promote his advantage and their disadvantage if they sailed and three thousand miles separated them from the assets which had cost severe privations to all and blood to many. On April 11 the Commodore assured Williams at Nantes that he would leave with the first favorable wind—after settlement of prize money matters. On April 12 he gave orders for the payment of 800 louis d'ors (about half of 24,000 livres) to the officers and men of the *Alliance;* ten days later the log recorded, "The people received one month's pay." Shortly after this sop, Bancroft wrote Jones from Passy that he had been assured 100,000 livres were now ready at L'Orient as the result of Franklin's efforts to remove difficulties in the way of his sailing.

Before the arrival of this additional misinformation, an incident occurred at L'Orient which excited the crew of the *Alliance,* particularly those members from the *Richard,* to passionate resentment and prompted Jones to decisive action. They saw the embodiment of their valor, the *Serapis,* transformed from a superlative frigate into practically a hulk as workmen instructed by the Court destroyed storerooms, parapets, galleries, and all the interior construction, including an entire deck. De Chaumont had persuaded De Sartine not only to take the ship for the account of the King—dispensing with the public sale required by American practice and ignoring whatever might be the wishes of Jones and his men—but also in the same spirit to convert her into a merchantman or other vessel according to his own non-professional judgment and choice.

Jones realized the fury to which this new incitement might rouse his men—those of his previous command who were still half-naked and almost penniless and those formerly under Landais who were disposed to both faithlessness and rebellion. He decided to write no more but to go to Paris in order to effect his business face to face as he had done with decisive results when the *Bonhomme Richard* had been bestowed upon him. All his friends at L'Orient concurred in his resolution. As for Arthur Lee, who among others was awaiting passage, he neither asked nor received his advice.

Although prize money and wages for the crew were the controlling motive, a more personal reason also impelled him. He had already received acclaim for his cruise from many sources, including Franklin, but none from the French Ministry or King, however close his connection had been with them. If, indeed, he had not remonstrated concerning the Ministry and its agents with regret but nevertheless with sailor-like frankness in letters to De Chaumont, La Vauguyon, and De Lironcourt as well as to Franklin, the continued failure of official France to accord him any word of appreciation would seem to have been both ungracious and uncivil; but under the circumstances the reticence from Paris was very understandable. Understandable, too, was his disquiet, without attributing to him an inordinate love of public acclamation. Granted that his sailors were justified in demanding a pittance for their pains, he was warranted in desiring at least an honorable token for the trials of his valorous leadership. "I was on the point of sailing back to America," the Commodore explained, "without any appearance of obtaining justice; without the least acknowledgment, direct or indirect, that the Court was satisfied with my services! Under these circumstances, in a moment of despair, I came to Court to demand satisfaction."[18]

Jones had good reasons for going to Paris, but perhaps better reasons for remaining at L'Orient. Wages or no wages, prize money or no prize money, his *Bonhomme Richard* men might have bitterly complained but would without doubt have continued loyal to him. The *Alliance* men formerly under Landais, however, had been estranged by their own past behavior and doubly estranged by their present suspicious antagonism towards the new commander and all others whom they associated with their delayed prize money; his absence would leave them free to nurse their grievances and his return possibly empty-handed might spur them to treachery. Arthur Lee, now on the scene, made plotting his forte, and he hated Jones only less than Franklin; his activities already promoted a storm which the Commodore foresaw. Gillon, too, a state naval officer from South Carolina, who was an ally of Lee, found that his interests brought him at this period to the same port. And Landais, who had fared badly in Paris at the hands of Franklin, as will duly appear, chose in the hope of faring better to come to L'Orient at the same time that Jones was leaving it.

Whatever dangers might threaten from these sources in his absence, the speed of Jones' journey to Paris promised a forthright return, which would enable him to cope ably with any emergency. The trip from L'Orient to Paris was almost three hundred miles and required approximately three days; the mood of Jones appears in his headlong rush and its immediate occasion. "This morning at four o'clock," Bancroft explained in a note to Franklin on April 17, "I was awakened by the arrival of Captain Jones and M. de Montplaisir from L'Orient. The latter went forward to Paris, but Captain Jones not having stopped since he left L'Orient is lain down for a little sleep. I shall call him in about half an hour and as soon after as he can dress I suppose he will wait on you. He brought me the enclosed letter from Mr. Wharton, which will inform you of almost all that I yet know except that the King's officers at L'Orient have begun to cut up and pull down a considerable part of the internal partitions of the ship *Serapis,* which has much incensed the discontent of the *Alliance's* crew."[19]

Nothing seemed likely to turn Jones from such centered purpose as the manner of his journey indicated, unless it were love or fame. As for fame, he had shown modesty and restraint when it came to him in Holland, particularly at Amsterdam, although applause might to be sure assume very much larger proportions at Paris. As for love, he had practically renounced any interest in women during the period at the Texel, but his earlier life, his recent poem to Mlle. Dumas, and his cavalier statement in the Netherlands, "I must wait a more favorable opportunity to kiss the hands of the fair,"[20] augured a courtliness and possibly a passion for which the poetic side of his nature hungered. And although the shadows at L'Orient were a warning to him to return quickly, he may not have realized that, however difficult it had been to extinguish the flames aboard the *Bonhomme Richard,* it might prove even more difficult to quench fire of another kind if he happened to kindle it in fulfilling his gallant intention only "to kiss the hands of the fair."

Chapter XXXVII

Landais and Franklin
Duel with Words

A T PASSY, Landais with his sword rattling after the rebuff by Cottineau and the challenge to Jones had finally presented himself as instructed before Franklin on November 8 of the preceding year, 1779, while the Commodore had continued at the Texel preparatory to his dash through the English Channel and his cruise to Spain. It did not require the outstanding knowledge of human nature which the American Minister possessed in his mellow age to recognize the guilt of the Frenchman before a word had passed from his lips. But he had summoned Landais with the promise as well as the disposition to do him justice, he himself was answerable in America to Congress, and the question remained in his mind not as to the wrongdoing but the extent of it.

Jones, it is recalled, had refrained from arresting Landais or convening a court-martial to try him at the Texel. He was occupied at the time mainly with the precarious situation of his ships and prisoners. He considered without doubt the lack of support given him in the earlier case of Simpson. He wished to afford no ground for suspicions which had already been circulated by his enemy of coveting the command of the *Alliance* for himself. As the most practical reason of all, he lacked a sufficient number of American officers of suitable rank to conduct the trial.

Although Jones might well have placed Landais under arrest when opportunity had served, Franklin otherwise had greater freedom and responsibility to act. He had been impelled not only by the first charges made by the Commodore in his long account of the cruise and by those of other officers, but also by remonstrances from De Sartine with special reference to the frightful loss among the marines under Chamillard, incident to the aloofness of the *Alliance* during the exposure of the *Richard* to the fire from both the *Serapis* and the *Countess of Scarborough*. The American Minister's authority was implicit by reason of his outstanding office in Europe and explicit also in view of instructions regarding Landais from the Navy Board "to follow such orders as he may receive from Your Excellency, which he is strictly to obey."[1]

Preliminary to the examination, Franklin subjected to closer scrutiny than before the history of Landais' naval career, including his record in the French marine as well as his short service under an American captain's commission. It must have occurred to the Minister, regardless of the wish of the United States to reciprocate the good will of France, that Deane had been gullible and members of Congress even more at fault when Landais had gone to the United States as the captain of a merchantman and had received the command of the best American frigate available. Perhaps Franklin himself had been negligent in not making the matter more his own business when the Frenchman had visited him before initially sailing from Europe. The Americans had accepted Landais solely on the basis of his own representations, which it may be concluded were neither modest nor honest.

Although the French officer had claimed that his wish to enter the American Navy was due to injustice in his profession at home and to the desire to change his religion in America, he had in fact found it necessary to withdraw, if he was not actually dismissed by De Sartine, from service in his native country. The reason, as Franklin was to state bluntly to Landais himself, applied similarly to his American connection: "The same temper which *excluded* him from the French marine would weigh equally with me." Although he had claimed to have been a captain of a ship of the line in the French service, the vessel in question was an old transport condemned and disarmed as unfit for war, and his other appointments as a capitaine de brûlot and as an assistant to the captain of the port at Brest were only subaltern grades not in the line of promotion of the corps of officers in the marine.[2] And although Deane had been foolish enough not only to make him promises of a command but also to agree to his stipulations for a gratuity upon his arrival in the United States, Richard Henry Lee and Samuel

Adams, who particularly censured the first American Commissioner in France,[3] strangely outdid him in foolishness by showing great deference to Landais.[4] Thanks to the assertiveness of the Frenchman, if not also to other ill-founded motives on their own part, they had accepted him at his own valuation, had been his chief instruments in gaining for him the command of the *Alliance,* and had offered a bonus of 2000 dollars, which with characteristic punctilio and arrogance he had refused to accept on the ground that the agreement with Deane provided for 12,000 livres or 2400 Spanish milled dollars.[5]

Against this background, Franklin now set about the inquiry with Landais before him. Jones and his officers then at the Texel were not available as witnesses. Likewise the twenty-five detailed charges had not yet arrived because of the delay that had followed the advice of La Vauguyon to send them by a safer means than by post. Regardless of the wish of De Sartine as the official representative of one of the two nations concerned that Landais should be brought to justice, the French Minister was not disposed to act and the accused Captain denied his right to do so on the ground that his present commission was from America. Nevertheless, with sufficient evidence at hand to undertake an investigation and with only Bancroft and De Chaumont as onlookers, Franklin proceeded to examine Landais in private.

To the pardonable incoherence and inaptness of the Frenchman's English when no interpreter happened to be available for speech or writing, he added a contentiousness which had nothing to do with the medium of language. He never lacked a subterfuge, however superficial, distorted, or absurd it might be. If he had not been so self-assured in his actions and his defense of them, and had not been in a position to impress them as convincing upon some of those with whom he became associated, he would deserve consideration only from the summary and burlesque points of view which his semi-madness merits. But while he was potentially almost as capable of discord as a madman rampant, he remained at large and outwardly rational. The perversions of which he was capable have characteristic illustration in an early statement he had addressed to Franklin regarding the *Bonhomme Richard-Serapis* battle. While Jones had lost more than half his men and his ship had foundered, Landais had proclaimed as evidence of his skill instead of admitting as proof of his cowardice and depravity: "All that I suffered in the engagement was in my sails and rigging, with a few shots in our hull; and this was of but very little damage."[6]

Whatever Franklin may have thought of such self-betrayal, he remained disposed to hear Landais with judicial fairness. On the basis of the accusations already before him, he questioned the Captain concerning four main charges: disobedience to orders, grave injury to the *Bonhomme Richard* by gunfire from the *Alliance,* failure to assist the *Richard* early in the engagement, and negligence in permitting the merchant fleet to escape.[7] His answers reveal the degree to which he was unscrupulous in resorting to disingenuity and cunning to obscure the issues set before him. He had an argument for every point like a duellist's guard for every thrust, but the guard in almost every instance was a gesture instead of an actual defense.

Landais claimed, first, that the charge of disobedience of orders from Franklin and therefore from Jones was not valid. The short preliminary cruise, he held, had released him by virtue of the Minister's instructions from serving under the senior Captain when the main enterprise followed;[8] and the further instructions to sail alone if the *Richard* was not soon in repair after the collision of the two ships freed him from control when Jones proved to be ready quickly enough to have all the vessels proceed together.[9] With even less truth he argued his independence on the ground that all the ships except the *Alliance* were privateers, and with even more captiousness when, Frenchman as he was, he called for an English dictionary to prove to Franklin that the term *cruise* in his orders did not include coastal raids in the plans of Jones. Not the least of his arguments in maintaining his defiance of the Commodore—in fact, the only valid one, for which he had to thank De Chaumont, who had good reason to squirm in his chair—was the concordat. And on this score, Franklin, too, deserved no credit.

As to the charge that the *Alliance* had raked the *Richard* as well as the *Serapis,* the basis for even greater resentment towards Landais than his other deeds, again he had his ready explanations. His crew would not have obeyed him, he maintained, in case the orders

had been to fire upon his consort; and Franklin replied that it was
not likely. He had brought with him a certificate signed by officers
of the *Alliance:* "That every time we went for to rake the *Serapis,*
Captain Landais and Mr. Buckley called all the lieutenants for to
tell the gunners to take care not to fire upon the *Bonhomme Richard* and always explained which was the *Serapis* and which was the
Bonhomme Richard that there might be no mistake."[10]

Landais' claim to innocence in this regard faced many contradictions. There was the cumulative testimony of most of the *Richard*
officers concerning the shots suffered on the unengaged side as
well as those in the bow and stern. There were the incriminating
affidavits of some of the very *Alliance* officers who had signed the
statement in support of their Captain.[11] There was a characteristic
assertion by Jones: "None but a fool, a madman, or a villain
would have raked at that distance, while a friend and an enemy
were made fast alongside of each other."[12] Landais chose grape-
shot which would scatter. He was at such a distance as would cause
it to spread the more. The coördination of commands to fire with
the changes in the course of the ship made accuracy the more difficult and so involved the greater danger, especially because, as he
himself said, "All the guns were fired at her [the *Serapis*] one by one
as we went along." Even according to four of his own officers,
Degge, Buckley, Larcher, and Parke, "several people on board the
Alliance told Captain Landais at different times that he was firing
upon the wrong ship, and others refused to fire."[13] These as well
as other factors point to conflicting views and conduct on the part
of the Captain and his officers as to their cannonade under the
uncertain conditions of manœuvre and observation, in particular
by moonlight, as the *Alliance* sailed erratically along the unengaged side of the *Richard* and across bow and stern of the two
ships joined like one. At best the Captain had shown himself
utterly incompetent as an ally.

With presumption as well as guile, Landais far from acknowledging that he had been criminally negligent by his failure to come
early to the assistance of the *Bonhomme Richard,* not to speak of
aiding her throughout the engagement, claimed that he had "reduced both the ships to surrender." He did not fail to submit a
complicated explanation, including diagrams, of the manifold

manœuvres of the *Richard* and *Serapis* in addition to those of the *Alliance*, although it varied in some essentials from the consistent accounts of officers from the other vessels concerned and was irreconcilable with the opportunities for observation from his own vessel removed most of the time from the scene. He admitted that the *Countess of Scarborough* raked the *Richard* in the early part of the battle while she was already engaged with the *Serapis;* but notwithstanding his own ship was the fastest of the American squadron and she had been in position to fight first, he had failed to challenge the *Serapis,* had not shielded the *Richard* from the *Countess of Scarborough* after she had closed with the stronger British antagonist during the early period when the *Pallas* had not yet reached the scene, and had let the *Pallas* herself contend with the *Countess of Scarborough*. Nor was his falsity less when, in order to mitigate his dilatory movements, he pretended that the period of the engagement was only two and one-half hours; and when he laid claim to going "with all possible speed to the assistance of the *Bon Homme Richard*," regardless of his tacking at pleasure and coming down under his topsails.[14] Still the volubility of Landais concerning manœuvres, wind, and tide served his purpose of puzzling Franklin and arousing the Minister's diffidence as to his judgment in a question which assumed as great complexities of navigation as the Captain's ingenuity could give it.

The loss of the British merchantmen, which was very close to the heart of De Chaumont and which in fact did not appear as an issue in the twenty-five charges later submitted by Jones,[15] was again, like the concordat, a boomerang to the merchant of Passy. The effrontery of independence that De Chaumont had encouraged in Landais had disorganized the strategy of attack off Flamborough Head so as to prevent a speedier, less costly victory and better opportunities to deal with the Baltic fleet under convoy. Granted the lateness for overtaking the merchant vessels after the engagement had ended and the intervention of fog which shortly had followed, it was idle as well as ludicrous for Landais to contend that Jones had not given signals after the battle to follow these ships inasmuch as the Frenchman had disregarded orders flagrantly throughout the cruise and even treasonably during the combat. And it had been impossible for the commander of the *Richard* to set the example for pursuit in the pandemonium of his rioting, burning, sinking ship.

Landais was not at all daunted by the course of the inquiry; on the contrary, as Franklin had neither the disposition, professional knowledge, nor detailed information to gainsay many of his assertions, the Captain felt the greater assurance. As a naval officer, he had shown himself, in nautical parlance, a "sea lawyer."

The later receipt at Passy of the twenty-five detailed charges and the testimonials sent by Jones from the Texel on November 13[16] added formidably to the weight of evidence against Landais for insubordination, cowardice, and treachery, and also fully revealed, in connection with them, his confirmed cynicism. Franklin handed him a copy of these accusations, and he answered them in writing in terms of even less validity but greater challenge than in his verbal replies.[17*] The more definite the charges were the more vague and confusing was his defense. His new arguments ranged from the puerile to the fantastic, the captious to the blatant, the cunning to the demented. Characteristically in answer to the evidence that he had disregarded signals, "particularly the signal of preparation and for the line," he crazily avouched: "They could not pretend that wherever the *Alliance* was, she was not upon a line, as a line might be imagined from one of the ships to the other, wherever they were."[18] Similarly, in attesting to his scrupulous care not to attack the *Serapis* from one side while the *Bonhomme Richard* engaged her on the other, he unwittingly revealed his unblushing cowardice if not downright madness: "Captain Landais never passed on the off side of the *Serapis;* he owns it. . . ."[19]

Guilty as Landais now was in the eyes of Franklin, the Minister wished to have as little as possible to do with him because his authority to remove naval officers was not express, his shoulders bore the weight of more important business, and his distaste for wranglings was as great as this Captain's proclivities for them. The Doctor therefore furnished him with funds upon the understanding that he was to take passage for America, according to his own request, in order to have his case decided by the proper powers at home. Franklin preferred indeed not only to avoid responsibility for a decision upon the officer's conduct but also for his supersedure in the command of the *Alliance*. On March 4 he wrote the

President of Congress, "In the absence of Captain Landais from the *Alliance,* Commodore Jones took command of her," omitting to explain that Landais had come to Paris at his own orders. He stated further, "Captain Landais has not applied to me to be replaced in her," omitting again to make clear that he himself had shown no disposition to reinstate him, but instead had recommended that Jones or some other officer appointed by him should assume the command.[20]

In these circumstances, Landais and presumably Lee, who was soon to serve as his habitual counselor, did not suffer Franklin to wash his hands of the matter, in fact to assume authority and disclaim responsibility, in so simple a fashion. On March 11, 1780 the displaced Captain, still in Paris, wrote to him: "You called me by your order from the command of the American frigate *Alliance.* . . . You have kept me here these four months past I don't know what for. If it could be said in America 'tis my fault if I had not the same command again by not having not [sic] asked it should be given me back. . . . I therefore beg as a right Your Excellency give me the command of the *Alliance* again. . . ."[21] Franklin recognized in this letter a turn in the situation which required resort to his dexterous hand. He replied to Landais: "It is really surprising to be now told that the officers and crew like you for their Captain and that they hate their present commander, of whom however they have not made the slightest complaint, and to have now, for the first time, a demand from you of being replaced in that ship, made only when you know she is just at the point of sailing." In so far as an earlier request justified Landais in any way, Franklin intentionally or unintentionally overlooked such an application made in the preceding month on February 10.[22]

The guilt of Landais, however, had been so flagrant and his manner so audacious that Franklin expressed his personal contempt unreservedly and admirably: "No one has ever learned the opinion I formed of you from the inquiry made into your conduct. I kept it entirely to myself—I have not even hinted it in my letters to America, because I would not hazard giving to anyone a bias to your prejudice. By communicating *a part of that opinion* privately to you, I can do no harm, for you may burn it. I should not give you the pain of reading it, if your demand did not make it neces-

sary: I think you then so imprudent, so litigious, and quarrelsome
a man, even with your best friends, that peace and good order, and
consequently the quiet and regular subordination so necessary to
success, are, where you preside, impossible; these are within my
observation and apprehension; your military operations I leave
to more capable judges. If, therefore, I had twenty ships of war
in my disposition, I should not give one of them to Captain Landais."[23]

The Minister now saw also the need to explain in some detail
both to Congress and to De Sartine the part that he had played
in conducting the investigation. To the former he set forth some
of the specious arguments of Landais, especially in regard to disobedience of his own orders, but explained that the absence of
Jones and all the witnesses, the conflicting testimony, his own
limited understanding of seamanship, and his uncertain authority
made it both impracticable and improper for him to render judgment. At the same time he forwarded the evidence, including the
full complaint of De Sartine, and conceded a point to the credit
of Landais which was tantamount to damning him: "I will only
take the liberty of saying in favor of Captain Landais that, notwithstanding the mortal quarrel that rose between them at sea, it
does not appear to me at all probable that he fired into the *Bonhomme Richard* with design to kill Captain Jones. . . ."[24] It was
sometimes characteristic of the Doctor to convey in gentle language of understatement a telling blow.

The finesse of Franklin was further evident in his report to De
Sartine, who might reasonably have been disposed to complain of
the indecisive inquiry because the loss of the marines, of the *Bonhomme Richard* herself, and of the merchant fleet concerned
France, which had financed the armament, even more than America. The spirit of conciliation, especially the policy of having national interests take precedence over private quarrels, governed
Franklin in deed as well as word. He ventured the opinion that,
if the *Alliance* really had fired upon the *Bonhomme Richard,* the
act must have been the result of accident not design; and that, even
if Landais had ordered his men to fire upon the ally, it was impossible that they would have obeyed him. Of the hostility between Landais and Jones and the consequences to which it might

have led, he added specifically: "The inquiry, imperfect as it is, has, however, had one good effect, the prevention of a duel in Holland between the two officers, which might have proved fatal to one or both of them, and would at best have occasioned much inconvenient rumor, scandal, dispute, and dissension prejudicial to our affairs."[25] Politic as the Doctor was in screening the facts from the public, his half-confidence towards De Sartine was politic too.

After these precautions to allay the storms which Landais was prone to precipitate, Franklin practically dismissed him from his mind, especially as he understood that the accused officer was on his way to America. He seemed to be so fully of the opinion that his concern with him was at an end that he set aside a letter of April 12 from Degge and other officers of the original *Alliance* crew petitioning for prize money and wages and for the return of their former Captain. Although Franklin advanced at this period 24,000 livres for the crew at the instance of Jones, he otherwise ignored for the present this message which Landais very likely had urged in view of the Minister's earlier remark to him that his former officers and men had not shown the least desire for his reinstatement. Jones himself consistently appreciated the dangers that brewed from the malcontent unpaid crew, but he remained unaware of such preliminary collusion to regain the command of the *Alliance*.

In the meantime Landais was following his own further devices unknown to both Franklin and Jones. He had become as incensed against the former as the latter, having accused the Minister of gross prejudice upon the refusal to return the frigate to him and having felt the sting in the unvarnished exposure of his own character. Franklin followed his plain-speaking by a request for a summary end to their intercourse: "I have passed over all the charges made or intimated against me in your letters and angry conversations because I would avoid continuing an altercation. . . . Our correspondence, which cannot be pleasant to either of us, may, therefore, if you please, end here."[26]

"Such an insidious, insulting letter," exclaimed the righteous and civil Landais, "could be devised, digested, and wrote [sic] but by His Excellency, Captain Jones, or their equals." When he transcribed it, the Frenchman was careful of course to omit from the copy for the reading of others the earlier portion which would have revealed him as he was. In his revengeful frame of mind, he found, while still in Paris, none that could have proved more attentive listeners than Arthur Lee and Ralph Izard, who were now without political appointments in Europe, and Gillon, the officer with the title of Commodore in the State Navy of South Carolina, who had found the American Minister less hospitable towards some of his ambitions than he desired and was readily disposed to join the others in their hate of him. With Landais as a new member of their company, they met and dined together on several occasions. During their confidences, Lee the spokesman upheld the Captain, who reported with self-approval: "He conceived how wrongly I had been used by my enemies in France."[27]

After this preface in Paris, they adjourned to continue their proceedings in L'Orient. The removal to the new scene of action appeared the less suspicious because Lee coincidentally chose to return to America, although his preference for passage in the *Alliance,* regardless of earlier unfriendly services to Jones, was somewhat singular; Gillon wished at this port to gain the *Serapis* for himself and to enlist some of the *Alliance* seamen and some of the exchanged American prisoners cared for by Jones; and Landais left the capital ostensibly to take passage in a ship bound for America but in fact to reappear incognito at L'Orient to effect his plotting with the greater secrecy.[28] Therefore nothing could have been more favorable to his purpose than the absence of Jones from the *Alliance* upon his departure for Paris and Passy.

◇◇

Chapter XXXVIII

Glory and Romance Surround Jones in Paris

IN AN INTERLUDE, strange in his career but consistent with his character, Jones was to assume a rôle attended by some of the most distinguished honors and introductory to several of the greatest humiliations of his life. The commander of the *Alliance* had come to Paris on an urgent mission; but however attentive to the mission at first, he was prone to become less mindful that it was urgent, especially when the Parisian ladies admired him in the drawing-room and stood in awe of his reputation on the quarter-deck. The men—jealous officers apart—equally acclaimed him. Paris had awaited the American whose victory was the more signal in contrast with the mimic-like skirmishes of the formidable French and French-Spanish fleets opposed to the British during the recent expeditions off the coast. The *Bonhomme Richard-Serapis* battle was, as Franklin had stated, the chief topic in Paris and Versailles for several days after the event, and the French awaited the coming of Jones with impatience.

The obscurity of the Commodore's arrival at the residence of Franklin at four a.m. indicated that his first thoughts were certainly not of glory awaiting him in Paris but of saving the *Serapis* as soon as possible from hands of destruction. He wished to confront De Sartine, and Franklin offered to accompany him. The Minister of Marine had too long experience with the American officer not to be wary now of assuming a false position. He was plainly resentful at the open criticism which had come recently to his ears from the Commodore's pen, and on this occasion it induced him to adopt an unfriendly attitude. "He gave us," Jones described, "a reception as cold as ice, did not say to me a civil word, nor even ask me if my health had suffered from my wounds, and the uncommon fatigue I had undergone."[1] The wounds were presumably unimportant (a breastplate he had worn in the battle may have served as an opportune precaution), and solicitude for them was scarcely an object to a fighter who was little disposed to chronicle his sufferings; but De Sartine's distant manner boded ill to Jones and his men.

Either the Minister shortly had a change of heart, or more likely the initial acclamation of the French public and the welcome of the King himself had their due influence upon him. After the winds of favor turned in Jones' direction, "The Minister of the Marine," as the Commodore later explained, "paid me the most marked attention." Apparently the later attitude caused him for some time to forgive if not to forget the earlier. To Congress and to friends he reported, perhaps in part for reasons of public expediency, that the Minister gave him "a most friendly welcome" and that he showed a readiness to meet all his requests in regard to the prizes.[2] Jones understood that he had De Chaumont alone to thank for the alterations of the *Serapis;* De Sartine countermanded the orders which had led to them and agreed that those prizes which had not yet been sold, including the two ships of war, should be advertised and disposed of, as the crew insisted, not by private purchase for the King but by public sale.

These promises following upon the new graciousness of the Minister, in addition to the welcome from other sources which were already surrounding him, appear early to have blunted his intended insistence upon all the interests of his men. "It became me, therefore, to be very modest," he said regarding De Sartine. The Minister was probably not unaware of Jones' attractive but dangerous susceptibility to friendly affections which suspended in part his judgment. If De Sartine's earlier conduct is a criterion, he was not averse to taking advantage of the officer's present diffidence, especially in view of the financial straits of his marine department and in the light of De Chaumont as his agent. In the meantime, with faith on the one hand and praises on the other, Jones turned his face, presumably with only a few days in view, to Versailles and Paris.

Nothing frivolous or effeminate occupied his mind. When, for instance, upon his first arrival in France as commander of the *Ranger,* his American fellow Captain, Thomas Thompson, had recommended to him "the pleasures which paris afourds," he had followed the suggestion only to the extent of referring sarcastically to his "sister officer." Now, even with a triumphant entry to distinguished society before him, he did not fail to employ his personal favor for the benefit of the United States more than for himself. Better naval means and possibly higher rank were his ambition, as he urged with both candor and truth, in order to render the greater services and to achieve the brighter glory. However modest Jones became in view of the acquiescent manner of De Sartine, he had "improved this moment and the favorable disposition of Government to ask for and obtain the *Ariel* to assist the *Alliance* in transporting the clothing, etc. for our armies."

He had to be sure much of the resourcefulness and subtlety of the diplomat in combining pleasure with profit, and it is not to be doubted that he had even a greater share of courtliness and attractiveness than most diplomats, especially in the eyes of the ladies. To the extent that he possessed such a magnetic personality, it is the more readily understood but not thereby excused that he may have felt the temptation to link the delicate thread of gallantry or love with the tougher cord of public interests.

Among acknowledgments of appreciation, especially from the Court, the secondary reason for which he had professed to come to Paris, one of the first and foremost was from the King himself. At Versailles His Majesty expressed "his satisfaction at the zeal and courage" which he had displayed in Europe for the support of the common cause, and at the same time announced his intention to confer upon him certain tokens of distinction.[3]

Even Marie Antoinette, in her anomalous position along with the King as a scion of monarchy in a France turning swiftly to republicanism and allying itself with America, was moved to see and admire this champion of a country founded on principles alien to those she had known. The Queen presented him with a seal; it fittingly pictured Neptune holding his trident and the Arms of France, and this emblem in turn bearing on its crown an American eagle; it displayed also the flags of France and the United States draping naval guns.[4] She further honored the Commodore, it was reported, by an invitation at the opera house to sit in her box.[5] It was said in addition that she expressed a wish, characteristic of her freedom and fancy, to attach a waving plume to his hat.

The opera house and the theatres afforded, in fact, the setting for the most picturesque honors which awaited Jones. For several successive nights he was crowned with laurel wreaths amid plaudits of thousands who had anticipated his coming.[6] On one occasion the director of a spectacle had arranged to have a crown descend upon him by a theatrical device, "but the Captain happily fore-warned of this exaggerated purpose begged humbly that it should not take place." The same director, playing the rôle of the Count d'Estaing in the *Siege of Granada,* came in his costume as an actor to conduct Jones back to his coach. On the boulevards, as at the theatres and the opera house, acclaim followed him.[7]

The most laudatory praises were from a select body, the Lodge of the Nine Sisters (the Nine Muses), a Masonic lodge in Paris to which belonged two of the foremost men of their age, Voltaire and Franklin. Masonry had attained such prominence during the second half of the eighteenth century in both America and France as to have listed among its members almost all the important men of the Revolution; Washington himself joined the Fredericksburg Lodge No. 4 A.D. & A.M. in the town which Jones associated with his earliest impressions of his adopted country. In France the order became so popular that women formed Lodges of Adoption, which generally had, however, only a spurious standing. Yet these lodges attracted many of the most prominent persons of their sex. A few years later Count Cagliostro took advantage of the vogue to seek to impose upon the Masons, as he was accustomed to impose upon the rest of the world, by the establishment of lodges in which he and also his wife professed to restore the sublime rites of Egyptian Masonry.

As the Freemasons were of such widespread reputation, even international in accord with Jones' taste on occasion for citizenship of the world as well as of the United States, and as the Lodge of the Nine Sisters was conspicuously select at the same time, he not unnaturally became interested in membership at Paris. He had taken, it will be recalled, the first two degrees, doubtlessly also the third, and so had become a Master Mason, at the Lodge of St.

Bernard in Kirkcudbright when his name initially may have appeared as Paul Jones.[8] In 1777 while the *Ranger* was being outfitted, he had visited in Portsmouth the local lodge to which his second lieutenant, Elijah Hall, belonged and also in Boston St. John's Lodge in company with this officer.[9] More recently, on the eve of the *Bonhomme Richard* cruise, he had applied for affiliation with the Lodge of the Nine Sisters so that now the occasion for his attendance in Paris was apt.

This lodge dedicated by name and by talents of its members to the humanities received the new brother on May 1, 1780 with a eulogy by M. de la Dixmerie, its foremost orator.[10] "I cannot begin your praises better," he stated, "than by naming you as the subject of them. I can even say that they are finished when I have named you. . . . The Order of the Masons draws its origin from ancient chivalry, which in turn draws its own from ancient initiates since Hercules, Theseus, and similar heroes were introduced to the Mysteries of Eleusis. . . . May not the same then be suitable for you, T.·. C.·. F.·., you who cease to fight only after conquering, you for whom every new enterprise is the signal for a new triumph? Your deeds are celebrated even among your enemies; all Europe speaks of them with enthusiasm; and I am at this moment only the feeble echo of your renown. . . . One of the most famous poets has said, 'To conquer without peril is to triumph without glory. . . .' You became simultaneously pilot, gunner, sailor, without ceasing for one moment to be captain."

From Jones the valorous, versatile commander, the orator turned to his distinctive counterpart. The eulogist had in mind the literary aptitudes of Jones, ranging from his sinewy, expressive, and rhythmic prose to his aspiring verse and from his early experience as an actor to his extensive reading and his readiness of quotation from poets like Shakspere and Thomson. "You courted Apollo," he continued, "before you enrolled yourself under the flags of Mars. You proved the falsity of an assertion, hazarded by a celebrated writer, against an art to which he was indebted for all his glory. According to him, letters not only corrupt manners but also enervate bravery. He forgot that the poet Tirthée inspired the Spartans with the courage they had lost, and that only after having inflamed them by his verse he led them to conquer by his example.

He forgot that Alexander possessed all the learning of Aristotle, and carried the *Iliad* constantly with him. . . . In short he failed to foresee that the intrepid Jones, after having signalized his spirit and his genius in the peaceful pursuit of letters, displayed with such great splendor his courage and other talents in the awesome art of combat. We will by no means forget that you combine with your native genius to sing of great deeds a quality indeed even still more rare—that of doing them."

If the latter half of these praises is exaggerated, even for the occasion of honoring a newcomer among their ranks and at the flood tide of enthusiasm for his achievements, it seems necessary to search the annals of Anglo-Saxon history to find, in persons like Sir Walter Raleigh, naval geniuses who joined the pen with the sword more brilliantly than Jones. And although M. de la Dixmerie was serious, he was not too serious; he did not fail elsewhere to relieve the high strain of eulogy by a lower chord of humor, which at the same time pictured some of the military talents of his subject:

> Jones who is fighting has fertile resources
> Turns the tables upon his confident foes;
> As coquettes surprise by their facile recourses,
> One conquers he thinks, but is conquered he knows.[11]

The lodge took the opportunity to honor Jones by the hand of an artist more inspired than the tongue of the orator. It engaged one of its members, Houdon, the sculptor who executed busts of Franklin, Washington, and Voltaire, to portray the Commodore. The work did ample justice to the genius of this artist in mirroring his subject as he was in life. "It has been remarked," said Jones himself, "that it does no discredit to the talents of Mr. Houdon."[12] Both Jefferson and Madison later held that it was an excellent likeness. In this bust which can be accepted as interchangeably true and artistic, it is possible to see Jones in the prime of his personality, with features neither youthful and unformed nor aging and attenuated, with the stamp of his surmounted cumulative trials since boyhood upon his face in dynamic emphasis, and with the battle of the *Bonhomme Richard* and the *Serapis* newly engraved upon him less in the guise of the conqueror than of the aspirant athirst for new conquests.

The contracted and protuberant brows revealing the energy and concentration of his thought reinforced by feeling; the slightly lidded and averted eyes confessing his secret pondering and aspiration, his circumspect searchings, and his canniness; the lines and hollows of the jaw, mouth, cheeks, and nose indicating his keen and vibrant physical forces in blend with the emotional and mental—all these attributes harmonize to unfold the fighter and man that he now had become.

The apt portrayal by the hand of Houdon, "the true master of his epoch," as he was described, has its lasting confirmation by other contemporary artists, especially Jean-Michel Moreau, who made an engraving of Jones likewise in May, 1780. Although the latter adopted a somewhat more informal style and his subject a corresponding manner, the resemblances to the bust even accentuate some of the distinctive traits so as to prove the more that Houdon in his bust of Jones, as typical of his busts and monuments of others, achieved his fame not by idealization of life but by fidelity to it. As for Moreau, one of the most eminent Franch artists of the eighteenth century and a special designer and engraver for Louis XVI, the quality of his engraving of the Commodore and its fitness for his subject are not inconsistent with the quotation from Molière's *Gloire du Val de Grâce* which honors the picture:

> Tels hommes rarement se peuvent présenter,
> Et quand le Ciel les donne, il faut en profiter.[13]

The Houdon bust had followed definitely from Jones' membership in the Lodge of *Les Neuf Sœurs;* a more indirect result was its part in the expansion of the circle of his friends, especially among ladies. As they had lodges of their own, the notable reception which he had received doubtlessly came to the ears of many among them. Of the Duke and Duchess of Chartres, who had previously interested themselves in his naval plans, the former was Master of all the Masonic Lodges in France and the latter, along with many other titled ladies, was actively connected with the Lodges of Adoption. He now renewed his acquaintance with them and with the matron of honor to the Duchess. There were other centres from which his friendships quickly developed, such as De

John Paul Jones

Tels hommes rarement fe peuvent préfenter,
Et quand le Ciel les donne, il faut en profiter.

à Paris chez l'Auteur rue du Coq St. Honoré, près le Louvre.

**ENGRAVED PORTRAIT OF JOHN PAUL JONES, 1780
BY J. M. MOREAU LE JEUNE**

Possibly the first likeness after Jones' victory over the "Serapis" and before the bust portrait by Houdon. A rare etching. Courtesy of the New York Historical Society (Naval History Section), New York City, which owns a print from the plate.

Genêt, the first secretary of the foreign department, Madame de Chaumont and her family exclusive of her husband, and to some degree Franklin; but perhaps his best entrée was his own name as truthfully as the orator of the lodge had said it was his euolgy.

In the complex transition period of France which marked his sojourn in Paris, these years following the notorious manners and morals of the Age of Louis XV, French ladies as a class undoubtedly conformed to the accounts of discriminating persons of their own sex and mirrored themselves by the behavior of characteristic persons of the other. One of the daughters of the diplomat M. de Genêt, Madame Campan who passed half her life at Court as a governess of the children of both Louis XV and Louis XVI, described the customs in the reign of the latter as compared with the former not as better but different. "By a strange abuse," she said, "the evils seemed to find an alibi in the philosophical ideas which gained acceptance from day to day. Their new partisans professed such noble principles, thought, discoursed so well, that they were not called upon to act comformably. A husband had the license to be fickle, a wife unfaithful, among those who spoke with regard, with enthusiasm, of the holy duties of marriage. Love of virtue and of humanity dispensed with good practices. . . . Diderot the bold author of *Philosophic Thoughts,* also the licentious author of *Indiscreet Trinkets,* aspired to the glory of Plato but did not blush to imitate Petrone."[14]

Of manners, closely linked as they are to morals, Abigail Adams, whose pen was less prejudiced than that of her husband, the former American Commissioner in Paris, and at the same time as graphic as his, drew several pictures with the objectivity of a foreigner and a person of the same sex as those she criticized. On the one hand, when in Franklin's company she first saw the free conduct and the slatternly appearance of Mme. Helvetius, the elderly widow of the celebrated French philosopher, Mrs. Adams felt even more distaste than astonishment. As to Franklin's assurance that in this lady "I should see a genuine Frenchwoman wholly free from affectation or stiffness of behavior and one of the best women in the world," she did not fail to comment privately in terms which need not be attributed to her puritanical upbringing: "For this I must take the Doctor's word; but I should have set her down for a very bad one, although sixty years of age and a widow." On the other hand, this American woman admired the accomplishments and charm of her sex in the Parisian setting: "The dress of the French ladies is like their manners, light, airy, and genteel. They are easy in their deportment, eloquent in their speech, their voices soft and musical, and their attitude pleasing. Habituated to frequent the theatres from the earliest age, they became perfect mistresses of the art of insinuation and the powers of persuasion. Intelligence is communicated to every feature of the face and to every limb of the body, so that it may with truth be said every man of this nation is an actor, and every woman an actress."[15]

The venerable affection which Mmes. Brillon and Helvetius inspired in Franklin is well known. The fascination which French women had for a celebrated Briton, Dr. John Jeffries, the first aeronaut of the eighteenth century to cross the English Channel, affords a better basis for comparisons. The achievement of this pioneer flyer several years after the Revolutionary War placed him in a position as a hero somewhat similar to that of Jones. Granted that Jeffries had a difficult task not to become somewhat dazzled by the radiance of beauty and favor which surrounded him, he said of the French ladies, "What would I not give to be able to transport such easy, engaging manners, joined with such wit and delicacy, to England?"[16]

Perhaps, in view of the brilliant setting, Jones was to keep his feet fairly well planted on the earth. His early years of poverty and struggle had precluded female society of any consequence, at the outbreak of the Revolution he had renounced it, life at sea had isolated him and continued his aloofness. Now doors were open at every turn and the atmosphere was in harmony with his innate cosmopolitanism, freedom, boldness, and charm. The extent to which the sailor could give place not only to the gentleman but also to the poetically inclined devotee of accomplished ladies appears at this time characteristically in the diary of Grimm, the correspondent of Catherine the Great: "This brave corsair who has given so many proofs of the strongest heart and the most distinguished courage is none the less a man of the world, of great intelligence and sweetness. It is a curious thing that he makes many verses characterized by delicate sensibility and grace."[17] Even a romanticism similar to Rousseau's, if not influenced by it, was traceable in his recent preference of one sister to another as a possible wife: "She is really a fine woman—yet . . . I should prefer the younger because one might prevent some little errors from taking root in her mind, which the other seems to have contracted."[18] Only Jones' deep-seated instincts of ambition, duty, and action, it seemed, might prove powerful enough to restrain him from devotion to love not less ardent than dedication to war.

The ladies of the nobility and gentry whom the Commodore came to know during his romantic May in Paris and its suburbs grew both numerous and in some instances intimate; and although his expected return to L'Orient foreshadowed a smaller number, it also promised proportionally closer bonds. For the present, at least, his taste was catholic; some of the women were young, others comparatively old; some were single, a greater number were married, and one was the natural daughter of Louis XV; some were beautiful, others were wise, one was certainly coquettish, and one gave token of a heart like that of Heloïse. Yet they had a common quality—all admired him.

There was Madame de Saint Julien who wrote him with honest tenderness, expressing on one occasion her deep regret that she had been absent when he called, asking him to pity her for this mischance by coming soon again before his departure, and greeting him "with all her heart." When Jones failed to respond suitably to her encouragement, she chided him after her fashion by stating that it was very unfortunate he had not words as well as bravery, for the two go well together as promise does with performance.[19]

Less intimate but equally hospitable was Madame Thilorié and her sister Madame de Bonneuil. Vigée Lebrun, the noted artist, described his visits to them: "I often went to supper at the house of Mme. Thilorié, sister to Mme. de Bonneuil, with that celebrated sailor who rendered so many services to the American cause and did so much harm to the English.

"His reputation had preceded him in Paris, where everyone knew the number of battles in which he had triumphed with his little squadron over the ten-times superior forces of England. Nevertheless I have never met so modest a man. It was impossible to get him to talk about his great deeds, but on all other subjects he willingly talked with a great amount of sense and wit."[20]

There were additional ladies of whom he saw more. He naturally was busier in making calls than in writing—while in Paris. As for poems, he later informed Dumas, "I got many little pieces addressed to me while near the Court, but I made very little return."[21] He may have discreetly intended this information for the daughter of his friend at the Hague, "the Virgin Muse," more than for her father. His intimacy grew with Barbantane Hunolstein at the residence of the Duchess de Chartres; with Madame la présidente d'Ormoy, a writer of romantic novels and of operas; with Madame Tellisson whom the Commodore soon held in such estimation as to promise to prepare for her an account of his services in the Revolution.[22] He was, in fact, to correspond with all of them after his return to L'Orient. Finally there were two others, the Countess de La Vendahl and the Countess de Nicolson, who began to be particularly in the foreground of his thoughts.

The Countess de Nicolson later confessed to Jones in the fullness of her affection that she had seen and loved him simultaneously: "No, never, I feel, never did I love until that moment at once so dear and fatal to my peace when fate revealed you to my ravished sight. That moment fixed my destiny forever." Exactly when and where "that moment" occurred during the Commodore's six weeks in Paris and its environs remains uncertain. He was to address her as "the all accomplished Delia," and she was to write to him under this poetic anonymity of his choice. Perhaps it was also she to whom he referred as "la belle comtesse" in several letters to Madame d'Ormoy which conveyed his special appreciation for having met her among the hospitable author's circle of friends. Possibly, however, they saw each other first through her relatives, particularly her soldier brother-in-law, William Nicolson, or her husband, Count Murray de Nicolson. The Nicolsons were of a large family in Scotland and England, some of whom had emigrated to Holland and France, especially in the wake of the Scottish uprising in 1745, so that the warm friendship which Jones inspired among its foreign members from the beginning must have had its basis in a common patriotism as well as in personal admiration.

In May, during the early course of his friendship with them,

he received their cordial invitation for a visit at nearby Sennon-
ville: "I have the pleasure to write you, sir, in the name of three
persons, the lord of the chateau, Madame de Nicolson, and myself
to urge you to come to pass twenty-four hours with us. You need
not doubt having such a reception as is fitting; if your affairs do
not permit this engagement, we shall come to Paris next Friday and
shall be delighted to find you there again."[23]

Several weeks later, during Jones' continued absence from
L'Orient, Murray de Nicolson himself wrote him a further message, which he probably sent, however, before the nature of the
attachment between his wife and the Commodore had matured
enough to expose itself. In his fairly correct English, with an added
word or two of French, indicating his blended nationality as well
as language, he conveyed his respects and good wishes: "You can't
imagine, sir, how much I regret haveing been deprived of the
plaisir I promised myself in seeing you this afternoon. I went out
only at seven o'clock in the belief that the multitude of your occupations had employed all your moments.

"As I am to go out of town after tomorrow, if I can't have the
pleasure of wishing you innumberable victories, as it is your way
of employing your time, may I pray you to think that no one can
take more part in the new cargo of laurels that you will not fail to
convoy with your return."[24]

A closer link connecting Jones with Delia was her brother-in-
law William Nicolson, whom he considered taking with him as a
marine officer for the *Alliance*. As late as June 2, 1780 when the
Commodore had not yet returned to his ship, the Marquis de Puy
Ségur, a friend of the Nicolsons, wrote him that he considered it a
privilege for the officer to serve under his command. Delia herself
seems to have appreciated this employment of her relative chiefly
in terms of the proximity it afforded him to the man she loved.
As for Jones, it is not unlikely also that he chose Nicolson less for
any particular talents as a marine officer than as an intermediary
between the countess and himself.

Jones now had to return, as will appear, abruptly and speedily
to L'Orient. The Countess de Nicolson wished for the present to
have at least a portrait, but the time was short for engaging a suitable artist and for sittings.[25] And however ardent her affection al-

ready was, the *Alliance* and America called and images of numerous other ladies newly known to him during the past six weeks crowded upon his imagination. Ironically for Delia, who was beautiful and accomplished, according to Jones' testimony, as well as in love at first sight, according to her later admission, another woman had attracted him more strongly—the Countess de La Vendahl.

Coincident with the progress of these early relations with Delia, business which came to be combined with pleasure led Jones' steps frequently to the home of M. de Genêt. This secretary of the foreign department, the Commodore explained somewhat unbecomingly to Bancroft, was the more to be cultivated because he had the ear of the Ministry. It is not improbable that the same practical motives which first prompted Jones to visit him weighed equally, although more indirectly, with the Countess de La Vendahl, who likewise called at his residence. And De Genêt, who had social amenities as well as political influence, especially in naval matters, was very likely not disinclined to divert into social channels some of the political pressure upon him of the one as well as the other. The opportunity to do so was the more favorable because, it seems, he had at hand for his purpose two daughters, one of whom was Madame de Marsan; a circle of family friends; Miss Edes, a young Englishwoman whose stepfather was employed in the difficult task of arranging the exchange of war prisoners[26] (a subject particularly close to the Commodore); and both the countess and Jones with common professional interests.

In this circle Miss Edes was the more detached and curious as an English lady whose country knew Jones the sailor only too well but Jones the man very little except in gross caricature. She sent animated letters to friends at home concerning her observations at Versailles, and they duly appeared in the British press. Although her style assumed a journalistic coloring, the accounts digressed little from truth. In her first letter joining the names of Jones and the Countess de La Vendahl, his age as three years older than he probably was may indicate only her general impression; it is consistent in any event with views that he was born earlier than 1747. Her reference to "Mademoiselle G . . ." as the recipient of an accompanying poem points conformably to the social group of the

De Genêt family and to Mademoiselle de Genêt as the honored person.[27] The correspondent wrote trippingly: "The famous Paul Jones dines and sups here often; he is a smart man of thirty-six, speaks but little French, appears to be an extraordinary genius, a poet as well as a hero; a few days ago he wrote some verses extempore, of which I send you a copy. He is greatly admired here, especially by the ladies, who are all wild for love of him, as he for them; but he adores Lady — [the Countess de La Vendahl] who has honored him with every mark of politeness and distinction."

> Verses addressed to the ladies who have done me
> the honor of their polite attention
> Presented by Paul Jones to Mademoiselle G—
> Insulted Freedom bled—I felt her cause,
> And drew my sword to vindicate her laws,
> From principle, and not from vain applause.
> I've done my best; self-interest far apart,
> And self-reproach a stranger to my heart;
> My zeal still prompts, ambitious to pursue
> The foe, ye fair, of liberty and you;
> Grateful for praise, spontaneous and unbought,
> A generous people's love not meanly sought;
> To merit this, and bend the knee to beauty,
> Shall be my earliest and latest duty.[28]

The Countess de La Vendahl gave particular encouragement to the author of such gallant verses.[29] She wrote him what he described as an "elegant panegyric." In the spirit of chivalry she bestowed upon him a ribbon, to which he was to refer as a reason for his ambition to prove himself worthy of the title of her knight. She asked of him a detailed account of his recent naval engagements. She induced him to show her a copy of the eulogy at the Lodge of the Nine Sisters and drew him out as to his possible attendance on future occasions and his return to France. She gave him a miniature of herself, and it was probably this token which inspired his lines "on a black profile" to Maria, who may with poetic license be Marguerite, her Christian name. The profile, which he considered altogether unworthy of the subject—perhaps not only as a poetic fancy but also as a practical fact, for in the verses he referred to it as a "vile profile" and in a letter he was to beg her for a picture—impelled him to wish for both the brush of an Apelles or a Raphael and the pen of a Homer to do justice to her:

> The loveliest form, the fairest face,
> The brightest eye, the gentlest mind,
> And every virtue, charm, and grace
> Should be to endless fame consigned.[30]

The most distinctive emblem from the countess was a portrait of Jones in a miniature which she painted herself.[31] It represents him in rich naval uniform adorned with two medals, one of which, an eight-pointed star, was in anticipation of the award of the Order of Military Merit, already mentioned by De Sartine as an honor contemplated by the King. Although the countess was at some time a student of the Dutch painter Van der Huydt, the assurance by Janette Taylor, the niece of Jones, that it was the lady's own workmanship, the comparatively scant time for the execution of the painting, and especially the imperfections indicate reasonably that she herself was the artist and that Van der Huydt at most retouched it. The hair and ear are less finished than the face, and the face itself has the general contours but by no means the strongly marked individualistic features which make the Houdon bust and the Moreau engraving expressive of the living John Paul Jones of May, 1780. However much the miniature may have been painted to the accompaniment of the smiling presence of the countess and however much the bravest are the tenderest, it is difficult even in this instance to conceive of the warrior almost wholly erased by the lover, and that lover less distinguished than conventionally handsome. But of course the spirit, not the talent, of the artist and giver was here most in question, and Jones to all appearances judged accordingly.

As Miss Edes' earlier commentary had proved decidedly acceptable to her British readers, she continued her piquant account: "Since my last, Paul Jones drank tea and supped here. If I am in love with him, for love I may die; I have as many rivals as there are ladies; but the most formidable is still Lady — [the Countess La Vendahl], who possesses all his heart. This lady is of high rank and virtue, very sensible, good natured, and affable. Besides this, she is possessed of youth, beauty, and wit, and every other female accomplishment. She drew his picture (a striking likeness) and wrote some lines under it, which are much admired, and presented it to him, who, since he received it, is, he says, like a second Narcissus, in love with his own resemblance; to be sure he is the most agreeable sea wolf one would wish to meet with."[32]

Abruptly, Jones' Maytime wooing of the Countess de La Vendahl, along with his growing interest in the Countess de Nicolson, suffered interruption. Franklin had asked the Commodore in the previous February when he expected to be able to sail, and now the Minister sent him summary instructions, in accordance with a letter of March 28 just arrived from the Board of Admiralty for the return of the *Alliance,* to "carry the same into execution with all possible expedition."[33] The request from the Board was the more urgent because four American ships of war which had been detached to guard Charleston left most of the coast open to depredations of the enemy and also because Washington's army was increasingly in need of the supplies which were expected by the *Alliance* and by merchantmen under her convoy.

In fact Jones needed no prompting to speed to L'Orient—provided his heartstrings did not constrain him to delay. With the close of the month he had tried to terminate his professional business in Paris and Versailles, although it assumed an aspect concerned more with the possibility of future expeditions under his command than with the pressing questions of his crew's prize money and wages.

His expectations for new signal services began to be almost roseate. In addition to the promise of receiving the *Ariel* for transportation of extra American supplies, he had hopes of a second squadron under his command, combining both French and American ships in accordance with the fertile strategic plans which he had laid in May before Vergennes. Although the terms of possible coöperation were vague, De Sartine provided Jones with a letter to the President of Congress which evinced a disposition on the part of Louis XVI to aid in support of such a squadron and which more particularly not only recommended him strongly to Congress but also signified the King's warm regard by proposing to present him with a sword as well as the Cross of Military Merit.

"I am convinced, sir," De Sartine stated in his letter of May 30 to Samuel Huntington, the President of Congress, "that the reputation he has so justly acquired will precede him, and that the recital of his actions alone will suffice to prove to his fellow citizens that his abilities are equal to his courage. But the King has thought proper to add his suffrage and attention to the public opinion. He has expressly charged me to inform you how perfectly he is satisfied with the services of the Commodore, persuaded that Congress will render him the same justice. He has offered, as a proof of his esteem, to present him with a sword which cannot be placed in better hands, and likewise proposes to Congress to decorate the brave officer with the Cross of Military Merit. His Majesty conceives that this particular distinction, by holding forth the same honors to the two nations, united in the same interests, will be looked upon as one tie more that connects them. . . . If after having approved the conduct of the Commodore, it should be thought proper to give him the command of any new expedition to Europe, His Majesty will receive him again with pleasure, and presumes that Congress will oppose nothing that may be judged expedient to secure the success of his enterprises."[34]

Along with this testimonial, Jones secured another on the next day from Franklin to present upon his arrival in America. It was in signal contrast with the peremptory orders from the same hand to sail at the earliest opportunity; the Minister stated with simple eloquence that "his bravery and conduct have done great honor to the American flag" and that, although the recommendation was at the Commodore's request, "his actions are more effectual recommendation and render any from me unnecessary."[35]

With the letters in his pocket, containing both the urgent command for his return with the *Alliance* and the distinguished testimonials for the purpose less of honors than of new enterprises after his arrival in America, Jones was at the very point of departure from Paris. But he still lingered for hours which lengthened into several days, hesitating to take the decisive step from the warm intimacy of the present to the cold separation of distance, years, and fortunes of war, hesitating in particular uncertainty while his heart urged him to stay and his mind commanded him to leave.

A new circumstance called for his return to L'Orient even more

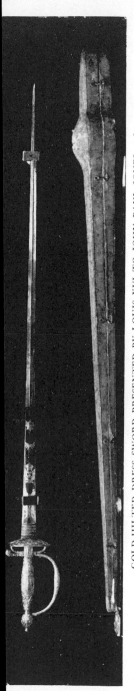

GOLD-HILTED DRESS SWORD PRESENTED BY LOUIS XVI TO JOHN PAUL JONES. 1780

Presented to Jones in commemoration of his victory over the "Serapis," September 23, 1779, at the same time the King of France awarded him the Order of Military Merit with the rank of Chevalier. Presented to the U. S. Naval Academy by Edward C. Dale. In Chapel Crypt.

DIES OF THE GOLD MEDAL AWARDED TO JOHN PAUL JONES BY CONGRESS. 1787

Commemorates the "Bonhomme Richard's" victory. Congress authorized the American Minister to France, Thomas Jefferson, to have the medal struck and to send the dies to this body, but they were not received. Augustin Dupré made the steel dies. The French Government returned the dies to the American Government August 20, 1939. They are now in the Chapel Crypt at the Naval Academy.

loudly than the orders from Congress and the added emphasis of
the American Minister bade his return with the *Alliance* to America. Landais, of whom in recent months Franklin had chosen to be
unmindful and Jones had been uninformed, suddenly threatened
danger to their affairs. They learned for the first time that he had
gone to L'Orient shortly before Jones had come to Paris and had
been plotting in the secrecy of disguise to regain command of the
Alliance. Now, following the letter to Franklin in which Lieutenant Degge and other officers had requested him to reinstate their
former Captain, arrived a second from Landais himself addressed
from the port, in which he peremptorily challenged the right of
the Minister to withhold the ship from him. When Franklin
showed Jones this denial of his authority as Minister, the Commodore quickly set forth at last for L'Orient.

Against his better judgment, however, he left without having
first effected the payment of the wages and prize money for which
the crew, especially the men of the *Alliance* as distinct from those
of the *Bonhomme Richard,* had long been clamoring. Ironically he
had gained the wish of the suspicious men to have the prize ships
sold not to the King but to the public only to find this means result
on the one hand in longer delay and on the other in less responsibility of the Ministry and more of De Chaumont, to whom the
concordat had provided that the commercial agents should remit
the proceeds. Some of the ships were still unsold and the funds
from others remained in the hands of this one person with whom
Jones had not had friendly relations during his sojourn. "He could
not," the Commodore said, "look me in the face, and fled whenever chance brought us near each other."[36]

Although the curious turn of circumstances made it doubtful
whether Jones could have secured the money for his men before
his departure however much he might have insisted, this public
consideration apparently had dimmed in his mind before the
glamour of his personal experiences in Paris. The procrastinating
compliance of De Sartine, the honors past and prospective from
the Court, the acclamation of the French populace, the hope for
a second squadron under his command, and the growing preoccupation with the Countess de La Vendahl—all contributed, as far as
his objective in behalf of the seamen was concerned, to take the
wind from his sails.

How immediately and how much the Countess de La Vendahl had power over his thoughts upon the departure, at the price not only of temporary forgetfulness of Delia and other ladies but also of greater circumspection in preparing to cope with Landais, is evident in a letter which bares his heart more passionately to a woman than any other discoverable from his pen. Married as the countess was, his professions gained somewhat in honor and devotedness in the light of his belief, whether or not mistaken, that she was unhappy with her husband. Probably, too, the free manners of the Paris in which he had just lived heightened the spontaneity natural to him. Still it appears that the lady herself more than his personal liberty and contemporary French customs impelled the Commodore enroute to L'Orient, when he stopped at Nantes on June 7 for business reasons, to write her with a vibrant accent of tenderness and passion:

"Nothing short of my duty to the glorious cause of freedom in which I have the honor to be engaged could have induced me to leave Versailles a little hour after I parted from you while my heart urged me to stay that I might have the happiness to see you the next morning. I will not attempt to describe here the sentiments that you have inspired in my mind, for words would not do justice to the affections of a breast like mine that is all alive to the divine feelings of gratitude and sensibility. I shall only say that my best abilities shall through life be exerted to merit a regard from you that is founded on private esteem; and if I have the good fortune to deserve your elegant panegyric by my future services, I can faithfully assure you it shall not be owing to my want of endeavors.

"You have made me in love with my own picture because you have condescended to draw it. If it is possible for you also to bestow the portrait I have solicited [apparently the one with the lock of hair now in the Museum of the United States Naval Academy], I will wear it round my neck and always think how I may merit so great an obligation. You may lay me under any charge you please and I will promise on my honor that your confidence shall not be misplaced. I am deeply concerned in all that respects your happiness; therefore I have been and am much affected at some words that fell *in private conversation* from Miss Edes the evening before I left Versailles. I am afraid you are less happy that I wish and am sure you deserve to be. I am composing a cipher for a key to our private correspondence so that you will be able to write me very freely and without risk. . . .

"I beseech you to accept the within lock. I am sorry it is now eighteen inches shorter than it was three months ago. If I could send you my heart itself or anything else that could afford you pleasure, it would be my happiness to do it. Before I had the honor to see you I wished to comply with the invitation of my lodge. I say this in answer to your question on reading the address with which I was honored; and I need not add that I have since found stronger reasons that have impelled me to seek after the means of visiting France again as soon as possible."[37]

◇◇

Chapter XXXIX

Landais Conspires and Threatens at L'Orient

WHATEVER machinations might be brewing at L'Orient, Jones calmly resumed command of the *Alliance* on June 10, 1780 after his business detour to Nantes where his friend Williams resided and where his ardent letter to the Countess de La Vendahl had been despatched to Paris. He now turned to expedite the final preparations for sailing home shortly with full cargoes aboard both the *Alliance* and *Ariel* in accordance with the urgent instructions from Congress which Franklin had shown him.

In the view of the officers and crew of the *Alliance* he had come back empty-handed—empty-handed without their prize money and wages, regardless of his success in saving the *Serapis* from destructive hands and in arranging for a public sale. Even in the opinion of a minor *Bonhomme Richard* officer like Fanning (granted his flippancy), he had very likely spent at Paris for his own pleasures some of the proceeds which belonged to them. According to the original crew of the *Alliance,* what with calumnies whispered in their ears as well as their instinctive suspicions, he was guilty of far greater wrongs.

Since Lee had come to the port on March 13 and Landais had followed a month later, the secret incitements against Jones had grown especially during his absence. These conspirators had represented to the officers and men who had been under the displaced Captain that they, belonging to an American Continental frigate, had served in a squadron of French privateers, and could hope for justice from such unscrupulous connections only by obtaining it before their ship sailed for home. De Chaumont, of course, had given occasion by the concordat for this plausible deceit and had reinforced it by his continued refusal to pay even part of their prize money. By the same token, Jones and Franklin, according to the delusion of the crew, were in league with the Frenchman and divided the spoils with him.[1] So they saw in Landais not only the shield to their cowardice but the avowed protector of their rights if he were again their commander. And as Landais strengthened the purpose of the crew, so Lee and Gillon fortified that of Landais.

In his demands to Franklin, this unpredictable Frenchman had early insisted twice upon reinstatement to the command of the frigate, but severely as the Doctor had replied he had taken no further note of his movements during six following weeks. The third challenge, without doubt one of the most peremptory communications which the Minister ever received from any man, had followed on May 29 from L'Orient under the signature of Landais but presumably with the correction if not in the writing of Lee or another counselor. It had arrived, as previously indicated, while Jones was still in Paris, and Franklin had handed it to him. "I have been waiting," Landais coolly began, "ever since I came to L'Orient for your order for me to retake the command of the frigate *Alliance,* thinking you would have reflected how she was taken from me."

"I should look upon myself," he continued, "as culpable to remain a tame spectator while my authority on board her is usurped by another. Since I have been placed in that command by a resolve of the Honorable Congress, it appears to me upon consideration that nothing can authorize Your Excellency in this proceeding of displacing me. I am persuaded that even the Congress themselves would never pretend to exercise a power so arbitrary as to overthrow their officers without trial, were their reasons ever so well founded—much less upon a parcel of scandalous charges intended to cover the ignorance and misbehavior of a man who would freely sacrifice the reputation of the officers and men of a whole fleet to establish himself . . . and if your Excellency is still determined to withhold me from my station, you must be answerable for any disagreeable consequences that may take place which I should wish to avoid."[2]

This third demand from the accused officer to Franklin to retake the *Alliance* had been to Jones his "first intimations of Landais' ideas on that head,"[3] and it had sufficiently alarmed him, as already seen, to induce his immediate return to the coast. The Minister had not, contrary to what might have been expected, asked at once the interposition of the French Government so as to have its port authorities take such opportune action as might prove needful. He did reply to Landais, however, with even greater sternness and finality than before in terms expressing equal surprise that the rebellious officer had not long ago set forth on his passage to America and that he had been waiting at L'Orient during the long elapsed period to resume the Captaincy. "I charge you," he concluded, "not to meddle with the command of the *Alliance,* or create any disturbance on board her, as you will answer the contrary at your peril."[4]

Another pronouncement from Degge and other officers of the *Alliance* reached Franklin coincidentally with the third challenge from Landais and indicated his prompting. If diplomacy could bring the *Alliance* crew to reason, the Minister's words, paternal and outspoken, deserved success. When he patiently explained, however, that wages were generally a matter of settlement in America and the business of the prizes was not in his hands, it would have been well to make clear at the same time to the suspicious seamen that the agents for these prizes were De Chaumont and less directly Gourlade & Moylan rather than Jones. Otherwise, he effectually laid bare the inconsistencies between the previous repeated complaints of the crew against Landais and their present insistence upon his reinstatement.

He impressed upon them his endeavor to interpret their motives to Congress and the public with more charity than justice: "I have related exactly to Congress the manner of his leaving the ship, and though I declined any judgment of his manœuvres in the fight, I have given it as my opinion (to Congress) after examining the affair that it was not at all likely either that he should have given orders to fire into the *Bonhomme Richard,* or that his officers would have obeyed such an order had it been given them. Thus I have taken what care I could of your honor in that particular. You will, therefore, excuse me if I am a little concerned for it in another. If it should come to be publicly known that you had the strongest aversion to Captain Landais, who had used you basely, and that it is only since the last year's cruise and the appointment of Commodore Jones to the command that you request to be again under your old Captain, I fear suspicions and reflections may be thrown upon you by the world, as if this change of sentiment may have arisen from your observation during the cruise that Captain Jones loved close fighting, that Captain Landais was skilful in keeping out of harm's way, and that you therefore thought yourselves safer with the latter."[5]

Lest he chafe their weaknesses too sorely and they fly the more to Landais as their protector against the American public as well as Jones and his dangerous battles with the British, Franklin proceeded to soothe them, whatever grave doubts rose in his mind: "For myself, I believe you are brave men and lovers of your country and its glorious cause; and I am persuaded you have only been ill-advised and misled by the artful and malicious misrepresentations of some persons I guess at. Take in good part this friendly counsel from an old man who is your friend. Go home peaceably in your ship. . . ."[6]

How little this advice was to influence the *Alliance* crew, more apt for mutiny than battle, became manifest in still another communication to the Minister before his previous answer could have arrived. This statement, supported by the signature of fifteen officers including Degge, is not less suave and hypocritical than arrogant. "We have reason to think," they affirmed, "there never was a ship's company of officers and men more unanimous for a captain than the *Alliance's* in this instance for Captain Landais . . . it was always our opinion that he was a capable and good captain; his behavior in the engagement was such as certainly evinced it. . . ." They even undertook in their superior wisdom to imply that the Minister had exceeded his authority and that he should abide by their correction: "We would also beg leave to represent to Your Excellency that, according to the customs and regulations of our Navy, we hold ourselves bound to obey him and no other as commander while our engagement continues, unless he is removed by the forms prescribed in our rules."[7]

A concluding dictatorial letter, signed by about one hundred and fifteen men of the frigate and clearly inspired by Landais, induced Franklin at last to resort to action. The French Government agreed to send at once an order to apprehend and imprison Landais and to provide Jones with whatever assistance he might require. Ironically, among their demands the sailors made claim to prize money for the ships arbitrarily sent by Landais to ports from which the Danish Government had directly returned them to England; but it was characteristic of the self-assurance of the Frenchman to try to divert guilt from himself by laying it in modified, flagrant form at the door of others.

An account of the terms dictated by these seamen to Franklin and the Minister's remarks upon them reached Jones shortly after he returned to L'Orient. This report indicated the climax to which the mutinous spirit was rising: ". . . a letter declaring that they would not raise the anchor nor depart from L'Orient till they had six months' wages paid them and the utmost farthing of their prize money, including the ships sent into Norway, and until *their legal Captain P. Landais* is restored to them. . . . That he has been concerned in that mutiny he has been foolish enough to furnish us with proofs, the sailors' letters being not only inclosed under a cover directed to me in his handwriting, but he has also in the same writing interlined the words *their legal Captain P. Landais,* which happens to contain his signature."[8]

Franklin recognized the seriousness of the situation. "You are likely to have great trouble," he added to the Commodore. "I wish you well through it. You have shown your abilities in fighting; you have now an opportunity of showing the other necessary part in the character of a great chief—your abilities in policy." However devoted Franklin, as both a public servant and a friend, showed himself towards Jones, the Commodore was to have the more reason to ask in the light of the advice whether the adviser in this emergency evinced corresponding talents in action as complementary to policy.

The intrigue went to further lengths, hidden in part from Jones now at L'Orient as well as from Franklin at Passy. Lieutenant Degge, other *Alliance* officers, and *Alliance* men became more and more the willing tools of their two leaders, the Captain smarting without a ship and the civil agent Lee without a political appointment. They sent to Landais, if he is to be believed, two "declarations in his favor and invitations to him to come on board."[9] To crown the plotting which their former Captain aimed to effect with them, but without the knowledge of the *Bonhomme Richard* officers and men, he sent Lieutenant Degge these instructions on June 12: "I order you to keep the said frigate till I have received an answer from His Excellency to whom I wrote on the subject. You may assure all the officers of my promise and tell them and all the crew that I will take the command as soon as the answer will be arrived. I expect Dr. Franklin cannot deny it to me, unless he has an order to the contrary from Congress. . . ."[10] It would appear from this ill-written, optimistic message as if Landais were requesting the *Alliance* for the first time from the Minister and had every reason to expect a favorable decision from him.

Lee and Gillon prepared the ground particularly on this day that Degge received instructions from Landais to share his confidence with the *Alliance* officers and men. "It cannot admit of a doubt, sir," Lee encouraged the Frenchman, "that an officer entrusted with the command of a ship by a resolve of Congress is bound to keep, guard, and defend such ship till he sees a resolve of Congress for devolving that trust upon another; and consequently that it is your duty to keep command of the frigate *Alliance* confided to you by a resolve of Congress till you know that the same authority has given that command to some other person."[11]

Gillon instigated him more precipitantly: "You are in honor and duty bound to directly take and keep command of the said *Alliance*. I moreover think that you are answerable for that ship if you do not directly take command of her."[12] In fact "the redribboned Commodore," as Jones was to describe this officer in the State Navy of South Carolina, considered himself so important that he tried at the same time to force his designs upon De Sartine and Franklin. To the American Minister he stated that he was strongly of the opinion that Landais should either be allowed to resume the command of the *Alliance* or be shown the order from Congress forbidding such a step.[13] To the French Minister he declared, on the basis of his claim to be the American naval officer of highest rank in Europe, the opinion that Landais was the rightful commander of the frigate.[14] He took occasion to urge further his personal interests to Franklin for the purchase of the *Serapis* and to De Sartine for the enlistment of American seamen, especially those of a cartel of one hundred prisoners from England who owed their liberty and care to Jones.[15]

Although the involvement of Franklin and Jones with Landais placed them in the forefront with him, there were others, scarcely unobserved, behind the curtain who set the stage; and some of them had as a special purpose the employment of the two naval officers as cat's-paws to satisfy personal enmities and to promote political ambitions in disregard of the best interests of America. In time Landais unwittingly brought by degrees to the light with him the treachery of Lee, the malice of Gillon, the bad judgment of Deane, the chicanery of De Chaumont, the double-dealing of De Sartine, the partisanship of John Adams, and even in America the overweening of Samuel Adams.

◇◇

Chapter XL

Landais Usurps the *Alliance*

THE CONSPIRACY of Landais and his seconds closed nearer and nearer from various quarters, but no overt mutinous attitude or acts came to the notice of Jones for several days in the course of his final occupations before weighing anchor. When officers and men, however, raised some question as to his authority on June 12, the Commodore summoned them on deck and read his orders from Franklin and his own commission, on the basis of which he had assumed command of the frigate. In answer there was not a word of protest. And when later on the same day the instructions from Landais to Degge did not escape his surveillance during their confidential transmission to some of the *Alliance's* officers, Jones was ready at once to act himself or to have proper authorities act for him.

If the Commodore had been in a port where he was to expect no assistance from friends or allies but needed to depend upon his own judgment and resources, he would have demonstrated the same celerity, circumspection, and boldness which he had invariably shown against the enemy at sea. In the present instance he saw and preferred an alternative to taking the matter directly in his own hands. His initiative was the less free because the authorities at the port were, of course, French, Landais was a French subject as well as an American officer, and he had no specific order at this time from either the American Minister or the French Government to deal summarily with him.

The policy of Franklin had indeed an unfavorable influence. Although the Minister had represented to De Sartine that his inquiry had borne at least the fruit of preventing a duel in Holland between Jones and Landais, it now seemed more likely that his efforts had served only to whet the rancour of the Frenchman for an encounter under aggravated circumstances at L'Orient. Certainly the Doctor had shown himself neither quick nor decisive in the new emergency to guard against such a combat.

Left for the present to his own circumscribed resources, Jones preferred to employ himself to better purpose in the war than to cross swords in a brawl with a half-madman, especially in view of other modes of dealing with him. With the more reason he did not choose "to have any particular dispute with Captain Landais after the charges I had given in against him and for which, with the approbation of the Government, Doctor Franklin had displaced him seven months before and given him money to bear his expenses to America for trial."[1] Apart from these restraints, it seems improbable that his recent honors, his new naval prospects, and his recently aroused feelings for the Countesses de La Vendahl and de Nicolson now preoccupied him so as to affect materially his judgment and energies in the crisis at hand.

After Jones had secured a copy of the portentous letter to Degge, he went without delay on June 12 to Thevenard, the commandant of the port, showed him Landais' seditious orders, and requested his decisive interference.[2] The commandant urged pacific measures. He went to Thevenard a second time the next morning and "desired him to send for Captain Landais and put him under arrest until the pleasure of Government should be known."[3] With canniness he wished not only to place Landais in custody but to do so before any possibility of a coup, although the instructions to Degge, as far as he knew them, conveyed no suspicion of one. A second time Thevenard gave peaceable advice to Jones, who stepped ashore on this morning to arrange for the despatch of the *Ariel.*

For once the Commodore allowed himself through the persistence of another to be unready if not exactly to be taken by surprise. An hour later, when he did not suspect that Landais would attempt to go on board the *Alliance* and he had even less reason to believe that Thevenard would not bar his way in the event of such an effort, the commandant actually sent for this officer against whom he had been warned twice, and let him set foot aboard the frigate.[4]

On the decks of the *Alliance* were most of Landais' own officers and men, who received him with three loud huzzas. They had awaited his coming by a prearranged stratagem for execution while Jones was in L'Orient and some of the *Bonhomme Richard's* officers were ashore and others below at their midday dinner.[5] At the acclaim, the *Richard* men aboard the ship rushed to the deck where they found Landais walking to and fro with papers in his hand and the other members of the crew at stations for getting under way.

The usurping Captain announced before all the assembled crew that he took command by orders of Congress, trying to impress them especially by instructions months ago from the Navy Board at Boston, which was wholly uninformed of the incidents that had since occurred.[6] "All you who do not acknowledge me to be Captain of this ship," he stated to the *Bonhomme Richard* officers in his uncertain English, "you must directly to the shore go, taking along with you your baggage. . . ."[7] These officers, powerless, saw no resource except to comply, and accordingly all of them, with the exception of one or two, shortly left the ship.

But Landais afforded no choice to the *Richard* seamen; he forbade them to leave, expecting no doubt that he could compel if not win their obedience.[8] At once they refused duty, and chose to become prisoners in the hold rather than to serve under him. And now the *Alliance* crew unmoored ship, not without the help of several men-of-war lying in the harbor, which might have been expected to be sufficiently under the orders of Thevenard if not to thwart at least not to aid them. Within an hour the frigate made sail and came to anchor in the road towards Port Louis. Pending his final preparations, Landais sent a message to Franklin, piously stating that he had taken command in accordance with the advice of principal Americans at L'Orient and the wishes of the officers and crew and requesting him to forward his despatches for Congress. Nor did he fail in these circumstances to insist upon payment of the prize money.[9]

In the meantime Dale and other *Bonhomme Richard* officers brought the news to Jones in L'Orient. He had no authority over armed forces at the port, and Thevenard had already demonstrated the little wisdom and power that were at the American's service. Jones managed, however, to secure an armed galley and one or two other small craft which Dale and others manned, and he instructed them to proceed to the *Alliance* and demand her return. But their effort was futile; if the Commodore had gone with them at the head of the impromptu band, there was little doubt, one of them averred, that they would have fought to the death.[10] Although they wisely did not sacrifice themselves in vain, Jones was furious at the outlook of the mutiny. Powerless, he had the advice of friends to send a despatch to the Court, but determined to go himself and speedily set forth as night fell.

While the Commodore hastened to Paris, the orders of the French Ministry to take effective measures against Landais should have reached the port authorities at L'Orient, provided the requests made by Franklin and promised to him on the 12th had been fulfilled. After Jones' arrival at Versailles, an extended delay of forty hours was the reward for his journey almost without rest before he could gain an answer to his urgent message.[11] But his waiting in the antechambers of the Court must have weighed less heavily upon him than might otherwise have been the case because of some arrangements for his portrait desired by the Countess de Nicolson[12] and probably some further communication with the Countess de La Vendahl, either directly or through De Genêt.

Finally De Genêt, the Foreign Secretary as well as his friend, informed him that the Court had sent an express with the necessary orders to the King's officers at L'Orient to cope suitably with Landais and the *Alliance*. Whether as the result of a visit by Jones to Passy or of the last self-righteous communication from the usurping Captain, Franklin also sent further commands to Landais and to the crew, directing the former "to quit the ship immediately" and the latter to obey "the Commodore" as the officer in command "until further orders shall be given by the Honorable Congress." But Landais did not scruple to withhold the message to the officers and men as well as to ignore the one to himself.

Only fifty-four hours after leaving Versailles, Jones was back at L'Orient early on June 20 at the most crucial moment when the *Alliance* was at the verge of an inglorious end.[13] Strangely, despite the assurances which Franklin had received a week earlier, despite those which Jones had received within three days, no express had come from the Court to stop Landais by force. An impressive display of strength by ship and fort would have brought Landais and his fellow-conspirators summarily to reason unless they were utter madmen, but such means were not available. Nor was a King's order to arrest Landais reinforced by sufficient strength to take him. Thevenard, however, had adopted measures of his own against the *Alliance,* which had been warped and towed from the road as far as the citadel of Port Louis. Here the commandant had placed a barricade across the channel, some troops had arrived at the fortress, and cannon pointed menacingly at the frigate. An armed galley and other small craft were also at hand. Thevenard's orders were "to fire on the *Alliance* and sink her to the bottom if they attempted to pass the barrier."

This fateful destruction to which Thevenard invited the *Alliance* was as little to Jones' taste as the commandant's careless if not criminal permission to Landais to board the frigate. The former pacific disposition of the port officer had turned to an ill-directed militancy, which threatened to complete his earlier folly by a far-reaching disaster. The force which Thevenard directed, unlike the more authoritative and formidable power that the Court might have shown, did not overawe the *Alliance* but rather challenged her. And Jones probably read better than any other, not excepting Franklin, the minds of Landais and Lee as the former called the men to quarters in acceptance of the challenge and characteristically directed Blodget the purser "to run Parke [the Captain of Marines, formerly of the *Ranger*] through the body if he detected any treachery in him."[14]

If Landais had been disposed, as many sincerely believed, to sacrifice the *Bonhomme Richard* and her men when he had Jones alone as his enemy, he would be even more unscrupulous at seeing the destruction of the *Alliance* and her cargo as a means for revenge not only against Jones but also against Franklin, towards whom his hate was now even greater.[15] If patriotism for America did not weigh with him in the former case, there certainly was no reason to believe that it would govern him in the present one. With respect to his cowardice as a possible restraining influence, his abandonment of the command of the ship to run below for his pistols during the preliminary expedition, combined with his scrupulous avoidance of close fighting in the main cruise, evinced clearly enough that he would provide for his personal safety.

Whatever consideration Lee had for his country became

blinded in view of a temper not less maniacal than the Frenchman's. Behind Jones, who refused to be the tool of the implacable Virginian and therefore barred his path, was his archenemy Franklin, whose high office he had coveted only to find it necessary for him to resign even a subordinate one. Lee had already transmitted an elaborate document to Jones, who "had never even hinted that his opinion or advice would be acceptable," stating with a pretense of judicial impartiality that "Captain Landais must answer at his peril for the frigate entrusted to him till he receives an order of Congress to deliver her to another."

In their mad mood for revenge, Landais and Lee were only too likely to give provocation; Thevenard, indecisive as well as unofficial in his alternating attitude of leniency and ruthlessness, was equally prone to sink the *Alliance*. As long as the barrier before Port Louis prevented the passage of the frigate, the challenge remained for Landais to cut the boom and for Thevenard to fire the large cannon of the fort that would destroy the ship. The French commandant and his guard at Port Louis as well as the French Captain and his reckless crew did not have particular scruples, it may be believed, for the safety of the frigate and her stores.

The feelings of Jones were greatly at variance with theirs. A welter of blood was cheap to him if necessary in the sacrifices of war against the national enemy, but a drop was dear in dissensions among countrymen and allies, especially when it might promote discord at home and abroad. His sensitiveness to personal affront was not less pronounced than his championship of public honor, but he was disposed now, as formerly, to renounce private revenge, however deep the insult and great his mortification, in favor of the preservation of the *Alliance* and her supplies, sorely needed in America. Indeed, it was impossible for him to be even a passive witness of the destruction of this frigate which he had found abominably dirty, hopelessly crank, and criminally neglected in every part, but had restored to cleanliness, improved in trim, and perfected with an artist's love from bow to stern and keel to masthead. It was this ship too, which he had commanded at the escape from the Texel, in the face of winter storms, Dutch insults, and British squadrons, with honor to the American flag second only to that won by the *Bonhomme Richard*.

Therefore his instinctive and inevitable decision at the return posthaste from Paris was to countermand orders that threatened momentarily the loss of the frigate and of American and French blood. Following his instructions, sailors aboard a French boat shortly cut the boom; and the *Alliance* passed Port Louis and came to anchor again under the isle of Groix. "Your humanity," Jones wrote the next day to Franklin, "will, I know, justify the part I acted in preventing a scene that would have rendered me miserable for the rest of my life."[16]

The Commodore's action may still seem hasty, for there was no obvious danger dependent upon the barrier laid across the passage. His foresight had prompted him more than his lack of patience. Little as Thevenard had previously justified his confidence, he now warranted it even less. When the boat from the fort had approached the *Alliance* to cut the boom, the officer and his men "gave the compliments of the commandant to Captain Landais."[17] Not Landais alone but Thevenard also proceeded to connive at the embarkation of Lee's "carriage, baggage, and family," regardless of the displacement of stores for Washington's army.[18] In spite of warnings given to the port authorities concerning Lee, who has been characterized as "the most insolent and haughty creature living,"[19] he enjoyed social and business courtesies in L'Orient. Landais himself received aboard a new suit of sails, which had been prepared especially by Jones, and even a full stock of liquor.

After his pains to prevent destruction of the *Alliance,* Jones resorted to "everything that persuasion or threatening could effect" to regain her. He sent a long plea as reasoned as impassioned to Parke, who apparently favored Jones against Landais but could bring little influence to bear upon the other *Alliance* officers, all of whom, except himself, supported the usurper from the beginning.[20] He sent to the *Alliance* copies of messages from Franklin regarding prospects of receiving immediately some of the prize money and accompanied them with his own exhortations. Whatever might be the results of these efforts to recover the ship, he entrusted to Dale the duty of requesting from Landais his privately owned barge, his other personal property, and particularly the *Bonhomme Richard* sailors.

The Frenchman proceeded to add insolence to insolence. He ignored some of these further communications, withheld others from the *Alliance* officers and men, refused to return the barge, and adopted a high-handed course regarding the *Bonhomme Richard* seamen. The behavior of these sailors in defiance of Landais and in fidelity to Jones testified to their stanchness as eloquently as the battle off Flamborough Head had borne witness to their valor. The unauthorized Captain resorted to both deceit and cruelties. He promised to let them return to L'Orient if Jones made a written request for them. They hastened to beg the Commodore to do so, and added the warning not to believe any assurances by Landais that they were willing to go to sea with him; already prisoners in the hold, they reiterated their determination not to serve under his orders.[21]

Jones undertook to reinforce his demand by the express authority of the United States and France; he emphasized that the shipping of public stores and clothing required the transfer of these men from the *Alliance,* which had her complement without them, to the *Ariel,* which had urgent need of their services. Landais then sent ashore less than one-third of these *Bonhomme Richard* sailors, and addressed to their commander a contemptuous note stating that they were such as he did not find necessary for the interests of the United States on board the *Alliance.* As for the others, he continued to keep them in the hold; and in his further efforts to bend these men to his will, he subjected them to irons and half rations.[22]

Although Jones in L'Orient grew under added provocations the more tenacious in his efforts to recover the *Alliance,* Franklin in Passy became the less desirous of occupying his mind with this naval problem, which had already caused him greater aggravation than his duties as Minister seemed to warrant. Still it is likely that he might have been disposed to bring new and greater pressure upon Landais through the French Government, if not in his own name, provided John Adams had seconded his authority. He placed the situation in full concerning the officer before his former fellow Commissioner, who had returned to Europe by appointment of Congress to negotiate a peace treaty with England when the occasion should be ripe and who was now biding his time in Paris. As the period of the request by Franklin for an opinion coincided with the trespass by Adams upon the province of the relations of the American Minister with Vergennes, and as the intrusion was also so little to the taste of the French Minister as to lead to his remonstrance and its transmission to Congress,[23] the nature of the advice from Adams assumes in this instance the greater irony.

Regardless of the cumulative charges from the hand of Franklin against Landais, regardless of even his own earlier diary record attesting to the incapacity of this naval officer, Adams offered an opinion as disingenuous and prejudiced as it was to prove unwise. This peace Commissioner, who once admitted that he was fit only for making war not peace,[24] recommended in this instance "the mildest measures," having in mind the retention of the ship by Landais and the transfer of the evidence against him to Congress, on the ground that the jurisdiction of Franklin was restricted. "I cannot think," he wrote, "that the instructions of the Navy Board to Captain Landais to obey the orders of the Minister Plenipotentiary contain authority to remove him, without his consent, from the command of a ship committed to him by Congress. . . ."[25] In one regard, however, his opinion was not without foundation; he questioned the assertion by the Minister that Landais "relinquished command of the *Alliance* and voluntarily withdrew his effects"—an assertion that has already appeared unjustified and that reflected more craft than frank responsibility. Adams pointedly said, "I have not observed among these papers any clear evidence of Captain Landais' consent to leave the command of the ship."[26]

Otherwise his views do him no honor. They recall his part during Jones' Captaincy of the *Ranger* when he along with Lee had dishonored the commander's draft, unduly supported Simpson after his arrest, and seemingly connived at the unexpected sailing of the sloop of war for America. His attitude in this second instance not only linked him with Arthur Lee and Landais in Europe but was later to associate him, as to this Captain, with Samuel Adams and Richard Henry Lee in America.

John Adams apart, practically all persons who sent their testimony to Franklin laid the blame uncompromisingly upon Landais,

Lee, and Gillon. Williams referred to "the pernicious counsels of a certain industrious genius" [Lee]; Moylan to the threats by Landais against him at his delivery of certain messages aboard the *Alliance* from the Minister; and even De Chaumont to the encouragement by Lee and Gillon for revolt of the *Alliance* crew. A group of merchants and naval officers at L'Orient, including Samuel Wharton and Thomas Bell, hastened to deny a report that they approved Landais' conduct. All of them insisted, on the contrary, that they condemned and lamented his usurpation. They declared that it endangered and delayed their shipment of supplies for the United States Army in conjunction with the American and French governments. The cargoes, valued at two million livres, were to have been sent in vessels under the convoy of Jones, whose "discretion and unexampled bravery" had given them confidence for a safe passage, but they now felt "the utmost doubt and anxiety for the arrival of the public stores and our property."

Regardless of these testimonials in favor of Jones, Franklin was the more chary of further involvement with Landais and Lee, and in fact with any maritime business, after Adams had given his views. He had earlier declined to buy the *Serapis* for the American Navy. Now, although this ship recently built by the British Admiralty at the cost of 50,000 guineas was purchased at public sale for the account of the King at the sacrifice price of 240,000 livres ($45,000), he refused Jones' plea, however close it was to his heart, to ask the French Government to lend her for transportation, along with the *Ariel*, of the remaining public stores, which had increased in proportion to the private property taken aboard the *Alliance*. He confirmed the accusations of Wharton against Lee and Landais, but implied also his irritation at Jones: "We are accountable at home. . . . You can have no conception of the vexation these maritime affairs occasion me. It is hard that I who give others no trouble with my quarrels should be plagued with all the perversities of those who think fit to wrangle with one another. I wish you a good voyage at last and that I could mend your company."[27]

Franklin reflected even more unfavorably upon Jones. In a message to Dumas, the Minister's defense of his policy, his direct censure of Jones for the first time, and his aloofness from implication with both naval officers did not reveal him in a distinguished light: "I am less committed than you may imagine in the affair between Jones and Landais. The latter was not dispossessed by me of his command, but quitted it. He afterwards took it into his head to resume it, which the former's too long stay at Paris gave him an opportunity of effecting. Captain Jones is going in the *Ariel* frigate to America, where they may settle their affairs as they can."[28]

Jones was as nettled to accuse Franklin as Franklin was to accuse Jones. While the statesman confided in one mutual friend, Dumas, the officer chose another, Bancroft. He complained that no orders from the Court had preceded him to L'Orient, that the commandants of the port and road "acted rather like women than men," that he could "even now undertake to stop the *Alliance* without losing the joint of a finger," that "there was some secret understanding between them and Lee," that "I am without having any complaint against me suffered to be sacrificed and dishonored in the face of all Europe."[29] Then, in references by cipher, particularly to Franklin, his heightened resentment expressed the sway of his active over his deliberative instincts: "If 299 sits still in this matter, I shall pronounce him and 868 philosophers indeed! I am no philosopher here but am stung to the soul to find that my honest endeavors are not supported."[30]

Bancroft showed the letter to Franklin. Although the ensuing rebuff from the Doctor to Jones had considerable fitness in view of the Commodore's reflections upon his friends, it came from him with less propriety than would have been the case if on the one hand he himself were not the accuser of the officer before Dumas and on the other he had secured the active intervention of the French Government. "You complain of your friends, who are in no fault," Franklin said in his candid manner. "They spare you, and have not even hinted that if you had stayed on board where your duty lay, instead of coming to Paris, you would not have lost your ship. . . . Hereafter, if you should observe an occasion to give your officers and friends a little more praise than is their due and confess more fault than you can justly be charged with, you will only become the sooner for it a great captain." Of these officers and friends, he presumably had in mind, not without some measure of reason, Ricot and Cottineau as well as himself.

Yet the Commodore later explained to him in extenuation: "It was a private letter, and, so far as I can remember, is the only one mentioning your name that I would not have freely submitted to your perusal."[31] Jones' message to Bancroft had been, indeed, almost as personal as Franklin's to Dumas, and therefore the sententious philosophy of the author of *Poor Richard's Almanac* might apply largely to his own conduct.

There was less reason on other grounds for Franklin's assumption of aloofness as well as injury, whatever excuse lay in his immediate aggravation, his manifold other occupations, his advanced age, and his gout. As the sole American Minister in France, his authority still embraced maritime affairs; consequently Jones could resort only to him. More important, regardless of the aspersions by Franklin concerning the quarrels of other people, the seizure of the *Alliance* involved him indirectly as much as Jones directly. It was against Franklin that Lee had struck in giving his advice to Landais; it was against Franklin fully as much as Jones that Landais had acted in following it. And if the Doctor had allowed De Chaumont less of a free hand beginning with the concordat, the *Alliance* crew would have been paid at least part of the prize money, Jones almost certainly would not have gone to Paris, and the mutiny could not have materialized.

Jones was not less self-assured than repentant after receiving the Minister's rebuke. Since recriminations were in order, he had several arrows to his bow and shot one in particular: "I need not remind you that I never sought after the command of the *Alliance*. But when I had taken it upon me, not only in obedience to yours, but to the orders of the King as herein enclosed, it was natural for me to expect to have my authority supported; and you know that Captain Landais' letter to you in the latter end of May for orders to retake the command of the *Alliance,* which, when you showed it to me, gave me the first intimations of his ideas on that head, was sufficiently alarming to have required the immediate interposition of Government. . . ."[32] It is to the remonstrant's credit that, although his wish had been to move Franklin to action by his criticism to Bancroft, the provocation to fix responsibility made him address his words fearlessly not to Bancroft, Dumas, or any other but Franklin himself.

In spite of these unhappy circumstances, the generous feelings of the Commodore for Franklin welled quickly and repeatedly from his heart. Coincident with the Bancroft letter, they were manifest notably in his account to Robert Morris of the recent happenings, which at the same time indicated that the Landais-Jones controversy had resolved itself into a phase of the Lee-Franklin feud. Jones explained to this other friend whom he cherished as deeply in America as Franklin in France: "I thank God that I am of no party and have no brothers or relations to serve, but I am convinced that Mr. Lee has acted in this matter merely because I would not become the enemy of the venerable, the wise, and good Franklin, whose heart as well as head does and will always do honor to human nature. I know the great and good of this kingdom better perhaps than any other American who has appeared in Europe since the Treaty of Alliance, and if my testimony could add anything to Franklin's reputation, I could witness the universal veneration and esteem with which his name inspires all ranks . . . envy itself is dumb when the name of Franklin is but mentioned."[33]

As the *Alliance* was almost on the eve of sailing, he added not without prevision of the calumnies which Landais and Lee might succeed in spreading abroad in America against him, especially upon their return before his own: "My ambition to act an eminent and useful part in this glorious revolution is unbounded. I pledge myself to you and to America that my zeal receives new ardor from the opposition it meets with and I live but to overcome them. . . . Let not, therefore, the virtuous Senate of America be misled by the insinuations of fallen ambition. Should anything be said to my disadvantage, all I ask is a suspension of judgment until I can appear before Congress and answer for myself."[34] In further anticipation of a possible duel with words instead of with guns, the Commodore addressed a short but pertinent message to the President of Congress and to the recently constituted Board of Admiralty, which conveyed his "truest pleasure" that Congress had at last created such an indipensable naval body and which did not fail to present also an ironic, challenging glimpse of Landais' cowardice in the *Bonhomme Richard-Serapis* battle by a reference to the *Alliance* as having been governed with more wisdom than to incur danger from cannon balls.[35]

While Jones, unlike Franklin, continued unremitting in his efforts to thwart Landais, whether by such anticipatory accounts to America or by warning messages to the *Alliance* still at Groix, the usurping Captain had the folly as well as effrontery to insist again upon payment of the prize money from the American Minister. In fact, he made the settlement a condition of his sailing as if it were a whip-hand over Franklin, who simply ignored his threats, apart from one pointed answer that revealed the Frenchman's bad judgment in so far as all his claimed prizes had been illegal, subject to indemnity, or restored by so-called neutrals to their owners. As the crew had revolted largely because he had posed as their champion, his failure was gall to both him and them. Not less unavailingly than arrogantly he demanded also that Jones should be reprimanded because of conversing with officers and men of the *Alliance*.

Landais not only ignored final orders from Franklin but refused to take military stores in the name of the French Court and denied a passage to Count de Vauban who was said to have important dispatches for Rochambeau.[36] With unconscious irony, on July 7, 1780, he informed the Doctor of his purpose to get under way at once, as he saw no prospect of fair treatment in France and was determined to seek justice in America. And despite the entreaties to Jones and Franklin[37] and in turn the repeated efforts particularly by the former, the brave and faithful *Bonhomme Richard* men in the hold of the *Alliance,* half-starved, poorly clothed, penniless, manacled, and guarded, pictured the cruelty—apart from the other vices—which Landais on this day of sailing carried with him to the United States as witness for justice that he demanded. The fate of these sailors personified also the bad judgment, the prejudice, and the plotting among those who initially had given this officer an important American command and later had seconded his viciousness.

Chapter XLI

◇◇

The Countess de La Vendahl Cools the Commodore's Passion

THE SAILING of the *Alliance* for America left Jones by no means inconsolable at L'Orient, although he had termed the brazen seizure by Landais as "the greatest hardship of my life" and had insisted that he was "not a philosopher here." But now that the frigate was gone, the Commodore with habitual resilience turned his eyes newly to enterprises, to honors, and by no means least to the ladies whom he had abruptly left in Paris much against his inclinations.

In fact the occasion must have appeared to him especially propitious for tarrying awhile in France as both love and ambition beckoned. The King had fulfilled his promise to bestow upon him a sword and the cross of the Order of Military Merit even before the *Alliance* sailed. On June 28 De Sartine had announced that they were about to be transmitted to him, adding in regard to the decoration that he had no doubt the United States would consent to this mark of recognition to an American citizen and in regard to the sword that the King "has the greatest confidence in the use you will make of it for his glory and that of the United States."[1] Jones had hopes, too, that these honors might lead more tangibly to the acquisition of ships, notwithstanding Franklin had refused to intercede with the French Government for the loan of the *Serapis* as a merchant vessel to transport the surplus stores at L'Orient and as a frigate to constitute one of a squadron after the Commodore's return to America.[2] Scarcely less pleasing than these military honors and prospects was the likelihood of renewed and close association particularly with the Countess de La Vendahl and the Countess de Nicolson, which his ardent letter from Nantes to the one and his recent sittings for a portrait for the other now ostensibly indicated.

There were more immediate, practical reasons which again made delay of his departure necessary even in the small *Ariel*. The ship had to be rigged and armed, the new supplies stowed aboard, the greater part of a crew enlisted to take the place of the members from the *Bonhomme Richard* who had been dragged away in the *Alliance,* exclusive of the forty-five officers and the group of men sent ashore. And again the problem of prize money and wages rose ominously. De Chaumont lately had his bills to the amount of 300,000 livres protested in Amsterdam, and De Montplaisir, his financial agent at L'Orient, still failed to furnish any part of the funds due to the officers and men.

Jones repeated to Franklin that the crew expected payment before sailing, and gave more definite warning to Bancroft that, if they suffered disappointment, he as their Captain would lose his credit in both Europe and America and a second revolt would not be unlikely. It cannot be said that he failed in the new situation to try to obviate as expeditiously as possible this unremoved difficulty in the way of carrying the stores of the *Ariel* promptly to America.

Under such diverse circumstances, the magnificent golden sword from the King finally arrived at L'Orient, and Jones contemplated entrusting it to the woman who was now foremost in his thoughts— the Countess de La Vendahl. Her guardianship would derive its full meaning from the worth the Commodore attached to this emblem, which signalized his present glory and whetted him to new achievements, which he declared a more handsome trophy than that presented to Lafayette and a recognition Tourville himself would have been proud to boast of, and which bore the memorable inscription "Louis XVI, the rewarder of the valiant avenger of the sea avenged." As a token from the Commodore, it would be as unique as the owner was distinguished, and also an eloquent commentary upon the mementos which had already passed between them: the miniature and panegyric from her to him; and the lock of hair, the cipher for secret correspondence, the poem of the black profile, and the impassioned letter from him to her.

But the valor which had won the sword did not insure corresponding judgment and worth in the use that Jones in the first instance was to make of his trophy, particularly since he was disposed to proffer it at the slippery threshold of love. Fortunately before he tendered the sword and while he looked with expectant eagerness for a reply to his words spoken and unspoken at Nantes, the countess deflated his fancies of love almost as much as Landais had wounded his pride of glory. To be sure his aspirations in the realm of love were not so sustained and uncompromising, even if they were sometimes as high, as in that of war.

The lady rewarded him for his pains in having sent her the impassioned letter and a packet with tokens of his sentiment by an answer intended not only to make clear that their romantic interlude was at an end, but also that she was now ready, the ground having been prepared, to proceed to the realistic business at hand. Perhaps she had abruptly set her mind against an honest courtship because of unexpected publicity, in particular from Jones' naïve acceptance of Miss Edes as a confidant and the Englishwoman's journalistic flair. Perhaps the Count de La Vendahl summarily taught his wife her place. Perhaps a discreet measure of gallantry was to her taste provided it stopped short within limits which she considered appropriate. In addition to her vanity for conquest, it is most probable that the lure she exercised over Jones developed for a business purpose in the interest of her husband. That she was sufficiently artful to deceive him as to her design does not prove that he was painfully unpracticed and weak in the hands of a woman beautiful, calculating, and coquettish.

She well might have persuaded herself that her conduct was right and his wrong. And that because she knew he thought her unhappy with her husband he was doubly at fault for his presumption. And if the names of other ladies whom he admired, like the Countess de Nicolson, came to her ears, as they very likely did, that he was trebly so and deserved to suffer the most dexterous turn of her art. Therefore she stated tellingly in reply that in sending his letter and packet to her he must have mistaken the person and address. And to disillusion him further as to her husband, she added that he was passing through L'Orient and that she would appreciate having Jones "pay him every civility." The count came indeed as she had indicated, and he impressed upon the Commodore his desire as a French officer to have the American's aid for advancement in his profession, possibly by means of a joint enterprise. He was no second Lafayette for such an undertaking, but the part of his hearer was scarcely to inform him or his wife to that effect. It was not exactly amiss that Jones, who however worthy was never averse to advance his own projects through the influence of important personages, male or female, should unexpectedly find himself not the petitioner but the one petitioned. Whatever his feelings, he had received instruction.

His tutoring prepared him for requital better than might have been expected in view of his sudden and pointed humiliation. He remained the courteous gentleman; he returned good for evil; and if he assumed a vein of frequent irony which curtained his mortification, his wounded affection, and an honest longing to retain her friendship, he likewise was practical as well as acidulous enough not to be disinclined to have the count and countess in turn exert whatever influence they might have at Court to advance the combined enterprise in question.

So with silence as to his injured feelings and with the philosophy that woman, like the buyer, is proverbially right, he assured the countess of his unassuming motives respecting the letter and packet, of his personal and professional esteem for her husband, and of the value of the cipher for *military* secrecy against the *British enemy*. Yet rather strangely in view of her downright repulse, some flickerings of his past warmth must have impelled him now to offer to place his treasured sword in her keeping—earlier he surely would have been disposed to tender it without qualification to her possession. On the whole, Jones fenced very adroitly from the beginning to the end of his answer of July 14, 1780 to his roguish correspondent:

"Since I had the honor to receive your packet from Versailles, I have carefully examined the copy of my letter from Nantes, but am still at a loss, and cannot conceive, what part of the letter itself could have occasioned your imagining I had mistaken the address. As for the little packet it contained, perhaps it might better have been omitted; if so, it is easily destroyed. If my letter has given you even a moment's uneasiness, I can assure you that to think so would be as severe a punishment as could be inflicted upon me. However I may have been mistaken, my intention could never have been to give you the most distant offence.

"I was greatly honored by the visit of the count, your husband, and am so well convinced of his superior understanding that I am glad to believe Miss Edes was mistaken. I admire him so much that I should esteem myself very happy indeed to have a joint expedition with him by sea and land, though I am certain that his laurels would far exceed mine. I mention this because M. de Genêt has both spoken and written to me on the subject, as from the count himself.

"I had the honor to lay a project before the King's Ministers in the month of May, for future combined expeditions under the flag of America, and had the satisfaction to find that my ideas were approved by them. If the count your husband will do me the honor to concert with M. de Gênet . . . I should be greatly proud to owe my success to your own good offices; and would gladly share with your husband the honor that might result from our operations.

"I have within these few days had the honor to receive from His Majesty the Cross of Military Merit, with a sword that is worthy the royal giver, and a letter which I ardently wish to deserve. I hold the sword in too high estimation to risk its being taken by the enemy; and therefore propose to deposit it in the care of a friend. None can be more worthy of that sacred deposit than you, madam; and if you will do me the honor to be its guardian, I shall esteem myself under an additional obligation to deserve your ribbon and prove myself worthy of the title of your knight. . . .

"If I am to have the honor of writing you from beyond the seas, you will find that the cipher I had the honor to send you may be necessary; because I would not wish all my informations to be understood in case my letters should fall into the hands of the enemy. I shall communicate no idea in cipher that will offend even such great delicacy as yours; but as you are a philosopher, and as friendship has nothing to do with sex, pray what harm is there in wishing to have the picture of a friend?"[3]

With the Countess de La Vendahl checkmated in this fashion for the present, it is not surprising that Jones now cast about to soothe his pride if not also his heart. He did not neglect, however, to try at the same time to forward his professional relation with the count following his personal intimacy with the countess. He explained to the Chevalier de Baudouin, who had influence with the French Government, and of course to De Gênet, who had "the ear and confidence of the Ministry," the plan to have the Count de La Vendahl join him in an expedition, of which the count would have command of the land forces; nor did he fail to express a high opinion of "that gallant and able officer." To what extent the recommendation was due to his honest estimate of the French soldier and to what degree it depended upon his wish to retain the favor of the soldier's wife, he kept to himself.

The suspicion arises that Jones was even disposed to some extent to serve others as the Countess de La Vendahl had served him. On the same day, July 14, that he sent his diplomatic reply to the countess, it is understandable that he wrote also to appease his disappointment, if not for other reasons, to some French-women who had been neglected or forgotten during his preoccupation with her. "For shame, Paul Jones, how could you let the fairest lady in the world, after writing you two letters, wait so long for an answer," he exclaimed in self-criticism to Barbantane Hunolstein, the sister of Count de Vauban as well as the matron of honor to the Duchess de Chartres. "Are you so much devoted to war as to neglect wit and beauty? I make myself a thousand reproaches, and believe I punish myself as severely as you would do, madam, were you present here. The truth is that I have been willing that the extraordinary events that have taken place here with respect to the frigate *Alliance* should be communicated to you rather by others than by myself. . . ." Not the whole truth as this excuse is, the reticence concerning the Countess de La Vendahl may be pardonable, although the ink of the letter to her of the same date had probably just become dry.

But a second missive to Madame Hunolstein about three weeks later bears a less generous construction. The superlative praises assume in retrospect the appearance of flattery, and the flattery gives place within this short period not only to indulgence of a

catholic taste for other women but a self-interestedness that recalls the professional ambitions of the countess, although not in
her artful but his open manner and certainly with a patriotic as
well as personal motive. After further regrets and repentance for
his former silence towards the lady, he turned to the business in
his mind which it was his purpose to have her promote in view
of her close association with the Duke and Duchess de Chartres:
"I have the greatest desire to give the world further proofs of my
grateful zeal for the interests of the King, the Government, and
this generous-minded nation by my actions against the common
enemy of France and America. Will you, my dear madam, honor
me with your interest that an application may be made by Government to Congress that I may henceforth during the war be employed in the most active and enterprising services."

Madame Hunolstein transmitted his messages to the Duke and
Duchess, hoped that he would have his deserts and even his wishes,
and thanked him for his kindness to her brother. She maintained,
however, an eloquent silence concerning the incongruity between
his gallant prefaces and their professional sequel.

In contrast with these Frenchwomen towards whom Jones came
to have blended motives, Madame Tellisson occupied, it seems, a
rôle apart. This friend, who knew Franklin and Necker the
French financier,[4] and who appears to have been erroneously
identified as Madame Thilorié,[5] the sister of Madame de Bonneuil, both of whom were the Commodore's cordial acquaintances
in Paris,[6] won his marked respect and courtesy. Although their
relationship at this period was limited in time and intimacy, he
felt more free to tell her of his difficulties with the *Alliance,*
especially in regard to De Chaumont, and of his reasons for having
gone to Paris than he seemed in his communication with most
men as well as women. Undoubtedly his opinion of her "elevated
mind" and her sympathetic understanding influenced his deference at her attention and his consequent hearty pleasure upon her
request for a promise to write to her "a particular account of my
service in this Revolution and of my late expedition."

Even the more confidential words of his present letter to her
indicate a greater public than personal interest: "Money is essential in war; in love, you will tell me perhaps the case may be other-

wise. I have still in contemplation to return to France soon after I arrive in America, for I have the most ardent desire to give the Court, the nation, and my friends further proofs of my gratitude by my services in the glorious cause of freedom that France has so nobly espoused in concert with America. The singular honors I have lately received from the King have made the deepest and most lasting impression on my heart, and it shall be my constant care to deserve the continuance of His Majesty's esteem. Although my departure is near, yet I hope to have the honor of a letter from you before I sail. I hope my conduct will always merit your good opinion, and that you will honor me in consequence with your attention, and permit me to consider you as one of my best friends."[7] Whether or not she was Madame Thilorié, Madame Tellisson named in the superscription of this message and Madame T— in the message itself[8] give no indication here, according to the tone of Jones' words, of being the Madame T— whom he was to know with not less respect but very much greater warmth seven years later.[9]

As the preparations aboard the *Ariel* approached completion in the latter part of July, the new exertions that Jones now made to secure the command of a second squadron, along with his preceding efforts in which he had not scrupled to enlist the aid of female friends, Madame Tellisson excepted, warrant the more generous view of his motives in so far as he foresaw an unpromising situation upon his return to America. The United States did not have the means to employ him suitably; it was possible that the country would not even have the desire to do so if he were to judge by past experience of special influence and party politics. The detachment of most of the American ships of war which had escaped capture or destruction to the duty of guarding Charleston increased his doubts. So he again made many applications in France, having of course greater prestige and a larger circle of friends in the present exigency than in the trying period when his resolution had won the *Bonhomme Richard* squadron. Still the postponements for sailing with the supplies sorely needed in America and the loss of the *Alliance* in relation to these delays, however understandable they were, naturally did not create a favorable impression.

He made known to Bancroft his endeavors to secure not only the *Serapis* but also another ship, the *Terpsichore,* to join the *Ariel.* His more special requests were to De Genêt and De Sartine, to Maurepas and Vergennes. De Genêt said that there was no hope of securing the *Terpsichore.* De Sartine offered little encouragement and indeed considered him pertinacious. Maurepas, who exercised less authority than his office indicated, replied in promising terms conditional upon his return to America in the *Ariel* and his arrival again in France with such ships as Congress might furnish him. Vergennes refused at this time to commit himself.

Apart from the response of Vergennes as the most influential French Minister, the petition to him by Jones invites attention for the self-portraiture from both personal and professional standpoints. His naval strategy appears to be sound and distinctive: "It is absolutely necessary, my lord, to destroy the foreign commerce of the English, especially their trade to the Baltic, from whence they draw all the supplies for their marine. It is equally necessary to alarm their coasts, not only in the colonies abroad, but even in their islands at home. These things would distress and distract the enemy much more than many battles between fleets of equal force. . . . We are in a position to surprise their coasts and take advantage of their unguarded situation under the flag of America as can never be done under the flag of France."[10]

Although his patriotic zeal needs neither asseveration by himself nor commentary by others, his claims of utter personal effacement require some qualification. In one breath he stated: "I should be happy to carry with me to Congress the interest of this Government for my promotion. . . ." In the next breath he corrected himself: . . . "especially that I may be henceforth constantly employed in the most active and enterprising services . . . to promote the interest of our glorious cause. This, my lord, would be my supreme ambition, actuated by no mean views of self-interest, but inspired by the purest principles of gratitude and philanthropy. . . ."[11] Recognizing that the higher the office the greater may be the opportunity for service, but also that promotion has a personal as well as public aspect, it appears that the Commodore protested too much.

Within a week of his solicitation to Vergennes on August 2, 1780 and in fact before replies from this Minister and others, Jones might have weighed anchor for America if the question of prize money and wages had not still remained undetermined. While Franklin wrote on August 9 to Congress, "Jones goes home in the *Ariel,*" with the understanding that he was about to sail, the Commodore informed at the same time De Genêt as well as the American Minister that he was indeed ready but that he would not sail before learning upon what banker in Paris to draw for the balance due his *Bonhomme Richard* crew both with him in the *Ariel* and on board the *Alliance* in chains. The financial straits of De Chaumont were growing worse as the result of varied speculation, and the grievances of Jones against him continued to develop. The Commodore did not feel his moral responsibility the less because the remaining *Bonhomme Richard* officers and men, unlike the crew of Landais in the *Alliance,* were not now at the point of revolt.

A personal concern, too, remained to be settled before his mind could be at peace at the decisive step that meant the separation of three thousand miles. Since his letter to the Countess de La Vendahl, craving at least her friendship in lieu of her love and offering the distinguished golden sword to her care in his absence, she had maintained for more than three weeks an ominous silence. "I am uneasy at not hearing from my fair friend Lady La Vendahl," he wrote on August 9 to De Genêt. "My last letter to her was of some consequence and went from hence the 14th ult. . . ."[12] The same post that sped his anxious inquiry to Paris apparently brought an immediate reply of August 5 from the countess herself only to confirm his foreboding that she had rejected alike his love and his sword.

In turn a meaningful silence of six weeks on his part followed her refusal of even bones and scraps to his disappointment. Although much, particularly in the way of another lady, transpired in his life during this long interval before he replied, his more immediate feelings were still discernible in his answer to her repeated rebuff, in which his style is graced by time and reflection with the greater irony, coolness, and courtesy.

The sly countess could not have failed to note an acidulous undercurrent in his phrases from first to last, especially as to the sword, her English, and her husband: "I was honored with the very polite letter that your ladyship condescended to write me the 5th of last month. I am sorry that you have found it necessary to refuse me the honor of accepting the deposit mentioned in my last; but am now determined to follow your advice and be myself its guardian. A day or two before I wrote to you last I had received a challenge from Sir James Wallace, who, in the *Nonesuch,* a ship of the line, copper bottomed, and of superior swiftness, declared he waited in sight for my departure. Had I commanded an equal force I hope you will believe I would have employed my time otherwise than in writing you any proposition for the safety of a weapon that I should have hoped to use immediately with success. . . .

"I have received a letter from the first Minister very favorable to the project I mentioned to you; and you may depend on my utmost interest with Congress to bring the matter to issue. I am sure that assembly will with pleasure say all yourself or the Court could wish respecting the count, if my scheme is adopted. . . .

"N.B. . . . I was selfish in begging you to write me in French, because your letters would serve me as an exercise. Your English is correct and even elegant."[13]

The greater part of a year was to elapse before the countess wrote him again, and a period almost three times as long before he was to respond. It cannot be supposed that the glamorous attraction during their intimacy in Paris, which had now twice undergone so great a change from warmth to coldness, however dignified by courtesy and respect, could fail to lose its character still further at the third stage as their relations hardened even more from spontaneous sentiment to deliberate ambition.

But before the initial estrangement had lengthened into weeks, not to consider years, and before in fact the countess had made known her refusal of the sword, Jones had already entered upon a course which demonstrated that he could act with a speed and versatility in love not unlike his talents in battle. For another lady, contrasting diametrically with the Countess de La Vendahl except as to her titled name, was already in the mind's eye of the Commodore. While the crew of the *Ariel* awaited the money due them or at least the certainty that it would be transmitted to

America, and the acquisition of additional ships for both commerce and war remained in abeyance, Jones became perhaps the less conscious of his own responsibility for continued delay of the frigate under his command, especially as his non-military preoccupation increased. On the one hand the freighted, rigged, and armed *Ariel* tugged at her moorings in readiness to sail; on the other hand the Countess de Nicolson had suddenly given her heart to the Commodore.

Chapter XLII

The Countess de Nicolson: "God, She Would Willingly Be the Lowest of Your Crew"

F ROM THE occasion when the Countess de Nicolson, on the one hand, first saw Jones and simultaneously became enamoured of him in Paris until the time when the Countess de La Vendahl, on the other hand, first repulsed his courtship by her initial letter to L'Orient, he in turn must have limited his interest in the former chiefly because of his infatuation for the latter. He had already complied with the desire of the Countess de Nicolson for a portrait and had apparently begun to entertain the thoughts which prompted future praises of her like "the all accomplished Delia" and "thy matchless heart." Subsequently, the romantic name of Delia, which he chose for her from love poetry in general and a lyric poem in particular, symbolized the simple and free warmth which she felt and inspired. With the artless letters she was to write him, he treasured a "Song written by Major André at Philadelphia," indicating both the source of her idyllic name and aspects of their youthfully spontaneous affection:

> Return enraptured hours
> When Delia's heart was mine,
> When she with wreaths of flowers
> My temples did entwine:
> No jealousy or care
> Corroded then my breast

But visions light as air
Presided o'er my rest.

.   .   .   .

Now nightly round my bed
No airy visions play;
Nor flow'rets wreathe my head
Each vernal holiday.
Far, far from these sad plains
The lovely Delia flies,
While racked with jealous pains
Her wretched lover dies.[1]

The period which set the seal to Delia's love for Jones, marking
the ecstatic height of their passion for each other, occurred when
she made a visit to L'Orient in company with her brother-in-law,
who was preparing for his duties as a marine officer in the *Ariel*.
"I realize that in all my life I have lived only during those five
days," she was later to confess concerning this sojourn. All her
letters indeed, which she wrote in French, were to derive a greater
intensity, if not actually to spring, from this occasion, after which
the Commodore was no longer a cherished image but a more
treasured reality to her. The words from her heart, equally expressive in phrase and untaught in form, assumed often a quality
vibrant like poignant music in utterance of the swiftly changing
chords of her emotion through the medium of her naïve prose.

Whatever its quality, prose was tame to the aspiring spirit of
Jones in celebration of Delia upon this occasion. He turned to
verse. Still the results were signal for him; his poem achieved a
more passionate beat, a bolder imagery, and a greater melodic
rhythm than in other instances. To be sure Delia was to admire
the lines. She was to hold them in the greater esteem because they
pictured allegorically the "soft flames" of a passion both virile
and tender, deepened by her momentary jealousy and his master-
ful power and faithfulness, and prophesying a joyous reunion upon
his return from America to France in the cause of "Freedom's
standard" and on the "wings of love":

I.

When Jove from high Olympus goes
To Ida and the fair below,

All heaven laments—but Juno shows
A jealous and superior woe:
In vain to her all power is given,
To female weakness ever dear;
She scorns the sovereignty of heaven,
Her God, her Jove, seems all to her.

II.

But when the Thunderer returns,
And seeks his skies (so Homer sings),
Soft flames the impatient goddess burns!
She hastes to meet the King of Kings:
Swift as the light her chariot flies,
Her swifter wishes fly before;
Still joyous in the middle skies
She meets the cloud-compelling power.

III.

Prolific nature feels the embrace,
Superior blossoms, fruits, and flowers
Spring up—all heaven wears a brighter face
And fragrance in profusion showers.
Celestial raptures who can *tell?*
Ours all divine are only *felt;*
What bold presumptuous strains shall swell
With transports which the gods can melt!

IV.

Thus when thy warrior, though no god,
Brings *Freedom's* standard o'er the main;
Long absent from thy blest abode,
Casts anchor in *dear France* again;
O, thou more heavenly, far more kind,
Than Juno, as thy swain than Jove,
With what heart's transport, raptured mind,
Shall *we* approach on wings of love![2]

Upon Delia's return from L'Orient to Paris, her first letter early in August was resonant not only with her delight at the poem, but especially with her joys and fears awakened by the visit:
"Pardon me, oh my beloved, if I am indiscreet; but I am op-

pressed with fears—fears which I felt at L—, and which observing your extreme delicacy on this subject, I never dared to express to you; but I am told that neither you nor your crew have yet been paid. In the name of that ardent love which consumes me, write me if I can be of use to you. I have diamonds and effects of all sorts, which may be readily converted into cash. Command your mistress; it will make her happy. Her heart pants to fly to your support.

"Twenty times, when in your arms, I have wished to speak to you to this effect, but feared to offend you. . . . Nothing but the hope of being beloved gave me strength to tear myself from you. When I lost sight of you, I was on the point of expiring with despair. . . . Alas, I thought that I beheld you for the last time, and I wished to put an end to all my sufferings; death would have been acceptable when I left your arms without a hope of seeing you again.

"Dear and adorable Jones, what would I not give if you could remain a little longer in France. Oh God, I am dying to rejoin you, never again to be separated; but I feel an agonizing presentiment at my heart that tells me that never again shall I be blessed with seeing you. . . .

"You ask my indulgence for your verses, adorable Jones. How dear is your modesty to my heart. But never had anyone less cause for it; everything belonging to you is enchanting. Those incomparable lines, which portray so well your noble mind and all its elevation, made me shed a flood of tears. Dear Jones, you are unequalled in your perfections, and never was mortal adored as you are worshipped by my devoted heart."[3]

The incoherence of her second letter pictured in itself her distraught feelings and her shaken health at the fear of approaching separation. She set aside as one of the least of the obstacles that should bar their path any questions of rivals. She returned again and again to her one and only thought of being with him. She panted for this fulfillment not after his expected return from America but now with all the immediacy of her throbbing love and with indifference for herself whether they would be rich or poor, live in Paris or elsewhere, inhabit a luxurious home or a cottage:

"I am in the greatest anxiety concerning your health, my only love. Dear Jones, if you be ill far from me, what will become of your being in mine. Mon Dieu, I am unhappy. And my angel, my adorable Jones, when shall we rejoin no more to be separated. Oh my sweetheart, I love so I realize that I am not able to live until your return. My extreme affection, my poor health, and above all my mortal fears concerning the fate of all that is dear to me make me die a thousand times a day and will end at last all my sorrows. They are inexpressible. Ah, I know by the torments of my heart that I love, I have loved, only only you, and if I lose you I realize that I lose life. Jones, dear lover, excuse your unhappy Delia, pardon her weakness, remember that she adores you, and that she dies if she loses you, or if you forget her. Can you tell me of rivals when I long to die for love of you, and if it is possible I should love you beyond the grave. Everything which is not Jones is abomination to me. . . .

"I received your letters of the 18th and 19th, and I confess to you that I am at a loss as to what I should counsel you. I should like to be able to give you a crown, and never was a mortal more worthy of wearing one. But my adorable sweetheart, I have thought little of my fortune, and I realize with despair that I am not able to make you happy in this regard or to live with you in an opulent manner. As for me, I should be only too happy with a cabin and my lover. But I should never require any sacrifices from you; you were not born to live in obscurity, and I must never suggest it to you. At the same time, you can yourself decide what you desire that I do and be assured of my eagerness to effect all which seems fitting to you. I love you with idolatry and for yourself alone, and my sole yearning is to live my life with you; but I wish that you be happy.

"You have never told me of your circumstances. It is very plain that you know only my affection for you and the tokens I have given you, but you are unaware of the sentiments of my soul and of all that it is capable in your behalf. If you are wholly without means and you feel moved to leave your service through dissatisfaction, you should come at once to France and count upon my heart which adores you and which will bring to bear all the resources in my power to make you forget the injustices of men.

"My health has in truth suffered somewhat, but that is of no consequence. Never has anything given me as much pleasure—what do I say. I aver that in all my life I have lived only those five days which have passed, alas, like a dream and which leave only the sad memory of a vanished happiness. . . ."[4]

The blasting of her despairing hopes for some last-minute resource to rejoin Jones in the present followed upon the receipt of a letter from him before her own could have arrived at L'Orient. His sailing for America was fixed and seemingly impending, and he offered no decisive and immediate solution to bring them together, which indeed was impracticable if not impossible without an inglorious end to his naval career. While she vowed again and again her dedication to him in his absence, her grief at the loss of seeing and being with him daily came to a climax in her exclamation, "God, she would willingly be the lowest of your crew":

"Your letter of — which reached me on Sunday the 20th of August lacerates my heart and increases my despair. I kissed with desolate poignant grief the traces of your precious tears and shed a flood of the bitterest drops that ever flowed from a breaking heart. I am weighed down with my sorrows and my mind is plunged in a chaos of doubts and fears. No, never I feel, never did I love until that moment at once so dear and fatal to my peace when fate revealed you to my ravished sight. That moment fixed my destiny forever.

"Yes, my dear adorable lover, on you alone depends that destiny, you alone have the power to make my happiness or misery. Please excuse this candid confession, my dear Jones, and be assured that believing you incapable of anything ungentle, I love, honor, and worship you. Never otherwise should I have revealed so freely all your power over every faculty of my being. I adore you, I repeat again; and no other mortal ever possessed such sway over my heart. This, my dear and only lover, is my pledge of faith. I am yours—and yours only—for life. Therefore be at peace, take courage, and let us trust that kind heaven will reunite us and guide the fortunes of two beings who love faithfully and who pure in heart deserve to be happy. Take care of your life and remember that mine depends on it.

"I ceaselessly pray to heaven for your safe arrival in America.

If you are satisfied in your service with that country, continue in it; if not, leave it and rejoin her who loves you. The whole world may forsake you, but her heart is yours for eternity. I swear it by that sacred flame which will never be extinguished in me. You ask how you can make me happy? Take care of yourself, love me, find a way we can live our lives together, and never forget that my existence is in your own—and that the moment which deprives me of you will put an end to all my yearnings. Your health is dear —ten thousand times dearer than my own. . . .

"Dear Jones, adieu, I am forced to leave you. The chevalier assures you of his respect and friendly sentiments. He sets out tomorrow evening. Alas, happier than his unfortunate sister, he will soon see you. God, she would willingly be the lowest of your crew."[5]

Notwithstanding the traces of his tears which Delia professed to find on the pages of the letter she had just answered, it is possible that Jones felt a surfeit of love for the present. The tremendous abandon of her confessions must have been somewhat alien to his sailor's temperament, which was, after all, very much less tenuously poetic than virile, roving, and uniquely dynamic in a practical, pulsating world of men. The promptings of such a nature governing his life as a whole explained to all appearances his conduct in the present instance. They furnished a palpable reason why he neglected at this period to write to Delia for about two weeks, while she watched and counted to her growing consternation and dismay the arrival of post after post.

More specifically, they explained his social expansiveness during the very time that she was preoccupied with their private relation. Granted his greater public obligations as both officer and man, the picture of him offset against her in the height of their passion is incongruous. Almost on the eve of weighing anchor for Groix, preparatory to sailing at last, he was absorbed for some days in the preparations and pleasures of an elaborate farewell entertainment aboard the *Ariel* on September 2. He invited many prominent ladies and gentlemen in L'Orient to have dinner on the quarter-deck and to witness later a sham naval battle, largely in imitation of the *Bonhomme Richard-Serapis* engagement.

The brilliance of the occasion measured in some degree the

extent to which Delia was temporarily forgotten. Even the blunt log of the *Ariel* chronicled on September 1: "People employed fitting the quarter-deck for a grand entertainment; received sixteen cases of wine."[6] And on September 2: "Expended two cases of number 7 and 20; fired salutes, exercised great guns and small arms; the Captain kicked Mr. Fanning, midshipman, and ordered him below."[7] The reference to Fanning is not the least significant of these remarks, for as the only record in all the logs of Jones' ships concerning such informal physical punishment, it must indicate the presumption of the midshipman, which the Commodore summarily corrected in this and probably other instances, and which the young culprit resented sufficiently to color his semi-historical narrative, in so far as it relates to his commander, with considerable smartness, misrepresentation, and malice.

With due allowance for the spirit and style of Fanning as a commentator, he provided a graphic account of the entertainment that centered about Jones:

"The quarter-deck of our ship was covered with the most elegant carpet; the plate alone which was made use of on this singular occasion was estimated to be worth two thousand guineas . . . for nearly twenty hours preceding the serving up of dinner we were almost suffocated with garlic and onions, besides a great many other stinking vegetables. . . . The next day was ushered in by thirteen guns, and the dressing of the ship with the thirteen stripes and the colors of all nations who were friendly to the United States. Captain Jones and his officers were all dressed in uniform, with their best bib and band on. . . . At a quarter before three o'clock in the afternoon the ship's boats . . . were despatched on shore to bring on board the company. Jones received them as they came up the ship's side, and conducted them to their seats on the quarter-deck with a great deal of ease, politeness, and good nature.

"Dinner was served up at half past three p.m. The company did not rise from table until a little after the sun set, when Captain Jones ordered his first lieutenant to cause all hands to be called to quarters, which was done just as the moon was rising. . . . At eight o'clock it began, and lasted about an hour and a quarter. Such a cracking of great guns, swivels, small arms, cowhorns, blunderbusses, etc., such a hissing and popping of hand grenadoes, stink pots, powder flasks was now heard as they fell into the water alongside as was never the like in the harbor of L'Orient seen or heard. . . . The fight over, a band of music . . . now played their part and all was glee and harmony."[8]

Under such circumstances, it is the less surprising that Jones in L'Orient heard from Delia in Paris:

"Six posts and still no tidings from you. My heart sinks at the thoughts of so cruel a neglect. Are you ill or have you ceased to love me? Heavens, the idea chills my heart. No, I cannot believe you so ruthless; you cannot wish my death. Is it possible that absence had ruined my happiness? Alas, if absence has lost me your heart, it has not made me feel the same way towards you, for you are now a thousand times dearer to me than on that black day of our parting. Your letters, your assurances of attachment, my heart's favor—all have served to deepen my affection; and now perhaps I must renounce forever all those fond hopes that have made me cherish life.

"But I may be wrong to despair. Yes, I am too sensitive and fearful. The loving and tender Jones is as faithful a lover as he is a valiant warrior and zealous patriot. Those rare qualities are united in the object of all my thoughts and affections. To doubt his constancy would be an injury—nay, a crime. Excuse dear lover, my apprehensive terrors; I will compel my foolish heart to be more tranquil. Judge of the excess of my love by my agonized dread of losing your esteem—your heart."[9]

As the silence of the Commodore still continued, the forebodings of the countess became confirmed in grief:

"Mon Dieu, my maid has come from the postoffice and there is no letter at all. Heavens, by what cruelty am I deprived of the only consolation which remains to my despair and to my regrets. Alas, have you had the cruelty to sail without desiring to bid me adieu, without giving witness of the least sorrow at separation from me or of regret for all the ills I have suffered since the cruel moment when fate gave you to me? Alas, if I was not very happy, my heart was without trepidation, and my indifference served in the place of happiness. Instead, as at present, I die of grief. . . .

"I have also pride, and I feel the courage to renounce everything which makes me care for life. All my existence would have been devoted to you for eternity, but I must believe myself loved and cherished in return, and I realize that I ought to be if the purest and most refined sentiments are worthy of preference. If on Tuesday I receive no letter at all from you, I will not importune you any more by mine. . . .

"Believe me, however, that if I did not have for you the greatest esteem, I should never have entrusted myself nor have laid bare my heart to you as I have done. In spite of everything, I count upon your uprightness that no one will ever see the testimony I have given you of a sentiment, alas, stronger than I am, stronger than my reason, and of which the torments render me the most pitiable mortal in the world. . . .

"I would have sacrificed everything for the blessing to please you and would have given my life to be loved by you, but I was not born happy. May you forever be exceedingly so, even at the price of all my peace. I am not able to continue. My eyes are covered with a mist, all is troubled and confused in my heart, and nothing remains clear except my profound grief and my frightful despair with which the fear of having lost you overwhelms me."[10]

Finally some reassurances came from Jones, who had now proceeded from L'Orient to Groix. They removed her most pressing fears, for which she confessed a reason not less apt than naïve in the excess of her love. But she allayed her present despair only to feel premonitions of new dangers from rivals in America:

"In my last letter I fear that I let you know too much the grief and torment of my heart. Excuse me, oh, my dear Jones, I was not myself. My mind was agitated, and my heart was torn. Dear and feeling friend, you do not know my trials, my grievous suffering. Ah, can I love the adorable Jones and not die from fear of losing him. . . .

"Your happy country, to which you proceed, without doubt will regard you as its military deity. It cannot know how much you preside over my heart and all its affections. You are born to have admirers who love you and await you with impatience. Dear and adorable Jones, among all the testimonies of their devotion, will you keep my memory and say to yourself there breathes a being who depends upon me for all her happiness or the most grievous torments? Adieu, too dear and too dangerous lover for

my peace. May fate always be as propitious towards you as my
heart. . . . Adieu, adieu, receive with kindness all the vows of
your tender and faithful sweetheart."[11]

Further vows, in turn, arrived from him, and Delia felt increased
confidence, although her yearning grew and his protracted delay
at L'Orient induced her modest but suspecting inquiry:

"I have just received, my most dear lover, your letter of the 18th.
How tender it is and expressive of the most touching and delicate
feelings. Every line paints a sentiment. Oh, my dearest Jones,
what will be the joy, the transport of your Delia when she beholds
again the author of those adorable letters.

"The only consolation to which my grief is susceptible is to
receive them—to read them again and again—to ponder over
them—to contemplate your picture. And though it does not re-
semble you, my fond imagination supplies its deficiency—and I
sit for hours, my eyes bathed in tears, gazing on this faint resemblance of the most beloved of men, while my heart, where your
cherished image is indelibly graven, is torn with despair and your
absence.

"It has been impossible for me, my lover, to write you for some
days. I have been very ill, and am yet extremely weak. The various
sorrows I have of late experienced, and your absence, the severest
of them all, have greatly contributed to my recent indisposition.
But I am better—thanks to your inestimable letters and the deli-
cious assurances in them of our reunion and your continued
affection.

"You do not mention the cause of your long stay at L'Orient.
I greatly fear that this detention will prevent your return—at
least for a long time. If this happy letter whose destination I envy
reaches you before your departure, give me some information on
this subject. The deep and earnest interest which I feel in all that
concerns you alone prompts this request; but if it is an indiscreet
one, do not gratify it. . . .

"Adieu, too dear and amiable Jones, receive the vows of that
ardent love which will continue till the last moment of my existence, and which offers the most fervent prayers that happiness
and success may always attend you. Adieu, adieu."[12]

At last the extremity of her feelings, rendered more and more poignant by alternating emotions of faith and jealousy, and complicated without doubt by estrangement from her husband, made her distracted at the unpromising contingencies of separation:

"The two letters I have received from you give me life, give hope to this lacerated heart which seems now too ready to fly away from this bosom and which will love you till its last breath. Oh, my angel. . . . If I had had the happiness to have known you longer, I might dare to hope you would not easily forget me. I implore you to forgive me for these groundless fears. If I did not restrain them, you would receive many letters which would reveal the sufferings of a heart where you reign despotically, but I trust in your goodness, although your Delia is jealous of you to the point of distraction. To love without jealousy is not to love, and I know by these torments that I love now for the first time in my life, for never has a human being caused me such trepidation.

. . . "I would sacrifice the whole world for you if that were possible. When I heard this summer of the loss you had sustained, I would have offered you, had I dared, 80,000 livres which I had to invest, but when I returned to L'Orient I found that the person who attends to my affairs had completed the contract, and because I am under his legal control, I saw to my chagrin that the paper had already been signed by my husband. I must also tell you that he is doing all in his power to keep me in France. Even then, my angel, the courage which I owe to you gave me the power to recover those contracts with the result that the income from that source is now available.

"Dear love, on leaving you at L'Orient, I thought seriously of getting this money and other portable effects to return and share your lot, whatever it might be. That would have been entrancing indeed to me—I should have seen you. But unable to carry out these intentions or to aid you in anything, I remain here disheartened, until heaven takes pity on your unfortunate Delia and brings you back to restore her to life.

"Adieu, dear and adorable Jones. May heaven preserve him I love and lead him to happiness. Think sometimes of me, for if I lose you, all is over forever. I fear to trust these tear-stained lines to the journey. I press the marks of your tears to my heart and my lips. Oh God, how I am unhappy."[13]

In the shelter of the island of Groix, the *Ariel* was already riding at anchor for several weeks since she had slipped her cables at L'Orient on September 4, 1780. Jones still waited for favorable winds and weather, although other considerations, not the least of which was Delia, contributed to his tarrying. In the name of love, the countess was ready enough to sacrifice at once, even if she protested too much in some respects, her marriage to the count and her moral scruples and conventions in, to be sure, a morally unconventional France. Likewise in the name of love, Jones gave no evidence of willingness to lose at this time what were more precious to him, his glory and patriotic service.

That, despite Delia's repeated entreaty, he took this stand now in the exigencies of war seems to prove him the less romantic lover but the more principled man. His later course, especially in the light of assurances implied and made, remained uncertain. Still what his ultimate decision would be, not only the *Ariel* pointing her prow seaward but a sailor's promise and the heart-free farewell celebration were portents.

Chapter XLIII

Aboard the *Ariel:* at Groix; the Hurricane; the Passage to America

JONES actively employed his pen for professional objects in the cabin of the *Ariel* as well as observed the wind and weather from the quarter-deck during the close of September and the beginning of October, 1780, while the ship even yet lay under the shelter of Groix. He continued his tireless efforts to provide for his future as an officer in the European naval theatre in anticipation of his hoped-for return. If his preoccupation with the Countess de Nicolson had become less, naval duties and plans also demanded his more immediate attention.

Now four merchantmen from Philadelphia arrived at L'Orient, bringing enthusiastic reports of his reputation in the United States. This news heartened him to write again to Maurepas at the expectancy of sailing on September 21 that Congress and all America were warmly his friends and that his hopes thereby increased of securing the frigates and men necessary for his projected enterprise under the combined auspices of the United States and France.

The next day he addressed himself also to De Sartine with the same object in view, stressing in particular how De Chaumont had continually been his evil genius. "Two years, my lord," he said, "has that harebrained man been employed in marring every idea of mine that was calculated to promote the common cause. . . ."[1] He undertook to prove that the Frenchman had cumulatively thwarted his aims, in which the smaller links connected with the larger, even to such a far-reaching extent as to associate his drawbacks

with the successful British defense of Gibraltar. Although expressing this conviction now only to the Minister of Marine, he was
to present it later to the King himself: "It is known that Admiral
Rodney was delayed in England more than two months because
the Baltic fleet remained at Scarborough for this period. This
fact shows of what importance the Baltic fleet is to the English
Navy. If this fleet had been captured, it is probable that Admiral
Rodney could by no means have succoured Gibraltar."[2] The condition is as speculative as the inference from it is long; yet the
conclusion is the more reasonable in so far as it applies to a naval
genius who achieved the miracle of the *Bonhomme Richard* victory
and to a series of situations not unlike the human system having
one part interrelated with many others so as to effect extremes
of good or ill.

The resentment of Jones against De Chaumont, with its long
history beginning shortly after his arrival in France and related
to the protracted quest for a ship, the evils in the wake of the
concordat, and the loss of the *Alliance,* rose even higher in indignation as he was about to sail for America without settlement for
any of the prize vessels. As for wages, the members of the *Bonhomme Richard* with him received at last payment in part from
the French Government through the coöperative efforts of Franklin. The Commodore had vowed earlier that, if De Chaumont
continued to offer idle excuses, there would be no further leniency
towards him. He had also exposed the subterfuges of the Frenchman to his agent De Montplaisir of L'Orient. Finally, as the
situation remained unchanged, Jones reported the financial chicaneries to De Genêt, Bancroft, and Franklin not less explicitly
than he had expressed the naval hindrances to De Sartine. He
forwarded as evidence "papers and vouchers" to De Genêt. He
assured Bancroft, "I have done with him [De Chaumont] now, and
sent to Court such proofs of his baseness as will I hope prevent
his doing further public mischief."[3] He similarly wrote to Franklin
of having borne the Frenchman's "base conduct too long" and of
turning now to decisive action.[4]

Almost throughout the prize money and wages problem, especially after the *Bonhomme Richard* crew were carried against their
will to America in the hold of the *Alliance,* Jones showed unremit-

ting sympathy for his men, unconnected with any professional ambitions. Of course he interceded in their behalf with Franklin, whom he now seemed to regard with even greater veneration than earlier. But he also plainly told Gourlade & Moylan, the agents of the sailors by their own choice, that the company was responsible for seeing them treated fairly. He reminded De Montplaisir, "I beg leave to observe that the men who belonged to the *Bonhomme Richard* and have been carried away by force in the *Alliance* are not to be forgot on that account. I engaged these men, they fought bravely, and I must see them done justice."[5] More feelingly he confessed to Bancroft: "I am obliged to force away my much-injured officers and men to depart almost naked. And how shall I face the poor fellows in America who for attachment to me were carried away *in irons* in the *Alliance?*"[6] It will be recalled, too, that by the terms of the concordat he owed no legal responsibility; his moral concern, therefore, does him the greater honor.

At last on October 7, 1780, two-thirds of a year after Jones had arrived in the *Alliance* at Groix following the dash from the Texel and the short cruise in Spanish waters, he sailed in the *Ariel* bound for America under seemingly favorable conditions of wind and weather. But the next morning, before the ship had made her way beyond sight of the Penmarque rocks, a most dangerous ledge off the French coast between Brest and L'Orient, the wind shifted, became a gale, and drove towards this treacherous lee shore.

By six p.m. the hurricane was already furious enough to cause Jones to house the guns.[7] He wore ship in an effort to bring her head to the wind, but she failed to hold the course. The frigate, caught in the troughs of the towering seas, shoaled her water very fast, and the Commodore himself made the soundings as they alarmingly dropped from fifty fathoms. He gave orders to lower the foretopmast, take in the mizzen staysails, and reef and then furl the mainsail. She could no longer carry any canvas; the lack of sea room prevented her scudding before the wind; helpless before the mountainous seas, she was on the verge of capsizing or of being driven on the rocks.

By eleven p.m., the lower yardarms dipped repeatedly under water, the gangway was flooded, and the waist became full. The water in the hold overflowed into the cockpit, regardless of frenzied use of the chain pumps. As one of his last expedients, Jones let go the best bower anchor in thirty fathoms. Although he paid out the bower cable to the bitter end, the anchor failed to hold; with a second cable spliced to the first, the ship still was not able to bring her head to the wind. Now at the peak of the tempest, she continued to drag her anchor and drifted even closer to the ledge in the uncertainty of utter darkness.

With the heavily laden frigate in less than thirty fathoms, Jones spliced a third cable to the second and paid out two-thirds of its length; and yet the *Ariel* seemed destined for the Penmarque reefs.[8] He cut away the foremast to lessen the wind's pressure— at last, ceasing to drag her anchor, she brought up and rode head to the wind. As if to aggravate the precarious dependence upon riding to the single anchor and its lengthened cable, the foremast in going overboard took along with it the stream and kedge anchors. To endanger the ship in another form, the mainmast had worked loose and out of its step, "reeled like a man drunk," and threatened to "break off above the deck or make a hole through the hull." Before Jones could cut the starboard shrouds in order to have the mainmast fall to port without additional injury to the ship, it carried away and fell to starboard, taking along the mizzenmast, which in turn took the quarter gallery with it. Only the bowsprit remained; all the masts were gone. Only the continued holding of the bower anchor stood between them and the Penmarque rocks for three nights and two days until the tempest subsided.[9]

In reliance upon his jury masts erected as soon as possible after the storm had spent most of its fury, Jones cut the cable at one o'clock in the morning of the 11th, and the *Ariel* sailed back in heavy seas to France. At evening she hove to in the road of Groix, and on the following afternoon anchored again in the harbor of L'Orient. It was an historic hurricane, carrying destruction on land as well as by sea over most of Europe,[10] from which the frigate had escaped with no loss of life and minor damage to her stores.

Even Fanning, who recounted that "the ship labored so hard, rolled so deep, and would bring up so sudden," said of her Captain, however much he was generally disposed to disparage rather than commend him: "Jones in all this time showed a great deal of presence of mind, and kept, with his own hands, sounding with the deep-sea lead."[11] Two of Jones' titled French passengers, De Vauban and Desoteux, were sufficiently impressed by his seamanship and courage to announce their readiness "to try again the wrath of Neptune along with you."[12] Samuel Wharton, one of the American passengers, wrote to Franklin of the last solemn farewells taken in expectation of imminent death and of the miraculous delivery from it when "the matchless skill and cool unshaken courage of Captain Jones prevented the ship from sinking."[13] Dale recalled in more professional and, if possible, more laudatory terms: "Never saw I such coolness and readiness in such frightful circumstances as Paul Jones showed in the nights and days when we lay off the Penmarques, expecting every moment to be our last; and the danger was greater even than we were in when the *Bonhomme Richard* fought the *Serapis.*" But Jones himself breathed no word of his conduct.

He did, however, praise very highly his officers and commend his seamen. "The gentleman passengers," he informed Franklin, "showed a manly spirit and true greatness of mind, even when death, in all its pomp, stared them in the face; and I am sure not one among them ever expected to see a returning sun."[14] He referred to "a ticklish situation" of his ship in one of several gallant letters to the romantic authoress, Madame d'Ormoy, whose circle of friends at Paris occasioned new compliments from him. For the reading of this imaginative writer, he added from the point of view of the poet rather than the sailor: "I know not why Neptune was in such anger, unless he thought it an affront in me to appear on his ocean with so insignificant a force. It is certain that, till the night of the 8th, I did not fully conceive the awful majesty of tempest and shipwreck. I can give you no just idea of the tremendous scene that nature then presented, which surpassed the reach even of poetic fancy and the pencil. I believe no ship was ever before saved from an equal danger off the point of the Penmarque rocks."[15] His artistic appreciation may be granted; but his modesty may require some qualification. He appears to invite the inference at least in this case, however just it is, that the miraculous escape was due to himself.

His sentiments addressed to Madame d'Ormoy bear witness to a growing passion, not too serious, for the regard of the female sex in particular as well as of man in general. It seems to have become a force infusing fresh spirit in his private and public ambitions. He characteristically remarked further to this woman who could understand his professions of chivalry: "I am extremely sorry that the young English lady you mention should have imbibed the national hatred against me. I have had proofs that many of the first and fairest' ladies of that nation are my friends. Indeed I cannot imagine why any fair lady should be my enemy, since upon the large scale of universal philanthropy, I *feel,* acknowledge, and bend before the sovereign power of beauty. The English nation may hate me, but *I will force them to esteem me too."*[16]

Perhaps such catholic professions, including all women, now justified in his eyes a less exclusive affection for the Countess de Nicolson than accorded with the more personal philosophy of her heart. In any event, he wrote to Madame d'Ormoy concerning such abstractions while Delia still looked in vain to hear from him in terms of greater concreteness. There may be the more excuse for the letters to the former because of references in them to her friends, including one named "the charming countess," and "la belle comtesse," conceivably Delia herself. Whoever may have been the countess in question, Delia remained without doubt important in his mind, according to an inquiry which he shortly addressed to Bancroft: "Pray have you seen my fair friend, the Countess of N—. She is, I understand, returned from Aix, and I am very anxious to hear from her."[17]

The time, however, since Jones had first planned to return to America had now through varied circumstances become so long that the countess for this reason if no other receded to the background of his immediate concerns. He had to make extensive repairs to the *Ariel* and to unload the damaged powder and arms, which were the most valuable of her stores.

In preparation of the vessel for service again, he evinced a characteristic liberality with the funds of the United States and a freedom with Franklin which reflect unfavorably upon his tendency to follow his own dictates with little restraint. The Minister, who knew the value of money better than the Commodore, reprimanded him considerately but severely: "I was dissatisfied with Mr. Moylan's proceedings in going on with so great and unexpected an expense for the *Ariel,* and never giving me the least notice of it till he drew upon me for the amount, near one hundred thousand livres, drawing, too, before sending the account. . . . However, on it being made to appear to me by Mr. Gourlade you had ordered the things I objected to, I supposing that if I refused paying for them he would sue and embarrass you, I sometime since accepted all his bills. But though I suppose you thought it for the good of the service, as you say you did, to order that great quantity of medicines for the 74-gun ship [the *America,* which Jones hoped to command in the United States], yet after I had written you of my difficulties, it still seems to me that you ought not to have done it. . . . and I have only to be thankful that you did not order all her other stores, sails, rigging, anchors, powder, etc. I think you must be sensible on reflection that with regard to me it was wrong, and it ought not to be expected of me to be always ready and able to pay the demands that every officer in the service may think fit to saddle me with. This affair, however, is done with, and I shall say no more about it."[18]

During the six weeks of refitting the *Ariel* generously, Jones did not neglect final efforts to secure a better command. His passenger De Vauban, whose sister Barbartane Hunolstein, it is recalled, he had requested earlier to intercede with the Duke and Duchess de Chartres, returned to Paris and made a special effort to secure in his behalf a larger and better frigate, the *Terpsichore,* in substitution for the *Ariel.* He undertook to use his influence at Court, and particularly his interest with the House of Orleans, formerly of Chartres, because of admiration for Jones rather than persuasion by him. Jones, of course, prosecuted this and other plans himself, urging them by letters especially to Bancroft, La Rochefoucauld, and the new Minister of the Marine, De Castries.

The most ardent and courageous advocate in his behalf, whatever her opportunities, was the Countess de Nicolson. Apparently Jones, who now had little time for love, did not shrink to enlist her aid for professional purposes. The rôle which he let her assume is the less to his discredit because her brother-in-law was an ambassador between them in business as well as love, and she seems to have tendered her endeavors as spontaneously as her affection. William Nicolson revealed in a message from the home of his sister-in-law in Paris the part that she was taking: "I should have had the honor to write you sooner, had I received any favorable news with regard to the ship you desire in your new memorandum. In that expectation I delayed from day to day, my sister-in-law having set to work the nobility most in credit at Court to carry it through. I have been at Passy to wait on Dr. Bancroft, who told me he would present me to His Excellency Dr. Franklin, but he thought it would be all in vain, nobody being able to prevail upon him to make any application to Government for it. We are nevertheless still in hopes to obtain the *Terpsichore* or some larger ship; but everyone here thinks your presence, sir, absolutely necessary at Paris, if your business at L'Orient could allow you. . . ."[19] Delia undoubtedly agreed that his presence was absolutely necessary and not improbably first made the suggestion.

Jones wisely refrained in the posture of events from going to Paris and from petitioning Franklin to promote this last-minute tenacious purpose. He knew well enough, despite his persistence, when it was useless to urge his views further. While such persuasions as those of De Vauban and even of Delia were still not completed, De Castries sent him a reply in consonance with those previously from De Sartine and other ministers, and he determined to forego continued applications. "I received a polite letter from the new Minister," he informed Williams on November 20, "which convinces me nothing will be done at present." So he set his mind undividedly upon a second departure in the *Ariel*.

Even at this time the prize money remained unpaid; but it had become increasingly clear that the insolvency as well as the subterfuges of De Chaumont was responsible for this situation. A year had already passed since Gourlade & Moylan had remitted to him upon his order the proceeds from the prizes. It is revealing that Jones on the one hand plainly made a final request to De Chaumont, and that Franklin on the other euphemistically wrote Jones that he understood the money was not yet received from the King. But Franklin was less tender as to the reputation of his neighbor at Passy upon writing to his nephew Jonathan Williams, who had mentioned the precarious credit of the Frenchman.[20] Franklin damned De Chaumont with faint praise and offered as his excuse for divulging the truth the apt occasion for a word of advice to his young relative: "He is not naturally inclined to chicaneries, but his embarrassments have made him say and do things inconsistent with his character, which I only mention as a caution to you never to go out of your depth in business, for the best swimmer may be seized with a cramp."[21]

Turning in the main from his interests in France to those in the United States as his second sailing impended, Jones anticipated his arrival by a letter to Robert Morris with particular criticism of the American Navy as seen from abroad. His convictions were the stronger because reports had reached Europe exposing in preliminary degree the fantastic passage to Boston of the *Alliance* under Landais, in which the Captain, the crew, and the passengers exhibited even a greater measure of madness, mutiny, and captiousness respectively than they had betrayed in Europe.

The purpose of Jones' message was less to prepare the way for his own vindication than to urge a naval establishment worthy of America: "A general reform is indispensable in the Navy. The great mass of the officers were never intended by nature to fill such important places; and what I have said from the beginning has proved true. They cannot support their rank with honor to themselves or their country. Our Navy has not only been put into bad hands, but it has been unwisely employed. It has served to enrich a few ignorant individuals, and has done almost nothing for our cause. If my feeble voice is heard when I return to Philadelphia, our Navy matters will assume a better face. The formation of the American Navy is an object of the highest importance . . ."[22]

A glaring incident of his own experience during this period, illustrating the dishonor suffered by the American Navy, impelled him to send also a stern report of it to the Board of Admiralty. Inspired by bravado and insolence, the master of an American merchantman, holding only a commission for a letter of marque, sought to flout the flag of the *Ariel* at Groix and L'Orient before the eyes of French officers as well as Jones and regardless of foreign ports. He tried to do so, too, in defiance of explicit naval regulations; what is more, he sought to justify himself by presumptuous criticism of Jones in reference to the Commodore's former surgeon, Dr. Brooke. Finally, he resorted to vicious language in consonance with his conduct.

Jones treated this master, Thomas Truxtun, who thoroughly digested his reprimand and later became a distinguished naval officer, first with moderate words and then with summary action:

"You passed some time ago with the merchant ship the *Independence* belonging to Philadelphia close upon the stern of the Continental ship *Ariel* under my command to the road of Groix, and you then showed no mark of respect to the Continental flag and commission, but went on with a long pendant flying and without lowering any sail or color or even showing any mark of politeness. In the port of L'Orient you were not satisfied with a long pendant, but you hoisted a kind of broad one. . . . When your vessel was yesterday under sail, she was steered, in my presence, very near the *Ariel,* in passing down to Port Louis. I then sent a boat with an officer to request you or your representative on board to take down the pendant in obedience to a law of Congress. The officer returned and reported to me that my boat's crew had been menaced by your people and that your mate said he had orders to treat with contempt and disobey any order or request to haul down the pendant. . . . I sent Lieutenant Dale with two boats armed with another polite message, and such orders as I will answer for having given. The pendant was then hauled down as he approached your ship.

"Should there be any occasion for it, I shall justify what I may write respecting my surgeon. In the meantime that subject is premature. I cannot answer your letter more particularly as there are in it several words that I do not understand, and cannot find in the dictionary. I hope I have said enough to show you your error. I will lay your letter to me before the Board of Admiralty with a complaint against you for having dared to insult, through my side, the Flag and Sovereignty of the United States. I shall receive no more letters from you on the subject. It is not me you have offended. You have offended the United States of America."[23]

Accordingly Jones forwarded the correspondence to the Board of Admiralty. In his comment he added: "Congress will judge what punishment is equal to such a crime when committed in sight of the flag and forts of an illustrious ally." The occurrence, unimportant in itself, represents in miniature by word and deed the unbounded honor of the United States for which he consistently strove in every form; it dwarfs in commensurate degree the vanity of personal glory that was his incidental indulgence.

Again the little *Ariel,* which thus upheld abroad the name of the United States, sailed heavily freighted on December 18 to attempt a second time her passage to America. Prompted by his chivalric sense of private and public fitness, Jones, according to his later journal for Louis XVI, "bade adieu to the beloved nation of France, where, though he had met with some difficulties, he had many reasons to be satisfied, and was charmed with the courteous behavior that so nobly marked the character of that generous-minded people." To Madame d'Ormoy, who had mentioned him in her correspondence with the King of Prussia, he modestly expressed his ambition and determination to be worthy of her praises: "If I have any merit, it consists in good will and perseverance. My abilities are poor, and I want experience, but opposition shall never cause my ardor to abate in pursuit of the glorious cause I have undertaken to support." As for Delia, ominously her brother-in-law does not appear again as an intermediary, and silence is the only record of her for a long period after this second sailing.

In contrast with almost every other occasion on which Jones put to sea, he sought a direct, uneventful passage, without interruption by an encounter with the enemy. His ship was encumbered and slow, the despatches she carried were important, her armament was of little force and her crew was small, and he himself was impatient to reach America after his years in Europe.

Whatever his wishes, he found his course challenged by the twenty-gun British ship *Triumph,* which showed herself an exceptionally fast sailer. At first he tried to avoid speaking with her, and night promised an opportunity to escape; but although the officers of the watch informed him repeatedly during the hours of darkness that the sail was no longer visible, daylight proved otherwise, revealing her in fact closer than during the previous evening. An engagement now seemed very probable.

Jones prepared at once for battle, but he did so secretly in order to gain as great an advantage as possible over the enemy. He cast overboard everything that interfered with the defense and safety of the ship. He kept the force of the *Ariel* hidden from view of her pursuer by particular care in the management of sails and helm. He avoided any warlike appearance or visible preparation. As an encounter became almost inevitable, he strategically conveyed the impression of weakness by firing a light stern chaser occasionally and of alarm by crowding sail. He did not allow the British ship to approach, however, until shortly before evening so as to reserve the possible alternative of having the *Ariel* show her heels under cover of the second night; then, having scrutinized her force carefully, he shortened sail, resolved and ready to engage her.

When the two ships were within hail of each other, the *Ariel*, as well as the *Triumph* commanded by Captain John Pindar, hoisted English colors. The next tactical move in Jones' plans failed because of the blunder of a quartermaster who had been instructed to lower the English flag and hoist the American at a given signal. He had permitted one end of the halliards to escape him so as to be unable to change the colors at the chosen favorable moment for a prearranged advantageous manœuvre and for a simultaneous discharge of the first broadside under the American standard.

Jones turned to another expedient as if nothing untoward had happened, although the quartermaster's mistake enabled the *Triumph* to range along the lee side of the *Ariel* where a battery bristled and glowed in readiness for immediate action. Nonchalantly he engaged the British Captain in a protracted conversation of almost an hour, learning as much as he could concerning the enemy's affairs in America. He pretended at length to be doubtful whether Pindar truly was of the British Navy, and demanded that he satisfy him by coming on board the *Ariel* to show his commission. Pindar discreetly refused, and wisely, too, stated that Jones in turn had not satisfied him as to his ship and identity. Doubtlessly he bore well in mind on this occasion the ruse in war to have ships display the flags of countries other than their own before battle and then to hoist their own standards at the moment an engagement actually began.

Under these circumstances, Jones announced that he would allow five minutes for compliance with his demand. Pindar replied that he "would answer for twenty guns, and that he and everyone of his people had shown themselves Englishmen." At the expiration of this short period, Jones, as he himself described, "backed a little in the weather-quarter of the enemy, ran close under her stern, hoisted American colors, and being within short pistol shot on the lee beam of the enemy, began to engage. It was past seven o'clock, and as no equal force ever exceeded the vigorous and regular fire of the *Ariel's* battery and tops, the action while it lasted made a glorious appearance. The enemy made a feeble resistance for about ten minutes. He then struck his colors. The enemy then begged for quarter and said half his men were killed. The *Ariel's* fire ceased; and the crew, as usual after a victory, gave cries of joy. To 'show themselves Englishmen,' the enemy filled their sails, and got on the *Ariel's* weather bow before the cries of joy had ended on board the *Ariel*. Captain Jones, suspecting the base design of the enemy, immediately set every sail he could to prevent her escape; but the enemy had so much advantage in sailing that the *Ariel* could not keep up, and they soon got out of gun shot. The English Captain may properly be called a knave, because, after he surrendered his ship, and begged for and obtained quarter, he basely ran away, contrary to the laws of naval war and the practice of civilized nations."[24]

After this matching of wits along with arms, in contradiction to the customs of war as well as in accordance with them, Jones had the satisfaction at least of able support in the battle, except for the fumbling as to the flag. "Never," he related, "was I in any preceding action so much pleased as in this of the *Ariel* with the . . . fire of the tops and deck guns . . . which proves the advantage of having good officers, for there never was a more indifferent crew than that of the *Ariel*."[25] This tribute to the former *Bonhomme Richard* officers, recalling also their comrades, the *Bonhomme Richard* seamen who had staunchly suffered the cruelties of Landais for the sake of their commander, was a fitting seal to the valor and loyalty of all those that had previously gone through the ordeal of fire, steel, and flood with him, and now had scant clothes and few dollars.

And so the *Ariel* continued her course, not without precautions from the beginning to the end of the passage against a conspiracy among British members of the crew to take the ship; but a careful watch, a special guard with fixed bayonets, and confinement of the ringleaders in irons quelled the potential mutiny. Fortunately, too, Jones escaped two British frigates which had been cruising off the capes of the Delaware to intercept him upon secret advice of his second sailing after the accident of the first.[26] At length the *Ariel* ran safely up the bay and river, and she moored at the port of Philadelphia on February 18, 1781, more than three and one quarter years after Jones had set sail in the *Ranger* under a crowd of canvas from Portsmouth for France. He was now close to the doors of Congress in Independence Hall, where some of its members wished to hear him and he zealously wished to be heard.

Part 5

Triumphs, Honors, and Leadership
in the United States

◇◇

Chapter XLIV

"Drag the Wretches into Open Day"

THESE ACTS are new in the world and are too glaring to be hushed up. I will drag the wretches into open day and hold them up to the world for such as they are,"[1] Jones had declared concerning Landais, Lee, Gillon, and the treacherous officers in their service when he still had been at L'Orient in the *Ariel* before his second sailing and already had received reports from across the ocean of the fantastic dissensions which had marked the return of the *Alliance* to America. The same lawless spirit which had impelled them to conspire against Jones and Franklin had not unnaturally stirred them to turbulent quarrels among themselves.

What previously had been masked as common resentment against alleged injustice of Jones and Franklin was now to be disclosed as arrant individual selfishness and knavery. Before Jones proved able to confront these accusers at home, however, their conduct had become so flagrant that the subterfuge of supposed madness of Landais and the shield of influential partisans in Congress were of little avail in hiding the truth. Prophetically Franklin had been apprehensive for the safety of the *Alliance* after her sailing for America under the French commander because this ship as governed by him had "ever been infected with disorder and mutiny." His fears were fully realized, although they assumed a form which even he had scarcely anticipated. She arrived in America to be sure, but only after a passage almost as wayward as a derelict's. Typical of her course, she had sailed for Philadelphia but came to Boston, and when she reached port Captain Landais was brooding in his cabin and Lieutenant Degge held command on the quarter-deck.

Riot had reigned cumulatively during the passage. The ship had not passed from view of Groix before Landais quarreled with Captain Parke of the Marines,[2] the officer who had been singled out for assassination as the only one previously opposed to the seizure of the command. Soon altercation began also with Lieutenant Degge; it rose in pitch when Landais rebuked him, in public as was his habit, for not keeping the ship nearer the wind. Incensed at what he considered the unreason of the command, Degge gave the crew orders precisely in contradiction to those he had received. The brawl grew into confusion as the lieutenant armed himself with a pike and the Captain rushed after him from one deck to another. With such scenes to whet the license of the incorrigible crew, including British seamen, the ship reached a state of still more ominous ferment.

Nor was the turmoil provoked by the officers and sailors alone. Lee was aboard, and his mere presence meant dissension. Like a proud woman with whom he was compared, Lee resented any circumstance, even under the necessary privations on a frigate, which did not cater to his egotism. Arrogant as Landais was in his own fashion, especially on board a ship where his authority was supreme, the Captain and the passenger were destined to come into conflict in spite of the mutual interests which had led them to join hands in conspiracy.

Yet the malevolence of the Captain was more in evidence than the presumption of the passenger when Lee objected to drinking from the water-butt in common with the sailors, including the sick and diseased, and when he insisted upon fresh water daily (instead of the usual salt water) for his ablutions.[3] The testiness of the one and the self-importance of the other were equally at fault and equally token of greater failings when Landais exclaimed against his passenger: "I will be helped first at table. You shall know not to pick the liver out of the dish; you shall take the first piece that comes to hand as I do. You shall not pick the prunes out of the plate, but take them as they come." On the occasion of a turkey dinner, "Landais rose in a passion," according to a French spectator, "and menaced Lee as if to kill him with his knife . . . he was indeed an infuriated madman."[4] In the same petty, demented spirit Landais reserved as his own property half

the pigs aboard intended for food on the ground that he owned
the boar which had begot them.[5] He particularly antagonized the
crew by refusing to delay the *Alliance* just an hour or two off the
Newfoundland Banks to permit them the long-anticipated opportunity of catching some fish and breaking the monotony of their
fare.

As for exercising command of the ship, Landais might as well
have been ashore. He retired for days to his cabin in waspish
aloofness; he gave no instructions to his officers and refused to
take counsel with them even at the very period of greatest peril
to the frigate. Fear arose among the officers and passengers alike,
especially in view of the British sailors aboard, that the disorgani-
zation would render the *Alliance* an easy prey to any hostile ship
of war she might meet. Some of them, fully conscious of their
guilty conduct towards Jones and Franklin, vowed that they would
prefer death to capture in the light of the ignominy which would
crown the circumstances under which the vessel had left L'Orient.
After two revolts among the seamen and after, to all appearances,
abdication of the command by Landais, the officers supported by
the passengers urged Degge to take command.[6] They represented
to him the pressing need not only to sail under his direction but
also "to make for the first port in America as the most sure and
almost the only method remaining of having the *Alliance* restored
to our country in safety."[7] Thus at Cape Ann on August 13 and at
Boston the nearest haven a few days later, the frigate under Degge
arrived safe at last while she was on the verge of a third mutiny.

Immediately the Navy Board in Boston learned with amazement
of the confusion on board the ship, and an incoherent message
from Landais accusing both officers and passengers served only to
incriminate himself. Following a report from Boston, the Board of
Admiralty in Philadelphia expressed "the greatest concern that
we see our flag disgraced by such extraordinary conduct, and we
shall not be satisfied until this dark business is thoroughly developed." Nor did it fail to express surprise that there had been
sixteen passengers and a large amount of private merchandise
aboard.[8] And regardless of a letter by Lee despatched at the first
possible moment to the President of Congress, in which he attributed the delay and the major difficulties to Franklin rather than to

Landais,[9] regardless too of Samuel Adams and Richard Henry Lee in Philadelphia, who were chiefly responsible for the appointment of the French officer, regardless further of John Adams in Europe, who had protected him, the Board now summarily gave the command of the *Alliance* to Barry.[10]

A court-martial of Landais, with Barry as president, soon ensued.[11] Thanks to the continued absence of Jones to witness against him, the warrant allowed for the examination of the conduct of Landais only from the time that he had seized the command of the *Alliance* at L'Orient. For the present at least, his behavior in the cruise with Jones was in abeyance. After a keen, judicious sifting of the evidence by Barry, who utterly exposed the guileful distortion of facts which had been habitual with Landais, the court declared him guilty in particular of disobedience to orders of Congress through its representative Franklin and of failure to watch over and govern the behavior of passengers, officers, and crew. Accordingly it adjudged him broke and disqualified from future naval service.

That the sentence was not more severe is attributable not only to the continued absence of Jones but also to the partially extenuating circumstances of Lee's influence upon the guilty officer. Barry did not fail publicly to link in dishonor with the name of Landais that of Lee and to emphasize the lawyer's wilful wrongdoing: "That said Peter Landais, Esq. in coming away without leave as aforesaid took the advice of the honorable Arthur Lee, Esq. a gentleman learned in the laws and late high in office, and so far is entitled to favor."[12]

Lee as well as Landais was fortunate by reason of the tempest which had prevented Jones in the *Ariel* from reaching America in the course of these proceedings. It is to be asked why, in the light of Barry's pronouncement upon Lee and the letters printed in support of it, the censure by the court-martial was not precedent to further investigation of his conduct by civil authority.

An indication of the force of the testimony by Jones against Lee if he had been in America appeared in his indictment written from Europe after an early account of the riotous passage of the *Alliance* had recrossed the ocean to him. Whether in sincerity, as a pretense in support of Landais whom he was shortly to abandon to his fate, or as is most likely for his own protection, Lee had attested during the investigation that the French captain was mad. "They pretend Captain Landais was mad," replied Jones from L'Orient. "But if that be true, I say he did not become mad on the passage between France and Boston. If he was formerly mad, which is perhaps the fairest way to account for his conduct while under my command, how will these officers and *Mr. Lee* at their head justify their having been in mutiny to replace him in command of the *Alliance* a few days before the frigate sailed from France to America?"[13]

That question, along with the further one concerning the private carriage and other property which had even displaced sorely-needed military supplies, did not at this time have its answer. Indeed, however revealing the replies, such unwelcome queries might well have been put to Arthur Lee, and other queries likewise regarding Landais to John Adams, Richard Henry Lee, and Samuel Adams.

Still the antagonism towards Jones as the ally of Franklin was too deep-seated for any confession of error even in spite of the official unmasking in part of Landais' conduct. Let Samuel Adams as representative speak several years later for him and at the same time reveal himself to Richard Henry Lee: "I beg leave once more to trespass upon your time by calling your attention to my friend Captain Landais. You and I patronized him when he first came into this country: and I have never for a moment repented of the small share I had in his promotion in the American Navy, although he has met with the fate which sometimes has been the lot of honest men, through the errors, to say the least, of courts.

"He has long suffered as other virtuous men had by a faction on the other side of the Atlantic which found means to extend itself to this country, and as you very well remember to the very doors of Congress! But enough of this."[14]

In the same vein he declared himself the advocate for prize money and other payments from the Government in behalf of Landais who had been discharged, as if his claim were prior to that of multitudes who had served honorably. "This Jones," he ended in suspicion apropos of prize money, in echo of the disgraced officer, "Captain Landais looks upon as his inveterate enemy, and he has not the least confidence in him."[15]

◇◇

Chapter XLV

Vindication and Honor
in America

WHEN "THIS JONES" in the scornful phrase of Samuel Adams, "such a person as Captain Paul Jones" in the corresponding terms of Arthur Lee, and "this emigrant foreigner of the South" according to those of John Adams, now stepped ashore from the *Ariel* at Philadelphia on February 18, 1781, about six weeks after the sentence by the court-martial, he was not averse to confronting political detractors on land in America as squarely as he had met enemies on the sea abroad. Barry as president at the trial had taken the road towards justice, and Jones, newly-arrived, prepared to follow its course to the end, although his reiterated purpose was to avoid party politics in adherence to his single aim as a naval officer.[1]

His presence promised dramatic revelations. The conduct of Landais in the *Bonhomme Richard* cruise and of Lee in the departure of the *Alliance* remained fully to be divulged at home. Jones had transmitted some of his charges against Landais when still in Europe, and in devotion to Franklin even more than in consideration for himself he had intended personally to represent "that wasp [Lee] in true colors."[2]

Even on the day following his arrival, Congress ordered that "the difference between Captain J. P. Jones and Captain Landais and also the detention of clothing be referred to the Board of Admiralty." Coincident with this procedure was a request that Jones should "attend Congress on Monday next to lay before them every information in his power relative to the detention of the clothing and arms belonging to the United States in France." Significantly the resolution added "that the doors of the Congress be open during such examination."[3] A manœuvre worthy of note was that Samuel Adams, whose forte lay in relentless publicity, in this instance opposed the glare of truth, for he was the leader in a postponement, in effect a withdrawal, of the motion for a public hearing.[4] Surely it was not Jones whom he wished to protect from open dishonor, but Landais his appointee, Lee his protégé, and himself the enemy of Franklin.

Tokens of esteem in America for Jones, not less than those which he had received in Europe, began to crowd upon him, whatever doubts some members of Congress, unprejudiced as well as prejudiced, may have retained concerning some aspects of his services abroad pending his answers in writing to a list of forty-seven exhaustive questions in lieu of the public testimony.[5] Before his answers to these questions of the Board of Admiralty, Congress was moved to appreciation by the recommendations which he had brought with him from Europe, notably the letter from De Sartine attesting to the high regard of Louis XVI,[6] and by the assurances in person of the French Minister, the Chevalier de La Luzerne, in America.[7] Therefore within a week after his return to the United States, February 27, 1781, it passed a resolution expressing a high sense of his "distinguished bravery and military conduct . . . particularly in his victory over the British frigate *Serapis* on the coast of England, which was attended with circumstances so brilliant as to excite general applause and admiration. . . ."[8]

The United States further paid to Jones an honor which was shown to no other American. "His Majesty's offer of adorning Captain Jones with a Cross of Military Merit," the resolution continued, "is highly acceptable to Congress." A message from Samuel Huntington, the President of Congress, to Franklin reiterated this view. Jones did not fail to record that His Majesty had expressed the hope that the decoration and with it the gold sword bestowed upon him would represent one of the strongest links between the two nations.[9] The distinction was especially unique in that Congress appears to have deferred final ratification of the Articles of Confederation for several days, until March 1, in order to permit him to accept on the preceding February 27 an honor such as these Articles forbad except by express Federal consent. At a reception which the Chevalier de La Luzerne gave to the members of Congress and the principal citizens of Philadelphia, the Minister invested Jones with the Order of Military Merit in the presence of the assemblage.[10] It was not, however, without some criticism based on the democracy of America that he thereby assumed on occasion the title of *chevalier* and wore the decoration of the order.

At the same time the vindication and honor which had begun so signally to attend his public services included a victory over his private enemies. Although the concerns of America at war overshadowed whatever personal animosities remained in his heart, Jones did not fail to expose in his terse replies to the forty-seven questions of the Board of Admiralty, in regard to the whole period from his sailing in the *Ranger* from Portsmouth to his arrival in the *Ariel* at Philadelphia, the true nature of the conduct towards him of Landais, Lee, and De Chaumont.[11] And although Franklin in a moment of impatience during the *Alliance* crisis had stated that Jones and Landais might settle their quarrels as they could, he later had sent to Congress a detailed account in support of the Commodore, which together with other letters made his case well-nigh overwhelming.

As for the delay in the return of the *Alliance* and the absence of expected clothing and stores in her, which particularly concerned Congress, Jones pointedly made clear the part of De Chaumont as a half-political, half-commercial intermediary who chiefly occasioned the first circumstance by withholding prize money and contributed to the second by failing to fulfill his mercantile obligations.

As for the assumption by Landais of the command of the *Alliance* (in addition to its bearing upon those circumstances for which he shared responsibility with De Chaumont), Jones explained that he himself had taken command "at last by the authority and repeated order" of Franklin, that he had also "all the authority that could be given him by the Ambassador of France," and that he conceived his own authority as commander in chief might justify him if he had acted on the basis of it. His plans, nevertheless, to sail in due time and with large cargoes in the *Alliance, Ariel,* and several merchant ships under his convoy were to his "great mortification . . . entirely defeated by Mr. Lee, Captain Landais, and his party." In explanation he added in terms as brief as trenchant: "Mr. Lee and the rest of his council can best answer why he sailed contrary to my orders as well as the orders of Mr. Franklin."

Why Lee was not brought to answer, but instead, in reward for past conspiracies and in view of new ones, was soon to gain a seat in Congress, intrenched again to plague Jones and Franklin, his political allies could best unravel. In contrast with the attitude of this group, the report of the Board of Admiralty is noteworthy as an official judgment upon Jones' personal relationships with those who had sought to frustrate his public services as well as upon these public services themselves. It exonerated Jones and Franklin from any implications arising from delay and non-arrival of clothing and stores, and attributed to them rather "the closest attention to that business."[12] It placed the blame flatly upon the shoulders of De Chaumont and Landais and explained that further prosecution of the latter for his conduct prior to his seizure of the *Alliance* was now withheld because he had already been dismissed from the service.[13] Finally it declared in praise of Jones that: "ever since he first became an officer in the Navy of these States, he hath shown an unremitted attention in planning and executing enterprises calculated to promote the essential interest of our glorious cause. . . . That he hath made the Flag of America respectable among the Flags of other nations. . . ."[14]

In view of the findings and recommendations of the Board of Admiralty, Congress itself, April 14, 1781, lauded the Commodore in specific and signal terms: "That the thanks of the United States in Congress assembled, be given to Captain John Paul Jones, for the zeal, prudence, and intrepidity with which he hath supported the honor of the American flag; for his bold and successful enterprises to redeem from captivity the citizens of these States who had fallen under the power of the enemy; and in general for the good conduct and eminent services by which he has added lustre to his character, and to the American arms. . . ." The resolution likewise praised his officers and men. Finally it recommended "that a medal of gold emblematical of the victory obtained over the *Serapis* be presented to Captain John Paul Jones. . . ." This last honor, however, was challenged and marked *negatived*.[15]

As if in dissent from these conclusions of the Board of Admiralty and these praises of Congress, Samuel Adams at once made a motion for an inquiry into "the cause of the detention of the prize money due to the seamen in the service of the United States in Europe and America."[16] It reflected obviously his continued suspicions not only of Jones but more particularly of Franklin. At the time of the *Bonhomme Richard* cruise, he already had raised the question "whether it was a project of private men so artfully contrived and conducted that they can declare the property to be either public or private as may best suit their interest."[17]

Samuel Adams notwithstanding, the greatest of the testimonials in favor of Jones came from Washington. Perhaps some scruples arising from earlier insinuations of his responsibility for the unreceived supplies of the Continental Army, incident to his difficulties at L'Orient and his prolonged stay in Paris, prompted Jones to write to the Commander in Chief; a more palpable reason may have been his ardent desire to have the General's support for his future naval service. The reply of Washington derives its value from the special import of his words as well as from his name:

"My partial acquaintance with either our naval or commercial affairs makes it altogether impossible for me to account for the unfortunate delay of those articles of military stores and clothing which have been so long provided in France.

"Had I any reason to have suspected you of being accessory to that delay, which I assure you has not been the case, my suspicion would have been removed by the very full and satisfactory answers which you have, to the best of my judgment, made to the questions proposed to you by the Board of Admiralty, and upon which that board have, in their report to Congress, testified the high sense which they entertain of your merit and services.

"Whether our naval affairs have in general been well or ill conducted would be presumptuous in me to determine. Instances of bravery and good conduct in several of our officers have not, however, been wanting. Delicacy forbids me to mention that particular one which has attracted the admiration of the world, and which has influenced the most illustrious monarch to confer a mark of his favor, which can only be obtained by a long and honorable service or by the performance of some brilliant action."[18]

The rank of Jones in the Continental Navy was still another and more specific matter which concerned his prestige. The standing as eighteenth on the list of captains since October 10, 1776 had been his greatest grievance against Congress, and he now looked for its correction. Although on the one hand he modestly expressed his devoted appreciation for the laudations tendered to him, on the other he later said, "I was far from thinking that such *pleasing expressions* were all the gratification I had to expect." Rank remained fixed in his mind now that he was home. "Rank, which opens the door to glory," as he was to declare, "is too near the heart of every officer of true military feeling to be given up in favor of any other man who has not, by the achievement of some brilliant action or by known and superior abilities, merited such preference."[19]

As Congress neither promoted him for his special exploits nor restored him to a standing based at least on seniority according to his position as the first lieutenant highest in the list in 1775, he followed the suggestion of some members to present his claim in writing. The Government referred this application of May 28, 1781 to a special committee of three members, one of whom informed him shortly of a report in his favor that in their opinion he had merited advancement to the rank of rear admiral.[20]

At this juncture James Nicholson, who had become first in the list of captains of 1776, especially through the influence of Richard Henry Lee, happened to learn of the claim and interposed strenuous objections to Congress. His record in the Revolution, aside from a noteworthy combat with a strong privateer the *Watt,* includes chiefly the loss of two newly built frigates under circumstances which may well reflect upon his judgment. With another Captain, Thomas Read, whose services are comparatively obscure but whose rank had been fifth on the list of 1776, Nicholson stated in his petition "the absurdity of Captain Jones' claims"—claims which in contrast with his needed no explanations for the loss of even a single ship.

Nicholson likewise sent to Captain Barry, who had just returned from a special voyage in the *Alliance,* a graphic but flippant, distorted, and slipshod account of his efforts to thwart Jones. This recital appears upon scrutiny to be more damaging by its form and substance to the reputation of the accuser than the accused:

"I shall without any apoligy relate to you what has been transacting in this quarter relative to rank for this week past, it still hangs over our head & requires every exertion of interest to prevent its taking place. The attempt has been bold and daring and is only equalled by the man who made it.

"The Chevalier ever since his arrival in this city has devoted his time, privately, by making personal application to the individual members of Congress to give him rank at the head of our navy, and after interesting (by being an accomplished courtior) every member who was week, or of his own stamp, in his favor, hands into Congress a narritive of his services from the beginning of time containing the best part of a quire of paper, and attended with a modest petition setting forth the injustice he had done him in the establishment of rank and desire of redress, &ca.

"This had the desired effect, and he had a committee of Congress consistg. of Genl. Vernon, Mr. Mathews, and Mr. Clymer appointed to enquire into his claim and to make report, they accordingly did and in his favor. Congress was upon the point of taking the report up, and I have too much reason to believe would have gratified the hight of his ambition had we not by the greatest accident discovered it. . . .

"I immediately took my hat and with very little ceremony waited on the President of Congress at his house, & informed what I had heard, he received me politely & told me my suspisians were just, I therefore desired as my right that Congress might delay determining on it until Cap. Reade & myself in behalf of ourselves & the absent brother officers equally concerned should have an opportunity of being heard, which he promised me his interest to have done, and that day Capt. Reade & myself threw in our remonstrance to Congress a copy of mine you have enclosed, the consequence of which the committee was ordered to reconsider it and to give us notice to attend.

"We accordingly did & found Cap. Jones without doors in

conference with two of them, Cap. Jones did not attend, I desired the chairman would send for him, the reason I assigned was that I would say many things in his presence that I would not in his absence, he sent word that he would wait on us but never came, we found the President and Mr. Mathews predetermined in his favor, but Mr. Climer otherwise, after pointing out the absurdity of his claim. . . .

"I say after pointing out this to them, the Presidt. appeared to be convinced, but if so in reality I wont pretend to say. We had a good deal of conversation with the committee, Mr. Mathews alone seemed his most strenuous advocate and in my oppinion behaved obstinate and ungentiel.

"I said many things pretty severe of the Chevaliers private as well as public carrector too odious to mention and yet unnoticed, upon the whole we acquited ourselves well. . . ."[21]

As Nicholson not only appealed in this manner to Barry, the most meritorious of these fellow officers, but also rallied all the other captains whom he could against Jones, and they were still many inasmuch as seventeen had ranked higher than he, Congress was not disposed to disturb a hornet's nest if it could be avoided. To be sure escape was difficult, for Hancock had even admitted to Jones the hurry and incomplete information which had attended the standing of the officers. Under these circumstances his application, with the petitions also of Nicholson and Read, was referred again to a committee, which scarcely could and in fact did not ignore the truth.

In a report faintly humorous as a naïve confession of the influences of hidden politics, the members stated that they had been "unable fully to ascertain the rule by which that arrangement [the October 10, 1776 order of captains] was made, as the relative rank was not conformable to the times of appointment and dates of commission and seems repugnant to a resolution of Congress of the 22nd of December, 1775." They admitted that, on the basis of seniority, the time of Jones' appointment as a captain entitled him to be fifth in standing and that on the same basis his appointment as a lieutenant warranted Whipple's rank as first and his as second. They made no effort to judge services as well as seniority, but concluded with a recommendation that Congress should appoint a commander in chief of the Navy. Still the buzz of the hornets must have sounded ominously, for "on account of the thinness of Congress," a seemingly disingenuous reason in view of no later procedure, the report received the endorsement "Not to be acted upon."[22]

Before these findings suffered oblivion, however, it remained to appoint an officer to command the *America*. The construction of this sole first-rate ship of the line built by the United States during the Revolution was, like the *Ranger,* under the direction of John Langdon as naval agent in New Hampshire. He had laid her keel at Portsmouth in June, 1777 and expected to complete her in five months,[23] but she was still on the stocks four years later. It was true, as Nicholson boasted in his efforts against Jones, that Barry had been appointed to her in 1779; it was also true, as he failed to reveal, that Barry had gone to Portsmouth only to be informed by Langdon that he had no money to complete the ship and that this officer had satisfied himself, after his return to Philadelphia to report to Congress, that the Government was financially unable to continue the construction. Barry, therefore, not unwisely, considered other assignments.

Although Nicholson professed that he was now asked whether he himself would accept the command of the *America,* the question does not prove the offer; and his motives, in the event of an offer, indicate that he had little patriotic inclination for bestirring himself to finish the ship at last. His assertions in this case invite the greater doubt because of his statements in general, warped by jealousy, and his specific declaration, prejudiced as it obviously was, that Morris was convinced of the justness of his views concerning the appointment of a suitable officer to command this ship of the line. For after Morris, the recently-appointed Secretary of Marine, had received authority on June 23 to take immediate steps to launch and equip the *America,* his hearty endorsement of Jones for the command was preparatory to the choice of him in Congress three days later by unanimous vote.[24]

"Thus Congress took a delicate method to avoid cabal and to do justice," wrote Jones with a truth that needs the greater emphasis in view of Nicholson's self-confessed resort to "every exertion of interest" against him and his sneers implying that the *America* was a gift horse. "It was more agreeable," Jones continued, "to be so honorably elected captain of the line than to have been, as was proposed by the committee, raised at once to the rank of rear admiral, because Congress had not then the means of giving him a command suitable to that rank." He had now marked his return to the United States not only by signal honors for his naval services but also by moral victories over Landais, Lee, and Samual Adams, which had their culmination in his command of the *America*.

◇◇◇

Chapter XLVI

Commander of the *America*, the First Ship of the Line

"FROM THE beginning almost to the end," Jones was to explain to Louis XVI, "I never lost sight of my purpose to form by dint of my perseverance a combined squadron of French and American frigates supported by America."[1] The *Bonhomme Richard* expedition with the victory over the *Serapis* had set the pattern for him; his object ever since had been a more formidable and better-composed squadron under the American flag and, if his spirit was to determine, even a greater conquest. He presented his views, supported by the letters brought from the French Ministers, especially to Robert Morris, who at the dissolution of the Board of Admiralty was now, as Agent of Marine, in effect a Secretary of the Treasury and Navy combined. As the war was reaching its late stages and the *America* was still far from completion, Jones felt the more urgent desire to expedite his plans. Although the Government owed him $15,000 for advances, particularly in connection with the *Ranger,* it had paid no part of his salary or subsistence; in fact, his only remuneration for six years as an American officer had been a small share of prize money. He left Philadelphia for Portsmouth, nevertheless, as speedily as possible, with his accounts approved but unpaid and under the necessity of begging from Congress an advance of £400 for his immediate needs.

Jones stopped for a visit to Washington and Rochambeau encamped at White Plains, during which he satisfied his pride so far as to wear his French decoration, but decided after hints not to do so for the present in New England states. He then hastened to Portsmouth only to find to his disappointment that, after four years under the direction of Langdon, the *America* remained less than half finished. The Navy Board at Boston had used for other purposes the funds which Morris had provided for the ship.[2] As the winter was approaching, the lack of materials on hand lengthened the normal delay due to the lack of money. The many demands upon Morris for the secret expedition of the Continental troops against Cornwallis in Virginia contributed to the stringency. Although Jones began construction at once, he wisely wished at this early stage of his superintendence to adopt a decisive course— either to abandon the work or to prosecute it with vigor. Possibly this initial attitude was only to spur the admiralty authorities in Philadelphia to greater activity; in any event, after his decision to persevere, he bent to the task of completing the *America* with his characteristic tenacity.

Along the path of this fierce purpose, if not across it, stood John Langdon. Urbane, diplomatic, practical, esteemed, this New Hampshire naval agent, who superintended prizes, built ships for personal business as well as for public objects, and had both the training and the taste for the policy of a merchant, did not see eye to eye with Jones ever athirst for naval exploit and glory. To be sure Langdon had given a thousand dollars, pledged his plate for three thousand more, and sold seventy hogsheads of Tobago rum at the best available price upon the call to withstand Burgoyne, and yet his purpose was seemingly more expedient than self-sacrificing in the light of his explanation that, if the British won, this wealth would be lost anyway.[3] The variant points of view of Jones as naval officer and Langdon as businessman did not account altogether for the cleavage between them. There were the further differences which had previously arisen during the equipment of the *Ranger,* and the unforgotten injuries which Jones had suffered through the appointment of Simpson, the fellow townsman and relative of the naval agent, as first lieutenant of this sloop of war.

Jones, it is recalled, had gained the *Bonhomme Richard* squadron only after he had vowed that he would die rather than return to the United States without a command and without honor; now it was to be expected that he would not turn back from Portsmouth before completion of the *America,* however difficult the means and however opposed Langdon the contractor might be. Dilatory as the work upon the ship had been from the outset, the merchant not unnaturally expected to be paid, and promptly too. Before the arrival of Jones, Langdon's remonstrances to the Admiralty Board in Philadelphia had become numerous. The replies had lamented "the reduced state of the public treasury"[4] and referred him on occasion to the naval authorities in Boston. To Morris he had also expressed regret for the discharge of the workmen on the one hand and for the inevitable ruin of the ship if she were not soon put afloat on the other.

It is to be concluded, nevertheless, on the basis of Langdon's warning which shortly followed, that the loss would have resulted not from warped timbers on the stocks, as he had previously implied,[5] but from his intention to cast off the uncompleted ship in order to use his facilities for private business. "If any measures are taken I should be glad to be informed of it speedily," he declared; "otherwise my shipyard must be employed in another way and I fear the seventy-four must be lost to the Continent."[6] This avowal presents him in a light somewhat at variance with that of the patriot in the Burgoyne campaign, differentiates him sharply from Morris, the fellow merchant, with whom he has been compared, and offers a clue to the impatience, to say the least, which Jones in his zeal was increasingly to feel towards him.

Perhaps the slow progress of the *America,* bridling the urgency of Jones' combined ambition and patriotism, contributed to turn his attention again to an interest which had taken little of his time at the call for action. The first subject of this minor distraction— at least seemingly the first—was again the Countess de Nicolson. A letter to her on Christmas day at Portsmouth broke a silence, whatever his excuses, of six months, and it had an uncertain warmth despite protestations which contrasted with her impulsive ardor:

"I wrote, my most lovely Delia, various letters from Philadelphia, the last of which was dated the 20th of June. On the 26th of that month I was unanimously elected by Congress to command the *America* of seventy-four guns, on the stocks at Portsmouth, New Hampshire.

"Since I came here I have not found a single good opportunity to write to Europe. I have not since heard from your relation I left behind, but suppose he is with the Army. This situation is doubly irksome to me, my lovely friend, as it stops my pursuit of honor as well as love!

"It is now more than twelve months since I left France; yet I have not received a single letter from thee in all that time, except the one written in answer to my letter at taking leave. That one is a tender letter indeed, and does honor to thy matchless heart! I read often and always with transport the many charming things that are so well expressed in thy letters; but especially the last. Thy adieu has in it all the finer feelings, blended with the noblest sentiments of the heart. Providence, all good and just, has given thee a soul worthy in all respects to animate nature's fairest work.

"I rest therefore sure that *absence* will not diminish, but *refine* the pure and spotless friendship that binds our souls together, and will ever impress each to merit the affection of the other. Remember and *believe* my letter at parting. It was but a faint picture of my heart. I will find opportunities to write, and be everything thou canst wish."[7]

Even less auspicious for his fidelity to Delia than this objective message, whether or not her own protracted silence had an unpromising influence, were indications that he was turning his serious thoughts elsewhere. "I say nothing to you at present of my affair of the heart, but wait impatiently to hear much on that subject from you," he wrote three months later to John Brown, the former Secretary of the Board of Admiralty, concerning an American young woman, presumably from Philadelphia. She was, it seems, "the fair Miss xxxx" of this city, whom "rigid duty and stern honor" had prevented him from wooing except in his bantering phrase, "by proxy." Alluding to this private subject as well as discussing at length the situation of the *America,* he added confidentially: "I shall rely on your advice, and, as I know it will come from the heart of friendship, I shall make no scruple beforehand to promise you to treat it with great respect and attention."[8]

Presumably his thoughts were not unduly preoccupied either by this renewed uncertain "affair of the heart" in America or by Delia in France. He devoted himself to extensive study of books

by the best authorities on naval warfare as well as to daily supervision of the *America*. And in the same breath with his concern
for the ship and for news of the Philadelphia young woman from
his confidant, Jones revealed himself somewhat in the guise of a
popular cavalier in the New Hampshire seaport, reminiscent of
his part in Paris: "I reached Portsmouth just when they began
to light candles after tea, and the dancing did not end till after
two in the morning." Consistent with this rôle, a request soon followed: "You will oblige me, my dear Brown, if you can send me
. . . a piece of good linen for shirts and a piece of cambric for
stock. I have muslin for ruffles, but thread and buttons are wanting.
. . . I should not have given you this trouble but that I find no
linen here except such as is both bad and very dear. . . ."⁹ To
complete his courtly outfit, he wrote not without at least one very
acceptable reason to another close friend in Boston, the former
naval officer Hector McNeill: "Excuse the liberty I take of enclosing a guinea which I pray you to invest in good hair powder. . . .
Entre nous there is none of that luxury to be had here, except such
as is impregnated with luxurious mites."¹⁰ The bachelor took his
diversion, perhaps his solace, as if he anticipated that the *America*
would shortly become his all-absorbing purpose.

In the spring of 1782 Jones hoped at last to speed the *America*
to completion so that at the coming of autumn he might sail with
her to France, as Morris himself proposed, and look forward to
realization of the encouragement already given him abroad for
the command of a second squadron of the two nations under the
flag of the United States. He would then prove himself an admiral
not on parade but in action. As his efforts, regardless of obstacles,
grew apace, those of Langdon declined; their relations approached
a crisis. "I am apprized," Morris in Philadelphia wrote conciliat-
ingly to Langdon in Portsmouth, "of a coldness subsisting between
you and the Chevalier. This gives me much concern and I desire
that it may be forgotten. You can, I believe, be of mutual aid to
each other, and it would be a great misfortune that the public
service should suffer by being deprived of the abilities of either."

Morris did not forbear to offer reproof: "The Chevalier informs
me that the gundeck of the *America* has been partly laid with short
planks. This I suppose has been owing to unavoidable circum-

stances, but I am very sorry, first because they are not so proper for the purpose as longer plank would have been. He has also mentioned to me several useful hints with regard to this vessel which he will readily communicate to you, and I promise myself they will meet with your attentive consideration." The Agent of Marine implied further criticism for failure to heed the professional skill of Jones: "He is a gentleman of worth, and as he has seen many ships knows well how to manage a ship in action, and as he is appointed by Congress to the command of this particular ship, his sentiments are worthy of attention. I must therefore request you to consult him on the subject and comply with his wishes more especially when they tend to economy as well as utility." The friendly disposition of Morris gave the greater pointedness to his mild-mannered correction of Langdon's self-sufficiency.

Notwithstanding the assurance from the naval head that Jones would do all in his power "to establish and cultivate a right understanding" and that funds would be available, Langdon took offense at these tempered efforts for coöperation in matters of which Jones had special knowledge and experience. Again and again the agent for the *America* requested to resign. In turn Morris repeatedly urged him to persevere so as not to expose the ship to ruin by displacing her, partly completed, from his shipyard.

At the same time, frankly and boldly, letter followed letter from Jones to Morris in Philadelphia and to Brown as his deputy in Boston. The measure of his exertions appeared typically during a threat by Langdon to stop the construction: "I wrote you, my dear Brown, by the last post, mentioning Colonel Langdon's intention to discharge all the carpenters last Saturday. . . . I had determined to try all my art of persuasion on Colonel Langdon and to call in the auxiliary aid of General Whipple and others to induce him to continue. If he had obstinately persisted in discharging the carpenters, I was resolved to have continued them at my own expense till I had heard from the Minister, being persuaded that to stop now would be to lose the *America*.

"Perhaps all my arguments would have failed, had he not by Friday's post received a remittance of ten thousand dollars. Even that has not operated to augment the number of carpenters nor even to set a single caulker to work. All it has effected is to continue the few men employed when you were here; and part of that number are and have been for some time past taken off to fit out his private vessels."[11]

Jones believed, too, that he had discovered an ulterior motive in the conduct of Langdon; whether or not these suspicions were well-founded, some of the words and acts of the agent tended to support them. "I now see also the reason why 'resigning' and 'getting clear of the business' are so much talked of," the subtle as well as outspoken sailor explained to Brown, who supported him in his determination to retain the workmen. "The scheme has been deeply laid, and if the successor [to Langdon] that has been recommended should be accepted, I think the coffers would be drained, and a double fence to knavery would be erected."[12]

Jones assumed various responsibilities for the ship to which the government agent, who felt free early in the war to condemn "the cursed disingenuity and ingratitude of mankind,"[13] turned his back in the spirit of "getting clear of the business." While Langdon was threatening to end operations because of the lack of funds, Jones showed himself resourceful as well as resolute to complete the ship by asking Gouverneur Morris to organize a subscription for this purpose and by suggesting that the subscribers might share in prize money from her future services.[14]

More importantly, he saved the *America* from imminent peril following the secret learned by American spies and transmitted by Washington that the British planned to set her afire on the stocks. Langdon did nothing in the emergency. The government of New Hampshire likewise did nothing. "It was not possible for me," Jones related, "to obtain a single soldier. As I had neither arms nor powder nor bullets, no means were possible for me to employ except to secure aid by my own funds. And so I did. I likewise engaged the two builders to keep guard, alternately, every night over the ship with a party of the carpenters whom I agreed to pay also at my expense. As it was necessary to set an example, I took command of the guard every third night during the whole period of construction. By this means I prevented the enemy from burning the *America*, inasmuch as several times some large boats with muffled oars approached, but the enemy did not dare to come ashore when they discovered that the guard stood watching in readiness for them."[15]

Two celebrations aboard the *America* contributed to allay temporarily the conflict between Jones and Langdon. One occurred on the anniversary of the Declaration of Independence and the other on a day proposed by France and accepted by the United States as her ally to observe the birth of the Dauphin. Aboard the *America*, Jones gave special recognition to France for the heir to the throne because he appreciated of course that country's part in the Revolution and also felt particularly the honor which he owed to the Crown. For the interest of Louis XVI he was to describe in detail the elaborate entertainment on board the ship, which attracted all the populace of Portsmouth and which "ended at midnight with a royal salute from the *America*."[16] He knew well how to gain favor by the *argumentum ad hominem* when it suited him to do so; yet if his words in this instance were flattering, he offered them to the King of that country which had already enabled him to serve the United States far more signally than himself.

The satisfaction and the infinite care of the naval architect as artist, of which the persevering renovations that he had previously made in the *Ranger* and the *Alliance* were token, seemed even more characteristic of him in the building of the *America*, despite his impatience for action and his difficulties with the business agent. While Langdon was properly the contractor, Colonel James Hackett employed his talent as the master builder, and Jones brought to bear his inspired superintendence based on all his years of experience and study in judging the structural, sailing, and fighting qualities of ships. He declared that "the workmanship was far superior to any before seen in naval architecture."[17] He changed particularly the plans for the upper works of the *America*. He increased materially her combat strength by a breastwork, pierced with gun ports, circling the quarter-deck, gangway, and forecastle, by means of which all the cannon on them could be fought on either side—"an advantage possessed by no other ship of the line." He likewise planned symbolic sculptural figures, which according to his own complimentary description expressed dignity and simplicity. Whatever were the merits of the naval ornament which was customary, his judgment upon the beauty in line, the trim, and the deceptive strength of the *America* appears to warrant full acceptance: "This ship, though the largest of seventy-four guns in the world, had, when the lower battery was sunk, the air of a delicate frigate; and no person at the distance of a mile could have imagined she had a second battery."[18] Now with this last cunning advantage, Jones must have been pleased to visualize far in advance the strategy as well as formidableness with which he hoped to sail the British seas in the *America* as his flagship at the head of an allied squadron.

Even one who had by no means shown himself partial to Jones evidenced the integrity and vision to have come to appreciate the talents which the *America* at completion would enable him to display. From The Hague, John Adams tendered an enthusiastic endorsement: "The command of the ship *America* could not have been more wisely bestowed, and I am impatient to see her at sea where she will honor her name. Nothing causes me more surprise and regret than the inattention of my countrymen to their Navy. . . . I assure you indeed that, if I could see the prospect of a dozen ships of the line under the American flag and commanded by Paul Jones, I apprehend that the event of a battle with the English, of equal force, would redound to the glory of the United States and lay the foundation of their prosperity in such a way as altogether to compensate for the continuation of the war."[19]

But it was less the approach of the close of the Revolution, following the surrender of Cornwallis at Yorktown, than an unlucky accident after Jones' unswerving perseverance for sixteen months that suddenly extinguished his hopes on the eve of their realization. In September, 1782 the *America* was practically finished; only her armament, rigging, and sails remained to be provided. When a French ship of the line, the *Magnifique,* one of the squadron under the Marquis de Vaudreuil at Boston, suffered wreck in the harbor, Jones urged Brown to engage Morris to secure opportunely the ship's cannon and other equipment for the *America.* "You will follow up this object," he pleaded, "if you regard my happiness."[20] Ironically the accident to the *Magnifique* by no means facilitated the outfitting of the *America;* it resulted, instead, in the sudden transfer, even without Jones' knowledge, of his own ship to the Marquis de Vaudreuil. Congress had already bestowed her upon France, "testifying on this occasion to His Majesty the sense they entertain of his generous exertions in behalf of the United States." Whether the burden of the *America* in view of the financial stress of the United States[21] or the fitting occasion to offer such a token of gratitude to the ally was the governing motive, Jones suddenly found all his exertions for a suitable ship as the nucleus for a French-American squadron vanish into nothingness.

Although the presentation of the *America* to France did not even refer in any way to his part in her construction and to his appointment to her, he persevered energetically for two months longer to see the ship afloat. What with a ledge of rocks, currents which prevented the use of stockades, and a circuitous, restricted space on the river by the shipyard on Rising Island, the launching was not the least of the difficulties in the history of the *America*. "When everything was prepared," according to his impersonal description, "Captain Jones stood on the highest part of the brow or gangway that ascended from the ground to the bow of the ship. From that position he could perfectly see the motion of the ship, and determine by a signal the instant when it was proper to let go one or both of the anchors which were hung at the bows, and slip the end of the cable that depended on the anchor, fixed in the ground on the island. The operation succeeded perfectly to his wish, and to the admiration of a large assembly of spectators."[22] After a display of the flags of the two allies and the mooring of the ship in safety, he presented her on the same day, November 5, to the Chevalier de Martigne who had commanded the *Magnifique*.

The labors of Jones had not been without appreciation in some quarters where they were best judged. When Robert Morris announced to him the transfer of the ship, he did not fail to add that "nothing could be more pleasing to me than this disposition excepting so far as you are affected by it." The grace with which Jones accepted his loss, particularly in view of his regard for France, had its mirror in further expressions by Morris to Congress as well as to him. In answer to a letter from the officer, now without a command, the Secretary of Marine replied that "the sentiments contained in it will always reflect the highest honor upon your character";[23] and in a message to the President of Congress he enclosed an extract from Jones' letter and commented, "I cannot resist the desire of laying sentiments which do him so much honor before my sovereign."

From Brown too, who had returned from Boston to Philadelphia, came words of promise to Jones. He mentioned "your active genius," "the ready disposition of the Agent of Marine to hear and adopt your plans," and his own hopes that "you may have command of a capital ship yet this fall."[24]

Optimistic as were these expressions on public matters, those on the private concern of which Jones had made Brown a confidant, his interest in the lady who was an acquaintance of his friend, were in contrasting, equal degree unhopeful. The incommunicativeness of his confidant on this score had finally induced Jones to write: "There is one delicate subject of a *private nature* on which you remain silent, though I wrote you at Boston that I expected to hear much from you on that head. Your silence, I fear, carries with it a disagreeable meaning." Now, along with his remarks occasioned by the *America*, Brown replied, in reference to a forthcoming marriage: "As to the delicate subject of a private nature which you hint at, it is all over . . . therefore think no more of it."[25]

Regardless of the good will with which he had completed the *America* and presented her to the French commander, regardless too of his ensuing reticence concerning "the delicate subject of a private nature," the coincident loss in the one case and disappointment in the other were not without apparent further meaning to him. "When the *America* was taken from me," he confided later in a statement intended for the Agent of Marine, "I was deprived of my tenth command. Will posterity believe that out of this number the sloop of war *Ranger* was the best I was ever enabled *by my country* to bring into actual service?"[26]

His public grievance lent itself thus to chronicle, but his private regret remained chiefly for philosophic inscription in his mind. This latest, briefly felt rebuff to his affections, along with his estrangements past and pending, already marked a disappointment in love which in its number corresponded approximately with half the total of his ten lost ships. It may well have hastened his steps to Philadelphia and influenced his thoughts of return to Europe.

Whatever were his future memories of Portsmouth, he was not to forbear at a chosen time to inform the King: "May I be permitted to say that if I had not in any way been commissioned to superintend the construction and preservation of the *America,* if I had not sacrificed eighteen months of my time and secured by my purse all the means to preserve her from the enemy for this period, this ship of war would never have appeared upon the list of the royal marine of France."[27]

Viewed in the light of this devoted service, the readiness with which Jones accepted his loss of the *America* again revealed his unselfish dedication to the cause of his country. He was happy to attest his gratitude towards that ally which, after her part in the fall of Cornwallis, promised to insure the freedom of the United States. In the same spirit, on one occasion he soon addressed Franklin with reverent appreciation for his public career: "You are beloved; and will ever, while virtue is honorable, be revered as a father and saviour of your country."[28] And on a further occasion, in one of his last messages to this aged friend, he voiced his feelings as to the presentation of the ship: "It was thought that act of Congress would give me great pain, but those who were of that opinion did not well know my character. It would certainly have afforded me more satisfaction to have retained that command and to have rendered thereby useful services to the common cause; but as things were circumstanced, it was a sacrifice I made with the pleasure to testify my grateful regard for France and my invincible attachment to the interests of the two allied nations."[29]

Chapter XLVII

◇◇

The Leader of the American Navy at the Close of the Revolution

EVEN ONCE more the *Indienne,* in place of the *America,* fleeted across the horizon of Jones' ambition as the chief ship of a proposed squadron under his command. Both Morris and the Chevalier de La Luzerne, influential well-wishers both American and French, considered the occasion opportune to secure this oft-sought powerful frigate for him. Gillon her present commander, who in malice had propagated the report that the *Bonhomme Richard* was a privateer,[1] and like Lee had supported Landais against Jones, later had managed to charter this ship from the Prince de Luxembourg after her transfer to him from the King.[2] The generosity of Colonel John Laurens, Gillon's compatriot from South Carolina, with funds from French loans which Franklin chiefly had negotiated, was responsible for this unworthy disposal of the frigate repeatedly promised to Jones and repeatedly withheld from him.

The *Indienne* had now arrived at Philadelphia for repairs at the expiration of half the period of her lease to Gillon. In violation of the terms of the charter, he had made no payments whatever from proceeds of a number of valuable prizes; nor did he provide funds for necessary repairs in port.[3] Morris and Luzerne, acting on behalf of the owners, prepared to be generous towards Gillon by absolving him from many obligations on condition that he resigned further pretensions to the ship. The State officer from South Carolina chose to elude them and sent the *Indienne* to sea. Promptly several British men-of-war on the lookout captured her. And with the loss of this frigate, following upon the surrender or destruction of almost all the ships of the Continental Navy, except the *Deane* and the *Alliance,* because of financial straits, naval policy, and ineptitude of officers, Jones' last hope of even an ordinary frigate in the Revolution from the hands of the American Government glimmered and died.

With no immediate prospects of activity in his profession under the flag of the United States, he petitioned Morris as the Agent of Marine to support his request that, unless Congress had some employment of greater importance for him, he might embark as a volunteer with the French squadron under the Marquis de Vaudreuil. His unflagging pursuit of marine knowledge and experience promised to find an unusual opportunity as De Vaudreuil expected to join the fleets of D'Estaing, his superior in rank, and of Don Solano, the Spanish Admiral, for a major naval and military attack upon the English at Jamaica. De Sartine, it is recalled, had thwarted his earlier similar request in France to accompany Count d'Orvilliers; Morris in contrast now did all in his power to advance his purpose to qualify himself as an admiral as well as to gain such an appointment. The Agent of Marine supported his application by a letter to Congress in which he stated his concern that "the present state of our affairs does not permit me to employ that valuable officer"; Morris also urged compliance with this wish of Jones on the ground that it would enable him "to become still more useful if ever he should be again called to the command of a squadron or fleet."

Not the least indebtedness of the United States to Morris derives from the heartfelt appreciation which this financial Hercules, bearing too the burden of the Navy, manifested towards Jones as expressed in his concluding terms: "I should do injustice to my own feelings, as well as to my country, if I did not most warmly recommend this gentleman to the notice of Congress, whose favor he has certainly merited by the most signal services and sacrifices."[4]

Jones proceeded promptly to Boston, at which the squadron lay, after Congress had expressed its approval fittingly and both Morris and Luzerne had provided him with letters to the Marquis de Vaudreuil. The Admiral received him with distinction aboard his own ship the *Triomphant*. And as Jones knew well the West Indies, especially Jamaica which the combined fleets planned to capture, and as he held d'Estaing in the highest regard as a naval strategist, his anticipation was the more eager. "I had the flattering hope," he said, "of finding myself in the first military school in the world, in which I should be able to render myself useful, and to acquire knowledge very important for conducting great military operations."

The cruise began inauspiciously with violent storms and contrary winds which prevented temporarily the junction of two of the French ships of the line at Portsmouth with those at Boston. After a passage to Porto Rico where De Vaudreuil conducted extensive naval evolutions for ten days and sighted some scouting vessels of the nearby British fleet under Hood and Pigot, the squadron arrived after further misadventure, including the wreck of the *Burgoyne* of seventy-four guns and the loss of many of her officers and men, at the rendezvous of Porto Cabello on the South American coast. Here both Don Solano and D'Estaing had been expected, but neither had yet come. It was understood that D'Estaing would have a combined fleet of seventy ships of the line and an army of eighteen thousand troops for his formidable operations against the British.[5]

De Vaudreuil and his officers, including Jones, felt increasing disappointment and concern as they waited at Porto Çabello for the delayed arrival of the Spanish and French Admirals. Nor were there tidings as the period lengthened. The American volunteer had the more leisure, however uneasy, to contemplate his future, especially in the light of the possibility of approaching peace.

Shortly before sailing with the squadron, he had received a message from the Countess de La Vendahl accompanying a letter from De Genêt, in which she reminded him of his promise concerning a naval-military project previously contemplated by him and her husband with the hoped-for countenance of the Court. Jones now explained his loss of both the *America* and the *Indienne* as a nucleus for the allied squadron in question: "Nothing could add more to my disappointment than a supposition on your part that I had not pursued these objects with constant zeal," he averred. "Invincible obstacles alone have prevented the full operation of my schemes, which, until lately, have always been supported by hope. I now think the war at an end; but if it should continue, I shall not voluntarily remain out of the busy scene, and I am still of opinion my former projects might be adopted with public utility. I can, however, promise nothing, but that my principles are invariably the same. I hope to return to France, and am persuaded you will rather feel compassion for my disappointment than withdraw from me any part of your esteem."[6] Tact consistent with his former manœuvre to checkmate her duplicity, disappointed love turned to faithful friendship, and readiness on his part as well as hers to use private influence for professional advantage—all of these motives in varying degree seemed to underlie this anxious explanation.

While the ships lay idly at anchor in Porto Cabello week after week, he looked also to other friends in Europe whom, unlike the Countess de La Vendahl, he could address as man to man. Among them the most intimate was Lafayette. At the outset of his superintendence of the *America,* he had considered joining the French patriot at Yorktown, who after the surrender of Cornwallis had replied on the eve of his return to France: "Your coming to the army I had the honor to command would have been considered as a very flattering compliment to one who loves you and knows your worth. I am impatient to hear that you are ready to sail; and I am of opinion that we ought to unite under you every Continental ship we can muster, with such a body of well-appointed marines as might cut a good figure ashore, and then give you plenty of provisions and *carte blanche*."[7]

Now Jones explained to him the final setbacks to such plans, especially the transfer of the *America.* Still he looked forward to serve possibly with Lafayette as well as D'Estaing, in the opinion that the former had joined the latter at Cadiz: "This would afford me the greatest pleasure, did not my love of glory give place to my more ardent wish for peace, and that you might have the happiness to carry over the olive branch to a country that already owes you so much gratitude."

After two months the apprehension occasioned by the failure of Don Solano from Havana and D'Estaing from Cadiz to arrive at the rendezvous came to an end with the French frigate *An-*

dromaque bringing news of peace. "The most brilliant success and the most instructive experience in the art of war," said Jones, "could not have given me a pleasure comparable with that which I felt when I learned that Great Britain had been compelled to recognize the sovereignty and independence of the United States of America."[8] His sincerity is undoubted, notwithstanding peace barred the principal door to the limitless fame in his profession to which he had dedicated himself. Still other avenues, even in the ways of peace, might open, and he turned his face towards them.

Following this sequel to the extensive prospects of the expedition, which finally explained the long delay and ultimate abandonment of the allied fleet concentration at Porto Cabello, the squadron of De Vaudreuil sailed for Cap Français on April 8, 1783, the day after news of the end of hostilities. From here Jones shortly took passage for Philadelphia, bearing with him from both De Vaudreuil and De Viomenil, the highest naval and military officers of the squadron, letters of generous recommendation and distinguished praise.

Ill-health had come to Jones as well as to many others in the trying months of inaction and uncertainty. A fever induced especially by the tropical marshes at Porto Cabello affected him throughout the summer and ended only in the autumn by a remedy of cold baths.[9] During the interim of recuperation at Bethlehem, Pennsylvania, a favored resort for rest of military and naval officers, he gave token that his unhesitating bravery could manifest itself on land as well as by sea. Here Jones saved a traveller from robbery if not from murder by his quick threat "to clear the deck for action," which was sufficiently ominous to the offenders not to provoke a conflict with the ready officer.

The end of the war marked, too, what promised to be one of his last visions, first conceived concretely in the person of Dorothea Dandridge and in recent months contemplated more abstractly in the form of "some fair daughter of liberty," to adopt a rural, philosophic life on an attractive estate with the woman of his choice. He newly had in mind a large farm not in Virginia as formerly but in New Jersey, near New York whose growth he expertly anticipated; but neither his prize money nor his funds owed by the Government were yet available to purchase it. If marriage still remained for him more a pleasing prospect than an actuality, it became doubly so when he would have found it necessary, at least for a period, to adopt a modest manner of living such as Delia had proposed when she vowed that a cottage along with him comprehended all her wishes.

But the image faded even more from his thoughts before new hopes for activity in his naval career. He prepared to offer his services on the one hand to collect abroad the prize money due his officers, men, and himself, and on the other hand to lead the American Navy during peace with wisdom not less than he had served during war as its exemplar in valor. Nor did he lose sight of the intention, for private as well as public reasons, which he had frequently expressed to return again to France.

Interwoven with his wish to establish a new Navy of the United States on lasting foundations, totally unlike the basis of the crumbling Continental establishment as typified by Hopkins its first leader, was his unforgotten endeavor to have due recognition in rank. The disposal of the *America* had largely offset the partial amends which the command of this ship of the line had afforded him. It is true that Congress had voted Jones high praises, but the members nevertheless had denied him the proposed gold medal as well as the office of Commander in Chief of the Navy. Granted that his enemies were primarily responsible, he still remained at the end of the war, according to the official naval list, just the eighteenth Captain, except in so far as others were no longer in the service.

This trend of Jones' thoughts had been evident by implication when he had written to Morris from Porto Cabello at the prospect of peace that De Vaudreuil and other high officers of the squadron were receiving promotions. Now in Philadelphia, with the war at an end, he prepared for the Agent of Marine, even if he did not at this time actually submit to him, a long account, parts of which he had offered before, concerning both his rank and his recommendations for the American Navy of the future. "It is the custom of nations, on the return of peace," he began, "to honor, promote, and reward such officers as have served through the war with the greatest 'zeal, prudence, and intrepidity.' And since my country has, after an eight years' war, attained the inestimable blessing of peace and the sovereignty of an extensive empire, I presume that (as I have constantly and faithfully served through the Revolution, and at the same time supported it, in a degree, with my purse) I may be allowed to lay my grievances before you, as the head of the marine. I will hope, sir, through you, to meet with redress from Congress. But as any personal honor occupies only a part of my thoughts, I shall introduce in this letter such ideas as occur at present and regard the establishment of our future marine."[10]

The leadership which Jones was prepared to assume in building the Navy is measurable not alone by this communication intended for Morris; it had developed in his practice and by his recommendations throughout the war. From the time that he had brought to an issue the inveigling of seamen by the avaricious privateers and opposed the inefficiency and malice of Hopkins, until his revelation of the viciousness of Landais and the treachery of Lee in his report to the Board of Admiralty—not to consider his disclosure of the indifference of the well-known official, Langdon, to the fate of the *America* in his accounts to Brown and Morris—in short, from the beginning to the end of the Revolution, he had condemned and striven to remove glaring defects in naval policy, administration, and personnel.

"In the course of near seven years' service," he had declared at Portsmouth to McNeill in Boston, "I have continually suggested what has occurred to me as most likely to promote the honor of our marine and render it serviceable to our cause; but my voice has been like a cry in the desert . . . but were I used ever so ill I determine to persevere till my country is free."[11] To his outstanding credit he had fulfilled his vow, not without full realization, however, of his company: "The whole result to counterbalance the dishonor of the flag and the loss of the Navy only appears to have augmented the purses of the agents, besides enabling a few of the actors, perhaps not the first in merit or abilities, to purchase farms, etc."[12]

Now Jones dispensed with buying a farm, and now, too, his country was free; but he continued to serve the United States generously, regardless of his private and public reasons for dissatisfaction. So his long memorandum expounded some of his views for the Navy, limiting them by his doubts whether Congress wished to hear, and, even if it chose to do so, whether the finances of the nation would permit it to act. Of his many recommendations, the establishment of naval academies aboard ships and at stations for the training of officers was typical of his foresight. His most valuable proposal as the first preliminary to the founding of American sea power was the thorough study of foreign naval systems as a valuable background for the newly born nation. He suggested for this object "sending a proper person to Europe in a handsome frigate" to form friendly relations and to visit the marine departments of particular countries. If Jones had himself in mind as such an ambassador of good will and professional purpose, he was apparently better qualified for this post, by talents and friendships abroad, than any other American. And if the vanity of the officer remains in question, his purpose clearly dominated over his pride, according to the further remark, "I think it can be done, though perhaps not with the same dignity, without a frigate."[13]

It is presumable that if Morris saw fit at this period to submit Jones' composite recommendations for the Navy to Congress, they suffered the same final endorsement which had been the fate of the proposal to advance his naval standing—"not to be acted upon." Regardless of the failure by Congress to promote the public objects in this account addressed to the Agent of Marine, Jones urged well his private cause, which he here presented in detail and summarized in spirit. In an eloquent plea for justice in rank, which in his expressive phrase "opens the door to glory," he did not fear to conclude: "If I have been instrumental in giving the American flag some reputation and making it respectable among European nations, will you permit me to say that it is not because I have been honored by my country either with proper means or proper encouragement?"[14]

Some members of Congress, especially those identified by past antagonism towards Jones, did not end with the war their undeviating opposition, which evidenced the greater prejudice by its contrast with the eulogy of Morris and the judgment of Washington. In addition to his earlier praises, Morris at the close of his career as head of the Navy, in which capacity he could speak of

Jones with greater authority than any other man, paid him what he termed "this last feeble testimony . . . unequal to your deserts. I now take the last opportunity which I shall ever have of expressing my sentiments officially upon the zeal, activity, fortitude, and intelligence which you have exhibited on so many occasions in the service of the United States." Washington, too, who had already described Jones' achievements as having "attracted the admiration of the world," offset more directly than Morris the prejudice in Congress by his remark on the occasion of a visit to Princeton by the naval officer. Jones asked Washington to do him the honor to read certain papers in regard to his standing. "His Excellency told me in returning them," Jones recounted, "that he must confess he could not see upon what principle of justice Congress had acted respecting my rank." Not without indulgence in irony at the expense of Congress, the officer commented in the light of this opinion: "I have, however, said nothing to that great body on the subject."[15]

In such a mood towards the governing body of the United States, perhaps Jones was disposed to set out the sooner for France as agent to collect the long-delayed prize money won in the *Bonhomme Richard* cruise. His application to render this service to the former officers and seamen of the squadron and to recover what was due to himself actually had to be passed upon by Arthur Lee. This enemy of Jones and Franklin—his deeds abroad were followed, *mirabile dictu,* by a seat in Congress—was now one of a committee of three to act upon it; fortunately the two other members, Duane and Huntington, were disposed to be just to the officer and recognized that he was the most eligible person to unravel the complications of the prize money. How Lee was thwarted in this committee must be evident from his presumptuous statement in confidence to Samuel Adams upon the appointment of Duane as the chairman in another affecting Morris: "Such a choice seems to point out that Congress did not mean the inspection should be productive of public good."[16] Under the circumstances Lee saw fit to acquiesce, especially since he insured the honesty of the agent by the requirement of a bond for $200,000.

With these preliminaries completed, Jones looked to a new rôle in time of peace. Apart from the potential reawakening of interests in France as an offset to his purpose to live in the country of his citizenship and services, not the least influence, if any personal as well as professional bias was to prompt him to remain abroad, would be the unhappy memory of his unchanged formal rank as the eighteenth American naval officer in the Revolution. As it happened, however, that five of the captains formerly above him had been dismissed from the Navy and four of the others had resigned, died from natural causes, been lost at sea, or been killed in action, he was now in fact the ninth in standing. To be sure even this position grossly ignored both his seniority and his services. Indeed his private injustice remained unheeded like his more important public warning at this period of the need to build a fleet so as to be forearmed in case of emergencies and, in short, always to be prepared for war by sea.[17]

Part 6

Public Missions and Private Interests in France
and Denmark; the Russian Appointment

◇◇

Chapter XLVIII

The French Prize Money Triumph; Finale to Delia

THE RECOVERY of the prize money in Europe was to Jones less a matter of profit than principle. Thwarted more than three years earlier in his efforts to win for the officers and men the reward which the gallantry of his *Bonhomme Richard* crew had merited manyfold and which, withheld especially through De Chaumont, had favored the machinations of Landais and Lee respecting the *Alliance,* he was now resolved on the one hand to redeem the faith which his followers in the *Richard* had reposed in his leadership, and on the other hand to prove even to his enemies that he had conducted the squadron not, as hostile tongues whispered, in the spirit of disguised privateers, but in that of a Continental officer devoted to the highest honor of the American flag. Whatever incidental purposes the renewal of his extensive associations abroad might promote, he was prepared to use the pen of the diplomat with as much intelligence, adroitness, and tenacity as he had employed the sword of the warrior. With such determination following upon his unamended status in rank and upon the limitations in means which had circumscribed his action and glory in the closing years of the war, Jones sailed on November 10, 1783 from Philadelphia for his return to France.

In a backward glance concerning his future associates in America, he wrote from Delaware Bay to an intimate friend, General A. St. Clair: "The Chevalier de la Luzerne and Baron Steuben have proposed to obtain a vote of the Society of Cincinnatus for my admission at the first general meeting. If I am elected a permanent member of the Society, my friend and attorney, John Ross, will pay seventy-five dollars, the monthly pay of a colonel, which rank I hold by virtue of my election to command the *America*. I shall place great dependence for my admission on your interposition."[1]

The Society of the Cincinnati, founded on the fraternity among officers and statesmen of the Revolution and in the spirit professedly of the Roman patriot from whom the name was derived, came to have several thousand original members, of whom the first President General was Washington and the first President in France was D'Estaing. This select organization, difficult to reconcile in some respects with the principles of the Declaration of Independence, in whose name its members had fought, raised very considerable opposition. Jefferson strenuously opposed it as contrary to the Constitution; Samuel Adams did likewise; John Adams with rather characteristic inconsistency first disapproved and then approved of its nature; Franklin termed it "an order of hereditary knights" but later accepted honorary membership; Washington proposed without avail to remove the hereditary aspect in its by-laws. Jones was thoroughly alive to the issues which it raised, but upon his election he did not show himself averse to such a mark of recognition for his achievements.

Aboard the ship, a fellow passenger was Major L'Enfant, the French engineer later known for his layout of the national capital, who happened to have been on a mission of the Society of the Cincinnati in America, and who may have prompted Jones' application on the eve of sailing. The vessel was the *General Washington*, formerly captured by and recaptured from the British and now distinguished as one of the few ships retained by America after the war, in which Congress had made provision for the prize agent. The Captain was Joshua Barney, formerly in command of the *Hyder Ally*, who in an engagement with the British had recaptured the *General Washington*, in sight of a strong frigate as a second potential enemy, by marked bravery and stratagem in manœuvering his vessel athwart the bows of his opponent and raking her until surrender. In his preoccupation, Jones entered little into the spirit of gayety which was natural at this time to L'Enfant; but he often paced the quarter-deck at night with Barney in reminiscence of their common interests during the Revolution.

Absorbed in moods of reflection and even melancholy, Jones

was intent upon his arrival in Europe as early as possible. To see again the Countess de Nicolson rather than to effect his public commission may have been his foremost, quickening thought, although correspondence had lapsed between him and Delia since his restrained letter of Christmas Day of 1781 from Portsmouth, despite the promise of his earlier poem, not to consider his letters, concerning the haste of her warrior when he would "cast anchor in dear France again."

He decided to disembark on the shores of England in view of unfavorable winds for France, however unfriendly the British might be supposed to have been at this period towards him. A contributory influence undoubtedly was the public despatches in his charge for Adams in London as well as for Franklin in Paris. Barney remonstrated at his wish to set foot on the coast of England "anywhere that he could first make land" because of knowledge that his destination was France and that his reputation in Britain boded ill. "As to that," Jones answered, "I shall very probably be in Paris before you—but it is infinitely more important to me to see a certain person in England [apparently Adams]; and I am too well acquainted with every foot of it, and know too well how to steer my course to apprehend any personal danger . . . and it will not be the first time if I have to traverse all England with the bloodhounds upon my track."[2] From the nearest port, Plymouth, Jones hastened by postchaise to London, in which he found Adams. In five days he was at Paris; the despatch of his journey aroused the curiosity of the *London Chronicle,* which stated that "it appears Jones arrived on 5 December at 9 p.m. and left at 3 a.m. on the 6th December, and consequently was only six hours in London."[3] Whatever his urge, it certainly was not fear.

Almost ten days elapsed in Paris before he received from Franklin formal authority as agent for the prize money due from France and Denmark, and several followed in addition before his first definite step towards soliciting payment from the former. However dilatory the French Court may have been, this interval points the more definitely to the conclusion that a private interest, presumably the Countess de Nicolson, if not his public zeal in delivering the despatches for the American Ministers, was the chief cause of his precipitate haste to disembark from the *General*

Washington at Plymouth and to speed from Plymouth to London and from London to Paris.

His devotion to Delia, however, seems to have cooled almost at her door. "Is it possible," she wrote him in an undated note, apparently soon after his arrival, "that you are then so near me and that I am deprived of the sight of a mortal who has constituted the misery of my life for four years? O, most amiable and most ungrateful of men, come to your best friend, who burns with the desire of seeing you. You ought to know that it is but eight days since your Delia was at the brink of the grave. Come, in the name of heaven!"⁴ The road of their ardent love had reached a laggard, unhappy turning to make necessary this exhortation, but Jones may possibly have had grounds for recriminations if he had been disposed to address them to the lady.⁵ Shortly beyond this crossways was the end of their relation, although he treasured the memory of Delia sufficiently to preserve all her passionate letters and the final note to which his pen added the distinctive reference to "her" in an otherwise bare statement: "From her apartments in the boulevard."⁶ And the rest on his part, as in the early case of Dorothea Dandridge, was silence.

Now Jones launched his diplomatic campaign for the recovery of the prize money. The background was unpromising in both France and Denmark. Thomas Barclay, the American Consul General, had been unable to collect a penny of this indebtedness from the former nation during two and one half years. Franklin had received an offer of £10,000 from the latter but had refused it on the ground that the ships *Union, Betsy,* and *Charming Polly* returned illegally to Britain from Bergen in Norway were worth several times this amount. He refrained altogether from any direct intercession in behalf of the claim upon France, heartily disliking as he did, especially after his experience with Landais, all naval complications.

The beginning of the negotiations by Jones was politic. Only a courtier in manner and an officer with knowledge of all the financial intricacies of the *Bonhomme Richard* expedition, such as he was, could have had his advantages. The first manœuvre was his attendance on December 20 at a dinner of the King of France and his Ministers. De Castries and De Vergennes received him, he reported, "with many attentions, and when I submitted to them the letters from M. le Chevalier de la Luzerne, who explained to them part of the commission with which I was charged, and in which he related several matters which were complimentary to me, both assured me that I had no need of recommendations to dispose them to render me justice and to esteem my character."[7]

Courtesies were one thing; payment of the prize money, particularly in view of the deflated French treasury, was wholly another. When De Castries proceeded to take no action during more than a month, Jones gently but expressly brought the business to his attention. "As nearly four years and a half," he concluded, "have already elapsed since those captures were made, I rely on the kind promise you gave me that the prize money shall now be immediately settled."

The diplomatic interchange was now fairly started. De Castries submitted a statement which Jones met squarely. In business fashion the French authorities had proceeded to make the indebtedness as small as possible; the American agent, however, was equipped to counter them with detailed information, expressive phrases, and moral fervor. His prestige, too, helped to enforce his views.

Jones took special care to dispel the shadow which De Chaumont tried to cast over these negotiations as the last chapter of the *Bonhomme Richard* cruise. De Castries withdrew all the papers from De Chaumont after the American agent exposed that "the commissary had taken possession of all the proceeds from the sale of the *Countess of Scarborough* and from the merchant vessels, and he had retained them during more than four years without rendering any account to the captors for either the principal or the interest. He wished to retain these funds from the prizes because the King, according to him, was indebted to him for 109,179 livres."[8] With a declaration that many of the sailors had been perishing from cold and hunger while the commissary withheld these funds, Jones boldly added: "Whether M. Le Ray de Chaumont is indebted to the Government or the Government is, as he says, indebted to him, is a matter that ought not to regard the captors, but they have a right to claim the protection of Government to force him to render the money with interest." And in support of some of his accusations of chicanery against De Chaumont, he brought to bear formidable evidence from Franklin and Lafayette.

The attempt to set against the account of the prize money the expenses for the care of the British prisoners at the Texel again rallied Franklin to declare to Jones in his support: "I certainly should not have agreed to charge the American captors with any part of the expense of maintaining the five hundred prisoners in Holland till they could be exchanged, when none of them was exchanged for the Americans in England, as was your intention, and as we both had been made to expect." Jones presented his corresponding views to De Castries not with less reason than the philosopher but also with the passion of the fighter: "I will not now complain that the prisoners which I took and carried to Holland were not exchanged for the Americans who had been taken in war upon the ocean, and were long confined in English dungeons by civil magistrates as *traitors, pirates,* and *felons.* I will only say, *I had such a promise* from the Minister of Marine. It was all the reward I asked for the anxious days and sleepless nights I passed, and the many dangers I encountered in the glad hope of giving them *all* their liberty. . . ."[9]

Persuasion as well as reason was indeed necessary, for it remains that the cruise, although under the flag of the United States, had been complicated by the French as well as the American, the private as well as the public, aspects under which the ships and their maintenance had been provided. "Whatever understanding there may have been between the two governments *respecting the expense of the armament,"* Jones urged upon De Castries, "it makes not the least difference to the captors. I but ask for justice for the brave men I commanded, and I expect no less from a generous mind like yours." Again the eloquent agent appealed to him on the ground that the present niggardliness of the Ministry put to shame the past liberality of the Sovereign: "It was an act of the King's free bounty, and His Majesty is too generous to lessen it by any afterclaims that are beneath his dignity." Finally he presented, in consistency with an earlier recital of his services in Europe, the most telling argument in behalf of his officers and men: "Permit me, my lord, to conclude by saying that no equal expense in the war was made with so great effect, or had such good consequences, as that made by the ships I commanded in the Texel; since Holland was thereby drawn into the war, without which the world would not have been this day at peace."[10]

By virtue of these persuasive efforts, Jones influenced De Castries to compute the prize money on the basis of the American instead of the French laws, allowing the officers and crews one half the value of merchant and the whole value of war vessels; likewise he gained the withdrawal of the Government claims especially for repairs of the *Serapis* and *Countess of Scarborough,* for expenses in maintaining the British prisoners at the Texel, for a levy in favor of a French veterans' hospital. And when the Minister desired further security from the agent to be given by the French banker for Americans, M. Grand, before payment of certain wages in addition to the prize money, Jones denounced the indignity of a second bond from him and succeeded also in setting aside this demand.

Still another difficulty almost snatched the prize money from him in the period between its authorization on July 15, 1785 and its later payment. "I find," Jones wrote from L'Orient to Jefferson, who recently had succeeded Franklin as the American Minister in Paris, "that a French merchant, M. Puchilberg of this place, who opposed Dr. Franklin and did all in his power to promote the revolt that took place in the *Alliance,* has produced a letter of attorney, which he obtained from the officers and men of that frigate when their minds were unsettled, authorizing him to receive their share in the prizes." After he had surmounted the dangers of this potential swindler and several new obstacles, which in combination with all that had preceded bear an analogy in number although not in kind with those of the *Bonhomme Richard* expedition, he received at last on August 18 and September 5, 1785 the gross total of 181,039 livres, about $35,000, which was of decidedly greater value then than today.

Whether there was justice in the amount awarded by the French Government is an enigmatic question. "His Majesty has generously renounced, in favor of the captors, the proportion (one half) of the sale of the merchant prizes, which by the laws of the flag of America he might have retained," Jones reported to Jefferson in 1786. If the general expenses of the *Bonhomme Richard* cruise are ascribed wholly to the King, as well as the ships and armament which he gratuitously provided, wages and other disbursements might be considered his obligation. In this view Jones claimed and received also 15,000 livres in part payment of wages for American seamen. But six years later he was to apply in their behalf for further arrearages and at a moment of provocation to allude to his own claim of 7000 livres as salary, to his loss three times in the service of all his personal effects, and to the sale of the *Serapis* to the King for "a seventh of the price which the ship of war cost the British Government before the capture."[11]

Against this financial background, the agent drew a picture of French officers in America who, he declared, had received at the end of the war "a gratification of five years' pay, the Order of Cincinnatus, and a lot of land; and they enjoy grades superior to what they could have attained under other circumstances." Doubtlessly Jones recalled that even Landais, disgraced as he was, although less than he should have been, had received a large advance for his share in the indemnity claimed from Denmark, involving a situation, too, for which he deserved more censure than reward.

It was especially with Samuel Adams, Lee, Gillon, and—in so far as he was disposed to regard him at all—Landais in mind that Jones took satisfaction in the recovery of the prize money from France, in addition to his more important object in behalf of his sailors. "I was anxious," he had disclosed to Jefferson, "to force some ill-natured persons to acknowledge that, if they did not tell a wilful falsehood, they were mistaken when they asserted 'that I had commanded a squadron of privateers!' And, the war being over, I made it my first care to show the brave instruments of my success that their rights are as dear to me as my own."[12] Now indeed Jones could answer his own question when Landais had usurped the *Alliance* and enchained the sailors who had fought in the *Bonhomme Richard* and refused to recognize any captain other than their own: "How shall I face the poor fellows in America who for attachment to me were carried away *in irons* on the *Alliance?*"

Chapter XLIX

Fate of the Sailors' Money; the Interrupted Mission to Denmark

THE FINAL history of the 181,039 livres recovered from the French Government on the verge of bankruptcy assumed certain ironical aspects in the light of Jones' avowal to defend with paternal care the interests of his *Bonhomme Richard* crew. It was not to be a simple matter for the funds to pass from the hands of several intermediaries into those of the officers and men in America.

As for Jones' own reimbursement, Congress had provided that he was to receive "the commissions usually allowed in such cases out of the money which he shall recover, as agent for the said prizes, in full compensation for his services and expenses." What these commissions should be or what consideration was due the particular difficulties and the special qualifications of the agent had been undetermined. He deducted 13,000 livres as his portion of the prize money, an amount which had no relation to his remuneration as agent. In a report to John Jay, who was now Minister of Foreign Affairs, Jones informed him in May, 1786, following settlement of minor claims of sailors other than Americans and pending instructions from the United States, that a gross amount of 157,483 livres was now ready in his hands. "I say nothing," the agent remarked with more fairness than modesty, "of the amount of the allowance that ought in justice to be made for the great expense, trouble, and time I have devoted to this business from the first of November, 1783. A commission on the sum recovered will certainly be no indemnification for my expenses, far less a recompense for my time and trouble."[1] He made no allusion to the recovery of his own share and to the moral victory for the sailors and himself.

Considerably earlier Jefferson had a plan for the disposal of the prize money in the custodianship of Jones. As Jefferson well knew that the American Government after the war was needy like the French, and he felt indeed the stringent circumstances even in person as the chief Minister abroad, the envoy made a recommendation in January, 1786 to the Board of Treasury for the use of this fund: "I take the liberty of suggesting whether the expense and risk of double remittances might not be saved by ordering it into the hands of Mr. Grand, immediately, for the purposes of the treasury in Europe, while you could make provision at home for the officers and soldiers, whose demands will come in so slowly as to leave the use of a great proportion of this money for a considerable time, and some of it forever."[2]

The Board of Treasury accepted the proposal by Jefferson regardless of the possible delay if not default in payment to Jones' seamen in view of the hand-to-mouth Government finances. In fact it was with special emphasis that the Board advised the use of this money for salaries to him and other ministers in Europe: "We have scarcely the means to defray the ordinary expenses of the civil government and to remit sufficient sums to pay the salaries and contingent expenses for the foreign ministers, so much so that if it were not for the intelligence you have given us of the moneys paid to Capt. John Paul Jones on account of the prizes taken by the squadrons under his command, it would not be possible for us to make provision for this object for the present year. We agree with you that it would be attended with a saving and accommodation to the public to permit these moneys to be used for the expense of the foreign ministers in Europe and to appropriate an equal sum for this object to be paid to the proper claimants in America, for which object we shall be careful to make the proper provision." If the Government straits were as dire as these correspondents represented them, and they felt warranted to jeopardize the pittances due the sailors, it appears unwise as well as strange that the salary of a minister was the liberal amount of more than $11,000.

Under the circumstances, Jefferson seemed disposed to give

precedence over the naval veterans to several ministers abroad including himself and to insistent French officers formerly in the American Army. Along with the authority to receive "the whole amount of the moneys" from Jones, the Board informed him of its desire regarding the agent's own share 'to leave the negotiation of this matter to your arrangement." Let it be said at once to the credit of Jefferson that his personal accounts for salary, including expenses, for his services several years as Minister were to remain long unpaid by the Government and that in his "negotiation" with Jones he simply and generously asked him to exercise his own judgment in reserving for himself the amount which he considered fitting.[3] Accordingly Jones deposited with Jefferson the balance of the prize money after reserving for himself, in addition to his share as the Captain of the *Bonhomme Richard,* 47,792 livres as his expenses in lieu of the commission to which he was entitled in due course.[4] He made no reference to the 15,000 livres entrusted to him approximately at this time on account for the wages of American sailors, due from France, who had been paid in the United States at the close of the Revolution.[5] The total remaining to the credit of the officers and men of the *Bonhomme Richard* expedition was only 112,712 livres.

The charges by Jones for expenses, nearly $11,000 for two and one half years, were liberal; but they aggregated, as he was to explain, not more than the salary allowed the American Minister in Paris for a single year.[6] If there is any objection to them, it should have as a basis less the amount *per se* than the payment to himself before his sailors and the relation between the high expenses and the comparatively small sum recovered. Granted the lack of sufficient ready funds of his own for current outlays, his reimbursement does not strengthen his ardent professions in the interests of the seamen. And it was not the first time, as the circumstances of the adventure with the mutineer and of the administration of his brother's estate signify, that he took care in financial matters not to think of himself last. His own further explanations and those of Jefferson, however, should tend to offset even these reflections upon his generosity.

Perhaps Jones was more ready to proclaim to Jefferson his motives of principle after having paid himself than he had been to state them to Jay upon hinting without effect the material reward that his services as agent merited. "I cannot bring myself to lessen the dividend of the American captors by making any charge either for my time or trouble," he now asserted to the former. "I lament that it has not yet been in my power to procure for them advantages as solid and extensive as the merit of their services. I would not have undertaken this business from any views of private emolument that could possibly have resulted from it to myself, even supposing I had recovered or should recover a sum more considerable than the penalty of my bond."[7] It was true, as Jones' attitude towards recovery of the claim against Denmark soon indicated further, that money was invariably of little importance to him in comparison with glory; but when money happened to be his immediate object, he always proved himself liberally disposed towards his own interests.

It now remained for Jones to have official confirmation of the deduction of his share in prize money, particularly the portion for his stated expenses. The agent naturally expected such support from Jefferson, from whom he had received warrant for an allowance based on his own discretion and to whom he exhibited his voluminous correspondence in negotiation and made clear the special talents that he had brought to the task. But the situation assumed an unpleasant turn for Jones inasmuch as he had rendered impracticable any later reconsideration by Jefferson in regard to the amount allowable for his expenses by having already used what he had withdrawn, and the Minister unavowedly may well have considered the sum excessive although it had actually been expended. Jefferson professed, upon re-examination of the terms in which the Board of Treasury had empowered him, not to have authority to accept the deductions as final. Jones readily acquiesced in view of his assigned reason and remained content with endorsement.

Jefferson expressed himself to Jones cordially: "I am perfectly ready to transmit to America any accounts or proofs you may think proper. Nobody can wish more that justice be done you, nor is more ready to be instrumental in doing whatever may insure it. It is only necessary for me to avoid the presumption of appearing to decide where I have no authority to do it."[8]

To Congress he wrote in a rather non-committal and a less personal vein: "I communicated to Commodore Jones your order for the balance in his hands. As he was entitled to a part of the money he had received, and it was reasonable to suppose he must have been living here on that resource, so that he could not be expected to pay the whole sum received, I desired him to state his account against that fund as he thought just himself, to pay me the balance on account, reserving to you a full right to discuss the propriety of his charges, and to allow or disallow them as you pleased, so that nothing that passed between us should either strengthen or weaken his claims. . . .

"He desired me at the same time to forward to you the papers, Nos. 1-12, which will show the objections and difficulties he had to encounter, and which could have been obviated by nobody else. There certainly was no other person whose knowledge of the transactions so well qualified him to negotiate this business, and I do suppose that this fund would have lost some of its capital articles in any other hands. This circumstance, with the real value of this officer, will, I doubt not, have their just influence in settling his claims. There is no doubt but that he has actually expended the money charged to have been expended."[9]

As Jones—admitted that his expenses were liberal—had won the funds primarily in behalf of the sailors and as Jefferson had converted them to less needful uses which endangered this important object, perhaps the warrior deserved better than such aloof although even-handed justice from the diplomat. Yet in a sense the latter had exercised necessary wariness, and his circumspection was to his credit. There was no need to give Arthur Lee and others on the Board of Treasury any pretext at all for sowing new suspicions in Congress of fraud and conspiracy among American representatives in France.

Pending confirmation at home, Jones had already embarked as far as circumstances permitted, after the order by De Castries for settlement of the prize money due from France, on the task of recovering the claim upon Denmark. There had been various difficulties in the way of his undivided attention to this second undertaking subsequent to De Castries' order: not only the meddling of a sailors' agent, Puchilberg, the deposit of authentic rolls of the seamen, the request for additional security, and the delayed payments by the French treasury but also the likelihood that his return to America would be necessary to transfer the funds to the United States Government. In these circumstances he had proposed that Bancroft in London, with the support of John Adams, now Minister to Britain, should solicit the prize money through the Danish Ambassador in the English capital. This avenue had proved unpromising by reason of the absence of the Ambassador. Adams then had advised recourse to the Danish envoy in France, but he too had not been in Paris either earlier or later when Jones had sought to present his claim to him. These difficulties were not inconsistent with the subterfuges which had followed several years previously the intercession by Franklin.

Franklin had contented himself chiefly with a memorial to the Danish Prime Minister which combined moral philosophy with views of international law pertaining to the rights of belligerents in neutral ports. These English prizes, he held, had sought shelter in Bergen under stress not of combat but weather and were entitled "as they conceived to the common rights of hospitality established and practiced by civilized nations." It will be recalled, however, as to alleged stress of weather that the instructions at L'Orient to Jones, for which the American Minister was largely responsible, had recommended Bergen simply as a port for prizes and that in acting upon these orders not the discretion of Jones but the heedlessness of Landais had prevailed.

"The United States find themselves," Franklin had continued more convincingly, "stripped of their property and the same given up to their enemies on the principle only that no acknowledgment had yet been formally made by Denmark of the independence of the United States, which is to say that there is no obligation of justice towards any nation with whom a treaty promising the same has not been previously made. This was indeed the doctrine of ancient barbarians, a doctrine long since exploded."[10] Although the Doctor gave warning in 1779 of future hostility of America notwithstanding her "present infant state," he refused to act further towards enforcing his demand for indemnity of the vessels valued at £50,000 except to declare later that a treaty of commerce, which Denmark began to solicit at the end of the war, was conditional upon suitable payment for the ships. "Those ministers are wise," he admonished, "who look into futurity and quench the first sparks of misunderstanding between two nations." But Denmark had replied in flattering terms and paid nothing, apart from her offer of £10,000.

Habitually direct and now more keenly aware than before of the obstacles and delays at courts by reason of his most recent experience in France, Jones made the decision to go in person to Denmark. As his early return to the United States was seemingly unnecessary because of the tentative settlement with Jefferson concerning the proceeds from the first claim, he turned to give his undivided attention to the second project. Jones set out, with the approval of the American Minister, for Copenhagen in the spring of 1787 after having waited several months longer to see in Paris the long-absent Danish Ambassador, Baron de Blome. *En route* he stopped abruptly at Brussels. There Jones learned from the bankers, in whose care he had arranged for letters, unfavorable news as to his private financial affairs involving funds necessary for his present journey to Denmark. Of greater concern was the absence of information that the Board of Treasury in America had yet confirmed the deduction for his expenses from the French prize money.

Now the results impended from Jefferson's protection of himself more than of Jones. Arthur Lee in Congress occupied a new strategic position, thanks to his allies and brother, for his suspicious eyes and sinister designs. Intrenched with Lee was his former confederate Izard. John Lovell complacently wrote of them to Samuel Adams: "Your friends are both now in Congress, and I am happy in assuring you they appear to me to be two of the ablest and best of our counselors."[11] In view of such well-wishers, Lee the member of important committees was prosecuting his hostile intentions against Franklin and Morris as well as Jones. He had passed upon his appointment as agent for the prize money, not neglecting the surety of the $200,000 bond; and he was now entrenched to pass upon his administration of this office. What Lee's decision would be was a foregone conclusion.

Still another matter may well have given Jones anxiety at this juncture. What with Lee in a position of authority at home and the Government well-intentioned but on the verge of bankruptcy, the disposal of the prize money, however innocently Jefferson may have suggested it, promised ill for the sailors. The intentions of Congress were good enough when it had passed a resolution on June 7, 1786 that the funds payable by Jones to the order of the Board of Treasury should be "distributed to the officers and men entitled to receive the same."[12] But almost a year had passed and the sailors had received none of their prize money, regardless even of the assurance given to Jefferson by the Board of Treasury that they would "appropriate an equal sum for this object" and "be careful to make the proper provision." The delay was ominous.

Consistent with this ill-boding situation, an impulse in behalf of his faithful followers of the *Bonhomme Richard,* as well as the need for confirmation of his services and the lack of ready funds for his stay in Copenhagen, impelled Jones to a sudden decision. Instead of continuing his journey to Denmark, he determined upon a precipitate passage to America.

Chapter L

Personal: Silver Plate Again; Prelude to Madame T—; Ledyard

BEFORE THE unpremeditated trip to America, various personal interests in Paris, along with the negotiation for prize money, not unnaturally occupied Jones in the long period that he contended with the formalities and complications of ministers. He found suitable occasion for these concerns especially during the interval between the award from France and its payment and during the dilatory procedure which beset his initial efforts to secure a settlement from Denmark. Such subsidiary private occupations called forth in particular some of the interwoven qualities of the man and the warrior.

The silver plate of Lord Selkirk involved a point of honor of special importance to him which had not been settled prior to his return to France after the war. On the one hand he labored tenaciously to gain the prize money honorably due his sailors; on the other hand he now as well as previously "scorned to profit by such a pillage" as that which had happened at St. Mary's Isle. He had sought to ease the conscience of the earl as to acceptance of the property from him rather than a public body like Congress by assurances that his sailors were "easily satisfied" upon his purchase of their share of its value, and that Franklin, in the name of Congress, renounced in this instance whatever portion of the proceeds might be due to the Government. But when Schweighauser, the agent appointed by Lee and Adams, had both sought to evaluate the plate at the preposterous sum of £3000 and tried to deduct in his own interest one-twentieth of the Captain's portion of three-twentieths, Jones had written in a fury to Williams, who unhappily for the Captain's business purposes had become the son-in-law of the Swiss merchant: "I will not abate the thousandth part of a sol of the three-twentieths of prizes, which no man in America ever presumed to dispute as being my just and proper right, and which no rascal in Europe shall dispute with impunity."[1]

The scruples of Selkirk to receive the plate at the expense of Jones and from the hands of a personage denounced as a pirate in Britain; the absence of the officer in America for several years instead of the six months which he had expected; the difficulties of transit for such a commodity as the plate from one belligerent country to another—all had resulted, after the altercations with Schweighauser, in protracted delay of its return. Again in Paris, Jones lost no time in expediting the transfer. And Selkirk now readily became complaisant, especially as the reports he had received of his character were highly favorable. "You will see," a friend confided to the earl, "that the offer was entirely a piece of gallantry of Jones to Lady Selkirk."

In scrupulous fulfillment of his purpose, Jones agreed to forward the silver to a relative of Lady Selkirk, the Countess of Morton in London, although expressing his regret to both the earl and his wife that he "could have wished to have ended this delicate business by delivering the plate to you at St. Mary's Isle in Scotland." His final letter of February, 1784 conveyed in implicit as well as explicit terms to Selkirk, "I bore no personal ill will, but the contrary, to you"; and it made clear once more his honest, if injudicious, purpose, "As I have endeavored to serve the cause of liberty through every stage of the American Revolution and sacrificed to it my private ease, a part of my fortune, and some of my blood, I could have no selfish motive in permitting my people to demand and carry off your plate."[2] Thus the silver had a further interrupted but safe journey by way of Calais, Dover, London, and Dumfries to its home at St. Mary's Isle, where, according to tradition, it arrived with the tea leaves that had been in the kettle at the time of the pillage still untouched.

With the justice of time, Jones gained honor by the strange misadventure. Lord Selkirk praised the scrupulous concern of the officer to return the plate as soon as possible after it had been taken and the "extraordinary good discipline" of his sailors even in their commander's absence—circumstances of which he gave assurance "I have mentioned to many people of fashion and on all occasions, sir, both now and formerly."[3] D'Estaing, the most noted French Admiral, took occasion to praise the conduct of Jones in this incident; and De Calonne, the Finance Minister, permitting the transportation of the plate from L'Orient to Calais free from duty, commented upon its return: "That action, sir, is worthy of the reputation which you acquired by your conduct, and proves that true valor perfectly agrees with humanity and generosity."[4]

Several years later the son of Lord Selkirk, Lord Daer, happened to meet Jones at a dinner in Paris. "I made him a speech from you," he wrote to his father, "expressive of your obligations to him, for the order in which his men were kept at the landing. I told him how you had first answered his letter [the one returned by Lord Le Despencer]. He said he had got your second, and began apologizing for not having answered it. I told him there was no occasion, it had not been expected he should. He seems a sensible little fellow. He is not dark as I had heard."

It was in time of peace and in a social atmosphere that others as well as Lord Daer revised preconceptions and prejudices which they had entertained of Jones. The wife of John Adams, who for all her discernment seems to have shared with her husband a trace of instinctive dislike born of the earlier Adams-Lee-Landais ties, described him to a female relative Miss Cranch in December, 1784 during her residence in Paris.

"Chevalier Jones you have heard much of; he is a most uncommon character," she began with her graphic but depreciating pen. "I dare say you would be as much disappointed in him as I was. From the intrepid character he justly supported in the American Navy, I expected to have seen a rough, stout, warlike Roman—instead of that I should sooner think of wrapping him up in cotton wool, and putting him in my pocket, than sending him to contend with cannon balls. He is small of stature, well proportioned, soft in his speech, easy in his address, polite in his manners, vastly civil, understands the etiquette of a lady's toilette as perfectly as he does the mast, sails, and rigging of his ship.

"Under all this appearance of softness he is bold, enterprising, ambitious, and active. He has been here often, and dined with us several times; he is said to be a man of gallantry and a favorite among French ladies, whom he is frequently commending for the neatness of their persons, their easy manners, and their taste in dress. He knows how often the ladies use the baths, what colors best suit a lady's complexion, what cosmetics are most favorable to the skin. We do not often see the warrior and the abigail thus united."[5]

Her picture of the abigail deliberately obscures that of the warrior. Despite the fact that Mrs. Adams' own Christian name was Abigail, that her description indicated a forgivable preoccupation of many of her sex, and that the trials of Jones may now have revealed him to her as past his physical prime, there remained a hostile slur in her gossipy characterization of the officer as a lady's maid. Perhaps she was the more satirical in her estimate because it was only by degrees that her husband, in contrast, overcame even those brusque political manners which had antagonized Vergennes.

Socially accomplished Jones undoubtedly had become. He had behind him his experience with the Countesses de La Vendahl and de Nicolson, and was on the eve of a new passion. He had now his friendships at Court, his standing with the Ministry, and even his recognition by the King. "I went to Court much oftener, and mixed with the great much more frequently, than our Minister Plenipotentiary," he was to comment in candid explanation of his expenses, describing himself not as an agent but "as a general officer and a special minister from Congress."

Jones appeared in a consistent rôle according to the recollection of Dr. John Jeffries the balloonist, who received brilliant entertainment and high honors in Paris in recognition for his sensational flight in January, 1785 from Dover to France. At Passy, Jeffries met "the celebrated and brave Commodore Paul Jones, from whom I received many compliments on my enterprise, and returned them, he deserving them much more than I." Apropos of talented and gay Frenchwomen skilled in repartee, he came upon "Commodore Paul Jones at the opera masque ball." And a second time at Passy, he dined there with Dr. Franklin and others including "Commodore Paul Jones who was very attentive, candid, and complimentary to me, and who brought me to Paris in his chariot."[6]

In addition to Jones' mood for society, his consistent regard for Louis XVI and the Court, in contrast with the Ministry, may have prompted the initial friendship between him and the woman whom he was to designate as Madame T—. He may also have entertained a professional view as well as a personal relation. It was during his present residence in Paris that his intimacy began with this natural daughter of the former King, Louis XV. Although this sovereign, notorious for his mistresses, had bestowed upon the mother of Madame T— "a very large fortune on her daughter's account," the mother, according to Jones, "has never since shown her either justice or natural affection." With Louis XV dead approximately ten years, he undertook through another woman who had influence with Louis XVI to secure an audience for her; "I had the pleasure," he recounted, "to be instrumental in putting her in a fair way to obtain redress."[7] Whatever bearing Jones' entrée at Court and his zeal to improve his favor with Louis may have had upon his interest in a natural daughter of French royalty and whatever additional significance may lie in more definite identification of her,[8] there was no doubt of his growing affection for Madame T—.

Chariots, masque balls, and in particular the incipient passion for Madame T—, which was seemingly to become the most serious of his life, must explain in large part the special drain at this period upon his financial resources, although the depreciating implications of Mrs. Adams concerning his special interests are to be discounted. As his outlays for any part of his current expenses were not payable at this stage from the prize money, he continued to be dependent wholly upon his own funds. His needs must underlie his particular urgency and resourcefulness.

He felt impelled to write on August 25, 1785 to his former trusted friend John Ross in Philadelphia, in whose keeping he had placed his private business: "I have no favors of yours to acknowledge since that dated in March, 1784 inclosing a bill for half a year's dividend on my bank stock. You then promised to send me immediately the remainder of the goods of mine in your hands that were unsold, but you have not performed that promise, although many opportunities have offered directly from Philadelphia to the ports of France. You knew that I was under great embarrassment here for want of those goods. . . .

"Your professions of attachment and friendship for me led me to expect a more delicate attention from you than is commonly to be looked for from one merchant to another. But you are silent, and have not given me the least account of the situation of my bank stock, notwithstanding the important and alarming alteration of that institution by the loss of the charter. . . . You may believe that it is my situation alone (and the circumstances of your long and unaccountable silence) that extorts from me this letter. My feelings are hurt, and I have been reduced to great difficulties; therefore you must excuse the plain dealing."⁹

This message placed in the confidential hands of another friend Jonathan Nesbitt, preparing to sail from France to Philadelphia, was to be delivered only if firsthand investigation warranted the step and it proved desirable to remove his affairs from the keeping of Ross. How kindly Jones continued to feel toward this bondsman for the prize money, regardless of pressing circumstances and impulsive words, was apparent in his later expression that, if he had lost the friendship of the Philadelphian, there had been provocation enough but nevertheless he would be "sorry, very sorry."

With money looming before Jones as a matter of increasing consequence, he turned his fertile mind, especially in the interim between the award and the settlement for the prizes, to means of commercial profit. Like his strategy as an officer, his plans for mercantile enterprise were bold and brilliant. He proposed the business of purchasing furs on the northwest coast of America and of selling or trading them for merchandise in China; the chief officer whom he planned to employ for the projected voyages by the route of the Cape of Good Hope was the well-known John Ledyard, the American who had been a lieutenant of Captain Cook on his last voyage around the world.

Jones sought to enlist the support of the Court of France on the one hand and of Robert Morris on the other; and in the event of aid by neither he was resolved to undertake the enterprise on a more limited scale with only the coöperation of Ledyard. The scepticism which the novel plan awakened in France, the delay in receiving approval from Morris, and his own straitened finances at the time most opportune for the purchase of ships resulted in postponements. But the promising venture appears to have been abandoned in the main because of the possibility of international complications. The non-support, if not the opposition, of his influential friends in the United States and France may have followed from the unfavorable news which he himself reported: "I wrote to Madrid, and by the information I have from thence, it appears that Spain is too jealous to permit any commercial speculation in the neighborhood of California."[10] And so the vast possibilities of a business relation between two such hardy and farseeing spirits as Jones and Ledyard, entertaining visions which the fur traders were later to make true, ended because of patriotic scruples and the lack of public or private means.

There was also a more underlying reason. Five years earlier Jones had explained to his Virginia friend Dr. Read, who had asked his influence for a commercial undertaking: "Military affairs have engaged my whole attention. I am as much a stranger to trade as if I had never been concerned in it. I have served as a volunteer in the American Revolution, and to this moment have neither received pay nor subsistence from the public. My property in the many prizes I took before I left America went through the hands of agents who did great injustice to the captors; and it has since melted away by the depreciation of the Continental paper money. Gain has never been my object, and since I came to France hard blows and honor have been my sole income."[11] More recently, in the same spirit, he had returned the silver plate to Lord Selkirk. Even now money was an afterthought; and although love might be reborn in the person of Madame T—, his greatest passion continued to be glory.

◇◇◇

Chapter LI

Ambitions for a New Navy; Tribute to Louis XVI

THE ABSENCE of opportunity was alone responsible in so far as Jones during this period in France did not achieve, in addition to his success in the uncongenial task as prize money agent, a memorable rôle as leader of a new American Navy. From the beginning to the end of the war he had proposed many reforms and effected some of them in the Continental Marine, and he had set an example of heroism which no other naval officer had equalled. With the Revolution at an end, he had warned: "We cannot, like the ancients, build a fleet in a month, and we ought to take example from what has lately befallen Holland. In time of peace it is necessary to prepare, and be always prepared, for war at sea."[1]

But both the Government under the Articles of Confederation was impotent to collect taxes for the founding of a new Navy and the political leaders were divided in their views even as to its expediency. If the office of Agent of Marine and Morris as its incumbent had remained, there might have been better prospects. In June, 1783 he had replied to a resolution of the House of Delegates in Virginia: "That although it is an object highly desirable to establish a respectable marine, yet the situation of the public treasury renders it not advisable to purchase ships for the present nor until the several states shall grant such funds for the construction of ships, docks, and naval arsenals and for the support of the naval service as shall enable the United States to establish their marine upon a permanent and respectable footing." In this situation, whatever were the hopes of Morris, the Government was to sell even the few remaining ships of the Continental Navy, including the *Alliance,* and to release from active service its dwindled group of naval officers.

The Revolutionary Navy which Jones more than any other captain had founded, improved, and inspired was now dead. Likewise more than any other officer he strove to revive it. Congress had not provided him with a frigate to conduct the better his investigation of European naval programs. It had not even given him official sanction to prosecute this study without a frigate or supplied him with personal expenses to do so. It had, in effect, now that men of his profession were no longer in immediate need, discarded him regardless of his uncompromising devotion and sacrifice. There have been few men who without their profession were equally without the breath of their nostrils. It would be altogether understandable, then, if he were at times to avert his eyes by instinct from almost hopeless expectancy of active naval service even in peace as a citizen of the United States and as a champion of her liberties to visions of a high command aboard splendid ships of war in the navies of France and even Russia.

In the meantime he sought as well as he could to found a new, lasting American Navy. His first support in the United States for this object appears indeed to have been more French than American. "On my arrival in Paris," as he explained to De Castries in May, 1784 apropos of the prize money and a naval program at the same time, "I had the honor to present a letter from the Chevalier de La Luzerne, mentioning that part of my business in Europe is to collect materials for forming a system for the future marine of America. You had, my lord, the goodness to promise me copies of everything respecting the government and manner of supplying the marine of France; and I should esteem it a great favor if you would now give orders in consequence."[2] It may well be true that whatever naval secrets he gained from this course in behalf of the United States were in such confidence as to render it expedient and even necessary not to commit them to writing.

From some American authorities, too, he had an informal commission. Alexander Hamilton requested Colonel Wadsworth of New York to secure detailed, technical information concerning the navies of various countries, and he in turn forwarded the inquiry to Jones. "I have sent this to you," he wrote early in 1784, "as the best able to make inquiries, and pray you to write him on the several articles of this request, as I know nobody in America so likely to make good use of them. I do not despair of seeing an American Navy; and my hopes will increase when I see such men as Hamilton at the head of our naval affairs in America, which may possibly not be far distant. I will not apologize for giving you this trouble. You have so eminently distinguished yourself as a naval officer, and so warmly and unremittingly pursued the true interest of America that I am certain I can commit these inquiries to no one so able and willing to make them."[3] It may be supposed that, in correspondence between Hamilton and Jones, the statesman appreciated the views of the officer, according to his later advocacy in *The Federalist* of strong armed forces.

It was to Jefferson in particular that the personality and sentiments of Jones were to become increasingly persuasive. Their proximity in Paris, the one as Minister and the other as special agent, afforded them special opportunities to know each other. The flouting of the United States by the Barbary pirates, knowing well America's naval impotence, incited Jones to protest loudly to Jay, the Minister of Foreign Affairs, and particularly to Jefferson. He wrote urgently on July 31, 1785 to the latter upon learning that Algiers had just captured two American ships and was holding the crews in bondage: "This event may, I believe, surprise some of our fellow citizens; but, for my part, I am rather surprised that it did not take place sooner. It will produce a good effect if it unites the people of America in measures consistent with their national honor and interest, and rouses them from that ill-judged security which the intoxication of success had produced since the Revolution."[4]

Jefferson in turn, apparently not by coincidence, communicated a week later with Adams in London concerning a new envoy to Algiers: "Dr. Bancroft or Captain Jones occurs to me as the fittest. If we consider the present object only, I think the former would be the most proper; but if we look forward to the very probable event of war with those pirates, an important object would be obtained by Captain Jones' becoming acquainted with their ports, force, tactics, etc."[5] Jefferson's bias towards preparedness in this and other instances and his further relations with Jones as to the Barbary States promised that the officer would bear an important part in future naval policy.

The trust which Colonel Wadsworth had reposed in Jones appeared more conspicuously in the case of a mission which Jefferson confided to him comparatively early in their association. The French scientific expedition under the command of Captain de la Perouse, which was to sail from Brest in August, 1785, happened to be of concern to the American Minister because of his fear that it might be a disguise for the establishment of factories for the fur trade or of colonies on the northwest coast of America. "If they would desire a colony on the western side of America," he reasoned, "I should not be quite satisfied that they would refuse one which should offer itself on the eastern side." Wishing to satisfy himself, he requested Jones, who happened at the time to be at L'Orient in regard to the prize money, to learn what he could without exciting suspicion. "His discretion can be relied on," remarked Jefferson. Accordingly Jones secured a full account of the preparations, which tended to remove the Minister's misgivings. Jefferson forwarded the detailed report to Jay, commenting as to his informant: "He refuses to accept of any indemnification for his expenses, which is an additional proof of his disinterested spirit and of his devotion to the service of America."

Such convictions testifying to the public-mindedness of Jones tended to become the stronger by reason of the personal good will which he won. He sent replicas of his distinguished Houdon bust executed in 1780 to his chief political and military friends, a few at this period and a larger number in the future—but it is not known that he forwarded any to his relatives in Scotland. Of those to whom he presented replicas early, Jones included Jefferson, whose acknowledgment he answered: "I offered the bust to you as a mark of my esteem and respect for your virtues and talents . . . it receives its value from your acceptance of it, with the assurances you give me of your particular esteem."[6] To Carmichael, now an envoy to Spain, he confided: "Like yourself I have done my best to support the dignity of human nature through every stage of the American Revolution. . . . My reward has been the esteem of the good and virtuous, and I wish my bust could tell posterity that while I lived there was no man more ambitious to deserve your friendship."[7]

His anger flared at a supposed affront not less than his heartiness expanded in fraternal compliments. A tax, possibly an oversight, for the importation of several busts to America, one of which "as a mark of my affection" was for Robert Morris, evoked his outburst: "They are not merchandise; and I flatter myself that my zeal and exertions for the cause of America will not be requited with such a mark of dishonor. I would rather hear that the busts were broken to pieces than consent that they should be subject to a duty."[8] Like Hotspur indeed he was on occasion jealous in honor; sudden and quick in quarrel.

This fieriness, however, did not disturb his course. It was not long before he presented a bust also to Washington, and implied along with his expressions of gratitude even heights of ambition not incomparable with the attainments of the General who distinguished him: "Your determination to 'place my bust with your own' confers on me a greater honor than I ever before received— an honor which I shall ever be ambitious to merit. But what man can hope to vie with the talents, the virtuous perseverance, and exertions of a General Washington." Perhaps Jones, behind the veil of his self-depreciation, presumed a little upon the special courtesy extended to him.

The most elaborate and telling instance in which a token of Jones' personal esteem was calculated to redound to his professional advantage occurred upon the presentation of his journal to Louis XVI. Although in a private capacity, it was to a great extent a public act on his own initiative, for he had been a medium for professions of good will between the United States and France and was ambitious to continue in this distinctive position. He presented with the memoirs a letter on January 1, 1786 in a courteous ambassadorial and laudatory personal tone, not lacking some of his verses:

"History gives the world no example of such generosity as that of Your Majesty towards the young republic of America; and I believe there never was a more flattering compliment shown by a sovereign to his allies, than when Your Majesty determined to arm and support a squadron under the flag of the United States.

"Words cannot express my sense of the preference I obtained when Your Majesty deigned to make choice of me to command that squadron.

"Your Majesty has as much reputation for knowledge and the desire of information as you have for wisdom and justice; but besides that consideration, I conceived it to be my duty to lay before Your Majesty an account of my conduct as an officer, particularly from the date of the alliance between Your Majesty and the United States. As Your Majesty understands English, I have perhaps judged ill by presenting extracts of my journal in French; my motive was to give Your Majesty as little trouble as possible.

"Accept, Sire, with indulgence, this confidential offering of my gratitude, which is an original written for your particular information. . . .

"The Congress of the United States has, with great justice, styled Your Majesty 'the protector of the rights of human nature.' With the Order of Military Merit, Your Majesty conferred on me a gold sword—an honor which I presume no other officer has received; and 'the protector of the rights of human nature' will always find me ready to draw that sword and expose my life for his service.

> "Protector of fair freedom's rights,
> Louis thy virtues please thy God!
> The good man in thy praise delights,
> And tyrants tremble at thy nod.
> Thy people's father, loved so well,
> May time respect! When thou art gone
> May each new year of history tell
> Thy sons with lustre fill thy throne."[9]

The journal embraced Jones' history during only those years which he considered might be of special interest to the King, and it included only a version written impressively in the third person. The most distinguished letters of commendation which had been addressed to the officer were in an appendix. In the course of preparation these memoirs had received warm praises from Malesherbes and D'Estaing. Jones had labored over the style with the care of an artist; the completed manuscript was simple and terse, poised and impassioned. Although the English original was his own composition, André, the future editor of *Mémoires de Paul Jones,* containing the same material in a French book published in 1798, "translated it under his eyes" into the French language. Jones had in mind only five manuscript copies; he did not intend to publish this special journal presumably for the reason, if no other, that it was addressed to the King and to France rather than to America.

"I believe he would have liked very much to become an admiral of the French fleet. I even heard that when he returned to Paris a second time he made a request of this nature to Louis XVI,"[10] related Vigée Lebrun, who, as already seen, often met Jones in company with her friends and should have had reliable grounds for her opinion. In fact both the journal and the future history of the officer strongly support her view. Without professional employment and with little prospect of any in America, and indebted to the King for the glory of the sword and the decoration and for the squadron which had afforded him his greatest opportunity, Jones was disposed and adept enough to color the journal, "this confidential offering of my gratitude," so as to appeal to the particular sympathies of Louis for his own advancement as well as for the interests of the United States.

His most characteristic plea in this regard was to depict himself now in the journal, as he had done earlier in the long address to Lady Selkirk, "less as an officer of Congress than as a man who fought for the cause of humankind."[11] In the same spirit, attesting his fidelity to the United States, even to the extent of refusing a commission in the French marine during the Revolution, Jones did not fail, however, to remind the King that it was possible to consider him in the service of His Majesty since February 10, 1778 when he had proposed the expedition to America undertaken by D'Estaing, or in any event since the following June when Franklin had intimated the wishes from Versailles to have him undertake a project under the auspices of France. Still in seeking the favor of France, he breathed no word in disparagement of the United States; on the contrary, he bore witness by his deeds to his abiding ardent patriotism as an American: "Personal advantage never was the spring of my public acts; I had more noble motives; and far from enriching myself by the Revolution in America, I have consecrated to this great object the ten best years of my life, without interruption, as well as my tranquillity, a portion of my fortune, and my blood."[12]

The political storm which was progressively besetting the

régime of Louis had without doubt an adverse influence upon any opportunities for Jones as an Admiral in the French Navy. Nevertheless, the esteem in which the King held the tribute from his pen became apparent after the French Revolution upon the discovery of the royal copy of the journal among the possessions most treasured for safekeeping in the palace of the Tuileries.[13]

◇◇

Chapter LII

Madame T—; New Triumphs and Unique Honors

IN AMERICA on his second arrival from the Continent in the summer of 1787, Jones learned that the Board of Treasury, with Lee as one of its members, had not yet approved his charges against the prize money, and that a recess of Congress indicated further delay in making the decision. He discovered also, to his dismay, that his sailors, promises and resolutions notwithstanding, remained unpaid. The private business regarding his bank stock and mercantile investments, which had given him concern, came to a more timely but not a noticeably favorable conclusion. He became reconciled with his friend Ross, and the merchant was later to receive one of his busts. But his cash resources continued uncomfortably limited for his liberal purposes, especially to the extent that they were to vex him in his relations with Madame T—.

The opportunity was his, in the meantime, to try again to secure the recognition and advancement as a naval officer which he had failed to gain during his previous return to the United States. His relinquishment of the *America,* his uncorrected rank in the official list of captains, his proposed Congressional gold medal which had not been awarded to him, and above all his disappointment in not having commanded a second, larger squadron of American and French ships during the Revolution were not forgotten. He had proved an able advocate in his own behalf previously, and he was not less skilful and forward now. The manner, in fact, in which he sought to induce both Congress and the King to vie with each other in according him honors would have done credit to a business man thoroughly accustomed to bargaining, even if what he sought was only his due.

With such views in anticipation of his return to Europe for the pending negotiations in Denmark, he expressed his wishes to John Jay, who as Minister for Foreign Affairs had succeeded Morris as one of the most influential statesmen in America: "It would be highly flattering to me if I could carry with me to France a letter from Congress to His Most Christian Majesty, thanking him for the squadron he did us the honor to support under our flag. And on this occasion, sir, permit me, with becoming diffidence, to recall the attention of my sovereign [his designation in this instance for the United States Government] to the letter of recommendation I brought with me from the Court of France, dated 30th May, 1780. It would be pleasing to me if that letter should be found to merit a place on the journals of Congress. Permit me also to entreat that Congress will be pleased to read the letter I received from the Minister of Marine when His Majesty deigned to bestow on me a golden hilted sword, emblematical of the happy alliance—an honor which His Majesty never conferred on any other foreign officer. I owed the high favor which I enjoyed at the Court of France, in a great degree, to the favorable testimony of my conduct, which had been communicated by His Majesty's Ambassador, under whose eye I acted in the most critical situation in the Texel, as well as to the public opinion in Europe. And the letter with which I was honored by the Prime Minister of France, when I was about to return to America, is a clear proof that we might have drawn still greater advantages from the generous disposition of our ally, if our marine had not been lost whilst I was, by perplexing circumstances, detained in Europe, after I had given the Count de Maurepas my plan for forming a combined squadron of ten or twelve sail of frigates, supported by the *America,* with a detachment of French troops on board, the whole at the expense of His Majesty."[1]

This catalogue concerning himself would no doubt more fittingly have come, if at all, from another pen. Jay had due regard for Jones' services and for the gratitude owed to the King, but he was not disposed to recommend compliance with all his desires, in particular the one for publicity of his letter from the Court of France. "Sovereigns being equal," Jay counseled, "and this letter being a deviation from that propriety which such equality seems to prescribe, the self-respect of Congress opposes their gratifying the Chevalier's wish to enter it at large on their journals." Jones was not averse to a precedent in his favor. Although the objection of the Minister for Foreign Affairs on the score of dignity seems rather vain, the wishes of the officer were not conspicuously modest.

Indeed the part which Jones on occasion attributed to himself as the blunt, outspoken sailor sometimes changed its aspect seemingly to that of the politician. In the Journal for the King, he had sought to emphasize his service, in effect, with France; now he stressed, not without a better case, his consistent career under the banner of the United States: "It is certain that I am much flattered by receiving a gold sword from the most illustrious monarch now living; but I had refused to accept his commission on two occasions, before that time, when some firmness was necessary to resist the temptation. He was not my sovereign. I served the cause of freedom, and honors from my sovereign would be more pleasing. Since the year 1775, when I displayed the American flag for the first time, with my own hands, I have been constantly devoted to the interests of America. Foreigners have perhaps given me too much credit, and this may have raised my ideas of my services above their real value—but my zeal can never be overrated."

While merit offset in large part his egoism, habitual championship of American prisoners almost wholly counteracted the impression of his self-centered ambition: "I should act inconsistently if I omitted to mention the dreadful situation of our unhappy fellow-citizens in slavery at Algiers. Their almost hopeless fate is a deep reflection on our national character in Europe. I beg leave to influence the humanity of Congress in their behalf, and to propose that some expedient may be adopted for their redemption. A fund might be raised for that purpose, by a duty of a shilling per month from seamen's wages throughout the Continent, and I am persuaded that no difficulty would be made to that requisition."[2]

Pending the results of this appeal to Jay and the decision of the Board of Treasury, Jones received a letter, forwarded by Jefferson, which divulged that Madame T— was now in the forefront of his mind, regardless of the distance from New York to Paris. Even his ardor for the Countess de Nicolson previously had cooled because of separation by the Atlantic, as he had written her one lukewarm letter in half a year from Portsmouth and offered excuses; but he was now to despatch his fifth eager message to Madame T— within only a few months of his departure from Paris.

Secrecy had suited the plans of Jones in regard to his connection with Madame T—. He had wished to secure for her first the moral prestige of the present King and the material influence of a goodly fortune from the same source. But the death of an important intermediary at Court had suddenly rendered his procedure more difficult. Madame T—, also, had confided her letter for Jones to the care of Jefferson for the purpose of imparting this unfortunate news, so that it became more desirable than opportune for him to dispel any suspicions of the Minister of a clandestine relationship which might prove embarrassing.

Even then Jones preferred not to make his connection with Madame T— public; his account of September 4, 1787 from New York to Jefferson was *"in confidence,"* explaining, without mention of her name, that "she is a daughter of the late K— and of a lady of quality" and that the present King was disposed, in view of the mother's injustice and the friend's intercession with him, to provide suitably for her. "But the letter you sent me," Jones added, "left the feeling author all in tears! Her friend—her protectress—her introductress to the K— was suddenly dead! She was in despair! She lost more than a mother! A loss, indeed, that nothing can repair; for fortune and favor are never to be compared to tried friendship. I hope, however, she has gone to visit the K— in July, agreeable to his appointment given her in the month of March. I am persuaded that he would receive her with additional kindness, and that her loss would, in his mind, be a new claim to his protection; especially as he well knows and has acknowledged her superior merit and just pretensions. As I feel the greatest concern for the situation of this worthy lady, you will render me a great favor by writing a note, requesting her to call on you, as you have something to communicate from me."[3]

The consoling letter which Jones sent in turn to Madame T— through the medium of Jefferson revealed his intimate concern for her at the loss of the friend and protectress:

"No language can convey to my fair mourner the tender sorrow

I feel on her account! The loss of our worthy friend is indeed a fatal stroke! It is an irreparable misfortune which can only be alleviated by this one reflection, that it is the will of God, whose providence has, I hope, other blessings in store for us. She was a tried friend, and more than a mother to you! She would have been a mother to me also had she lived. We have lost her! Let us cherish her memory, and send up grateful thanks to the Almighty that we once had such a friend.

"I cannot but flatter myself that you have yourself gone to the King in July as he had appointed. I am sure your loss will be a new inducement for him to protect you, and render you justice. He will hear you, I am sure; and you may safely unbosom yourself to him, and ask his advice, which cannot but be flattering to him to give you. Tell him you must look on him as your father and protector. If it were necessary, I think, too, that the Count d'A—, his brother, would, on your personal application, render you good offices by speaking in your favor. I should like it better, however, if you can do without him.

"Mr. Jefferson will show you my letter of this date to him. You will see by it how disgracefully I have been detained here by the Board of Treasury. It is impossible for me to stir from this place till I obtain their settlement on the business I have already performed; and as the season is already far advanced, I expect to be ordered to embark directly for the place of my destination in the north. Mr. Jefferson will forward me your letters. I am almost without money, and much puzzled to obtain a supply. I have written to Dr. Bancroft to endeavor to assist me. I mention this with infinite regret, and for no other reason than because it is impossible for me to transmit you a supply under my present circumstances.

"This is my fifth letter to you since I left Paris. The two last were from France, and I sent them by duplicates. But you say nothing of having received any letters from me! Summon, my dear friend, all your resolution! Exert yourself, and plead your own cause. You cannot fail of success; your cause would move a heart of flint! Present my best respects to your sister. You did not mention her in your letter; but I persuade myself she will continue her tender care of her sweet godson, and that you will cover him all over with kisses from me; they come warm to *you both* from the heart!"[4]

The sympathy and encouragement in these words set them apart from the facile, gallant terms in which Jones had frequently indulged. His very hesitation to have her seek the support of the Count d'Artois, the brother of the King, seemed to indicate less any scruples concerning the conduct of this gay and courtly personage than his own special solicitude in her case. In so far as his concern may have been for himself apart from her and their bond, it related apparently to his ambitions at the French Court and his hopes of professional advancement through the King.

According to Jones' comments to Bancroft, he mentioned the death of the intermediary whom Madame T— mourned as "also a great grief and loss to me, as I had in that lady a valuable friend."[5] According to his condolence to Madame T—, the expression, "She would have been a mother to me also had she lived," bore a less professional implication. In fact it was personal enough to imply that his intimacy with Madame T— would have rendered their common friend the foster mother of them both, and perhaps indeed that an actual marriage contemplated with Madame T— would have been the basis for the adopted relationship. This second surmise has the greater plausibility because of the "sweet godson" towards whom he felt such affection as to wish her to "cover him all over with kisses from me . . . warm to *you both* from the heart!" Especially in view of his indirection in references to Madame T—, the phrases from his pen lead to the impression that the child was his own.

The supposed mystery of Madame T—, whose name Jones preferred not to disclose, has resulted in a great deal of conjecture. There is practically no reason for believing that she was Madame Tellisson. This name first appeared in the superscription of the letter which Jones wrote on July 24, 1780 from L'Orient, although in the body of it he used merely the title Madame T—.[6] The communication, already quoted in part, was in a friendly and respectful but not particularly intimate tone; the subsequent letters in question were, as has just been seen and as will be further evident, in a contrastingly personal and warm vein. While it is possible that the first relation may have grown into the second, there are substantial reasons for its improbability. The identification of the earlier correspondent does not reasonably fit the later. Madame Tellisson, as already indicated, knew Franklin and the family of Grand, the French banker. She was an influential woman, according to a request which the poet Aimé Ambrose Feutry made to Franklin for an introduction to her through Madame Grand for presenting a petition to the statesman Necker.[7] Likewise, on the authority of the niece of Jones, Janette Taylor, who had no reason for bias in this matter, the earlier Madame T— (Madame Tellisson) was not the later.[8] Miss Taylor stated reliably as to this later correspondent: "There is no mystery about Madame T—. She was acknowledged by the King to be the daughter of his predecessor, and she was known in Paris as the widow of an English gentleman. . . . This lady who resided with Madame T— was an English woman, not her own sister [as Jones referred to her], but the sister of Madame T—'s late husband."[9]

Whoever Madame T— may have been more specifically among the numerous offspring of whom Louis XV was father, she occupied Jones' thoughts even to a greater degree than before as he marked time in awaiting action upon his professional concerns and looked forward to his return to Europe. With Lee as a member of the Board of Treasury, its long delay led inevitably to an adverse decision. The Board recommended that Jones should return 38,000 livres as the difference in amount between the charges for expenses and the commission of five per cent, that he should likewise remit a suitable sum from his alleged share of the prize money as the commander of the *Richard,* and that he should provide new bondsmen and receive a predetermined percentage for the business to be completed in Denmark.[10]

Jones hastened to reply to the chairman of a committee to which Congress referred the report of the Board of Treasury. He emphasized that he had served not as an agent but a special envoy, and that his position had occasioned greater expenses than those of the American Minister but his charges on a yearly basis were only about one-third as large as the Minister's salary. He claimed without contradiction: "The credit with which I am honored as an officer, in the opinion of Europe, and the personal intimacy I have with many great characters at Paris, with my exclusive knowledge of all circumstances relative to the business, insured me a success which no other men could have obtained."[11] Finally his defense turned to offense; and Congress had reason to dislike if not to fear a more direct reference to the unredeemed pledge of several of its members for prompt payment to his sailors: "The settlement that I made with the Court of France had first Dr. Franklin's, and afterwards Mr. Jefferson's approbation, in every stage and article of the business; and I presume it will be found, at least as far as depended on me, to merit that of the United States."[12]

As Jones had been provoked to take issue with the Board of Treasury in respect to some details of his own services, he availed himself of the occasion to criticize this body in particular and Congress in general regarding Landais and naval regulations. It was not without authority as well as candor that he said: "The Board seems very zealous for the interests of that broken and disgraced officer. I shall say nothing in opposition to his interests; but I am possessed of ample testimony that, if he had been tried on my accusations (instead of being broken and disgraced for bringing away the *Alliance* from France, after his suspension by Franklin), the judgment of the court-martial would have been of a more grave and serious nature—a glaring proof, among many others, that we had no system for the government of our Navy, and that we need not at this date be so tenacious of its vaunted ordinances."[13] Doubtlessly these sentiments were displeasing to Lee and Samuel Adams and helped to open the eyes of members of Congress to the activities of such colleagues present and past.

As for Landais, he lived in Brooklyn on his small pension. Striding the streets of New York and threatening with the attendant rattle of his sword that if there was bad blood in Congress he would draw it, the convicted officer made a final vain effort to provoke a quarrel with Jones. In New York he happened to see Jones, with his back turned to him, speaking on a sidewalk with a friend. Jones ignored his approach and did not hear his remark at a short distance as he spat in the street, "I spit in his face." Landais seized the occasion to circulate reports that his enemy had proved himself craven. Jones then published a statement, signed by his witness, to contradict the arrogant remarks, and added his decision not to condescend to take notice of any future words or acts of Landais.

The verbal counteroffensive of Jones' letter to a committee of Congress—not without reference to Landais under circumstances more fitting than those of a wisely avoided street brawl—had a due effect upon its five members to whom the findings of the Board of Treasury had been referred. There was no Lee or Adams upon this committee. The chairman in particular, Edward Carrington of Virginia, was disposed to support Jones. He made a motion in Congress to confirm the financial settlement as it stood in the light of these circumstances: "Whereas . . . finding that M. Le Ray de Chaumont, in whose hands the greatest part of the prize money had been placed, had become insolvent, he [Jones] was reduced to the necessity of abandoning so much of the property as lost, or turning his views upon the Court of France, . . . as the business was found to stand upon ground materially different from that which was contemplated by either Congress or the said Captain Jones at the time of his appointment, it is just and reasonable that the full value of the services and expenses which he has necessarily incurred for the benefit of the claimants be deducted from the property recovered."[14]

Neither Arthur Lee nor his brother Richard Henry was at hand in Congress, and Samuel Adams was no longer a member to act against this direct attack upon their position. But a new scion of the family, Henry Lee, Jr., who had recently been elected to Congress also from Virginia, was intrenched at the breach. And as an ally he had William Grayson, likewise from Virginia. Lee made a motion, seconded by Grayson, to set aside Carrington's; it provided for paying from the Federal Treasury the amount of the expenses in excess of the commission.[15] The past and prospective delay of the Board of Treasury, with Arthur Lee of course as one of its members, in fulfilling the promise to pay the prize money to the sailors was a gauge of the fate in store for Jones in the event of success for this subtle manœuvre. But Lee and Grayson alone voted in favor of it; the original motion by Carrington passed by a large majority. At last on October 11, 1787 the controversy over Jones' charges had reached an end successful and honorable.

The outlook for the sailors, too, assumed a more favorable turn. Congress may well have read between the lines of Jones' defense of the settlement in France an implication concerning the interests of his men: "I presume it will be found, at least as far as depended on me, to merit that of the United States." Lee and Osgood of the Board of Treasury rather than Congress, however, appeared to be responsible for the postponement in paying them. They had reported that it was "not practicable to make a division of what has been received agreeably to the Act of Congress of the 7th June, 1786" until the settlement with Jones.[16] Apparently, then, the prize money was now available in America; Jefferson stood exonerated, by the result as well as his intention, from any design against the sailors; and it remained only to distribute the funds among them. Now, along with final approval of Jones' services, Congress passed a resolution "That the monies paid by Captain John Paul Jones into the hands of the Hon. Thomas Jefferson be distributed by the Board of Treasury as soon as may be among the captors."[17] Although Jones again could hope to face his *Bonhomme Richard* officers and men, the indecisive phrase "as soon as may be," the delegation of the final procedure for payment to the Board of Treasury hostile as it was, and above all the continued presence of Lee on the Board were ominous.

As for Jones himself, the full measure of his victory was still to appear. The recent diplomatic letter to Jay as well as the plain-spoken remonstrance to the committee under the chairmanship of Carrington now bore fruit. Congress, sitting in New York, on October 16, 1787, "Resolved unanimously that a medal of gold be struck and presented to the Chevalier John Paul Jones in commemoration of the valor and brilliant services of that officer in command of a squadron of American and French ships under the flag and commission of the United States. . . ."[18] This medal, distinguishing him alone among naval commanders of the Revolution, was the honor which had been denied him in 1781 and which he now deeply appreciated. He took special note that it had been bestowed for signal services upon five other officers only (Washington, Gates, Wayne, Morgan, and Greene), and that his recognition, unlike that of the others, occurred not on an occasion of enthusiasm but in memory of achievements eight years after they had taken place. Aside from his ambition for advancement to the rank of rear admiral, to which Congress gave further consideration at this time, Jones prized this gold medal as greater recognition than any other he had received in America. He no longer had reason to feel any resentment at the former stigma of his rank as eighteenth Captain; none could now question his position as the foremost American naval officer alike in standing and accomplishment.

A further resolution of Congress was of more practical value towards realization of his limitless aspiration as a naval commander. It was an official request from the United States to the King of France, which promised to achieve a purpose of Jones' unofficial journal to him. It tended to prove also, candidly solicited as it was from Congress, that whatever professional opportunity he might covet in France incident to the lack of a navy at home, his loyalty as an American officer and citizen was unchanging. In accordance with this resolution by Congress, Jay provided him with a suitable letter for presentation to Louis XVI. "As it is his earnest desire to acquire greater knowledge in his profession," wrote the Secretary for Foreign Affairs, "we cannot forbear requesting of Your Majesty to permit him to embark in your fleets of evolution, where only it will be probably in his power to acquire that degree of knowledge which may hereafter render him more extensively useful."[19]

While Jones now awaited passage for Europe, Congress took occasion to define more clearly the conditions for negotiating the claim upon Denmark in consonance with the recommendation of the Board of Treasury for less discretionary power by the agent. It placed authority for conclusion of the business in the hands of Jefferson, providing that he should send Jones or any other deputy to the Court of Denmark to transact it subject to his own confirmation. The provisions specified in particular "that the person employed shall . . . be allowed five per cent of all expenses and demands whatever on that account." This commission was reasonable inasmuch as the claim amounted to as much as £50,000; but whether the provisional powers of the agent were wise remained to be seen.

The impatience of Jones had been straining at its leash for many months. Now that his affairs were completed with success and notable honors, he was characteristically ready to sail at the first opportunity. At this juncture the protracted absence of word from Madame T— gave wings to his thoughts of return. "The last French packet brought no letter to me from the person whose happiness is dearer to me than anything else," he wrote to her. "I have been on the rack of fear and apprehension, and am totally unable to account for that silence! My business is done here, and the moment of my return to Europe approaches. My sentiments are unchanged, and my impatience can better be imagined than expressed. I have been honored here beyond my own expectations. But your silence makes even honors insipid. I am, however, far from blaming you; want of health, or some other misfortune must have interposed. If this reaches you, remember me affectionately to your sister and her godson. May Heaven avert all trouble from you."[20]

Nevertheless the seemingly headlong lover retained his canny circumspection—the same cool mastery of mind even during heights of excitement which explained in large part his invariable naval victories. When Jones wrote to Madame T— on October 24, he despatched also a message to Jefferson: "I should have embarked in the packet that will sail for Havre tomorrow morning; but an account having arrived here that the English fleet is out, and was seen steering to the westward, and that a British squadron is cruising in the North Sea, has induced me, with the advice of my friends, to postpone my embarkation till the next opportunity, an American ship, about the beginning of next month."[21]

He must have felt legitimate reasons, as a passenger on an inconsequential boat, for avoiding British ships at sea, if not British people on their soil. Perhaps a fictitious "Supplement to the Boston Independent Chronicle," ascribed in part to Jones, but written and distributed anonymously near the close of the war by Franklin with the facility of his journalistic training, newly fanned embitterment against the officer. According to this satirical picture of cruelties by the British, a chief of the Seneca Indians in their pay sent eight packages containing a thousand American scalps to an English governor for shipment to King George in token of mercenary faithfulness; and accompanying the imaginary news item in a second edition was a supposed letter by Jones which proved Britain, not himself, worthy of the name *pirate*.[22] On his previous passage to Europe in 1783 he had recognized but braved continued hostility. On the present occasion he preferred to be discreet, notwithstanding too the delay under his care of official despatches from Jay and even of special letters from Washington. Biding his time almost three weeks longer, he embarked at New York in an American vessel bound for Holland, whose Captain agreed to set him ashore in France.

As the shores of America disappeared below the horizon, little could he imagine the time and other circumstances of his return to the United States. He had ostensible reasons for optimism. Professionally, his letter to Madame T— spoke for him, "I have been honored here beyond my own expectations." As to his sailors, he had done far more than his duty and hoped to serve them further in Denmark. But if he could not presage in any way his next return to the United States, neither was he able to foresee that, thanks to the delaying tactics begun by the Board of Treasury, including Lee in particular, only a small number of the seamen who had bled with him and only heirs of some of the others would receive payment of the French prize money as many years later as fifty.[23] Personally, his bond with Madame T— appeared more strongly forged than any other. Still if the fortunes of life and the faith of some representatives of the Government were to be so unpredictable, love warranted no prophecy, concerning his part or Madame T—'s, to whom he had just written as "the person whose happiness is dearer to me than anything else."

Chapter LIII

◇◇

A Vision of Russia

ADMIRAL of a Russian fleet—this was a fantasy which had floated across the horizon of Jones during his previous residence in France. It seemed, however unsubstantial, to influence his steps now at his return. His precaution to avoid the British gave place to indifference towards them when, in order perhaps to scout this dream of Russia, he landed in England instead of France under the pretext of adverse winds. He even proceeded to London; indeed, according to his own assurances, "passed some days with my friends there and went to Covent Garden Theatre." This leisurely detour was in any event at variance both with his professed reasons of safety for sailing from America in the second instead of the first ship available and with his apparent haste for the sake of the despatches and of Madame T—. Then followed his arrival in Paris on December 12, 1787 in secret expectancy.

At once he sent a cryptic message to Jefferson: "I am just arrived here from England. I left New York on the 11th of November, and have brought public despatches and a number of private letters for you. I would have waited on you immediately, instead of writing, but I have several *strong reasons* for desiring that no person should know of my being here till I have seen you, and been favored with your advice on the steps I ought to pursue. I have a letter from Congress to the King, and perhaps you will think it advisable not to present it at this moment. I shall not go out till I hear from or see you. And, as the people in this hotel do not know my name, you will please to ask for the gentleman just arrived, who is lodged in No. 1."[1]

Some encouragement for his vision of Russia undoubtedly was the cause of his initial hesitation to proceed with his plan to gain experience by embarking with the French fleet. But he waited **to** hear from Jefferson how far this vague prospect regarding Russia had developed and how feasible it might prove. The thought of such foreign service was itself not new to him; the possibility of its realization was another matter.

A preliminary manœuvre, to which Jones had not seemed disinclined, occurred nearly three years earlier to secure his services for Russia. The Scotchman Earl Wemyss on February 18, 1785 had informed a member of the Russian Court who apparently solicited information: "Since coming to Paris I have made the acquaintance of my compatriot, the celebrated Commodore Paul Jones. Your highness knows that he is a brave and great sailor. More than that, my lord, he is an agreeable man, full of all sorts of attainments. I can see that he does not love the inactive life and, without having actually spoken to him of service, I feel that he would not be averse to it, although he is very well off. If your highness finds it advisable to write of him to the Court of Russia, if there is occasion, I undertake to discuss it with him."[2]

A month later Wemyss wrote again in advocacy of the officer: "As you desired, I have sounded the Commodore Paul Jones and learned the following: He is very well off for money; he has the Cross of Military Merit and the Cross of Cincinnatus; he could enter the service here as a high ranking Captain; when America forms her Navy he is sure to be Commander in Chief; he is regarded as one of the best of sailors. Your highness will remember his battle with the *Serapis,* the English man-of-war which he captured. He has taken others. He is modest, polite, and very intelligent. I am sure that if the Empress of Russia cared to offer him advantageous terms, he would prefer the service of Her Imperial Majesty to every other."[3] But Russia was preparing, not actually engaged, in one of her numerous wars in 1785, and so the negotiation temporarily lapsed.

In 1787, however, Russia had characteristically begun a second war with Turkey. Her Navy in particular was chaotic and inept; therefore she buttressed it with foreign officers of every description and from every country. A few were of outstanding prestige, some were in search of occupation, most were unscrupulous mercenaries. Russia had secured the services of the talented Dutch Admiral Kinsbergen in the First Turkish War; she now had the able Scotch

Admiral Greig for her Baltic fleet; and Jones seemed a promising leader in this new emergency for the operations in the Black Sea. Under these circumstances M. de Simolin, the Russian Minister to France, had expressed to Jefferson on numerous occasions during Jones' absence in America the desire of his country to secure his services.

The author of the Declaration of Independence and of letters which evinced his abomination of autocracy had listened to this proposal in behalf of that very autocratic nation Russia. When Jefferson came to the hotel at which Jones stopped upon his arrival in Paris, conflicting considerations must have moved him. He knew that Jones wished activity and thirsted for new, broader experience in his profession; he realized likewise that more extensive training would make him a greater asset to the United States when her hoped-for Navy should be established. But did he know Russia and her rulers? In a diatribe regarding contemporary kings as "all body and no mind," he was to describe every one of them as either imbecile or mad—except "old Catherine, who had been but too lately picked up to have lost her common sense."[4]

In the interests of both the United States and of Jones, Jefferson explained to him the views of Simolin, who according to the comment of the Captain himself "appeared anxious to succeed in prevailing on me to go to Russia to command the fleet against the Turks in the Black Sea." Jones felt indebted to the American Minister, in fact, not only as the primary source for his information but also as the intermediary who put the proposal "in train." If Jefferson was non-committal enough to leave the decision wholly to the person most concerned, another counselor gave Jones express advice even to the extent of marked preference for the Turks: "Speaking to a man of very high rank at Paris," Jones admitted, "I repeated to him what had been communicated to me by Mr. Jefferson. He replied that he would advise me to go to Constantinople at once rather than to enter the service of Russia."[5]

Such counsel and Jones' own scruples gave him pause. He avoided a meeting with De Simolin, notwithstanding the flattering professions which Jefferson had reported from him. He neither believed that the proposal was likely to materialize, looking upon it "as a castle in the air"; nor was it pleasing to his conscience. At this early stage, unmoved by the compliments to which he was susceptible, Jones honestly said, "I did not wish for any employment in foreign service."

Almost at the moment of Jones' departure for Copenhagen, he received a note from Lewis Littlepage, a Virginian then in Paris who was chamberlain to the King of Poland, urgently requesting the officer to breakfast with him the next morning as he had "matters of the utmost importance to communicate." When Jones went to see Littlepage the same night, he learned that De Simolin desired very much to speak with him before his journey and looked forward to breakfasting with both of them on the following day. Whatever hesitation Jones may have felt because Littlepage himself had pursued a wayward course in Europe and adopted a virulently hostile attitude toward John Jay who formerly befriended him, he accepted the invitation for the meeting at this crossroads of his career.

The chivalric sense of gratitude, not unrelated to vanity, which was natural to Jones sometimes prejudiced his reason when he received appreciation and praises from the lips of the powerful. Russia was seemingly powerful; and De Simolin, who was also personally well-disposed to liberalism in France, represented this Russian prestige. "M. de Simolin said the most polite and obliging things to me," Jones himself related rather naïvely; "that having known me well by reputation while he was Ambassador in England and since he had come to France, he had already proposed me to his sovereign as commander of the fleet in the Black Sea, etc., and that he expected Her Imperial Majesty would make me proposals in consequence. I did not yet look upon the affair as serious; but I was much flattered with the politeness of M. de Simolin, and endeavored to express to him my sense of it."[6] Presumably with unconscious art and no unworthy intention, Littlepage too played even more upon his professional pride, to which he was especially susceptible. "When he [De Simolin] left the house," Jones continued, "Mr. Littlepage assured me that he had written to his Court that if Her Imperial Majesty confided to me the chief command of her fleet in the Black Sea, with *carte blanche,* he would answer for it that in less than a year I should make Constantinople tremble."

The stimulant of professional and personal tribute having been injected into the veins of Jones, De Simolin proceeded to write to Besborodko the Russian Foreign Minister in a politic but at the same time an enthusiastic manner:

"Your Excellency will undoubtedly recall the name of the Chevalier Paul Jones who in the last American war did great and annoying deeds with small means. He is now in Paris and about to go to Copenhagen to settle the accounts of the last American war. He is, in the opinion of everyone, one of the greatest sailors of the time. To rare boldness, valor, and intelligence, he adds a great deal of prudence, circumspection, and disinterestedness, and seeks nothing but glory.

"This sailor is in the prime of life, has very fine manners, and a good fortune before him. But his spirit urges him to great deeds and he sees in our war with the Porte an opportunity to gather new laurels. The Minister of the United States at this Court, Mr. Jefferson, with whom the said Chevalier is on close terms, has sounded him as to his inclinations and confided to me that he prefers the service of the Empress to every other, if Her Imperial Majesty pleases to accord him a rank equal to that of vice admiral in France, which corresponds to that of rear admiral with us. . . .

"Mr. Jefferson, who knows the character of the said Chevalier, pointed out that on great and dangerous missions this officer, who is as spirited as he is disinterested, will be better employed as chief than under the orders of a superior. In the Black Sea this officer will make the Seraglio tremble. The day before yesterday I made the acquaintance of this officer, who delighted me. He confirmed what Mr. Jefferson had told me of his desire to serve our great and august Sovereign by obtaining the rank of rear admiral, leaving the other conditions of his journey to Russia to the good pleasure of the Empress."[7]

Where had the circumspection, recognized by De Simolin himself, now flown? To be sure Jefferson had urged that Jones should receive a separate command, knowing well his history in relation to Hopkins, Simpson, and Landais in the American service and without doubt fearing even worse confederates in the Russian. But Jones himself was disposed to depend upon "the good pleasure of the Empress," tempted by the rank of rear admiral, thinking that this confidence reposed in a sovereign at least as generous as Louis XVI, and trusting to that resourceful spirit of his which, at the failure of other expedients, fell back upon a dauntless valor.

If Jones was eager, the leaders of Russia were not less so. Catherine followed closely, by unofficial as well as official means, the negotiations to secure him for her Navy. Baron Grimm, her ingratiating German correspondent, who eight years earlier had noted at Paris the curious combination in Jones of the hardy warrior and the poet, particularly caused the Empress to bestir herself to win his services. Even her first words to Grimm for engaging the officer convey an impression of the gracious manner as well as the diplomatic subtlety which she could adopt: "Come, come, your recommendations are not so far on the rocks; friend Paul Jones will be well received and welcome; such personages are not refused; but have the kindness not to make a great noise about it, so that no one may prevent our getting him."[8]

Potemkin, also, who for the moment may be described as the foremost companion of Catherine in her private and public life, showed himself somewhat aloof but nevertheless civil and professionally well-disposed. As Commander in Chief of the military and naval forces in the Black Sea, he personified along with the Empress the Russian policies in the wars against the Turks. "I have been informed, sir," he wrote to De Simolin, "of the contents of the despatch which Your Excellency sent to St. Petersburg relative to the desire of the Chevalier Paul Jones to serve Russia, and I know that Her Imperial Majesty is agreeable to his services. . . . Assure the Chevalier Jones that as regards his entrance to the service, I will do all in my power to place him comfortably and to advantage, and that I will certainly procure opportunities for him to turn his abilities and valor to account."[9] The pressing need of Potemkin for Jones undoubtedly promoted his readiness to have him. Perhaps for this reason in particular he affected to be lukewarm himself in describing the attitude of the Empress as "agreeable."

Catherine made the decision to engage Jones within two weeks after the recommendations by De Simolin. Her haste was obviously connected with her realization that Russia was so much opposed by other nations, openly by some and secretly by others, as to endanger her success in securing him. When the prospect of having him matured, De Simolin replied to Potemkin that he was "one of those geniuses whom nature rarely produces." Had it occurred to De Simolin that he might have overreached himself for the purposes of autocratic Russia by his honest praises as well as his flatteries? "Scratch a Russian," said Napoleon, "and you will find a Tartar." If Jones the genius who loved his independence of both speech and action should scratch Potemkin the Russian and Catherine the Russo-German, was it not possible that the one would revert to the Tartar and the other to the Vandal?

◇◇

Chapter LIV

The Comedy in Denmark

THE ASPIRING spirit of Jones was on the wings of his ambition after the interview with the Russian Minister in Paris. The mission to Denmark promised to restrain it only a few short weeks. The claim for the ships, returned by Denmark to Britain, which Landais had sent in the name of the squadron to Bergen in Norway, belonging at that time to Denmark, had less personal meaning to him than the prize money negotiation with France, although Franklin and Congress had represented it as based on a gross violation of international practice. The vindication of his honor in opposition to De Chaumont and in disproof of the charge that the squadron had been a group of privateers was less intimately involved. The funds already reclaimed from France were token of his regard for the interests of his officers and men; the larger amount demanded from Denmark would be welcome enough, but the principle in question was not so immediate to him. It remained true, as Jones often had proved by deed even more than declaration and was disposed to demonstrate in the present instance, that he felt "extremely tenacious of the *honor* of the *American flag.*" But undeniably he now saw this duty, which was also his pride, colored by the flag rank visualized as his in Russia.

When Jones finally departed for Copenhagen on February 5, 1788, he carried with him various letters to forward his negotiations. While the claim against France, however complicated, had been primarily a matter of adjustment and collection, that against Denmark presented the more difficult problem of indemnity for an unfriendly act by a nation which had confessed itself at fault only to the extent of an unacceptable offer of £10,000 for settlement nine years previously.

Although Congress had given Jefferson discretionary powers to

LETTER IN PARTIAL CODE IN THE AUTOGRAPH OF
JOHN PAUL JONES

*This draft was addressed to Thomas Jefferson, the American Minister at Paris,
under the date of March 11, 1788, from Copenhagen. Jones wrote many of his
letters in this fashion, using a small dictionary with numbers written in opposite the words as his code. Courtesy of the Masonic Library, Boston, which
owns this draft.*

choose another envoy for this undertaking, he had accepted Jones without the slightest consideration of an alternate. Indeed the heartiness as well as respect which the successor to Franklin felt towards Jones was rapidly becoming not less than the generous sentiments which his predecessor had shown, however variant they appeared. It was not diplomacy alone for the purpose of having weight with Count de Bernstorff, the Danish Minister for Foreign Affairs, that caused Jefferson to address a letter to him, in the care of Jones, which made clear his own implicit faith, whatever that of Congress might be, in the negotiations entrusted to his agent: "No one could be so adequate to this business as the Commodore Paul Jones, who commanded the squadron which took the prizes. . . . As the natural patron of those who fought under him, whatever shall be satisfactory to him, will have a great right to that ultimate approbation which Congress have been pleased to confide to me."[1]

But with the letter from Congress for the King of France un-delivered in his pocket as well as with another in expectancy of greater import from the Empress of Russia, Jones chafed from the beginning in Copenhagen even as a plenipotentiary. Preoccupation with the new trend of his affairs as a naval officer, in addition to his physical exposure on the journey, may account for the unusual confession to Jefferson in his first message from the Danish capital: "I have been so much indisposed since my arrival here the 4th . . . that I have been obliged to confine myself almost constantly to my chamber. I have kept my bed for several days; but I now feel better and hope the danger is over." It was not a good omen that a warrior of his restless spirit should now be checked by a body which seemed to have lost some of its former hardiness.

Well or ill, haste governed him in Copenhagen, regardless also of the two and one half years which in contrast he had spent during the prize money negotiation in Paris. Almost at once he visited the French Minister to Denmark, Baron de la Houze, with whom he hoped to present a joint claim inasmuch as the squadron had consisted of allied ships. Shortly he saw Count de Bernstorff, who from the outset was as intent upon ignoring the American demand as the envoy became in directing his attention to it. De Bernstorff had a special weapon, his flattery, to parry the pressure of a glory-loving agent; Jones was by no means averse to compliments, as his recent relations with De Simolin attested perhaps too well, but the Danish brand lacking the professional aspect of the Russian had only a temporary hold upon his interest. "I was much flattered with my reception," he admitted to Jefferson; "and our conversation was long and very particular respecting America and the new constitution, of which I presented a copy." But incidental matters aside, he did not fail to add, "It was a day of public business, and I could not do more than present your letter. I shall follow the business closely."

A wide detour by way of the Danish Court seemed to be the most passable road to his financial objective. The French Minister presented him to the King, his family, and the chief personages of Copenhagen. Jones even dined in state with them. The King, as he described, was complaisant, the Prince Royal affable, the Princess Royal charming, and the Queen Dowager civil and attentive. This diplomatic route having been travelled not without satisfaction to his self-esteem and to his regard for the dignity of the United States, he looked to the business sequel.

De Bernstorff of necessity took notice of the claim at length and promised an early decision in answer to the letter delivered from Jefferson and to his own urgent request. When no determination was forthcoming within a few days, Jones reiterated his wishes, reminding the Minister of his promise. His private affairs had now interposed even a greater reason than previously for pressure in terminating the negotiations, although they had scarcely begun. The likelihood of an offer from Russia had turned into reality.

He proceeded, therefore, to inform De Bernstorff on March 24 with importunity tempered by diplomatic flourish in key with his entertainment at the Court: "You must be convinced that circumstances do not permit me to remain here; but that I am under a necessity to return to France, or proceed to Russia. . . . The promise you have given me of a prompt and explicit decision from this Court . . . inspires me with full confidence. . . . I felicitate myself on being the instrument to settle the delicate national business in question with a minister who conciliates the views of the wise statesman with the noble sentiments and cultivated mind of the true philosopher and man of letters."[2] The compliments could not offset the disadvantage of a claimant who was in haste to end the negotiations. It was apparent that Jones was more intent upon a decision than upon success. De Bernstorff was prepared to avail himself of his strategic position.

While waiting impatiently for the Danish Minister to act, Jones made little pretense at bargaining for conditions at his entrance in the service of Russia. A courier from St. Petersburg had already arrived at Copenhagen in the latter part of March, bringing the offer from the Empress. The Russian Minister to Denmark, Baron de Krudener, presented it to Jones with "the most flattering expressions." The praises of De Krudener were indeed even more designed to lure Jones than those of De Simolin: "My sovereign will learn with pleasure the acquisition which she has made in your great talents. I have her commands for your acceptance of the grade of captain commandant, with the rank of major general, in her service, and that you should proceed as soon as your affairs permit; the intention of Her Imperial Majesty being to give you a command in the Black Sea, and under the orders of Prince Potemkin, from the opening of the campaign. The immortal glory by which you have illustrated your name cannot make you indifferent to the fresh laurels you must gather in the new career which opens to you. I have the honor of being on this occasion the interpreter of those sentiments of esteem with which for a long period your brilliant exploits have inspired Her Imperial Majesty. Under a sovereign so magnanimous, in pursuing glory you need not doubt of the most distinguished rewards, and that every advantage of fortune will await you."[3]

In these honeyed phrases came the invitation from Catherine, and Jones could not find it in his heart to do otherwise than accept. His chivalry towards those who honored him, in this instance a woman as well as a sovereign, had its influence. If he forbore, at the same time, to make stipulations, his experience impelled him to emphasize the justice of the standing to which he aspired and the particular importance in his case of an undisputed separate command.

Foresight and even prophecy governed his reply to De Krudener, intended for the Empress herself: "The very favorable sentiments with which my zeal for the cause of America, rather than my professional skill, has inspired Her Imperial Majesty fills me with an

COPY OF THE PHOTOSTAT OF JOHN PAUL JONES' APPOINTMENT AS A CAPTAIN BY CATHERINE THE GREAT

The signature is that of Catherine. By virtue of a later document Jones hoisted his flag as a Rear Admiral in command of the Russian squadron in the Liman. (From the John L. Senior Moscow Papers in the Naval Academy Museum)

Order to our Admiralty College:

Having admitted Captain-Commander Paul Jones to our service, we have graciously commissioned him as Captain of our Navy with the rank of Major-General, and we have ordered him assigned to our Black Sea Navy, and to that effect we have issued an order to General Field Marshal Prince Potemkin Tavrickesky.

[Ekaterina]
Catherine

St. Petersburg,
February 15, 1788.

irresistible desire to merit the precious opinion with which Her Majesty deigns to honor me. . . . You will discover, I presume, that my talents have been considerable; but that, loving glory, I am perhaps too much attached to honors, though personal interest is an idol to which I have never bowed the knee. The unbounded admiration and profound respect which I have long felt for the glorious character of Her Imperial Majesty forbids the idea that a sovereign so magnanimous should sanction any arrangement that may give pain at the outset to the man she deigns to honor with her notice, and who wishes to devote himself entirely to her service. A conjoined command is hurtful, and often fatal in military operations. There is no military man who is so entirely master of his passions as to keep free of jealousy and its consequences on such occasions. Being an entire stranger, I have more to fear from a joint authority than any officer in Her Majesty's service. But I cannot conceive that Her Majesty could deem it expedient to *divide the command* in the Black Sea."[4] These were only words; the die was already cast.

If Jones had been disposed to act more slowly, relying in particular upon Jefferson to negotiate in his behalf, he might have stood, at least in theory, on more solid ground at the threshold of Russia. The terms of the appointment had been under the supervision of De Simolin as well as De Krudener. Jones did qualify his acceptance of the offer from the latter to the extent that he proceeded in addition to inform Jefferson: "There seems, however, to remain some difficulty respecting the *letter* of M. de Simolin's proposal, though it is accepted, in substance, with an appearance of great satisfaction." He was fully alive to his step, notwithstanding "an irresistible desire to merit the precious opinion with which Her Majesty deigns to honor me." Still the scale weighed so heavily in favor of Russia that he not only had made his unalterable decision but also prepared to put it into speedy effect in the face of the unfinished Danish negotiations. "I find myself," he explained further to Jefferson, "under the necessity of setting out for St. Petersburg, through Sweden, in a few days instead of returning first, as was my wish and intention, to Paris. I hope in the meantime to receive a satisfactory answer [from Denmark], which I shall duly communicate to you."

De Bernstorff remained artfully silent. Jones was like a bridled horse, stamping for the race. A successful issue to the claim, which the negotiations of Franklin had not achieved and which had now pended almost a decade, required patience even in the most skilful of agents. But that quality was not evident in the message which Jones sent to the Danish Minister on March 30, a week after he had already received the appointment from Russia: "Your silence on the subject of my mission from the United States to this Court leaves me in the most painful suspense; the more so as I have made Your Excellency acquainted with the promise I am under, to proceed as soon as possible to St. Petersburg. This being the ninth year since the three prizes reclaimed by the United States were seized upon in the port of Bergen, in Norway, it is to be presumed that this Court has long since taken an ultimate resolution respecting the compensation demanded by Congress. I have remarked, with great concern, that you have never led the conversation to the object of my mission here. A man of your liberal sentiments will not, therefore, be surprised or offended at my plain dealing when I repeat that I impatiently expect a prompt and categorical answer in writing. . . . Both my duty and the circumstances of my situation constrain me to make this demand in the name of my sovereign, the United States of America. . . . You are too just, sir, to delay my business here; which would put me under the necessity to break the promise I have made to Her Imperial Majesty, conformable to your advice."[5]

That De Bernstorff took advantage of Jones' position, not without craftily recommending the Russian offer at this time to further his advantage, does not imply that he would have failed to find another avenue of escape. Addressed in categorical terms, he now glossed over the issue with effusive compliment and sheer subterfuge. In spite of the years which had passed since the claim was first made, he had the assurance to say in his reply of April 4: "Nothing can be further from the plans and wishes of His Majesty than to let fall a negotiation which has only been suspended in consequence of circumstances arising from the necessity of maturing a new situation, so as to enlighten himself on their reciprocal interests, and to avoid the inconvenience of a precipitate and imperfect arrangement." This diplomatic verbiage was his manner of obscuring the question of indemnity behind the temptation of advantages which might accrue to the United States from a commercial treaty with his country. As Jones with characteristic directness had come to Copenhagen, De Bernstorff arbitrarily claimed that the negotiations should properly be conducted in Paris where they had been begun, but where, ironically, the Ambassador had been elusive. For his final ministerial sleight of hand, he held, notwithstanding the explicit and confiding authority from Jefferson, that it was not possible to negotiate with Jones because "his want of plenipotentiary powers from Congress was a natural and invincible obstacle."

Jones considered his mission at an end. If the period of negotiation had been months instead of weeks, there is no evidence that he would have been more successful. But from the point of view of Denmark, the curtain was not altogether ready to close upon the little diplomatic comedy in Copenhagen. The Court had enacted the prologue; De Bernstorff the Minister had assumed a leading rôle in the play itself; it remained for the Court to present the epilogue. And on the day before Jones was to leave for Russia, a messenger from the Prince Royal came to invite him to participate.

"The Prince Royal," as Jones was to describe the scene, "had desired to speak with me in his apartment. His Royal Highness was extremely polite, and after saying many civil things, remarked that he hoped I was satisfied with the attentions that had been shown to me since my arrival and that the King would wish to give me some mark of his esteem.

" 'I have never had the happiness to render any service to his Majesty.'

" 'That is nothing; a man like you ought to be excepted from ordinary rules. You could not have shown yourself more delicate as regards our flag, and every person here loves you.'

"I took leave without farther explanation. I have felt myself in an embarrassing situation on account of the King's patent, and I have as yet made no use of it. . . ."

On the part of Denmark, the obtrusion of the patent, granting him fifteen hundred crowns annually, was consistent with the subterfuge of the Minister towards Jones. And the future attitude of the country towards payment both of the pension to him and of the claim of the United States was to be such as might have been expected on the basis of the past.

As to Jones, the acceptance of the pension in his half hour with the Prince Royal, whatever its extenuating circumstances, was perhaps one of the most compromising acts of his life. Still it has been misrepresented as to both his motives and the situation. If the patent was offered as a bribe, the means did not serve the end as far as he was concerned. The presentation of it was to all appearances *after* the close of the negotiations with him—not, as has been said, *at the same time* as the ending of them. The termination, moreover, was in effect not Jones' but De Bernstorff's; and all the letters between them, which the envoy transmitted to Jefferson, confuted the slightest suspicion of a hidden purpose. Although Jones failed to mention the proposed patent to the American Minister at this period on the eve of his departure for Russia, he did not make any effort for a long time to draw upon the gift following its receipt a few days after his later arrival in St. Petersburg. And before any step for this purpose, he was to give further thought to its propriety.[6]

The temporary weakening of Jones' sense of fitness under the influence of egoism, inflated by the blandishments of the Russian Ministers and the Danish Court, especially the Prince Royal, had rendered him the more susceptible to temptation. These fine words had reached their height in such expressions as "A man like you ought to be excepted from ordinary rules" and "Every person here loves you." Flattery tendered to himself sometimes assumed in his ears a sincere complimentary ring. The effect of the beguiling attentions upon his vanity was characteristically evident, regardless of regret at the failure of the negotiations, in a final message on April 8 from Copenhagen to Jefferson: "I have, however, the melancholy satisfaction to reflect that I have been received and treated here with a distinction far above the pretensions of my public mission." In short, along with his public trust, he saw himself in a private light not without complacency; and in this view he allowed his thoughts to be not the less faithful to the United States but the more preoccupied with that personal recognition which he accepted as only his due. Yet none understood better than he himself the measure of his weakness—and at the same time of his strength which freed it from harm: "Loving glory, I am perhaps too much attached to honors, though personal interest is an idol to which I have never bowed the knee."

With his face turned towards Russia, Jones had little time or inclination to meditate over the patent. He did not fail, however, in this last message to Jefferson from Copenhagen to review his mission to Denmark. The envoy made clear, what might readily have been forgotten, that although the business remained uncompleted he had been in Copenhagen at his own expense, and that the failure of Congress to allow him plenipotentiary powers had afforded De Bernstorff his chief pretext for setting aside the negotiation. It was also not a vain or presuming thought which, considered in the light of his success as prize money agent in France, now caused him to remark to the American Minister: "While I have the consolation to hope that the United States will derive solid advantages from my journey and efforts here, I rest perfectly satisfied that the interests of the brave men I commanded will experience in you parental attention and that the American flag can lose none of its lustre, but the contrary, while its honor is confided to you." It remains that, however earnest were to be the efforts of the Minister to fulfill these final wishes for "parental attention" to the interests of his affectionately remembered *Bonhomme Richard* sailors, only Jones could probably have won their prize money in Denmark as he had already won their due in France —by fighting for it.

Part 7

The Rear Admiral in Russia

Chapter LV

The Advocacy by Jefferson and the Dash to Russia

J ONES SOUGHT the good offices of Jefferson particularly in support of his drastic step as a citizen of the United States entering the service of a foreign power. "I ask for nothing," he wrote to him from Denmark; but one of his hints was broad enough. "If Congress should think I deserved the promotion that was proposed when I was last in America, and should condescend to confer on me the grade of rear admiral from the day I took the *Serapis,* I am persuaded it would be very agreeable to the Empress. . . ." Again his modesty seemed more affected than real; still, to his credit, Congress had tried his patience long enough by having since 1781 twice considered and unaccountably set aside his advancement to this rank.

A further request, indeed an entreaty, transcended considerations of his standing and mirrored the warrior who had fought for America simply because he loved her. Now, at the moment of leaving for Russia, he felt poignantly the conflict between his previously uninterrupted service under one flag and his anticipated war activities under another. Jones realized too that, apart from the approval of an eminent American like Jefferson, he had not secured in his haste the express permission of the United States to accept the offer of Russia, although on two previous occasions he had taken pains to solicit the consent of Congress even for the purpose of embarking for experience with the fleets of France in time of peace. "Yet America is independent, is in perfect peace, has no public employment for my military talents," he reasoned. "But why should I excuse a conduct which I should rather hope would meet with general approbation?" With eloquence of passion he further urged upon Jefferson: "While I express, in the warm effusion of a grateful heart the deep sense I feel of my eternal obligation to you, as the author of the honorable prospect that is now before me, I must rely on your friendship to justify to the United States the important step I now take, comfortable to your advice. You know I had no idea of this new fortune when I found that you had put it in train before my last return to Paris from America. I have not forsaken a country that has had many disinterested and difficult proofs of my steady affection; and I can never renounce the glorious title of *a citizen of the United States!*"[1]

Jefferson was faithful to this trust reposed in him. The common affection of the statesman and officer for their country strengthened the bond between them. The Minister did not fail to write in his behalf to Americans in highest authority.

"I am glad our Commodore Paul Jones has got employment, and heartily wish him success," Washington was to reply from Mount Vernon to the American Minister in Paris. "His new situation may possibly render his talents and services more useful to us at some future day. I was unapprised of the circumstances which you mention that Congress had once in contemplation to give him promotion. They will judge now how far it may be expedient."[2]

The Minister set forth in full the position of Jones to Secretary for Foreign Affairs Jay. He did not commit himself but revealed clearly enough his favor: "The Empress has engaged Commodore Paul Jones in her service. He is to have the rank of rear admiral, with a separate command, and it is understood that he is in no case to be commanded. He will probably be opposed to the Capitan Pacha in the Black Sea. He received the invitation at Copenhagen, and as the season for commencing the campaign was too near to admit time for him to ask and await the permission of Congress, he accepted the offer, only stipulating that he should be always free to return to the orders of Congress whenever called for, and that he should not be expected to bear arms against France.

"He conceived that the experience he should gain would enable him to be more useful to the United States, should they ever have occasion for him. It has been understood that Congress has had it in contemplation to give him the grade of rear admiral from the date of the action of the *Serapis,* and it is supposed that such a mark of their approbation would have a favorable influence on his fortune in the North."[3]

To Colonel Carrington of Virginia, who it is recalled had been most influential in the confirmation by Congress of the prize money settlement in France, Jefferson showed himself an outspoken advocate of Jones as the American naval leader of the future: "I wish it corresponded with the views of Congress to give him the rank of rear admiral from the taking of the *Serapis*. I look to this officer as our great future dependence on the sea, where alone we should think of ever having a force. He is young enough to see the day when we shall be more populous than the whole British dominions and able to fight them ship to ship. We should procure him then every possible opportunity of acquiring experience."[4]

However indecisive Congress might continue to be because of partisan politics, the present influence and the future power of Jefferson held the highest possibilities for Jones when the United States was to establish her Navy. Not even Franklin had been so interested and active in promoting his career.

In the meantime that career, not without the recommendation of a statesman as astute as Jefferson, called him to Russia without further delay. And why not Russia, he reasoned, he whose fearlessness and circumspection in war had been equal to every emergency, despite the absence of certainty as to the pivotal conditions of a rank and a command which should leave him free from the entanglements of divided authority and disputed responsibility? Russia, in the person of Catherine, had been the patron even of literary geniuses like Voltaire. Russia had been friendly towards the Masons. Russia had been indeed the leader in that movement towards freedom of the seas, aimed especially against Britain, which had assumed the benevolent face of the Armed Neutrality. Even more, Catherine awaited him, he was informed. The chivalrous Jones could not refrain at least from going to St. Petersburg "to thank the Empress for the favorable opinion she had conceived of me."

His bridges behind him to America having been cared for with affection as well as expediency, he was not the man to keep the Empress waiting. He had intended and wished to return first to

Paris. But he forbore even to see again Madame T—, whose silence during his last stay in the United States had made "even honors insipid."

The swiftest dash possible to Russia was now his aim. The route by Paris would have been the most roundabout of all. Even that through Germany was too circuitous for him. From Copenhagen he went as directly as possible to Stockholm, regardless of some difficulties placed in his way by Elliot the English Minister who during the Revolution had "filched Dr. Lee's papers in Berlin." At Stockholm he stayed only one night, and want of time prevented him, as he said, from appearing at the Court.

His choice was the shortest passage, like that the crow flies, to St. Petersburg by way of the Gulf of Bothnia. But the ice barred him from the outset at the port of Gresholm, above the Swedish capital, from which he hoped to bridge the passage to Finland by the Aland Islands. He made several attempts by boat, but all his efforts were unavailing. He considered the overland route along the east side of Sweden and the west of Finland, but the condition of the roads rendered it impracticable. The sailor turned again to his element the sea in challenge to every obstacle.

At Gresholm for the second time, he hired two boats, both undecked, the larger thirty feet long and the smaller half that size. He engaged, too, some Swedish sailors, not telling them his purpose. He did not fail to have with him, in addition to a small compass in the larger boat, the lamp of his travelling carriage and his pistol.

At dawn he again tried several times to make the direct crossing eastward, but the floes barred him from gaining even the first island. He then steered for the south, keeping along the coast of Sweden the rest of the day as with difficulty he found room enough to pass between the ice and the shore. He gave the boatmen no inkling of any plans more hazardous.

Pistol in hand, towards night he compelled the astounded sailors to steer to the east and enter the crashing ice in the Baltic Sea regardless of their frail craft. Now the second boat served its purpose. When the floes made the way of the larger impassable, all the men entered the smaller and dragged the larger over the caked ice; when in turn the smaller was blocked, the expedient was reversed. The wind was fair, and he hoped to land in Finland the next day. But as they approached the distant shore now in sight, the expanse of solid ice again barred the passage. If it was impossible to reach Finland by this route, it was equally impossible because the wind was strong and directly adverse to regain the Swedish side.

No decisive course remained except to circle the ice to the south in order to make for the Gulf of Finland. He chose this expedient and settled down to the fight with nature and the possible defiance of the men. He kept his pistol always at hand. To chart his new route the better, he fixed in position his travelling lamp on this second night so as to throw a gleam upon the compass. In the darkness the smaller boat crashed and sank, but the men in it escaped to the larger. Two additional nights as well as days followed in the one open boat, which, surviving with difficulty the fate of the other, completed at last a circuitous journey of four to five hundred miles to Esthonia.

The four nights and days passed in vigilance over his boatmen and in endurance of intense cold were probably his greatest test of sheer physical courage. His unrecovered health on the occasion doubled the abandon of the exploit. He had confessed to Jefferson before his departure from Copenhagen that he still felt the effects from his "inexpressible sufferings" due to his exposure on the journey to Denmark. It is inconceivable that he did not feel with greater poignancy this repeated, deeper shock to his constitution. But whatever were the effects, he now chose to seal his lips.

Jones landed at Revel in Esthonia, favorably situated for his short, final journey to St. Petersburg, at which he arrived on April 23, 1788. He paid the men liberally for their undreamt-of services and for the loss of their boat; he likewise provided them with a good pilot and with provisions for the homeward passage, which they were to undertake when conditions became favorable. At Revel he was made aware of the amazement with which the natives looked upon his performance. No one had ever shown the hardihood to attempt, let alone the genius to achieve, such a feat except in large vessels. It was considered "a kind of miracle."[5] But this was only a token of the warrior's zeal and powers in the name of Catherine of Russia.

Chapter LVI

◇◇

Catherine the Russo-German
Prepares for War

CATHERINE II of Russia, so-called the Great—who was she that Jones should aver: "If my heart had not been enlisted for Her Majesty, I would never have drawn my sword in her cause"? In the setting of eighteenth century Russia, she bore sway over the vast conglomerate empire molded principally by the military aggression of its Germanic founders from Scandinavia, the ruthless cruelty of its assimilated invaders the Asiatic Tartars, the superstitions of its adopted Greek Orthodox Church, and the typical Eastern treachery and plunder of its Muscovite despots. The Court of Catherine at St. Petersburg remained at best, beneath a veneer of European liberalism and culture, semi-Oriental and semi-barbaric. The shallow influence of refinements from the West, in particular from Germany and France, reluctantly accepted by the nation through the determined policy of Peter the Great, found its most conspicuous exponent in Catherine, herself a German by birth, when after two generations she followed him on the throne.

What raimant of royal splendor, what jewels of Eastern brilliance, what allurement of Oriental feminine graces, what domination of autocratic power were not on parade to dazzle each new arrival at the Court and to flatter the latest newcomer into believing that his reception was the most notable of all. With the rôle of the designing woman in the absolute sovereign, Catherine the German actress entered upon her Russian stage to extend her welcome to Jones.

No flatteries to the vanity of Catherine could be greater than the manner in which the officer had sped to her, spurred as he had been because "the Empress expected me from day to day." How

madly inspired his exploit was and how fitting it seemed for a
Leander who swam the Hellespont to his Hero rather than for
even a death-defying warrior, must have been transparent to this
woman who, regardless of her age, gloried in personal supremacy.
Although in retrospect Jones was to confess, "I would not re-
attempt my passage from Gressalham to Revel, under like circumstances, for a thousand times the sum I received and spent in her
service,"[1] in her presence the price seemingly was cheap to him.

He had his first audience with the Empress on April 25, the
second day following his arrival, when Count de Ségur, now the
French Minister to Russia and formerly a volunteer in the
American Revolution, presented him to her. During the next
twelve days at St. Petersburg, he enjoyed her special attentions as
well as those of the Court in general. And she did not fail to remove
his concern as to rank by showing him that, after her earlier order
of February 15 to Potemkin, she had issued a later one of April 4:
"We graciously command that as soon as the Captain of our fleet,
Major General Paul Jones, presents himself before you, he be
given the rank of rear admiral and be employed in accordance with
your best judgment in the Black Sea fleet."[2]

Jones refrained from setting any conditions. She addressed him,
he once said, as if to inspire the trust given to a mother. She impressed him with the seeming riches of her vast empire. She
moved him, too, by her personality as a woman. "I shall never be
able to express," he confided, "how much greater I find her than
fame reports. With the character of a very great man, she will
be always adored as the most amiable and captivating of the fair
sex."[3] It was less Jones the canny, circumspect warrior than Jones
the warm-hearted man dedicated to his new loyalty who further
described his association with the Empress before he turned to the
Black Sea: "I was entirely captivated, and put myself into her
hands without making any stipulation for my personal advantage.
I demanded but one favor, 'that she would never condemn without hearing me.' "[4] Pliant as he was in her presence, this one seemingly modest request, which ordinarily would not have required
the asking, might be considered the wisest and most daring that he
could have made. It was in effect a challenge for freedom of speech
and of the press and for impartial trial by court—none of which
could be assumed in Russia.

But her apparent marked anxiety in his behalf made him feel that any suspicion, even in Russia, would be ungrateful. The guardedness against a divided or subordinate command which he had earlier shown during his discussion of terms with De Simolin and De Krudener had become thoroughly known to her. Now he was too favorably disposed either to turn back or even to insist upon any explicit agreement in this essential matter. Yet potential difficulties as a foreign and unfriended officer appeared from the beginning. His arrival became the signal for English officers in the service of the Russian Baltic fleet, who had heard a report that he was to be their commander, to announce that they would resign their commissions rather than serve under him. Such assertiveness in Russia, unheard of among native if not foreign officers, terminated peacefully, however, because the Scotch Admiral Greig remained as one of the commanders of the fleet in the North and Jones had been assigned from the outset to that in the South.

Whatever real difficulties might be in the making, the gracious assurances of Catherine seemed to smooth them away. Just before his departure for the Black Sea, the Empress sent him a message enclosing another concerning the professions of good will from Potemkin: "As I believe that this letter may help to confirm to you what I have already told you verbally, I have sent it, and beg you to return it, as I have not even made a copy be taken, so anxious am I that you should see it. I hope that it will efface all doubts from your mind and prove to you that you are to be connected only with those who are most favorably disposed towards you. I have no doubt but that on your side you will fully justify the opinion which we have formed of you, and apply yourself with zeal to support the reputation and the name you have acquired for valor and skill on the element in which you are to serve."[5]

With Jones on his way to the Black Sea on May 7, Catherine could retire for the present from the stage where her part was "to make a striking impression" and enter her dressing room to put aside her disguises as far as he was concerned. It was the second recent occasion, on a scale more complex than the first in Denmark, that Jones had found himself an unsuspecting actor in what may be considered a private theatrical performance. As the Empress was already fifty-nine years old, it may be supposed that the rôle for her ambitions of a public nature was as practiced as that of her well-known personal vanities. Divesting herself in some measure, perhaps now that her audience had departed, of the one along with the other, she could see her life as it was with more than usual candor offset by the fearless openness of such a person as Jones. In her mental mirror she must have stumbled across at least a few obstacles in its hidden closet of memories, not to be sure because of her conscience but the further pursuit of her policies. She could be no exception to the intrusion of thoughts, if only for a moment, which bore intimately upon her past and future.

They told of the arrogance, evident in her hostile distended lips, heavy-set jaw, and long blunt nose, and of the treachery, reflected in her veiled and even furtive eyes—features which had developed their particular cast while she usurped the Russian throne, held it against all rivals regardless of right or wrong, and extended its sway with unsated lust for power. There was her deep-laid conspiracy leading to the murder of her husband, the Emperor Peter III, over whose living as well as dead body she had seized the Government with her stout arms. There was her imprisonment of the lawful inheritor of the empire, Ivan Antonovich, who died conveniently for her at a desperate attempt to escape after almost a crazed lifetime of suffering. There was even her unnatural cruelty towards her son Paul, deprived as he was not only of the rule of Russia but also of his freedom and domestic peace.

Abroad, not less than at home, her deeds had been of the same color. Westward against Poland, northward against Sweden, eastward and southward against Turkey, her course was marked by incitement of internal conflict so as to provide her with pretexts for intervention and seizure of territory. In Poland her greed had only been whetted by the First Partition of 1772. She had placed upon the throne of this traditional enemy a discarded lover, Stanislas Poniatowski, who was to serve as a puppet for her future machinations. As for Sweden, she had bribed and fomented dissensions among the nobles, who were to be of timely help to her in the approaching war with Gustavus III. Against Turkey, her double-faced aggressions in the name of Orthodox Christianity had succeeded especially in accordance with her plotting and encouraged her to pursue them more boldly. In her designs upon Georgia, she had won the great victory of Tchesme by the skill of foreign naval officers, who received little credit for it. In laying her grasping hands upon the Crimea, she had gained ascendancy over the rival Turks by setting up a khan of her choice, granting him large estates in Russia, overrunning the region with her soldiery, and assimilating it in her great maw. As the digestion was to her taste, she began to look beyond from the new vantage point by the Black Sea.

Behind the warfare of the Empress lay her strategy of inviting other countries to participate in the spoils, behind her corruption of these nations hid her betrayal of them, and behind this treachery smirked her religious and moral professions. She, the Machiavellian woman and the German, taught even her adopted Russia as well as Europe in general the later conceptions of the Balance of Power, which undertook to justify the seizure of the weaker nations by the stronger, provided that the division of the spoils among the interested aggressors was on an equitable basis.

Even her liberal theories of government and her patronage of the arts had been first a plaything and then a business, and were finally becoming a sham. As an obscure princess in a petty German duchy and as the wife of Peter before her usurpation, it had been pleasing to contemplate distantly the republican theories of Montesquieu. After she had clambered upon the throne, it served to gloss her reputation in the West to patronize French authors; it was "useful," as she herself revealed, "to have such acquaintances." And now when American Independence had been achieved and the French Revolution showed its first signs of birth, her subjugation of the Russian serfs to the meanness of slaves, her expulsion of Masonry from her borders, her exile and torture of Russian liberal writers were in process of realization.

The very compliments of the beneficiaries who hungered for her roubles but remained little interested in her company were often left-handed and not infrequently venomous. Voltaire said, "France persecutes the philosophers and the Scythians patronize them"; and again, "What is one to do? We must needs take our friends as they are, with all their defects." Diderot turned from gross flatteries to the deepest rancour: "The most dangerous enemy of a ruler is his wife, if she can do anything but bear children." D'Alembert, invited to come to Russia, dipped his pen in vitriol: "In that country it is too easy to die of a colic." But none of these repulsed her bribes in following a consistent path as tellingly as the Comte de Turpin who replied: "The medal could not be accepted by the Comte de Turpin were it worth a hundred thousand ecus. My principles and those of all French gentlemen would not permit me to receive any present from a foreign power."[6]

The thoughts of Catherine turned more pleasurably to contemplate the glittering promise of the future than the obtrusive shadows of the past. This future happened to follow the road which Jones had taken to the Black Sea. The Empress herself, less than a year and a half earlier, had travelled in reality most of the same route which on occasion she must have retraced in imagination.

Her ambitions had become audacious. Following her first Turkish war, she had absorbed the Crimea and gained a foothold on the shores of the Sea of Azov. Now her goal was not merely the adjacent regions to the west but more particularly the lands of the Porte across the Black Sea. For this dream she had the vanity of Potemkin as well as her own to excite all her arts and arrogance. Potemkin himself was to become the ruler of Dacia, a kingdom to be seized comprising Moldavia, Wallachia, and Bessarabia. The Empress already had decorated him with the title of "the Tauricien" for overrunning the Crimea (Taurida) with fire and steel, and for the conquest in contemplation she intended piously to honor him with the rank of a prince of the Holy Roman Empire.

But Potemkin and Dacia were the lesser of the two links which she prepared to weld with mendacity not less hypocritical than ruthless. For the greater link, her second grandchild born in 1779, whom she had named Constantine and now spoke of in anticipation as Constantine II and whom she had provided with a Greek nurse and proclaimed with classic poems, was destined by her to rule over Constantinople and the Greek mainland as a Christian emperor in the line of Constantine I. And although she blandly gave assurances that neither the one nor the other realm should form part of Russia, Catherine the benevolent meant to hold sway over a new Holy Roman Empire and be the so-called defender of Eastern Christendom.

Her pretentious excursion from St. Petersburg to Sevastopol, the furthermost point of her dominions in the South, had been outwardly a festive tour but subtly a political manœuvre that marked the beginning of her second Turkish War to satiate her predatory lusts. The showmanship was admirable. An untold number of serfs performed the labor of building the scenic background not only without a rouble for wages but at the cost of long abandonment and decay of their distant homes. Potemkin was the slave driver who cracked the whip over them and their families. Catherine assumed the rôle of actress after the manner of Cleopatra.

The cortège set out with 15 carriages, 124 sledges, and 40 supplementary vehicles. Her own carriage had 30 horses, and 560 were in readiness at each post. Accompanying her were the Ministers de Ségur from France, Fitzherbert from England, and Cobentzel from Austria; the Chamberlain of Austria, the Prince de Ligne; and Momonoff, the twelfth of her lovers, euphemistically called favorites, with whom she lived unabashed, sometimes with a strict public decorum and sometimes with a license which prompted even the blasé Russian Court to marvel.

Along the route, the combined political and social galaxy grew in size and distinction. The Emperor Joseph of Austria arrived, despite his determination to stay away, travelling in his favorite guise as Count Falkenstein. King Stanislas Poniatowski of Poland, Catherine's long discarded second lover changed into her present political vassal, also saw fit to come. Of course Nassau-Siegen, the satellite of court and camp, and Potemkin, who was responsible for the expedition, were conspicuously present.

The holiday spirit presided over by Catherine was intoxicating to her flatterers. Although she remained soberly intent upon pushing every political advantage, the personal homage was also immeasurably pleasing to her feminine vanity. "Her vanity must be tickled," said Joseph; "her vanity is her idol; boundless luck and the extravagant flattery of all Europe have turned her head; one must go with the crowd."[7] To please and impress her, Potemkin as the showman had created along the imperial itinerary kaleidoscopic, fantastically conceived illusions of fertile lands instead of deserts; prosperous, contented natives in their villages instead of miserable burlaks droning their mournful songs on the Volga; idyllic gardens and grottos and illuminated mountains instead of desolate plains. With a measure of truth, however highly colored his palette was prone to be, De Ségur painted his impressions: "From fairyland I should not have been able to see, as in our triumphal and story-like procession, at each moment new objects of wonder—fleets suddenly created, squadrons of Cossacks and Tartars from the depths of Asia . . . enchanted palaces, temples of Diana, alluring harems, nomadic tribes, camels and dromedaries wandering in the desert . . . dethroned princes of the Caucasus, persecuted kings of Georgia, all, offering their homage and their prayers to the Queen of the North."[8]

The display was the greatest when the cortège embarked upon a fleet of ornamented galleys on the Dneiper and sailed in triumph as far as the Russian stronghold of Kherson. At this stage, before the intended passage to the Black Sea, were signs in Greek: "The Road to Constantinople." Not less significant was a squadron of Turkish warships on guard beyond the river's mouth, near territory including the fort of Oczakow still possessed by the Sultan, which abruptly interrupted this route by sea. But the overland course remained open across the Crimea to Sevastopol, at which a Russian fleet lay not alone for parade. The ostentation of the passage on the Dnieper excelled even the earlier journey over the plains, just as the rococo descriptions of the Prince de Ligne tended to greater exaggerations than those of the Prince de Ségur: "The gauzes, lace, trimmings, garlands, pearls, and flowers which adorned the curtains of the pavilions erected on the bank of Her Majesty's vessel looked as if they came from the *Traits Galants* shop in the Rue St. Honoré; they were the work of the Russian soldiers who are turned into dressmakers . . . or what you will by the touch of a rod."

"The touch of a rod" and the well-known superstitions of Potemkin, this magician, were of the same hollow mockery. His supposed miracles have made the term "Potemkin's villages" synonymous with sham splendor. Such transformations as he achieved on the desert steppes, said one onlooker, "were caused by tyranny and terror, and will entail the ruin of several provinces." "Everything seems easy when money and lives are squandered," said another. "The master orders; the bands of slaves labor. They are paid little or nothing; they are badly fed; they do not dare to let escape a murmur and I know that for three years past, under the new governments, overwork and unhealthfulness of the marshes have killed fifty thousand men while no one pities them and no one even mentions the matter."[9]

To be sure Catherine was too decorous and genteel to do one or the other. She chose, moreover, to humor Potemkin by not seeing beyond the village façades and to assume a manner easy and even gay among her distinguished company. Indeed "the Semiramis of the North" travelling in the direction of a warmer sun appeared to adopt the more expansive nature of her noted Egyptian namesake from the South. Accordingly she was so good humored as to suggest that De Ségur should recite some light verse which he had composed. Knowing something of the history of the Empress and wishing to adapt himself to her spirited mood, the French Ambassador chose a well-bred tale, which was "in truth a little free and gay, but decent enough in its phrases to be well received at Paris by the Duke de Nivernais, by the Prince de Beauvau, and by ladies whose virtue equalled their amiability."[10] The modest Catherine, however, rightly could not tolerate such an offense even to the purity of her thoughts, especially in the very presence of Momonoff, only the twelfth personification of her own virtue. She drew herself up, threw back her head, assumed her most dignified expression, and interrupted De Ségur with a totally irrelevant question.

Certainly she had more weighty matters to occupy her mind beneath the mask of an airy manner. The war brewing against Turkey required her shrewdest foresight, and she now had opportunely at her beck the foreign diplomats and rulers of Europe who were most important for Russia's designs. Catherine wanted to feel confident before invading the territories of the Porte that Poland would not rebel in retaliation for the past while she would be preoccupied, that she could cajole France and England to turn a blind eye towards her brigandage, and that Austria in particular would remain faithful to the alliance with her.

Thus she had King Poniatowski pay homage as a vassal by spending "three months and three million roubles to see the

Empress for three hours." Surrounded by her other international attendants, she subtly tried to probe them. " 'You know,' she exclaimed, as if in innocence, according to the Prince de Ligne, 'that your country, France, without knowing why, always protects the Turks.' Ségur turned pale, Nassau blushed, Fitzherbert yawned, Cobentzel was upset, and I laughed."[11] Her suspicion, lightly uttered but darkly felt, was not less shrewd than prophetic as she searched the faces of the ministers from both France and England. Catherine felt reassured at least regarding the Emperor of Austria, about whom she had long woven her political and personal toils. He knew her for what she was but could not help himself. On the one hand she lured him with the bait of territory and on the other hand flattered his *amour propre*. Potemkin, too, had urged her to turn from Prussia and Frederick the Great with his commonplace nephew, Frederick William, to Austria and the accomplished Joseph, who attracted her the more by travelling incognito and by sleeping in a common tent on a sack of straw. At the same time she bargained with this Joseph concerning lands which belonged to neither of them, planning to give him a sop for his pains and to seize for herself and Potemkin the greater part of the Turkish Empire. And so Catherine prepared to wage a second war against the Porte; the decision once made, she had ready pretexts in the name of the Christian charity which she credited to herself and of the insolence, truly her own, which she attributed to the enemy.

As a suitable close to the tour and introduction to the hostilities, Catherine in coquettish humor seemingly prepared the ground for the appointment of Nassau-Siegen as one of her admirals in reward for his knight errantry. He and the Prince de Ligne, self-confessed "amateurs and perhaps connoisseurs," received her permission, in the assured words of the Chamberlain of Austria, "to go and reconnoitre Oczakow and ten Turkish vessels which . . . have been stationed most unfairly as if to stop our voyage. . . . When she saw their position on the little map that had been made for her, Nassau offered his services to get rid of them. The Empress flicked the paper, smiled, and gave it back to him. I think that was a pretty beginning for the pretty little war which I hope we shall have soon."[12]

After the return of Catherine to St. Petersburg from her journey of state, she soon realized indeed that one knotty problem had been overlooked. It was easier to foment the war than to win it. The recent camouflages of Potemkin, mock bravery of Nassau, and impertinence of De Ligne did not promise to prevail against the Turks. Usually foreign officers gained the victories while Russians and special favorites wore the decorations. In the past, the English had been the actual leaders at Tchesme; in the present, Greig the Scotsman commanded the Baltic fleet—and Jones the American served as her practical solution of the pressing need to change the war in the region of the Black Sea from masquerade to reality.

Jones now arriving at the scene from which Catherine had returned, with his martial spirit the more devoted because of the faith-inspiring reception in St. Petersburg, continued to have comparatively little understanding of this Empress for whom he was to fight. Both the lesser and greater evil deeds at her door and the distant shadows cast by them had been relatively foreign to his immediate observations and his honest if nearsighted objectives in Russia. In characteristic artful and autocratic fashion, the crimes of the Empress within the borders of the country were veiled as much as possible in mystery. Those beyond its confines were recognized none too clearly in a Europe which itself had no squeamish conscience, notably in the case of Prussia and Austria, already the plunderers with her in the First Partition of Poland. Her political ambitions, moreover, especially in the direction of Turkey, were only now rising to their climax.

In St. Petersburg, Jones had been blissfully unaware of the fundamental, uncompromising antagonism between her nature and his. It was certainly not regarding the blackest deeds entombed in the consciousness of the Empress that he could have jarred in particular upon her; it was in other directions that he had struck discordant notes. She must have smiled ostensibly in approval and laughed secretly in autocratic contempt when he had "demanded but one favor, 'that she would never condemn without hearing me.'"

She must have assumed the same attitude when he had become eloquent in praise of democracy and the United States. "I presented the Empress," he was to inform Lafayette, "with a copy of the new American Constitution. Her Majesty spoke to me often about the United States, and is persuaded that *the American Revolution cannot fail to bring about others and to influence every* other government."[13] Ironically, while she had baited her hook, Jones had failed to discern how abysmally divided were his advocacy and her abomination of the American precedent. Apparently he had not known, for example, how Francis Dana, the highly respected envoy sent from the United States to Russia in 1781, had received no recognition of any kind from Catherine, endured subterfuge after subterfuge as he waited at her doors, and crowned his mortification by conforming to a diplomatic custom of adulation for her superlative public and private virtues.[14] Perhaps Jones, too, even in spite of his one demand upon entering her service and his pressing personal reasons, would wait for a hearing in vain.

Further ironical implications were in the same letter to Lafayette. It contained Jones' prophetic warning concerning dangers inherent in the office of President of the United States: "I am glad that the new constitution will be, as you tell me, adopted by more than nine states. I hope, however, they will alter some parts of it; and particularly that they will divest the President of all military rank and command; for though General Washington might be safely trusted with such tempting power as the chief command of the Fleet and Army, yet, depend on it, in some other hands it could not fail to overset the liberties of America. The President should be only the first civil Magistrate. . . . These are not my apprehensions alone, for I have mentioned them to many men of sense and learning since I saw you, and I have found them all of the same sentiment." Such foresight in behalf of the United States, however, failed to be accompanied by a circumspection at all comparable in behalf of his own future in Russia under the dictatorship of the German Empress.

◇◇

Chapter LVII

The Russian Toils Begin
to Close

FACE TO FACE stood Jones, the newly appointed Russian Rear
Admiral, with Potemkin, the Russian Prince Marshal, in
command of all the empire's armed forces against the Turks and
personally at the head of the campaign for the capture of Oczakow,
strategically situated on the Black Sea, near present-day Odessa.
The American, for the first time in a naval service other than
that of his chosen country, had made a twelve days' journey of
almost a thousand miles as speedily as possible across the wild
Russian steppes from the palace of the Hermitage (Sarscosello)
in St. Petersburg to the pretentious but disease-ridden military
depot at St. Elizabeth. The two men scrutinized each other in
anticipation not only of their destined close relationship but even
more of the potential clash between their utterly dissimilar personalities. Jones was to record in the journal of his Russian campaign that the Commander in Chief received him "with much
kindness." He was even to write to Lafayette, urging the patriot
to come to Russia: "You would be charmed with the Prince de
Potemkin. He is a most amiable man, and none can be more
noble-minded."

Was it the extraordinary cunning of this Russian in playing
upon the strings of human nature, whether in the art of love with
Catherine or of insinuating relations with men, that explained
such a surprising description even at the outset? Or was it the
wilful blindness of the American, duped by the Empress, his passion for glory, and his tenacity which knew no retreat, that hid the
truth behind what he wished and found expedient to see? Both
the one and the other influence must have hypnotized him. Mas-

querade and blandishment were to be sure essential expedients behind the monstrous sway of Catherine, the German courtesan, but an erratic primitive force often not less craftily persuasive and commanding was the more strange phenomenon behind the dominance of Potemkin, the aboriginal Russian savage. A French volunteer at the scene of the war, Count Roger de Damas, although not disinterested and therefore favorably disposed towards him, sometimes spoke out with at least a measure of candor: "Potemkin was capable of the most perfect graciousness and courtesy, and of the most morose rudeness and insolence; alternately prompted by his vanity and his heart, he sometimes inspired gratitude, devotion, and hatred at the same moment."[1] What those who owed nothing to and sought nothing from him thought of his insidious complexity is best seen and judged by his life.

Potemkin needed to be scratched very little to reveal himself not merely the proverbial Tartar but also the veritable barbarian who in his self-centered caprice and passion sweeps away all reason and turns to every device of treachery and ruthlessness. The only characteristic which the Russian and the American had in common was that each was typical in a sense of his own country and at the same time strikingly individualistic. Otherwise their traits were as unlike as two links in the chain of human evolution separated by thousands of years.

Jones was of medium build, finely proportioned, lithe and arresting in feature and limb. Potemkin was ungainly in his height, bow-legged, and disfigured by a squint in one eye and blindness in the other, seemingly the result of an arrogant quarrel. Jones had the muscular firmness of a deer and the intellectual tenseness of unflagging concentration upon his profession. Potemkin had the flabbiness of a debauchee and the unreliability of a mind subject to sudden and gross passions. Jones, notwithstanding the rude conditions of a sea life, had a refined sense of personal order and attractiveness, reflected in the art with which he governed the trim of his ships and the good discipline which he instilled as far as lay in his power among his officers and men. Potemkin presented an example of Eastern squalor, which his profusion of diamonds as playthings, his richly-braided uniforms, and his numerous fancy decorations served only to exaggerate in view of his frequently unwashed, uncombed, bare and hairy-legged, slippered and negligently robed, fingernail-biting, and altogether slovenly appearance even before the Empress as well as others of less exalted station. Jones was as frank in his personal relationships as he was subtle and grim in his professional strategy and resolution. Potemkin was as wily and unscrupulous in the one as he had so far shown himself lacking in plan and perseverance in the other. Jones had risen to eminence by unfailing skill and bravery. Potemkin had leaped to power as an accomplice of Catherine and the Orlofs at her seizure of the throne, as the "favorite" who stood apart from all his predecessors and successors by the magnitude of his audacity and cunning, and as the outstanding pander to her lust both of the body and for military conquest. And when his trickery had overreached itself in the attempt to change his position of favorite into that of husband by veiling his ambition behind the pretense of piety, the overthrown pseudo-lover turned all his savage forces to the satisfaction of his avarice, vanity, and despotic will.

It is a just if double-edged compliment to both Potemkin and Catherine to recognize that they had for each other a mental as well as physical attraction. He was "her pupil" whom she had trained for affairs of the empire, "her phenomenon," and "one of the greatest, oddest, and most amusing originalities of this iron age." "This clever fellow," she emphasized, "is amusing as the very devil." As she showed a partiality for him among her thirteen favorites and her other more casual lovers ending in number only with her death, he is most entitled to be considered the male counterpart of her own lawless nature. He resembled her in spirit as she was in the portrait by Lampi before the painter betrayed his art to expediency by smoothing over the hypocrisy of her eyes and especially the sinister wrinkle on her long, blunt nose.[2] He resembled her as she found herself, according to her own admission, despite her celebrated ease and urbanity, a Medusa in the eyes of her salon.[3] He resembled her when she viewed herself the accomplished actress as objectively as on occasion she described him: "He looks like a wolf." It was she who not only made possible but encouraged the life of Potemkin. His career required both the topsy-turvy, brutal, and rapacious orbit of Russia and the more organized German inner orbit of dissimulation and ruthlessness represented by Catherine herself.

De Ségur, the French Minister, did Potemkin no injustice: "He was colossal like Russia. In his mind, as in that country, were cultivated districts and desert plains. It also partook of the Asiatic, of the European, of the Tartarian, and the Cossack; the rudeness of the eleventh century and the corruption of the eighteenth; the polish of the arts and the ignorance of the cloisters; an outside of civilization and many traces of barbarism. In a word, if we might hazard so bold a metaphor, even his two eyes, the one open and the other closed, reminded us of the Euxine always open, and the Northern ocean so long shut up with ice."

Notwithstanding the potential dangers to which Jones was exposed at the hands of Potemkin as well as Catherine, the interests of both dictated a policy that would enable him to exercise his talents. The amiability of the Empress in St. Petersburg had already enlisted his loyalty; the behavior of the Commander in Chief at the American's arrival in St. Elizabeth was ostensibly in the same spirit and had a similar effect. The continuation of such an attitude, however, presented greater early difficulties to Potemkin than to Catherine. He was not less intriguing but more readily swayed by fluctuating emotions. He was prone to be jealous because his military ascendancy was liable to question in the presence of so able an officer as the new Rear Admiral. And first and last he coveted for himself, almost to the exclusion of consideration for others, the crowning honor of the Order of St. George and a dukedom of several conquered provinces.

In so far as he was not secretly prejudiced against Jones, who was the Empress' not his appointee, and to the extent also that he was not too self-absorbed to give thought to him, Potemkin had courtiers, military adventurers, and compatriots ready with their envious persuasions against the foreign Rear Admiral. They swarmed around the Prince Marshal as the personage who, next to the Empress, was most powerful in Russia. Indeed Potemkin's assumption of independence seemed at times to indicate that, at least in his own opinion, he was her equal and even her superior. Not without unconscious truth she playfully addressed him on occasion as "my master." Therefore one of the first and most conspicuous arrivals at St. Elizabeth had been the courtier the Prince de Ligne, who was presuming and self-complacent enough to expect to be a chief of staff of the allied forces, Russian and Austrian, and in particular to rule over Potemkin. Such anticipated power did not fail to include furtherance of the interests of the Prince de Nassau, his relative and close friend, who to be sure had likewise hurried to the Russian military scene.

The cajoleries of De Ligne were not as innocuous as they may seem. He had encouraged the sovereigns of Austria and Russia to enter into their grasping bargain to dismember Turkey, regardless of the watchful eyes of France, Prussia, and Great Britain, and the threat of retaliation by Sweden. Although in the service of Austria as a soldier and pseudo-diplomat, he prided himself upon being an international citizen, seemingly in order both to assume the least responsibility and faithfulness and to gain the greatest rewards. In this practice he had for example Nassau the condottiere. When war had been declared, De Ligne had vowed that it was the greatest happiness of his life. To Catherine, he characteristically expressed himself: "I write not to Your Imperial Majesty, but to a heavenly being." Such adulation was always very acceptable to her vanity, and she proceeded with a cynicism ill-disguised behind her humor to ask this very amenable tool "to play the spy" upon Potemkin, in whom she otherwise pretended to repose the utmost trust. To the unctuous, knee-bending courtier, Catherine and Potemkin were valuable for the objects of the Emperor Joseph and for himself; to Potemkin and Catherine, he was especially serviceable as a pawn for their Austrian interests.

When the news of the coming of Jones had reached the Russian headquarters, it had been to De Ligne an ill wind. As an interloper himself, he feared that the Rear Admiral might be another. And he had also the ambitions of Nassau-Siegen to advance. Thus in an account to the Emperor Joseph, De Ligne referred to Jones sneeringly and attributed to others the malice which he in particular showed in anticipation towards him: "The jealousy felt here at seeing a volunteer—German, French, or Spanish, it matters not—in charge of all this is extreme, and will increase when it becomes known that Potemkin has persuaded the Empress to take Paul Jones into the service of Russia as Major General or Vice-

Admiral. He will arrive here next week; an excellent acquisition, so they say. We shall see; but I think him only a corsair."[4]

Both Nassau and De Ligne were absent from St. Elizabeth during Jones' short stay at the headquarters of Potemkin, and the Commander in Chief said nothing of them. He explained simply to the newly arrived Rear Admiral that it has been his purpose to have him command the fleet at Sevastopol, a recent object of attack by the Turks, but that a new movement of the enemy to reinforce Oczakow determined his present decision to give him command of the naval force intended to oppose one hundred and twenty Turkish war vessels and armed craft now in the estuary of the Black Sea, formed by the rivers Dneiper and Bug, known as the Liman. Jones accepted the change "as a mark of confidence"; indeed at this time he knew neither what he had escaped in the Black Sea at Sevastopol nor what was in store for him in the estuary. The Prince Marshal assured him that he would bring forward his troops without loss of time to coöperate by land with the forces by sea for the capture of Oczakow, and he entrusted to the Chevalier de Ribas, a Spanish member of his staff, the mission to place the Rear Admiral in his command.

On the journey to the Admiralty headquarters at Kherson, Jones learned definitely for the first time from Ribas that Nassau-Siegen had received from Potemkin the commission to head a division of the vessels in the Liman known as the flotilla, which comprised the smaller craft manœuvred by oars and adapted especially to the shallow waters of the estuary, in contrast with the Rear Admiral's squadron of large ships, which dependent on sails presented every difficulty because of the narrow navigable channels and the shoals. It was De Ligne who boasted that the appointment to the flotilla had resulted from his influence. De Ribas assured Jones, however, that "all the forces of the Liman, comprehending those of the Prince de Nassau, would be under his orders."

Not Nassau alone now awoke suspicions in the mind of Jones. He and De Ribas proceeded to Kherson, the arsenal which had beckoned Catherine to Constantinople, but which on the present occasion received him with decidedly less favor. Jones found here Rear Admiral Mordwinoff, the chief of the admiralty, another potential rival whom he had little reason to expect in view of the repeated stipulations made and assurances received for an un-trammeled command. Whether the discipline of the Russian Navy was unworthy of the name or Potemkin and others connived at the challenge, Mordwinoff looked upon the arrival of the American as an affront to him. "He did not affect," said Jones, "to dis-guise his displeasure; and though he had orders from the Prince Marshal to communicate to me all the details concerning the force in the Liman, and to put me in command of the silk flag belong-ing to my rank as rear admiral, he gave himself not the least trouble to comply therewith."

After this inhospitable reception on one day, he proceeded with De Ribas to a mutinous greeting on the next. He set out from Kherson early in the morning to take command of the armament of the Liman, which was at anchor in the roads of Schiroque near the mouths of the Dneiper and Bug Rivers. He went on board his prospective flagship the *Vladimir* (Wolodimer) just when the senior officer, Brigadier Alexiano, had assembled all the com-manders to draw them into a cabal against his authority. "This man," Jones described, "was a Greek by birth, as ignorant of seamanship as of military affairs, who under an exterior and man-ners the most gross, concealed infinite cunning, and by an im-pertinent roughness of discourse had the address to pass for a blunt honest man. Though a subject of Turkey, it was alleged that he made war with the Mussulmans by attacking their com-merce in the Archipelago on his own authority and that he had followed this means of enriching himself." Leaving this former pirate to storm, to threaten that all the other officers would resign if he himself did so, and to represent to Potemkin the sacrifices that he suffered because of the newcomer who was to supersede him, Jones proposed to De Ribas that they should take a small boat to reconnoitre the Turkish positions. He had also in mind "to give time to those angry spirits to become calm" and to afford himself an opportunity to make his plans in the light of the un-promising trend of circumstances. Accordingly, at his return from this first scouting expedition, Jones directly boarded the *Vladimir,* found his officers contented at least in appearance, and hoisted his flag.

It remained for the Rear Admiral to see Nassau-Siegen, whom

he had not met since their slight, unpropitious acquaintance ten years earlier, and to learn the truth as to the appointment, the supporters, and the purpose of this adventurer and courtier in relation to his own command. Even the name of the Prince de Nassau-Siegen was tainted with false appearances as well as his birth with an illegitimate strain. Equally typical of him was his marriage to a Polish woman whose wealth for the repair of his broken fortunes reconciled him to her limitations in personal appearance and to her earlier divorce. Still, to do him justice, her incredible flights of imagination, devoid of even a vestige of common sense, and her self-assurance, however falsely grounded and overbearing, were not in disagreement with his own exaggerated tastes.

"The moment cannon were discharged anywhere, he ran to the noise," the Duke de Levis, a contemporary, described him. "He was everywhere, but his abilities were as ordinary as his boldness was great. His military travels so prompt and rapid resembled to be sure the journeys of paladins, and when he arrived after traversing some five hundred leagues, either returning from or going to battle, everyone expected to see a knight of the Round Table. He appeared and the romance vanished; his presence was a disillusionment. Not the least splendor, not the least brilliance, not even liveliness; his arrival was cold, his manners were common, and his conversation was flat."[5]

The ambitions of Nassau in Russia represented only one of his many ventures, which were practically without thought of the country and the cause; but his present enterprise had possibilities of becoming the most extraordinary in his life, associated as he was to be with Jones, however little the connection pleased the American. He had sailed with Bougainville around the world, an unusual experience in his time, but to Jones was so ignorant as a sailor as not even to have learned the points of the compass. He had directed a French expedition against the island of Jersey, but had both failed to capture his objective and lost his ships seemingly through lack of care after their return to port. He had been in command of the newly invented floating batteries at the Spanish-French attempt to capture Gibraltar, but because of inadequate preparations on his part, as well as other reasons probably beyond his control, had not succeeded in making the breach which had been his boast. He had in his wanderings seduced the Queen of Tahiti—according to his report; this success may be granted to him as in character and as in recommendation to his not ill-assorted wife. Now he was prepared to climax his achievements and to carry Jones with him on their victorious current.

His eagerness to serve Russia was a tribute to his honorable views, as he understood them, of fidelity and disinterestedness. He had initially come to Russia on a diplomatic mission from France in behalf of peace for the Turks but now chose a military appointment from Russia to make war against them. There were personal reasons for the change which so honest a man had to weigh against public considerations.

Nassau had found particular inducements to come to Russia, in which millions of serfs starved but the favored few partook in the scramble for diamonds, ravished territories, and human beings valued at ten roubles per head. Thanks to De Ségur, whose nice moral discrimination sometimes became clouded behind his personal leanings and his love of the picturesque and dramatic, Nassau considered it most profitable to make a pretense of fighting for love of this country. "When I was in Russia," De Ségur later recalled, "true to our sworn fraternity, I obtained for him from the Empress, whom he had never seen and who was even prejudiced against him, the gift of an estate in the Crimea, and permission to transport to the Black Sea under Russian colors the products of his dominions in Poland. Out of gratitude for these favors, he offered to serve Her Majesty against the Turks."[6] And what was the basis of this "sworn fraternity" of earlier years between De Ségur and Nassau? As the former himself could not conceal, it was dishonest and boorish behavior of the latter in Paris, ending in an extravagant duel between them and less deserving a quixotic "sworn fraternity" than an inveterate contempt.

Thus the French Minister had disposed Catherine favorably towards Nassau, although she herself had already written of him to Potemkin: "Strange that you should have taken a fancy to Nassau. He has everywhere the reputation of a crazy fellow." But Nassau was a courtier in his own fashion who had little to learn even from a master like De Ligne. He had exercised his best arts as a flatterer in the favorable atmosphere of the gay journey in the Crimea. He had used to special personal advantage his position as a French envoy, along with De Ségur, who had some scruples to urge the favorite goal of Catherine to achieve a quadruple alliance of France, Spain, Austria, and Russia so that she might be the more free in her designs against Turkey. Such agents, especially those who might be expected to respond politically to gifts of lands, serfs, and other acceptable rewards in which she specialized, were always welcome. And the feminine susceptibilities of the Empress began also to respond favorably to Nassau's exceptional swagger and his good build. She proceeded to encourage him: "I very much love persons who, like you, combine great merit with distinguished valor."[7]

While Catherine had De Ségur to recommend Nassau, Potemkin had De Ligne to exalt him, not to consider Kaunitz and Cobentzel, other Austrian diplomats who seconded their personal friend. The Prince Marshal not less than the Empress considered the possible political value of Nassau in relation to Austria as well as France. Therefore he exercised the more patience, however sceptical-minded, at hearing the vaunts of De Ligne in favor of his fellow-adventurer. De Ligne eulogized Nassau for "his tenacity in negotiation, like the shot of a gun"; for "his reputation, his consideration, and his logic"; for his assured ability to make a successful breach in the fortifications of Oczakow; for his intrepidity. Concerning the last-claimed virtue, De Ligne related at the camp that he owed his life to this brave warrior, who on the very day of arrival had rescued him, as he lay asleep in the sun during a fever, by cutting a snake about to strike into as many as twenty pieces. Not less indeed than twenty pieces, according to the courtier, whose meticulous truth in this detail renders the whole story the more believable and gives the greater credence to a similar, widespread tale that his friend had vanquished a tiger.

Whatever the wily Potemkin thought of such praises of Nassau by his advocate, he had looked about to find a position suitable for him. No one had seemed to relish Nassau as a fellow officer in the Russian Army. The only alternative had been the Navy. It had been remarked that Nassau's "fantastic star, indeed, had almost made a sailor of him, when it led him around the world with

M. de Bougainville. 'Almost a sailor, is he?' answered Potemkin. 'I have something that will suit him then! I'll give him the flotilla and prove to him that there is no other way of employing him so usefully and successfully in the service of our cause and his own vanity.' In another hour the command had been offered and accepted."[8] And so Nassau "almost a sailor," ignorant even of the points of the compass, was to share the naval forces of the Liman with Jones after such a cavalier, fantastic decision typical of both Russia and Potemkin.

Not without premonitions based on his former slight acquaintance with Nassau as well as on his first association with Potemkin, Mordwinoff, and Alexiano, Jones met the newly appointed leader of the flotilla in order to concert operations in the Liman. "You know my esteem and friendship. It will end only with my life," were Nassau's first velvety professions. To be sure he also expressed his fearful determination, in bad French and worse spelling, to advance against the Turks only when Jones protected him. But if a trace of cowardice already escaped from his pen, evidence of his self-assured rivalry was not far behind when he asserted that his command of the flotilla was *carte blanche*.

While De Ribas had given Jones reassurances, Potemkin and De Ligne were the source of his perplexity and disappointment. With the courtier at his elbow, the Prince Marshal had bestowed upon Nassau the unqualified command of the flotilla, adding compliments in regard to his "great experience and generally recognized intrepidity"; and he appears to have justified the appointee's inflated accounts to his wife in Poland, telling of "an absolute authority" and of promises for his employment in "a distinguished rôle." Nor did Nassau fail to inform her at this time, "I am not able to tell you how much I love the Prince Potemkin."[9]

It was the finesse of Potemkin to encourage Nassau in such fashion and to mislead and be silent towards Jones. In any case a divided command was inimical to efficient leadership; in the case of Nassau, whose explosive temperament and naval incompetence were obvious for any capable commander in chief to see, it was courting disaster. And in view of Jones' reiterated efforts to be his own master, especially in a foreign land where he did not even know the language, the policy of the Prince Marshal was the more disingenuous. Having done all in his power by inconsiderateness and design to thwart coöperation, Potemkin soon had the assurance to write him regarding harmony with Nassau: "I regard this concert as the basis of all the good services which your talents and acknowledged courage enable you both to render to my country."

The vessels for the operations in the Liman were to Jones, the expert seaman, not less foreboding than the persons with whom he had to act. And Nassau and Alexiano at once, before the Rear Admiral had time to consider in detail for himself both his means and the navigation dangers of the Liman, did their best to weaken his confidence and mislead his judgment in preparing for the campaign. Balanced against their concern for personal safety in the treacherous waters of the Liman was their artful purpose to lure him into error and to arrogate to themselves the appearance of leadership and the merit of honors.

Considered apart from their motives, however, the representations of these intriguers were scarcely capable of exaggeration. The Russian Navy was in many respects in a worse state than the Army. The latter had at least a tradition of violent, aggressive fighting against neighbors; the former was comparatively alien to an unskilled people within borders which even since the conquests of Peter the Great had been largely land-locked as well as icebound. And even the Navy created by this uncouth Russian giant was characteristically Russian in being more impressive in size than effectiveness.

It had improved little with time. The personnel consisted largely of conscripted serfs who knew nothing of the sea and of foreign adventurers who were not less ignorant of their calling than unprincipled in their quest for gain. And the vessels were, if possible, less reliable than the men. Their serviceability appeared to be inversely proportioned to the huge sums expended upon them because of corruption on the one hand and inefficiency on the other. The ships were of such timber as to rot and make them worthless within six years. For defense, many of the frigates could not be expected to sustain the first broadside; for offense, there was in some instances such difference between the bore of the cannon and the size of the shot that a rude device of covering the latter with pitch to equalize them was so likely to result in explosions as to strike fear in the hearts of the boldest gunners.

For the flotilla as well as the squadron, the heavy armament was ill-designed for use on the shallow Liman. The ships of the squadron were fortunate to sail with their bottoms a few inches above the shifting sands of the estuary. The vessels of the flotilla, although better suited for the scant depth, were a nondescript assortment, most of which had been built for the non-military object of the holiday cruise of the Empress down the Dnieper and had now been converted and armed with cannon by an English engineer for purposes of war. And both the squadron and flotilla were clumsy and slow—inferior in the all-important matter to Jones of sailing qualities.

Nor was it true that the Russians were blissfully ignorant of the failings of their Navy. Alexis Orlof, whom Catherine had acclaimed as the hero of Tchesme, had been wary enough—apart from his objection to be under the orders of Potemkin—to refuse inviting disaster by acceptance of the command of the Sevastopol fleet. Rear Admiral Woynowitch, who was then placed at the head of it, had shown himself afraid, seemingly not without reason, to accept the challenge of the Turkish ships in the Black Sea. A storm, in lieu of a battle, made trial of this Russian fleet from Sevastopol, which may well have suffered the more because of bad construction and worse seamanship.

The misfortune in the Black Sea had also put Potemkin to the proof as the Commander in Chief ashore and afloat, and he had been found ridiculously wanting. He was in some respects a child as well as a barbarian who had undertaken the war especially to decorate himself with the pretty badge of the Order of St. George— a child, who faced with this mishap to the Sevastopol fleet, with some criticism in St. Petersburg, and with unexpected opposition from the Turks aided by the French (the devil had taught them, he said in a more resentful than comic mood), became spiritless, affronted, and wished to retreat before he had begun to fight. He threatened in his messages to Catherine to surrender his command and even to evacuate the Crimea, which was in his hands except for the danger to it from strategic Oczakow. In reply she humored and petted him: "You are tired and ill, you never would have thought of it. . . . You are impatient as a five-year-old boy, while the work requires unshakable patience. Adieu, my friend, neither time nor distance nor anyone in this world can change my feelings towards you."[10] Yet she had been as extravagantly capricious in giving him his military position as he was fantastic in occupying it.

If guile were a desirable attribute of his office, however, the Prince Marshal was certainly well-fitted for it, according to the first few days of the reception of Jones. Apart from De Ligne, Alexiano, Mordwinoff, and others in their train, also apart from the nature of the vessels for operation in the Liman, Potemkin, as the superior officer to whom the new Rear Admiral was responsible, and Nassau, as the independent officer with whom the joint needs of the squadron and flotilla required that he should act in concert, beset him with desperately ominous circumstances. Was it in smiling irony that Potemkin, "this clever fellow," who was "as amusing as the devil," according to Catherine's description, now sent the Empress his version of the initial fulfillment of both her and his assurances to Jones: "Rear Admiral Jones has arrived and I sent him to the fleet. He now has a chance to show his experience and bravery. I have given him every chance and facility."

The career of Jones in Russia might well have ended before it had really begun if he had not already taken a bulldog stand, typified by his memorable reply in the *Bonhomme Richard* battle, "I have not yet begun to fight," and soon to be confirmed by his further declaration, "I saw that I must conquer or die. For me there was no retreat."[11]

◇◇◇

Chapter LVIII

The First Victory Despite
the Snares of Intrigue

WHEN JONES had scarcely hoisted his flag as Rear Admiral in the *Vladimir* on the Liman, Nassau made known to him what was his own first and most important naval policy. It coincided with sentiments which this unexpected associate, to whom the American found himself tied, had already conveyed in messages to his wife after Potemkin had given him his command. As Nassau expressed his thoughts unreservedly to her, his confidences were the more revealing.

He assured his wife, on the one hand, that she ought to be an eyewitness to his forthcoming attack upon the Turks, "one of the most beautiful sights that it would be possible to see,"¹ and in particular that she should feel no alarm at all for him because there would be no close fighting and no danger. From the repeated assurances there appeared very much greater concern on his part for his personal safety than for her fears in behalf of it; and the protestations reflected as little the spirit of a soldier's wife as of a soldier.

He equally emphasized to her, on the other hand, to all appearances with brazen disregard for the incongruity and with approval on her part not less than repetition on his, a contemplated campaign of barefaced lies. It was natural to him and especially adapted to his Russian setting. "I expect to have," he explained, "the opportunity at the least cost to make the world talk of me; as a person follows my trade only for that purpose [he conveniently ignored his fattening Russian bribes of the present, not to consider those of the future], you see that I ought to be very well satisfied."² Undeterred by his shameless exposure and imposture at the same time, he revealed himself in a further confession even more explicitly shameless: "Although my undertaking may not be dangerous at all, it will nevertheless be brilliant, for I will make so great a noise that the fanfare will be resounding."[3]

Accordingly Nassau broached to Jones the subject of making war without taking risks. He was strangely modest enough at this time, outwardly at least, to consider sharing his exalted laurels with the Rear Admiral. To the surprise of this parade-warrior, however, he suffered a rebuff at the first suggestion. "The Prince of Nassau-Siegen, whom I had known slightly at Paris," Jones recorded, "told me that if we gained any advantage over the Turks, it was necessary to exaggerate it to the utmost; and that this was the counsel the Chevalier de Ribas had given him. I replied that I never had adopted that method of making myself of consequence."[4] After this caustic answer, Nassau was soon to set about his policy, whatever might be the exact course that it would assume when opportunity served him. Because Jones had refused to lie with him as a confederate, Nassau's simple, secret plan was to lie against him as an enemy. Nothing could be more logical to his mind.

With such a preface, Jones and Nassau on the Liman, the one in command of his squadron and the other of his flotilla, proceeded to open the active campaign for the capture of Oczakow, this stronghold which challenged the Russian ambitions to control all the Crimea and the Black Sea and to achieve the first objective towards conquest of Constantinople. "The squadron," as Jones said, "had a formidable appearance but little real strength." It consisted of thirteen frigates, sloops, and smaller craft and of one ship of the line, the flagship *Vladimir*. The flagship carried less than half her complete armament and some of the other vessels fewer guns than had been intended for them because of their poor naval construction and the shallow and treacherous waters. Nassau's flotilla was at least not only more manageable than Jones' squadron, but also as greatly superior in strength to the corresponding light vessels of the Turks as Jones' ships were inferior to those of the enemy opposed to him. It remained that as a whole both the armament and the sailing qualities of the Russian forces under the two commanders were unequal to those of the adversary

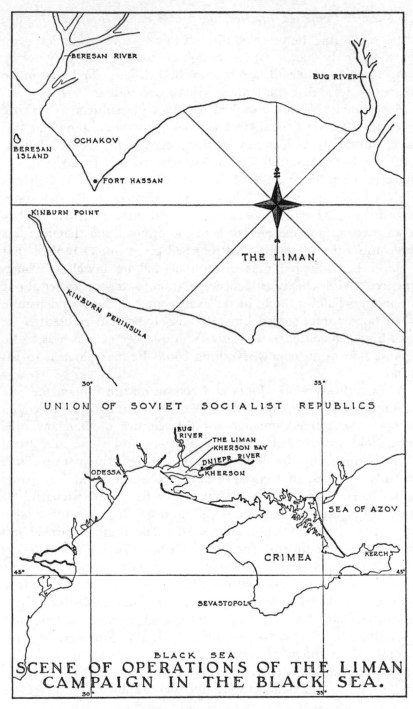

SCENE OF OPERATIONS IN THE LIMAN, 1788

under the Capitan Pacha, a tried and distinguished leader, and therefore dictated the more reasonable forethought in opposing him.

To the north of the Liman, guarded by Jones and Nassau, was Potemkin with his troops, whom they expected shortly to cross the Bug River and close upon the enemy. To the west was Suvorof, the eccentric and savage Russian General (infamous in history for blood-lust in overrunning Poland after the Second Partition), who had repulsed the Turks shortly after war had been declared in a bitterly fought attack upon his position at Kinburn, a pointed strip of land on the southern shore projecting into the only and narrow channel between the Liman and the Black Sea. On the shore opposite Kinburn, somewhat further within the estuary and upon the side where Potemkin advanced, Oczakow towered with the Turkish Fort Hassan at its foot. And outside the immediate field of operations, the Russians had their naval depot at Kherson by the closed eastern end of the Liman and their second fleet at Sevastopol on the Black Sea. Similarly by the Black Sea, at Beresane Island and other bases, the Turks stationed reinforcements of ships and men, intended to brave the passage through the Liman and bring succor for the defense of Oczakow.

While Nassau often turned his eyes to his publicity program, Jones consistently devoted his professional skill to a well-analyzed, coördinated plan between the two naval units on the one hand and the naval and military forces on the other. But inasmuch as he neither was vested with the authority of a commander in chief nor received practical orders for coöperation from Potemkin, his mode of fighting remained subject to incalculable difficulties. He failed even to have reports concerning the actual position of the Prince Marshal's army so as to govern his own movements the more wisely. He forbore to be swayed by the sudden haste of Nassau to advance with all their naval forces against the Turks only a few days after his associate had feared to adopt a comparatively safe station with the flotilla alone pending the arrival of the squadron after embarking its quota of soldiers.

Envisaging the progress of the campaign, Jones advised on his own initiative the placement of a battery at Kinburn Point, which, unlike the more removed defenses of Kinburn itself commanded by General Suvorof, promised to contribute effectively towards blockading against the Turks the nearby narrow passage from the Black Sea to the Liman. Suvorof recognized at once the importance of the suggestions and proceeded without delay to erect both a battery and a block fort, realizing that they should have been in this position at the beginning of the war.

For want of better means to insure unity of action, Jones assembled a council of war in accordance with a custom from the time of Peter the Great. He urged in an address the resolute patriotism of the officers and particularly the importance of setting aside all personal considerations to achieve wholehearted coöperation between the squadron and flotilla. He proposed many questions of a tactical and strategic nature for proceeding against the enemy, and Nassau distinguished himself by bold but incoherent suggestions. He further desired a second council to determine definitely the modes of attack and defense and to arrange a general system of signals to be sent from one vessel only; but the opposition of Nassau and Alexiano was such that these two objects for centralized leadership did not materialize. The only decision among them related to the choice of a defensive position in the Liman for both the squadron and flotilla pending the approach of the Army under Potemkin.

The two naval forces, therefore, drew up in formation, four verstes in advance of their previous stand, across the whole breadth of the Liman in a line from north-northeast to south-southwest, according to Jones' plan to proceed westerly in conjunction with the expected movement of the troops on the nearby shore. The alignment enabled them to protect Kherson and the passage of the Bug by Potemkin in the rear, to come to the support of Suvorof in case of an attack upon Kinburn in front, and to guard the country on both sides of the Liman.

The vessels had scarcely taken their appointed places before Nassau was seized with one of his impulses to move forward again, although he had been a party to the agreement for adopting the present position. Suvorof, too, urged Jones to advance so that the forces should serve primarily for the safety of his position: "You are well enough with the two squadrons, but you know well that under the circumstances the *radical* of the operations regards Kinburn, a principal, efficacious, and unequivocal point, and one on which all our cares and pains should be directed. . . . Enough said for a soldier who has never been a seaman." Yes, but the soldier, not less than the supposed seaman at the head of the flotilla, tried to dictate to Jones. In the Rear Admiral's view, Kherson had become a more strategic objective of the Turks than Kinburn, and he refused to accede to the desires of Suvorof and Nassau. At the present stage he was convinced of the wisdom to wait and even of the danger to the point of disaster to rush ahead. A special reason also prompted his desire to lure the Turks to advance against him up the shoal waters. And in the meantime Potemkin the generalissimo continued neither to invest him with authority suitable to his responsibilities, nor to bring up the land forces to act in concert with those at sea, nor to issue any orders for coördinated action.

Delay and negligence on a scale peculiar to Russia and even more peculiar to Potemkin were new to Jones but only typical of the conduct of the war from the beginning of the operations against Oczakow by the amateur soldier-favorite of Catherine. The Prince Marshal had boasted during the triumphal Crimean journey that one hundred thousand men were ready to march against the Turks. When De Ligne had asked him after the beginning of the war how soon he expected to proceed against Oczakow, Potemkin had replied: "Eh, my God, there are eighteen thousand men in the garrison, and I have not so many in my whole Army. I lack everything; I am the most unfortunate man if God does not help me."[5] The courtier resented his inability to lead the Prince Marshal "by the nose," as in cynical repartee the latter bluntly charged him with trying to do and the former frankly admitted his intention of doing. Accordingly De Ligne flattered Potemkin on one day and exposed him not without malice on the next to his Austrian friends in Vienna—but wisely for his interests not to Catherine in St. Petersburg. How Potemkin the pious Russian trusted in the help of God to the exclusion of help by himself must have explained in large part the slowness of the campaign as influenced, for example, by conditions at the camp in St. Elizabeth, according to the disgruntled courtier's report, with due allowance for exaggeration: "The horses and men are in fine condition! Two hundred per battalion on the sick list; but that will not last long. If they continue to be as ill-treated as they are now, they will all be dead soon."

After Jones had waited in vain during more than a week for the expected movement of the Army of Potemkin or at least for orders to insure unified action of the Navy, he finally arranged with Nassau to have the latter move forward at two o'clock in the morning of June 6, 1788 to cut off the enemy's advance guard near the Liman shore by one of the villages neighboring Oczakow. The adverse wind as well as the shallow waters and the sand bars close to the land rendered it impossible to employ the large vessels of Jones' squadron in addition to the galleys, gunboats, and other craft propelled by oars of Nassau's flotilla. Far from achieving success, Nassau retired at daybreak, without making the smallest resistance, before a very inferior force of the Turks; they chased him with their cannonade even into the midst of the squadron, which had advanced to the position that had been chosen. The precipitate retreat inspired the enemy so much that in the course of the night they drew up their flotilla as if to give battle.

At sunrise the next morning the enemy made sail, and it was now the turn of Brigadier Alexiano to reveal his capacity as a naval officer in fitness with his earlier aptitude for conspiracy. Although he had "given his voice," as Jones took occasion to explain, "in favor of the position we now actually held," the brigadier had so little command of himself, not to consider abilities for the command of others, as to run "upon the deck of the *Vladimir,* half naked, exclaiming like a frantic man, in French and Russian, that the Turks were going to attack and board us, and that we would be blown to pieces for having been so foolish as to leave our former position." The onset of the Turks, nevertheless, proved to be a false alarm.

At Jones' suggestion, he and Nassau proceeded to reconnoitre the squadron and flotilla of the enemy. Their advance prompted the Turks to begin a brisk attack against the right wing of Nassau's boats. He was at a loss, finally deciding to adopt a close formation and await the assault. Jones insisted that it was most important, on the contrary, "to raise the anchors with the utmost despatch and to form in line of battle to meet the Turks." Nassau with his flotilla was on the verge of a shameful defeat, perhaps the destruction of his vessels. "If I had kept quiet on the 7th June," Jones was to remark, "his business would have been soon transacted." Whatever his fellow commander deserved then and especially later at his hands, the Rear Admiral exerted himself as if the flotilla were his own. Leaping into a boat, Jones hastened along the line to direct the squadron and above all to bring forward the remainder of the flotilla, which had been posted on the left and in the rear. As the wind was adverse, he had these vessels towed by various craft attached to his squadron. He began an "oblique movement formed in front line, with the intention of cutting off the retreat of the enemy."

While the Turks favored by the wind advanced with a second division of their flotilla under the Capitan Pacha, Nassau deserted his endangered galleys on the right wing. Not daring to lead these vessels himself, he sent Brigadier Corsacoff to do so, who in the crisis had them retreat. In the endeavor to rally this right wing during his manœuvres on the left, Jones then despatched Alexiano to succeed Corsacoff; but his conduct in this instance scarcely did him more credit than his earlier extravagance in the *Vladimir*. He contented himself, to Jones' mortification, "with waving his hat in the air, and shouting from behind the lines, 'Fire, my boys, on the kirlangitch of the Capitan Pacha!'"

In the meantime, Jones on the other side led on his flanking attack. With the reinforcements which had come up under his orders, he arrived within cannon shot of the enemy, opened fire, and advanced steadily in an oblique line to cut off a possible retreat. Nassau having abandoned his own post, at which a leader was greatly needed, accompanied Jones, with whom he was as utterly useless as he made himself obtrusively conspicuous before him. "When the line led on by the Rear Admiral," as Jones himself described in his journal of his Russian services, "came to close fire with the enemy, their flotilla was thrown into the utmost confusion. Our reserve gave no further way, and the enemy was placed under a cross fire. The Capitan Pacha availed himself of the only resource he had left; the wind being in his favor, he set every sail to withdraw his force. Had he remained a half hour longer, he would have been surrounded. Two of his vessels were burnt in this affair. The flotilla of the enemy was composed of fifty-seven vessels, and we chased them up to their fleet."

Now that Jones had won the victory, it was time for Nassau to claim it. Had not his flotilla alone engaged the enemy? Had not he displayed himself in front of the Rear Admiral so as to give the appearance of directing the manœuvres? Had not he already prophesied to his wife this "beautiful spectacle. I have truly never before seen any so beautiful"?[6] Had not he indeed also "gazed during the battle upon her picture, which had brought him good luck"?[7] Had not Jones himself, seemingly in his zeal to serve Catherine and Potemkin, in his desire to propitiate his fellow commander for the sake of the common cause, and in his modest courtesy, really proved rather his weakness and given away, so to speak, his birthright? There was a letter from the Rear Admiral's own hand to Potemkin which in the eyes of Nassau proved as much by such terms as "I did my best to help the Prince make the necessary manœuvres. . . . The Prince showed great coolness and intelligence. . . . I had the honor to act as his aide-de-camp, and he took all my suggestions in good part."[8]

Nassau had his cue and he meant to follow it with a vengeance. Not without sincerity he had prepared his wife for "the great noise" which he would make. There were, too, supporters enough in the fertile soil of Russia. De Ligne loved him and had aptitudes similar to his own. Alexiano was his unscrupulous fellow conspirator. Potemkin favored him as an officer whom he himself had chosen, and nothing pleased the Prince Marshal more than to have the Empress hear of high-sounding victories from so skilful a trumpeter. Whether they were true or false was of little moment. Indeed he himself invented on occasion even greater victories in the Caucasus based on nothing at all, which actually surpassed as fiction his noted sham villages.

Accordingly Nassau hastened to the camp of Potemkin, who was the first willing confederate in accepting his version of the engagement. Above all, he sent messages proclaiming his naval triumph to most of the civil and military notables in France, to others whose list was too long for him to enumerate, and to the Empress of Russia. The more he wrote, the greater became his assurance and pretense. To build his reputation was especially to undermine the name of Jones.

"Paul Jones had changed very much," he boasted to his wife. "Fortune has taken from him that intrepidity which people said that he possessed. If I had not been obliged to combine the movements of my squadron with his, I should already have attacked again the Capitan Pacha; but with the indecision of this Rear Admiral, whose vessels have need of being protected by mine, I fear indeed that I may not gain a second complete victory, unless I have a man other than Paul Jones, with whom I am greatly dissatisfied. You see what three-fourths of reputation is!"[9] Nassau slandered, a sham seaman as he was, the abilities as well as the valor of the Rear Admiral, and adopted malicious epithets after the manner of De Ligne: "The corsair Paul Jones was very famous; but I fear greatly that at the head of a squadron he is not in his place."[10]

In contrast with these frontal attacks, Potemkin employed a flanking movement which was suitable to his more wily, complex nature and his more complicated position. He wrote letters to Paris and Vienna and St. Petersburg attributing the success to Nassau. To Catherine he praised Jones in some measure at the beginning, but proceeded to place him in shadow more and more by such expressions as "Nassau was the real hero and to him belongs the victory."

Still to have triumphs to boast about it was very desirable even in Russia, if not altogether necessary in that country, to have someone win them; and in view of the dearth of native talent, Potemkin considered Jones an excellent tool. Therefore it was necessary for the present to conciliate him. With his affectation of sincerity, the Prince Marshal wrote to the Rear Admiral: "The part you have taken in concert with the Prince of Nassau in uniting your forces with his and acting thus against the enemy, cannot, sir, but give me most particular pleasure. This junction is as necessary as useful for the service of Her Imperial Majesty, and particularly at this time. I recommend it to you, therefore, sir, in the strongest manner possible, in assuring you that on every occasion it will do me the greatest pleasure to appreciate to the Empress the services you may render the country." He addressed him, indeed, a second time on this day after the engagement: "The zeal and intrepidity manifested by Your Excellency in the affair against the Turks, on the 7th of this month, in aiding the Prince of Nassau, merit a just distinction, and I return you my thanks. I am persuaded that such undertakings will contribute much to the honor and glory of the Russian arms."

Jones expressed in answer—with the modesty and consideration which Nassau was quick to turn to his own account—his deep satisfaction with Potemkin's assurances, reiterated his disinterested motives, and even went out of his way to state that "Alexiano helped to establish order in the latter part of the engagement, and so if there are favors to bestow, I ask them for him; for myself I still have not the least claim to them." Perhaps he found it inevitable to add adroitly concerning the occasion for his own part in the engagement: "I saw the first division of Her Majesty's flotilla in disorder and in a critical situation." This remark, which probably came to the attention of Nassau, must have been wormwood to him in the presence of the Prince Marshal.

"Your star is bright . . . Prince Potemkin is much your friend," Littlepage, who had just arrived at the Russian camp, wrote to Jones. But only a few days passed before the first enthusiasm of Potemkin must have cooled, and the Rear Admiral was acute enough to realize how the winds of his future in Russia were veering.

The understatement of Jones not less than the fiction of Nassau had been accepted by Potemkin for reasons of his own. And Nassau, now even more self-assured than before, was already making his demands for a farther advance up the Liman, in spite of strategic considerations and of standing orders, scant and equivocal to be sure, from Potemkin. As this issue closely concerned his professional judgment and the whole future of the fleet and the campaign, Jones took his stand squarely against him and prevailed. Already the Rear Admiral began to suspect, as his words later expressed, that he served as "the cat's-paw to draw the chestnuts from the fire for them."[11]

If Jones had known the fate of the few letters which he had sent by post to his friends outside of Russia, not to consider the tenor of those which Nassau and Potemkin had penned and which had arrived in due course, his scepticism would have increased many-fold. He was altogether unaware for the present that Russia, with Potemkin as the particular censor in his case, secretly suppressed all his letters sent by mail, however free they were from any offense to this country—except the truth.[12] Jefferson especially waited in vain for a message; but when he heard in Paris the warped reports of the first Russian victory, the statesman commented with his usual penetration: "The Russians were commanded by the Prince of Nassau, with whom our Paul Jones acted as a volunteer, and probably directed the whole business."[13]

◇◇◇

Chapter LIX

Jones the Naval Genius; Nassau the Braggart Mercenary

THE STRATEGY of Jones, not less than his decision and valor, was now especially to distinguish him. The recklessness of the Prince de Nassau as seen in his blind haste to advance against the Turks rendered it the more conspicuous. Even the Count de Damas, the youthful friend and follower of Nassau, admitted that "his patience would not suffice for the sustained effort of directing an extensive plan of campaign."[1] Although the reputation of the Turks in war was not impressive, their fleet was more formidable than that of the Russians, their commander, the Capitan Pacha, was of proved abilities, and their desperation was so great that they intended to board the vessels of Jones and Nassau and even to set fire to their own in order to burn those of their adversary. They, like Nassau, had more impetuosity than skill; but their situation, unlike his, urged a speedy assault because of the forces by land as well as by sea which were closing upon them.

The importance of choosing the most favorable moment to fight weighed so much upon Jones that he requested De Ribas to send papers to Potemkin regarding his controversy with Nassau in order to "prevent any too hasty step." He desired to attack the Turks in the Liman at the same time that the Sevastopol force of Rear Admiral Woynowitch would meet the enemy's other ships in the Black Sea. But such concerted action seemed beyond the capacity of the Russians. He desired, further, to follow the instructions of Potemkin, in agreement with his own wary views, to defer an offensive movement until the Prince Marshal's army crossed the Bug so that sea and land forces might act in coöperation. But whether through cowardice, perversity, or sheer sloth, "the Prince," as Jones later noted caustically, "never had any intention of passing the Bug while the Turkish squadron was in the Liman. I do not presume to suggest his reason. . . . I had this from Brigadier Ribas and many others in his full confidence." Jones desired, finally, to lure the Turkish ships of large draft up the shoals of the Liman so that the enemy, not he, might suffer the imminent danger of running aground, just as he had already set a snare for them at the narrow outlet of the estuary by means of the battery and block fort placed at his suggestion on the point of Kinburn.

Before either Potemkin with his troops or Woynowitch with his fleet showed the initiative to act in conjunction with Jones, the Turks decided at last on June 16, favored by the wind, to advance up the Liman against the Russians. Jones' patience had been greater than theirs, not to consider Nassau's; the squadron and flotilla of the enemy, however, had just reinforced Oczakow from the Black Sea and strengthened themselves with troops from the garrison so that they saw no special reason for further delay. "The plan of the Capitan Pacha," Jones learned, "was to bear down full sail on the vessels of our flotilla, and run them to the bottom by the shock of the encounter of his large ships. He also proposed to burn our squadron by throwing in fire-balls (*grappins*) and setting fire to certain trading vessels which he had prepared as fireships." The Turkish Admiral did not give due consideration to a possibility which he had little reason to foresee, but which materialized in accordance with Jones' purpose to have the ships of the enemy, not his own, thread the shallows of the Liman in all the haste of an onset.

As the whole Turkish squadron and flotilla advanced at noon to attack and board those of the Russians, the flagship of the Capitan Pacha steered directly for the *Vladimir;* but when within a mile it ran aground and all the vessels which accompanied it dropped anchor. The fresh wind, which continued unfavorable for the Russians, especially in the narrow as well as shoal waters, caused Jones to warp the right of the line so as to draw up their forces in an obtuse angle as most effective for a cross-fire. The wind fortunately shifted to north-northeast during the night. At daybreak the Rear Admiral made the signal to attack the enemy, and his own squadron promptly set sail. "The Turks," Jones reported, "got in confusion the instant this manœuvre was perceived. They raised their anchors or cut their cables with the greatest precipitation, and not the shadow of order remained in their fleet. Our squadron advanced in line of battle with an imposing and formidable appearance so that the Turks knew not how weak it really was."

Laggard now, however forward before, Nassau with his flotilla was very slow in weighing anchor, and Jones had to stop the squadron twice to wait for him. Nassau even continued to lag behind after Jones had arrived close enough to open fire on the enemy. Nassau's flotilla failed particularly to perform its duty to oppose that of the adversary on the right flank of Jones' squadron in the shallows near the Liman bank where the larger ships could not sail.

The bold advance by Jones not only resulted in confusion among the Turkish vessels as a whole, but caused the officer second in command among them to run his ship on a sandbank and to become the expected prize of the Russians when they should find the time to claim it. Jones, now ready for close fighting, ordered that the *Vladimir* should be "steered within pistol shot of the vessel of the Capitan Pacha," which had been set afloat in the course of the night. The Turkish flagship again ran aground upon a sandbar. Hardly had this new accident happened before Alexiano in the *Vladimir* gave orders, beyond Jones' hearing and in Russian, to let go the anchor. Motivated without doubt by jealousy towards the Rear Admiral at his immediate prospect of taking the flagship, the flag, and the admiral of the Turkish fleet, this Greek with a pirate's history pretended that there were only fifteen feet of water within a short distance ahead. Even the Captain aboard the *Vladimir*, Zefaliano, made a sworn statement which proved the treachery. The ill-timed powerlessness of the flagship was sufficient to thwart the leadership of Jones against additional vessels of the Turkish squadron, which quickly availed themselves of their opportunity to flee.

While the Russian flotilla still lagged behind, one of Jones' frigates, the *Little Alexander,* sank at the side of the *Vladimir* after being struck by a bomb from the enemy's flotilla at the same moment that Alexiano's plot engaged the attention of the Rear Admiral. In the emergency, Jones commanded Alexiano to rally some vessels of their flotilla so as to dislodge those of the Turks on the exposed right wing near the shallows. He himself hastened in a boat to the left wing where Nassau was with his reserve to tell him of the fate of the *Little Alexander* and to urge, even beg, him to oppose the dangerous concentration of the Turkish flotilla. Jones' fellow-commander, remaining behind his batteries, quietly ignored the obvious public duty, apart from the personal obligation in view of his rescue from imminent disaster at the time of the engagement on June 7. The Rear Admiral then found Corsacoff, who with Alexiano took as many vessels of the flotilla as he could gather and chased those of the Turks even to the walls of Oczakow. If the manœuvre had been effected in due time, the *Little Alexander* would have been saved and the Turkish flotilla might reasonably have been defeated or captured.

To be sure Nassau had his own purpose in disregarding his duties. The jackal was now lurking near his disabled prey. The safety of the Rear Admiral's squadron was of no moment to him; its loss, on the contrary, would emphasize his expected glory. While the Turks had been unharmed, he had remained consistently in the background. Now that two of their ships lay stranded at an angle sharp enough to prevent the use of their guns—ships which Jones not only had opposed and brought to their present helpless condition but also had lured to the advance that had endangered them—it was time for Nassau to show his type of bravery. Although he himself, of course, continued to remain behind, the commander of the flotilla sent forward at last the greater portion of his vessels, not certainly against any substantial number of the enemy's flotilla which might have replied with their own batteries, but against the two helpless ships.

Nassau proceeded to show himself, after his fashion, even more humane than intrepid. Although the ships and men were at the mercy of the Russians and begged for their pity, it was not his intention to take any thought of the lives of human beings or the preservation of ships however valuable. His boasts could be louder if he made it appear that his victory was in a grim, close-range contest of cannon balls. In accordance with his earlier explanation to his wife concerning the personal safety of his expected mode of fighting, he had the crews of his vessels cowardly and heartlessly throw a fearful kind of incendiary missiles called brandcougles, thanks in particular to a French engineer whom De Ségur had recommended to him, which caused a grewsome carnage by setting fire to the Turkish ships with such of their imploring crews as could not escape. And long after one of the flags of the Capitan Pacha, shot down from the mainmast of his flagship, had come into the possession of some Cossack sailors, the Zaporavians, he snatched the trophy as his own (Jones who had his hand upon it at the same time permitted him to do so rather than to begin an altercation) and proceeded to send it to Potemkin as a mark of his valor.

A further engagement on the next day seemed probable, and Jones made whatever preparations were in his means to insure a decisive victory. The fateful stranding of the two ships of the Turkish squadron on the one hand and the escape of the Turkish flotilla under the walls of Oczakow on the other impelled him to be both the more scrupulous to continue to avoid accidents to his own squadron and at the same time the more eager to attack with his ships where Nassau's vessels of lighter draught should have fought. His presence of mind in combination with his daring now manifested itself in a manner reminiscent of his stand alone on the shores of Whitehaven under the focussed eyes of the astounded multitude. "How imbecile does the human mind become under the influence of sudden panic!" he philosophized. "The Rear Admiral, an hour after the affair, advanced in his boat, and took soundings all along the Turkish line, opposite the walls of Ocza-kow, and within reach of case shot, and not a single gun was fired upon him."[2]

It may well have been in the ensuing night that he accomplished a feat even more ingenious, novel, and intrepid, which at the same time revealed the human bond that moved his sailors, Russian now as well as American before, to be ready on occasion to die fighting with him. Jones came at nightfall to one of the vessels of Nassau's flotilla to prepare to reconnoitre the Turkish lines, and the occasion was to be to a Cossack member of the crew, Ivak, a lifelong memory, in the words of an officer to whom he later told it:

"Pavel [the Russian for Paul, the name by which Jones had introduced himself] was dressed the same as others, but his weapons were better. He looked very impressive and brave, had some grey hair but remained decidedly strong, and it was obvious at once that he was an expert in what concerned him. As soon as he stepped into the vessel, he began to arrange everything in the way he thought best. He examined the sails, the guns, the ammunition, having help from the interpreter only to the extent of his ability to translate. He then had a small boat hoisted aboard, attached a little rudder to it, chose a pair of good oars, wrapped about them some pieces of cloth, and after various other minor preparations sat down for a rest.

"It had grown dark, supper was served, and Pavel seated himself with us around the table. He ate and made jokes through his interpreter just as if he were one of us. After our meal he gave us a double ration of spirits; we became really good-humored and started to sing, but the song proved to be a very sad one. It is a strange way in which man is created that even when he seems to be happy his heart is often sad as if with the presentiment of some misfortune. Our Pavel listened very attentively as though he were trying to understand the meaning of the song; yet it seemed that clouds of sadness passed over his face, although he tried hard to conceal his mood. Well, it is no shame to shed a tear when one is in a strange land.

" 'It is time,' cried Pavel, jumping to his feet suddenly."

Jones chose Ivak among his fellow sailors after "he examined us as if he wished to pierce through our characters"; and the two entered the little boat, the former at the rudder and the latter at the oars. They made for the Turkish lines, brazenly met some enemy boats, and subtly drew from the Turks their countersign. "Never in all my life," continued Ivak, "have I seen a man such as he was. When he wished, he was like honey, and when necessary like stone.

"We soon reached the enemy's fleet. It looked like an entire town as it lay at anchor, a whole forest of masts. We were asked for the countersign and Pavel himself gave it. We kept moving among the ships like a sea gull. Some threatened us, others paid no attention—we crawled along silently in some places, in others we passed boldly. When finally beyond range of the enemy's fire, we removed the cloths from the oars and rowed quietly to the galley of Prince Nassau with our information. Not one of the Turks had suspected us."[3]

◇◇◇

Chapter LX

Jones Wins the Battles; Nassau Usurps the Honors

AT DAYBREAK on June 18, 1788 Jones aboard the *Vladimir* learned from reports sent by Suvorof concerning the essential services rendered during the night by the block fort and batteries which the Rear Admiral's prevision had caused to be erected at Kinburn Point. The sequel now proved how unwarranted had been the opposition of Potemkin, whose jealousy rather than judgment had governed his attitude because he had not proposed the defenses himself. The Turkish squadron, put to rout on the 16th by Jones and having endeavored to escape from the Liman to the Black Sea in the night of the 17th and 18th, had run aground a number of its vessels, varying in accounts from six to nine, in the attempt to pass through the shallow channel and at the same time to keep beyond the range of the Russian guns on the Point, which had maintained a continuous fire against them.

With the assurance that these stranded Turkish vessels were as helpless as the two others of June 16, it was only necessary to take possession of them as if they were the game which a hunter who had proved both his strategy and marksmanship allows his retriever to bring to him. Jones himself wished to send several frigates for this purpose; but since it was obviously safer if not essential to employ vessels more manageable and of less draft, he deferred to the warning of Alexiano, who with prejudice if not treachery in this case assured him that the risk for large ships would be great because the current in the channel was "like that of a milldam and the bottom was so bad that anchors would not hold." It was resolved accordingly to proceed with vessels of the flotilla, and Alexiano, who, as Jones remarked, "had his private reasons," set out with Nassau.

The Admiral objected to the employment of all the flotilla for the easy task of taking possession of the powerless stranded craft. His opposition was the greater because the Turkish flotilla remained at full strength under the cannon of Oczakow and continued to threaten the Russian squadron, whose right wing was within cannon shot. It was best to attack first this flotilla, now without the support of the routed squadron; but in any event it was as necessary as convenient to detach a sufficient force from Nassau's flotilla to guard against an attack upon the vulnerable but strategically-placed right wing of the Russian squadron.

While the stranded vessels lay on the sand spit near Kinburn, the antagonism between Nassau and Jones came to a verbal duel. "He permitted himself," Jones recounted, "to say many uncivil things; among others, that *he* was always wanted to protect *my* squadron with *his* flotilla. As he had often said such things since the affair of the 7th, I told him it was improper for him to say this and for me to hear it. That the squadron was respectable, as belonging to the Empress and having conquered Her Majesty's enemies. He bragged that *he* had taken the two ships. I told him that I saw nothing extraordinary in that because they were aground and, of course, captured before he came up. He said that he would write what I had uttered to Prince Potemkin; and that *he* knew better than *I* did how to take ships! I told him that without impugning his skill he was not ignorant that I had proved my ability to take ships which *were not Turks*. He got out of control of himself, and threatened to write against me to the Empress and Prince Potemkin. As for that, I told him, if he was base enough to do it, I defied his malice. He left me three half-galleys, one small battery, and one chaloupe, which I placed under our right wing, and has not spoken to me since. Before this ridiculous dispute, our combination was unnecessary; otherwise I would have put up with still more for the good of the service. I feel no rancour against him; and though he said in a bitter tone that I would be rejoiced to see him beaten, he little understood my heart!"[1]

Pell-mell went Nassau with his flotilla, except the few boats left with Jones, against the Turkish ships aground. But while the

Russian craft dashed upon them in the Liman channel, Nassau and Alexiano took the precaution in their swift chaloupes to turn aside to Kinburn at a safe distance from the carnage wrought by the steel and flame which their craven orders now let loose. The Russians fired brandcougles without mercy. "Vainly the wretched Turks made the sign of the cross and begged for quarter on their knees!" Jones was informed. "About three thousand of them burned with their ships." It was chance alone that saved from fire two of these vessels, a corvette and brigantine, however valuable all of them would have been for the Russian Navy. It was likewise the absence of any kind of order or plan that occasioned extraordinary confusion in Nassau's flotilla so that such loss as there was among his men, although not great in view of the negligible opposition by the enemy, resulted in part from Russian bullets.

The braggadocio of Nassau, which had begun after the first engagements of June 6 and 7 and now assumed greater and greater proportions after the victories of June 17 and 18, was to resound in most of the courts of Europe. Even the obvious contrast between the losses of the Turkish squadron, which was the particular opponent of Jones, and the absence of damage to the Turkish flotilla, which was the corresponding adversary of Nassau, did not in the least restrain his claims. The extent of his barefaced knavery as it grew day by day is measurable by the accounts to his wife in Poland. On June 17 he wrote: "It was the flotilla which I commanded that did everything." On June 18: "My flotilla fought alone. We have destroyed six vessels, of which the crews of four are burned." On June 19: "I am, in short, content with myself! Three battles in which I have taken or destroyed with cannon balls four vessels of 64 guns, five great frigates of 36 to 40, a sloop of 30, a brigantine of 14, and three small boats, all of which were led by the Capitan Pacha, who had three or four times as great a force as I possessed. . . . It was fitting that I should have great success; I always acted against the advice of the commander of the squadron who has achieved nothing. Paul Jones has learned that there is indeed a difference between commanding a privateer and a squadron. The reputation, however, which he had usurped would have crushed me if I had not succeeded."[2]

Next Nassau proclaimed, on June 20, not only that he had won the three battles himself, but that the Rear Admiral had been a liability instead of an asset: "I was also obliged to protect the ships of the squadron of another, who always held me responsible for all the mishaps which might happen to him. Oh! what a poor man is Paul Jones! He has surely made a mistake to come here on such a day. I am master of the Liman. . . . I know that persons disapprove of my disputes with Paul Jones. I am going to write to Prince Potemkin to complain in the matter. I will state to him that my exertions have impaired my health and that I expect to withdraw after the siege. I do not wish any longer to expose myself to compromising my reputation."[3]

That the reputation of Jones was "usurped" and that his own needed care against "compromising" illustrate the degree of effrontery with which Nassau could mock the truth and assume his innocent face.

Offset against the brazenness of Nassau, *I* and *my* were inconspicuous in the reports from the pen of Jones. He scarcely mentioned to Potemkin his personal deeds. In the absence of anyone whom he could praise heartily, he recommended for some of their services the Russian seamen, Corsacoff, and even Alexiano. Of Nassau's part, he said to the Prince Marshal with sufficient directness: "It is well known not to be difficult to take ships when they are aground, for a third of their force was enough to do it"; and "Our victory might have been complete if some persons had not stayed so long around the grounded ships, which were no longer able to escape us."[4] It was not without irony, perhaps unintentional, that apropos of the *Te Deum* which the Russians customarily sang in honor of a victory, Jones commented: "After all, Providence has done a great deal for us and we cannot be too grateful." And now that Jones had seen the Turks in action and had driven their squadron into the Black Sea to join their other forces, he was ready to pursue and bring them to a major battle as a climax to the campaign. "I beg you," he said to Potemkin, "to give me opportunities for using without delay such means as Your Highness may think it wise to accord me for the good of the service."[5]

Jones had revealed Nassau more than enough to Potemkin, who, as Littlepage had remarked, loved him. But as the impudent boasts of the commander of the flotilla echoed louder and louder across the Liman, Jones expressed himself to those who he thought might listen more understandingly. He sent a report, according to the custom, to the Admiralty of the Black Sea at Kherson, in which was the characteristic understatement: "I believe that the estimate of the prizes is slightly exaggerated."[6] He was to expose explicitly to De Ribas the gross falsehoods regarding the number of vessels, burned and captured, and their sizes, and to reveal his associate's hideous cruelty and his double-dealing with the Court of Constantinople: "Never was bravado more impudent than that of M. de Nassau. To depart from truth costs him nothing. He had the effrontery to deceive the Prince Marshal . . . in saying he had burnt six ships of the line and taken two. These pretended ships of the line were nothing other than the merchant vessels called caravellas. . . . Humanity recoils, indignant and affrighted, at beholding so many wretched creatures perish in the flames without any necessity. But these are small marks of the goodness of heart and gratitude which M. de Nassau is pleased to show to prove himself worthy of the kindnesses he lately received at Constantinople. Now he is with the Russians where he has found his market. The same motives which induced him to come here may lead him back to Constantinople."[7]

Whatever the truth, the victories as heralded by Nassau stirred the dormant monkish superstitions of Potemkin which were inherent in his half-savage nature. The Prince de Ligne, humorous and gay not less than fulsome as a courtier, described the manner in which Potemkin exhibited his grotesque religious instincts upon receiving his favorite officer's reports:

"It was at the camp of Novo Gregori that we heard the news of the victory of the Prince of Nassau over the Capitan Pacha. Potemkin sent for me, embraced me, and said: 'This comes from God. Look at that church; yesterday I consecrated it to St. George, my patron, and the news of this victory at Kinburn comes the next day. . . .'

"We received the news of two more naval victories of the Prince of Nassau. 'Well, my friend,' said the Prince to me, flinging himself on my breast, 'what did I tell you of Novo Gregori? Here it is again. Is it not a signal? I am the petted child of God.' Those were his very words; and I repeat them to make known the most extraordinary man that ever lived. 'How fortunate,' he added, 'that the garrison of Oczakow is running away. I march at once; will you come with me?'

" 'Can you doubt it?' I cried. And we started.

"Instead of going straight to the fortress, which I counted on reaching with the whole cavalry in two days, we spent three by the waterside, catching and eating fish, and we went to pay a visit to the victorious fleet."[8]

Surfeited with his fish, Potemkin accompanied by his chief followers at length arrived at Kinburn and proceeded indeed to pay Jones a visit aboard the *Vladimir*. As the Prince Marshal had learned in part from Jones and without doubt in greater fullness from others regarding the outbursts of hostility between the two commanders, he engaged De Ligne and Littlepage to persuade Nassau to make an apology to the Rear Admiral. "I accepted it with sincere pleasure," Jones described. "We embraced in the presence of this honorable company, and I believed him as sincere as myself." Forgiving Jones always was, and often he proved himself patient; but in this instance he appeared naïve. Devotion to his professional objects made him the more tolerant and credulous.

Potemkin remained rational and wily enough, despite his superstition, to look for future victories to Jones rather than to his chosen officer and patron saint. On the one hand he sought the reconciliation of the Admiral and complimented him upon his recent services. On the other hand he sent to Catherine a message which in some respects outdid the art of lying as practiced by Nassau the master: "The flotilla of the Capitan Pacha is smashed. Six ships of the line are burned, two are stranded . . . thirty are destroyed, and the others are hiding behind the guns of Oczakow. Among the ships destroyed are the Capitan Pacha's and the Vice Admiral's. Three thousand persons are taken prisoner, about as many were killed, but our losses were small. Suvorof inflicted much damage on the enemy with his shore batteries. Prince Nassau was tireless in his efforts. It was all his work."[9]

Chapter LXI

Singlehanded Gallantry before Oczakow; Hostile Fabrications

Now THAT Jones had virtually won command of the waters of the Liman despite the arbitrary lack of coöperation by Potemkin's Army, the Prince Marshal at length crossed the Bug River with his troops and appeared on June 27 along the shores of the estuary. He had spent fifteen days in passing from one bank of the river to the other, and then made "the very shortest marches he could manage."[1] Whatever were his errors of omission while at a distance from the operations by sea, his errors of commission promised to be greater during his nearby presence.

A minor incident presaged that the recent friendly professions among the commanders, including Potemkin as well as Nassau, had for the most part little meaning. The Prince Marshal had given Jones orders to recover cannon, anchors, and other effects from the vessels sunk by Nassau and Alexiano. When he proceeded to perform this duty, Alexiano became furious because of his concern that the Rear Admiral would profit by this task and because Potemkin, at his insinuation, had given a similar order to him. Nassau became even more irate, totally ignoring his past apologies; although the transport chosen for the salvage had been empty and unused, he made the petty charge that it belonged to his flotilla. Potemkin, to crown the comedy, not only forgot his instructions to Jones, but proceeded with his Russian imperiousness to try to bully him. At his direction, De Ribas prepared a message to the Admiral: "His Highness is very sorry that Your Excellency has directed a change in what he had resolved upon.

In such cases, the Prince Marshal, notwithstanding the goodness of his heart, is severely rigid, and I make it a point to inform you of it, sir, that you may be on your guard for the future."[2] Jones replied that he could recall to Potemkin the place, the time, and the words of the order to him, that he had no thought of personal profit from the prizes, and that "I know but one manner of conducting myself; and as I can never depart from it, fear nothing."[3] Rebuffed, the Prince Marshal confessed to Littlepage that he had censured Jones "very malapropos"; but he lacked the honorableness to admit at least his mistake, not to consider his arrogance, to Jones himself.

In the face of the newly aggravated relations for which he was increasingly responsible, Potemkin commanded Jones to give Nassau and his flotilla "every assistance that might be useful" in making an attack on July 1 to capture or destroy the Turkish flotilla which lay under the walls of Oczakow. The Prince Marshal himself, now in position with his troops, was to make a diversion to promote the undertaking. The circumstances were indeed curious. Nassau had assumed all the praises, but his proper opponent, the Turkish flotilla, was still intact. Jones had received little credit, but the Turkish squadron had fled the Liman. Jones was to help Nassau, but not only were the two commanders at swords' points but the Rear Admiral's squadron could not enter the shallow waters near Oczakow.

For the benefit of the service, Jones tried once more to coöperate with Nassau. On June 17, Nassau's flotilla had been late and behind; now on July 1, he was equally at fault. The flotilla advanced at one in the morning but at dawn was still far too distant to make the necessary attack. When Jones met Nassau in his swift and luxurious chaloupe, which the Empress had used on her trip to the Euxine in 1786 and which now was especially suitable for him in the event of flight, the Admiral asked whether he did not think it time to begin the assault. "Is it of me you thus inquire?" answered Nassau. "I have nothing to say to you on the subject." "After a reply so uncivil and so publicly made," commented Jones, "it was impossible I could have any further intercourse with him."[4]

Still the Admiral did his best with the few small boats attached to his squadron and with his own valiant arm. He used the craft to haul into position some vessels of the flotilla and set the example himself in one of the chaloupes. He persisted in this task, regardless of the enemy's gunfire, when the current carried rather too far to leeward several of the batteries and double chaloupes. He advanced considerably in front of Nassau's forces in order to seize five of the Turkish galleys, exposing himself between the cross-fire of the Russian flotilla on one side and that of Fort Hassan, the Turkish flotilla, and the guns of Oczakow on the other.

While companions fell about him, he boarded and overcame one of these galleys and had it towed out of danger. He then boarded and overcame the galley of the Capitan Pacha, still nearer the enemy's shore batteries. Tenaciously he retained possession of this second capture, although a too eager young and clumsy officer cut the cable before orders to do so. While the vessel could not be hauled within the Russian lines, it drifted closer and closer to the Turkish shore. However much personally exposed to danger from the cross-fire of the nearby bastions and flotilla of the enemy, he despatched a lieutenant to the *Vladimir* for an anchor and cable to kedge the prize to a place of safety.

It was unendurable to Alexiano and Nassau, in their chaloupe far within the Russian lines, to contemplate the triumph of Jones in bringing home the galley of the Turkish Admiral. Therefore Alexiano, swearing that the exploit must not succeed and conspiring with Nassau, sent a Greek canoe with instructions to set the galley afire while Jones was temporarily occupied with towing some of the floating batteries into position. "The wretched beings who were chained in the galley of the Capitan Pacha perished there in the flames!" Jones lamented; but their fate could have been only an additional "beautiful" spectacle for which Nassau was to congratulate himself in his accounts to his wife.

Apart from the deeds of Jones performed without regard to personal danger, the attack of the Russian forces was insignificant. The reason lay in Nassau's fear to fight at close quarters and his absolute incapacity for command. Only the three other galleys which Jones had made his objectives and two additional vessels were destroyed. On the first occasion that Jones had stood aside from the main operations, Nassau with his flotilla suffered a signal failure.

His boasts, nevertheless, reached their ultimate stage. The Count d'Artois, brother of Louis XVI; the Count de Montmorin, successor to Vergennes as French Foreign Minister; De Ségur in St. Petersburg; and many another were to hear from Nassau afresh.[5] Never dreaming of the irony with which truth, sooner or later, in one form or another, inevitably reasserts itself, he declared anew to his wife: "No more Turkish war vessels exist on the Liman! Those which I attacked, in the presence of the Army, under the walls of Oczakow, have afforded another beautiful battle. . . . I have effected in my life a great achievement. I have reached the goal which I wished to attain; my name will pass to posterity. . . . Prince Potemkin who came here yesterday said that my victories were more brilliant than the famous day of Tchesme, at which fireships did all the destruction, as compared with the blows in battle that enabled us to overcome the Capitan Pacha."[6]

How Nassau, Alexiano, and Potemkin himself had turned the previous achievements of Jones to their own advantage was soon obvious tangibly. On the basis of their reports and the recommendations of the Prince Marshal, the Empress sent gifts and awarded honors, some earlier and some later, with a characteristically Russian partial as well as ostentatious hand. Nassau on July 7 learned that he had been promoted two grades; later he received a valuable estate and several thousand peasants in White Russia, the military order of St. George of the second class, a golden sword with a row of diamonds, and the anticipatory appointment as vice admiral at the taking of Oczakow. Alexiano, too, became the owner of an estate and of peasants and gained a promotion of two grades. Potemkin received a magnificent golden sword decorated with large diamonds and emeralds and encased in a shield of gold, which bore an inscription hailing him, along with other titles, as the victor on the Liman.

Jones had bestowed upon him the subordinate order of St. Anne; it was not a Russian but a Holstein decoration, and not conferred by the Empress but by the less valued hand of the Grand Duke Paul as Duke of Holstein. The Admiral considered it, as he said, "an honor with which I am highly flattered, and with which I could have been perfectly satisfied, had others been recompensed only in the same proportion, and according to the merit of their services." What wounded him most was that all the officers of the flotilla received promotions of one grade, gratuities of a year's pay, medals and golden swords, while those of his squadron, although superior in naval experience and more distinguished in services, won no recognition at all. However disappointed, they agreed in deference to Jones to make no complaint for the present on his voluntary promise to demand justice for them at the end of the campaign.

These were only minor, obvious indications of the growing intrigue which surrounded the Admiral. Potemkin continued to confiscate whatever letters, regardless of their contents, Jones addressed beyond the borders of Russia. He required him, on the one hand, not to send further naval reports to the admiralty at Kherson; he subtly tried, on the other hand, to have him subscribe to the official lies which had originated with Nassau regarding the number and especially the nature and size of the Turkish vessels sunk. When Jones showed his repugnance, Potemkin was too crafty to press him. Having attempted to seal the world inside as well as outside Russia against the truth of Jones' pen, he undertook to hoodwink it with the falsity of Nassau's and his own. And so even a comparatively discriminating diplomat in St. Petersburg like De Ségur credited what was told him of the striking victories of Nassau and the contrasting inconsequence of the services of Jones. Catherine herself, astute enough in her diplomacy of state, but inordinately vain and gullible when her favorite supporters were involved, had painted for her more amazingly distorted pictures of the campaign in the Liman.

But the truth still had some avenues of escape from Russia so as to expose the dupery. Jones' earlier habit of securing testimonials was to be of timely value. His accomplishments, as recorded by him in his *Journal of the Campaign in the Liman,* had through his care the documentary witness of a number of his captains, accompanied by the signature of his official Russian secretary.[7] Even an Irishman in the Russian service, obviously not prejudiced in his favor, admitted in a letter to his father in Dublin: "Be his crimes what they may, he is a most excellent and intrepid marine officer, whose valor on this and the subsequent attack has obtained him vast honor."[8]

The most damning evidence of all, perhaps, against his enemies, in regard to the events which had already transpired, came likewise firsthand and unbiased from the English historian Eton: "It is a difficult thing at all times to discover truth amidst the misrepresentations of courts, of ministers, of commanders. Should anyone write, for instance, the history of the last war between Russia and Turkey, he would take for his guide, in relating the first event, the siege of Oczakow, the accounts published by the Court of St. Petersburg, and the reports of the commanders. There he would find a brilliant victory, gained by Prince Nassau over the Turkish fleet in the Liman; but if he could get the reports made by Paul Jones to the admiralty of Kherson, signed by all the commanders of the fleet, he would find that no engagement took place (except a distant cannonade); that the Turkish ships ran aground by their ignorance and bad manœuvres; and that Nassau with the flotilla, instead of taking possession of them, set them on fire. This journal, which I have read and taken an extract from, was forbidden by Prince Potemkin to be sent to Petersburg, and the whole campaign, as it stands on record, is nearly a romance. . . . I was at the opening of the trenches, and at the storming of the place, and therefore can speak of facts to which I was an eyewitness."[9]

This striking judgment of Eton has greater instead of less authority by contrast with the views of both De Ségur and of another contemporary writer of Russian history, Tooke. As for De Ségur, he had the assurance not only to credit Nassau with all that the adventurer claimed but also to say, "In vain the Englishman Eton strives to diminish the brilliance of this battle by accepting the observations of Paul Jones who was blinded by jealousy." To judge between the two witnesses it is necessary only to remember that De Ségur, at the distance of St. Petersburg, was the bosom friend of Nassau, lived on terms of equal intimacy with De Ligne, and felt greatly flattered during a long period by the personal attentions of Catherine for her political purposes; that Eton, for years a consul in Turkey, a secretary of a British mission to St. Petersburg, and an observer at the Liman, was not likely for these reasons as well as his nationality to be biased at this time in favor of Jones.

As for Tooke, his obvious prejudices against Jones were so great as to render all his assertions worthless. He described him as "the English pirate and renegado Paul Jones" and his part in the American Revolution as one of "atrociousness." With his inaccuracy regarding the Rear Admiral in Russia on a par with his hate of him as an American officer, he stated that Nassau was appointed to "the command of the naval armament on the Euxine" and Jones to "a command in the Cronstadt fleet."[10] As the most flagrant instance apparently of his inaccuracy and hate alike, Tooke ignored altogether the services of Jones on the Liman, whether good or bad, as if they had never happened.

Although the extravagant reports of Potemkin and Nassau were of the same color beyond Russia as their claims within it, many (with such exceptions as De Ségur and Tooke) saw them in a different light. There was in particular Jefferson, who in Paris had still received no word from Jones and looked with increasing suspicion upon the announcements which emanated from Russian sources. "One side alone is heard," he wrote to John Jay. And that one side, as he noted, overreached itself by its contradictions: "The Russian accounts of their victories on the Black Sea must have been greatly exaggerated. According to these, the Capitan Pacha's fleet was annihilated; yet themselves have lately brought him on the stage again, with fifteen ships of the line, in order to obtain another victory over him."[11] The attempts to discredit Jones seemed in fact only to make him rise the higher in the esteem of the American Minister to France, who was soon to be the Secretary of State under Washington. It was during this period that he said of the unforgotten *Bonhomme Richard* Commodore and patriot: "I consider this officer as the principal hope of our future efforts on the ocean."[12]

◇◇◇

Chapter LXII

"The First Duty of a Man Is to Respect His Own Character"

MORE AND MORE like an Asiatic despot in the surroundings of a luxurious court, Potemkin assumed his sway at his headquarters on a cliff overlooking the shores of the Black Sea. As extravagant as his vanity and presumption were his self-indulgence and capriciousness. He ordered two detachments to proceed by different routes from St. Petersburg, each with its quota of plate and other private supplies, so as to insure the arrival of one of them to satisfy his desires. He sent two officers of high standing, one to Florence and the other to Paris, for perfumes and jewels intended for a niece who was expected at the camp. Indeed he invited several of his nieces, especially a favorite Varinka, to be with him at the scene, as if his purpose were a kind of harem in accord with his Oriental tastes and principles. These were only minor aspects of the extremes to which his half-savage, exotic instincts were to impel him, but they became expressive of the wilful egoism which threatened to govern his conduct during the remainder of the operations on the Liman. Jones now had to deal closely with this satrap.

The action of July 1 proved to Potemkin, if any doubts had persisted in his mind, the incapacity of Nassau. It gave him an inkling, too, that Jones had made his decision not to be a gullible or base tool for the reputation of others. At this turn of the campaign, Potemkin sent Nassau to Sevastopol to learn the results of an encounter between the Russian and Turkish fleets in the Black

Sea. Rear Admiral Woynowitch with a force very much weaker than that of the enemy had fled to port; "the affair," as Jones commented, "was neither close nor warm." In the meantime the Prince Marshal inconsiderately gave the control of the flotilla to Ribas, who had neither experience nor ambition for such a command. When it was discovered that Nassau had left the vessels in the greatest confusion, with not "five soldiers belonging to the same company" in any galley or gunboat and most of them unaccounted for, Potemkin seemed the more inclined to follow the recommendation of Ribas that Jones should lead the flotilla for the next assault upon Oczakow.

"On the afternoon of July 17th, the Prince Marshal fairly proposed to give me the command of the flotilla," Jones recounted. "His Highness informed me his intention was to have Oczakow attacked a second time. I replied that I was disposed to execute with zeal whatever he might think proper for the good of the service; but that to attack with advantage it was necessary to come to close quarters, and to advance in better order than on the 1st of July. He was of the same opinion, and requested me to come ashore next day that we might concert together the plan of attack.

"I did not fail to comply with the orders of the Prince Marshal, but His Highness spoke no more of the flotilla. I remained to dinner and supper, and afterwards returned on board of my ship. The Prince de Nassau having returned some days before from Sevastopol had intrigued with the Prince de Ligne; and the Prince Marshal had restored to him the command of the flotilla."[1]

The vacillation and final course of Potemkin were equally in character. The public interest appeared to him of little consequence in comparison with his private ambitions. It was always possible to manufacture news of fictitious victories with a confederate like Nassau, and it was consistent to retain in command this officer of whom he had written that the successes were "all his work." Moreover a powerful courtier like De Ligne, who had the ear of the Empress, was to be propitiated. De Ligne did not dare to describe to Catherine the Marshal's weird manner of carrying on war because of his fear to antagonize him; but he wrote plainly enough to the Emperor Joseph: "The antechamber intrigues, of which the Russians are thinking much more than they are of the enemy, will continue to keep them useless to us. Her Majesty the Empress knows nothing of what is going on; she is ignorant, though I have written it by post to our Ambassador [Cobentzel] that her troops have made the most shameful of campaigns. She is thinking only of rewarding them, preparing ribbons and medals for battles that will never be fought."[2]

Offended as De Ligne was by the cabals of others, those of his own in behalf of Nassau, for instance, did not trouble his easy conscience. "They have made the Prince of Nassau pay dear for his victories," he wrote further to Joseph. "Part of his fleet has been given to Paul Jones . . . to whom the Prince intends to entrust the chief commission for the bombardment whenever it takes place."[3] These views in favor of De Ligne's comrade, along with the testimony of Jones himself, indicate clearly enough that the return of the flotilla to Nassau is attributable to the courtier's own "antechamber intrigues."

In lieu of the flotilla, on July 20 Potemkin placed, nevertheless, twenty-one gunboats and five bomb vessels under the command of Jones with the view of a forthcoming attack. His design, however, may well have been only to lure him to fight again for the elevation of Nassau and himself. As if in disclosure of ulterior motives, he gave the Admiral a commission at the same time to undertake a very dangerous enterprise which had negligible connection with the campaign. It is not to be unduly suspicious of the Prince Marshal to believe that he was disposed to take satisfaction in case Jones should be killed. Even if the best construction be put upon his motives, he had in mind spectacular feats, craved by his barbaric instincts and not inconsistent with burning ships and men described by Nassau as "beautiful." Doubtlessly he desired also to provide suitable diversion at his headquarters, which were now further assuming the atmosphere of a court to be graced by his nieces, but which bored him with no more important interest on mornings than to polish and play with his great quantities of diamonds.

In accordance with the half-mad commission from Potemkin, in which De Ligne and Nassau may have had a secret part, Jones undertook to capture two enemy gunboats stationed close by the fort of Hassan Pacha. He set out at night with five armed chaloupes for the venture itself and with an equal number of gunboats for emergency defense in case of a Turkish sortie. Of the two enemy vessels, Jones attempted to seize the one in the more difficult position and sent an officer, Lieutenant Edwards, to take the other. The first was high aground on the sands, adjoining a Turkish entrenchment and battery; and he found it impossible to set the gunboat afloat under the terrific fire from all the lines and batteries on the shore. The second gunboat, however, lay just afloat, although by the very walls of the fort. Edwards had already boarded this vessel and cut the cables; but after one of his two chaloupes had fled and several of his men had been wounded, he left through fear of being deserted by the second chaloupe. The lieutenant had already disappeared in the dark night when Jones arrived to support him. In defiance of the encircling enemy and in spite of the wounds suffered by some of his men, the Admiral boarded the gunboat, hauled it away, and brought it within the Russian lines. The next morning Potemkin found the prize vessel stationed directly in his view from the windows of his headquarters overlooking the nearby shore.

Nassau in turn now desired to satisfy his egoism at the expense of Jones, and Potemkin appears to have connived at his purpose. The commander of the flotilla hoisted a vice-admiral's flag in his luxurious galley and expected the Rear Admiral to salute it.

"The first duty of a man is to respect his own honor" declared Jones about a month later in a trenchant letter to De Ribas, intended for the reading of Potemkin, in answer to "a kind of note without date which purports to be from you, but which I do not recognize as your handwriting."[4] De Ligne may well have meddled in anonymous fashion in behalf of Nassau, especially in the light of his characteristic defense of his bosom friend and his condemnation of Jones upon writing to the Emperor: "In spite of a private letter from the Prince, who feared the wrongheadedness of Paul Jones, the latter has refused to salute the flag of the Vice-Admiral."[5] To be sure the American refused most decisively.

Whether or not Potemkin as well as De Ligne actively supported the so-called Vice-Admiral, Jones stated to De Ribas as the Prince Marshal's representative, in terms ranging from calm to impassioned, the history of his connection in Russia, including the recommendation of De Simolin that he was to serve as Commander in Chief on the Black Sea and the understanding that his only superior officer was to be the Prince Marshal. Of the flotilla commander in particular he asserted: "As I can never bring myself to resolve on having any connection with a man so detestable as M. de Nassau, I can never acknowledge him for my superior. If he has received the rank of vice admiral, I will say in the face of the universe that he is unworthy of it. It is now ten years since he wished to serve under my command. I have known him without knowing him. I knew that he was foolish, but I did not believe, before proving it, that his character was base to the bottom; the only military merit he possesses is effrontery."[6] This present instance of Nassau's insolence failed utterly—in a few days he lowered the flag. "How should he have done so," Jones pointedly remarked, "if he had been Vice-Admiral"?[7]

The decisive refusal of Jones to compromise his self-respect commanded the recognition of Potemkin, however much he was in connivance with his favored officer. The Admiral's gunboat exploit, his rescue from wreck ashore of certain vessels among a number with which the Marshal had meddled, and his demonstrated skill in blockading Oczakow made him also the more valued for future operations. Now the refusal of Woynowitch to fight the Turkish fleet in the Black Sea on the ground that his forces were not powerful enough to oppose it led to the tentative offer August 19 from Potemkin that Jones should go to Sevastopol to take the command.

Jones recognized well enough the gift horse; it did not dazzle his eyes as an impending fulfillment of his original expectation "to command *all* the naval force in the Black Sea."[8] Potemkin had disregarded his urgent desire to have his signals in English translated into Russian, he had made no effort to arm certain auxiliary ships at Kherson to serve as reinforcements for those at Sevastopol, and he had done nothing otherwise to strengthen a fleet which had been too weak for the attack before and was even weaker now. Under these circumstances the Prince Marshal, who was delaying his own military operations before Oczakow month after month to the wonder of all Europe, crazily wished him to be ready to sail and fight on the day after his arrival at Sevastopol. Like a soldier, Jones was altogether ready "to fulfill his orders"; but not like a rash and capricious Russian, he refrained from having it appear that he "sought to be sent." This sanity cooled the ardor of Potemkin, who did not revert to his suggestion; he proceeded, however, as Jones described, to send "positive orders to Woynowitch to meet the Turks," but this officer "always found reasons for not dealing further with the Capitan Pacha."

Very soon Nassau's sense of fitness in war showed itself equally fantastic. Possibly he had a special liking for watermelons, similar to Potemkin's for fish and Suvorof's for oranges, which was accountable for the untimely disruption of strategic plans. In any event, just when it happened on August 30 that the Turks captured a mere boat loaded with watermelons belonging to merchants of Kinburn, Nassau chose his hour to attack Oczakow with the flotilla in order to "punish the Turks" for this outrage.

The assault upon the defenses was almost as ridiculous as his immediate reason for it. He expended a great deal of ammunition to little purpose. He distinguished himself characteristically not in fighting the Turks but in conspiring against Jones. A rash Greek lieutenant had in a minor way disregarded explicit instructions not to advance with his boats before orders; he happened to be under the direction of Littlepage, who had secured from Potemkin the permission to command a number of Jones' gunboats. Nassau not only in perverse inconsistency later succeeded in having this lieutenant advanced in rank while Jones wished him punished, but also with unblushing deceit pretended that the consequences of this Greek officer's disobedience "had prevented him from taking the whole Turkish flotilla." It was the turn of Littlepage to marvel at his trickery: "But what does honor to the presence of mind of the Prince de Nassau is his having profited by this small circumstance to make a story out of it, and ascribe to it the bad success of his expedition. How? Can fourteen shots, fired almost out of gunshot distance, have deranged the operations of his line, which was acting, or rather *ought to have been,* against a part of the town absolutely opposite? Truly his prudence is praiseworthy. I remember, that, in the affair of July 1st, the fire of all his flotilla did not prevent Paul Jones from going in front with his chaloupe, and withdrawing from the flames a Turkish galley, which was struck by several of our bullets while he was towing her."[9]

Experience had now taught Littlepage to be less ready with easily given advice to Jones than when he had previously urged him: "For God's sake, my dear friend, be prudent. . . . Prince Potemkin has conceived a high regard for you, but *he loves Nassau.*" He could likewise better understand what Jones had replied: "I have put up with more from Nassau than, under other circumstances, I could have done from any man who was not crazy. I can no more reckon upon his humor than on the wind."[10] In the present circumstances of his combined military and political rôle, Littlepage resolved to leave Russia, although Potemkin urged him to remain. "I have nothing to lose or gain here," he wrote to his friends in Poland; "for I am neither engaged in the war as a *necessary* man like Paul Jones nor as a *necessitous* one like the Prince de Nassau." To Jones himself he offered parting advice: "Adieu, my dear General, take care of yourself, and be cautious in whom you trust. Remember you have to sustain here a political as well as a military character; and that your part is now rather that of a courtier than a soldier." To this realistic warning, Jones appended a note typical of his inflexible principles: "I never was made to play that part."[11]

In the clash of personalities, this issue touching the fixed course of the Rear Admiral not to compromise grew the sharper. The capricious incapacity of Potemkin on the one hand and his Asiatic self-willed arrogance on the other were increasingly manifest in his rôle as a military chief. The inconsequence of Nassau's attack upon the Turks on the occasion of the captured watermelons had not improved the Marshal's ill-humor, and the persistence of Woynowitch in ignoring his commands further aggravated it. He therefore directed Rear Admiral Mordwinoff to assemble a council on board the *Vladimir* to consider combining the ships in the Liman and the Black Sea, without even apprising Jones of his purpose. Jones ignored an affront which might have justified him in placing Mordwinoff under arrest and proceeded to make the only important suggestions at the conference, which related both to the preliminary need to attack and rout the advance guard of the enemy and to other means to escape the Turks in effecting the junction with the Sevastopol fleet.

Potemkin soon issued tentative orders to Jones to attack this advance guard on the island of Beresane and also to capture Fort Hassan Pacha, but ended by countermanding his instructions in both cases. He directed him likewise to isolate Oczakow but insisted upon placing the ships in accordance with his vagaries. He permitted Nassau to carry out his part of the operations in a haphazard manner but gave little attention to Jones' judgment. Accordingly the blockade became so ineffective that the Turks passed in and out with impunity. As if to climax his failings as a naval strategist and to satisfy his smoldering antagonism towards Jones because he no longer drew the chestnuts from the fire for them, Potemkin chose the day after Nassau had made a final vain effort against Oczakow to order the Rear Admiral to return the boats of the flotilla which had been attached to his squadron.

After this seal to repeated failures in attacking the strongholds, the relations between Potemkin and Nassau came to a crisis despite the earlier affectionate professions between them. Both repressed the news of the concluding defeat attributable to themselves as emphatically as they had heralded the victories attributable to Jones. "The flotilla," Nassau's follower Damas admitted, "suffered great losses; several ships were disabled, and a large number of men killed."[12] Nassau accused Potemkin and Potemkin accused Nassau. Especially galling to Nassau, who had boasted of a vast opening which he could blast in the walls of Oczakow, was the inquiry of Potemkin as to how many breaches he had made in Gibraltar. Before their recriminations, De Ligne had already left the camp in a highly disgruntled mood; and in his absence as a mediator, Nassau was soon to follow. "He shut himself up in a tent for three days," Damas related, "and never went near the Prince, whom he was expecting every moment to make advances or promise to adopt some more resolute plan of action. But Prince Potemkin's character was incapable of bending, or yielding to anyone's remonstrances, especially when they were made with vehemence. He made no advances whatever to the Prince de Nassau, and even neither asked what he was thinking nor what he was doing. The Prince de Nassau, in a greater rage than ever, wrote to ask for his passport; he received it in answer to his demand, and without any further explanation or delay set out for Poland."[13]

The riddance of Nassau from the naval scene was no indication that Potemkin was awakening to his own flagrant weaknesses and turning to correct them; it did not foretoken that his attitude towards Jones would be less censurable. Even Damas, as a partisan as well as an eyewitness of the Marshal, said of him and his campaign: "Nowhere, save in Russia, and to no general save an empress' favorite, would this futile sacrifice of time and men be permitted with impunity. And only a general who was his sovereign's lover could arbitrarily bestow military commands without any regard for order, seniority, or rank." The recent aloofness of Jones from operations under the commander of the flotilla was, without doubt, responsible indirectly for the breach between Potemkin and Nassau, inasmuch as it had brought to an end the victories which they had exploited exclusively in their own interests. And applicable to his future stand against the one scarcely less than to his past defiance of the other was his declaration: "The first duty of a man is to respect his own character."

◇◇

Chapter LXIII

Jones Challenges Potemkin

STUNG BY THE mortifying reverses of the campaign as well as intoxicated by his power, Potemkin was confirmed in his wayward dictatorship. Inevitably a vindictive mood was to vent itself upon Jones, under whatever pretext the Prince found nearest at hand. The scrupulous devotion of the Rear Admiral to his duty had protected him from open affront; therefore the guile which was the favorite resource of Potemkin and which from the outset had peeped from behind the curtain of his hypocrisy began more obviously to expose its face.

A second absurd enterprise like that which had resulted in the captured gunboat was now the Marshal's inspiration. Certainly it might provide new amusement as a tale for his recently arrived married nieces, who could not be expected to remain satisfied merely with jewels, perfumes, and the free attentions of Damas as well as of himself. It would serve especially as a fitting climax to the capriciousness at the scene of war, consistent with the Prince's imperious and lawless passions and with such accidental influences as Nassau's watermelons, Suvorof's oranges, and his own fish.

Thus when Jones went to headquarters on October 10 to return, according to orders, all boats which had been attached to his squadron, Potemkin took occasion to express "the strongest desire to pitch overboard a large piece of artillery placed on the forepart of the vessel of the Turkish squadron which stood farthest out and had run aground."[1] As to a general with such confirmed fancies, even the declarations of courtiers rather than soldiers like Nassau and De Ligne may be accepted as true that he was the most unmilitary man living.

Philosophically Jones agreed to undertake this second nonsensical venture. But with the reasonable assumption that he should employ his own time to better purpose against the Turks, the Admiral entrusted the exploit to Lieutenant Edwards, who on a number of occasions had given ample evidence of his abilities. Nevertheless Edwards failed in this night enterprise, explaining to Jones that a very large number of men who were in the vessel opened fire upon him and that he had been poorly supported by his followers. The Admiral then made the offer to Potemkin to conduct the exploit himself during the next night, and the latter held him to his word. As it was already eleven o'clock of this night when Edwards returned with the information and as both the violent wind and strong tide were unfavorable, Jones would have deferred the attempt if he had not been committed.

He set out with five armed canoes as the moon rose at two o'clock in the morning, but left behind several larger craft in order that the passage might be as swift as possible. Great as was his haste, daylight came and the rowers were fatigued before he reached within two-thirds of a mile of the stranded boat with the "large piece of artillery"; accordingly he decided to avoid a needless alarm and to try again the next night with more promising prospects. In advance of his report, however, Potemkin sent him the curt order "to abandon the enterprise, for he had entrusted it to other ships."

The Prince Marshal now had for his purposes one pretext marked against Jones, and he shortly found another. Thanks to his orders, the plan of the blockade against Turkish reinforcements for Oczakow from the nearby island of Beresane had become ineffective. Thanks also to his orders, several Turkish vessels escaped just at this period because Jones could not at the same time both overcome the mistakes of the instructions to him for the blockade and keep vigils at night for freakish exploits. Therefore Potemkin, in ire at the cumulative failures of his own delay, perversity, and imperiousness throughout many months, issued a further command to Jones on October 13 which was not only brusque but insulting.

It touched the warrior at one of his tenderest points, his bravery: "As it is seen that the Capitan Pacha comes in his kirlangitch from the grand fleet to the smaller vessels, and as before quitting this he may resolve to attempt something, I request Your Excellency, the

Capitan Pacha having actually a greater number of vessels, to hold yourself in readiness to receive him courageously, and drive him back. I require that this be done without loss of time; if not, you will be made answerable for every neglect."[2] To this order Jones affixed his private note: "A warrior is always ready, and I had not come there as an apprentice."[3]

The Admiral had effected and wished to continue his successful blockade at the more exposed and dangerous position in the road of Oczakow, as compared with the passage of the Liman, to which Potemkin had ordered him to withdraw. And it was Nassau, not he, who had permitted the whole Turkish flotilla to escape. The day after the message from the Marshal with its insult added to injury, Jones replied that the officers, gunners, and seamen of twenty gunboats and bomb vessels formerly under his command for the blockade should be returned to him if he was to be "answerable for every neglect." He also maintained an opinion, at variance with Potemkin's, that neither the transfer of men nor stormy weather justified even a temporary withdrawal of his ships from their position in the blockade in view of both practical and psychological advantages which might accrue to the enemy. In behalf less of himself than his followers, he added with respectful independence such a counterblast as was unique in the military annals of Russia and particularly in the absolutism of a Potemkin. "In case the Capitan Pacha decides to undertake anything before his departure, I can assure you in advance that the brave officers and crews which I have the honor to command will do their duty "courageously," in spite of the fact that they have not been rewarded at all for the very important services which they have already rendered the empire under my eyes. I pledge my honor to explain myself frankly concerning this delicate matter at the end of the campaign; in the meanwhile I shall say only that it was upon the sacred promise which I have given them to call for justice in their favor upon Your Highness that they have consented to conceal their grievances and keep their silence."[4]

The freedom nurtured in the blood of Jones in Scotland and in America had at last asserted itself unassumingly but inevitably against one of the two linked, outstanding exemplars of Russian despotism. In political life, De Ségur prided himself upon his retaliation against the arrogant wiles of Potemkin, who elevated himself by humbling all persons whose conduct was on a basis of equality. If the Russian received him with studied carelessness in a slovenly dressing gown, the Frenchman attended his most formal functions in similar apparel; if the former purposely caused him to wait in antechambers, the latter left a message that he was unable to delay and promptly departed. But the Prince Marshal had as much to gain as the Minister of France by friendly relations in the fencing of international diplomacy, and so he came to terms. In the autocratic military sphere, no one, not even noted generals like Romanzoff and Suvorof, however flagrantly downtrodden, presumed to oppose his word or glance. Catherine herself, who at this very time was in desperate danger from the Swedes threatening at the gates of St. Petersburg, dared only to soothe him. It remained for Jones, without the benefit of personal or political intimacy such as De Ligne enjoyed sometimes to good purpose, to challenge the Marshal with the galling truth of his pen.

Potemkin had scarcely credited the reality of the one letter from Jones before he received another from him which was to his dictator's spirit a new affront in degree like Ossa piled on Pelion. While a gale prevented the immediate execution of orders for the withdrawal of his blockading ships from the road of Oczakow to the passage of the Liman, the Admiral expressed his readiness to obey them but at the same time enlarged upon his own views and on October 16 added: "Every man who thinks is master of his own opinion. Mine is fixed that the return of these vessels can only result in an effect to our disadvantage in the morale of the enemy."

The immediate issue now before Potemkin had nothing to do with naval policy; it was only a question of unreserved obedience. The glint of challenged tyranny in the eyes of the Prince Marshal is readily imagined as he sent Jones the next day a summary command and emphasized it by terms similar to those which had already given offence: "Should the enemy attempt to pass to Oczakow, prevent him by every means, and defend yourself *courageously*."[5] To this command as to the earlier, the Admiral appended a private note: "It will be hard to believe that Prince Potemkin addressed such words to Paul Jones."[6]

Intimations shortly followed that these flagrant orders from

Potemkin were just preliminary to more hostile action. The Admiral was not the less sure that he had conducted himself in accordance with his professional and personal honor, but he had learned forbearance and discretion in a hard school and reflected that he had replied "with perhaps too much freedom and warmth." The prospect was not in the least pleasing. He therefore took pains to make clear in detail without delay on October 18 that no fault attached to him for the failure on the single night to throw overboard the cannon of the Turkish vessel and for the escape of enemy craft through the blockade. He even humbled himself to make an apology, which could be expected only to make a despot more despotic: "Your Highness is so just in every circumstance that you will excuse the ardor which escaped me in my letter of the 14th. I wish very much to continue my service. I do not need to recall either the promises or the offers which have been made to me. I am altogether disposed to do everything which can be required of a man of honor in my position; and if you find me any asset for the Imperial Marine, it depends only on you to have me remain in Russia. But in view of the fact that I have come here not at all as an adventurer nor as a charlatan to repair a ruined fortune, I hope in the future to experience no humiliation and to find myself soon in the position which was promised me when I was invited to enter the Navy of Her Imperial Majesty."[7]

So honest a man like Jones became dangerous to Potemkin, dangerous indeed to the whole network of intrigue woven into the military organization of Russia. Even his apology had an air of accusation. Even as he showed himself deferential in one breath, he bluntly exposed the errors and double-dealing of his superior officer in the other. His fearless bravery made him outspoken, and his candor unmasked in many ways both the farcical and subtle lies which surrounded him at every turn. The frigate *Alexander* had been lost under his eyes, but it remained unalterably one of the ships of the Russian Navy in the list of the marine. He had prepared an official account of his operations in accordance with admiralty regulations, but Potemkin had required Mordwinoff to suppress it. Ominous of the fate of his letters from Russia was the continued absence of letters for him to Russia. In short, the ruthless means by which Potemkin had seized and held his power tolerated only confederates who, if they possessed talents like Jones', also required in particular guile like Nassau's and subservience like a Russian peasant's. Now the Prince had found his desired pretexts to remove the Admiral, and without further ado he sent Mordwinoff aboard the *Vladimir* on October 20 to assume command of both the squadron and flotilla.

It was impossible for Potemkin to be straightforward even at the removal of the Admiral. His final lies are by reason of their enormity the unconscious tribute which his disguised malice paid to the talents and achievements of Jones as the naval officer to whom was due all the honor of the campaign on the Liman. On the one hand he had sent on October 18 an order to Jones: "According to the desire of Her Imperial Majesty, your place of service is fixed in the Northern seas"[8]—and the Rear Admiral was credulous enough to accept the source as authentic especially since it was attributed to the Empress. On the other hand he had written on the same day to Catherine with a brazen lie in regard to Jones almost in every phrase and with a concluding admission of his own subterfuge towards him, which might well have enlightened the Empress as to his subterfuges towards her—but from a favorite like Potemkin and to a favorite's mistress like Catherine, such trifles could not have mattered. Accordingly he stated: "The sleepy Admiral Paul Jones has missed the transports to Oczakow and could not burn the ship which the Don Cossacks burned. He was brave while he was a pirate, but he has never been at the head of many ships. No one consents to serve under him. Hence I have decided to send him to St. Petersburg under pretense of a special expedition to the North." How the reputation of Jones soon suffered in St. Petersburg appears from a variant account in the diary of the Empress' secretary, Khrapovitski: "He is brave for gain. He was a pirate. He never was in command of many ships. He is afraid of the Turks. Nobody wishes to serve under him, and he doesn't want to serve under anybody."[9]

A stratagem of Potemkin's treachery was to find the cue for his lies in the truths on which Jones most prided himself. He sought with the guile for which he had a perverted aptitude to turn the outstanding virtues of the American patriot into equally conspicuous vices, especially when his intrigue served to hide his own evil acts behind the alleged corresponding misdeeds with which he slandered the Rear Admiral. As one instance among many, Potemkin distorted Jones' championship of the officers and crews of his squadron to secure justice for them from him into the accusation that they refused to serve under the Admiral; and this charge spread not only to Catherine and her secretary in St. Petersburg but also among certain hostile persons in the Prince's Army by the Black Sea. Never hesitant to confront falsehood, Jones secured testimonials from several of his chief officers certifying to the contrary; but dread of retaliation by Potemkin, not any question as to the validity of their statements, moved these officers to demand the return of the originals in Russian and to leave only less formal evidence in his hands. They proved, as Jones said, that "men sometimes dare not render homage to truth";[10] they set in relief the fearlessness of the American against the dark background of Russian duress as the all-pervasive whiphand to make the false prevail.

At first Potemkin's artifice to free himself handily from Jones even without a confrontation seemed the more likely to succeed because of the bait which promised that the Rear Admiral would be employed by the Empress in a capacity of greater importance in the Baltic Sea. Admiral Greig of the Cronstadt fleet had just died, and Sweden was now at war with Russia, so that the order to proceed to St. Petersburg had an appearance of reasonableness. But when Jones reflected that it was too late in the season for a campaign before the next year in the icebound Baltic, he felt grieved to have been deprived of his command so near the close of naval operations on the Liman. He was pitiful at first in appealing to a cynic whose only motives were the aggrandizement of his own power: "I will not say that it is difficult to find more skilful sea officers than myself; I know well that it is a very possible thing; but I feel emboldened to say that you will never find a man more susceptible of a faithful attachment or more zealous in the discharge of his duty."[11] He was naïve, also, a few days later in volunteering to continue his services at the pleasure of the Prince, especially in gratitude for his order of St. Anne, in any suitable line until the end of the campaign. Potemkin, enacting his little plot to its conclusion, informed him through his secretary Popoff that, since he had been recalled by the Empress, it was necessary for him to go.

If Jones had his lapse into entreaty as undeserved as useless upon his final requests to remain, he rose to the full stature of his self-respecting independence upon taking his leave. At headquarters, he discovered that Potemkin sought to avoid a confrontation, and in his absence he spoke freely to Popoff, telling him "all that was on my mind." The secretary reported the words to Potemkin, who, although vexed at first, decided to speak with the Admiral. "Without failing in the respect due to him, I spoke to him freely enough," Jones recounted. "I told him he had played an unfair game at the opening of the campaign in dividing the command in the Liman in the existing circumstances of the country; and that if I had not resolved to sacrifice my own feelings in order to manage the persons he had given me for colleagues, the campaign would have taken a very different turn. He replied, 'Agreed; but it is too late now.'

"He then said that he would be glad to see me fixed in Russia, and that he was disposed to give me *solid proofs of his esteem,* both now and in the future. I showed him the testimonial of the Captain of the *Vladimir* and some other papers to convince him that he had neither done justice to me nor to the squadron. He said the Prince of Nassau pretended all was done by himself; 'but I have never,' said he, 'been deceived in him. I have always known him for what he is.' "[12]

Such admissions from Potemkin himself, in view of the contradictory words from his pen as well as his not less contradictory deeds, expose his guile in deep-dyed colors. Whether sincerely repentant even for a moment or only seemingly so in order to trick Jones to undertake a new thankless task, he proposed that the Admiral should equip and command a squadron which was being built at the port of Taganrog. Jones' experience with the *America* in the Revolution had been beset with sufficient disappointments; another of a similar nature with Potemkin as his master and with Russian ineptness and corruption at every turn threatened to involve infinitely greater difficulties. There were also more persuasive considerations.

He had already brought the campaign on the Liman near its victorious end; and in this instance as in every other of his life, in significant contrast with Potemkin's, what he began his will was to finish. If the Prince barred his path in this regard, there was the apparently imperative summons of the Empress, notwithstanding the lateness of the season, which he had little means to recognize as merely a ruse. Above all, Potemkin had played "an unfair game," as Jones had been bold enough to tell him outright; and the American had his reasons for suspecting that the Russian was not disposed even in the future to play a fair one. Russia in the person of Potemkin had broken a point of honor, and Jones possessed both a long memory and a tenacious spirit to resent such an offence. "I had been brought to Russia," he repeated, "to take the chief command in the Black Sea."[13] As his last acts before leaving, his refusal of the offer at Taganrog and his request for justice to the officers of the squadron were indicative of his moral triumph.

The outcome which saw his departure had been preordained by the irreconcilable professional and moral traits of the two men. Potemkin had the despotic authority of Russia behind his treacherous self-will, which became the more malignant because he was opposed by a singlehanded warrior in a foreign country who was immeasurably his superior in professional abilities and in personal character and who was steadfast enough not to compromise either the one or the other under any circumstances of the insatiable egoism of a jealous tyrant. When Jones bearded the Prince at the final interview, chiding him for the influence of enemies, he answered: " 'Don't believe that anyone leads *me!* No one leads me'; and getting up and stamping with his foot, he added, 'Not even the Empress.' "[14] If De Ligne and Nassau and Alexiano and others of their kind did not in fact have influence upon him, his treachery towards the Admiral was simply the more shameless. The passionate declaration of Potemkin was an index to his preposterous insolence, which underlay most of his vices and failures and which was not less the basis for ultimate vindication of Jones as both officer and man for challenging him.

In a small open galley Jones started on November 9 for Kherson on the first stage of his route to St. Petersburg. Exposure to what he described as "the excessive cold" for three days and nights of this trip to the eastern end of the Liman resulted in a dangerous illness which affected his chest, apparently connected with injury from the earlier dash for Russia on his circuit of the ice-caked Baltic to Revel; the day after his arrival the Dnieper River froze; and it was December 6 before his health permitted him to proceed to St. Elizabeth. Here he learned that the Russians had just taken Oczakow by storm.

His removal from the scene of war newly served to emphasize for him with better perspective how basically he as an officer of European and American traditions stood apart from a military head like Potemkin with his Asiatic and Russian heritage. Aside from crude mistakes in the military operations after his departure, which did not prove to be very serious only because the Turks failed to take full advantage of them, the inhumanity of Potemkin towards his Russian soldiers and sailors and in turn of these Russians towards the Turks was abhorrent to Jones.

Thousands of Russians, not to consider horses, died from want, disease, and exposure in their tents to the exceptional cold of the early winter of 1788. The prolonged inaction of the Prince Marshal was merely one instance of his criminal indifference to the lives of those who served under him. Damas, who himself suffered unbearably from the cold even with a spirit-lamp in his tent night and day so as to obtain a few moments of rest in his sleeping-bag, said of the Commander in Chief: "The person of Prince Potemkin was inviolable; he was himself the Empress' soul, conscience, and authority, and in consequence considered himself independent of all the laws of duty and reason."

The savagery of a general like Suvorof and of a horde of Zaporavians who were a branch of the Cossacks was in particular agreement with his own. At the assault upon Oczakow, success resulted less from strategy than from the strange unreadiness of the Turks, the cruelty of the Russians, and most of all the prodigality of Potemkin with the lives of his soldiers. The Russians lost, according to Potemkin, less than a thousand officers and men; according to one more reliable source, the number was several times as great, and according to another, it was twelve thousand. As for their enemy, "I have been assured," said Jones, "that from eighteen to nineteen thousand Turks perished on that day."

The manner of their death has far greater significance than the number who met their end. With his superstition if not hypocrisy hand in hand with his ruthlessness, Potemkin had arranged to make the attack on the feast of St. Nicholas, and he not only chose a removed place for his personal security but ejaculated, "O Lord, have mercy upon us!" He figuratively meant, it appears, mercy upon himself rather than upon the Russians, still less upon the Turks. Damas, who took part in the attack, referred to the scene as "the most horrible and unparalleled massacre"; he avowed, "It was not until every drop of Turkish blood was shed that the Russian soldiers would consent to stay their hands." But the perverted piety which Potemkin instilled in the hearts of his Russians and which does him still greater ignominy appears in an account that De Ségur received from another witness of higher authority: "The ferocity of the Russian soldiers was such that two days after the assault, finding some Turkish children hidden in underground hovels, they seized them, threw them into the air, impaled them on the points of their bayonets, and cried: 'At least these will never do harm to Christians.' I had these facts from the worthy Prince d'Anhalt, who in telling them to me still trembled with horror."

In absolute contrast was the humaneness of Jones, which distinguished him all the more because he had found himself, among the naval not less than among the military Russian forces, in such an environment of blood. And doubtlessly the jealous purpose to drag him down to this level and at the same time to hide it from the eyes of the world was to inspire the machinations which spread the reports that he was "a cruel and brutal man" and that during the American Revolution he had "even killed his own nephew." The calumniators did not trouble themselves even to learn that at this period he had no nephew of a sufficiently mature age who could have been the victim of such a crime.

To judge by his conduct in the Liman campaign, his mercy was not less than his valor in Russia as well as in America, although his opportunities to practice it had been limited. It was not he but Nassau, Alexiano, and their accomplices who had used brand-cougles to set afire the Turkish ships, even when they were help-less. It was he, not they, who had taken most of the Turkish prisoners and who had refrained, even in his exploits upon capturing enemy galleys, to endanger lives by resort to the ready but savage expedient of these incendiary missiles. It was he who had not suffered even a single ship to run aground in the treacherous waters so as to have her officers and men become a prey to cruelties of the Turks like those which they had suffered at the hands of the Russians. Finally it was he who had written to Jefferson in a letter sent by private means but long delayed in transit: "I leave to Mr. Littlepage to inform you particularly of the military events that have taken place here this campaign. I can take no delight in telling over tales of blood. God knows there has been too much of it spilt! Scenes of horror have been acted under my eyes in which, however, I have the happiness to say that I had no part."[15]

It was as natural for Jones to be humane, in addition to brave and honorable, as it was for Potemkin to be savage, in addition to dictatorial and treacherous. The culminating barbarities which had attended the capture of Oczakow by the Prince newly forecast that the fortunes of Jones, to the extent that they might remain in the keeping of the ruthless Marshal, would not be better in the North than they had been in the South. Neverthless the Admiral preferred that, when he enlightened the Empress concerning his services, Potemkin himself should be at hand. He pursued leisurely the last stages of his journey to St. Petersburg until such time as it was expected that the Prince had arrived at the capital. Although he understood correctly enough that the ambition of the Empress was "to be esteemed the most magnanimous of sovereigns," it was an unpromising characteristic instance of the duplicity of Potemkin that the recommendation which the Admiral had received from him to be presented to Catherine certified only to "his ardor and zeal"—not at all to his talents and achievements.[16] Jones knew his own character when he said, "I love virtue better than reward."[17] He still did not thoroughly know Potemkin the Russian whom he had dared to challenge, and he knew even far less Catherine the Russo-German whom he looked to, ironically, for redress.

◇◇◇

Chapter LXIV

The Russo-German
Girl Decoy

CONFIDENT and resolute, Jones reached St. Petersburg on December 28, 1788, expecting full justice and even generosity at the hands of the Empress. Although he had previously known how European courts sometimes blew alternately hot and cold, his faith in believing that Catherine would fulfill her apparent promise, in his favorite phrase "not to condemn me unheard," disarmed suspicion that even in the half-Asiatic environment smiles might be the mask of guile and soft words of calumny. Nassau, too, was now in St. Petersburg, De Ligne the Austrian Chamberlain was in correspondence with his friends at the Russian Court, Cobentzel the Austrian Ambassador was in personal and political sympathy with both of them, and Potemkin himself was soon to return, when Jones on the third day after his arrival received an invitation to the Hermitage, Catherine's palace in the capital. In his own words, "Her Imperial Majesty did me the honor of granting me a private audience."

The customary showmanship was in order pending the completion of Russian political strategy. In lieu of a naval appointment in the Baltic such as Jones had reason to expect on the basis of the explanation falsely assigned by Potemkin for his transfer to the North, Catherine confined herself to the flattery of this "private audience," which was pleasing to the condescension of her feminine vanity and might increase his devotion to her and her country, whatever course she should see fit to adopt after the return of the Prince Marshal. And now that she had acted her part of preliminary duplicity, one of her political tools was to perform his. Foreign Minister Besborodko supported Jones' expectations by the assurance that a command of greater importance than that of the Black Sea was intended for him; presumably it was to be in the Baltic, in the war against Sweden.

Nassau had a more meaningful audience with the Empress, whether or not Jones was informed of it, within a day or two after his own. Closely linked as Russian public affairs were with the private life of an egoist like Catherine, repercussions which the Admiral was to feel in his profession were the more likely. And in recognition that one of Nassau's greatest boasts was his seduction of the Queen of Tahiti and that Catherine had her procession of favorites (in the phrase of De Ligne, "it was court etiquette to be the Empress' lover"), the triumphant account which the mercenary adventurer sent even to his wife paints him as a swaggering gallant and as a potential enemy of the Admiral in a new setting.

"It is not possible to express words more flattering and better suited to honor me," he wrote to Madame de Nassau concerning the reception of Catherine. "After my audience, I dined with the Empress at a little table reserved for eight, and in the evening she received me in her bedchamber, which she did not leave; in this way I have returned to the earlier pace of my living."[1] His favor was such that soon he presided at a chapter of the outstanding Order of St. George, received a diplomatic mission to Spain in an effort to bring about a quadruple alliance to include this country along with Russia, Austria, and France, and had promises of a Russian command in the Baltic through which he planned "to achieve great deeds." But it is not unlikely that the intimacy between Nassau and Catherine, as set forth even in his letter to his wife in Poland, explains her subsequent arrival in St. Petersburg and some of the complications among the three which were to ensue.

While Jones awaited with such patience as he could muster a decision concerning his future service, his enterprising mind was busily occupied. Turning his thoughts to mutual advantages of the United States and Russia, he presented to Vice Chancellor Ostermann a plan for a commercial treaty between the two countries; he likewise suggested it to Potemkin after his arrival at last in St. Petersburg about February 15, amid a royal celebration for the capture of Oczakow. But the Marshal considered such a proposal premature, especially since he professed to believe that it would antagonize Britain, with which the Russian wars of aggression made friendly gestures the more important.

Now that Potemkin was at Court, the falsity of the pretext under which he had sent Jones away before the end of the campaign on the Black Sea become obvious as weeks passed and the Admiral received no intimation of a new command. It may readily be imagined how envenomed were the aspersions which both Potemkin and Nassau, the one practically a partner in the rule of Russia and the other a rising favorite, whispered in the ears of Catherine against Jones. And apart from their persuasions, innumerable instances of her own combined pride, caprice, and ruthlessness make it appear that what she heard only whetted her own Russo-German taste for treachery. From the time that she had usurped the throne of Russia, her lovers, her statesmen, her soldiers, her sailors, and even the writers and artists whom she patronized—all of them, unless they were meek, stolid, or bureaucratic, rose today only to fall tomorrow or the day following. High abilities combined with self-respect grew repugnant to her after they had served a purpose, for they might in some measure put in shadow her own egregious vanity and autocratic power.

When self-protection and even fear happened to impel the Empress, her hostility was invariably the more unscrupulous. Now she, with Potemkin as a political partner, must have begun to feel, scarcely less than he had already experienced, particular embarrassment at the blunt truthfulness of Jones. In St. Petersburg the Admiral learned that his naval services had been misrepresented even more flagrantly than he had before believed. "I either deserved to lose my head," he declared, "or the plans of the operations on the Liman, which had been got up in St. Petersburg during the winter, and which I saw with astonishment in the office of M. Popoff, ought to be burnt. I assert that they are false even in the most trifling details."[2] Closer to the door of Catherine, and attributable to her active policy rather than to her connivance, was the systematic confiscation of Jones' letters, of which he became increasingly aware in the capital. To the Empress who was ambitious for the good opinion of the world in step with the infamy which she merited, it proved to be more and more uncomfortable to have in her midst an honest man who dared to speak out.

Of Jones' letters, those in his correspondence with Jefferson were typical. Even after his return to St. Petersburg he found that messages sent to him by post from the Minister still failed to arrive safely.[3] Following earlier letters, including one from the Liman which he had sought to transmit privately by Littlepage, Jones wrote to Jefferson twice from St. Petersburg, on January 26 and 31, 1789; the first communication, similar in essentials to the second, indicates some of his immediate interests:

"Having written you fully respecting the Denmark business by Mr. Littlepage, with the papers necessary to finish it, I now have the honor to transmit you the extract of my journal that you wish to communicate to the Academy of Inscriptions and Belles Lettres on the subject of the medal with which I am honored by Congress.

"I have only at present to inform you that I returned here from the Black Sea a short time ago, by the special desire of Her Imperial Majesty; but I know not yet my future destination.

"I congratulate you on the establishment of the new American Constitution. Among other good effects, a marine force will naturally result from it. If there is still a disposition to send a force against the Algerines, would it not be a good thing to conclude a treaty with this country, and make the war a common cause in the Mediterranean? The Turks and Algerines are together, and acted in conjunction against us before Oczakow. A treaty might now be concluded, permitting Her Imperial Majesty to enlist seamen in America, and assuring to America, after the peace, a free navigation to and from the Black Sea. If you approve of this idea in general, various other things will necessarily be engrafted in the treaty, and I flatter myself I may obtain the command of the force destined to act in conjunction with that of the United States."[4]

Significantly by "courier of France," Jefferson answered on March 23: "Your favor of January 31, from St. Petersburg came safe to hand and is the only proof we have received of your existence since you left Copenhagen. I mention this that, reflecting how and what you have written heretofore, you may know how and what you may write hereafter. I shall put nothing in this letter but what is important to you and unimportant to any government through which it may pass."[5] This indirect reflection upon Catherine and her postal seizures, which had occurred regardless of the absence of military or political secrets in Jones' letters, was not less applicable to the suppression of liberty of speech and of the press in Russia.

The American Minister took occasion to mention at the same time his own intended recommendations to Congress for energetic action against the pirates of Algiers and his own lack of success for the present in urging the claim against Denmark, even to the extent of not obtaining "one word of an answer of any kind." He further explained, as to Jones' personal affairs, his arrangements with the medalist Dupré for the engraving of the gold medal which had been awarded by Congress, and also with Houdon for the completion of eight replicas of the bust, as the Admiral had requested, for gifts to American friends.

Jones seems, however, not to have heard in regard to one subject of special private concern. In the early message of September 9 entrusted to Littlepage, he had asked Jefferson anxiously: "I pray you to inform me, if you possibly can, what is become of Mme. T—. I am astonished to have heard nothing from her since I left Paris. I had written to her frequently before I left Copenhagen. If you cannot hear of and see her, you will oblige me much by writing a note to Monsieur Dubois, Commissaire du Regiment des Guardes Français, vis-à-vis la Rue de Vivienne, Rue neuve des petits Champs, desiring to speak with him. He will wait on you immediately. You must know that, besides my own purse, which was very considerable, I was good natured, or, if you please, foolish enough to borrow for her four thousand four hundred livres. Now M. Dubois knows that transaction, and as she received the money entire from me for the reimbursement, I wish to know whether she has acquitted the debt? When that affair is cleared up, I shall be better able to judge of the rest."[6]

The openness of Jones' inquiry to a man whom he regarded as highly as Jefferson further reflects his honorable feelings towards Madame T—, whatever may have been her unrevealed final conduct towards him. It was probably not a simple coincidence and certainly not a matter of mere form which explains the closing words of the Minister's letter: "I shall be glad to hear from you as often as possible, and have the honor to be with very great esteem. . . ."[7] Nor, by contrast, was the characteristic gentlemanly connection of the Admiral with Madame T— without relevance to what was now to befall him in St. Petersburg in relation to a person of the female sex.

Suddenly, on March 30, an incident occurred which led to a charge on the next day before the police court of the city that Jones had forcibly violated a very young girl, Katerina Stepanova, daughter of a colonist and his wife, Stephen and Fredrica Sophia Koltzwarthen.[8] According to the report of the head of the police, Major General and Cavalier Nikita Ivanovich Ryleyev, the girl testified:

"That she was in her tenth year, and that on the 30th day of last March, she, Stepanova, was sent by her mother to sell the colonist's butter, which she carried with her. As she was walking along an unfamiliar street in the first district, somebody knocked and called to her, Stepanova, from a first floor window. Who it was that knocked, and whose house it was, she does not know. She, Stepanova, entered the court, and went into the apartment—on that floor. She sold to an unknown man twenty-five kopecs worth of butter. At the same time an unknown man-servant entered the room and called her, Stepanova, to his master who lived in the same house on the second floor, not saying who his master was, to sell some more butter.

"Having consented, she followed the lackey to the other floor, and entered an anteroom. Opening the door for her, the lackey asked her what the price of the butter was. She told him then that the price of the butter was fifteen kopecs. The lackey raised three fingers, and, addressing himself in Russian to his master, who was standing in the antechamber, told him about the fifteen kopecs. His master was dressed in a white uniform, the front of which was embroidered in gold and decorated with a crimson ribbon and a gold star.

"She, Stepanova, entered the room, but the lackey remained behind the doors. The master proceeded to lock the entrance doors, with what she does not remember, then took from her, Stepanova, one piece of butter, for which he paid twenty-five kopecs, put the butter on the stove, and when she, Stepanova, wanted to leave the room, seized her around the waist and dealt her a blow on her chin, whereupon her lower lip was cut by the teeth, and the chin became crimson with blood. Pressing her mouth with a white handkerchief, he carried her from that room, through another, into a third room . . . with violence assaulted her.

"Though she, Stepanova tried to call for help, her mouth was pressed tight with the handkerchief, so that nobody could hear her, until she lost her memory. . . . The man spoke Russian very badly. He urged her not to tell her mother, and threatened that if she should talk he would stab her. He nodded his head, and asked her to come again, beckoning with his hand. But when it became evident to him that she could not understand him at all, he opened the doors for her, and she left the room. She did not meet the lackey who brought her there, and upon leaving the apartment she did not say anything about what had happened to any strangers.

"On coming home, she related to her mother Sophia Fiodorova everything that had happened to her. She then went to the pastor, and told him about it. The pastor commanded her to go to the registered midwife. The midwife examined the girl, and found that she really had been assaulted. Then she Fiodorova, to ascertain who had committed this deed, went to the house, named "Pokhodyashina," there lived the Major General Paul Jones. She also added to her testimony that a man who was secretary to Paul Jones told her to come on the next day when he would show her who had assaulted her daughter. He also added that were a thing like that to happen in the German land the culprit would be hanged."

The self-styled secretary, who in fact happened to be a lackey of Jones, was a German native, Johann Gottfried Bahl; and the police recorded, in turn, his version of the circumstances:

"On the 30th he saw in the servants' quarters the colonist girl with the butter. He led her to his master, the Admiral Paul Jones. He brought her over to the antechamber where his master was. He told his master that the butter was fifteen kopecs apiece, and showed him three fingers. To that his master replied in French that he could bargain himself, and told him to go. He went away, shutting the glass door after him. Shortly after, he came out, and saw that the outer wooden doors of his master's chambers, the room where the girl with the butter had remained, was shut. Whether it was locked or not he did not know.

"He peeped through the keyhole and saw the Rear Admiral Paul Jones in dressing gown. Before that, when the Admiral was buying the butter, he had his uniform and orders on. However, the girl with the butter, who had followed him to his master's and had remained there, he did not see. Fearing that the door might be suddenly opened, and he, Bahl, discovered peeping, he ran away. He had not heard any calls for help. An hour and a half later he, Bahl, went out into the court to talk to the coachman Ivan, who was waiting at the perron for his master Paul Jones. He, Bahl, asked Ivan whether he had seen any girl coming out of the rooms. The coachman answered that she had just left and that she walked around the court.

"At this information, Bahl went back to the servants' quarters, when shortly afterwards he was followed by the colonist girl. She entered the court through the back entrance. Her eyes were red from weeping, her face was swollen, and her lips were covered with blood. She came in to get the jug in which she carried the butter, and also her gloves. When he asked her where she had been, she at first stammered, and then said that she had been selling butter. . . .

"When he, Bahl, went as usual into his master's bedroom to fix the bed for the night, he carried with him a lit candle. While he was making the bed, he noticed some small blood stains on the floor, something he had never seen there before. Where the blood came from, he did not know; as to the said girl he had never seen her at Paul Jones' before."[9]

Along with the declarations of Bahl, the mother, and the girl herself, were statements by an alleged staff surgeon Nilus and midwife Krestina Litkerova that she had been assaulted.

In the face of this seemingly formidable array of testimony, the situation of Jones was fantastic in that he had scarcely begun to collect his evidence in defense before the attorney whom he had employed, Monsieur Crimpion, or indeed any other lawyer, was expressly forbidden at his peril by the governor of the city "to meddle with my cause."[10] The injunction seems the more preposterous because of Jones' inability to speak Russian; nevertheless it apparently simplified the one-sided court procedure in Russia for the object of prejudging him. Although the adverse testimony of others was in full and one of his servants, as Jones said, was "kept prisoner by the officers of police for several hours, two days successively, and threatened with the knout," his own evidence was seemingly disregarded and unrecorded as immaterial on the basis of this Russian reason, equally ironic and extravagant: "The explanation issued by Rear Admiral Jones was in the French language."[11]

To be sure such a travesty of legal justice was characteristic of the nation and especially of Catherine. The despotism manifested itself, for example, in the fate of a founder of Russian liberal schools, Novikof, as the result of his influence upon the Empress' son, the Grand Duke Paul. Catherine not only tyranically disregarded his right to the throne during her life but also plotted to thwart it in anticipation of her death.

"The phantom of a conspiracy in favor of Paul," it is related, "haunts and exasperates her. Novikof has unluckily lent some books to the heir to the throne. They are immediately seized; whereupon it is found that one of the volumes contains extracts from Thomas à Kempis. No matter! After having brought the accused to judgment, she pronounces the sentence herself without going on with the trial: fifteen years' imprisonment in the fortress of Schlüsselburg; the burning of all the publications of the Muscovite society . . . the closure of all the Freemasons' lodges in Russia.

"Nor is this enough: judged and condemned already, Novikof has to submit to further, endless interrogatories. . . . She has by this time forgotten a phrase which she wrote between 1744 and 1764, and which is preserved among her autograph notes: "Was there ever a more barbarous way of procedure, and more worthy of the Turks, than that of beginning by the condemnation in order to come finally to the examination?"[12]

This high-handed mockery of the processes of law was scarcely surprising towards Russian subjects throughout a land in which, as Ratishtchef, the martyred author, described a village to which he was exiled, "All is silence; everyone trembles; it is the abode of despotism."[13] But the tyrant's heel was likely to encounter some difficulties in the case of an American, a patriot scarcely less regarded as an adopted citizen of France than of the United States, and above all a fighter whose honor, as he himself averred, was a thousand times dearer to him than his life. The unskilful contradictions of the petty and disreputable witnesses against Jones, the force of his own discoveries before the police prohibited his defense, and the timely championship of his cause by De Ségur soon threatened to tear the mask from the charges and to have them betray both those who had made and those who had engineered them.

In spite of extravagant pressure at the police court, the evidence of all the persons employed at the house occupied by Jones, with the exception of the German Bahl, strongly contradicted the testimony against him. The most trustworthy of these witnesses, judged by his intelligence and position, was the Titular Councilor Dmitrevski of the College of Foreign Affairs, who served as his interpreter and secretary. "On the 30th day of March," he testified, "while doing some work in the said Rear Admiral's house, I noticed through the window of my room a little girl, carrying butter. It was about eleven, or half past eleven o'clock, when she entered the court. Noticing her in the court, I called her into my room where I ordered a lackey to lead her to the Admiral. This I had always done in the past, for the Admiral always chose his own butter. The said girl returned in about an hour and a half or more, and came through the same back entrance through which I had called her in. She came to get her gloves and her jug. When I asked her where she had been such a long time, she answered that she had been selling butter. While bidding me farewell, she told me that the Admiral had bought only one piece of butter for fifteen kopecs. She then went away. When she had returned to my room, I had not noticed any change in her."[14]

These statements, strengthened by those of a seaman Yakovlev and a coachman Vasilyev, both on duty with the Admiral, point to many self-incriminating assertions by the accusers, in particular their contradictions. Specifically, as for the girl, she falsely pretended not to have been at the house before and not to have seen Jones previously while selling her butter; she falsely stated the circumstances of her arrival and departure; she made typical irreconcilable remarks concerning the amount of her sale; and she offered the excuse of her youthful age, which itself was falsely represented, for the incongruities of her testimony, but gave no counterbalancing reason for confidence in either her good faith or her mental and moral fitness in making the grave charges. As for Bahl, he leaped to his conclusion, unwarranted even by his own statements, that Jones was guilty, and as a self-appointed judge he gave his verdict to the girl's mother, who accepted it at once for making her own accusations. He not only cast suspicion upon his own character and his evidence by the confession of peeping, but also contradicted testimony of far greater dependability in regard to such essentials as the appearance of the girl after the alleged attack, the period of her absence with Jones, and the person who brought her into the house. As for the girl, her mother, and Bahl in common, details of their charges conflict. Even as for the police court itself, the gross manner in which it presumed to change what each of the three accusers said into what each should have said so as to make their testimony consistent exemplifies the most corrupt collusion of the officers of the law.

Regardless of these clear indications of a far-reaching vile conspiracy, the case became the more threatening to Jones as the police department transferred it to the jurisdiction of the State Admiralty College, and he remained grotesquely shorn of all the rights at law allowed to a defendant in any civilized country. And true to the sycophantic traditions of the courtiers at the Russian Court, among whom favor or disfavor immediately followed the smiles or frowns of the Empress and her underlings, Jones found himself avoided with studied care by supposed friends who had previously shown him every respect. It appears that in this dark crisis, when the interdictions in St. Petersburg left him without private as well as legal aid, De Ségur proved to be his one outstanding supporter.

Although egoism and studied dramatization tend to distort the recollections of De Ségur, his firsthand account of generous efforts in behalf of Jones, however inaccurate in some particulars, is memorable for its Russian setting. Apropos of the fall of Catherine's favorite Momonoff, bringing in its train his abandonment, completely and at once, by the courtiers, the French Ambassador found occasion on the one hand to condemn the servility throughout a nation with an absolute government and on the other hand to call to mind "an example still more striking . . . to engrave deeper than ever in my heart the love of a noble liberty, despite all the storms which its enemies, and even its friends, cause to be raised too frequently around it." This example was Jones. After telling of his situation, particularly that "no one spoke to him, people avoided recognizing him, all doors were locked to him," De Ségur described his own part:

"I went to see him. He was moved to tears by my visit. 'I had not wished,' he said to me, pressing my hand, 'to go to your door and expose myself to a new affront, which would have been more painful to me than all the others. I have braved death a thousand times; today I yearn for it.' His expression and his weapons, placed upon the table, made me suspect a sinister purpose.

" 'Recover,' I told him, 'your calm and your courage. Do you not know that human life has its storms like the sea, and that fortune is more capricious than the wind? If, as I hope, you are innocent, brave this squall; if, unhappily, you are guilty, speak to me with complete freedom and I will do all that I can to extricate you, by an immediate escape, from the peril which threatens you.'

" 'I swear to you upon my honor,' he answered, 'that I am innocent and the victim of the most infamous calumny. These are the facts: A young girl came to my house in the morning a few days ago to ask if I could give her some linen or lace-work to mend; she made me advances quickly and indecently enough. Astonished at such brazenness at her age, I felt pity at her behavior; I urged her not to enter upon such a wretched course; I gave her some money and dismissed her. But she obstinately made up her mind to remain.'

" 'Impatient at this insistence, I took her by the arm and put her outside the door; but at the moment that the door opened, the little profligate tore her sleeves and her neckerchief, made a great outcry, claimed that I had outraged her, and threw herself into the arms of an old woman who called herself her mother and who certainly had not hidden there by chance. The mother and the daughter made the house echo with their cries, departed, and proceeded to make a charge against me. You know the whole situation.'

" 'Very well,' I answered, 'but has anyone been able to tell you the names of these adventuresses?'

" 'The porter knows them,' he replied; 'here are their names in writing, but I do not know their address. I wished to present a statement concerning this ridiculous affair first to the Minister and then to the Empress herself; but all access to them has 'been forbidden to me.'

" 'Give me that paper,' I said to him; 'recover your usual resolution; be confident; leave the matter to me; we shall shortly see each other again.'

"Immediately upon my return home, I directed some discreet agents, skilful and unfailing, who were devoted to me to secure information regarding these suspected women and to discover what manner of life they led. I was not long in learning that the old woman was a female accustomed to carry on a vile traffic of young girls whom she passed off as her daughters. . . ."[15]

Detailed evidence of a conspiracy came to light not alone by means of the disclosures of De Ségur and the contradictions and hollowness of the testimony itself before the courts of the police and the admiralty. There were supplementary but not less pertinent revelations, especially as to the character of the German Bahl and of the mother and the girl, who according to their names, the neighborhood of their recent home in Russia, their status as colonists, and their association with the lackey appear also to have been German.[16] In an eloquent appeal to Potemkin, in which he stated that "this deceit has brought me into disfavor with Her Imperial Majesty," Jones not only entreated the intercession of the Prince Marshal but also divulged his additional discoveries:

"This woman has never concealed that she has been directed from the beginning of the affair by a man wearing decorations and that she had no other aim in all her efforts than to gain money. Finally she has confessed that my servant has known her daughter for three months and that he had often trifled with her. We have learned besides that on the very day of the alleged violation the girl had been at the house of a lady named Thevis after she had left my home, that she did not in the least have an agitated appearance, that no one noticed on her any mark of violence, that this girl herself said to this lady that she would make no resistance to surrendering herself to a man.

"My coachman and postilions have seen her leave very quietly; she returned later by the rear door; but it is not possible to judge the time she was absent. However she made no complaint, took her gloves which she had forgotten, greeted my secretary, and left again very peacefully by the same rear door. And the coachman who had been at the front entrance of the house has seen nothing of either her arrival or her departure by the rear door.

"By the accompanying certificate of the father attested by the pastor of the [German] colony, it appears that the girl is older than the mother states in her sworn statement, and this statement also contains other matters equally false and equally easy to refute. It is said, for example, that I had a conversation with the girl in Russian, and it is impossible that anyone has heard me speak two words in this language, inasmuch as I do not know it at all.

"Finally, my Prince, the husband of this woman declares that she has run away from his home, that she has lived in St. Petersburg with a young man, that she has stolen his daughter from him to make her, apparently, a spectator of her debauchery. These facts are certified by the pastor of the colony; and the Pastor Lambe of St. Petersburg declares in his affixed certificates that he has never seen this woman at communion—which proves that she is without religion as well as without morals. And it is this person who has dared to accuse me, who has been believed, and upon whose authority I see myself exposed to public disgrace!"[17]

"The charge against me is an ignoble fraud," Jones continued. "I love women, I confess, and the pleasures which one enjoys only with their sex, but any enjoyments which it would be necessary to take by compulsion are horror to me. I am not able even to think that one can gratify his passions at the expense of their freedom and their modesty; and I give you my word as a soldier and as an honest man that, if the girl in question has not at all passed through other hands than mine, she must still have her virginity."[18]

It was De Ségur who on April 25 forwarded a letter from Jones to Potemkin, possibly this one of April 13, and emphasized anew the evil reputation of the mother and her utter unworthiness as a witness. He plainly referred to instigators who might be hidden behind their agents: "In the name of the friendship of which you have given me such frequent proofs, come to the aid of this brave officer and free him from a trial whose publicity and continuance discredit a reputation won by the most brilliant valor. . . . He has enemies and powerful ones. In the last war I often heard them accuse him of actions the falsity of which I can as Minister certify."

And in explanation of his special defense of Jones, this Minister who had taken a part in the Revolution declared: "I owe him this service as an American, as a companion in arms, and as a Chevalier of an order of the King."[19]

A misleading version of a part of De Ségur's letter has contributed to present Jones in a light which is the more unfounded in view of the proneness of the Minister to exaggeration and even very evident inaccuracy. According to Valentine Thomson's *Knight of the Seas,* the objection of the Minister on principle to a trial as "fâcheux," is made to appear "disastrous," and his generalization that "il rend publiees les egarements de la vie privée" is particularized as "it would make public the missteps of his private and dangerous life."[20] The meaning of De Ségur, even if his knowledge is not discounted, implied less regarding any information he may have had as to Jones' personal conduct in general or in particular than regarding the notoriety in any case incident to a public investigation of private affairs, especially of an eminent person. Actually he wrote: "I beg you to obtain permission from Her Majesty to save Paul Jones, a celebrated man, from the shame of a trial, always vexatious when it makes public the errors of private life, and always formidable when the accusers are counseled by enemies."[21] No slur upon Jones is implicit in these words under the conditions in which they were written; even less do they suggest that he was guilty of the specific charge against him.

The conviction of Jones with not less fantastic barbarism in arriving at the verdict than viperous insolence in bringing the charge against him seemed to be his fate as several weeks passed but Potemkin did not deign to heed the appeal of either the Admiral or the Minister. A final resource was an attempt at explanation to the Empress, who had remained aloof and seemingly had approved the so-called legal procedure. Officially cut off from all normal avenues of approach, Jones possessed as his only means a letter to her; but even if she was not disposed to ignore his entreaty, this expedient seemed doomed to frustration by her underlings, especially in view of the custom of flagrant confiscation in Russia. De Ségur once more as his second, however, had assured him that Catherine required, under severe penalty, that all letters addressed personally to her should without fail reach her hands; accordingly on May 17 Jones sent a message by post:

"I have never served but for honor, I have never sought but glory, and I believed I was in the way of obtaining both when I accepted the offers, made me on the part of Your Majesty, of entering your service," he began eloquently. After review of the declarations of De Simolin in Paris, the drama of his zeal in undergoing "a thousand dangers" in arriving at Revel, his implicit confidence in her following the assurance "never to condemn me unheard," and the evidence of the merit of his services on the Liman—after this picture of promise, he painted with the greater effect the deep shadow of treachery in Russia:

"Such was my situation when, upon the mere accusation of a crime, the very idea of which wounds my delicacy, I found myself driven from Court, deprived of the good opinion of Your Majesty, and forced to employ the time which I wish to devote to the defense of your empire in cleansing from myself the stains with which calumny had covered me. . . .

"Understanding neither the laws, the language, nor the forms of justice of this country, I needed an advocate, and obtained one; but, whether from terror or intimidation, he stopped short all at once, and durst not undertake my defence, though convinced of the justice of my cause. But truth may always venture to show itself alone and unsupported at the foot of the throne of Your Majesty. I have not hesitated to labor unaided for my own vindication; I have collected proofs; and if such details might appear under the eyes of Your Majesty, I would present them; but if Your Majesty will deign to order some person to examine them, it will be seen by the report which will be made that my crime is a fiction, invented by the cupidity of a wretched woman, whose avarice had been countenanced, perhaps incited, by the malice of my numerous enemies. Her husband has himself certified and attested to her infamous conduct. His signature is in my hands, and the pastor, Braun, of the district has assured me that if the College of Justice will give him an order to this effect, he will obtain an attestation from the country people that the mother of the girl referred to is known among them as a wretch absolutely unworthy of belief."

It is ironical that he further entreated the justice which was his right, that he expressed devotion and paid compliments which were suitable to an unseeing lover, that he found himself in such circumstances as might have recalled how on occasion, in the words of Hamlet, virtue itself of vice must pardon beg. "Take a soldier's word, madam," he declared fervently; "believe an officer whom two great nations esteem and who has been honored with flattering marks of their approbation (of which Your Majesty will soon receive a direct proof from the United States). I am innocent; and if I were guilty, I would not hesitate to make a candid avowal of my fault and to commit my honor, which is a thousand times dearer to me than my life, to the hands of Your Majesty."

Like the warrior that Jones invariably proved himself, he always stood ready, however convincing was his pen, to write in terms of deeds in the profession of arms. "If you will deign, madam," he concluded, "to give heed to this declaration, proceeding from a heart the most frank and loyal, I venture from your justice to expect that my zeal will not remain longer in shameful and humiliating inaction. It has been useful to Your Majesty, and may again be so, especially in the Mediterranean, where, with insignificant means, I will undertake to execute most important operations, the plans for which I have meditated long and deeply. But if circumstances, of which I am ignorant, do not admit the possibility of my being employed during the campaign, I hope Your Majesty will give me permission to return to France or America, granting as the sole reward of the services I have had the happiness to render, the hope of renewing them at some future day.

"Nothing has been or will be able to change or efface in my heart the deep feelings of devotedness with which Your Majesty has inspired me.

"To you, madam, I am personally devoted. I would rather have my head struck off than see those ties broken asunder which bind me to your service. At the feet of Your Majesty I swear to be ever faithful to you, as well as to the empire of which you form the happiness, the ornament, and the glory."[22]

Although it could be wished that these vows of consecration had been for more worthy objects, they enlarge the great obligations which the Empress owed to him. Did Catherine excuse herself for a court charge against which the defendant had not been allowed to record his own testimony, much less to engage a lawyer even in a foreign country? Did she recognize the dastardly nature and source of the accusation as special reasons for doing justice to his name? Did she undertake to expose publicly the miscreants, not merely the mother, the girl, and the lackey, but in particular those behind them? Did she even express an apology of any kind to the foreign officer whom she personally had invited to Russia? She made no amends at all.

It is to be asked even more pertinently not what the Empress failed to do but what she did. She brought to an end the pending trial undoubtedly because the exposure by Jones of the intrigue, without thanks due to her, Potemkin, or the Russian legal system, was already so transparent that even the grossest hypocrisy could no longer mask the truth. She had reason to appreciate in making this retreat from connivance if not complicity in despotic practices that, if he had been convicted in the face of his innocence, a serious loss to Russia would have followed in the good opinion of Europe, especially of France, which she courted and greatly valued for reasons of both her vanity and political manœuvres. De Ségur especially had weight with her, concerned as she was with the advancement of a prospective quadruple alliance and flattered as she felt with the attentions of so accomplished a courtier. Above all, despite her later flagrant disparagement of Jones' services in Russia, she feared his prowess as a naval officer in case he should turn in time of war from friend to foe.

How her malignant hypocrisy masked her licentiousness, evidently indicating that the gross measure of the one was proportioned to the other, appeared in a declaration to Grimm, her German confidant in Paris: ". . . there was a charge against him for attempted violation, which by no means did honor to either his excellence or his humanity or his justice or his generosity, and after this little happening it would have been difficult to find among the sailors anyone who wished to serve under the Rear Admiral."

Without doubt the crude ordinary Russian seamen, not to consider such leaders as the illegitimate Potemkin and Nassau, least of all Catherine herself, who at this time was turning from her twelfth favorite Momonoff to her thirteenth Zouboff, would have blushed to have any association at all with a man, however highly respected and honored throughout the United States and France and even among many in Britain, whom a procuress, her profligate daughter, and a lackey (the girl's favored friend) accused. She did not undertake to conceive the bounds of their outraged susceptibilities if he had been tried and found guilty. Indeed their purity and honesty must have been such, according to Catherine, that the very breath of scandal, whatever its source, spelled guilt to their shocked eyes; and perhaps it was such transcendent social morality of Russia and her ruler that explained, in the last analysis, the procedure of Russian law which enabled a court both to dispense with the testimony of a defendant and his employment of counsel and to change the evidence to please itself. In short, the bare-faced pretense that the most despicable calumny was tantamount to the guilt of Jones became the last refuge of hypocrisy and deceit.

◇◇◇

Chapter LXV

The Conspirators

A "COMPLOT," as the Admiral himself described the intrigue against him, indicated that a number of persons were involved, although to be sure some appeared to be more implicated than others. Both he and De Ségur referred early in the charges to numerous enemies in general; later their terms became more specific. Jones mentioned "a man wearing decorations." De Ségur and the younger De Genêt, who followed him as the French representative in Russia, named especially Potemkin.[1] It was De Ségur who announced: "This celebrated sailor, knowing better how to conduct himself in the midst of his battles than in courts, has offended by his frankness some of the most powerful people, and among others the Prince Potemkin. His enemies and his rivals had profited by his momentary disgrace to hasten his destruction."[2] In a more sweeping although somewhat less definite declaration in a letter to Franklin, Jones was to refer again to these "enemies and rivals"[3] against the background of "the dark intrigues and mean subterfuges of Asiatic jealousy and malice." And later, writing naïvely to Potemkin, whom he still failed to recognize as one of these enemies, the Admiral mentioned the evil reports of the Prince Marshal's manner of conducting the campaign against Oczakow and referred to a political plot against the Prince himself: "You know it was the echo of another intriguer at the Court of Vienna."[4] This intriguer against Potemkin was De Ligne;[5] practically without doubt his fellow intriguer against Jones from the Court of Vienna was the Austrian Ambassador in St. Petersburg, Cobentzel.

The English in Russia appear to have been innocent although sometimes falsely accused bystanders. Catherine's brigandage against Poland as well as Turkey was in the face of the opposition of European countries, particularly of France and Britain. Now that Russia found herself at war, suddenly and critically, with Sweden as well as with Turkey and that Austria, her ally, had suffered very serious reverses in Bannat and Bosnia, the two allied nations were disposed to try especially to propitiate Britain. Therefore in the knowledge that the part of Jones in the American Revolution was not forgotten, the intrigue had its inspiration in an attempt to court the favor of the British by affording them the satisfaction of witnessing his downfall. The purpose failed utterly; the British scorned such a despicable sacrifice and, in fact, turned to Jones with sympathy and friendship.

The truth of the exposure of the primary motives and actors in the conspiracy had further, more direct support from the declarations of informed persons. Even De Ségur, who had no love for the English during this period of rivalry, remarked with frankness: "This atrocity, which must be imputed to some envious cowards, was, I believe, very unjustly attributed to the English officers of the Russian Navy and to the merchants their compatriots. These, in truth, did not disguise their hostility towards Paul Jones; but it would be unjust to make fall upon them a base intrigue, which was perhaps the work of only two or three persons who remain unknown."[6]

The convictions expressed to Jefferson by Littlepage, whose informants in the course of his diplomatic journeys to courts of Europe gave him special opportunities to unravel the cabal, point more definitely to the perpetrators as well as their designs: "Some political motives, I have reason to think, concurred in depriving Admiral Paul Jones of the fruits of his services: he was thought to be particularly obnoxious to the English nation, and the idea of paying a servile compliment to a power whose enmity occasions all the present embarrassments of Russia induced some leading persons to ruin him in the opinion of the Empress by an accusation too ridiculous."[7] Jones himself, likewise in a declaration to Jefferson, was to recount some of the details: "Chevalier Littlepage, now here [in Paris] on his way from Spain to the North, has promised me a letter to you on my subject, which I presume will show the meanness and absurdity of the intrigues that were practiced for my persecution at St. Petersburg. I did not myself comprehend all the blackness of that business before he came here and related to me the information he received from a gentleman of high rank in the diplomatic service, with whom he travelled in company from Madrid to Paris. That gentleman had long resided in a public character at the Court of St. Petersburg, and was there all the time of the pitiful complot against me, which was conducted by a little-great man, behind the curtain.

"The unequalled reception with which I had, at first, been honored by the Empress had been extremely mortifying and painful to the English at St. Petersburg, and the courtier just mentioned, finding that politics had taken a turn far more alarming than he had expected at the beginning of the war and wishing to soothe the Court of London into a pacific humor, found no step so expedient as that of sacrificing me! But instead of producing the effect he wished, this base conduct, on which he pretended to ground a reconciliation, rather widened the political breach, and made him to be despised by the English Minister, by the English Cabinet, and by the gentleman who related the secret to the Chevalier Littlepage."[8]

Like white against black was the testimonial reply of Jefferson which offset the calumnies mentioned in the Admiral's letter and his accompanying papers to prove his innocence. The newly appointed Secretary of State wrote not only in his own name but also in that of Washington, now the President: "No proof was necessary to satisfy us here of your good conduct everywhere."[9]

The conspiracy as a whole against Jones must have sprung from an Austro-Russian group, including Nassau who had close bonds at the Austrian Court not only with De Ligne but also with Kaunitz, the Foreign Minister, and Cobentzel, the Ambassador to Russia. It seems that the personal hatred of Nassau towards the Admiral coincided in choice of a victim with an unscrupulous political motive of Cobentzel, who by reputation was a fit accomplice of the braggart. The Ambassador, according to representative reports, had "a mean and unwieldy figure"; he was long an intimate, oily sycophant at the heels of Potemkin and Catherine; he had a passion for planning and acting plots on an amateur's stage, and may well have had a bent to apply them to life; despite a pretense of uprightness, he "believed that in politics all means were justified if they proved successful";[10] and he "followed as far as indecency his favoritism in everything towards England."[11] The parallel purposes of Cobentzel and Nassau may well have had on the one side the support of Potemkin, against whom the Admiral had committed the unpardonable sin of upholding his self-respect, and on the other side that of Catherine, who with Nassau now in high personal and military favor, apart from her other reasons, could be depended on to have no hesitation in overthrowing the opponent of the former flotilla commander on the Liman.

The malevolence of Catherine towards Jones was potentially baleful, in particular as judged by his almost certain tragic fate if he had been not an American but a Russian and if she had not become disconcerted before the conspiracy had run its full course. Her history leaves no room to inquire whether she was unscrupulous enough to destroy his career and life; the only question is whether she had such a motive and considered it expedient. To all appearances her capricious, despotic will found greater incitements to obliterate him from the scene of her autocratic sway than many another who suddenly fell her victim. Her policy of connivance, her diabolical tacit consent to the secret crimes of ready accomplices who fulfilled all her wishes, whether of kidnapping, imprisonment, exile, or murder, points with unerring directness to her complicity as well as responsibility in the light of the malice from her pen, her special friends, counselors, and lovers who were Jones' enemies, and the narrow margin by which he escaped the full force of the conspiracy under the deep shadow of her despotism.

As if to offset the grim reality of the perfidious intrigue and its actors, a legend has been evolved which pictures a supposed romance of Jones with a Princess Anna Kourakina, represented as a maid of honor of the Empress; Catherine herself appears in a rôle coloring the love tale with tragedy, and the story in its entirety takes the form of a background for the fortunes which overtook the Admiral in Russia.[12] This fable is as chimerical as gratuitous for establishing the part of Catherine and of others in the conspiracy.

The so-called "secret romance" misinterprets for the second time a statement from De Ségur, already noted, by which the morality of Jones' relations with women appears in an unjustifiably shadowed light.[13] It depends further upon a series of coincidences which would make truth not merely stranger than good fiction but more exaggerated than bad fiction. In contradiction to history, Catherine is in love with Jones; in contradiction to credibility, Nassau as well as the Admiral is in love with the Princess Anna; and Catherine is jealous of Anna and Nassau of Jones. It is equally unbelievable that the Empress thwarts a marriage of the Admiral and the maid of honor, which she supposedly fears would lead to revelations of her own immoral private life, by means of the conspiracy of the procuress and her daughter, causing shame to Jones and disillusionment to Anna. The legend is admittedly based on a "suppositional diary"; not one authenticated document supports the tale. Amorphous as fiction and baseless as history, it neither adds to nor subtracts from the intrigue which brought the Russo-German girl to Jones' door to peddle butter and mend linen or lace.

Whatever was Catherine's exact part in the conspiracy, it may have been a mere coincidence but not less likely a tie for association that she, German by birth and training in youth, had for company not only the Russian and Austrian intriguers but also the three agents, the profligate girl herself, the procuress mother, and the foresworn servant Bahl, who all were German. Curiously, even Grimm, her most abiding sycophantic confidant, was also German, and it was to him that the Empress felt disposed to reveal herself most brazenly in regard to Jones. Of all her tricks against the Admiral, she was later—not yet certainly—to unmask herself to this confidant, with the cynical remark, "I have emptied my bag."[14]

◇◇

Chapter LXVI

The Two Years' Leave
of Absence

POTEMKIN the barbarian, De Ligne the courtier, Alexiano the pirate, Mordwinoff the boor, Suvorof the madman, De Ribas the tool, Cobentzel the intriguer, and Nassau the ass in lion's skin—this rapacious pack had enlisted and most of them remained in the service of the Empress, lurking and snarling at the heels of Jones. It was scarcely possible for him to exaggerate the extent to which these enemies in varying degree had striven by word and deed to undermine his professional and personal reputation. And he continued to be insensible to the evil of the woman at their head even after she had set aside the trial as a matter of expediency, not for his sake but hers. He was still unable to conceive the particular strain of treachery hidden behind her feigned nobility of character, especially because of his unremitting naval ambitions in pursuit of glory within her hands for fulfillment.

Even during the prosecution in St. Petersburg, his zeal had been such as to impel him to formulate new plans for Russian naval strategy; after the charge had finally come to an end, he turned with special resourcefulness to his public interests. "The great object of a Russian fleet in the Mediterranean," he stated in a note to the Minister of State, Besborodko, proposing a blockade in the next campaign against the Turks, "is to endeavor to cut off the communication between Egypt and the coast of Syria with Constantinople, from whence they procure their corn, rice, coffee, etc. This operation will oblige them to withdraw a very considerable part of their fleet from the Black Sea. To encompass this end, I ask a *carte blanche*, and only, exclusive of small boats, five large vessels, like the East Indiamen which are purchased in London after they have made three voyages, and which carry from forty to fifty guns. They are strong vessels and good sailers. . . ."[1] No slow, crank, and half-rotted Russian frigates or ships of the line for his enterprise and no Nassau and Potemkin as his associates were the primary conditions on which his will was set more expressly than ever before while a new *Bonhomme Richard* cruise, of larger scope and greater marvel, shaped itself in his imagination.

This plan, which Besborodko had promised to submit to the Empress and which was related to another that he himself had recommended, elicited no response for six weeks. Then the only reply to Jones proved to be an announcement on June 27, 1789 that was little to his taste for action and most disappointing at the moment of his expectancy to prepare for a brilliant campaign. Catherine had given him a leave of absence for two years.

The Minister as well as the Empress now refused him the opportunity to express himself face to face. Even their Asiatic duplicity, it appears, was not brazen enough to meet his eyes and counter his words. "I presented myself at your hotel the day before yesterday," Jones was reduced to write Besborodko on July 14, "to take leave and, at the same time, to entreat of you to expedite my commission, my passport, and the leave of absence which Her Majesty has thought fit to grant me. Though I have perceived on several former occasions that you have shunned giving me any opportunity to speak with you, I made myself certain that this could not occur at a last interview; and I confess I was very much surprised to see you go out by another door, and depart without a single expression of ordinary civility addressed to me at the moment of my departure to console me for all the bitter mortifications I have endured in this empire. Before coming to Russia, I had been connected with several governments, and no minister ever either refused me an audience or failed to reply to my letters."[2] Jones might have spared himself this comparison if he had recognized that the Russian Minister not only had the crudest origin and upbringing but also that his policy was as craftily unscrupulous and his appearance as inveterately gross as Potemkin's.

Nevertheless a confederation against the Barbary countries, particularly Algiers which at this time still held in bondage a number of sailors from the crews of two American ships captured in 1785, was a final object which the Admiral brought to the attention of the Minister on the eve of his departure from Russia and his expectancy of close associations with the United States. The redemption of American prisoners was, of course, not a new incitement to his efforts against the pirate nations, but perhaps they were not the less because the Dey of Algiers, who with the Turks was waging war against Russia, had offered "a reward of two thousand sequins to him who shall bring the head of Mr. Jones with or without the body." And as one of the topics of Jones' recent correspondence with Jefferson had been retaliation against Algiers, he now took occasion to add to Besborodko: "The United States having concluded a treaty of friendship and commerce with the Emperor of Morocco are about to propose to the different powers of Europe a war with the other Barbary States, and to form a confederation against these pirates till they shall be annihilated as maritime powers. It is proposed that even the event of war between the contracting parties shall not disturb the confederation. It would be worthy of the august sovereign of this empire to place herself at the head of an alliance so honorable, and of which the consequences must be so useful to Russia."[3]

His deluded wish to be a spokesman from Russia to the United States for such a league was even more disregarded than his earlier recommendation for a political and commercial treaty between the two countries. As in the case of the Armed Neutrality of 1780 proposed by Catherine, which had concerned the historic question of the rights at sea of neutral nations in time of war, she was very ambitious for the prestige of arbiter in Europe, but at the test of leadership showed regard exclusively for Russia's profit and her personal vanity. The political efforts of Jones, even more than his military, were without appreciation of the diplomatic artifice and the ruthless selfishness which governed the Empress. He was in need of the realism of the former British Ambassador, Sir James Harris, who stated that while Catherine showed herself "gracious to me beyond measure," she was attempting "by this extraordinary affability to mislead me."[4] And of Russia as well as her ruler, the Ambassador wrote: "The friendship of this country partakes of its climate—a clear brilliant sky with a cold freezing atmosphere . . . all words and no deeds, empty profession and shuffling evasions."[5]

The respect of Catherine and her accomplices for Jones' military prowess continued to be in proportion to their hostility towards him. The spring and summer campaigns of 1789 against Sweden as well as Turkey were in progress; and treacherous as the leaders in Russia had shown themselves, they took precautions to guard against retaliation, if not treachery, on the part of the Admiral as to his possible enlistment in the cause of an enemy. They therefore put difficulties in the path of his departure after the earlier period of delay culminating in the two years' dismissal from active duty; one month then transpired before he received his passport, and another elapsed before he could secure payment for the year of his service and investigate an order which seemingly contradicted an earlier provision for his emoluments during the two years' leave of absence. "I was detained in St. Petersburg," he himself revealed, "until the end of August in order to hinder me, as I have heard, from proceeding into the service of Sweden."

At length, Jones left the country in which the measure of the dastardly treatment of him may be essentially judged by the earnest friendship and respect that in contrast it promoted in the eyes of his enemies in war, the British, and by the final tokens of the generous feelings of the two French diplomats, De Ségur and De Genêt. De Ségur seldom used his facile pen to better purpose than now as he provided Jones with several testimonial letters, directing in his emphatic style particular attention to the innocence of the Admiral in the face of the Russian conspiracy. He did not fail also to write to the same effect to the recently appointed French Foreign Minister, Montmorin, adding, "I would wish the enclosed article, the authenticity of which I guarantee, should be inserted in the *Gazette of France,* and in the other public papers which are submitted to the inspection of your department. This article will undeceive those who have believed the calumny, and will prove to the friends and to the compatriots of the Vice Admiral that he had sustained the reputation acquired by his bravery and his talents during the last war. . . ."[6] Not less explicitly in his exposure of the intrigue against Jones and not less warmly in his support of him, De Genêt gave the Admiral a letter to his sister, the well-known Madame Campan, who had wide influence as the close friend of Marie Antoinette. Recalling Jones' temporary but propitious connection with the elder De Genêt at the prospect of outfitting a second French-American squadron in the Revolution, he referred to him as "a man whom my father loved and esteemed, and to whom I am personally attached."[7] Jones had well repaid France for the opportunity she had afforded him in the Revolution; now in turn the representatives of France in Russia memorably served the American.

Nothing in the wake of Jones' departure from St. Petersburg appears to have signalized more clearly an ultimate reason for his misfortunes in Russia, behind the curtain of the charges concerning the Russo-German girl, than the continued rising glory of Nassau in the esteem of the Empress. As in the Liman against the Turks, so in the Baltic against the Swedes, Nassau was at the head of a large flotilla; and fortunately for himself he had under his command several capable foreign captains such as Winter from Holland and Varage from France. "The Swedes," he boasted, "will have perhaps some officers better taught than those which I possess, but I will bring it about that valor will achieve everything."[8]

Through his captains, it seems, he gained initially some partial successes. Catherine hastened to proclaim him "truly heroic." Nassau proceeded to write a letter to his opponent, Gustavus III of Sweden, who, although something of a braggart in his own right, must have found himself altogether outdone by the author of the fables in regard to the campaign on the Liman. "I have been surprised," he declared to the King, whose description of an engagement was at variance with his own characteristic exaggeration, "that a person has had the audacity to place a name as respectable as that of Your Majesty at the end of an account filled with errors and untruths."[9] The King bided his time for a reply.

"The confidence which the Prince de Nassau inspires in the Empress is without bounds," said De Genêt.[10] "She has embraced him, overwhelmed him with praises," reported De Ségur.[11] She provided without question all the armament which he asked for to equip his vessels; she bestowed upon him a pension of three thousand roubles instituted by Peter the Great; she sent him two dressing robes such as Potemkin had received from her at Oczakow, remarking that they had afforded great comfort. Only the recent presence of Madame de Nassau in St. Petersburg seems to have occasioned a discordant note. Thus the Empress awaited new and greater triumphs from the Admiral whom she personally had exalted to his present pinnacle. Indeed she had now promoted him to the command of all the fleet in the Baltic—the successor to Greig was not Jones but Nassau by right of her sovereign will. And Jones, passing from the borders of Russia to Poland on the first stage of his journey westward, had such echoes ringing in his ears.

Catherine had not afforded Jones even at his departure the opportunity of a private audience, at which he had hoped to express his convictions with plain-spoken fearlessness. She merely had bidden him a conventional *"bon voyage"* and so at length had belied the one promise upon which he had always reckoned— "never to condemn me unheard." How her inordinate feminine vanity went hand in hand with her absolutism was evident later in her protestation to Grimm that, contrary to a report by Jones— in fact, a misstatement by De Ségur—she had by no means given him the privilege of a private audience at his leave-taking. Probably in part for this harmless lie as well as for important truths from De Ségur regarding the shameless intrigues against Jones in Russia, Catherine was later to brand her long-admired French Ambassador with the epithet "as false as Judas."[12]

Part 8

Chains of Inaction

◇◇◇

Chapter LXVII

Travels over Europe in Readiness for Recall

POLAND, which had already suffered the First Partition and had still to endure the Second and the Third, must have further revealed to Jones during his visit to the Court of Warsaw and to Littlepage that the treachery which had been his lot in Russia, both on the Liman and in St. Petersburg, should scarcely have occasioned his particular surprise. But he still persisted in believing that the attitude of the Empress herself was due less to her natural impulses than to her misinformation. Accordingly his first and chief object in Warsaw was to try to unfold to her eyes by correspondence the truth concerning himself, which in his opinion remained hidden from her by his enemies.

With this purpose he undertook to impress her by his important friendships in France and America, and adopted a tone of earnestness and reverence not just conventionally flattering but almost worshipful. He sent a shortened *Journal of the Campaign on the Liman* with "the proofs of every separate article," namely, with the many letters and notes of the *Pièces Justificatives*. He added separately his memoirs of the American Revolution, presumably based on the *Journal for the King*, which it had been his pleasure to show her upon his first arrival in St. Petersburg.

"Your Imperial Majesty," he addressed her in his accompanying letter of September 25, 1789, "having done me the honor to cause me to be informed by her secretary, M. de Khrapovitski, 'that she would be pleased to have a copy of my journal (which she had read) of the American war,' I have added some testimonies of the high and *unanimous* consideration of the United States, and of the private esteem with which I was honored by several great

men *to whom I am perfectly known,* such as M. Malesherbes and
the Count d'Estaing of France, and Mr. Morris, Minister of Finance and of the American Marine. I have the honor to present
it to Your Majesty with profound respect and *confidence.*

"I owe it to my reputation and to truth to accompany this
journal with an abridgement of the campaign of the Liman. If
you will deign, madam, to read it with some attention, you will
perceive how little I have deserved the mortifications which I
have endured, and which the justice and goodness of Your Majesty
can alone make me forget.

"As I never offended in *word,* or *speech,* or *thought,* against the
laws and usages of the strictest delicacy, it would assuredly be most
desirable to me to have the happiness of regaining, in spite of the
malice of my enemies, the precious esteem of Your Majesty. I
would have taken leave of the Court on the 17th July with a heart
much better satisfied had I been sent to fight the enemies of the
Empress, instead of occupying myself with my own private affairs.

"Trusting entirely on the gracious promise that Your Majesty
gave me, 'never to condemn me without a hearing,' and being devoted to you, heart and soul. . . ."[1]

He intended particularly for her reading a closing account of
the Liman campaign. It confutes in summary the various charges
and misconceptions concerning his professional services and his
private character. Not the least significant, coming from the pen
of the fighter that he was, are his terms in refutation of the
aspersions of cruelty, including those already noted in regard to his
nephew, with which, ironically, his enemies in Russia had had the
impudence to charge him. The man himself, often unrecognized
in the officer, appears not without faithfulness in his self-portrait:

"If my heart has bled for the Americans, above all, for those
shut up as victims in English prisons by an act of Parliament as
sanguinary as unjust; if I have exposed my health and life to the
greatest dangers; if I have sacrificed my personal tranquillity and
my domestic happiness, with a portion of my fortune and my blood,
to set at liberty these virtuous and innocent men, have I not given
proofs sufficiently striking that I have a heart the most sensitive,
a soul the most elevated? I have done more than all this. So far
from being *harsh* and *cruel,* nature has given me the mildest dis-

position. I was formed for *love* and *friendship,* and not to be a seaman or a soldier; as it is, I have sacrificed my natural inclination.

"As an officer, I loved good discipline, which I consider indispensable to the success of operations, particularly at sea, where men are so much crowded and brought into such close contact. In the English Navy it is known that captains of ships are often tyrants, who order the lash for the poor seamen very frequently, and sometimes, for nothing. In the American Navy we have almost the same regulations; but I looked on my crew as my children, and I have always found means to manage them without flogging.

"I never had a nephew, nor any other relation, under my command. Happily these facts are known in America, and they prove how cruel and harsh I am. I have one dear nephew, who is still too young for service, but who now pursues his studies. Since I came to Russia I have intended him for the Imperial Marine. Instead of imbruing my hands in his blood, he will be cherished as my son."[2]

Two weeks after Jones had sent the letter to the Empress, "sealed with my arms" and addressed in care of her secretary, Khrapovitski, he learned from De Ségur, who himself was now on his return to Paris via Warsaw, that his communication had been stopped by Besborodko, who had written to Potemkin to decide whether or not to deliver it to Catherine.[3] Even if the journals and the message came into her hands, Jones continued to await a reply in vain.

It was with the conflicting feelings of his allegiance to the Empress and of repulsion for the tyranny by Russia that he met at Warsaw that greatest Polish patriot who had fought in the cause of the American Revolution, Kosciusko. "As I shall be in relation with our friends in America," Jones wrote to him on November 2 at the moment of his departure from the city after a hospitable sojourn of two months, "I shall not fail to mention on all occasions the honorable employment and the respect you have attained in your country, and the great regard you retain for the natives of America, where your character is esteemed and your name justly beloved for your services."[4] But this generous tribute from one champion of liberty to another was not all for which the heart of General Kosciusko yearned; Jones left him his later address in

Amsterdam, the next important stage of his itinerary, and there the one warrior was to read the smouldering thoughts of the other.[5]

Before proceeding to Holland, however, the Admiral made a detour to Vienna, in which he desired, if possible, to see the Emperor Joseph. As Austria was the ally of Russia and Joseph played his unhappy part as the political and personal friend of Catherine, Jones presumably had faint hope that this ruler might intercede in his behalf with the Empress. Certainly he could have had no expectation of any naval employment by an Austria which lacked a fleet. But what support was to be looked for at a court where Cobentzel, De Ligne, and Nassau were powerful and where the Emperor in the year 1789 during the decline of his health wrote to Kaunitz of "the absurdity and impertinence" of Catherine and in the next on his deathbed dictated a message to her, "I shall never again see the writing of Your Imperial Majesty, which has been all my happiness"?[6]

Professionally, the sojourn of several weeks in Vienna was without significance; personally, it reflected further—coming, in contrast, on the heels of the Russo-German girl episode—his refinement in the choice of friendships among women and his abiding regard for nature and poetry. Addressing a letter on November 23 from Vienna to a mother and her daughter in Warsaw, Madame and Mademoiselle de Tomatis de Valery, Jones referred to his visit to several young women of the family and to his gift of some books of poems, and he incidentally mentioned an unrealized prospect of seeing the Emperor: "I went to pay a visit to the convent today, but was unable to have the pleasure of seeing Mademoiselle Caroline, who is slightly indisposed. I saw your two other daughters, who are very pretty and very interesting. They had given me hopes of having an audience of the Emperor; but I no longer expect it, as he sees no one and conversation is painful to him.

"I left the works of Thomson at the convent, and here are some remarks for Mademoiselle the Countess, who will have the goodness to accept these books as if I had had the honor of presenting them to her on her birthday. I have spoken to you several times of the beautiful poems called *The Seasons,* written by the delicate author whose works I have deposited with your sister for your acceptance. There is nothing in the English language that surpasses his thoughts and his happy elegance of expression. In the first and second volumes you will meet with some small parts where the margin is marked, or the words underlined; though, without that circumstance, the contents could not have escaped your particular attention. Adieu! I pay you no compliment. But I wish you all possible good."[7]

Disillusioned in Russia, the Admiral must have appreciated more than ever before the idyllic serenity of the Scottish scenes painted in words by his favorite Thomson. He presented as a gift the English volumes brought even to a distant land, but doubtlessly the lines from *The Seasons* with his often-quoted phrase "calm contemplation and poetic ease" still remained in his memory and sang in his heart:

> Oh, knew he but his happiness, of men
> The happiest he! who far from public rage,
> Deep in the vale, with a choice few retired,
> Drinks the pure pleasures of the rural life.
>
> . . . .
>
> Here too dwells simple truth; plain innocence;
>
> . . . .
>
> Calm contemplation and poetic ease.
> Let others brave the flood in quest of gain,
> And beat for joyless months the gloomy waves.
> Let such as deem it glory to destroy
> Rush into blood. . .[8]

In continuing his travels from Vienna, Jones set aside whatever interest if not temptation he had to observe close at hand the political attitude of the enemies of Russia and especially the naval forces which Sweden was mustering against her in the war undertaken by Gustavus III to recover the territory in Finland formerly wrested from his kingdom. The Admiral, who possessed various letters of introduction from De Ségur, had particularly in mind visits to Copenhagen, where he had been before; to Berlin, where a grand review of the Prussian Army offered a special occasion; and to Strasbourg, where he planned to call nearby upon the Duke of Württemberg, a friend of the Earl of Wemyss. But his own opinion and that of others led him to determine to proceed directly to Holland. "As it was well known," he said, "that I had left Russia dissatisfied, I thought it best to give my enemies there no handle against me. (They had insinuated that I would accept a command in the Swedish Navy.)"

To Holland, the scene ten years earlier of his dramatic experience at the Texel and his visits to The Hague and to Amsterdam, Jones retraced his steps early in December for various reasons, some of which were certainly financial, others presumably professional, and still others perhaps social. He chose for the present to bide his time here, pending a definite course.

Now that Jefferson had left France in September for America and William Short was chargé d'affaires in Paris, Gouverneur Morris, who was fulfilling important duties as an envoy of the United States in Europe, began at once to occupy an important place in Jones' orbit. "I arrived here the 9th without having gone to Strasburg, which I found would have taken me out of my way without any object of consequence," the Admiral stated in a message from Amsterdam to the successor, soon to be appointed, to Jefferson in Paris. "The kind letter you wrote me to Warsaw has been transmitted to me here. It is a new proof of your friendship on which I have always set the highest value and which I will to the end of my life be ambitious to deserve. . . ."

He proceeded to speak with confidence to the caustic but well-intentioned Morris concerning some of his private affairs after the manner in which it had been his habit to express himself to the kindly nature of Jefferson: "I thank you for the trouble you took about my bust for Madame de Ségur. I enclose for Mr. Short a list of the names of eight gentlemen to each of whom I promised to send my bust when last in America. . . . I should be glad to know if the gold medal with which I am honored is ready, though I would not have it sent. I must ask your permission to add your name to the within list. I pay you no compliment on this occasion, and if I did not love you I would not make you this offer. I left in the hands of Mr. Jefferson a small trunk with papers and two swords, one of which is that I received from the King of France and is of course of great value in my estimation. I hope Mr. Short will take particular care of those objects."[9]

Now relieved in Western Europe from the possibility of the interception of his letters, he resumed his open and frequent correspondence with Americans in the United States as well as on the Continent, and it is noteworthy that his first missive of December 20 addressed overseas was to Washington: "I avail myself of the departure of the Philadelphia packet, Captain Earle, to transmit to Your Excellency a letter I received for you on leaving Russia in August last, from my friend the Count de Ségur, Minister of France to St. Petersburg. That gentleman and myself have frequently conversed on subjects that regard America; and the most pleasing reflection of all has been the happy establishment of the new constitution and that you are so deservedly placed at the head of the government by the unanimous voice of America.

"Your name alone, sir, has established in Europe a confidence that was for some time before entirely wanting in American concerns; and I am assured that the happy effects of your administration are still more sensibly felt throughout the United States. This is more glorious for you than all the laurels that your sword so nobly won in support of the rights of human nature. In war your name is immortal as the hero of liberty! In peace you are her patron, and the firmest supporter of her rights! Your greatest admirers, and even your best friends, have now but one wish left for you—that you may long enjoy health and your present happiness.

"Mr. Jefferson can inform you respecting my mission to the Court of Denmark. I was received and treated there with marked politeness; and if the *fine words* I received are true, the business will soon be settled. I own, however, that I should have stronger hopes if America had created a respectable marine; for that argument would give weight to every transaction with Europe.

"I acquitted myself of the commission with which you honored me when last in America by delivering your letters with my own hands at Paris to the persons to whom they were addressed."[10]

Only a week later he wrote in terse expressive terms to Franklin, who was still to live for several months, as to his views of the past and future of his connection with Russia. Even in the shadow of his dying days, the former wise and benevolent Minister, who had zealously planned naval strategy with Jones the Captain and had thrilled at the brilliant victories won by his sheer will and genius, must have felt with vivid memory the ironic sadness of the warrior's present entreaty to him regarding Russian calumnies for "justification in the eyes of my friends in America, whose good opinion is dearer to me than anything else."[11] Even more, the ex-Minister must have relived with the Captain the momentous occasion of the signal honor of the American flag on this anniversary of the escape of the one frigate remaining under the colors of the United States, as Jones recalled it in a postscript in terms the more moving for their simplicity: "It is this day ten years since I left the Texel in the *Alliance*."[12]

Jones' memory harked back also, taking practical form, to such a home in the United States as his most admired poet, Thomson, sang of in Scotland, although with the passing of years it grew increasingly doubtful whether a wife would share it with him. "You mentioned to me at New York," he said in a letter to an old friend, Charles Thomson, the Secretary of the Continental Congress, "a small but convenient estate to be sold in the neighborhood of Lancaster. I think you said it had belonged to Mr. George Ross. May I ask the favor of you to inquire about it and favor me with your opinion about the purchase of it? I shall probably come to America in the summer, if the Empress does not invite me to return to Russia before the opening of the next campaign; a thing I do not expect."[13] And to John Ross, with whom, along with Bancroft, it is recalled that his surplus funds had been entrusted, he wrote in a similar vein: "I may perhaps return to America in the latter end of the summer; and in that case I shall wish to purchase a *little farm,* where I may live in peace."[14] In theory at least, Jones seemed to have come to agree with his poet, who said, "The best of men have ever loved repose," citing for example a soldier:

> So Scipio, to the soft Cumæan shore
> Retiring, tasted joy he never knew before.

In practice, however, the Admiral was little disposed, at least for the present, towards such a withdrawal from the perilous roads on which he had travelled with fearless challenge since his boyhood. His most persistent purpose in Amsterdam was to efface the last vestiges of the attempted stigma from Russia that had attached to his name; even to the Empress he had dared to say of his plain speaking, however repugnant to her, "I owe it to my reputation and to truth."

Thus following the efforts of De Ségur in his behalf and his own letters to friends in America, Jones communicated frankly with those diplomats in particular who had been spectators or agents of his departure under promising auspices for St. Petersburg. A reply from the French Minister at Copenhagen, the Baron de la Houze, was especially apt. Referring to the announcement which De Ségur had written for the *Gazette of France,* he declared: "This article, which has been repeated in many foreign gazettes, has entirely destroyed all the venomous effects which calumny had employed to tarnish the distinguished reputation which you have acquired by your talents and valor. In consequence, public opinion still continues to render you justice, and the most noble revenge you can take on your enemies is to gather fresh laurels. The celebrated Athenian general, Themistocles, has said: 'I do not envy the situation of the man who is not envied.'[15] No one more accurately indicated the ultimate, jealous roots of the intrigues against Jones and more becomingly suggested the course of action, "the most noble revenge," which the Admiral himself was disposed by nature to perfect.

Jones wrote with somewhat conflicting sentiments to Baron Krudiner, the Russian Minister in Copenhagen, who, like De Simolin in Paris, had flattered him. He confessed: "Notwithstanding the unjust treatment I received in Russia, the warm attachment with which the Empress inspired me at the beginning remains rooted in my heart." But he also declared unreservedly: "I have seen the credit of my services bestowed on others," and "I wrote several letters while in the Department of the Black Sea to my friend Mr. Jefferson at Paris, containing no detail of our operations, yet they were all intercepted."[16] The Baron's answer was rather typical of the combined evasiveness and blandishments which the Admiral had experienced at first in St. Petersburg. Despite the expressions, "It is with lively sensibility that I have received your mark of remembrance" and "I flatter myself as a good Russian that your arm is always reserved for us," the suave Minister offered no answer at all to the implications of the blunt disclosures.

It was in Amsterdam, the address communicated to Kosciusko, that the overtures to engage Jones in the service of Sweden against Russia, incidentally offering a matchless opportunity to oppose Nassau in command of the Russian fleet in the Baltic, placed the American in a strange position of conflicting desires. Kosciusko, with his English imperfect but his thoughts as an intermediary transparent, informed him on February 15, 1790 from Warsaw: "I had the honor to write you the 1st or 3d of Feb. I do not recolect; but I gave you the information to apply to the Minister of Svede at Hague or at Amsterdam for the propositions (according to what M. D'Engestrom told me) they boths had order to communicate you. I wish with all my heart they could answer your expectation. I am totaly ignorant what they are; but I could see you to fight against the oppression and tyranny. Give me news of everything."[17]

Jones was obviously troubled; he knew that his enemies were watchful for any act which might be interpreted as hostile to Russia. The punctilio of his reply, even if he did not feel unfavorably disposed, is understandable: "You propose, if I am not mistaken, that I should apply to a gentleman at The Hague, who has something to communicate to me. But a moment's reflection will convince you that considerations of what I owe to myself, as well as the delicacy of my situation, do not permit me to take such a step. If that gentleman has anything to communicate to me, he can either do it by writing, by desiring a personal conference, or by the mediation of a third person. I have shown your letter to my bankers, and they have said this much to the gentleman from whom they received it; but this message, they say, he received with an air of indifference."[18]

At this uncertain stage of the negotiations, Gouverneur Morris, whose varied business had brought him to Amsterdam, took a hand in bringing these preliminaries to a definite issue at the offices of the banker Van Staphorst, the place of delivery of Kosciusko's letters. In his diary, Morris noted on March 8: "This morning Jones comes in and keeps me late, as I had risen late also. . . . Go to Mr. Van Staphorst's and meet Jones as I intended. Adjust the means by which he is to receive a direct offer from the Swedish Ambassador or Minister here. They have made a kind of indirect application through Kosciusko. . . . This is very well."[19]

It is not manifest that the proceedings were equally well in the eyes of Jones, although he prepared an unpublished document at some indeterminate time after leaving Russia which indicated a disposition to sever his last ties with her. The paper not only revealed his vows "to preserve the condition of an American citizen and officer" and "never to draw it [the gold sword from Louis XVI] on any occasion where war might be waged against His Majesty's interest," but also expressed "a presentiment that in spite of his attachment and gratitude to Her Imperial Majesty, and notwithstanding the advantageous propositions which may be made to him, he will probably renounce the service of that power, even before the expiration of the leave of absence which he now enjoys."[20] There is no evidence, however, of any decision to make public this memorandum and still less of any definite step to enter the service of Catherine's northern foe.

Jones appears, on the contrary, to have pondered with care at the crossroads and to have arrived at a negative resolve. We seem to observe him weighing his position as he visits Morris on three successive days after the latter's intercession. His host's diary of March 9 and 10 invites only vague speculation: on the first day, "Jones comes in about eleven and stays till twelve"; on the second, "Take up Jones and Appleton [a former American consul at Calais], bring them home and give them a dish of tea. They sit with me till late." On the third day, March 11, however, it is possible to judge the trend of the Admiral's thoughts: "Jones comes in after dinner and sits with me. He has a plan for going round the Cape of Good Hope and laying under contribution the places subject to the Turk. Consider of it."[21] Inasmuch as Turkey was practically in alliance with Sweden and Jones was now revolving in his mind a strategic enterprise against the former, he had reached his determination—not to turn against Russia, whatever his provocations and his opportunities. This fidelity to the leaders of a nation who had shown themselves altogether unworthy of it casts at the same time a long ray of light into the distant past to make newly evident the steadfastness of Jones when he had fought in the cause of America not for the opportunism of an adventurer but for the love of honor and liberty.

With his conscience at peace on this question of his professional course, another problem of a financial nature remained for settlement while opportunity served in Amsterdam. Edward Bancroft the spy, still not exposed, had given him a rude private shock in 1787 by withholding funds, promised for placement to his credit with bankers in Brussels, on his first journey to fulfill his mission to Denmark and by being responsible in part for his sudden return at that time to America. Jones had advanced money to Bancroft, who was engaged in the business of introducing the quercitron bark among the woollen dyers, and estrangement developed after the breach of good faith.

Accordingly Jones now made a trip across the English Channel to London, in which the former spy from America had wisely settled for political as well as commercial reasons. It happened that Gouverneur Morris had likewise proceeded to London as an envoy of the United States, and he served as an opportune if not very willing arbitrator. Jones wished a settlement in accordance with the terms of the contract; Bancroft pleaded his inability for the present to pay more than half the amount due. After an agreement to a necessary compromise, Jones explained to Morris from Boulogne in the course of his return to the Continent that the delay interfered with his plans "respecting a particular farm I wished to purchase" in America through Charles Thomson, and he ventured to add the caution, seemingly not amiss as applied to a spy, that "the release to him ought to remain in your hands *in trust* till he shall have paid me what he owes." Perhaps the intrusion upon the time of Morris was inconsiderate, perhaps too the warning to him was gratuitous, but these circumstances did not lead to the only occasion on which he was to show himself irascible towards the Admiral. Apropos of the expenditure of his time, Morris confided to his diary, "I could dispense with this visit"; apropos of the caution, he wrote, "This is mighty absurd, for it had always been so understood of course, and I reply by asking if Jones thinks me a fool."[22]

Shortly after his return to the Continent, the Admiral won a triumph over the treacherous leaders of Russia even without retaliating in kind by unsheathing his sword in the service of Sweden. It was a moral victory especially over Catherine, who at whim enthroned and dethroned her military and naval chiefs; and over Nassau her most recent puppet who had risen to the zenith of power and pomp as a Russian commander only to plummet to the nadir of shame.

In the historic naval battle of Svenskund on July 12, 1790, Nassau suffered an irreparable rout at the hands of Gustavus III of Sweden, losing 53 vessels, 1400 cannon, and 6000 men as prisoners. Even in cowardly flight on a swift vessel carefully reserved for himself, he tried to disguise his fear and ineptness by theatrical posture and exclamation, brandishing a pistol in one hand and a sword in the other, and striding the deck in his white uniform and *cordon bleu* against the background of six sailors also in white with orange plumes and sashes. Although so cowering after the defeat that Catherine had to urge him to command himself, he did not fail with his usual effrontery, after Russia began to sue Sweden for a reconciliation as the result of the great naval loss, to issue challenges on his own part to the King. "I see," replied Gustavus, who was his match in words, not to consider deeds, "that I have made peace with Russia, but not with M. de Nassau."[23]

It was little consolation to the Empress with her Russo-German absolutism that in a letter to Nassau she set her hideous ego against truth as if to mask from herself as well as from the world the very substance of lies by her autocratic hocus-pocus: "You acted according to a plan approved by me and according to my orders; and having come from supreme authority, they cannot be submitted to any examination because, as long as I live, I will never allow that what I have ordered and found good in point of service should be subject to the revision of any soul who lives, as well as that anyone should arrogate to himself such an investigation. You are right, and you must be right because I find that you are right myself. It is a mode of reasoning doubtlessly aristocratic; but it cannot be otherwise without turning all sense upside down."[24]

Whether such logic as applied to international affairs was too feminine, too revolutionary, or too Russo-German, it now seemed progressively unpalatable to all the European nations and in similar increasing degree unfavorable to her wars with Sweden and Turkey. Svenskund was an excellent commentary upon the disastrous practical results of her philosophy. It served in particular to explain who had won the battles on the Liman against the Turks and what kind of absurdity and intrigue had governed the

Empress in ignominiously discarding a naval genius and arbitrarily choosing in his stead for her Commander in Chief an egregious imposter. She had herself primarily to blame that, in the North even to a greater extent than in the South, Jones did not stand her bulwark, but instead wasted his health and talents in the disquiet of his spirit as he turned from one city to another.

◇◇◇

Chapter LXVIII

In the Paris of the French Revolution

BORN AND accustomed to the strenuous activity of his long naval career, Jones returned in May, 1790 from London and Amsterdam to Paris, the hub from which his greatest opportunities as an officer had radiated ever since he had come to France, nearly twelve years previously, an American captain. He had not chosen to take the advice of Gouverneur Morris offered half a year earlier: "A journey to this city can, I think, produce nothing but the expense attending it; for neither pleasure nor advantage can be expected here, by one of your profession in particular, and, except that it is a more dangerous residence than many others, I know of nothing which may serve to you as an inducement."[1] This counsel, at best sincere, happened to be ill-considered and ironical.

Jones was not noticeably in a mood for pleasure, but it scarcely became Morris to volunteer a pessimistic view on this score inasmuch as he stumped about on his wooden leg with increasing gusto on the road of his smug, gallant attentions to Parisian women. In the shadow of the storming of the Bastille by the populace on July 14, 1789, the Admiral could expect perhaps less professional advantage than previously, but Paris was still the centre of his French political and military friends and patrons and of such seemingly important Russian connections as De Simolin, the Ambassador from St. Petersburg, and Grimm, the favorite correspondent of the Empress. Least of all was he likely to turn aside because of the perils of the rising French Revolution, even if Morris resorted to subtlety in warning him against them. Apart from America, he had not lost his love of France—France which had bestowed the gold sword as a symbol of peerless valor for the common liberties of the United States and her ally on the seas, and which had moved him to the unshaken vow to fight for her whenever she might have need of his prowess.

In Paris, the Admiral promptly spoke his mind to De Simolin as the first and most important Russian agent in the negotiations prior to his service with Catherine. "If I have not sought to avenge myself of the unjust and cruel treatment I met with in Russia, my forbearance has been only the result of my delicate attachment towards the Empress," he declared, presenting evidence of rejected offers from Sweden and frankly implying his devotion to Catherine rather than to her country. Jones followed the interview by a letter; he enlarged upon "the intrigue and slander resorted to by my enemies," recalled his recent plans by which "the Russian flag would have gained new laurels and the empire new advantages," and proposed a further enterprise reminiscent of his daring plans and deeds in the American Revolution regarding descents upon such cities as Leith, Edinburgh, and Liverpool.

"Today I have the honor," he explained, "to submit to Your Excellency another project; and since this plan can hurt no one, I flatter myself with the hope that you will do me the kindness of conveying this directly to Her Imperial Majesty.

"I propose to levy a contribution on Arabia, since that land is a part of the Turkish Empire. I have already studied this matter and have reason to believe that the contribution this land can yield will considerably exceed that already realized by the empire, showing that the project cannot fail to crown the flag with greater glory and prove very disadvantageous to the Empress's enemies.

"Religious secrecy is imperative to carry this project through. To disguise this enterprise it would be discreet to start from Europe, turn the Cape of Good Hope, and sail farther under the American flag. I have such a right in the capacity of an American officer and citizen. If the Empress approves this plan dictated by devotion to her service, I ask for the enterprise only two boats with fifty cannon, two frigates, and *carte blanche*. The boats' arms must be disguised, since the plan calls for simulating a commercial enterprise. The boats must carry merchandise. . . ."[2]

After almost two months passed without word from Russia concerning this or any other pertinent matter, it is not surprising that Jones, as a prolific correspondent, failed to refrain at the departure of an aide-de-camp of Potemkin from Paris for St. Petersburg to despatch a final letter for the Prince. Although Potemkin had climaxed his secret villainies against him by neglecting even to answer by courteous word, let alone by generous deed, the entreaty for support against the Russo-German girl conspiracy, the Admiral took the pains to recapitulate the true history of his career in Russia. He observed on the one hand respect and even undue deference, but turned on the other to blunt statement of his convictions. In effect his candor and forbearance set in the more severe light his condemnation of Potemkin as well as his other enemies. Potemkin must have snarled at the admonition: "The time will arrive, my lord, when you will know the exact truth of what I have told you. Time is a sovereign master. . . ."[3]

The capture of Oczakow had intoxicated the Prince to gratify even greater excesses of barbaric luxuriousness than his means had permitted and his ingenuity had conceived in the past. During his next campaign, with headquarters at Bender in Bessarabia, he had five hundred servants, two hundred musicians, a corps de ballet, a troupe of actors, one hundred embroiderers, and twenty jewelers.[4] His Asiatic personal extravagances have perhaps greater meaning in his history than his new military triumph in Bessarabia. Naturally his excesses of a savage led to his early, repulsive death in October, 1791. "Prince Potemkin," according to the French soldier of fortune, the Comte de Langeron, "killed himself. . . . I saw him, during a fever, devour a ham, a salted goose, and three or four fowls, and drink *kvass, klukva,* mead, and all kinds of wines."[5] As to Jones and his letter, it need scarcely be added that he received no answer during the fourteen months which passed before Potemkin epitomized by his death the harlequin, who was not less the Mephistophelian, first lieutenant of the Empress.

In the meantime the early course of the French Revolution presented a new conflicting challenge to Jones. He found himself on this epoch-making scene while still engrossed in his latest efforts to triumph completely over his wrongs in Russia and while his energies were becoming circumscribed by serious illness over which even his spirit found it progressively difficult to dominate.

In such terms as "the dignity of human nature," "the flag of freedom," and "the divine feelings of philanthropy," he had previously proclaimed in essence what the Declaration of Independence had defined as the inalienable rights of life, liberty, and the pursuit of happiness. The French now popularly heralded the same inherent principles as liberty, equality, and fraternity, and outstanding revolutionary authors like Paine, the English-American, and Rousseau, Diderot, Montesquieu, and Voltaire, the Frenchmen, had pictured them variantly in their philosophies. Whatever the form, the principles reflected revolt against the underlying social, political, and economic inequalities of monarchy in the eighteenth century. They found even more articulate expression in the reasoned ideals of the French Revolution than in those of the American; it remained to be seen, however, whether the latter did not surpass the former in translating these ideals into practical and temperate action. The application, in fact, of the new idealism was to be the touchstone to determine success or failure in France. For Jones, this application decided only in part his attitude towards the present upheaval; his points of view, private and public, were also in some respects conflicting now as contrasted with formerly in the American Revolution when he had championed a cause with the force of unqualified convictions.

He was tied above all by personal sympathy and gratitude to Louis XVI, who was a generous but particularly unfortunate king in a great crisis inherited from the grievances of the past. And, on the one hand, he had friends among the nobility like D'Estaing, Malesherbes, and Lafayette; on the other hand, he had bitter memories, not alone from St. Petersburg, of the evils of courts, and retained little faith in many leaders of the nobility such as those who crowded about the Duke of Orleans, formerly the Duke of Chartres, and fomented dissension in their self-interested hopes of having him dethrone if not succeed his cousin the King.

The tendency of the Revolution to excesses on the one side and standardization on the other served especially to prejudice Jones against its democratic appeal. The danger loomed of overthrowing authority only to substitute chaos and uniformity. He was not disposed to forgive, for instance, the indignities suffered by Louis when, in spite of the efforts of Lafayette, a mob of six thousand men and women and the National Guard several times as many tyrannically brought him and his family from Versailles to the confinement of the Tuileries in Paris and dubbed them "the baker, the baker's wife, and the baker's little boy." The Admiral looked for order in civil society which should suitably parallel the discipline on board a ship. A genius himself who had known only too well the hindrances of opponents not less arrogant than incapable, he had become progressively convinced that a government should encourage rather than level the widely differing mental, moral, and spiritual capacities of men. And as an obscure boy who had risen to international fame by his sheer tenacity and brilliance and who measured that fame not in terms of power or money but of honor, he was now not less one of the most humane of men but also one of the most glory-loving. He had not shown any disposition to renounce, as the National Assembly required of citizens, his decorations of a Chevalier of France, of the Order of St. Anne, and of the Society of the Cincinnati.

But in the flush of the Revolution when it promised to introduce a new era of national and even international harmony, enthusiasm was widespread among Frenchmen and foreigners alike. Louis was to be the just head of an enlightened constitutional monarchy. It was at the period of greatest expectation that Jones had recently returned to Paris, and he became apparently the leader of a delegation of Americans in the capital who on July 10, 1790 appeared before the National Assembly. In accordance with a custom to invite petitioners to be heard before the body, the President on this day announced that "M. Paul Jones, and a number of citizens of the United States of America, ask also to be admitted to the bar to express to the Assembly their admiration and to congratulate it upon its labors."[6] It was resolved to grant the request.

On the evening of the same day the American deputation was at hand, and in this as well as the previous instance the Assembly mentioned by name Jones alone. "The orator of the deputation," otherwise unidentified in the official record, was not Jones; the naval officer had neither practice in speaking French before a large body nor health to encourage him to be the American mouthpiece. It was William Henry Vernon who delivered the address,[7] but the Admiral probably offered him suggestions as to its nature if not its phrasing. The words appear, in any event, to have expressed his sentiments as a leader and as the most reputed of the Americans, especially in regard to the bond of the United States with France, the hoped-for rôle of Louis as the "first king of men," and the wish to participate in the approaching national fête to inaugurate a new constitutional government on the first anniversary of the taking of the Bastille:

"Impelled by admiration at the courage with which you have consecrated and spread the principles of liberty, the citizens of the United States who are here express to the National Assembly their keen appreciation and their deep respect for the fathers of a great people and for the benefactors of humanity. We realized that the force of truth is irresistible and that the speed of its progress is beyond conception; we believed that at last the blessings of liberty would be appreciated; that liberty would reclaim the rights of man with one voice which men would not stifle; that the kings, the gods of the earth, would become men; that religion would throw off its murderous shackles of intolerance and fanaticism in order to raise the sceptre of peace.

"You have accelerated all such changes, and we feel an inexpressible joy in coming before these heroes of humanity who have fought with such great success in the field of truth and of virtue. May you reap truth and virtue! May you reap the fruits of your efforts! May the patriot King, who shares the one, share the other! The Monarch who, in beginning his career, has spread the benefits of liberty to distant nations is worthy indeed to exchange the inherited glamour of arbitrary power for the love of his fellow citizens. Louis XVI, in the language of France, will be named the first king of the French; but in the language of the universe, he will be called the first king of men. (The hall resounds with applause.)

"We have only one petition to make, and it is to have the honor to assist at the august ceremony which should assure forever the happiness of France. When the French shed their blood with us for liberty, we learned to love them; today when they are free, we feel for them in our hearts the sentiments of brothers and of fellow citizens. It is at the foot of this altar of the fatherland where they come to renew the oath of loyalty to the nation, to the constitution, to the King that we swear eternal friendship to Frenchmen. (Here unanimous applause.) Yes, to all Frenchmen faithful to the principles consecrated by you; for like you, we cherish liberty, like you, we love peace. (The applause doubles on the left side of the Assembly.)"[8]

The response of the President of the National Assembly reflected the great enthusiasm of its members for both the memorable reforms which they sought to establish in the French Government and their warm appreciation of the bond with the French people which the unofficial delegation of Americans under the leadership of Jones had ardently expressed:

"It was in helping you to conquer liberty that the French learned to know it and to love it. The hands which broke your chains were not made to bear them. More fortunate than you, the French nation owes this conquest to the virtues and to the patriotism of her King; it cost you rivers of blood. Courage has broken your chains, reason has broken ours. It was in your country that liberty had established its throne; today it has the support of two peoples.

"The Assembly will see with pleasure at this fête, which is to give to the world a vivid spectacle of a great reunion of friends, the citizens of the United States who are present before it. Again may they greet their brothers, and may the two peoples form only one people in the view of the French."[9]

The President received hearty applause from the Assembly. Robespierre then rose to thank the Americans, but he suffered, in contrast, repeated increasing interruptions of disapproval so that his address was scarcely intelligible and ended abruptly. The rebuff of the revolutionist served to enhance the effect of the President's tribute to the Americans.

The fête of the federation commemorating the first anniversary of the fall of the Bastille, to which the Americans were thus invited with distinction, took place in a vast amphitheatre on the Champ de Mars. The inspired manner in which citizens, men and women alike, volunteered even with pick and shovel to complete the extensive preparations for July 14 attested to the spirit of the gala celebration itself. "What a vision!" it was proclaimed. "What a sublime spectacle! Two hundred thousand men surround the altar of the fatherland, they await their brothers, their legislators, and their king to affirm by their oaths a liberty, still in process of completion, upon the foundations of justice and faith. What holy sentiment dominates this immense multitude! How elevated the people are when they show themselves entirely devoted to their own grandeur!"[10]

Lafayette, who on this day was at the height of his popularity, first pronounced the oath of the constitution. As the last and most momentous of the ceremonies, the King swore his fidelity to it. Perhaps a phrase which Talleyrand, then the Bishop of Autun, is said to have uttered to Lafayette was ominous of the great contrast between the sublime appearances of the day and the dark realities of the morrow. When the Bishop ascended the stairs to the altar at the same moment that Lafayette descended them, he remarked, "Don't make me laugh."

After the conspicuous rôle of Jones at the most hopeful hour of the Revolution, a rôle of which Catherine heard with autocratic resentment even in St. Petersburg, it may seem surprising that he did not readily pursue a continued active part. As the storm became more threatening, he might have taken a public stand against the Revolution if not for it. There was one grave private reason for his aloofness for the present. Health failed him. His body now progressively paid the cost of the prodigal fire of his spirit; the attrition of his disappointments in Russia contributed not a little.

When he first went to see Morris after the latter's return from London to Paris almost half a year following his own arrival, his visit was in the spirit of good will as well as business regarding the arrangements with Bancroft. Morris to be sure had taken some trouble in London to terminate the partnership of the two former friends, and perhaps for this reason he now had the less patience in Paris for interest in Jones' health and society. "I continued my writing," he remarks on November 12, "but Paul Jones comes in and I give him his papers. He tells me he has been very ill." There are on the one hand the absence of a word of regret and on the other the irritation suggested by *but* on this and other occasions. Three visits followed at intervals of two days before they ceased for several months. On November 14: "Paul Jones calls on me. He has nothing to say but is so kind as to bestow on me the hours which hang heavy on his hands." On November 16; "Paul Jones calls. He has nothing to say." On November 18: "Paul Jones calls and gives me his time, but I cannot lend him mine." It is understandable that the convalescent, lonely, and saddened Admiral was not at this period the best company for the chief envoy of the United States in Europe, who had the merit of attending well to his correspondence and other duties in connection with his employers across the Atlantic. Still the time of Morris was not so precious as to prevent him from devoting much of it to an amour with a married woman, Madame de Flahaut, and to an almost daily round of calls upon titled personages for the sake of vanity more than for business. His remarks, although private, sound harsh by contrast with those that came, even during the Admiral's robust health, gently and admiringly from his predecessors Franklin and Jefferson. In an alien Paris increasingly rocked by the Revolution and dominated by new leaders, it was not through Morris that Jones could look for satisfying renewal of his American associations.

◇◇

Chapter LXIX

The Gentleman-Warrior and the Trickster-Empress with "Emptied Bag"

THE MELLOW friendships and the kindly family connections of Jones unfolded in the few remaining, shadowed years of his residence in Paris. They became manifest especially incident to the seriousness of his ill health, however little the warrior relished such a subject, in the course of explanations of his absence to persons who were obviously more interested than Morris in his company and his well-being. Madame T—, as well as the Countess de Nicolson, had vanished from his orbit, although there have been romantic reports to the contrary which are baseless.[1] An estrangement from the natural daughter of Louis XV resulted presumably because of confirmation on his part that she had cared for his money more than for him and also possibly because of the conviction on her part that his professional career, as judged by his direct and swift journey from Copenhagen to St. Petersburg without detour first to Paris, had meant far more to him than any personal relationship. His reputation and appeal, in any event, increased rather than declined among cultured Frenchwomen.

Jones' earlier association with Madame de Tomatis de Valery and her daughters, suggesting contemplative and serene moods of pastoral poetry and of convents, had come to a rather abrupt but apparently unavoidable end with his departure from Warsaw and Vienna for Amsterdam. To judge by four letters which he had soon afterwards received, two addressed to Amsterdam and two earlier forwarded from Strasbourg, another woman, Madame Le Mair d'Altigny, who was now at beautiful Avignon on the Rhone in southern France, felt particular regard for him. "I am infinitely flattered by the interest with which I have the happiness to have inspired you, and your good wishes in my concerns give me true pleasure," he had replied on February 8, 1790 from Amsterdam. "I am not come here on account of anything connected with military operations; and though I think it right to retain my rank, I have always regarded war as the scourge of the human race. I am very happy that you are once more above your difficulties. Past events will enable you to value the blessings of Providence, among which, to a sensible heart, there are none greater than health and independence, enjoyed in the agreeable society of persons of merit. As soon as circumstances permit, I shall feel eager to join the delightful society in which you are."[2]

Her reply, a fifth letter at the least, soon reached him now in Paris. But many months passed before his answer, revealing the curious threat against him of a mob at Harwich during his trip to England and the repercussions of the French Revolution in Avignon, as well as the seriousness of his ill health with its influence upon his intended visit to her: "I have received your charming letter of 2nd March. Having an affair of business to arrange in England, I went from Amsterdam to London at the beginning of May to settle it. I escaped being murdered on landing. From London I came hither, and have not had an hour of health since my arrival. I now feel convalescent, otherwise I would not have dared to write for fear of giving pain to your feeling heart. In leaving Holland my plan was to repair to Avignon in compliance with your obliging invitation. My health formed an invincible obstacle, but I still hope to indemnify myself on the return of the fine weather. I was for a long time very much alarmed by the disturbances which interrupted the peace of your city, and am very glad to see they are ended. I have learned, with lively satisfaction, that they have had no disagreeable consequence so far as regards you. Give me news of yourself, I pray you, and of those interesting persons of whom you speak in your last letter."[3]

The trace of formality in this correspondence, which tends to offset the cordiality of it, was absent from another with Mesdames Le Grande and Rinsby, at Trevoux, also near the Rhone at Lyon, which soon followed in a spirit more spontaneous. In the light of Jones' extended experience in both love and friendship, his message to them is in part a retrospect upon his private and public career as seen from his bitter view of "the nauseous draught of life":

"Madame Clement has read me part of a letter from you, in which you conclude that I prefer love to friendship and Paris to Trevoux. As to the first part, you may be right, for love frequently communicates divine qualities, and in that light may be considered as the cordial that Providence has bestowed on mortals to help them to digest the nauseous draught of life. Friendship, they say, has more solid qualities than love. This is a question I shall not attempt to resolve; but sad experience generally shows that where we expect to find a friend we have only been treacherously deluded by false appearances, and that the goddess herself very seldom confers her charms on any of the human race.

"As to the second, I am too much of a philosopher to prefer noise to tranquillity; if this does not determine the preference between Paris and Trevoux, I will add that I have had very bad health almost ever since your departure, and that other circumstances have conspired to detain me here, which have nothing to do either with love or friendship. My health is now recovering, and as what is retarded is not always lost, I hope soon to have the happiness of paying you my personal homage, and of renewing the assurance of that undiminished attachment which women of such distinguished worth and talents naturally inspire."[4]

The warmth of feeling that he was able to quicken has scarcely greater testimony, even in the impassioned vows of Delia, than in the response from Madame Le Grande, which beats with the sentiments of her heart and sparkles with the light of her understanding:

"I had given up the hope of receiving any intelligence of Your Excellency, and I acknowledge it cost me much before I could believe that the promise of a great man was no more to be relied upon than that of the herd of mankind. The letter with which you have honored me convinces me that my heart knew you better than my head; for though my reason whispered that you had quite forgotten us, I was unwilling to believe it.

"Madame Wolfe, as well as myself, is much concerned for the bad state of your health. I am sorry that, like myself, Your Excellency is taught the value of health by sickness. Come to us, sir; if you do not find here the pleasures you enjoy in Paris, you will find a good air, frugal meals, freedom, and hearts that can appreciate you.

"I am concerned to perceive that Your Excellency is an unbeliever in friendship. Alas, if you want friends, who shall pretend to possess them! I hope you will recover from this error, and be convinced that friendship is more than a chimera of Plato.

"Do me the favor to acquaint me with the time we may expect the honor of seeing you. I must be absent for some days, and I would not for anything in the world that I should not be here on your arrival. If I knew the time, I would send my little carriage to meet the stage-coach, as I suppose you will take that conveyance.

"Madame Wolfe expects the moment of your arrival with as much eagerness as myself (she says); but as I best know my own feelings, I am certain I go beyond her. Of this I am certain, that we shall both count the day till we have the happiness of seeing you. Come quickly then, I pray you."[5]

This kindly appeal of friendship and even a closer tie of blood did not seem able to interrupt for a short period his residence in Paris while his thoughts, accentuated by illness and disappointment, remained fixed primarily upon his profession. Almost a score of years had elapsed since he had last seen his relatives in Scotland; almost fifteen had passed since his mother had died, and in the interval his two surviving sisters, Janet and Mary, had grown to womanhood and married. Before and during the American Revolution, however, he had sent letters and funds to his family, and at Portsmouth in the *Ranger* he had made them the beneficiaries in his will. In Europe he had even confided to Franklin: "I think that Pope himself could not have taken more pleasure than I should 'to rock the cradle of declining age.' "

Notwithstanding such professions of devotedness to his mother and sisters, he assuredly did not practice them. Still in his niece Janette Taylor he has had an emphatic witness to his unchanging loyalty and affection towards his kin, even if his feelings were manifest only at a distance. "It was my intention at first," she declared as owner of many of Jones' papers, "to publish the whole of my uncle's letters to my mother, by which it would have appeared that his interest in his relations was uniform and ardent from the first to last, but as they contained reference to matters of a domestic nature which it might have wounded the feelings of some connected with me to see in print, and not wishing to have the letters garbled, on reflection I deemed it best to withhold them altogether. . . ."[6]

During his initial efforts to recover the claim against Denmark, he had sent a message to his sister Janet in March, 1787: "I have a great desire to see you; and I will exert myself for that purpose after I have finished my public business . . . do not write till you hear from or *see me*."[7] As he shortly made his unexpected trip to America and later did not turn aside even from Copenhagen to Paris at the call which sent him flying to St. Petersburg, it is understandable that he postponed indefinitely his visit to Scotland. From Amsterdam, in March, 1790, he had written again to Janet, addressing himself to both sisters: "It would be superfluous to mention the great satisfaction I received in hearing from two persons I so much love and esteem, and whose worthy conduct as wives and mothers is so respectable in my eyes. Since my return to Europe, a train of circumstances and changes of residence have combined to keep me silent. This has given me more pain than I can express; for I have a tender regard for you both, and nothing can be indifferent to me that regards your happiness and the welfare of your children. I wish for a particular detail of their age, respective talents, characters, and education. I do not desire this information merely from curiosity. It would afford me real satisfaction to be useful to their establishment in life.

"We must study the genius and inclination of the boys and try to fit them by a suitable education for the pursuits we may be able to adopt for their advantage. When their education shall be advanced to a proper stage, at the school of Dumfries for instance, it must then be determined whether it may be most economical and advantageous for them to go to Edinburgh or France to finish their studies. All this is supposing them to have a great natural genius and goodness of disposition; for without these they can never become eminent.

"For the females, they require an education suited to the delicacy of character that is becoming in their sex. I wish I had a fortune to offer to each of them; but though this is not the case, I may yet be useful to them. And I desire particularly to be useful to the two young women who have a double claim to my regard, as they have lost their father [Mr. Young, the first husband of Mary].[8]

He further showed himself highly ambitious for the training of his sisters' children, who included the son William and the daughter Janette of Janet Taylor and several daughters of Mary Lowden by her first and second husbands. William as his only nephew and the son of his favorite sister Janet attracted his special interest. Ironically the Russians had accused Jones of cruelty towards this boy of whom he had vowed in reply: "Instead of imbruing my hands in his blood, he will be cherished as my son." The Admiral had sent him the Latin inscription of the gold sword from Louis XVI as an exercise in translation and remarked that it "might some day be his." In addition to consideration of Edinburgh, Glasgow, and institutions in France for his studies, he had also in mind the prospect of sending him to St. Paul's School in London preparatory to transfer to Cambridge or Oxford.[9]

Jones felt almost equal regard for the education of his niece Janette. His varied advice might have come from the director of a girls' finishing school. It seems partly consistent with Abigail Adams' former description of him as "a most uncommon character"—not "a rough, stout, warlike Roman" but, to her somewhat jaundiced eyes, both "the warrior and the abigail." "I am very glad," Jones counseled, "your daughter understands music, which is a most advantageous accomplishment to a young woman who has a good ear and voice. I need not mention that Italian music has now the opinion of all good judges in its favor. Everything that regards the economy of a family should be comprehended in female education, and a woman should be able and have taste sufficient to make up with her own hands almost everything she wears, particularly articles of millinery. . . . The best reading is history. . . . Reading romances only serves to fill young heads with ridiculous visions. . . . Dancing is a necessary talent for youth, and drawing is a genteel and sometimes a useful accomplishment."[10]

The warrior had even further suggestions for the cultivation of girls, especially as it seems that he received encouraging appreciation from his youthful niece and her mother. "Your daughter interests me much," he wrote once more to Janet. "My desire is that her education be continued without interruption. I shall explain myself more particularly on this head hereafter." Janette the niece must have cherished throughout her life what he had said and planned. It was she in particular who was to repay her uncle by jealous guardianship over those letters and manuscripts which later came into her hands and by her championship of his name in a spirit, at once fiery, determined, and affectionate, testifying to their common blood. The accurate and trenchant style of her annotations for the early full-length biography of Jones based on material in her possession evidenced not the least of the attributes which she shared with him.

It is not surprising perhaps that Jones whose own ambition was audacious enough to "ascend the slippery precipices . . . even to the pinnacle of fame" should have been sufficiently enlightened and resolved to advance as far as possible the practical and cultural education of his nephew and nieces. But it is noteworthy in particular that this officer, since boyhood in surroundings of rude manners and of violent passions at sea, should have revealed the same spirit of mercy and forgiveness in regard to the domestic broils between his two sisters and their families that he had shown in battle and triumph typically by his zeal in behalf of prisoners, his abhorrence of uncalled-for bloodshed, and his return of a vanquished rival's sword. A future incident was to exemplify the present serious breach between the two families which he tried to remove. Of the numerous letters and manuscripts which Jones was to leave at his death, the Taylors later said in indignation against the Lowdens concerning the manner in which they were apportioned between them: "The papers were divided like snuff paper, by weight and measure, just as they happened to come to hand, without any regard to their value or to their connection one with another."[11]

When Jones learned from his sister Janet of the dissension between the Taylors and the Lowdens, it was a warrior enriched by large experience of forbearance and suffering, who, although seriously ill, wrote to her from Paris in December, 1790:

"I shall not conceal from you that your family discord aggravates infinitely all my pains. My grief is inexpressible that two sisters, whose happiness is so interesting to me, do not live together in that mutual tenderness and affection which would do so much honor to themselves and to the memory of their worthy relations. Permit me to recommend to your serious study and application Pope's *Universal Prayer*. You will find more morality in that little piece than in many volumes that have been written by great divines:

> Teach me to *feel* another's woe,
> *To hide the fault I see;*
> That mercy I to others show,
> *Such mercy show to me!*

"This is not the language of a weak superstitious mind, but the spontaneous offspring of true religion, springing from a heart sincerely inspired by charity and deeply impressed with a sense of the calamities and frailties of human nature. If the sphere in which Providence has placed us as members of society requires the exercise of brotherly kindness and charity towards our neighbor in general, how much more is this our duty with respect to individuals with whom we are connected by the near and tender ties of nature as well as moral obligation. Every lesser virtue may pass away, but charity comes from Heaven and is immortal."[12]

The thoughts which took form in such letters but significantly not in visits from Paris, his strategic centre, occupied at best a small portion of Jones' time while he still waited less and less hopefully for developments important to his profession. He determined to bring his uncertain situation to an issue when the two years' leave of absence was fast approaching its expiration. He had written without result from Warsaw directly to the Empress, from Amsterdam to one of her ambassadors and from Paris to another, and likewise from Paris even to Potemkin. In March, 1791, a year and a half after his last previous effort to explain himself to Catherine, he addressed to her a final message, which in contrast with the earlier was highly respectful but not adulatory and at the same time even more explicit concerning the unfulfilled promises on her part and the intrigues on the part of her subordinates. Along with the letter itself, the Admiral submitted his latest naval plan, which proposed to attack Britain in India in the event that complications over Turkey resulted in a declaration of war by her against Russia.

It was calculated to chafe the Empress to read that his reason for sending his present letter was the necessary assumption that his previous one had not reached her; the frank statement bore the unflattering implication as to her régime that his enemies had intercepted it according to the common practice.[13] In this second case, Jones did not deceive himself by reliance upon seals and Russian secretaries or ambassadors. He confided his message to Grimm, whose consistent servility to her promised to render a communication under cover of his own immune to the suspicions of self-appointed censors.[14] The letter was destined also to eradicate any flattering illusions she may have cherished in regard to her favorites Nassau and Potemkin. He had formerly sent extensive documentary evidence and now added: "I have in my hands the means to prove, incontestibly, that I directed all the useful operations against the Capitan Pacha."[15]

In Jones' concluding words to Catherine, there was more of the charity which he had preached to his sisters than the justice which his positive nature had often discerned, pronounced, and championed. His attitude also indicated once more that in the case of his Russian services both his loyalty and his ardor for glory had been and still were directed unwisely: "As I have my enemies and as the term of my parole is about to expire, I await the orders of Your Majesty, and should be flattered if it is your pleasure for me to come and render you an account in person. . . . I therefore pray you to withdraw me as soon as possible from the cruel uncertainty in which I am placed. Should you deign, madam, to inform me that you are pleased with the services which I have had the happiness to render you, I will console myself for the misfortunes which I have suffered, as I drew my sword for you from personal attachment and ambition, but not from interest. My fortune as you know, is not very considerable; but as I am philosopher enough to confine myself to my means, I shall be always rich."[16]

Even in the transmission of Jones' letter it was evident again that the Empress and her agents were of the same stripe. Grimm had inspired the faith of the Admiral by his suave and flattering professions; but the references to Jones in the accompanying note from the one German to the other indicate the duplicity which was a bond between the compatriots: "The Rear Admiral Paul Jones has entrusted to me the enclosed packet. I am ignorant of its contents, but as far as I have been able to have a glimpse, it contains a project or plan in which he doubtlessly has reserved a principal rôle for himself, but which he believes of great importance in case the war should continue, an importance which would increase if the Court of London proceeded to the point of taking an active part. As far as I have been able to determine, it would be a matter of disturbing them even in the region of their heart and of their sources of life, in India. The Rear Admiral dares to flatter himself that Your Majesty will deign to transmit to me some decision regarding his packet.

"The other waste papers ought to find their extinction in the imperial chimney."[17]

Grimm continued his double-faced course, smiling at Jones and ridiculing him and his "waste papers" to the Empress. The Admiral awaited a reply from Catherine with the impatience of a lover, and in the meantime presented the treacherous German with a replica of the bust by Houdon which he had praised. During an absence of Catherine's correspondent from Paris, Jones hastened to write him on July 9: "M. Houdon has sent to your house the bust which you have done me the honor to accept. Mademoiselle Marchais has informed me of all the obliging things you have said regarding my affairs. She has just told me that the answer of the Empress awaits you at Frankfort."[18]

And with his characteristic zeal he newly presented an outline for the construction of ships for the Russian Navy in accordance with architectural and engineering improvements and inventions at his disposal. These discoveries, he explained, were the secret knowledge of a certain shipbuilder, "a man here whom I have known for fifteen years." In addition were the results which he hoped for from studies in the distant past with Franklin and more recently by himself "to devise the construction of a ship which could be navigated without ballast, be ready for action at any time, draw less water, and at the same time drive little or not at all to leeward." As for the strange collaboration between two such ingenious men, he concluded: "We always encountered great obstacles. Since the death of that great philosopher, having too much time on my hands, I think I have surmounted the difficulties which baffled our researches."[19] Perhaps his views of startling inventions were sanguine; in any case he had much to offer in construction, materials, and armament for Russian shipbuilding in the light of the sorely inefficient vessels which had been under his command on the Liman.

The Empress received Jones' packet transmitted by Grimm, and she answered it through her German correspondent after her fashion and at her chosen time, which was in September, 1791, almost six months following his letter. Although at bay morally before the pressure of the blunt statements of Jones, she was so inveterately Machiavellian as scarcely to give heed to her own repellent falsity. But also at bay more tangibly before the pressure of military and political events, she was prepared to curb her brigandage at the threat of force, the only reality which her savage nature respected. Nassau had suffered a debacle against Sweden. Potemkin had died and broken the continuity of her carnage against Turkey. Joseph II of Austria also had died, and he had been succeeded by Leopold, who made a separate peace with the Turks inasmuch as he was susceptible neither to the personal nor to the political blandishments which she had exercised over his predecessor. Prussia gazed with a jealous and hostile eye upon her pillages. England resented her arrogance and looked with concern upon her attempts to disrupt the balance of power. The European nations in general did not succumb to her ruse to turn their attention to the French Revolution so as to allow her license to glut her lust for conquest over Turkey. As they knew her too well and threatened a coalition against her, she took steps through necessity towards peace. It was such a despot who now turned to comment upon Jones to her ingratiating fellow-German in her present mood and situation of a lawless beast which has only half slaked its predatory thirst and has been beaten back, snarling, to the protection of its lair.

"It seems to me that I have nothing to say in regard to Paul Jones: having emptied my bag and peace being almost concluded, he should be advised to go to attend his affairs in America"[20]—in these first words it is possible to read her confession that she had no defense against him, that the Russo-German girl episode was only one of the tricks which had come from her now emptied bag, and that only her dread of his enlistment in the cause of her enemies while war lasted had been her motive for the two years' leave of absence instead of an outright expulsion. As to this leave of absence, she did not hesitate at the approach of peace to reveal more plainly: "It was not indeed necessary further that he should become Turco-Swedish; now I think that a simple drudge could almost understand the manœuvre: the Rear Admiral was indeed put off with a pension somewhat after the manner, I think, in which France gave one to General Luckner."[21]

"GOD KNOWS WHAT THAT MEANS!"—this, in continuation, was her cry of affected innocence and surprise in answer to Jones' indirect remark upon the seizure of his letters by Potemkin and Bosborodko in accordance with the Russian practice. He *"accuses no one"*—this, with equal guile, was her citation from his own letters for her attempt to belie the contrary meaning of these words in their context in order that she might put a righteous face upon her own deeds and those of her lieutenants. "It is certain that he did not fight, because he was given order after order to advance and he never advanced, because of head winds as he himself admits"—this, again with similar artifice, was her alleged evidence based on her distorted interpretation of one of the Admiral's statements and apparently on Nassau's and Potemkin's testimony by which she pretended to prove conclusively that the services of Jones in the Liman campaign, as set forth in his letters and certified documents, were false. At bay, she had turned to her repertory of mocking scorn, unblushing cynicism, and rank hypocrisy.

"He says that he gave you the packet for me, sealed with his arms; that is how I received it, but he did not tell me of the audience which he asked for and obtained from the National Assembly; I do not know why"[22]—this, finally, among many other examples of her guilt-inspired subterfuges, was the utterance of the despot who trembled at the spectre in Russia of another French Revolution and who associated with it the bold and free voice of the Admiral.

Fear indeed was the first and last of her reactions towards Jones and the most revealing betrayal of her sins against him. Ironically she merited her name Catherine the Great, given to her by abject courtiers, as one of the most criminal despots of either sex, not only among the autocrats of the lands of her birth and her rule but also all those of history.

After reading the remarks of the Empress, Grimm appears to have become discreetly silent towards the Admiral. The Empress, moreover, had stated to him: "I hope that the peace will soon be concluded; but if it is not, I shall make known my intentions to Mr. Paul Jones."[23]

◇◇◇

Chapter LXX

Last Ties with America and France

THE DEVOTION of Jones to the United States was not the less even if during the two years' leave of absence from Russia he clung tenaciously to the connection which he should have spurned. At his dash from Copenhagen for St. Petersburg, he had avowed to Jefferson: "I have not forsaken a country that has had many disinterested and difficult proofs of my steady affection; and I can never renounce the glorious title of *a citizen of the United States!*" From the Liman he had declared again to the Minister: "I can in no situation, however remote I am, be easy while the liberties of America seem to me to be in danger." On his return to Amsterdam he had written to Franklin and to others concerning "my friends in America, whose good opinion is dearer to me than anything else." There is no reason to believe that these words did not come from his heart.

However loyal towards America and however concerned at the same time at the possible effect of the Russian plot upon his reputation, he looked long in vain across the waters for a favorable response to his sentiments. Although the months following his arrival in Amsterdam and Paris lengthened to considerably more than a year, he failed to receive, in his own phrase, "a single line in answer" particularly to his letters to the President, the Vice President, and Charles Thomson, the retired secretary of the Continental Congress. Nor did he see any prospect of suitable employment by America or France in either peace or war. Under these circumstances it was the more natural that he should continue to visit Gouverneur Morris, even if with greater frequency than the envoy seemed to relish, in order to learn especially of his distant friends and of the progress of the infant country in which he had the concern of one of its foremost liberators.

It was Jefferson and indeed Jefferson the new Secretary of State almost alone who remained his close link and his warm friend in America. Franklin was no more, and Robert Morris was engrossed in his financial ventures. But after the Admiral's departure from Russia, it was as late as March 20, 1791 before he communicated again with Jefferson. The annual pension of. fifteen thousand crowns granted to Jones three years earlier by the King of Denmark as well as the recent evidence from Littlepage to expose the Russian conspiracy may have occasioned his delay. Apart from recalling the particulars of the latter event, Jones explained for the first time the nature of the former and observed upon its fitness according to the advice of Gouverneur Morris and of Short. "Both gave me their opinion," he informed Jefferson, "that I may with propriety accept the advantage offered. I have in consequence determined to draw upon the sum due, and I think you will not disapprove of this step as it can by no means weaken the claim of the United States, but rather the contrary."[1] Whether or not Jefferson thought differently, he chose to remain silent; whether or not Denmark had expected Jones to avail himself of the patent, this nation continued to fail to make any payment during his life.

The Admiral gave such emphasis to other personal concerns as to suggest his somewhat vain preoccupation with them, particularly in view of the democracy in both the United States and the new France of the Revolution. "You will observe," he wrote to Jefferson, "that the Empress of Russia has decorated me with the great Order of St. Anne; and as I have appeared with that order ever since, I must beg the favor of you to obtain and transmit to me, as soon as possible, the proper authority of the United States for my retaining that honor."[2] This request bordered upon an imposition inasmuch as the American Constitution forbade the acceptance of titles by American citizens without the consent of Congress, although it had the encouragement of the circumstances under which he had received the decoration of Chevalier of France. In the present instance Jefferson was to reply with consideration but without enthusiasm: "I can only say that the Executive of our Government are not authorized either to grant or refuse the permission you ask, and consequently cannot take on themselves to do it. . . . In general there is an aversion to meddle with anything of that kind here."[3]

Jones also asked for the delivery of one of the Houdon busts to the State of North Carolina, apart from the eight copies which Jefferson with the aid of Short had forwarded to the Admiral's chosen friends in America, and exclusive of thirteen or more additional copies which Jones separately presented in both America and Europe. He now wished to comply with a desire of Robert Burton, a former member of Congress from North Carolina, who had offered a bust of him for the State to Governor Samuel Johnston as early as January 28, 1789 and had received a written acceptance. "As those men who have fought and bled for us in the late contest," Burton had said, "cannot be held in too high esteem and as Chevalier John Paul Jones is among the foremost who derived their appointment from this State and deserve to be held in remembrance to the latest ages, I take the liberty of offering to the State, as a present through you its Chief Magistrate, the bust of that great man and good soldier to perpetuate his memory."[4] Inasmuch as Jones mentioned to Jefferson a bust for North Carolina decorated with the Order of St. Anne and Mr. Burton offered his copy considerably earlier, it is probable that this new bust with the added order was to be presented in lieu of the earlier one. There is no evidence of its receipt. The interest of North Carolina to do honor to Jones points back in particular to his early connection with Joseph Hewes.

More in the spirit of a claim than a petition, Jones further saw fit to recall to Jefferson an event of national and international import of the Revolution. He appeared to feel that the United States had neither recognized its full meaning nor given him his due. His merit had been undoubtedly most distinguished, but his modesty was not equally without question, in his reminder to the Secretary of State: "I reserve for my return to America to produce to the United States full and unquestionable evidence, signed by the Grand Pensioner, that *my conduct,* in 1779, drew the United Netherlands into the war. This is saying enough to a man of your information; for it would be superfluous to enumerate the advantages that thence resulted to America, particularly the great event that took place under your own eyes, and which could not have happened if Holland had remained a neutral power." The certificate to which he referred, attested by M. F. Dumas in addition to Van Berckel and dated March 11, 1784 at The Hague, had presented Jones' achievements at the Texel most favorably. Exclusive of such aid as loans after the involvement of Holland, it scarcely had exaggerated the result of his part as stated by Van Berckel: "The English made use indeed of the stay and the conduct of the commander at the Texel as the ground for the first article of their declaration of war."[5]

Frank in some respects and vain in others, this significant letter to Jefferson was also generous. Once more, for instance, Jones called to his attention a subject which from the beginning of the Revolution had never failed to arouse his zeal and pity: "I continue to be sensibly affected by the situation of our poor countrymen at Algiers; the more so as I learn indirectly from the pirate, now here, who took the greatest part of them that, if they are not very soon redeemed, they will be treated with no more lenity than is shown to other slaves." Only a month previously he had asked William Carmichael, now at Madrid: "Pray can you inform me whether anything efficacious is in agitation for the relief of our unhappy countrymen at Algiers? Nothing provokes me so much as the shameful neglect they have so long experienced."[6]

It is a curious but revealing parallel between this message which Jones now sent to Jefferson, the Secretary of State, and that which he had written almost three years earlier to Jay, the Minister of Foreign Affairs, that they bore evident resemblances in frankness, vanity, and generosity, including similar allusions to the American prisoners in the hands of Algerian pirates.

At Paris, still in the shadow of Russian malevolence and in the midst of the ever-rising passions of the French Revolution, Jones must have welcomed a delayed message from Jefferson, who spoke in his public as well as private character and expressly in behalf of Washington as well as of himself. Although the Secretary of State was not encouraging in regard to foreign presents and titles, it was at this suitable time that he sent pleasing assurances from America which contrasted significantly against the dark backgrounds of Russia and France. Relative to the Admiral's full evidence exposing the Russian conspiracy, Jefferson now used his previously quoted words, "No proof was necessary to satisfy us of your good conduct everywhere"; and apropos of the political storm in Paris, he concluded, "Our new constitution works well and gives general satisfaction. . . . A state of tranquil prosperity furnishing no particular and interesting events to communicate to you, I have only to add assurances of my constant esteem and attachment."[7]

More and more awesome indeed became the fury of the French Revolution to Americans, who were able to contrast it with the peaceful freedom which their ally had helped to cradle in the New World. "An American," said Gouverneur Morris, whose lodgings were in sight of the Tuileries, the virtual prison of the King, "has a stronger sympathy with this country than any other observer, and nourished as he is in the very bosom of liberty, he cannot but be deeply afflicted to see that in almost every event this struggle must terminate in despotism."[8] Although prone to be royalist and highly skeptical of popular rule, Morris did not lack supporters of some of his prophecies among the few Americans, including Jones, who in Paris were firsthand observers of the Revolution. "This unhappy country, bewildered in the pursuit of metaphysical whimsies," the American Minister further declared, "presents to our moral view a mighty ruin. Like the remnants of ancient magnificence, we admire the architecture of the temple, while we detest the false god to whom it was dedicated. Daws and ravens and the birds of night now build their nests in its niches. The sovereign, humbled to the level of a beggar's pity, without resources, without authority, without a friend. The Assembly at once a master and a slave, new in power, wild in theory, raw in practice. It engrosses all functions though incapable of exercising any, and has taken from this fierce ferocious people every restraint of religion and of respect."[9]

In the later stages of the Revolution, Jones scarcely would have disagreed with this portrayal. He lost faith in the transformed appearance of France as the storm moved onward increasingly demagogic, factional, violent, bloody, and tyrannous over the King. If the American Minister was more conscious of the irony, the Admiral was more aware of the pity. But the former probably did not need to sharpen with his caustic pen the disillusioned views of the latter following, first, the defeated attempt of Louis and his family to flee from the Tuileries; secondly, the return of the King and his family from Varennes in charge of ten thousand riotous peasants, men and women, armed with muskets, clubs, and scythes; and thirdly, the suspension of the ruler by the National Assembly. "Paul Jones called on me this morning," wrote the diarist on July 5, 1791; "he is much vexed at the democracy of this country."[10] And considerably later, although in a nettled, ironical mood at criticism impugning his conduct towards Jones, Morris was to declare that his fellow-American "detested the French Revolution and all those concerned in it."[11]

"Without a friend," Morris had described Louis XVI. Jones was at least one exception. He remained loyal to him and to Lafayette, who occupied a difficult position between rival forces, both of which often ceased to trust his motives. During the fickle, gruesome course of the Revolution, tried, generous friends were a greater bond to the Admiral than republican principles without consistency, guidance, or practice. In March, 1791 he still looked forward when in better health to fulfill a purpose which his Russian services had long caused him to set aside; he wished to present to the King the letter with which Congress had honored him during his last return to America and "to embrace the first occasion to embark in the French fleet of evolution." And at the increasingly crucial need for the leadership of a fearless, magnetic warrior, when Louis was virtually a prisoner surrounded by threatening daggers and Lafayette was his precariously situated champion, Jones sent a characteristic message on December 7 to the latter:

"My ill health for some time past has prevented me from the pleasure of paying you my personal respects, but I hope shortly to indulge myself with that satisfaction.

"I hope that you approve the quality of the fur linings I brought from Russia for the King and yourself. I flatter myself that His Majesty will accept from your hand that mark of the sincere attachment I feel for his person; and be assured that I shall be always ready to draw the sword with which he honored me for the service of the virtuous and illustrious 'PROTECTOR OF THE RIGHTS OF HUMAN NATURE.' "[12] If Jones had had his health and if he had not been quixotically faithful to his ties in Russia, it is probable that he would have braved the revolutionary mobs of Paris which flouted even Lafayette, the popular hero. And at the same time he would have proved, in France as well as in America, his love of the freedom of democracy.

"When my health is reëstablished," the letter added, "M. Simolin will do me the honor to present me to His Majesty as a Russian Admiral." It was not alone Jones' desire to retain his title but also the strange compulsion exercised by the Empress which must have influenced him to make this declaration. Surely Grimm had been able to give him scant encouragement for the future. Catherine herself did not write to him. Even his salary, concerning which he had asked De Genêt to inquire, remained unpaid. The two years of the leave of absence had elapsed under such humiliating circumstances in time of war; the design both to cast him off and to temporize so as to prevent his service with an enemy accomplished its full purpose when on January 3, 1792 Russia and Turkey became at peace. Thus longer and longer a vain spur of ambition and a knight-errantry towards Catherine governed the man whose outstanding qualities normally included speed, decision, and independence.

The Empress had palsied his will. It is recalled that Jones had early prepared the statement that he would "probably renounce the service of that [the Russian] power, even before the expiration of the leave of absence which he now enjoys." From Amsterdam in December, 1789 he had declared to Franklin, "I can easily prove to the world that I have been treated unjustly, but I intend to remain silent at least till I know the fate of my journal." In February, 1791 he had still hesitated but emphasized to Carmichael his resolve, depending upon the effect of the evidence submitted for the Empress: "It contained such damning proofs against my enemies that it has undoubtedly been intercepted. As a sure occasion offers, I shall write again next month; and my letter will contain my resignation in case I receive no immediate satisfaction." In this next month he had expressed a similar determination to Jefferson: "Though the Baron de Grimm has undertaken to transmit to Her Imperial Majesty's own hands my last packet, I shall not be surprised if I should find myself constrained to withdraw from the Russian service and to publish my journal of the campaign I commanded: in that case, I hope to prove to the world that *my operations* not only saved Kherson and Crimea but decided the fate of the war." To others such as General St. Clair, Governor General of the Northwest District of America, he wrote in the same vein. But the man of action stood irresolute before the autocrat who mocked him to the end; although not a Hamlet disposed to thought more than deed, like Hamlet he nevertheless lacked gall to make oppression bitter.

He sacrificed to Catherine much of that glory to which he had dedicated his life and from which he drew the breath of his being. He refrained from publishing both the journal of the Russian campaign itself and the one hundred and forty pages of corroborative evidence, the *Pièces Justificatives,* which would have exposed the Empress as well as her lieutenants to widespread shame. In deference to her he chose to suffer misunderstanding by his contemporaries. His sacrifice, however, not without both weakness and strength, has served to reveal her despotic unscrupulousness on the one side and his military and moral honor on the other with the darkness of temporary eclipse offset by the permanent light of history.

In the course of these closing days at Paris, England brought to Jones' memory the past in relation to the present, apart from his special interests relating to Russia, France, and the United States. Even during the latter part of the American Revolution his hostility had become less sweeping after previous business friends in England had informed him of unfortunate misunderstandings on both sides. Recently in Russia the regret of the British at his departure from St. Petersburg had newly impressed upon him the more by contrast with his cruel, treacherous experience in that country that these new friends of the land of his birth were as a people not less just and humane than brave. And now with minds of larger perspective and with hearts more mature, he and Britishers met on increasingly reconciled, open terms. Lord Daer, the son of the Earl of Selkirk, it is recalled, had described him at his accidental meeting, "He seems a sensible little fellow. He is not dark as I heard"; he also acknowledged, in the words of Gouverneur Morris, "the polite attention of Jones in the attack on his father's house last war." But more indicative of mutual respect are, for example, the cordial relations of Jones with the Earl of Wemyss who had early sought to advance the Russian connection, and the particular interest of Admiral Digby who desired to become acquainted with him. Perhaps the best testimony that Jones held an enlightened view of Britain in his later years is the absence of disparaging remarks, apart from such a bare reference as that to a hostile rabble at Harwich. Generous in victory towards individuals whether they were private or public enemies, he was disposed to be even more generous towards a nation. And in turn the land of his birth has allowed him justice and even honor despite the passions of mobs and the scurrility of scribblers of tall stories.

It was not England which in any way corroded the last months of his life with bitter thoughts. Russia among nations, the French among ministries, and an American traitor among individuals rather assumed such a part. During his last half year following the peace with Turkey, silence remained his final answer to Russia, in spite of the evidence in his hands which gave him the power to be most articulate and damning. At the same time there were reverberations in his written words to testify indirectly that, although his nature was enriched by a spirit of forgiveness, it could glow even in his increasingly sick condition with that fire which had set him apart in dramatic moments of his life when the issue turned upon a point of honor.

Under the circumstances that aroused him in February and March, 1792 to make severe protests first to one minister of the French Marine and then to another, his suppressed resentment towards Russia even more perhaps than towards the French Ministry underlay his acerbity, sharpened by an immediate slight to his name at a time of aggravated illness. His limited pecuniary resources for present use may also have been at least a subconscious influence. He had written at the period of crumbling alike of the French Government and finances to Bertrand de Molleville, the Minister of Marine, in regard to wages still due on account to seamen and officers of the *Bonhomme Richard,* apart from the settlement of the prize money and an advance to him of fifteen thousand livres toward payment of the wages in question. De Molleville neglected to reply for six months, and then not only failed to accede definitely to his request but also brought him first to task, especially to provide evidence in strict business fashion of proper disbursement of these fifteen thousand livres.[13] The Admiral was incensed most of all that the Minister manifested a spirit which assumed ignorance of what his services had been to France and the United States as allies and even indeed of who he was.

Accordingly the heat of Jones' long rejoinder had its incitement in a far larger consideration of justice and honor than the immediate topic of the unpaid balance of the wages for the *Bonhomme Richard* crew. He did not fail to declare frankly the attitude, foreign to his habit, to which the provocations now impelled him to give rein. He spoke of himself as "one who has for many years been accustomed to the baseness and duplicity of some who are attached to courts," and specifically recounted his trying experiences with De Sartine and De Castries. But now as well as at all times in the past, he distinguished between the King and the Court. "I pray you, sir," he challenged, "to lay this letter before the King. It contains many things out of the general rule of delicacy which marks my proceedings, and which, on any other occasion less affecting to my sensibility, would never have escaped from my tongue or pen. . . . I have hitherto been the dupe and victim of my modesty. . . ."[14]

Incident to the rapid changes of the Revolution, M. de la Coste followed Bertrand de Molleville as the Minister of the Marine between the time that Jones had prepared his letter and decided to transmit it; he accordingly sent his communication with another conspicuously more tempered to the successor. The Admiral had been stirred to make demands in his own behalf, in addition to those for the *Bonhomme Richard* officers and men. In his second message, he made the further conciliatory declaration: "As to my personal pretensions, I never should have set up a claim on that score under circumstances less affecting to my sensibility. Of this I need offer no other proof than my silence in that respect for twelve years past. My losses and unavoidable expenses during my long connection with this nation amount to a large sum and have greatly lessened my fortune. I have given solemn proofs of my great attachment towards France and that attachment still remains undiminished."[15] The reticence which he set aside in his own interests was doubtlessly also not without his outlook upon the incapacity, the trials, and the portents of his illness.

At an even more serious stage of his broken health and with a sense of unfair, disillusioning treatment by an individual comparable in some measure to that which he had experienced from the French Court and the Russian Empress, Jones renewed on April 30, 1792 his correspondence with Edward Bancroft. If still without an inkling that his earlier highly regarded confidant was a traitor to America, he nevertheless had lost all faith in him as a friend and business associate. That Jones had considered it desirable two years previously to have Morris serve as a witness and referee at his negotiations with Bancroft was in itself sufficient evidence of his loss of regard for Franklin's former secretary. Now in marked contrast with his cordial assurances during the Revolution, the Admiral stated curtly and sternly: "I have this day drawn on you . . . for one thousand and fifty pounds sterling, being the amount that becomes due on your bond for principal and interest the fourth of next month. And that you may have no pretext for protracting the final settlement of this business, I have deposited your bond in the house of Sir Robert Herries & Company of this city. . . .

"I just take the liberty to remind you of your breach of promise. . . . The account you give me of your present fortune is so flourishing in comparison to what you wrote me two years ago that you can be at no loss to raise the sum now due to me . . . both reason and right entitle me to the use of mine, which I can no longer spare for your speculations."[16] It remained for the future, however, to unmask the traitor to his country as well as the deceiver of his friends.

Significantly the final glimpses of Jones' career, before the scene of his death, revealed him in relation to the United States. He continued to make occasional calls upon Morris, the official tie with and source of news from America; but illness and consideration progressively limited their number. On the day of the last reference of the diarist to a visit, he remarks, "Paul Jones comes but I send him away"—and the question springs to the mind whether Morris had been fittingly chosen as the American envoy who was soon to be the Minister Plenipotentiary to France. But on this same day, in a separate, later comment, he adds, "Jones dines with me"— and at second thought it appears that familiarity and not rudeness largely excuses the one statement in the light of the other.[17]

A more tangible as well as symbolic circumstance marked the next day, June 1, not abroad but at home. If any cordial to Jones' spirit were still able to give strength to his body, it was the tenor of a message which Jefferson now sent to him respecting the Americans held as captives for ransom by the pirates of Algiers. "The President of the United States," he explained, "having thought proper to appoint you commissioner for treating with the Dey and Government of Algiers on the subjects of peace and ransom of our captives, I have the honor to enclose you the commission [signed by both Washington and Jefferson] of which Mr. Thomas Pinckney, now on his way to London as our Minister Plenipotentiary there, will be the bearer."[18] Only thirteen prisoners now remained of the twenty-one who had been taken from two American ships in 1785; the ransom of them, according to Jefferson, had been and still remained complicated not by lack of humaneness and of funds but by considerations of policy.

The confidence of the American Government in Jones was evident in the shrewdness and intelligence which Jefferson indicated were essential in negotiation with a band of blackmailers. Unofficial attempts to redeem the captives had simply raised the price of the Algerines to unprecedented levels and encouraged them to look forward to the capture of additional American sailors, in preference to those of other nations, with the expectation of a better market for their piratical trade. The object now was to deflate these optimistic hopes by a low price for the redemption and to conclude at the same time an agreement of peace bought by tribute as a guarantee against future seizure of Americans. It was believed that adroit measures of the chosen envoy, free from interference, were so important to secure the best possible terms that knowledge of the commission rested solely with Washington, Pinckney, and Jefferson.

An additional reason weighed especially with Jefferson for choosing the Admiral. "As the duration of this peace," he added at the prospect of appeasing pirates, "cannot be counted on with certainty, and we look forward to the necessity of coercion by cruises on their coast, to be kept up during the whole of their cruising season, you will be pleased to inform yourself, as minutely as pos-

George Washington President of the United States of America

to all to whom these Presents shall come, Greeting.

Know ye that reposing special trust and confidence in the integrity, prudence and abilities of John Paul Jones a citizen of the United States, I have nominated and appointed him the said John Paul Jones a Commissioner for the United States, giving him full power and authority for and in the name of the United States of America, to confer, treat and negotiate with the Dey and Government of Algiers; or with any person or persons duly authorized on their behalf, of and concerning the ransom of all citizens of the United States of America in captivity with the said Dey, government, and subjects of Algiers; or with any of them, and to conclude and sign a Convention thereupon; — transmitting the same to the President of the United States for his final ratification by and with the advice and consent of the Senate of the said United States. In testimony whereof I have caused the seal of the United States to be hereunto affixed. Given under my hand at the city of Philadelphia the first day of June in the year one thousand seven hundred and ninety two, and of the Independence of the United States the sixteenth.

Go. Washington

By the President

Th. Jefferson

sible, of every circumstance which may influence or guide us in undertaking and conducting such an operation, making your communications by safe opportunities." However able as a diplomat, Jones remained first of all the circumspect naval officer—the naval officer indeed who even as a youthful lieutenant in the New Providence expedition of Commodore Hopkins had shown himself the pilot and strategist of the squadron as well as the commander of the *Alfred's* guns. It was second nature for him to cast his eyes upon navigable waters, harbors, ships, and in fact all that pertained to both defense and offense.

The selection of Jones by Washington and Jefferson was, therefore, eminently on the basis of sound reason. Their decision had also the supplementary support of the warm friendship which Jefferson especially retained for him. The same motives must consistently have prompted the additional offer: "Should you be willing to remain there, even after the completion of the business, as consul for the United States, you will be free to do so, giving me notice that no other nomination may be made." The salary was not large, in fact only two thousand dollars a year; but this secondary proposal indicated at least that the Secretary of State bore him well in mind for the future.

Misgivings overtook Jefferson, despite his detailed message. Pinckney still had not sailed on July 11, and on this day Jefferson wrote to him concerning the letter entrusted to his care: "It has been some time, however, since we have heard of Admiral Jones." And he proceeded to give the Minister further instructions to be followed "should any accident have happened to his life, or should you be unable to learn where he is, or should distance, refusal to act, or any other circumstances deprive us of his services on this occasion." His allusion to the absence of news " 'of' Admiral Jones" would seem to indicate not only that there were those in America to whom information would have been welcome but also that there was no one upon whom the responsibility in addition to the privilege to send it rested as much as upon Morris, the American representative in Paris. As to news from Jones himself, the answer was his impending fate.

It was not to be his happiness to read the message from Jefferson, which expressed intimate connection with the motive that had inspired some of the officer's most sustained efforts and daring exploits in the Revolution—the cause of prisoners. How it would have stirred him is recognizable in the pain which breathed in his earlier utterance in memory of the defeat of his purpose, despite his intrepidity at the Texel: "I will not now complain that the prisoners which I took and carried to Holland were not exchanged for the Americans who had been taken in war upon the ocean and were long confined in English dungeons. . . . I will only say *I had such a promise* from the Minister of Marine. It was all the reward I asked for the anxious days and sleepless nights I passed and the many dangers I encountered in the glad hope of giving them *all* their liberty."[19]

Chapter LXXI

◇◇◇

Death—"With His Feet on the Floor"

H E WALKED into his chamber and laid himself upon his face, on the bedside, with his feet on the floor"[1]—in this manner, even against death, Jones fought to the end, standing. There is generally no better index to a man's life, whatever his foes of years or suffering may be, than the instinctive forces with which he meets his last hour. Inasmuch as the Admiral sat in a chair instead of lying in bed on this day of July 18, 1792 while he wavered on the verge of dying, it must have been simply his nature to confront the one inevitable defeat in a posture which symbolized the spirit of "I have not yet begun to fight."

Alone, removed from the country of his citizenship and of his affection from boyhood, and comforted by no wife or relations, he now found his unswerving brilliant quest to "ascend the slippery precipices" of patriotic achievement and of glory descend abruptly to the cold blackness of a grave at the early age of forty-five years. At least several friends, French as well as American, were not lacking in Paris at this conclusion to his career. The most conspicuous among them were Samuel Blackden, a colonel of dragoons from North Carolina; Jean-Baptiste Beaupoil, a retired French officer and a former aide-de-camp of Lafayette, who himself was already absent with an army at his country's border; and Gouverneur Morris, who was now Minister Plenipotentiary. Blackden was the foremost among them; he had visited Jones daily during many months of his last illness and with Beaupoil had been sitting by him until eight o'clock on the evening of his death.

Shortly after this hour Morris arrived at Jones' lodgings with Vic d'Azyr, the Queen's physician. The Minister was so much in love with Mme. de Flahaut that he seems to have considered it necessary to take her along with them. They found Jones, in his standing position over the bedside, "dead, not yet cold."[2] The immediate cause of his end, which had followed almost constant ill health for about a year, was dropsy of the breast. But the development of this disease was preceded, if not also complicated, during the last two months by jaundice. These physical causes of his death likewise had connection doubtlessly with certain predisposing conditions of his professional life. He suffered, on the one hand, great exposure to cold and storms affecting his respiratory organs on such occasions as the journey to Copenhagen, the dash to Revel, and the return to Kherson. He endured, on the other hand, habitual struggles against almost insurmountable obstacles leading to his unparalleled exploits but also to the attrition of his vital forces, especially under the stress of his deep disappointments. The law of human compensation applied to his body as against his spirit, his death as against his victories.

Earlier on this last day, July 18, Gouverneur Morris had received "a message from Paul Jones that he is dying." The Minister went to see him in the afternoon; and during these final hours Jones managed to convey his barest wishes concerning the more important terms of his will, which Blackden had urged him for some time to execute. Morris prepared the document, with several Frenchmen as notaries and with Blackden, Beaupoil, and a third friend, Swan, as witnesses. He recorded separately, with his signature alone, an itemized statement of the property. The will named Robert Morris as Jones' only testamentary executor—Robert Morris whom he still cherished as the warmest supporter of his naval advancement as long as his operations had been confined to the Western Hemisphere.[3]

According to Gouverneur Morris' own admission, however, Jones asked him to share the office of executor; but he refused and indeed also tried at the same unhappy moment to persuade the Admiral to choose someone other than Robert Morris. When ten months later the Minister in Paris sent a copy of the will to the financier in Philadelphia and disingenuously explained the long delay of his letter, he remarked apropos of expected requests of Jones' heirs which in his opinion would be "somewhat troublesome": "A preview of this made me desire Jones to think of some other executor, but the poor fellow was so anxious, telling me that, as we alone possessed his full confidence, he could not think of losing the aid of both, etc. And as what he said, besides his natural stammering, was interrupted by the strugglings against death, I was obliged to quit my opposition."[4] The best that can be said of the Minister's "preview" at the hour of the dying man's entreaty is that it was in consideration for Robert Morris as well as for himself and that it strangely happened not to be ill-advised in the light of the executor's later circumstances.

To the credit of Gouverneur Morris for his sympathy if not his readiness to exert himself, he referred for a second time to Jones as "poor fellow": "I drew the heads of his will, poor fellow, the day he died and when his extremities were already cold." Indeed his end had been already so near that the testament did not possess the specific character which it would have assumed under normal circumstances. According to Blackden and Beaupoil, Jones had intended to divide his property into equal parts between his two sisters, but agreed to the suggestion of advisers for an equal division among all his heirs, including his various nieces and his nephew, most of whom were of the Lowden, not the Taylor, family. Nor did his dimming faculties enable him to fulfill any intentions as to specific bequests such as provision for the gold sword of Louis XVI, which he had written to his nephew William Taylor might some day be his. He died, his niece Janette Taylor was to recount, half an hour after the will had been made, and his signature was scarcely legible.[5]

The memorandum of his property is revealing not only in regard to his circumstances, especially in view of reports that he died without means, but also as a commentary upon some of the relationships, private and public, which had caused him unrest. The record included, among the private items, stock for $6,000 in the Bank of North America at Philadelphia, a Loan Office certificate for $2,000, lands in Vermont, shares in the Ohio and the Indiana Companies, and funds in the hands of John Ross, whom he twice referred to as his friend, and of Edward Bancroft, whom he contrastingly named without such personal reference. Although he mentioned unpaid dividends and interest for many years from such private sources, his public accounts more definitely expressed his grievances: "Upwards of four years of my pension due from Denmark, to be asked for from the Count de Bernstorff; arrearages of my pay from the Empress of Russia and all my prize money; the balance due to me by the United States of America and of sundry claims in Europe, which will appear from my papers." This sorrowful account at the imminence of death was, as Morris wrote, "taken from his mouth."[6]

It is not to be supposed that Catherine ever honored the indebtedness of Russia. Nor is it recorded that Denmark at any time paid the pension, although there was a measure of poetic if not legal justice in not recognizing this questionable gratuity. It is to the credit of France in the midst of political turmoil that Janet Taylor, who came to Paris after her brother's death and appeared before the National Assembly, succeeded in having her claims recognized and payment ordered, but she was obliged to flee before receiving the whole amount as the Revolution reached the stage when suspicion and the guillotine followed fast upon each other. Finally it is to the honor of the United States that he appears to have had no just claims of consequence against his country. The American Government was later generous to his heirs by advancing to them his share of the value of the prizes which had been sent to Denmark, although this nation never paid the demand for indemnity. The Government was further considerate towards these heirs by appointing his nephew, William Taylor, a midshipman in the Navy.

Certain demands against the estate of Jones led to legal proceedings for the sale of property available in Paris; but fortunately the provision of friends prevented the loss of the emblems of the Admiral's valor. Gouverneur Morris, whom no one could deny skill in business, wrote on October 22, 1792 to Mrs. Taylor and Mrs. Lowden: "I desired a gentleman to attend and bid for the different effects, which he did and thereby raised the prices considerably. The sword given to him by the King of France was not put up but is reserved for you. A mourning sword, that which he wore in the action of the *Serapis*, his Order of Merit and Cincinnatus I caused to be bought, and you can have them when you please at the cost, or if you prefer the price I will keep them, so that I pray you in this respect to act without any regard to the circumstance of the purchase or to my intention in making it."[7]

The gold sword of Louis XVI, the most valuable and prized memento, was to have a variable, unforeseen future. In due time the heirs of Jones presented it to Robert Morris, the legal executor, along with their thanks to him for the receipt of the certificate of the Danish pension, which they presumably did not recognize as

COPY OF LETTER FROM HEIRS OF JOHN PAUL JONES PRESENT-
ING GOLD SWORD TO ROBERT MORRIS

From Jones' brother-in-law, John Lowden, for the family, dated January 14, 1794, at Dumfries, Scotland. Courtesy of the Masonic Library, Boston, Massachusetts, which owns the copy.

valueless. "Our two families unite," they wrote on January 14, 1794, "in requesting that you would honour them with the acceptance of the gold hilted sword presented by the late King of France to the deceased, and we do so as a small token of our respect and gratitude to you, and that you may be possessed of a remembrance of the deceased, the suddenness of whose death had prevented him from making those acknowledgments to you which we are conscious he would certainly otherwise have done . . ."[8] Morris received the sword in America through Thomas Pinckney, the American Minister to Great Britain, to whom he stated, "I have presented it to Commodore John Barry, who will never disgrace it."[9] Barry, in turn, bequeathed the sword to Richard Dale, the gallant officer of the *Bonhomme Richard*.[10] It remained in the hands of his family until presented in 1938 to the United States Naval Academy.

If in regard to Barry and Dale the disposition of the most brilliant token of Jones' valor was not altogether to the taste of his heirs, the administration of the estate by Robert Morris was still less pleasing. He became immersed in greater and greater difficulties following his bold speculations; and only his sad, oppressed circumstances leading even to a debtors' prison can explain, although they cannot excuse, his remissness in the trust which marked the Admiral's last confident as well as grateful memory of him. But the descendants of Jones as well as he himself must have been satisfied that what he had lived for and bequeathed was not his ephemeral estate, his decorations, and his sword, but his imperishable name. Even so the final guardian of the sword in particular could not be more appropriate than the Naval Academy, the fulfillment even beyond Jones' dream for the selection, training, and inspiration of naval officers.

Part 9

From a Lost Grave to a Monument

◇◇

Chapter LXXII

The French Public Funeral; the Lost Grave; the Identification of the Body

THE ARRANGEMENTS for burial of Jones happened at a time in Paris when life was cheap, distinction under the monarchy was a source of danger, the violence of the Revolution drowned private incident, and France was aroused by external as well as internal conflict on the road to the long Napoleonic wars. Nor did the shadow of political turmoil alone contribute to obscure the circumstances attending the resting place of the Admiral. In keeping with the custom of Gouverneur Morris to haggle with overreaching tavernkeepers and servants in regard to their fees during his travels on the Continent, he may well have carried his views of thrift further than was suitable in the case of a warrior of such public reputation. "Before I quit poor Jones, I must tell you," he was to explain in his defense to Robert Morris, "that some people here who like rare shows wished him to have a pompous funeral and I was applied to on the subject, but as I had no right to spend on such follies either the money of his heirs or that of the United States, I desired that he might be buried in a private and economical manner. I have since had reason to be glad that I did not agree to waste money of which he had no great abundance and for which his relatives entertain a tender regard."[1]

Blackden, the closest friend in Paris, followed the dictates of affection and urgency. Morris himself does not seem to have acted except in so far as he determined not to use any appreciable part of Jones' property for funeral expenses. It was Blackden who, in the name of the Americans in France, appealed on July 19 to the National Assembly for suitable recognition of the officer, stating at the same time the formal measure taken for burial of a foreign Protestant in a country dominantly Catholic: "I announce to you that Admiral Paul Jones died last evening in Paris, that the American Minister has ordered the person at whose house the Admiral lodged to cause him to be interred in the most private manner and at the least possible expense. This person, on account of the formalities still existing relative to Protestants, found it necessary to apply to a commissary. He has done it; and M. Simonneau the commissary expresses his astonishment at the order given by the Minister, and says that a man who has rendered the most signal services to France and America ought to have a public funeral. He adds that, if America will not pay the expense, he will pay it himself. The friends of the Admiral await the orders of the Assembly respecting the mode of interment."[2]

A final halo of Jones' career still shone in Paris despite the menacing political clouds over the city. At this last opportunity, republican as well as monarchial France honored his memory. On the one hand, the payment of the expense of the public interment, 462 francs, by Pierre-François Simonneau, the commissary of Louis XVI for the foreign Protestant burial section, in lieu of similar provision by Morris, expressed the spirit and possibly the command of the King as a fitting and opportune tribute to the loyalty which Jones had always felt towards him in particular. On the other hand, the National Assembly applauded this recognition, and one of its members emphasized it by the resolve: "I request that the Assembly send a deputation to the funeral of Paul Jones to signalize the sacredness of freedom in religious opinion."[3] After overruling an objection that Jones was a Calvinist, the body decreed that twelve members should attend the funeral to mark its religious toleration at the same time that it honored Jones for "such important services to America and to France."[4]

It was thus an added distinction rendered by the new democracy of France to this American that it chose him as the first Protestant to symbolize the end of religious persecution during a long era of Catholic rule. Such toleration was not inconsiderable in Paris for persons other than Catholics, inasmuch as many had long received burial in privately owned land, in cellars without public knowledge, and in forbidden cemeteries by secret arrangements. That later first one and then another burial ground known as the cemetery for foreign Protestants was the place of interment for such deceased residents further evidences the discrimination and even desecration which had not ended even at the outbreak of the revolutionary movement for liberty, equality, and fraternity.

A more impressive ceremony followed than might have been expected under auspices which owed nothing to the representative of the American Government and which depended in the main upon a war-torn France. There were three chief groups to attend the funeral at eight o'clock in the evening of July 20 after proceeding from his home at 42 Tournon Street for the cemetery devoted to foreign Protestants.[5] The deputation of the National Assembly, accompanied by a detachment of grenadiers, appears to have had highly respectable personages, including a bishop and a vicar, among its twelve members, who in no sense expressed the radicalism often associated with that body. Another delegation came from the consistory of Protestants in Paris, among whom was the pastor, without affiliation with the Assembly, chosen to make an address. Finally, the gathering of friends and associates of Jones consisted of Americans in Paris and several Frenchmen, especially Blackden and Beaufoil, who had often been with him during his last illness; Simonneau, the commissary of the King; Colonel Mountflorence, a former major in the United States Army who, like Blackden, was from North Carolina; Joel Barlow, the poet; and Thomas Waters Griffith, an American traveller whose recorded recollections were slight and chiefly in error.[6]

Gouverneur Morris saw fit not to be present. "The American Minister," according to a current report, "could not attend the funeral as he had persons to dine with him that day!" Morris himself has noted in his diary how he passed the evening of July 20, even including a remark upon a curious incident of the weather which probably did not impress him as an evil omen: "I have a large company to dinner. After dinner go to visit Madame de Narbonne who is my neighbor, thence to the British Ambassador's; Madame is abroad. Thence to visit Madame de Guibert, sit with her a little while and go afterwards to Madame Le Couteulx's. Chat with her and to my surprise she declares for gallantry without the least scruple so that I conjecture rather the reverse. Return home early. The weather is pleasant this evening, but we had a storm in which the lightning struck very near me about seven o'clock."[7] It was at seven o'clock, as the funeral procession started from Jones' residence for the cemetery, that Morris was most conspicuously absent.

Grandiloquent as was the funeral address by Paul Henri Marron, the Protestant minister, it was also not without truth. Probably the clergyman himself did not exaggerate the tone of the address in delivery as much as has been done by the marks of exclamation in recording it. And in his private, clerical capacity, he may have appeared more radical than he really was on account of his public, revolutionary setting. Viewed in the light of the time and place, the purport of his sentiments was worthy of his subject:

"Legislators! Citizens! Soldiers! Friends! Brethren! And Frenchmen! We have just returned to the earth the remains of an illustrious stranger, one of the first champions of the liberty of America; of that liberty which so gloriously ushered in our own. The Semiramis of the North had drawn him under her standard, but Paul Jones could not long breathe the pestilential air of despotism; he preferred the sweets of a private life in France, now free, to the éclat of titles and of honors, which, from a usurped throne, were lavished upon him by Catherine. The fame of the brave outlives him; his portion is immortality. What more flattering homage could we pay to the manes of Paul Jones than to swear on his tomb to live or to die free? It is the vow, it is the watchword, of every Frenchman."

"Let never tyrants nor their satellites pollute this sacred earth! May the ashes of the great man, too soon lost to humanity, and eager to be free, enjoy here an undisturbed repose! Let his example teach posterity the efforts which noble souls are capable of making when stimulated by hatred to oppression. Friends and brethren, a noble emulation brightens in your looks; your time is precious; the country is in danger! Who among us would not shed the last drop of his blood to save it? Associate yourselves with the glory of Paul Jones by imitating him in his contempt of dangers, in his devotion to his country, in his noble heroism, which, after having astonished the present age, will continue to be the imperishable object of the veneration of future generations!"[8]

When the echo of Marron's discourse and of the volleys of musketry of the French grenadiers at Jones' grave travelled as far as Russia to the ears of Catherine, through either Grimm or the journals of Paris, her jaundiced pen sought to fix a final barb upon the memory of the warrior. The references to her as "The Semiramis of the North" and to her empire as the abode of "the pestilential air of despotism" sharpened to be sure her acrimony. It was natural for the obsessed tyrant, whose foremost fear was free men and nations, to vent her bitterness at the same time upon Jones and the French Revolution. "This Paul Jones," she affectedly scoffed, "was a very bad rogue and altogether worthy of being acclaimed by a mob of detestable rogues."[9]

The blessing of "undisturbed repose," which Marron the minister had wished for Jones, was not apparent, in either spirit or body, as the French Revolution rose to its peak. The little graveyard soon had its dead in layers of two and even three. Some of the bodies had their resting place within a foot of one another even without coffins of any kind. There were doubtlessly among them members of the Swiss Guard, largely Protestants, who bore him company within a month as the result of their heroic defense of the King at the Tuileries. Yet the fate of Jones beneath the earth was better than a lingering, impotent illness would have been above it only to learn that the Frenchmen whom he most cherished were the victims of barbarity—the King and D'Estaing of the guillotine before the populace, La Rochefoucauld of murder in the presence of his aged mother, Lafayette of cruelest imprisonment.

A century rolled by in the fortunes of France during which the graveyard underwent changes so great as to render it unrecognizable. With the passing of landmarks, variant reports arose that Jones had been buried elsewhere; one indicated Pére la Chaise and another the first burial ground for foreign Protestants, the Saint Martin Cemetery, which had in fact been closed in 1762. But new evidence followed to establish that the interment was at the only cemetery for foreign Protestants at the time of his death, that of Saint Louis, opened in the year of the closing of Saint

Martin in 1762 and closed itself partly in 1793 and completely in 1804. It was at the corner of what are now known as Rue Grange-aux-Belles and Rue des Écluses Saint Martin.[10] In denying an erroneous account, Jones' niece Janette explained: "He was interred in the old Protestant burial ground, purchased by Lord Viscount Stormont (afterwards Earl of Mansfield) when British Ambassador at the Court of France—it was situated near the Barriére du Combat, and is now, I believe, totally covered with buildings."[11]

General Horace Porter scrupulously retraced the place of burial during the period of his office as Ambassador to France.[12] In 1905 he undertook to effect the removal of the body of Jones to the United States. More than fifty years earlier John Henry Sherburne, the register of the Navy Department, who was the editor of letters of Jones which first revived interest in him, and who was also the son-in-law of Elijah Hall, the disgruntled second lieutenant of the *Ranger,* had set afoot the same undertaking but relinquished it. And in 1899 Julius Chambers, the journalist, gave the plan wide publicity, prepared a resolution which was introduced in Congress but died in committee, and held in fact that an agent whom he employed at his own expense discovered the exact location of the grave.[13] It was General Porter, the Ambassador in the footsteps of Gouverneur Morris after more than a century, who described the circumstances as he viewed them preparatory to his search for the body at the scene of burial: "Here was presented the spectacle of a hero whose fame once covered two continents, and whose name is still an inspiration to a world-famed navy, lying for more than a century in a forgotten grave, like an obscure outcast, relegated to oblivion in a squalid corner of a distant foreign city, buried in ground once consecrated, but since desecrated. . . ."[14]

At the outset of his difficult search in such a cemetery, Porter had not alone the encouragement of his own patriotic zeal, the proffered if not accepted official support of President Theodore Roosevelt for the expense, and the benefit of such discoveries as Chambers and others may already have made. He had also a special clue. Blackden had written to Janet Taylor shortly after the death of her brother: "His body was put into a leaden coffin on the 20th that in case the United States, whom he had so essentially served, and with so much honor to himself, should claim his remains, they might be more easily removed."[15]

The exploration of the burial ground by excavation and sounding disclosed five leaden coffins, of which the third in order of discovery, without a name plate, justified particular investigation. Three of the others had name plates which readily revealed that they did not contain the body of Jones; and the remaining one of the five, without an identifying mark, was of a man over six feet in height, who could not have been the object of search.

The body, according to custom, was not clothed in a uniform or any other readily identified raiment; it had only a winding sheet, a linen shirt, and a linen cap for the long, gathered hair. The cap, however, contained a monogram which appeared to be a "J" for Jones when it was held rightly and a "P", with an open loop, for Paul when it was inverted.

A detailed examination followed to compare the general characteristics, the height, the color of the hair, the proportions of the head and face, and the state of the internal organs, with various records of Jones' life. The authentic sources at hand in Paris for this purpose were the Trocadéro replica of the Houdon bust, the profile on the gold medal awarded by Congress, and reliable biographies.

Dr. Georges Papillault, professor in the School of Anthropology in Paris, who took an outstanding but disinterested part in the examination, wisely did not employ for his comparative measurements a second bust, known as the De Biron and represented to be of Jones, which in fact bears practically no resemblance to the warrior's strongly marked features. Nor did he try in excess of zeal to reconcile his findings with personal descriptions of the officer in accounts by Buell in *Paul Jones, Founder of the American Navy.* In 1905 this supposed biography was not generally recognized for what it is—a work of historical fabrication, as already indicated, which has just enough of a seasoning of truth to mask its predominant falseness. And finally he had the qualifications to appreciate thoroughly, in his comparison of the measurements of the head with those of the Houdon bust, the need to allow for the artistic method of the sculptor while following the scientific procedure of the anthropologist. "Six different dimensions of the body and bust," reported Papillault, "offer an approximation really extraordinary. Two experienced anthropologists measuring the same subject would often make as great differences."[16]

The autopsy performed by other specialists, Doctors J. Capitan and V. Cornil, who likewise were professors in the School of Anthropology, provided further evidence. Although some of the organs were poorly preserved so as to render analysis indecisive, a most important discovery was lesions of the kidneys, which "presented the appearance, very clearly, of chronic interstitial nephritis," a condition responsible for Jones' last symptoms and finally for his death. In addition, as General Porter stated, "Twelve American and French persons officially took part in or witnessed the work of identification, and their affirmative verdict, after six days passed in the application of every possible test, was positive and unanimous."

In the light of all the scrupulous procedure, including the determination of the exact area of the cemetery, the search of practically the whole of it, the elimination of four of the five leaden coffins by definite proof, the character of the monogram, the testimony of witnesses, and in particular the findings of specialists in anthropology and pathology, the identification was thorough. The cumulative evidence had its fitting summary in the deliberate opinion of Professor Papillault—the foremost authority of the investigation, who seemed disposed to understatement—that "the body examined is that of Admiral John Paul Jones."[17]

THE SARCOPHAGUS CONTAINING THE BODY OF JOHN PAUL JONES IN THE
CRYPT OF THE NAVAL ACADEMY CHAPEL

John Paul Jones 1747-1792 United States Navy
He Gave Our Navy its Earliest Traditions of
Heroism and Victory. Erected by Congress A.D. 1912

Chapter LXXIII

"In Life He Honored the Flag; in Death the Flag Shall Honor Him"

THE TRIBUTE to the memory of Jones more than a century after his death was in contrasting proportion to the neglect which his grave had suffered for this period. In July, 1905 a squadron of American warships brought his body to the United States after it had passed in an elaborate procession, with French military and American naval escorts, along the Champs Élysées in Paris. Commemorative services followed in April of the next year at the United States Naval Academy; President Theodore Roosevelt and the French Ambassador Jusserand participated in the outstanding patriotic ceremonies. And the body now rests in its distinguished setting in Annapolis.

The United States chose the imposing Chapel of the Naval Academy to treasure the memory of John Paul Jones. In the spacious crypt reserved for him alone lies the sarcophagus which contains his casket. The walls of the crypt itself display in recessed cases several intimate tokens of Jones' career: his gold sword presented by Louis XVI, his service sword, his captain's commission of October 10, 1776 signed by John Hancock, and the two steel dies for his gold medal authorized in 1787 by Congress. Nearby stands one of the original plaster busts of Jones executed during his life by Houdon in Paris.

Enclosing the sarcophagus in a large circle are eight monolithic white and black columns of Pyrenees marble in compliment to France, and on its surrounding marble floor are a number of in-

scriptions inlaid with letters of bronze. In front of the sarcophagus
appear the words: HE GAVE OUR NAVY ITS EARLIEST TRA-
DITIONS OF HEROISM AND VICTORY; and around it are
the names of the ships which he commanded during the Revolution: PROVIDENCE . ALFRED . RANGER . BONHOMME
RICHARD . SERAPIS . ARIEL.

The names of the frigates and sloops of war are a becoming
epitaph. They characteristically bring to mind not only his deeds
but also the spirit which animated them. The flagship *Alfred*
recalls the first lieutenant of Hopkins' squadron. His motives as
one of the earliest volunteers of the American Navy live again in
the words he once expressed to Samuel Huntington, the President
of Congress: "I have not drawn my sword in our glorious cause
for hire, but in support of the dignity of human nature and the
divine feelings of philanthropy. I hoisted with my own hands the
flag of freedom the first time it was displayed on board the *Alfred*
in the Delaware; and I have attended it ever since with veneration
on the ocean." The little *Providence* of twelve four-pounders and
of seventy men recreates the newly appointed, resourceful young
Captain on his first independent cruise who, apart from the capture of many prizes and the convoy of various vessels, eluded the
powerful frigate *Solebay* after a four-hour chase within musket
shot. He described the episode not without grim humor: "Our
hairbreadth 'scape and the saucy manner of making it must have
mortified him not a little." The *Alfred* and *Providence* in conjunction make live again his dynamic activity in command of the two
vessels when he combatted the demoralizing influences of the
privateers, signalized his successful enterprise by his effective ruse
for the protection of the valuable prizeship *Mellish,* and spurred
the inefficient naval authorities by characteristic words: "The affairs of America cry haste, and speed must answer them."

In France, the *Ranger* brings to memory his offensive strategy
in attacking Britain on her coasts as well as in her home waters,
and his humanity in behalf of American prisoners. It was a consecrated patriotic fervor which he voiced, for example, to Robert
Morris in gratitude to America, her people, and especially to him
upon the arrival in a French port: "I feel by a prophetic impulse
in my breast that I shall either manifest a grateful sense of your

friendship by my conduct in life or by meeting my death in the great cause." The *Bonhomme Richard* makes reappear the climactic fulfillment of this forecast, which the conquest over the *Drake* first realized in part. The challenging reply of the invincible warrior, "I have not yet begun to fight," to the demand for surrender of his beaten ship had a counterpart less dramatic but scarcely less expressive of indomitable courage in his decision to appeal to the King over the heads of toying French ministers and commissaries and even without obligation for particular timely support from Franklin.

At the Texel, the *Serapis* signifies the generosity that marked the surrender of a bitterly won private interest for the sake of what French diplomats, with the acquiescence of Franklin, represented as a public need. "I made on this occasion," declared Jones, "a greater sacrifice in the eyes of all Europe than any other officer in the Revolution. I sacrificed that military pride which prevents an officer in a neutral port from depriving himself of his prizes and his prisoners which have cost him so dear." The *Alliance* suggests to be sure the boldness of his memorable dash from the Texel under the American flag; but of more practical importance it also bears upon the involvement of Holland in the war resulting from such privileges from a neutral to a belligerent country as Jones' armed control of a Dutch fort for safeguarding his prisoners ashore. This unprecedented favor caused him to declare in triumph, "Huzza America!"

Again in France, the *Ariel*, finally, reflects in particular his magnificent seamanship. He himself was reticent, but Richard Dale spoke of it with greater authority than any other person except the commander aboard the frigate: "Never saw I such coolness and readiness in such frightful circumstances as Paul Jones showed in the nights and days when we lay off the Penmarques, expecting every moment to be our last; and the danger was greater even than we were in when the *Bonhomme Richard* fought the *Serapis*."

One additional name, the *Vladimir*, is missing among the inscriptions on the marble floor. Although the flagship of his squadron on the Liman in Russia was in no way connected with his services in America, it typifies his leadership under the most difficult circumstances in a manner comparable with his talents during his *Bonhomme Richard* cruise. And the acceptance of a command in Russia marked the naval officer's solemn and fulfilled declaration: "I can never renounce the glorious title of a citizen of the United States."

It is the victories of Jones, notably those during his command of the *Ranger* and the *Bonhomme Richard,* which won for him his immortality as an American. To account for them is to recall especially his love of America from the age of thirteen when he first saw the Colonies, his passionate devotion throughout the Revolutionary War in fighting for the principles of freedom of this country of his early "fond election," and his manifold stern obstacles practically throughout his life which steeled him to rise in crises to climactic heights of strategy, valor, and the will to win.

The loss of not a single vessel, slow or fast, small or large, on which Jones paced the quarter-deck (with the notable exception of the sinking *Bonhomme Richard,* from which he stepped by conquest to the command of the *Serapis*) sets off the more conspicuously the distinction of his naval achievements. Only his resourcefulness in the *Providence,* his initiative as first lieutenant and his speed as Captain in the *Alfred,* his perseverance in the *Ranger,* his versatile genius in the *Bonhomme Richard,* his circumspection in the *Serapis,* his boldness in the *Alliance,* his seamanship in the *Ariel,* and his independent policy in the *Vladimir*—only all these traits could have won such a record. And although the *America* passed to the keeping of France before he had an opportunity to command her at sea, it was his foresight and ardor in the face of great difficulties which made possible the preservation and completion of our first ship of the line.

To consider him at his best, this naval record, as compared with that of his American contemporaries, was peerless. Even to consider him at his worst, personally as well as professionally, there is nothing that detracts in large degree from his stature as evoked by these memories of his ships.

The severest accusations against him pertaining to his early manhood have counterbalancing aspects. If, for instance, as the master of a merchant vessel he withheld the wages of seamen to suit his instead of their pleasure, as a captain in the American

Navy he advanced funds to pay them from his own pocket. If it is true that he assumed the trusteeship of his brother's estate in Virginia, he was the only relative in America, communication during the war was difficult, the terms of the bequest were arbitrary, he himself sought to provide for his mother and sisters, and he reserved his own fortune for his kin.

The charges against some of the more professional aspects of his later years likewise do not weigh heavily against him. If his attempted attack upon Whitehaven seemed cruel and reflected an exaggerated antagonism towards the British people as contrasted, at least, with the British Government in power, it also was retaliatory, strategic, and praiseworthy in so far as he sacrificed minor personal to major patriotic considerations. If his professions as an American to Americans were not altogether consistent with others as a citizen of the world to Lady Selkirk, Lafayette, and Louis XVI, in deed as contrasted with word he always had an American commission during the war. And he not only scorned the command of privateers and letters of marque whether from the United States or France but also refused an appointment in the French Navy. In fact it was he who in the face of diplomatic subterfuge and pressure in time of great danger unswervingly upheld the honor of the American flag at the Texel; it was he who more than any other naval officer in the service of the United States helped to promote the vital wartime alliance between France and his boyhood-chosen country. If Jones made the greatest mistake of his career by acceptance of service in Russia, he had in mind the extensive professional experience which a large fleet would provide in preparation for very possible future American emergencies of war. His Russian engagement had the promotion and recommendation of Jefferson, the foremost representative of America in Europe. And whatever were the overtures of Jones to tyrants like Catherine and Potemkin, he did not lose either his professional or his personal self-respect. This was not little, for truth underlay the vow that his honor in his own eyes was a thousand times dearer to him than his life.

The limitations, finally, of his mature years regarding both his private character and its more indirect influences upon his career as a naval officer speak for as well as against him. If he was insufficiently drastic with enemies like Simpson, Landais, and De Chaumont, his forbearance reflected at least both his forgiving nature and the precedence which he gave to public over private interests. If he accepted a gift from Denmark under the allurement of flattery, later he saw it in its true light and at no time did it affect his views of America's claim. If he delayed unwisely in Paris with the result that Landais found an opportunity to seize the *Alliance,* at least the purpose of his journey in behalf of the penniless sailors was highly commendable, and his supporters, not excluding Franklin, were largely at fault for failing to deal effectively with the half-mad Frenchman. If love was the only influence which ever interfered conspicuously with his professional duty, conversely he proved himself more faithful to his professional duty than to love. If he never felt the ties of blood strongly enough to visit his relatives in Scotland during the last twenty years of his life, the war, the hostility towards him, and his later ill-health discouraged such a journey. If he had no close human bonds of wife or family, he felt a romantic and very sincere admiration for women, possessed a refined taste for the natural and simple in living, and included among his loyal friends and warm supporters Morris, Hewes, Franklin, Jefferson, and Washington among Americans and D'Estaing, Lafayette, and Louis XVI among Frenchmen.

Even the vanity and egoism which especially have been associated often with his name are less characteristic of him than they may seem. If he strenuously insisted upon his due in rank and always was ambitious to earn new marks of glory, it was only natural that a warrior who fought as valiantly and enterprisingly as he for the rights of America should exemplify some of the same traits of justice and ambition in his own behalf. His attitude had the greater reason on the one hand because flagrant political corruption chose him as a victim and on the other because his legitimate advancement was in the best interests of the country. And it is significant that he never permitted personal wrongs to interfere in the least with his faithfulness as an officer throughout the Revolution.

If he loved more to command than to obey, the devotion of his sailors in the *Alfred* and *Providence* and the valor of those in the *Bonhomme Richard* prove that he had qualities of mind and spirit which eminently fitted him for leadership. Particularly the *Bonhomme Richard* men who suffered imprisonment for his sake in the *Alliance* under Landais, Richard Dale who revered him, and the Russian sailors and officers who found him the best advocate of their rights bore witness that he could inspire not only loyalty but affection in the revealing intimacy of life at sea. Certainly the most striking evidence of his unselfishness, humanity, and sacrifice, all of which are inconsistent with a corrupting vanity, was his unexampled championship, in act apart from word, of American prisoners.

While the magnificent memorial of Jones at the United States Naval Academy vivifies his deeds and the patriotic devotion which inspired them, the statue in Washington helps to evoke his personality. This bronze figure close to the tidal basin in West Potomac Park, which is the work, unveiled in 1912, of the sculptor Niehaus, had as its model the bust by Houdon. It is indeed the genius of Houdon which was best able to recreate the genius of Jones—Jones who in the fire of his ordeals forged the more strongly the versatile and yet concentrated talents to which his richly endowed nature lent itself.

The statue aids in bringing to mind the man in addition to the Captain, Commodore, and Rear Admiral who had been born poor and obscure in a gardener's cottage in Scotland. It is he whom Grimm described not only as of "the strongest heart and the most distinguished courage" but also as of "great intelligence and sweetness." It is he whom Wemyss characterized on the one hand as "a brave and great sailor" and on the other as "an agreeable man, full of all sorts of attainments." It is he whom Vigée le Brun found "so modest a man" that it was "impossible to get him to talk about his great deeds, but on all other subjects he willingly spoke with a great amount of sense and wit." It is this gentleman-warrior who was small but well-knit, restrained but animated, urbane but rugged, studious but active, sympathetic but resolute, gentle but steel-like.

Nevertheless Jones, whose professional ambition, by his own avowal, was "infinite," revealed his nature decidedly less in the man than the warrior. It was especially the fighter who manifested himself by his stern beetled brows, the changing lights of his im passioned eyes, the dynamic assertiveness of his jaw, and even the militant poise and muscular lines of his face, shoulders, and back. It was especially the *fighter* who found in the liberty of America, in his affection for many of his fellow citizens, and in the dictates of his naval genius the transcendent aspiration to ascend "the slippery precipices" even to "the pinnacle of fame." Fittingly the memorial in Washington as well as the monument in Annapolis fulfills his heart's goal and does justice to his patriot's devotion. Fittingly this statue records in two inscriptions the spirit that attends his memory. The gratitude of America has its epitome in the symbolic terms, "In life he honored the flag, in death the flag shall honor him"; but the lion's never-daunted bravery of Jones will always remain best known in his immortal words, "I have not yet begun to fight."

STATUETTE OF JOHN PAUL JONES
(Full Size Figure in West Potomac Park, Washington)

This study model is by Charles Henry Niehaus the sculptor. Presented by his daughter, Miss Marie J. Niehaus. The monument stands at the foot of Seventeenth Street, N.W., near the Tidal Basin where the Navy Day exercises are held each October 27th—the anniversary of Theodore Roosevelt's birthday.

Appendices

◇◇◇

The Unfounded Claims of Illegitimate Parentage

I T IS TRUE that the name John Paul, Jr., did not appear in the parish register of Kirkbean Church, although the names and years of birth of his three sisters were on its pages. The register likewise did not contain, however, the names of his brother William in America or of the two children who died in infancy.[1] It seems that for reasons of their own his father and mother considered the baptism of the female children enough; certainly no accuser has presumed to believe that the church authorities refused to enter the names of the four other offspring, both older and younger, because of a persuasion that not one but all of them had been born out of wedlock. Nothing, indeed, apart from the aspersions upon the one son, is known to impugn the good name of John Paul, Sr. and his wife. And whatever minor meaning may lie in the absence of known allusions by this son to his father, he was only twenty years old when his parent died, and it was he who made filial provision for a headstone at the grave.

Some of the sceptical reports as to his origin include questions concerning the generally accepted year of his birth. They express the belief that it was not 1747 but several years earlier.[2] It is claimed, for instance, that if the date 1747 were correct, Jones would have been too young for his notable achievements. But without doubt his position as the master of the *John* before the age of twenty-five, even in view of the sudden death of two officers of the merchantman which attended his advancement, and his victory in the *Bonhomme Richard* against the *Serapis* at thirty-two are plain evidence of early maturity if not of genius. The apt choice of a youthful officer like Richard Dale in preference to others twice his age as the first lieutenant for the cruise culminating in the battle points to a case parallel with his own early attained stature as a commander.

A more tangible reason for the view that he was from three to five years older than the age commonly ascribed to him rests upon the memories of Douglas Hamilton Craik, a grandson of the laird of Arbigland and his successor. "Mr. Craik told me today," stated the rector of Kirkbean Church in 1842, "that he believed he [John Paul] was born several years earlier [1742]. He used to carry about the present laird upon his back, when he was a child."[3] On the basis of Douglas Craik's death at the age of eighty-two years in 1844,[4] Paul must have been twenty-two, in the event that his birth was in 1742 instead of 1747, before the child whom he bore upon his back reached the age of two at least so as to be suitable for play in this recalled manner. Although there is nothing to contradict the possible accuracy of this recollection, a child of tender years might well have looked upon a brawny youth of seventeen as likely to be twenty-two, and Paul himself probably found more leisure if not inclination for such sport at the earlier than the later age. Other reports that he was born several years before 1747 assume a vague if not fanciful form; in the light of incongruous declarations which accompany them, their unreliability becomes manifest.

Offset against these uncertain beliefs are the authoritative grounds for establishing the year of his birth in 1747 and support-ing by their consistency his legitimate parentage. Negatively, if he was born as early as 1742, it results that the events of his youth during the period from the beginning of his career as shipboy at twelve until his appointment as chief mate aboard a slaver in 1766 at an unspecified age are less accountable. Positively, on the one hand, a contemporary native of the parish of his birth, Patricia Malcomson, attested, "Paul Jones was nineteen years of age in 1766";[5] on the other hand and more important, the first biographi-cal accounts of his life based on the affirmations and documents in the possession of his niece Janette Taylor bore witness to the date July 6, 1747.[6]

The names more commonly associated with the surmises of illegitimate birth, regardless of the later date which renders them the less tenable, are George Paul[7] and the fourth Earl of Selkirk.[8] George, like his brother, John Paul, Sr., it has been noted, not only

learned horticulture but also came from Leith to Kirkcudbrightshire. He received employment at St. Mary's Isle, which lies picturesquely just below the town of Kirkcudbright and the mouth
of the River Dee and juts into the bay near the Solway Firth. According to the story of George Paul's parenthood, the child John,
naturally disliked if not disowned at Arbigland because of the
senior John Paul's suspicions, passed early years in the servants'
quarters at St. Mary's Isle. There, too, the Duke of Queensbury,
who observed young Paul in the garden on the occasion of a visit
to his distant cousin, the Earl of Selkirk, took a fancy to him and
promised his future patronage.

This explanation is unfounded in time and place. George Paul
left his position at the Isle before September, 1735, secured some
land in the environs of Kirkcudbright, and apparently engaged in
gardening on his own account until his death in 1751.⁹ As John
Paul was born at least seven years, probably twelve, after George
Paul had no further connection with St. Mary's Isle and as a few
additional years of John's infancy would have passed before the
supposed episode in the garden, there is no basis for the child's
presence there, following the lapse of so extended a period and on
the alien soil of the Isle many miles from Arbigland, as if he had
been transplanted as readily as one of his uncle's shrubs.

The further association of the name of the child under such
untenable circumstances with either the Earl of Selkirk or the
Duke of Queensbury¹⁰ has likewise no warrant. During the service
of George Paul at St. Mary's Isle, it did not belong to the Selkirk
earldom; the second and third Earls of Selkirk, in fact, possessed
no lands in Galloway. The family of Dunbar had purchased the
property in 1704, and the fourth Earl of Selkirk, who received the
title in 1744 and inherited the Isle in 1760, was the first through
whom the land and the Selkirk name stood united. Consequently,
along with the discredited parenthood of George Paul, the presence of the child in the "Selkirk" garden has no basis in fact; and
the interest of the Duke of Queensbury, at this place and time in
particular, remains without foundation.¹¹

In the spirit of this legend concerning George Paul, the in-
nuendo of several of his distant descendants is not the less vaporous
because of its ostensible authority. The insinuations by an American granddaughter and great grandson of George, Isabella and

William Burnie, would seem to be, Iago-like, the more damning in their artful reticence. "On my mother's side," wrote William Burnie, "I was descended from George Paul, the Earl of Selkirk's gardener, who according to the school histories when I went to school was the father of John Paul Jones. . . . One day in a talk with mother, I suggested that Paul Jones was not a Paul, but a Douglas (the Earl of Selkirk's family name). She said he was not a Douglas but a Paul, and that at some time she would tell me all she had heard about him."[12] To all appearances she neither did nor could tell more, and was in short a gossipmonger. At the paternal home in Kirkcudbright, two of her aged sisters, Mrs. Robertson and Miss Agnes Paul, happened to see William Burnie's statement; they looked at each other for a pause, and then one said to the other in setting it aside as a fantastic tale unworthy of a second thought, "That's just Isabella."[13]

To entertain the reports that the fourth Earl of Selkirk was the father is even less within the bounds of reason than to credit the story concerning George Paul. The earl, who was born Dunbar Hamilton in 1722, passed to be sure practically all his life at St. Mary's Isle. But it seems strange indeed to associate him in a clandestine relation with a woman, married, very much older than he, and the mother already of three children, who dwelt at Arbigland thirty miles by sea and twenty-five by land from his residence. It seems even stranger, if such a relation had existed, that the wife of the earl should have seen fit to make clear, to all appearances with candor, that she had previously known nothing of the child John Paul, alias John Paul Jones, when years later during the Revolution sailors from his ship made their extraordinary raid upon her home and carried away her silver plate only to have it chivalrously returned by their Captain.[14] It seems strangest of all to accept such an account in the case of a man who, in the years to which the birth, earlier or later, of John Paul must be ascribed, spent his time at college and at home in "the most retired manner" with his books, even to such a degree that he "came into the world more fit to be a professor than an earl";[15] who in terms not less definite and, apparently, sincere than those of his wife expressed his ignorance of him prior to the raid; and who in his own letters consistently revealed himself kindly and principled.

In manhood, the declarations of Jones himself after the publicity occasioned by the incursion from his ship upon the estate of Lord Selkirk disclosed further that he not only bore no relationship to the Earl but also that he had been fully aware of the non-existence of such a connection and presumably never had entertained any illusions to the contrary. When on one occasion he confided to a friend that it had not been his intention to attract Lord Selkirk's notice "either by my history or otherwise—except only as far as he might have been concerned in my scheme of bringing about an exchange of prisoners,"[16] it was evident by the context that his object had been public affairs and that whatever personal aspects might have been implied were not of a secret nature such as a question of his birth. When on another occasion, in answer to an inquiry prompted by cumulative rumors, he gave the assurance "I never had any obligation to Lord Selkirk except for his good opinion nor does he know me or mine except *by character*,"[17] it was even more understandable that both he and the earl honestly professed no association beyond what followed in the wake of the raid at St. Mary's Isle. If the officer thought otherwise, it is practically certain also that he would not have written openly after his descent at the Isle such an extraordinary letter on public and private themes as came from his pen to Lady Selkirk rather than to her husband.

Although no link connects his birth or childhood with Lord Selkirk, its absence does not preclude a casual association with the Duke of Queensbury. The contingency is the more possible because in his mature years as an American he was to claim former intimacy with British officers,[18] and he seems to have served for a short period in the Royal Navy. To recognize that an acquaintance with the Duke of Queensbury is conceivable is not, however, to associate it by any means with either the garden of the Earl of Selkirk or the earl himself, as report has been quick to do. Perhaps in consistency with Jones' own remarks concerning early British connections, those of an alleged "fellow-lodger" may in this regard be trustworthy: "His parents were in obscure situations. . . . By accident he was known to the old late Duke of Queensbury, who introduced him in early life to a commander in the British Navy."[19] Beyond this possible occurrence, the stories of the illegitimate birth of Jones have no consistent, rational support to render them credible.

◇◇

An Alleged Ending of the Romance between Jones and the Countess de Nicolson

AN EPILOGUE to the past love between Delia and Jones occurred possibly as the beginning of a new romance between her and William Temple Franklin, the Minister's young, handsome, and illegitimate grandson and secretary. But both the extent of the relationship and the identification of the Countess de Nicolson and her husband seem so questionable in this instance as not to justify the opinion that the final parting between Jones and the countess was due primarily to such a situation.

Doubtlessly Franklin's grandson knew the Countess de Nicolson, whether through Jones, his grandfather, or others. Perhaps their acquaintance began during the long absence of Jones in the United States when the countess must have been disposed to hear from so likely an American source as William Temple any news he might have of him. A certain Captain de Stark wrote to this grandson from Versailles on July 24, 1784: "I recall with pleasure the period of our familiarity at the home of Madame la Comtesse de Nicolson."[1] Beyond this association, William Temple was one of two parties involved approximately a year earlier in a sharp interchange of words concerning his possession of a miniature portrait of a lady. Her husband referred to her as "Lady Nicolson" and to himself as "Sir James Nicolson"; young Franklin mentioned them in the same terms.

Sir James addressed a first letter on August 12, 1783 to Benjamin Franklin himself: "Sir James Nicolson presents compliments to Doctor Franklin and is somewhat surprised to find out, only since his visit to the Doctor, that his grandson had been received, out of respect to the Doctor's great merit, by Lady Nicolson and that he had concealed her Ladyship's portrait in miniature, under pretence of putting a glass to it. Sir James insists on the restoration of it, as his Lady does on all letters that may have passed on the subject. He hopes that the Doctor will grant all the merit due to the present method he has taken, having no time to lose, being on his departure for England.

"N.B. An immediate answer expected, as the Doctor's grandson long before this refused complying with Lady Nicolson's request."[2]

On the next day Sir James followed his respectful note to the grandfather by a severe one to the grandson: "Under whatever pretence you received Lady Nicolson's portrait, which I found out by mere accident, it requires but little penetration to perceive the propriety of restoring it to her husband or her. The justness of the request must be obvious to any man of sense and delicacy, and therefore I am persuaded that I need add no more on so disagreeable a subject except that Lady Nicolson is very concerned to have been so imprudent and says that she has some things appertaining to you to send on receipt of hers, which I must entreat to be forthwith. Your grandfather's perspicuous merit is a sufficient explication of any *meaning* in my note or letter, which is merely to return what does not belong to you, as this is the first time I ever put pen to paper on such a disagreeable subject. I cannot help wishing as a *man of honor* that it may be the last. . . ."[3]

William Temple hastened to answer in a youthfully challenging vein: "I am, sir, by no means of your opinion 'that under *whatever* pretence I might have received Lady Nicolson's portrait it requires but little penetration to perceive the *propriety* of restoring it to her husband.' On the contrary, it appears to me that it requires but *very little penetration* to perceive the *impropriety* of such a measure, both with regard to her, to you, and to myself. A more proper and delicate method for all parties, according to my ideas of propriety (and the only one I shall ever comply with), would be for her to send me back my portrait first. This would convince me she did not wish me to retain hers. . . .I know of no method more eligible, and doubt not it will be adopted, if it is true that Lady Nicolson wishes to deprive me of the only token I have left of the friendship the family honored me with.

"This is the only answer I can or shall make in this puerile affair, which has already taken up too much of my time."[4]

The end of the correspondence probably attests to the skill of Benjamin Franklin in curbing the youthful blood of his grandson as well as in pursuing the difficult paths of the Minister at the Court of France. It is likely that both parties returned the portraits in their hands; certainly William Temple found other ladies to please him. But the significance of the incident in relation to Delia and Jones is more problematical.

It may be true that Count Murray de Nicolson and Countess de Nicolson were the names which they assumed interchangeably in France with Sir Jámes Nicolson and Lady Nicolson. But their genealogy is obscure because many titled families of the name *Nicolson* stemmed from England and Scotland, and because one branch settled in Holland and elsewhere on the Continent in 1693 and another came to France at the emigration of Jacobites and their sympathizers after Culloden.[5] According to Miss Valentine Thomson in *Le Corsair chez l'impératrice* and *Knight of the Seas,* the husband and wife with the French titles in the one case and the English in the other were the same.[6]

Whatever external evidence may indicate such identification, the letters themselves point to the likelihood of related but not the same individuals. Miss Thomson, on the authority of her own *Knight of the Seas,* read only the *Calendar of the Papers of Benjamin Franklin,* which contains summaries of the letters just quoted available in many libraries but not the manuscript letters in full available exclusively in the American Philosophical Society in Philadelphia.[7] While these letters show that Sir James wrote English with reasonable correctness and ease, the earlier note by the Count de Nicolson had several inaccuracies in spelling and several French phrases. And apparently inconsistent with the long-adopted residence of the Count de Nicolson in France, Sir James referred to "his departure for England," named an address at Passy near the home of the Count d'Estaing which differs from that previously indicated by the Count de Nicolson, mentioned "his visit to the Doctor" as if he were a comparative newcomer, and adopted a drastic tone towards William Temple as contrasted with the seeming aloofness of the husband in the serious relation between Delia and Jones. Likewise the phrase in Captain de Stark's letter, "chez Mme. la Comtesse de Nicolson" (at the home of the Countess of Nicolson), referred to a family circle and may well have included ladies in addition to the countess. Franklin's grandson himself alluded indefinitely to the portrait as "the only token I have left of the friendship the family honored me with." If, finally, the spirit of the letters from Delia to Jones, including the note upon his return to Europe, offers a reasonable basis for judgment of character rather than serves as an ironical commentary upon the pretences of love in France of the later decades of the eighteenth century, the Countess de Nicolson either was not Lady Nicolson or her relations with William Temple have little meaning.

It does not seem well-founded to establish the end of the romance between Jones and Delia on the basis of the alleged references to a man and his wife with interchangeable French and British titles and names and on the further ground of questionable inferences from this claimed identification.

Appendix III

Madame Tellisson and Madame T—

THE ASSOCIATION of the name *Madame Tellisson* with Madame T— has contributed to obscure the identification of both persons whom Jones designated as *Madame T—*. Although the name *Madame Tellisson* is established for Jones' earlier friend by his manuscript letter of July 24, 1780 in which the superscription appears in this form[1] and although various persons including Franklin knew her under this name,[2] Mrs. Reginald De Koven in *The Life and Letters of John Paul Jones* has been of the opinion that she was Madame Thilorié, the sister of Madame Bonneuil,[3] at whose home Vigée Lebrun the artist met Jones. Mrs. De Koven based her belief on the ground of a variant spelling. But she reached her conclusion in the face of the wide difference between *Tellisson* and *Thilorié* and on the assumption of an incorrect initial spelling of the name in a fragmentary first biography of Jones which was based upon the compilation by John Henry Sherburne and possibly upon some recollections from Lafayette. This *Life of Paul Jones,* published in London by John Murray in 1825, lacks the name of an author or editor, but has been attributed, as an initial literary venture, to Benjamin Disraeli.

As to the later Madame T— and Jones' romance, there are more serious and less accidental mistakes from other sources. They relate to the use of the Christian name *Aimée* as well as the surname *Tellisson* in reference to Madame T—. While *Tellisson* came into incorrect use partly by mistake, *Aimée* acquired vogue by deliberate falsification forty years ago through Augustus C. Buell in *Paul Jones, Founder of the American Navy.*[4] Lately the substitution of Trusson for Tellisson and the seeming corroboration of the name *Aimée* in *Knight of the Seas* by Valentine Thomson are erroneous in some of the premises and inconsistent with known facts in some of the conclusions.[5]

According to this recent untenable account of Madame T—, she was one of two sisters called Agnes and Afroidine—"the 'Aimée,' so named by Jones, and made known to the world through Jones's disclosure to Jefferson." Let it be understood specifically that she received this name *Aimée* not from Jones but from Buell, whose account of the naval officer is less a biography than a semi-historical novel and whose statements, it should be added, are known to many to be fabrications in uncounted details. And it need scarcely be said further that, contrary to the assumption in the recent account by Miss Thomson, there is no trace in the correspondence regarding Madame T— between Jones and Jefferson of the word *Aimée*.

Trusson, the substitution by Valentine Thomson for the surname of Madame T—, is almost as unwarranted as *Aimée* for her Christian name. Louis XV had numerous offspring by his many mistresses, and they are generally lost in the mazes of anonymity. On the authority of Jones, Madame T— was "the daughter of the late K— and a lady of quality;" in contrast, according to Miss Thomson, Madame Trusson the mother of Madame T— was "neither well-born nor wealthy . . . a lady's maid of the dauphin's mother." On the authority of Janette Taylor, the supposed sister of Madame T— was in fact a sister-in-law; in contrast, according to Miss Thomson, the identification of Madame T— as Madame Trusson rests in part upon the alleged evidence that the latter had two children who were the sisters—not the sisters-in-law—Agnes and Afroidine, one variantly called *Aimée*. On the authority of Jones' reference to the lady whom he greatly cared for and was naturally disposed to present with as much credit as possible despite his secrecy, she bore simply the untitled name *Madame T—*; in contrast, according to Miss Thomson these sisters allegedly identified with Madame T— must have acquired titles in the reign of Louis XV by "acts of nobility."

Nor are these matters the last in which the supposed history of Madame T—, evidently first falsified by Buell and recently misapprehended by Miss Thomson, must rest on grounds that have no warrant either in name or in deed. They resurrected her to preside romantically at Jones' bedside in Paris before his death.

◇◇

The Present Biography and Its Background

I T MAY BE desirable to indicate some of the more important material presented in the extended and new information of the present biography. The survey takes into consideration both the books concerning Jones mentioned in the introduction and bibliography and in the additional volumes, less formidable than their array seems, which comprise reprints and adaptations by new publishers and in some cases under the misleading names of new authors. These volumes include also biographical accounts of special purpose, among which the most distinctive for valuable phases are *Paul Jones, His Exploits in English Seas during 1778-1780,* published in 1917, by Don C. Seitz, and *John Paul Jones in Russia,* published in 1927, by F. A. Golder. Some data from Seitz and Golder are included in the estimate of the material presented here for the first time within the compass of a biography.

As to the early life of Jones, this additional information relates to the legitimacy of his birth which has been questioned again and again; to the circumstances of his change of name from John Paul to John Paul Jones; to his connection with the carpenter Mungo Maxwell of whose death he has been accused; to his membership in Freemasonry; to his adventures as a "pirate"; and to his first benefactors in America. Regarding his service under Hopkins, the first American Commodore, it concerns his special association with the ensign of thirteen stripes of the flagship *Alfred;* his part in the New Providence cruise; and his victorious controversy with the Commodore.

In his sphere abroad during the Revolution, the new material pertains to the mutinous officers and men of the *Ranger;* to the support of the insubordinate conduct of Lieutenant Simpson by the American Commissioners, Arthur Lee and John Adams, and the lieutenant's intimate friends, John Langdon and Captain Abraham Whipple; and to many aspects of the special *Ranger* exploits, including the descent upon Whitehaven, the raid at St. Mary's Isle, and the battle with the *Drake*. With the cruise of the *Bonhomme Richard* and its aftermath following the return of the *Ranger,* it bears upon obstacles overcome by Jones preliminary to the battle; upon views of his professional character entertained by Captain (later Admiral) Mahan; upon the battle itself; upon the crisis at the Dutch anchorage in the road of the Texel; and upon the seizure of the *Alliance* by Landais.

After his return to the United States in the final years of the Revolution, the data have reference to his success in supervising the building of our first ship of the line, the *America,* in the face of special opposition by John Langdon, the contractor; and to his triumph over powerful enemies political as well as naval.

As for the French ladies whom he knew over a span of years, the material pertains in particular to his association with Madame T—, Madame Tellisson, the Countess de Nicolson, and the Countess de La Vendahl.

In the Russian setting, it relates to the practiced slander and treachery of his fellow commander, the Prince de Nassau; to the guile of Potemkin and the Prince de Ligne; to the story of the often-supposed hidden skeleton in the closet of Jones' personal life as here revealed in full by the Russo-German girl conspiracy; to the evidence of the French Minister de Ségur in respect to this plot; to the special rôle of the Empress Catherine herself; and to the faith of Jefferson, the American Minister to France, in Jones professionally and privately.

Upon his residence in Western Europe and particularly in Paris during his last few years, the additional information applies, finally, to his part in the environment of the French Revolution; to his connection with the newly appointed American envoy in Paris, Gouverneur Morris; and to his personal distrust of his former friend, Edward Bancroft the British spy, undetected in the Revolutionary War and for a century after it.

Bibliography

Bibliography

I
MANUSCRIPTS

THE LIBRARY OF CONGRESS:

The Peter Force Collection of John Paul Jones Letters and Documents. The nine volumes are the largest and most valuable source for Jones' career in the Revolution.

The Papers of the Continental Congress, 1777-1789. Volumes 54, 58, 132, 147, 168, 193, and 639 in particular.

The Marine Committee Letter Book.

The Naval Records of the American Revolution.

The Benjamin Franklin Papers.

The Gouverneur Morris Papers.

Miscellaneous Records of Service in Russia.

"Documents mainly relating to charges of assault brought by Katerina Stepanova against Rear Admiral and Chevalier Paul Jones of the Russian Imperial Navy."

THE LIBRARY OF THE NAVY DEPARTMENT, WASHINGTON:

The Complete Logs of the Ranger *and the* Bonhomme Richard.

Pièces Justificatives.

Files of Letters and Records, including a document of December, 1913 from Captain John Hope, R.N., descendant of the Earls of Selkirk, to Captain Stockton, U.S.N. as to the parentage of Jones.

Court Martial Testimony at the Trial of Landais in America and miscellaneous data.

THE NAVAL ACADEMY MUSEUM LIBRARY, ANNAPOLIS:

The Robert Morris Letter Book.

The Letter Book of John Paul Jones from March, 1778 to July, 1779.

Janette Taylor Notes (in a copy of the biography by Robert C. Sands) from Jared Sparks Collection (Cornell).

John L. Senior Moscow Papers.

THE LIBRARY OF THE AMERICAN PHILOSOPHICAL SOCIETY, PHILADELPHIA:

The Papers of Benjamin Franklin. A storehouse of letters by, to, and concerning Jones during his operations in European waters.

The Bache Papers of Benjamin Franklin. Supplementary to the main Franklin collection.

THE UNIVERSITY OF PENNSYLVANIA LIBRARY:

The Papers of Benjamin Franklin. A collection similar to that at the American Philosophical Society but less extensive.

THE PIERPONT MORGAN LIBRARY (also THE NAVY DEPARTMENT and THE NEW YORK PUBLIC LIBRARIES):

The Selkirk Letters, copied from the Manor House, St. Mary's Isle.

Letters and Reports relating to the *Ranger* and the *Bonhomme Richard* from the British Admiralty Foreign Office and Custom House Records.

The Filkin Collection. Four voluminous notebooks of contemporary newspaper reports and miscellaneous information.

Correspondence with Washington and with Captain Hector McNeill (in the Morgan Library alone).

THE NEW YORK PUBLIC LIBRARY:

Letters of Samuel Adams.

Letters and Autobiographical Journal of Arthur Lee.

Knapp Notes and Documents; September, 1846.

Letters to Hector McNeill.

The United States Navy Board Letter Book, Eastern District, Boston; October 24, 1778 to October 29, 1779.

THE HARVARD UNIVERSITY LIBRARY:

Jared Sparks Collections: 16, 41, 54, 57, 132, and "Lafayette."

Arthur Lee Collections: 3, 4, 5, 6, 7, 8, 13.

THE HISTORICAL SOCIETY OF PENNSYLVANIA, PHILADELPHIA:

The Effing Papers.

The Dreer Papers.

Various Memoranda.

THE LIBRARY OF THE MASSACHUSETTS GRAND LODGE, MASONIC TEMPLE, BOSTON:

Correspondence with Edward Bancroft, Gouverneur Morris, Robert Morris, and John Ross; other material.

THE MASSACHUSETTS HISTORICAL SOCIETY, BOSTON:

The Massachusetts Historical Society Proceedings, October, 1921-June, 1922, Vol. IV (Hector McNeill Papers).

THE NEW YORK HISTORICAL SOCIETY:

Silas Deane Letters; Collections, 1886-90.

Peter Landais Letter and other data.

ST. MARY'S ISLE; KIRKCUDBRIGHT, SCOTLAND (the Selkirk estate):

Record from Sir C. D. Hope-Dunbar, Bart., Descendant of the Earls of Selkirk, to the author pertaining to accounts which associate Jones' early life with St. Mary's Isle.

II

CHIEF PRINTED SOURCES

Adams, John. *The Works of John Adams.* Edited by Charles F. Adams. Boston, 1851.

Adams, Samuel. *The Life of Samuel Adams.* Edited by H. L. Cushing. New York, 1904.

Allen, Gardner Weld. *Captain Hector McNeill of the Continental Navy.* Boston, 1922.

André. *See* Jones, John Paul. *Mémoires de Paul Jones.* Edited by le citoyen André.

Ashe, S. A. C. *Some New Light on John Paul Jones.* South Atlantic Quarterly. Vol. XVII, Jan. and Oct., 1918. Investigations in regard to the early years in America.

Bixby's Collection, W. K. Unpublished Letters of John Paul Jones from the Un-

published Originals in Mr. W. K. Bixby's Collection, including *the Recovery of the Body of John Paul Jones by General Horace Porter.* Edited by Horace Porter and Franklin B. Sanborn. Boston, 1905.

Buell, Augustus C. *Paul Jones, Founder of the American Navy: A History.* New York, 1900 and 1905. This book, fictitious as purported "history" or "biography, has been challenged from many informed sources. For detailed exposure, refer in this bibliography to *Paullin, De Koven,* and the Virginia Magazine of History and Biography.

Chambers, Julius. *News Hunting.* New York, 1921.

Chase, Thomas. *Sketches of the Life, Character, and Times of Paul Jones.* Richmond, 1859.
Memoirs seemingly based in small part upon the experiences of a sailor associated with Jones, but in fact in large part upon the biographical efforts of his grandson. Scarcely more reliable as a whole than some of many lurid pamphlets of Revolutionary times and later of which Jones became the sport.

Cooper, James Fenimore. *The Lives of Distinguished American Naval Officers.* 1846.

Cooper, James Fenimore. *John Paul Jones.* Graham's Lady's and Gentleman's Magazine. Vol. 23, 1843.

La Correspondance Littéraire. No. 8, 20 Mars, 1859; Paris. Detailed circumstances of the death and burial in Paris.

Dale, The Life of Commodore. The Port Folio. June, 1814.

De Koven, Mrs. Reginald. *A Fictitious Paul Jones Masquerading as the Real.* (Buell's *Paul Jones*). A pamphlet. The New York Times, 1906 (1928).

De Koven, Mrs. Reginald. *The Life and Letters of John Paul Jones.* New York, 1913.

Dixmerie, F.: de la (La Loge des Neuf-Sœurs). *Discours adressé par le premier orateur . . . a l'illustre F.: Paul Jones.* Du Deplacement des Mers. Genève, 1779 (?)
Tribute from Jones' Masonic lodge in Paris.

Fanning, Nathaniel. *Fanning's Narrative.* New York, 1806. Reprinted in the Magazine of History with Notes and Queries. Edited by John S. Barnes. New York, 1912. An interesting account, sometimes true and sometimes prejudiced and false, concerning the part of a midshipman under Jones.

Force, Peter. *American Archives,* 1843. Fourth Series, Vols. 1-6; Fifth Series, Vols. 1-3. Invaluable letters for Jones' career early in the Revolution.

Franklin, Benjamin. *Calendar of the Papers in the Library of the American Philosophical Society* (and of the University of Pennsylvania). Edited by I. Minis Hays.

Golder, F. A. *John Paul Jones in Russia.* New York, 1927.
An important collection of letters in relation to Potemkin and Catherine II.

Green, Ezra. *The Diary of Ezra Green.* Reprinted from the Historical and Genealogical Register for January and April, 1875.
The surgeon aboard the *Ranger.*

Hart, Charles H. and Edward Biddle. *Memoirs of the Life and Works of Jean Antoine Houdon.* Philadelphia, 1911.
Questions concerning the identification of the body recovered from Paris as that of Jones. pp. 125-172.

Henkels, Stanislaus V. (Collector). Pamphlet No. 1074. Philadelphia, 1912.

Herbert, Charles. *The Prisoners of 1776 or A Relic of the Revolution.* Edited by R. Livesey.

Hopkins, Esek. *The Letter Book of Esek Hopkins.* Edited by William Davis Miller from original manuscripts in the Library of the Rhode Island Historical Society. Providence, 1932.
Background in regard to the Commodore who thwarted Jones' command of the American squadron.

Hopkins, Esek. *Correspondence of Esek Hopkins.* Edited by William Davis Miller from original manuscripts in the Library of the Rhode Island Historical Society. Providence, 1933.

Jefferson, Thomas. *The Writings of Thomas Jefferson.* Edited by Andrew W. Lipscomb, Washington, 1907.

Jones, John Paul. *Mémoires de Paul Jones.* Edited by le citoyen André. Paris, 1798. The distinguished autobiographical account of his career in the Revolution prepared especially for presentation to Louis XVI. *"The Memoirs of Paul Jones,"* recorded André, "have been written in English by himself and translated under his eyes by the editor."

Jones, John Paul. *The Calendar of John Paul Jones Manuscripts in the Library of Congress.* Edited by Charles Henry Lincoln. Washington, 1903 and 1906.

Jones, John Paul. Niles Weekly Register. June 6, 1812-July 13, 1812. A version of Jones' memoirs of the Revolution. It may not be wholly authentic.

Journals of the Continental Congress. 1774-1789 especially.

Khrapovitski, A. V. D. *Diary.* St. Petersburg, 1874. A record by the secretary of Catherine II.

Landais, Peter. *The Charges and Proofs Respecting the Conduct of Peter Landais.* Printed by Francis Childs. New York, 1787. Includes observations and a biographical notice by the publisher regarding Landais.

Landais, Peter. *Memorial to Justify Peter Landais' Conduct during the Late War.* Printed by Peter Edes, Boston, 1784. Also a second, different volume with the same title, Boston, 1794.

Langdon, John. *Letters by Washington, Adams, Jefferson, and Others to John Langdon.* Edited by Alfred Langdon Elwyn. Philadelphia, 1880.

Lloyd, Malcolm, Jr. *The Taking of the Bahamas by the Continental Navy in 1776.* Pennsylvania Magazine. Vol. 49, 1925. Details of the cruise of Hopkins' fleet to New Providence.

Logs of the Serapis, Alliance, and Ariel. Edited by John S. Barnes for the Naval History Society, New York, 1911. Includes in an appendix a significant letter of June 24, 1781 from James Nicholson to John Barry.

Mackenzie, Alexander Slidell. *The Life of Paul Jones.* New York, 1846.

Madigan, Thomas. *Autograph Letters, Manuscripts, and Historical Documents.*

Memoirs of Rear Admiral Paul Jones. Edinburgh, 1830. The first full-length and authoritative biography, based on material from Jones' niece, Janette Taylor, and including a large part of the "Journal of the Campaign of the Liman." Reprinted in London, 1843, by Henry Washburn.

Le Moniteur Universel, Paris. Especially July 10, 12, and 16, 1790 and July 19, 1792. Jones in Paris of the Revolution.

Morris, Gouverneur. *A Diary of the French Revolution, 1778-1793.* Edited by Beatrix Carey Davenport. Boston, 1939.

Morris, Robert. *The Confidential Correspondence of Robert Morris.* S. V. Henkels' Catalogue No. 1183. Philadelphia, 1917.

Nassau-Siegen, Le Prince Charles de. *Un Paladin au XVIII⁰ Siècle . . . d'après sa correspondance originale inédite de 1784 à 1789* par Le Marquis d'Aragon. Paris, 1893. The self-exposure of this braggart.

Naval Records of the American Revolution, 1775-1788. Calendar prepared from the originals in the Library of Congress by Charles Henry Lincoln. Washington, 1906.

New Hampshire Documents and Records, 1776-83. Vols. VIII and XVII. Concord, N.H., 1874.

Correspondence between Jones and state authorities while outfitting the *Ranger*.

Niles Weekly Register, Vol. II, June 6, 1812—July 13, 1812. *See* Jones, John Paul.

North Carolina State Records. Vols. 9, 13, 14, 15, 17, 18, 21.
Apropos the extent of Jones' connection with North Carolina and the tradition concerning Willie and Allen Jones.

Paul Jones' Country: A Guide. Published by William Grieve. Dumfries.

Paullin, Charles Oscar, Editor. *Outletters of the Continental Marine Committee and Board of Admiralty*. Published by the Naval History Society. New York, 1914.

Paullin, Charles Oscar. *"When Was Our Navy Founded? A Criticism of Augustus C. Buell's 'Paul Jones, Founder of the American Navy.'"* United States Naval Institute Proceedings; Vol. 36, No. 1, Whole No. 133.

Remick, Oliver P. *Kittery and Eliot, Me. in the American Revolution*. Boston, 1901.

Repplier, Emma. *How Many Mutineers did Paul Jones Kill?* The Independent, April 12, 1906.

Robison, Joseph. Transactions and Journal of the Dumfriesshire and Galloway Natural History and Antiquarian Society, N.S. Vol. XX, pp. 179-185, 1907-08 and pp. 135-140, 1911-12.
Aspects of the Maxwell charges, the Masonic affiliation, and the change of name.

Rogers, Ernest C. *Connecticut's Naval Office at New London during the American Revolution*. New London Historical Society, 1933.

Sands, Robert C. *The Life and Correspondence of John Paul Jones including the Narrative of the Campaign of the Liman*. New York, 1830. Stereotyped by A. Chandler (D. Fanshaw, Printer); Copyright by Sherman Converse.
Miss Janette Taylor, who provided the original material and explained that she refused an offer "to insure me an independence for life," preferring "the respectability of the book to pecuniary advantage," said of her sacrifice in relation to the chosen publisher and author: "I find myself disappointed in the object for which I made it—a *correct* and superior work." In spite of the limitations in form and accuracy to which she objected, the book has been the greatest single published source for authentic information.

Scottish Notes and Queries, Vol. 1, Third Series, June, 1923.
Alarm caused by Jones on British coast.

Ségur, L. P. de. *Mémoires, ou Souvenirs et Anecdotes*. Paris, 1826.
Particularly an account of the Russo-German girl conspiracy.

Seitz, Don C. *Paul Jones: His Exploits in English Seas*. "Contemporary accounts collected from English newspapers, with a complete bibliography." New York, 1917.

Sherburne, John Henry. *The Life and Character of John Paul Jones*. New York, 1825. A second enlarged edition, 1851.
The first valuable published collection of letters; but a badly-organized compilation, not a biography.

Sherburne, John Henry. *The Life of Paul Jones* from Original Documents in the Possession of John Henry Sherburne, London. John Murray. 1825.
A short biography based almost exclusively on Sherburne but more readable than his compilation. Benjamin Disraeli, according to James R. Thursfield, was the author.

Shuldham, Molyneux. *The Despatches of Molyneux Shuldham*. Edited by Robert Wilden Neeser for the Naval History Society. New York, 1913.
Naval accounts in connection with this first British Admiral in American waters during the Revolution, including the log of Captain Biddle of the *Andrew Doria* and British reports of Commodore Hopkins' fleet.

Sloan, John. *Harvard Scrap Book*. July 25, 1905.
Local color concerning Jones' birthplace.

Sparks, Jared, Editor. *Diplomatic Correspondence of the American Revolution.* Boston, 1829.

Sparks, Jared. *The Life of Gouverneur Morris.* Boston, 1832.

Stevens, B. F. *Facsimiles of Manuscripts in European Archives relating to America, 1773-1783.* London, 1889-95. Valuable for the diplomatic history abroad of the Revolution in relation to Jones, especially as to Edward Bancroft the spy.

Stewart, Charles W., Editor. *John Paul Jones Commemoration.* Washington, 1907. The volume contains representative Jones letters, a chronological table, a bibliography, and in particular full information regarding the means of identification of Jones' body and its return to the United States.

Taylor, Janette. *New Light upon the Career of John Paul Jones.* Reprinted from the Proceedings of the United States Naval Institute; Vol. XXXIII, No. 2, Whole No. 122. Opinions upon controversial aspects of Jones' life by his niece.

Thomson, Valentine. *Le Corsaire chez l'impératrice.* Paris, Librarie Plon. No date. This biography omits most of Jones' life before his arrival with the *Ranger* in France. The information available through Jones' relatives and from other firsthand historical sources do not support some of the portrayed incidents.

Thomson, Valentine. *Knight of the Seas.* New York, 1939. As in the case of *Le Corsaire chez l'impératrice,* Miss Thomson here ignores almost the whole of Jones' life before his arrival in France. Her biography in English follows largely the form and spirit of her earlier one in French. In "Sources and Bibliography," she mentions her "fragmentary but strictly historical study of the romantic life of John Paul Jones." The present writer refers to his own preface, biography, and appendix for consideration of a number of questions of historical truth.

Virginia Magazine of History and Biography. Vol. 7, Jan. 1900; Vol. 8, 1900-01, pp. 442-445; Vol. 13, July, 1905. Adverse criticism of Buell's *Paul Jones* and other data.

Wharton, Francis, Editor. *The Revolutionary Diplomatic Correspondence of the United States.* Vols. I-VI. Washington, 1889. Along with the *Diplomatic Correspondence* edited by Jared Sparks and the *Facsimiles of Manuscripts* published by B. F. Stevens, these letters provide a broad background of Jones in relation to civil authorities, American and French, in Europe.

III
GENERAL REFERENCES

Abernethy, T. P. *Commercial Activities of Silas Deane in France.* American Historical Review. Vol. XXXIX, No. 3. April, 1934.

Adams, Mrs. John. *Letters.* Edited by Charles F. Adams. Boston, 1848.

Alger, Philip R. *The Naval Academy Miniature of John Paul Jones.* The United States Naval Institute. Vol. 31, No. 3, Whole No. 115.

Allen, Gardner Weld. *Naval History of the American Revolution.* Boston, 1913.

American Catholic Historical Researches. *John Paul Jones and John Barry.* Vol. 1, 1905, pp. 343-358; Vol. 2, 1906, pp. 242-273.

Anderson, William. *The Scottish Nation.* Edinburgh, 1864. Genealogy of the Nicolson family.

(Anonymous). *Secret Memoirs of the Court of Petersburg . . . the Reign of Catherine II.* Philadelphia, 1802.

Anthony, Katherine, Translator. *Memoirs of Catherine the Great.* New York, 1927.

Ashe, Samuel A. Court. *The History of North Carolina.* Vols. I, II.

Bachaumont. *Mémoires Secrets,* 1762-1787. Paris, 1809.

Barnes, James. *Personal Appearance of Paul Jones.* Appleton's Booklover's Magazine, July, 1905.

Barney, Joshua. *A Biographical Memoir.* Edited by Mary Barney. Boston, 1832.
Bazley, Basil M. *The Romance of Scotland.* Published by the London and North Western Railway.
Beazley, R.; Forbes, N.; and Birkett, G. A. *Russia.* Oxford, 1918.
Beer, A. and Ritter, J., Editors. *Fontes Rerum Austriacarum.* Vols. 53-54. Wien, 1901.
Bemis, Samuel Flagg. *Diplomacy of the American Revolution.* New York, 1935.
Bemis, Samuel Flagg. *A Diplomatic History of the United States.* New York, 1936.
Bemis, Samuel Flagg. *Edward Bancroft.* American Historical Review. Vol. 29, pp. 492-495; April, 1924.
Benjamin, Park. *Is it Paul Jones' Body?* The Independent. Vol. LIX; July 20, 1905.
Besenval, Baron de. *Mémoires.* Paris, 1846.
Best, Mary Agnes. *Thomas Paine.* New York, 1927.
Biddle, Charles. *Autobiography of Charles Biddle.* Edited by James C. Biddle. Philadelphia, 1883.
Bigelow, John. *The Life of Benjamin Franklin.* Philadelphia, 1874.
Blease, W. Lyon. *Suvorof.* London, 1920.
Boies, Bessie. *Edward Bancroft: A British Spy.* Univ. of Chicago, 1908.
Burke, John Bernard. *Peerage, Baronetage, and Knightage.*
Cambridge Modern History. Chapters V, VIII, IX, X, XIX, XXV especially.
Campan, (Madame). *Mémoires.* Paris, 1886.
Catherine II. *Memoirs of the Empress*—Written by Herself. Edited by A. Herzen. New York, 1859.
Catherine II. *Les Lettres de Catherine II au Prince de Ligne, 1780-1796.* Par La Princesse Charles de Ligne. Paris, 1924.
Cérenville, J. E. P. *Vie du Prince Potemkin.* Paris, 1808.
Clark, George. *Silas Deane.* New York, 1913.
Clark, Thomas. *The Naval History of the United States.* Philadelphia, 1814.
Clark, William Bell. *Lambert Wickes, Sea Raider and Diplomat.* Yale University Press, 1932.
Clark, William Bell. *Gallant John Barry.* New York, 1938.
Cokayne, G. E. *Complete Baronetage.*
Colonial Records of North Carolina, 1776.
Conyngham, Gustavus. *Letters and Papers relating to the Cruises of Gustavus Conyngham.* Edited by Robert Wilden Neeser for the Naval History Society. New York, 1915.
Cooper, James Fenimore. *History of the Navy,* Philadelphia, 1839.
Craik, Sir Henry. *A Century of Scottish History.* New York, 1901.
Cresson, W. P. *Francis Dana: A Puritan Diplomat at the Court of Catherine the Great.* New York, 1930.
Damas, Count Roger de. *Memoirs.* Edited by Jacques Rambaud. New York, 1913.
Dandridge, D. *American Prisoners of the Revolution.* Charlottesville, 1911.
Davis, Junius. *Some Facts about John Paul Jones.* South Atlantic Quarterly, Vol. IV, 1905 and Vol. V, 1906.
Deane, Silas. *A Narrative of the Objects and Proceedings of Silas Deane.* Edited by P. L. Ford. Brooklyn, 1891.
Deane, Silas. *Paris Papers, or Mr. Deane's Later Intercepted Letters. . . . Reprinted by James Rivington,* New York, 1782.
Deane, Silas. *An Address to the United States of America.* New London, Reprinted 1784.
De Koven, Mrs. Reginald. *Paul Jones' Body.* New York Times, Dec. 25, 1911.
De Koven, Mrs. Reginald. *Criticism of Phillips Russell's "John Paul Jones: Man of Action."* New York Times, March 1, 1928.
Dick, C. H. *The Kirkcudbrightshire Coast.* Transactions and Journal of Proceedings of Dumfriesshire and Galloway Natural History and Antiquarian Society. 1911-1912. pp. 135-140.

Doniol, Henri. *Histoire de la participation de la France à l'établissement des États-Unis d'Amérique.* Paris, 1886-1900.

Durant, John. *New Materials for the History of the American Revolution.* New York, 1889.

Ellet, Elizabeth F. *Women of the Revolution.* New York, 1850.

Embrey, Alvin T. *History of Fredericksburg, Va.* Richmond, 1937.

Encyclopedia Britannica, Thirteenth Edition. *Kirkcudbrightshire.*

Field, Edward. *Esek Hopkins.* Providence, 1898.

Fiske, John. The American Revolution. Boston, 1891.

Fleming, Mrs. Vivian Minor. *Historic Records of Fredericksburg, 1608-1861.* Richmond, 1921.

Forbes, Allan and Cadman, P. F. *France and New England.* Boston, 1927.

Footner, *Sailor of Fortune.* New York, 1940.

Frost, Holloway H. *Our Heritage from Paul Jones.* The United States Naval Institute Proceedings. October, 1918, Vol. 44, No. 188.
　Misleading to the extent that Buell is an accepted authority.

Gallovidian Annual, 1929. *"Bonnie Annie Laurie."* pp. 34, 40.

Grand Lodge of Massachusetts. *Facsimile of Application of John Paul Jones for Degrees in Freemasonry in Scotland,* etc. Abstract of Proceedings of Massachusetts Historical Society. Jan. 12, 1912.

Greenwood, Isaac J. *Captain John Manley.* Boston, 1915.

Griffin, Martin J. J. *Commodore John Barry.* Philadelphia, 1903.

Grimm, Baron F. M. von. *Lettres de Grimm à l'Impératrice Catherine II.* Publiées par Jacques Grot; Paris, 1791.

Gurn, Joseph. *Commodore John Barry.* New York, 1933.

Hackett, F. W. *Deck and Field.* Washington, 1909.

Hale, Edward Everett and Hale, E. E., Jr. *Franklin in France.* Boston, 1887.

Hart, Albert Bushnell. *John Paul Jones.* The Mentor. Oct. 16, 1916; Vol. 4, No. 17.

Hart, Charles Henry. *The Sword Presented by Louis XVI to John Paul Jones.* Proceedings of the United States Naval Institute, No. 122.

Hazen, Charles Downer. *The French Revolution.* New York, 1932.

Hendrick, Burton J. *The Lees of Virginia.* Boston, 1935.

Hume, Edgar Erskine. *Lafayette and the Society of the Cincinnati.* Baltimore, 1934.

Hunt, Gaillard. *The Works of James Madison.* New York, 1908.

Inglis, Francis C. *Notes on a Wax Medallion and Relative Autograph Letters of Paul Jones.* Edinburgh, 1906.
　Informative, but numerous errors.

Istoricheskii Viestnik. 1902: 1062-1085; 1895: 174-200.

Jameson, J. F. *St. Eustatius in the American Revolution.* American Historical Review; VIII, pp. 683-708.

Jeffries, John. *Diary.* Magazine of History, 1910.

Jesse, John Heneage. *George Selwyn and his Contemporaries.* London, 1844.

Jett, Dora C. *Minor Sketches of Major Folk.* Richmond, 1928.

Johnson, Guion Griffis. *Ante-Bellum North Carolina.* University of North Carolina Press, 1937.

Jones, Colonel Cadwallader. *A Genealogical History.* Columbia, S.C., 1900.

Jones, William Robert. *John Paul Jones and His History.* Chicago, 1927.

Kilby, John. *The Narrative of John Kilby.* With Introduction and Notes by Augustus C. Buell. Scribner's Magazine. Vol. 38, 1905.
　The account itself seems less questionable than Buell's commentary.

Knox, Dudley W. *A History of the United States Navy.* 1936.

Knox, Dudley W. *The Naval Genius of George Washington.*

Latimer, Elizabeth W. *My Scrap Book of the French Revolution.* Chicago, 1898.

Lee, Richard Henry. *The Life of Arthur Lee.* Boston, 1829.

Lee, Richard Henry. *Letters.* Edited by James Curtis Ballegh. New York, 1911.
Lee, William. *Letters.* Edited by W. C. Ford. Brooklyn, 1878.
Lee, William. *Reply of William Lee to the Charges of Silas Deane.* Edited by W. C. Ford. Brooklyn, 1891.
Levis, M. de. *Souvenirs et Portraits, 1780-1789.*
Ligne, Prince de. *His Memoirs, Letters, and Miscellaneous Papers.* Selected and Translated by Katharine. P. Wormeley. Boston, 1899.
Ligne, Prince de. *Mémoires et Lettres.* Paris, 1923.
Livesey, R. *The Prisoners of 1776.*
Maclay, Edgar Stanton. *A History of the United States Navy.* New York (Vol. I), 1897.
Mahan, Captain A. T. *John Paul Jones in the Revolution.* Scribner's Magazine. July and December, 1898.
Mahan, Captain A. T. *The Major Operations of the Navies in the War of American Independence.* Boston, 1913.
Massachusetts Historical Society Proceedings; November, 1912. *State Navies and Privateers in the Revolution.*
Master Mason, The. *The Search for the Body of John Paul Jones.* March, 1926.
Maxwell, Sir Herbert E. *A History of Dumfries and Galloway.* Edinburgh and London, 1896.
Mayo, Lawrence Shaw. *John Langdon of New Hampshire.* Concord, N.H., 1937.
McKerlie, P. H. *Galloway in Ancient and Modern Times.* Edinburgh, 1891.
Middlebrook, Louis F. *Maritime Connecticut during the American Revolution.* Salem, 1925.
Miller, Margaret. *Spy Activities of Doctor Edward Bancroft.* Journal of American History; Vol. XXII, 1928.
Moré, Comte de. *Mémoires.* Paris, 1898.
Moore, Frank. *Diary of the American Revolution.* New York, 1860.
Muir, Edwin. *Scottish Journey.* London, 1935.
Oberholtzer, E. P. *Robert Morris: Patriot and Financier.* New York, 1903.
Paullin, Charles Oscar. *Diplomatic Negotiations of American Naval Officers, 1778-1783.* Baltimore, 1912.
Paullin, Charles Oscar. *The Navy of the American Revolution.* Chicago, 1906.
Pennsylvania Magazine. Vol. 49, 1925.
Porter, General Horace; and Others. *Unveiling of the Statue of John Paul Jones.* Washington, April 17, 1912.
Potemkin. *Memoirs of the Life of Prince Potemkin, translated from the German.* London, 1812.
Potemkin. *The Life of Field Marshal Prince Potemkin.* The Royal Military Chronicle. London, 1812.
Preedy, George R. *The Life of Rear Admiral John Paul Jones.* London, 1940.
Proceedings of the Grand Lodge of Free and Accepted Masons of the District of Columbia for the year 1907. Washington, 1908.
Proceedings of the Grand Lodge of Free and Accepted Masons of Massachusetts: 1907, 1912, 1913, 1914, 1916.
Proceedings of the United States Naval Institute, Annapolis. No. 115, Vol. XXXI.
Rambaud, Alfred. *The History of Russia.* New York, 1897.
Renaut, Francis P. *Les Relations Diplomatiques entre la Russie et les États-Unis, 1776-1825.* Paris, 1922.
Revue de Paris. *Catherine II et Potemkine.* Année 41, May-June, 1934.
Rietstap, J. B. *Armorial Général,* 1887.
Roberts, Charles H. *A Sketch of the Life of George Roberts.* Concord, N.H., 1905. Not consistent with historical records.
Rush, Dr. Benjamin. *A Memorial of Dr. Benjamin Rush.* Published by Louis A. Biddle, 1905.

Russell, Phillips. *John Paul Jones: Man of Action.* New York, 1927.

Russian Imperial Historical Society. *Collections;* Vol. 27, 1880.

Russkaia Starina; 1876, pp. 1-58, 207-238, 239-262, 399-478.

Russki Vestnik; July 5-19, 1878.

Scots Peerage, The, Vol. 7. Edited by Sir James Balfour Paid.

Scribner's Magazine. Vols. LXX; XLVIII, new series.

Ségur, Comte L. P. de. *Tableau Historique et Politique de l'Europe.* Paris, 1803.

Sikes, Walter. North Carolina Booklet, No. 4 Raleigh, N.C., 1904.

Sloan, J. N. *The Carlyle Country.* London, 1904.

Smyth, Albert Henry. *Benjamin Franklin.* New York, 1905.

Soloveytchik, George. *Potemkin.* London, 1938.

Soulavie. *Mémoires Historiques et Politiques du Règne de Louis XVI.* Paris, 1802.

Sprout, H. and M. *The Rise of American Naval Power.* Princeton, 1939.

Stewart, Robert A. *The History of Virginia's Navy of the Revolution.*

Stuart, Margaret. *Scottish Family History.* Edinburgh, 1930.

Thursfield, James R. *Nelson and Other Naval Studies.* New York, 1909.

Tooke, W. *The Life of Catherine II.* London, 1799. Jean Henri Castéra is the original author; "Tooke's additions," according to the Dictionary of National Biography, "amount to more than half the work."

Tooker, Lewis Frank. *John Paul Jones.* New York, 1916.

Trevelyan, George Otto. *The American Revolution.* New York, 1899, 1903.

Unaflart, A. et Weiss, N. Extrait du Bulletin de la Société de l'histoire du Protestantisme français. Sept.-Oct., 1905.

United States Literary Magazine. Oct. 15, 1825, Vol. III. *Review of the "Life and Character of the Chevalier John Paul Jones by John Henry Sherburne, 1825."*

Van Tyne, Claude H. *The Causes of the War of Independence.* Boston and New York, 1922.

Victor, O. J. *The Life and Exploits of John Paul Jones.* New York, 1867.

Vigée Lebrun, (Madame). *Souvenirs.* Paris, 1882.

Waliszewski, Kasimir. *Le Roman d'une impératrice.* Paris, 1893.

Waliszewski, Kasimir. *The Story of a Throne: Catherine II of Russia.* London, 1895.

Washington, George. *The Writings of George Washington,* Edited by W. C. Ford. New York, 1890.

Watterson, Henry. *Compromises of Life.* New York, 1906.

Webster, Nestah H. *Louis XVI and Marie Antoinette.* London, 1937.

Wheeler, John H. *History of North Carolina,* Philadelphia, 1851.

Wright, Dudley. *Woman and Freemasonry.* London, 1922.

Reference Notes

Reference Notes

(Full titles, not obvious from the abbreviated notes, are in the bibliography. Whenever no mention appears of the sender or recipient of correspondence, the person implied is Jones.)

CHAPTER I

1 Sands, p. 13.
2 Sloan, *Harvard Scrap Book.*
3 Files, Navy Department Library.
4 Craik, Vol. 1, pp. 130, 131.
5 Ruskin, *Works,* Cook and Wedderburn edition, Vol. 35, pp. 544-5.
6 Craik, p. 49.
7 *Record* . . . Hope-Dunbar.
8 Sands, p. 13; Filkin II, p. 320.
9 *See* Appendix I.
10 ——
11 Sands, p. 22.

CHAPTER II

1 Franklin *Papers,* A.P.S., March 6, 1779.
2 Sands, p. 15.
3 Franklin *Papers,* A.P.S., March 6, 1779.
4 Peter Force *Collection,* I; J. to R. Morris, September 4, 1776.
5 ——, IX; "To the U. S. Minister of Marine at the Close of the War, 1782."
6 "U. S. Literary Magazine," October 15, 1825.
7 Langdon; April 4, 1778.
8 Correspondence with . . . Hector McNeill (Morgan Library); "*Ranger, Friday.*"
9 Russell, facsimile.
10 Sands, p. 451.

CHAPTER III

1 Sloan, *Harvard Scrap Book*
2 Sands, p. 18, 19.
3 ——, p. 22.
4 Robison.
5 ——
6 ——
7 ——
8 Sands, p. 21.
9 ——, pp. 18, 19.
10 ——, pp. 19, 20.
11 ——, p. 21.

12 Ashe, "Some New Light on J. P. J."; Sands, p. 22.

CHAPTER IV

1 Franklin *Papers,* A.P.S., enclosure March 6, 1779; Repplier.
2 ——
3 ——; Ashe, "Some New Light on J. P. J."
4 ——
5 Sands, p. 25; Peter Force *Collection,* VI, to Alex. Scott, Oct. 30, 1779.
6 Sands, pp. 25, 26.
7 *Papers* of Franklin, A.P.S., March 6, 1779.
8 ——
9 ——

CHAPTER V

1 Filkin; miscellaneous chapbooks.
2 Chase.
3 ——

CHAPTER VI

1 Franklin *Papers,* A.P.S., March 6, 1779.
2 ——; Sands, p. 25; Ashe, "Some New Light on J. P. J."
3 Ashe, "Some New Light on J. P. J."; Files, Navy Department Library.
4 Embrey; Stewart, R. A., p. 209.
5 Davis; "Virginia Magazine," July, 1905.
6 Davis; Embrey.
7 ——
8 ——
9 Davis; "Virginia Magazine," July, 1905.
10 Sparks *Collections,* 41, 132 (Harvard); Janette Taylor *Notes* (Cornell).
11 Sands, p. 63.
12 Sherburne, 1851, p. 53.
13 Peter Force *Collection,* IV, to John Plaince, March 9, 1779.
14 Franklin *Papers,* A.P.S., March 6, 1779.
15 Sherburne, 1851, p. 43.

16 Peter Force *Collection*, VI, to T. Scott, December 3, 1779.
17 Sherburne, 1851, p. 42.
18 Embrey.
19 Peter Force *Collection*, II, from J. K. Read, February 28, 1778.
20 ————.
21 Ashe, "Some New Light on J. P. J."
22 Peter Force *Collection*, II, from J. K. Read, February 28, 1778.

CHAPTER VII

1 Peter Force *Collection*, VI, to T. Scott, December 3, 1779.
2 ————, I, to Robert Smith, November 12, 1776.
3 Facsimile of Petition to Lodge of St. Bernard, 1770, from J. L. Senior's ms.
4 Peter Force *Collection*, I, to Robert Smith, November 12, 1776.
5 Ashe, *History of N. C.*, Vol. 1, p. 377.
6 Sikes.
7 Peter Force *Collection*, II, to Hewes, October 30, 1777.
8 Ashe, *History of N. C.;* Wheeler.
9 De Koven, Vol. 1, pp. 52-63; Buell; Jones, Cadwallader; Brady.
10 Robison.
11 Franklin *Papers*, A.P.S., March 6, 1779.
12 Ashe, "Some New Light on J. P. J."
13 ————
14 Mrs. R. T. Newcombe, Raleigh, N.C. to the author, March 16, 1938.
15 Peter Force Collection, II, to Hewes, August 17, 1777.
16 ————, I, to Robert Smith, November 12, 1776.
17 ————, I, to Hewes, January 12, 1777.

CHAPTER VIII

1 Franklin *Papers*, A.P.S., March 6, 1779.
2 ————
3 ————
4 Adams, John, Vol. 5, p. 492.
5 Franklin *Papers*, A.P.S., March 6, 1779.
6 Trevelyan, p. 365.
7 Franklin to Strahan, July 5, 1775, Historical Society of Pa.
8 Sherburne, 1851, pp. 41-3.
9 Peter Force *Collection*, I, Read to J., October 13, 1775.
10 ————
11 Ashe, "Some New Light on J. P. J." and "History of N. C.," Vol. I, p. 542.

12 Sikes.
13 Ashe, *History of N. C.*, Vol. 1, pp. 542-4.
14 Sikes.
15 Knox, *Naval Genius of George Washington*, Washington to Congress, January, 1776.
16 Greenwood, p. 9.
17 Allen, *Naval History of the American Revolution*, Washington to R. H. Lee, November 27, 1775.
18 Force, *Archives*, Series IV, Vol. 4.
19 Peter Force *Collection*, IX, "To the U. S. Minister of Marine . . . 1782."
20 Field, p. 78.
21 ————, pp. 75, 76.
22 Griffin, p. 25.
23 Peter Force *Collection*, II, to Hewes, August 17, 1777.
24 ————, IX, "To the U. S. Minister of Marine . . . 1782."

CHAPTER IX

1 Peter Force *Collection*, VI, to Huntington, December 7, 1779.
2 Force, *Archives*, Series IV, Vol. 4,—to the Earl of Dartmouth, December 20, 1775.
3 Rogers, pp. 130, 131.
4 Force, *Archives*, Series IV, Vol. 4, Newbern, N.C., February 9, 1776.
5 ————; Shuldham, pp. 120, 121.
6 Hopkins, *Correspondence of E. H.*
7 Force, *Archives*, Series IV, Vol. 4, p. 570.
8 Peter Force *Collection*, IX, "To the U. S. Minister of Marine . . . 1782."
9 Sands, pp. 32, 33.
10 ————, p. 35.
11 Peter Force *Collection*, I, to Hewes, May 19, 1776.
12 Rush.
13 Field, p. 134.
14 Sherburne, 1851, pp. 22-4.
15 Field, p. 100.
16 ————, p. 95 ff.
17 "Penn'a. Magazine," Vol. 49, 1925, Montford Browne to "My Lord," November 5, 1776.
18 ————, John Brown to "My Lord," May 2, 1776.
19 Sherburne, 1851, pp. 12, 13.
20 "Niles Weekly Register"; *Memoirs of Paul Jones*, London, 1843.
21 "Penn'a. Magazine," Vol. 49, 1925, John Brown to "My Lord," May 2, 1776.
22 Montford Browne to "My Lord," November 5, 1776.

23 ———, George Germaine to Gov. Browne, January 14, 1777.

CHAPTER X

1 Shuldham, "Log of *Andrew Doria*."
2 Force, *Archives*, Series IV, Vol. 5, Whipple to Hopkins, April 30, 1776.
3 Hopkins, *Letter Book of E. H.*, Hopkins to Hancock, April 8, 1776.
4 Shuldham, Wallace to Shuldham, April 10, 1776.
5 Hopkins, *Letter Book of E. H.*, Hopkins to Hancock, April 8, 1776.
6 Sands, pp. 36, 44.
7 Shuldham, Capt. T. Howe's report, April 6, 1776.
8 Shuldham, "Log of *Andrew Doria*."
9 Sands, pp. 47-8.
10 Shuldham, Capt. T. Howe's report, April 6, 1776.
11 Cooper, *Lives of Distinguished American Naval Officers*, Vol. 1, pp. 52, 53.
12 *Journals of the C. C.*, Vol. 5, August 15, 1776, Ford edition.
13 ———, June 13.
14 ———, August 9.
15 ———, August 16.
16 Sands, p. 37.

CHAPTER XI

1 Force, *Archives*, Series IV, Vol. 6, to Tillinghast, June 2, 1776.
2 Peter Force *Collection*, I, to Hewes, May 19, 1776.
3 ———
4 Gurn, p. 39.
5 *Papers of the C. C.*, No. 58, from Marine Com., August 6, 1776.
6 Sherburne, 1851, p. 29; Sands, p. 306.
7 Peter Force *Collection*, I, to Morris, September 4, 1776.
8 "Logs of the *Serapis*, *Alliance*, and *Ariel*," September 4, 1776.
9 Sands, p. 49.
10 ———, p. 51.

CHAPTER XII

1 Adams, Samuel, Vol. 3, January 9, 1777.
2 Rush.
3 Ségur, pp. 303, 304.
4 Sands, p. 304.
5 Clark, W. B., *Gallant John Barry*, p. 104.
6 Force, *Archives*, Series V, Vol. 2, Bartlett to Langdon, October 15, 1776.

7 Washington, Vol. 3, p. 389.
8 Clark, W. B., *Lambert Wickes, Sea Raider and Diplomat*.
9 Allen, G. W., *Capt. Hector McNeill of the Continental Navy*.
10 Peter Force *Collection*, II, to Hewes, August 17, 1777.
11 Force, *Archives*, Series V, Vol. 2, Whipple to Langdon, October 26, 1776.
12 ———, R. H. Lee to S. Purviance, Jr., September 16, 1776.
13 ———, September, 1776.

CHAPTER XIII

1 Paullin (Editor), *Outletters* . . . , Marine Com. to Hopkins, October 10, 23, and 30, 1776.
2 ———
3 Force, *Archives*, Series V, Vol. 3, Hopkins to Marine Com., November 3, 1776.
4 ———, Series V, Vol. 2, to Morris, October 17, 1776.
5 Peter Force *Collection*, I, to Morris, September 4, 1776.
6 Force, *Archives*, Series V, Vol. 2, to Morris, October 17, 1776.
7 Force, *Archives*, Series V, Vol. 3, Hopkins to Marine Com., November 2, 1776.
8 Allen, *Naval History of the American Revolution*, Vol. 1, p. 67.
9 Force, *Archives*, Series V, Vol. 2, from Hopkins, October 28, 1776.
10 *Papers of the C. C.*, No. 58, to Hopkins, November 2, 1776.
11 Peter Force *Collection*, I, to Robert Smith, November 12, 1776.
12 Hopkins, *Correspondence of E. H.*, Marine Com. to Hopkins, March 25, 1777.
13 Peter Force *Collection*, I, to Robert Smith, November 12, 1776.
14 *Papers of the C. C.*, No. 58 to Marine Com., November 12, 1776.
15 Peter Force *Collection*, I, "Subscribers" to Hacker, November 14, 1776.
16 Sands, p. 57.
17 ———
18 Peter Force *Collection*, VI, to Pres. of Congress, December 7, 1779.

CHAPTER XIV

1 Paullin, *Outletters* . . . , Marine Com. to Hopkins, January 21, 1777.
2 Hopkins, *Letter Book of E. H.*, Hopkins to Rev. Samuel Adams, October 1, 1776.

3 Peter Force *Collection*, I, to Marine Com., January 21, 1777.

4 ———

5 Force, *Archives*, Series V, Vol. 3, Hopkins to Marine Com., November 8, 1776.

6 Peter Force *Collection*, I, to Marine Com., January 21, 1777.

7 ———, to Tillinghast, January 20, 1777.

8 ———, from Tillinghast, January 23, 1777.

9 ———, to Tillinghast, January 20, 1777.

10 *Marine Com. Letter Book*, pp. 52-4.

11 Peter Force *Collection*, I, to Hewes, January 12, 1777.

12 ———

13 Sands, p. 62.

14 ———

15 ———, p. 63.

16 ———

17 Field, p. 175.

18 Hopkins, *Letter Book of E. H.*, Hopkins to William Ellery, March 13, 1777.

19 Peter Force *Collection*, I, to Morris, February 10, 1777.

20 ———

CHAPTER XV

1 *Marine Com. Letter Book*, pp. 52-4.

2 Henkel's "Catalogue, no. 1183," B. Harrison to Morris, December 25, 1776.

3 *Naval Records of the American Revolution*, Morris to Hancock, December 16, 1776.

4 ———, Morris and others to Hancock, January 16, 1777.

5 Henkel's "Catalogue, no. 1183," Hancock to Morris, January 17, 1777.

6 Mass. Historical Society, Morris to J. Wendell, May 16, 1778.

7 Paullin, *Outletters . . .* , Marine Com. to Hopkins, January 21, 1777.

8 ———, Morris to Hopkins, February 5, 1777.

9 *Marine Com. Letter Book*, from Morris, February 1, 1777.

10 Hopkins, *Correspondence of E. H.*, from Hopkins, February 16, 1777.

11 *Papers of the C. C.*, No. 58, Hopkins to J. Olney, February 28, 1777.

12 Sands, pp. 58, 59.

13 *Papers of the C. C.*, No. 58, from Hopkins, March 1, 1777.

14 Hopkins, *Letter Book of E. H.*, Hopkins to William Ellery, March 13, 1777.

15 *Papers of the C. C.*, No. 58, pp. 225-30.

16 Field, pp. 190, 191.

17 ———, pp. 205, 206.

18 ———, p. 158.

19 Adams, John, Vol. 3, p. 66.

CHAPTER XVI

1 Henkel's "Catalogue, No. 1183," William Hooper to Morris, May 27, 1777.

2 Adams, John, Adams to Benjamin Rush, January 24, 1813.

3 Peter Force *Collection*, I, to Morris, April 7, 1777.

4 Sands, pp. 67, 68.

5 Peter Force *Collection*, II, to Hewes, September 1, 1777.

6 Sands, pp. 67, 68.

7 Mayo, p. 146.

8. Peter Force *Collection*, II, from Wendell, October 29, 1777.

9 Franklin *Papers*, A.P.S., Wendell to Franklin, October 30, 1777.

10 ———

11 "N. H. Documents and Records," p. 691.

12 Henkel's "Catalogue, No. 1183," Whipple to Morris, August 28, 1777.

13 Peter Force *Collection*, III, August 15, 1778.

14 Sands, p. 69.

15 Langdon, John, *Letters . . .* , to Langdon, October 31, 1777.

16 Madigan, to John Brown, October 31, 1777.

17 Franklin *Papers*, A.P.S., Vol. 6, 214, to Commissioners, August 30, 1777.

18 Sands, p. 70.

19 Peter Force *Collection*, II, to Morris, August 24, 1777.

20 ———

21 Dreer *Collection*, to Whipple, December 11, 1777.

22 "Logs of *Serapis, Alliance,* and *Ariel*," edited by Barnes, to Wendell, December 11, 1777.

23 Peter Force *Collection*, II, to Morris, December 11, 1777.

CHAPTER XVII

1 Stevens, No. 217.

2 Sands, p. 73.

3 ———, pp. 73, 74.

4 ———, p. 72.

5 ———, p. 74.

6 Arthur Lee *Collections*, IV.

7 ———, III and IV; Lee, William, *Letters*, Vol. 3, p. 812.
8 Wharton, I, p. 551.
9 ———, p. 587.
10 Stevens, No. 754.
11 ———, No. 179.
12 Franklin *Papers*, A.P.S., VIII, 103.
13 André, p. 23.
14 Clark, Thomas, pp. 60, 61.
15 Jameson.
16 Stevens, No. 795; Franklin *Papers*, A.P.S., XLVIII, 159.
17 Green, March 23.
18 André, pp. 30, 31.
19 *Papers of the C. C.*, No. 58, to Hancock, February 22, 1778.
20 Sands, p. 78.

CHAPTER XVIII

1 Peter Force *Collection*, VI, to President of Congress, December 7, 1779.
2 Sherburne, 1851, p. 46.
3 Seitz, p. 7.
4 Sherburne, 1851, p. 47.
5 André, p. 32 ff.
6 "Letters and Reports . . . from the British Admiralty Office. . . ."
7 ———
8 Sherburne, 1851, p. 47.
9 André, p. 33 ff.
10 "Letters and Reports . . . from the British Admiralty Office. . . ."
11 Sherburne, 1851, p. 47.
12 André, p. 33 ff.
13 ———, p. 40 ff.
14 Sherburne, 1851, p. 48.
15 Mahan, "Scribner's Magazine," July, December, 1898.
16 Cooper, "Graham's Lady's and Gentleman's Magazine," Vol. 23, 1843.

CHAPTER XIX

1 "Complete Log of the *Ranger*," April 23.
2 Moore, p. 461.
3 Arthur Lee *Collections*, III, Franklin to Cooper, December 11, 1777.
4 Dandridge, p. 162.
5 André, p. 26 ff.
6 Maclay, p. 140.
7 Peter Force *Collection*, II, to Morris, December 11, 1777; Maclay, p. 139.
8 Peter Force *Collection*, II, to Morris, December 11, 1777.
9 Selkirk *Letters*, Lady Selkirk to Countess of Morton, April 23, 1778.
10 Sherburne, 1851, p. 52.
11 ———

12 Selkirk *Letters*, Countess of Selkirk to Mr. Craik, April 25, 1778.
13 ———
14 ———, Countess of Selkirk to Selkirk, April 24, 1778.
15 Niles.
16 Selkirk *Letters*, Daer to Blanc, May 27, 1778.
17 ———, Countess of Selkirk to Selkirk, April 24, 1778.
18 ———
19 ———, Countess of Selkirk to Countess of Morton, May 15, 1778.
20 ———, Countess of Selkirk to Mr. Craik, April 25, 1778.
21 Sherburne, 1851, pp. 51-4.
22 Selkirk *Letters*, from Selkirk, June 9, 1778.
23 ———, Selkirk to Le Despencer, June 9, 1778.
24 Jared Sparks *Collections*, Parlia. Reg. X, 63; Parlia. Reg. VIII, 36.
25 Selkirk *Letters*, to Selkirk, February 12, 1784; Lee, William, *Letters* (Extract from *Courier de l'Europe*, No. 34).

CHAPTER XX

1 Green, April 21; André, p. 32 ff.
2 "Log of the *Ranger*," April 11.
3 André, p. 32 ff.; Sherburne, pp. 45-51; Niles.
4 André, p. 40 ff.
5 "Niles Weekly Register."
6 André, p. 40 ff.
7 Peter Force *Collection*, III, n.d.
8
9 André, p. 40 ff.
10 Seitz, p. 19; Sherburne, 1851, pp. 45-51.
11 Sherburne, 1851, pp. 45-51.
12 Green.
13 Sherburne, 1851, p. 45-51.
14 ———, pp. 51-54.
15 Seitz, pp. 19-21.

CHAPTER XXI

1 Seitz, pp. 15, 16; Green, April 25; Sherburne, 1851, pp. 45-51.
2 Mayo, p. 116; John Paul Jones, *Calendar*, Wendell to Hope & Co., October 28, 1777.
3 Peter Force *Collection*, III, n.d.
4 Franklin *Papers*, A.P.S., XLVII, 106.
5 Sherburne, 1851, pp. 45-51; Franklin *Papers*, A.P.S., LXI, 95.
6 Franklin *Papers*, A.P.S., XLVII, 10.
7 ———, LXI, 95.
8 ———, LXI, 99.
9 ———, XLVII, 110.

10 Peter Force *Collection*, VI, to President of Congress, December 7, 1779.
11 Franklin *Papers*, A.P.S., XI, 49.
12 Seitz, p. 17.

CHAPTER XXII

1 Bemis, *Diplomacy of the American Revolution*, p. 15 ff.; Stevens, 754.
2 Jared Sparks *Collections*, to Commissioners, February 10, 1778.
3 Franklin *Papers*, A.P.S., IX, 132.
4 Franklin (Bigelow), Vol. III, pp. 32, 33.
5 Franklin *Papers*, A.P.S., XI, 96.
6 Sherburne, 1851, pp. 40, 83-5.
7 Jared Sparks *Collections*, "Memos," Lettre de Gerard à Vergennes, Phila., March 9, 1779.
8 Arthur Lee *Collections*, VI, R. H. Lee to F. L. Lee.
9 André, p. 23.
10 Sparks, *Diplomatic Correspondence of the American Revolution*, Deane to Commissioners of Foreign Correspondence, September 3, 1777.
11 Stevens, Vol II, No. 179.
12 Franklin (Bigelow), Vol. 3, p. 48.
13 Henkel's "Catalogue, No. 1183," Deane to B. Harrison, December 20, 1777.
14 Franklin (Bigelow), Franklin to A. Lee, April 4, 1778.
15 Adams, John, Vol. III, p. 197.
16 Peter Force *Collection*, III, Passy, May 25, 1778.
17 Adams, John, Vol. III, p. 157.
18 Sands, 100, 101.
19 ———, 109-11.
20 Sherburne, 1851, pp. 83-5.
21 Sparks, *Diplomatic Correspondence of the American Revolution*, Vol. I, p. 154.

CHAPTER XXIII

1 Sands, p. 102.
2 Langdon, John, *Letters . . .* , Adams to Langdon.
3 Franklin *Papers*, A.P.S., XLVII, 110.
4 Remick, p. 214.
5 Franklin *Papers*, A.P.S., LXI, 95.
6 ———, LXI, 99.
7 ———, X, 10.
8 ———, LXI, 96.
9 Force, *Archives*, Series 4, Vol. 4, December 4, 1775.
10 Franklin *Papers*, A.P.S., XXXVII, 100; Clark, W. M., *Lambert Wickes . . .* , p. 199.

11 Peter Force *Collection*, III, to Ross, September 6, 1778.
12 Franklin *Papers*, A.P.S., LXI, 97.
13 Sparks, *Diplomatic Correspondence of the American Revolution*, Vol. VIII, from Commissioners, June 3, 1778.

CHAPTER XXIV

1 Sherburne, 1851, p. 68.
2 Sands, p. 113.
3 ———, p. 115.
4 Franklin *Papers*, A.P.S., X, 24.
5 Sparks, *Diplomatic Correspondence of the American Revolution*, Vol. I, p. 401.
6 Bemis, *Diplomatic History of the American Revolution*, p. 66.
7 Arthur Lee *Collections*, V, to Commissioners, July 3, 1778.
8 Sands, p. 119.
9 Franklin *Papers*, A.P.S., VII, 90.
10 Sands, p. 118.
11 Peter Force *Collection*, III, August 15, 1778.
12 Sparks *Diplomatic Correspondence of the American Revolution*, Vol. II, August 15, 1778.
13 Sands, p. 122.
14 Stevens, No. 702.
15 ———, No. 218.
16 ———, No. 235.
17 Peter Force *Collection*, III, to Duke of Chartres, September 21, 1778.
18 ———, III, to Duchess of Chartres, October 19, 1778.
19 Buell.
20 Mass. Hist. Soc. *Proc.*
21 Peter Force *Collection*, III, to William Whipple.
22 Franklin *Papers*, A.P.S., X, 24.
23 Sands, p. 520.
24 Sherburne, 1851, p. 71.
25 ———, p. 59.
26 De Koven, Vol. 1, p. 357.
27 André, pp. 49, 50.
28 Franklin *Papers*, A.P.S., XI, 49.
29 Sparks, *Diplomatic Correspondence of the American Revolution*, Vol. I, p. 304.
30 ———, Vol. I, p. 311.
31 Green, August 20.
32 Peter Force *Collection*, III, to Whipple.
33 Green, August 21.
34 Sherburne, 1851, p. 84.
35 Sparks, *Diplomatic Correspondence of the American Revolution*, Vol. I, p. 312.
36 ———
37 Mayo, p. 138.

38 Peter Force *Collection*, III, to Bancroft, August 21, 1778.

CHAPTER XXV

1 *Letter Book of John Paul Jones*, to Bancroft, August 21, 1778.
2 Sands, p. 128.
3 ———, p. 129.
4 Peter Force *Collection*, III, to Chaumont, September 6, 1778.
5 Sherburne, pp. 75, 76.
6 Sands, p. 135.
7 ———, pp. 135, 136.
8 ———, p. 136.
9 ———, p. 137
10 Franklin *Papers*, A.P.S., to Franklin, October 27, 1778.
11 Sherburne, pp. 81-2.
12 Peter Force *Collection*, III, to T. Bell, November 15, 1778.
13 ———
14 ———, III, to J. Young, November 18, 1778.
15 ———, IV, to Williams, December 16, 1778.
16 Knapp, *Notes and Documents*.
17 Peter Force *Collection*, IV, to Chaumont, December 18, 1778.
18 ———
19 To Williams, December 16, 1778.
20 Peter Force *Collection*, IV, to Bancroft, December 18, 1778.
21 ———, IV, to Williams, December 21, 1778.
22 *Bache Papers* of Franklin, A.P.S., June 13, 1782.
23 Sherburne, 1851, pp. 86, 87.
24 ———, p. 87.

CHAPTER XXVI

1 André, pp. 55, 56.
2 Wharton, I, pp. 494, 495; *Bache Papers* of Franklin, Franklin to Williams, June 13, 1782.
3 Sands, pp. 125, 126.
4 Landais, *Memorial*. . . .
5 Cooper, *Lives of Distinguished American Officers*, Vol. I, p. 103 ff.
6 Franklin *Papers*, University of Pa., *Alliance* officers to Franklin.
7 Arthur Lee *Collections*, V, Mlle. Benoit to Arthur Lee (in French), Paris, n.d.
8 *Letters* of Arthur Lee (N. Y. Public Library mss.), A. Lee to S. Adams, August 2, [1781?]
9 Wharton, I, pp. 484, 534.
10 Lee, William, *Letters*, Vol. III, p. 812.
11 Durand, pp. 247, 593; Stevens, No. 733.

12 Arthur Lee *Collections*, VI, R. H. Lee to F. L. Lee, n.d.
13 *Letters* of Samuel Adams, R. H. Lee to S. Adams, September 10, 1780.
14 Sherburne, 1851, p. 54.
15 Franklin *Papers*, A.P.S., March 6, 1779; "Independent," April 12, 1906, by Emma Repplier.
16 ———
17 Stevens, Nos. 282. 288.
18 ———, 218, 235, 254; Bois; Bemis, *Diplomacy of the American Revolution*, p. 66.
19 Peter Force *Collection*, II, M. Livingston, April 11, 1778.
20 ———, II, J. Wharton (affidavit).
21 ———, IV, to Livingston, April 25, 1779.
22 ———
23 Lee, William, *Letters*, W. Lee to R. H. Lee, March 25, 1779.
24 Jared Sparks *Collections*, 16, to Franklin, March 6, 1779.
25 Franklin (Smyth), Vol. 7, Franklin to Lafayette, March 22, 1779.
26 Sands, pp. 151, 152.
27 ———, p. 154.
28 Arthur Lee *Collections*, VI, Franklin to Landais, April 28, 1779.

CHAPTER XXVII

1 Franklin *Papers*, A.P.S., to Franklin, July 4, 1779; Sherburne, 1851, pp. 95, 133, 134; "Log of the *Bonhomme Richard*," May 17, 18.
2 Sands, p. 156; André, p. 58; Sherburne, p. 125.
3 Wharton, Vol. 3, p. 90.
4 *Papers of the C. C.*, No. 168, to Williams, April 3, 1779.
5 André, p. 68.
6 Peter Force *Collection*, IV, to M. Livingston, April 25, 1779.
7 ———, IV, to Amiel, May 3, 1779.
8 ———, V, from Dale, May 22, 1779.
9 Adams, John, Vol. 3, p. 201.
10 Adams, Samuel, Vol. 4, S. Adams to J. Warren, July, 1778; S. Adams to R. H. Lee, December 17, 1785.
11 Adams, John, May, 1777.
12 Sherburne, 1851, p. 108.
13 ———, p. 93.
14 *Letter Book of John Paul Jones*, to Mme. de Chaumont, June 13, 1779.
15 Sherburne, 1851, p. 94.

CHAPTER XXVIII

1 Livesey, p. 228.
2 Sherburne, 1851, p. 333.
3 Sands, p. 159.

4   Sherburne, 1851, p. 97.
5   ———, pp. 85, 86.
6   André, p. 59 ff.
7   Franklin *Papers*, A.P.S., to Franklin, July 4, 1779.
8   Sands, p. 153.
9   André, p. 68.
10   Peter Force *Collection*, V, to Mme. de Chaumont, July 22, 1779.
11   Arthur Lee *Collections*, VI, Franklin to Landais, July 28, 1779.
12   Fanning.
13   Peter Force *Collection*, V, from Walsh-Serrant, June 14, 1779.
14   Sherburne, 1851, pp. 102, 103.
15   André, pp. 70, 71.
16   Sherburne, 1851, pp. 200, 201.
17   André, p. 59, ff.
18   ———

CHAPTER XXIX

1   "Logs of the *Serapis, Alliance,* and *Ariel,*" August 14, 1779; Peter Force *Collection*, V, to Bancroft, August 13, 1779.
2   Franklin *Papers*, A.P.S., XV, 124; Arthur Lee *Collections*, VI, Franklin to Lee, July 18, 1779.
3   André, p. 70.
4   *Letters and Reports* . . . from the British Admiralty Foreign Office . . . , Custom House, Records at Ayr, August 22, 1779.
5   ———, September 1, 1779.
6   Seitz, pp. 29, 30.
7   ———, p. 31.
8   Sands, p. 173.
9   André, pp. 71, 72.
10   Niles.
11   Sherburne, 1851, pp. 168, 169.
12   André, p. 72 ff.; Filkin, Vol. 1, p. 18.
13   Fanning, pp. 27-29.
14   "Log of *Bonhomme Richard,*" September 15, 1779.
15   Cooper, "Graham's Lady's and Gentleman's Magazine," 1843, p. 74 ff.
16   Sherburne, 1851, p. 106.
17   Seitz, pp. 36, 37; "Log of *Bonhomme Richard,*" September 18, 1779.
18   Cooper, "Graham's . . . ," 1843, p. 74 ff.
19   Files of the Navy Department Library: "Evening Despatch."
20   Filkin, 3, Scott to Miss Edgeworth, February 24, 1824.
21   ———, "St. James Chronicle," September 30, 1790.
22   *Scottish Notes and Queries*.
23   "Log of *Bonhomme Richard,*" September 19, 1779.

24   Sherburne, 1851, pp. 108-20.
25   Mahan, "Scribner's," July, December, 1898.

CHAPTER XXX

1   André, p. 116.
2   "Log of *Bonhomme Richard,*" September 23.
3   Filkin, Vol. IV, pp. 37, 38.
4   ———
5   André, p. 72 ff.
6   ———
7   ———, pp. 97, 98.
8   ———
9   Sherburne, 1851, pp. 124-6.
10   ———
11   ———, pp. 120-3; 124-6.
12   ———, pp. 124-6.
13   André, p. 76 ff.; Sherburne, 1851, p. 158.
14   Sherburne, 1851, p. 115.
15   ———, pp. 120-6.
16   ———, p. 121.
17   ———, pp. 124-6.
18   André, p. 76 ff.
19   Sherburne, 1851, pp. 108-20; 120-3.
20   Fanning, p. 36 ff.
21   Sherburne, 1851, pp. 120-3.
22   ———, pp. 108-20.
23   ———, p. 167.
24   ———, pp. 156-71.
25   ———, p. 166.
26   ———
27   ———, p. 159.
28   ———, p. 161.
29   ———, pp. 124-6.
30   Filkin, Vol. I ("Public Advertiser," October 20, 1779).
31   André, p. 76 ff.
32   Sherburne, pp. 124-6.
33   Rush.
34   André, p. 76 ff.; Filkin, Vol. I, p. 13.
35   Fanning, p. 41.
36   André, p. 94 ff.; Sherburne, 1851, pp. 108-120.
37   Sherburne, 1851, pp. 120-3.
38   André, p. 94 ff.
39   Sherburne, 1851, pp. 120-3.
40   *Letters and Reports* relating to . . . the *Bonhomme Richard,* Public Record Office—Admiralty 1-5315.

CHAPTER XXXI

1   Sherburne, 1851, pp. 120-3.
2   Sands, p. 186.
3   ———
4   Sherburne, 1851, pp. 108-20.
5   "Logs of the *Serapis, Alliance,* and *Ariel,*" September 14.
6   Sherburne, 1851, pp. 124-6.

7 Fanning, p. 51.
8 ———
9 Sherburne, 1851, pp. 108-20.
10 Seitz, p. 68.
11 "Logs of the *Serapis, Alliance,* and *Ariel,*" September 29, 1779.
12 Seitz, p. 53.
13 ———, p. 61.
14 ———, p. 55.
15 ———, pp. 61, 62.
16 ———, pp. 52, 53.
17 ———, pp. 51, 52.
18 Wharton, IV, p. 384.
19 Sherburne, 1825, p. 155.
20 Seitz, p. 77.
21 "Logs of the *Serapis, Alliance,* and *Ariel,*" October 3, 1779.

CHAPTER XXXII

1 Sherburne, 1825, p. 135; André, p. 104 ff.
2 André, p. 128 ff.
3 "Logs of the *Serapis, Alliance,* and *Ariel,*" October 6, 1779.
4 Sherburne, 1851, pp. 131-3.
5 *Letters and Reports . . .* from the British Admiralty Foreign Office, Foreign State Papers, 84-566.
6 Bemis, *Diplomacy of the American Revolution,* pp. 35 ff., 121 ff.
7 Sherburne, 1851, pp. 108-20.
8 André, p. 104 ff.
9 *Letters and Reports . . .* from the British Admiralty Foreign Office, Foreign State Papers, 84-566, October 29, 1779.
10 Sherburne, 1851, pp. 108-20.
11 Franklin *Papers,* A.P.S., to Franklin, October 8, 1779.
12 Sherburne, 1851, pp. 176, 177.
13 Peter Force *Collection,* VI, Franklin to S. Cooper, October 27, 1779.
14 Seitz, p. 87.
15 ———, p. 89.
16 ———, p. 106.
17 *Letters and Reports . . .* from the British Admiralty Foreign Office, Foreign State Papers, 84-566, Hague, October 8, 1779.
18 Seitz, p. 100.
19 Filkin, Vol. II, p. 286.
20 ———, Vol. I, p. 173.
21 ———, Vol. II, pp. 360, 361.
22 ———, Vol. II, p. 105.
23 Sands, pp. 211, 212.
24 Peter Force *Collection,* VI, from T. Scott, November 19, 1779.
25 ———, to Scott, October 30, 1779.
26 ———, to Scott, December 3, 1779.
27 Neeser, p. 191; Sands, p. 214.

CHAPTER XXXIII

1 Sherburne, 1851, pp. 103, 104.
2 ———, p. 180.
3 ———, pp. 148, 149.
4 Peter Force *Collection,* VI, to Bancroft, January 16, 1780.
5 Arthur Lee *Collections,* Franklin to Landais, October 15, 1779.
6 ———, VI, Landais to Franklin, n.d.
7 Sherburne, 1851, pp. 156-71.
8 *Papers of the C. C.,* No. 168.
9 Sherburne, 1851, pp. 149, 150.
10 ———, p. 151.

CHAPTER XXXIV

1 *Letters and Reports . . .* from the British Admiralty Foreign Office, Public Record Office, S. P. Foreign, 84-566, October 29, 1779.
2 Sherburne, 1851, pp. 129, 130.
3 Wharton, III, pp. 398, 399.
4 Henkel's "Revolutionary Manuscripts and Portraits, Cat. No. 683," p. 60.
5 Sands, p. 227.
6 Sherburne, 1851, p. 177.
7 André, p. 104 ff.
8 Sherburne, 1851, p. 247.
9 "Logs of the *Serapis, Alliance,* and *Ariel,*" November 18, 1779.
10 Fanning, p. 66.
11 "Logs of the *Serapis, Alliance,* and *Ariel,*" November 29-December 26, 1779.
12 Fanning, p. 70.
13 Sherburne, 1825, p. 190.
14 Peter Force *Collection,* IV, to Huntington, December 7, 1779.
15 Facsimile, n.d., Boston Public Library.
16 *Letters and Reports . . .* from the British Admiralty Foreign Office, State Papers, Foreign, 84-566, Yorke to Stormont, December 14, 1799.
17 Sands, pp. 237, 238.
18 Franklin *Papers,* A.P.S., to Franklin, December 13, 1779.
19 Peter Force *Collection,* VI, to Gourlade & Moylan, December 15, 1779.
20 ———, VI, to Williams, December 15, 1779.
21 *Memoirs of Paul Jones,* London, 1843, p. 215.
22 Peter Force *Collection,* VI, from Neufville, December 15, 1779.
23 ———, to Neufville, December 17, 1779.
24 Sands, pp. 241, 242.

CHAPTER XXXV

1   "Logs of the *Serapis, Alliance,* and *Ariel,*" December 27, 1779.
2   ———; Seitz, p. 144.
3   Sands, p. 243.
4   Cooper, "Graham's. . . . "
5   André, p. 104 ff.; Peter Force *Collection,* to Dumas, January 16, 1780.
6   "Logs of the *Serapis, Alliance,* and *Ariel,*" December 29.
7   Peter Force *Collection,* VI, January 16, 1780.
8   Sands, pp. 317, 318.
9   Memoirs of Paul Jones, London, 1843, Vol. 2, p. 334 ff.

CHAPTER XXXVI

1   "Logs of the *Serapis, Alliance,* and *Ariel,*" January 17, Sherburne, 1851, pp. 184, 185.
2   ———, January 19 and 20.
3   ———, February 19.
4   Sherburne, 1851, pp. 185, 186.
5   ———, p 188.
6   ———, p. 190.
7   "Logs of the *Serapis, Alliance,* and *Ariel,*" May 24, 1780.
8   Franklin *Papers,* A.P.S., to Franklin, November 20, 1779.
9   Sherburne, 1851, p. 192.
10 Franklin *Papers,* A.P.S., to Franklin, February 21 and 23, 1780.
11 André, p. 57 ff.
12 Sherburne, 1851, p. 97.
13 ———, 1851, p. 218.
14 Sands, p. 253.
15 Wharton, III, p. 535; IV, 22, 26.
16 *Papers of the C. C.,* No. 132, July 23, 1780.
17 Franklin *Papers,* A.P.S., to Franklin, April 4, 1780.
18 Sands, p. 256.
19 Franklin *Papers,* A.P.S., Bancroft to Franklin, April 17, 1780.
20 Sherburne, to Dumas, November 5, 1779.

CHAPTER XXXVII

1   Franklin *Papers,* University of Pa., Navy Board to Franklin, December 21, 1778.
2   Landais, Peter, *Memorial* . . . , Boston, 1794; Sherburne, 1825, pp. 213, 214.
3   Adams, Samuel, Vol. IV, S. Adams to J. Warren, October 11, 1778.
4   ———, S. Adams to R. H. Lee, December 17, 185.
5   Landais, Peter, *Memorial* . . . , 1794.

6   Hale, journal of Landais' cruise.
7   Landais, *Memorial* . . . , 1784.
8   Arthur Lee *Collections,* VI, Franklin to Landais, April 25, 1779; Landais, *Memorial* . . . , 1784.
9   Wharton, III, p. 548.
10 Landais, *Memorial* . . . , 1784, p. 43.
11 Sherburne, 1851, p. 161.
12 ———, 1851, p. 180.
13 ———, 1851, pp. 159, 161.
14 Landais, *Memorial* . . . , 1784, pp. 43, 53.
15 Sherburne, 1851, pp. 156-61.
16 Franklin *Papers,* A.P.S., to Franklin, November 13, 1779.
17 Landais, *Memorial* . . . , 1784, p. 68 ff.
18 ———, p. 64.
19 ———
20 Franklin to Huntington, March 4, 1780.
21 Franklin *Papers,* A.P.S., Landais to Franklin, March 11, 1780.
22 ———, Landais to Franklin, XVII, 63, February 10, 1780.
23 Sherburne, 1851, p. 173.
24 Wharton, III, p. 548.
25 Franklin (Smyth), Vol. VIII, pp. 47, 48.
26 Franklin *Papers,* University of Pa., April 12, 1782; Landais, *Memorial* . . . , 1784, p. 93.
27 Landais, *Memorial* . . . , 1784, p. 88.
28 Fanning.

CHAPTER XXXVIII

1   Sands, p. 257; Niles.
2   Peter Force *Collection,* VIII, to Dumas, September 8, 1780; Sherburne, 1851, p. 222.
3   Stevens, No. 727.
4   "Proc. of the Grand Lodge of Mass.," 1916, pp. 266, 267.
5   Fanning, p. 78.
6   Filkin, II.
7   ———, III; Bachaumont, XV, pp. 179-82.
8   Robison, pp. 179-85.
9   Library of the Navy Department, March 2, 1907.
10 Dixmerie.
11 Filkin, III, July 18, 1780 (Trans. from French).
12 Sherburne, 1851, p. 257.
13 "Scribner's," Vols. LXX; XLVIII, new series.
14 Campan, p. 21.
15 Adams, Mrs. John, January 20, 1785.
16 Jeffries, November 12, 1910.
17 Hale, Vol. II, p. 367.

18 Peter Force *Collection*, VI, to Bancroft, October 26, 1779.
19 ———, VIII, May 28, 1780.
20 Vigée Lebrun.
21 Peter Force *Collection*, VIII, to Dumas, September 8, 1780.
22 Peter Force *Collection*, VIII, to Mme. Tellisson, July 24, 1780; Sherburne, 1851, pp. 204-6.
23 ———, VII, from de Charlary, n.d.
24 ———, IX, from Murray de Nicolson, n.d.
25 ———, VIII, from Rouel, June 21, 1780.
26 Files of Letters and Documents . . . , Library of the Navy Department.
27 Sands, p. 288.
28 ———
29 Peter Force *Collection*, VIII, to Countess de La Vendahl, June 7, 1780.
30 Sherburne, 1851, pp. 330, 331.
31 Alger.
32 Sands, pp. 288, 289.
33 Sherburne, 1851, p. 191.
34 ———, 1851, pp. 193, 194.
35 ———, 1851, p. 195.
36 Peter Force *Collection*, VIII, to Dumas, September 8, 1780.
37 ———, VIII, to Countess de La Vendahl, June 7, 1780.

CHAPTER XXXIX

1 André, p. 128 ff.
2 Franklin *Papers*, A.P.S., Landais to Franklin, May 29, 1780.
3 Peter Force *Collection*, to Franklin, July 12, 1780.
4 Arthur Lee *Collections*, VII, Franklin to Landais, June 7, 1780.
5 Sands, pp. 263, 264.
6 ———
7 Franklin *Papers*, University of Pa., Degge and others to Franklin, June 7, 1780.
8 Arthur Lee *Collections*, from Franklin, June 12, 1780.
9 Arthur Lee *Collections*, VII.
10 Franklin *Papers*, A.P.S., Vols. V, XVIII, 131.
11 Landais, *Memorial* . . . , 1784, p. 100; Arthur Lee *Collections*, VII, June 12, 1780.
12 Arthur Lee *Collections*, VII, Gillon to Landais, June 12, 1780.
13 Franklin *Papers*, A.P.S., XVIII, 133.
14 ———, XVIII, 133a.
15 Arthur Lee *Collections*, VII, to Robert Morris, June 27, 1780; Hale, Vol. 1, p. 337.

CHAPTER XL

1 Arthur Lee *Collections*, VII, to Robert Morris, June 27, 1780.
2 Peter Force *Collection*, VIII, to Bancroft, June 27, 1780.
3 ———
4 ———; Sands, p. 267.
5 *Papers of the C. C.*, No. 193; Fanning.
6 "Logs of the *Serapis, Alliance,* and *Ariel,*" June 12; Franklin *Papers,* A.P.S., XVIII, 142 and 143.
7 Fanning.
8 ———; "Logs of the *Serapis, Alliance,* and *Ariel,*" June 12.
9 Franklin *Papers,* A.P.S., 142 and 143.
10 Fanning.
11 Jared Sparks *Collections*, 57, to Franklin, June 21, 1780.
12 Franklin *Papers*, A.P.S., VIII, from Rouel, June 21, 1780.
13 Jared Sparks *Collections*, 57, to Franklin, June 21, 1780.
14 *Papers of the C. C.*, No. 193.
15 ———
16 Jared Sparks *Collections*, 57, to Franklin, June 21, 1780.
17 *Papers of the C. C.*, No. 193.
18 Peter Force *Collection*, VIII, to Bancroft, June 27, 1780.
19 Stevens, Vol. I, Smith to Eden, February 23, 1777.
20 Jared Sparks *Collections*, 57, to Parke, June 20, 1780.
21 Franklin *Papers*, A.P.S., XLVII, 181.
22 ———, XIX, 2.
23 Wharton, IV, Franklin to Congress, August 9, 1780.
24 Durand, p. 238.
25 Franklin *Papers*, A.P.S., XVIII, 164.
26 ———
27 Hale, Vol. I, p. 337.
28 Franklin (Smyth), Vol. VIII, p. 122.
29 Peter Force *Collection*, VIII, to Bancroft, June 27, 1780.
30 ———
31 ———, VIII, to Franklin, July 12, 1780.
32 ———
33 Arthur Lee *Collections*, VII, to Morris, June 27, 1780.
34 ———
35 ———, VII, to President and Board of Admiralty, June 27, 1780.
36 *Papers of the C. C.*, No. 168, Lafayette to Admiralty Board, December 16, 1780.
37 Franklin *Papers,* A.P.S., XIX, 2.

CHAPTER XLI

1 Sherburne, 1851, p. 196.
2 Franklin *Papers*, A.P.S., to Franklin, June 23, 1788.
3 Sands, pp. 290-2.
4 Franklin *Papers*, University of Pa., II, 22, Aimé A. J. Feutry to Franklin, May 8, 1778.
5 De Koven, Vol. II, pp. 274, 275.
6 Vigée Lebrun, p. 208.
7 Peter Force *Collection*, VIII, to Madame Tellisson, Paris, July 24, 1780.
8 ――――
9 See Appendix III.
10 Sands, p. 285.
11 ――――, p. 284.
12 Franklin *Papers*, A.P.S., to De Genêt, August 9, 1780.
13 Sherburne, 1851, pp. 332, 333.

CHAPTER XLII

1 Peter Force *Collection*, IX.
2 Sherburne, 1851, pp. 324, 325.
3 ――――, 1825, p. 331.
4 Peter Force *Collection*, VIII, n.d.
5 ――――, VIII; Sherburne, 1851, pp. 320, 321.
6 "Logs of the *Serapis, Alliance,* and *Ariel,*" September 1.
7 ――――, September 2.
8 Fanning, p. 88 ff.
9 Peter Force *Collection*, IX; Sherburne, 1851, pp. 321, 322.
10 ――――, VIII.
11 Peter Force *Collection*, VIII.
12 ――――, VIII.
13 De Koven, Vol. II, pp. 172, 173.

CHAPTER XLIII

1 Sands, p. 293.
2 André, p. 116.
3 Peter Force *Collection*, VIII, to Bancroft, September 23, 1780.
4 Franklin *Letters*, A.P.S., XIX, 141.
5 *Papers of the C. C.,* No. 132.
6 Peter Force *Collection*, VIII, to Bancroft, September 23, 1780.
7 "Logs of the *Serapis, Alliance,* and *Ariel,*" October 9.
8 Fanning, p. 80.
9 Sherburne, 1851, pp. 212, 213.
10 Filkin, III.
11 Fanning, p. 80.
12 Peter Force *Collection*, VIII, from Nicolson, November 18, 1780.
13 Franklin *Papers*, A.P.S., XX, 26.
14 Sands, p. 296.
15 Sherburne, 1851, p. 331.
16 ――――

17 ――――, p. 211.
18 Franklin (Smyth), November 25, 1780.
19 Peter Force *Collection*, A.P.S., from Nicolson, November 18, 1780.
20 Franklin *Papers*, University of Pa., Williams to Franklin, December 27, 1780.
21 Franklin (Smyth), Franklin to Williams, December 27, 1780.
22 Etting *Papers*, to Robert Morris, November 8, 1780.
23 Peter Force *Collection*, VIII, to Truxton, October 21, 1780.
24 Sands, pp. 301, 302.
25 Sherburne, 1851, p. 214.
26 André, p. 134 ff.

CHAPTER XLIV

1 Peter Force *Collection*, VIII, to Morris, November 8, 1770.
2 *Papers of the C. C.,* No. 193.
3 ――――
4 Moré.
5 *Papers of the C. C.,* No. 193.
6 ――――; Court Martial Testimony at Trial of Landais, Capt. Parke's evidence, Navy Department Library.
7 ――――
8 Board of Admiralty to Navy Board of Eastern Department, September 5, 1780.
9 Arthur Lee *Collections*, VII, A. Lee to Congress, August 13, 1781.
10 Board of Admiralty to Navy Board of Eastern Department, September 5, 1780.
11 *Papers of the C. C.,* No. 193.
12 ――――
13 Etting *Papers*, to Morris, November 8, 1780.
14 Adams, Samuel, S. Adams to R. H. Lee, December 17, 1785.
15 ――――

CHAPTER XLV

1 Arthur Lee *Collections*, VII, to Robert Morris, June 27, 1780.
2 Peter Force *Collection*, to Bancroft, August 7, 1780.
3 *Journals of the C. C.,* Vol. XIX, February 19, 1781.
4 ――――
5 Sherburne, 1851, pp. 214-24, *Journals of the C. C.,* Vol. XX, March 28, 1781.
6 Sherburne, 1851, p. 196.
7 André, pp. 143, 144.
8 Sherburne, 1851, p. 194.

9 André, pp. 143, 144.
10 ———
11 Sherburne, pp. 214-24.
12 *Journals of the C. C.*, Vol. XX, March 28, 1781.
13 ———
14 ———
15 *Journals of the C. C.*, Vol. XX, April 14, 1781.
16 ———
17 Adams, Samuel, S. Adams to J. Lovell, March 30, 1779.
18 Sherburne, pp. 225, 226.
19 Sands, p. 304.
20 ———, pp. 307, 327.
21 "Logs of the *Serapis, Alliance*, and *Ariel*," Appendix B.
22 Sands, pp. 307, 309, 310.
23 Stevens, No. 182.
24 Sherburne, 1851, p. 228; Sands, pp. 328, 329.

CHAPTER XLVI

1 André, pp. 156, 157.
2 ———, p. 156.
3 "Granite Monthly," Vol. LXI, p. 142; Henkel's "Catalogue, No. 1183."
4 Paullin, *Outletters . . .* , Admiralty Board to J. Langdon, June 16, 1780.
5 Henkel's "Catalogue, No. 1183," Langdon to Robert Morris, April 20, 1781.
6 ———, July 6, 1781.
7 Peter Force *Collection*, VIII, to Countess de Nicolson, December 25, 1781.
8 Bixby's *Collection*, to John Brown, March 25, 1782.
9 ———, April 4, 1782.
10 Mass. Hist. Soc., to McNeill, March 21, 1782.
11 Bixby's *Collection*, to John Brown, April 15, 1782.
12 ———, April 25, 1782.
13 Henkel's "Catalogue, No. 1183," Langdon to Robert Morris, July 6, 1781.
14 Files of Letters and Records, Navy Department Library, "Bibliography ZB," to G. Morris, July 15, 1782.
15 André, pp. 157, 158.
16 André, pp. 158 ff.
17 ———, p. 163; Sands, p. 337.
18 ———, p. 163.
19 ———, No. XII, appendix.
20 Bixby's *Collection*, to John Brown, September 7, 1782.
21 Peter Force *Collection*, IX, from

22 John Brown, October 1, 1782.
22 Sands, p. 341.
23 Sherburne, 1851, p. 234.
24 Peter Force *Collection*, IX, from John Brown, October 1, 1782.
25 ———
26 Sands, p. 309.
27 André, p. 187.
28 Franklin, *Bach Papers*, A.P.S., to Franklin, August 8, 1881.
29 Franklin *Papers*, A.P.S., to Bancroft, February 28, 1783.

CHAPTER XLVII

1 Franklin (Smyth), from Franklin, August 12, 1780.
2 André, pp. 166, 167.
3 ———
4 Sherburne, 1851, p. 234.
5 ———, pp. 235-7.
6 *Memoirs of Paul Jones*, Vol. II, pp. 264, 265.
7 Sands, p. 333.
8 André, p. 174.
9 ———, p. 174 ff.
10 Peter Force *Collection*, IX, "To the U. S. Minister of Marine . . . 1782."
11 Correspondence with . . . Captain Hector McNeill (Morgan Library), to McNeill, May 25, 1782.
12 ———, November 15, 1781.
13 Peter Force *Collection*, IX, "To the U. S. Minister of Marine . . . 1782."
14 Sands, pp. 304-9.
15 Bixby's *Collection*, to General St. Clair, November 10, 1783.
16 *Letters* of Samuel Adams, N. Y. Public Library mss., A. Lee to S. Adams, August 6, 1782.
17 Peter Force *Collection*, IX, "To the U. S. Minister of Marine . . . 1782."

CHAPTER XLVIII

1 Peter Force *Collection*, to Arthur St. Clair, November 10, 1783.
2 Barney, p. 143, 144.
3 Filkin, Vol. II, p. 282.
4 *Memoirs of Rear Admiral Paul Jones*, Edinburgh and London, 1830, Vol. II, p. 278.
5 *See* Appendix II.
6 *Memoirs of Rear Admiral Paul Jones*, Vol. II, p. 278.
7 André, p. 178.
8 ———, p. 179 ff.
9 Sherburne, 1851, p. 247.
10 ———, p. 249.

11 Sands, pp. 538, 539.
12 Sherburne, 1851, p. 265.

CHAPTER XLIX

1 Sherburne, 1851, p. 262.
2 Jefferson, Vol. V, p. 265.
3 Jefferson, Jefferson to Commissioners of the Treasury, August 12, 1786.
4 Sands, pp. 358, 359.
5 ———, pp. 532, 533.
6 Jefferson, Vol. 7, p. 32.
7 Sherburne, 1851, p. 265.
8 Jefferson, from Jefferson, July 11, 1786.
9 ———, Jefferson to Commissioners of the Treasury, August 12, 1786.
10 Sherburne, 1851, pp. 276, 277.
11 *Letters* of Samuel Adams, N. Y. Public Library mss., J. Lovell to S. Adams, July 8, 1782.
12 Sherburne, 1851, p. 262.

CHAPTER L

1 *Papers of the C. C.*, No. 168, Vol. I.
2 Selkirk *Letters*, to Earl of Selkirk, Paris, February 12, 1784.
3 ———, from Lord Selkirk, London, August 4, 1785.
4 Sands, p. 355.
5 Adams, Mrs. John, p. 208.
6 Jeffries, January 11, February 11, 1785.
7 Sherburne, 1851, p. 337.
8 *See* Appendix III.
9 Correspondence with . . . John Ross, Mass. Grand Lodge, to Ross, August 25, 1785.
10 Sands, pp. 361-5; Jared Sparks Collections, 132, Duncan to Palfrey, October 3, 1825.
11 Sherburne, to Dr. Read, L'Orient, November 9, 1780.

CHAPTER LI

1 Peter Force Collection, IX, "To the U. S. Minister of Marine . . . 1782."
2 Sands, p. 354.
3 ———, p. 355.
4 ———, p. 357.
5 Jefferson, Vol. V, p. 55.
6 Sherburne, 1851, pp. 257, 258.
7 Naval Academy Museum Library, to William Carmichael, June 30, 1784.
8 Sands, p. 361.
9 Sherburne, 1851, pp. 344-5.
10 Vigée Lebrun, p. 208.
11 André, pp. 154, 155.

12 ———, pp. 187, 188.
13 Filkin, IV, "Le Hérois d'un Roman de Fenimore Cooper" by Charles Read.

CHAPTER LII

1 Sherburne, 1851, pp. 269, 270.
2 ———
3 ———, p. 337.
4 Sands, pp. 373, 4.
5 ———, p. 373.
6 Peter Force *Collection*, VIII, to Madame Tellisson, July 24, 1780.
7 Franklin *Papers*, A.P.S., Aimé A. J. Feutry to Franklin, May 8, 1778.
8 Sands, pp. 473, 474.
9 Janet Taylor *Notes* (Cornell).
10 *Journals of the C. C.*, Vol. XXXIII, edit. by R. R. Hill, September 29, 1787.
11 Sands, p. 375.
12 ———
13 ———, pp. 375, 376.
14 *Journals of the C. C.*, Vol. XXXIII, edit. by R. R. Hill, October 11, 1787.
15 ———
16 ———, July 19, 1787.
17 ———, October 9, 1787.
18 Sherburne, 1851, p. 272.
19 ———, p. 273.
20 Sands, p. 378.
21 ———, p. 379.
22 Franklin (Smyth), Vol. 1, pp. 174-6.
23 Sherburne, 1851, pp. 366-8.

CHAPTER LIII

1 Sands, pp. 379, 380.
2 Golder, Earl Wemyss to the Russian Court, February 18, 1785.
3 ———, March 20, 1785.
4 Langdon, John, Jefferson to Langdon, March 5.
5 Sands, p. 402.
6 ———
7 Golder, Simolin to Besborodko, January 23/February 3, 1788.
8 ———, Catherine to Grimm, February 22, 1788.
9 ———, Potemkin to Simolin, April 5/16, 1788.

CHAPTER LIV

1 Jefferson, Vol. 6, p. 417.
2 Sands, p. 384.
3 ———, pp. 387, 388; Library of Congress *Collection*, "Order to the Admiralty College," signed "Ekatrina," February 15, 1788.
4 Sands, pp. 391, 392.

5 Sherburne, 1851, p. 283.
6 Sands, pp. 393, 527.

CHAPTER LV

1 Sherburne, 1851, pp. 285-7.
2 Washington, Vol. XI, p. 319.
3 Jefferson, Jefferson to Jay, May 4, 1788.
4 ———, Jefferson to Carrington, Vol. VII, pp. 38, 39.
5 Sands, pp. 403, 404; Sherburne, 1851, p. 288.

CHAPTER LVI

1 Sands, p. 487.
2 Library of Congress *Collection*, order signed "Ekaterina."
3 Sands, p. 398.
4 ———, p. 404.
5 ———, pp. 396, 397.
6 Waliszewski, *The Story of a Throne*, Vol. II, p. 55 ff.
7 ———, Vol. II, p. 42.
8 Séglur, Vol. III, p. 236.
9 ———, Vol. III, pp. 149, 150.
10 ———, Vol. III, pp. 20, 21.
11 Ligne, Wormeley edit., Vol. II, p. 16.
12 ———
13 Sherburne, 1851, p. 288.
14 Cresson, *Francis Dana*. . . .

CHAPTER LVII

1 Damas, p. 59.
2 Waliszewski, *Le Roman d'une impératrice*.
3 Ligne, edited by Crès, p. 317.
4 Ligne, edited by Wormeley, p. 70.
5 Levis, *Souvenirs et Portraits*.
6 Ségur, Vol. 3, p. 72.
7 Nassau-Siegen, p. 138.
8 Damas, p. 23.
9 Nassau-Siegen, p. 206.
10 Golder, Preface.
11 Sands, p. 427.

CHAPTER LVIII

1 Nassau-Siegen, p. 225.
2 ———, p. 207.
3 ———, p. 209.
4 Sands, pp. 406, 407.
5 Ligne, edited by Wormeley, Vol. II, p. 52.
6 Nassau-Siegen, p. 239.
7 ———, p. 232.
8 Golder, Preface, to Potemkin, June 7, 1788.
9 Nassau-Siegen, p. 236.
10 ———, p. 237.

11 Sands, p. 429.
12 Sands, p. 463, 508; Jefferson, Vol. XIX, from Jefferson, March 23, 1789.
13 Jefferson, Jefferson to Cutting, Vol. 7, p. 83.

CHAPTER LIX

1 Damas, p. 36.
2 Sands, p. 419.
3 "Biblioteka dlia Tchenia," 1844, Vol. LXV, Sec. 3, pp. 1-46.

CHAPTER LX

1 Sands, p. 421.
2 Nassau-Siegen, p. 237.
3 ———
4 Golder, to Potemkin, June 18, 1788.
5 ———
6 Golder, to Admiralty of Black Sea, June 21, 1788.
7 Sands, p. 431.
8 Ligne, edited by Wormeley, pp. 53, 54.
9 "Russkaia Starina," 1876, TXVI, 473-5.

CHAPTER LXI

1 Ligne, Wormeley edit., Vol. II, p. 54.
2 Sands, p. 428.
3 ———
4 ———, 432, 433.
5 Nassau-Siegen, p. 241.
6 ———, pp. 240-2.
7 Sands, pp. 424, 457.
8 Hist. Soc. of Pa., "Letter from an Irish Gentleman in the Russian Service."
9 Eton, Preface.
10 Sherburne, pp. 305-7.
11 Jefferson, Vol. VII, p. 149.
12 ———, Vol. 7, p. 126.

CHAPTER LXII

1 Sands, pp. 434, 435.
2 Ligne, Wormeley edit., Vol. 2, p. 87.
3 ———, pp. 86, 87.
4 Sands, p. 429.
5 Ligne, Wormeley edit., Vol. 2, pp. 86, 87.
6 Sands, pp. 429, 430.
7 ———, p. 438.
8 ———, p. 440.
9 ———, p. 443.
10 ———, p. 415.
11 ———, p. 444.
12 Damas, p. 59.
13 ———

CHAPTER LXIII

1 Sands, p. 449.
2 ———, p. 451.
3 ———
4 Golder, to Potemkin, October 14, 1788.
5 Sands, p. 453.
6 ———
7 Golder, to Potemkin, October 18, 1788.
8 Sherburne, 1851, p. 301.
9 "Russki Vestnik," 1878, July 5-19.
10 Sands, p. 457.
11 ———, pp. 454, 455.
12 ———, p. 458.
13 ———
14 ———, p. 455.
15 Sherburne, 1851, p. 298.
16 ———, p. 301.
17 Sands, p. 469.

CHAPTER LXIV

1 Nassau-Siegen, p. 278.
2 Sands, p. 463.
3 ———
4 Sherburne, 1851, pp. 301, 302.
5 Jefferson, from Jefferson, March 23, 1789.
6 Sherburne, 1851, p. 298.
7 Jefferson, from Jefferson, March 23, 1789.
8 Library of Congress, "Documents mainly relating to charges of assault brought by Katerina Stepanova. . . ."
9 ———
10 Sands, p. 477.
11 Library of Congress, "Documents mainly relating to charges of assault . . . ," "No. 7132. . . ."
12 Waliszewski, *Story of a Throne*, Vol. 1, p. 280.
13 ———, Vol. 1, p. 283.
14 Library of Congress, "Documents mainly relating to charges of assault . . . ," "No. 7132. . . ."
15 Ségur, Vol. III.
16 Library of Congress, "Documents mainly relating to charges of assault . . . ," "No. 7132 . . ."; Sands, pp. 478, 479.
17 Golder, p. 141.
18 ———, p. 141.
19 ———, p. 143.
20 Thomson, *Knight of the Seas*, pp. 513, 514.
21 Golder, p. 143.
22 Sands, pp. 484-6.

CHAPTER LXV

1 Sands, p. 495.
2 Sherburne, 1851, pp. 307, 308.
3 *Memoirs of Paul Jones*, 1843, Vol. II, p. 208.
4 Sherburne, 1851, p. 312.
5 Ligne, Wormeley edit., Vol. II, pp. 51, 53, 63, 87; Waliszewski, *The Story of a Throne*, Vol. II, p. 50.
6 Ségur, Vol. III, p. 499 ff.
7 Sherburne, 1851, p. 319.
8 ———, 316, 317.
9 Jefferson, Vol. VIII, p. 245.
10 Ségur, Vol. II, p. 280.
11 ———, Vol. II, p. 27.
12 Thomson, pp. 551-87.
13 *See* Chapter LXIV, note 21.
14 Golder, Catherine to Grimm, September 1, 1791.

CHAPTER LXVI

1 Sherburne, 1851, p. 303.
2 Sands, p. 489.
3 ———, p. 491.
4 Cresson, p. 187.
5 ———, p. 189.
6 Sherburne, 1851, pp. 308, 309.
7 Sands, p. 496.
8 Nassau-Siegen, p. 304.
9 ———, pp. 339, 340.
10 ———
11 ———
12 Waliszewski, *The Story of a Throne*, Vol. 2, p. 54.

CHAPTER LXVII

1 Sands, p. 498.
2 ———, pp. 468-9.
3 ———, pp. 500, 501.
4 ———, p. 499.
5 ———
6 Waliszewski, *The Story of a Throne*, Vol. II, p. 45.
7 Sands, pp. 501, 502.
8 Thomson, James, "Autumn".
9 Mass. Grand Lodge, to G. Morris, n.d.
10 Sands, pp. 502, 503.
11 ———, p. 505.
12 ———
13 ———, p. 503.
14 ———, p. 504.
15 ———, p. 507.
16 ———, p. 508.
17 ———, p. 499.
18 ———, p. 500.
19 Morris, G., Davenport edit., March 8, 1790.
20 Sands, p. 497.

21 Morris, G., Davenport, edit., March 9, 10, 11.
22 ———, May 3, 5.
23 Waliszewski, *The Story of a Throne,* Vol. I, p. 85.
24 Ligne, Wormeley edit., Vol. II, p. 350.

CHAPTER LXVIII

1 Morris, G.
2 "The New York Times," January 21, 1926, to Simolin, May 31, 1790; Sands, p. 511.
3 Sands, p. 516.
4 Waliszewski, *The Story of a Throne,* Vol. I, p. 161.
5 ———; Vol. I, p. 190.
6 "Le Moniteur Universel," Paris, Bulletin d'Assemblée Nationale, 10 Juillet, 1790, p. 788.
7 Unaflart, A. et Weiss, N.
8 "Le Moniteur Universel," Paris, Bulletin d'Assemblée Nationale, July 10, 1790, p. 792.
9 ———
10 "Le Moniteur Universel," Paris, Bulletin d'Assemblée Nationale, July 16, 1790, p. 807.

CHAPTER LXIX

1 *See* Appendix III.
2 Sands, p. 512.
3 ———, pp. 512, 513.
4 ———, pp. 522, 523.
5 ———, pp. 523, 524.
6 Taylor, Janette, "New Light on the Career of J. P. J."
7 Jared Sparks *Collections,* No. 41.
8 Sands, pp. 513, 514.
9 Taylor, Janette, "New Light on the Career of J. P. J."
10 ———
11 Jared Sparks *Collections,* No. 132.
12 Sands, pp. 519, 520.
13 ———, p. 520.
14 Grimm, 15 (26) Mars, 1791.
15 Sands, p. 520.
16 ———, pp. 521, 522.
17 Grimm, 15 (26) Mars, 1791.
18 Sands, pp. 528, 529.
19 ———, pp. 529, 530.
20 Golder, Catherine to Grimm, September 1, 1791.
21 ———, September 16, 1791.
22 ———
23 ———

CHAPTER LXX

1 Sherburne, 1851, p. 317.

2 ———
3 Jefferson, Vol. VIII, p. 245.
4 *State Records of N.C.,* Vol. XXI, p. 527.
5 Sherburne, 1851, pp. 130-3; "Memoirs of Paul Jones, 1843, Vol. II, Appendix, p. 334 ff.
6 Taylor, p. 525.
7 Jefferson, Vol. VIII, p. 245.
8 Morris, G., Davenport edit.
9 ———
10 ———
11 ———, Vol. II, p. 469.
12 Sands, pp. 531, 532.
13 ———, pp. 532, 533.
14 ———, pp. 534-40.
15 ———, pp. 540-1.
16 Mass. Grand Lodge, to Bancroft, April 30, 1792.
17 Morris, G., Davenport, edit., June 27, 1792.
18 Jefferson, Vol. VIII, p. 353-64.
19 Sands, pp. 353, 354.

CHAPTER LXXI

1 Sands, p. 543.
2 Morris, G., Davenport, edit., Vol. II, p. 468.
3 Sands, pp. 541, 542.
4 Morris, G., Davenport, edit., Vol. II, p. 469.
5 Jared Sparks *Collections,* No. 132.
6 Sands, pp. 547-9.
7 Morris, G., Davenport edit, Vol. II, p. 470.
8 Mass. Grand Lodge, Heirs of Jones to Robert Morris, January 14, 1794.
9 Hart, C. H. "The Sword Presented by Louis XVI to John Paul Jones." Proc. of the U. S. Naval Institute, No. 122.
10 ———

LXXII

1 Morris, G., Davenport edit., Vol. II, p. 469.
2 John Paul Jones, *Commemoration,* p. 52.
3 "Le Moniteur Universel," Paris, July 19, 1792, pp. 86, 87.
4 Filkin I, p. 86.
5 "La Correspondance Littéraire," No. 8, 20 Mars, 1859, Paris.
6 ———
7 Morris, G., Davenport edit., Vol. II, p. 470.
8 Sands, pp. 545, 546.
9 Golder, Catherine to Grimm, August 15, 1792.

10 "La Correspondance Littéraire," No. 8, 20 Mars, 1859, Paris; Files of Letters and Records, Library of the Navy Department.
11 Taylor, Janette, "New Light on the Career of J. P. J."
12 John Paul Jones *Commemoration*, p. 50 ff.
13 Julius Chambers. *News Hunting*, p. 365, 366, 367. New York, 1921.
14 John Paul Jones *Commemoration*, p. 58.
15 Sands, p. 543.
16 John Paul Jones *Commemoration*, pp. 91, 92.
17 ———, p. 92.

APPENDIX I

1 Filkin, IV, William Murray to D. Macpherson, January 6, 1845; Inglis, *Notes on a Wax Medallion*. . . .
2 André.
3 Filkin, I, pp. 140, 141.
4 ———, I, p. 140, note.
5 ———, IV, record of Patricia Malcomson.
6 Janette Taylor *Notes* from Jared Sparks *Collection* (Cornell).
7 De Koven, Vol. I, p. 304.
8 Chase.
9 *Document* of December 1913 from Captain John Hope, R.N., descendant of the Earls of Selkirk, to Captain Stockton, U.S.N., Library of the Navy Department.
10 De Koven, Vol. I, p. 303.
11 *Document* of December 1913 from Captain John Hope, R. N. . . . to Captain Stockton; *Record* from Sir C. D. Hope-Dunbar, Bart., to the author.
12 De Koven, Vol. I, pp. 300, 301.

13 Document of December 1913 from Captain John Hope, R.N. . . . to Captain Stockton.
14 Selkirk *Letters*, Countess of Selkirk to Mr. Craik, April 25, 1778.
15 Paid, J. B. *Scots Peerage*, Vol. VII.
16 Franklin *Papers*, A.P.S., to Franklin, March 6, 1779.
17 *Papers of the C. C.*, No. 132.
18 Sands, p. 65.
19 "United States Literary Magazine," October 15, 1825, Vol. III.

APPENDIX II

1 Franklin *Papers*, A.P.S., de Stark to W. T. Franklin, July 24, 1784.
2 ———, *Letters* to William T. Franklin, Vol. V, August 12, 1783.
3 ———, August 13, 1783.
4 ———, William T. Franklin to Sir James Nicolson, August 14, 1783.
5 Anderson, Vol. III, pp. 253, 254; Cokayne, Vol. IV; Rietstap.
6 Thomson, *Knight of the Seas*, pp. 391-3.
7 ———, p. 596.

APPENDIX III

1 Peter Force *Collection*, VIII, to Madame Tellisson, July 24, 1780.
2 Franklin *Papers*, University of Pa., A. A. J. Feutry to Franklin, May 8, 1778.
3 De Koven, Vol. II, pp. 272-5.
4 De Koven, "The New York Times," March 1, 1928 and "A Fictitious Paul Jones Masquerading as the Real"; Paullin, "When Was Our Navy Founded?"; "Virginia Magazine of History and Biography," Vol. VIII, pp. 442-5.
5 Thomson, *Knight of the Seas*, pp. 418-20.

Index

Index